Canadian
Organizational
Behaviour

Canadian Organizational Behaviour

Second Edition

Steven L. McShane

Faculty of Business Administration
Simon Fraser University

Represented in Canada by

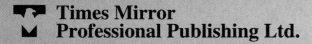
Times Mirror
Professional Publishing Ltd.

IRWIN

Toronto • Chicago • Bogotá • Boston • Buenos Aires
Caracas • London • Madrid • Mexico City • Sydney

Sponsoring editor: Evelyn Veitch
Product manager: Murray Moman
Project editor: Waivah Clement
Production supervisor: Dina L. Treadaway
Designer: Keith McPherson
Interior designer: Annette Spadoni/Keith McPherson
Cover designer: Keith McPherson
Cover illustrator: Rick McCollum
Art studio: ElectraGraphics, Inc.
Graphics supervisor: Heather D. Burbridge
Compositor: Carlisle Communications, Ltd.
Typeface: 10/12 New Baskerville
Printer: Von Hoffmann Press, Inc.

ISBN: 0-256-14573-3
Library of Congress Catalog Card Number: 94-79193

Printed in the United States of America

3 4 5 6 7 8 9 0 VH 2 1 0 9 8 7 6

Dedicated with Love and Devotion to Donna,
and to Our Wonderful Daughters,
Bryton *&* Madison

Preface

These are exciting times for the field of organizational behaviour. More than ever, business, nonprofit, and government leaders are applying OB knowledge to help their organizations reach new heights in effectiveness and employee well-being. The field of organizational behaviour has also forged new links with information science (electronic brainstorming, e-mail), engineering (concurrent engineering teams), architecture (culture, team dynamics), and other disciplines.

Canadian Organizational Behaviour, 2nd ed., builds on the success of the first edition by incorporating these new perspectives and applications of organizational behaviour knowledge. At the same time, this textbook continues to embrace the four distinctive philosophies that guided the first edition: Canadian orientation, theory–practice link, OB knowledge for everyone, and contemporary theory foundation. These core elements made the first edition of *Canadian Organizational Behaviour* a popular and highly rated book among students, and we hope they will make your journey through this field both meaningful and enjoyable.

Canadian Orientation

Canadian Organizational Behaviour, 2nd ed., has been written specifically for the Canadian audience, although it may be used effectively in other countries (just as American texts have been used in Canada and elsewhere for so many years). This book includes several Canadian cases and makes solid use of Canadian scholarship in organizational behaviour. The Canadian orientation is most apparent in the Canadian examples that appear throughout this textbook. For example, you will read about improving customer service at Marine Atlantic, reducing waste at Bell Canada, using team-based rewards at Sport Mart, making tough ethical choices at Sunnybrook Hospital, creating a team-based organization at GE Canada's Bromont plant, and overcoming colour-coded conflict at Canadian Airlines International.

Of course, *Canadian Organizational Behaviour,* 2nd ed., also includes numerous international examples, such as appreciating cultural values in Hawaii, managing the communication grapevine in Scotland, using stomach language in Japan, and building a circle organizational structure in Brazil. Still, Canadians don't know enough about themselves. Recent surveys report that Canadians expect universities and colleges to put more effort into communicating Canadian culture. This book serves the important goal of building the Canadian identity as well as introducing central concepts in organizational behaviour.

Theory–Practice Link

Canadian Organizational Behaviour, 2nd ed., relies on real-life examples to help students understand organizational behaviour concepts more easily. The value of this theory–practice link philosophy is well known among educators and trainers. Anecdotes effectively communicate the relevance and excitement of this field by bringing abstract concepts closer to reality. The stories found throughout this book also make interesting reading, such as how a public works employee in Saskatoon was motivated to work *less* hard, and how employees rebelled against a Nova Scotia company whose organization development sessions got too personal!

Organizational Behaviour Knowledge for Everyone

A distinctive feature of *Canadian Organizational Behaviour,* 2nd ed., is that it is written for everyone in organizations, not just traditional "managers." The philosophy of this book is that everyone who works in and around organizations needs to understand and make use of organizational behaviour knowledge. The new reality is that people throughout the organization—from systems analysts to production employees to accounting professionals—are assuming more responsibilities as companies remove layers of bureaucracy and give teams more autonomy over their work. This book helps all employees make sense of organizational behaviour, and gives them the tools to work more effectively within organizations.

Contemporary Theory Foundation

The first edition of *Canadian Organizational Behaviour* was respected for its solid foundation of contemporary organizational behaviour scholarship. By thoroughly searching the recent literature on every major OB topic, the second edition has maintained those standards. As you can see in the endnotes, each chapter is based on dozens of articles, books, and other sources, a large percentage of which have been published within the past five years. This literature update has produced numerous content changes throughout *Canadian Organizational Behaviour,* 2nd ed., which are described next.

Changes to the Second Edition

Canadian Organizational Behaviour, 2nd ed., includes many important additions and changes from the first edition. Several chapters have been reorganized. The writing style throughout the book has been streamlined so that important ideas are presented smoothly without bogging readers down with unnecessary details. Every chapter has been substantially updated with new conceptual and anecdotal material. In fact, over one-half of the *Perspectives* and almost all of the chapter-opening vignettes are new.

Based on a substantial literature search, *Canadian Organizational Behaviour,* 2nd ed., has numerous content changes and significantly updated references in every chapter. Here are some of the emerging concepts and issues discussed in this edition: appreciative inquiry, competency-based rewards, concurrent engineering teams, creative decision making, dialogue, electronic brainstorming, electronic mail, gender differences in communication style, network organization, organizational citizenship behaviours, romance of leadership, tacit skills and knowledge, team-based organizations, third-party conflict resolution, transformational leadership, virtual organization, and work–family stressors. This edition also adds established OB topics that did not appear in the first edition, such as creative decision making, social learning theory, and research methods in organizational behaviour (Appendix A).

Another change is that *Canadian Organizational Behaviour,* 2nd ed., gives more attention to the ethical and cross-cultural aspects of organizational behaviour. Ethical issues are described in the sections on organizational effectiveness, monitoring employee performance, stereotyping employees, making individual decisions, using peer pressure, engaging in organizational politics, and applying organization development practices. Cross-cultural issues are discussed around the topics of gender differences in communication (Chapter 6), the cross-cultural relevance of motivation theories (Chapter 3), cultural values in aboriginal organizations (Chapter 8), and the cross-cultural relevance of organization development practices (Chapter 15).

Finally, *Canadian Organizational Behaviour,* 2nd ed., includes several improvements to the experiential exercises and cases. Three-quarters of the experiential exercises have been replaced. Most exercises now involve interesting team-based activities, such as a not-so-trivial game about cultural gestures, a team-trust exercise, and an occupational stereotype exercise. There is a new section at the end of the book where additional cases have been added. These cases make excellent assignments, because most relate to concepts in several chapters. Several end-of-chapter cases are also new to this edition.

Learning Elements

Canadian Organizational Behaviour, 2nd ed., includes several learning elements to make your reading of this book more enjoyable and render the OB material more memorable.

Learning Objectives and Chapter Outline   Several learning objectives and an outline of the main topic headings are listed at the beginning of each chapter to guide you through the main points of the material to follow.

Chapter vignette and photos   Every chapter begins with a vignette about a Canadian organization that relates to some of the concepts presented in the chapter. A photograph accompanies each vignette to give the story more visual meaning. Most chapters include additional photos that visualize examples found in the text. A few cartoons have been added to provide more colourful interpretations of OB issues.

Perspective boxes and in-text examples   Each chapter includes three or four Perspectives—stories that describe specific organizational incidents in Canada and elsewhere. These anecdotes are strategically placed near the relevant organizational behaviour concepts, and the text clearly links them to these concepts. The text of each chapter also includes numerous real-life examples to further strengthen the theory–practice link.

Graphic exhibits   Graphic exhibits created with recent computer technologies are placed throughout each chapter to help you visualize key elements of OB models or integrate different points made in the text.

Margin notes and end-of-text glossary   This book minimizes unnecessary jargon, but the field of organizational behaviour (as with every other discipline) has its own language. To help you learn this language, key terms are highlighted in bold and brief definitions appear in the margin. These definitions are also presented in an alphabetical glossary at the end of the text.

Chapter Summary and Discussion Questions   Each chapter closes with a summary and list of discussion questions. The chapter summary highlights important material, whereas the discussion questions help you to check your understanding of the main points in the chapter.

Cases and Experiential Exercises   Every chapter includes one case and one experiential exercise. Several additional cases appear at the end of the textbook. The cases encourage you to use organizational behaviour knowledge as a tool to diagnose and solve organizational problems. The experiential exercises involve you in activities in which you either experience organizational behaviour or practise your OB knowledge in entertaining and informative ways.

Indexes   A corporate index, name index, and subject index are included at the end of this textbook to help you search for relevant information and make this book a valuable source for years to come.

Supplemental Materials

Canadian Organizational Behaviour, 2nd ed., includes a variety of supplemental materials to help instructors prepare and present the material in this textbook more effectively.

Instructor's Manual   The *Instructor's Manual* includes a wealth of information that instructors will find useful. For each chapter, the manual presents the learning objectives, glossary or highlighted words, a chapter summary, complete lecture outline (in larger typeface!), solutions to the end-of-chapter discussion questions, notes for the case and experiential exercise, and at least one supplemental lecture. It also includes a very large set of transparency masters, some cases and exercises not found in the textbook, and notes for the end-of-text cases.

Test Bank   The *Test Bank* manual includes dozens of multiple-choice and true/false questions for each chapter. It also includes several essay questions along with answers to these questions. All questions were written by the author and many have been tested in large class examinations. For example, for many of the multiple-choice questions there is information in the *Test Bank* manual indicating the percentage of students answering the question correctly.

Computerized Test Bank   The entire *Test Bank* manual is available in a computerized version for either IBM-compatible or Macintosh computers. Instructors receive special software that lets them design their own examinations from the test bank questions, edit test items, and add their own questions to the test bank.

PowerPoint® overheads   Instructors who adopt *Canadian Organizational Behaviour,* 2nd ed., can receive PowerPoint presentation files in either IBM-compatible or Macintosh formatted disks. These disks include a PowerPoint file for each chapter as well as PowerPoint Viewer software to display these files on any microcomputer with a Macintosh® or Microsoft Windows® system. Each PowerPoint file has several overheads relating to the chapter, complete with builds and transitions. Some files include photographs from the textbook. You can get more details about these PowerPoint disks from the Irwin representative in your area.

Video package   We live in the age of television, so it isn't surprising that students appreciate video programs to punctuate the lectures, cases, and other pedagogical devices used in the organizational behaviour class. Irwin has several organizational behaviour video programs in its library, copies of which are available to adopters of *Canadian Organizational Behaviour,* 2nd ed. You can get details from the Irwin representative in your area.

Acknowledgments

One of the best decisions I ever made was to move to Vancouver and join the Faculty of Business Administration at Simon Fraser University. This is a unique institution that quite correctly deserves its high ratings from the media and public. For their continued support, guidance, and friendship, I would especially like to thank my organizational behaviour colleagues at SFU: Mark Wexler, Rosalie Tung, Dean Tjosvold, Bob Rogow, Larry Pinfield, Stephen Havlovic, Carolyn Egri, Gervase Bushe, Stephen Blumenfeld, and Neil Abramson. I also owe a special debt of gratitude to Dean Stan Shapiro for being a superb role model, and for supporting me throughout this project.

Several colleagues from other colleges and universities across Canada provided valuable feedback and suggestions as reviewers of *Canadian Organizational Behaviour,* 2nd ed. Their comments significantly improved the quality of the final product. These colleagues are:

Donna Bentley, Northern Alberta Institute of Technology

Ronald Burke, York University

Beth Gilbert, University of New Brunswick, Saint John

Pat Sniderman, Ryerson Polytechnic University

Paul Tambeau, Conestoga College

Judy Wahn, University of Northern British Columbia

I would also like to extend my gratitude to the following colleagues who provided valuable input in the first edition of this book:

Brenda Bear, Northern Alberta Institute of Technology

Richard Foggo, Southern Alberta Institute of Technology

Brian Harrocks, Algonquin College

Jack Ito, University of Regina

Anwar Rashid, Ryerson Polytechnic University

John Redston, Red River Community College

The students in my BUS272 classes deserve special mention. They have been very supportive as I lectured on new OB concepts, introduced new cases and exercises, tested new examination questions, and experimented with computer-based overheads. My BUS272 class typically has over 200 people who come from all age groups and walks of life. I could not ask for a better setting in which to test out this book. Through their enthusiasm for this project and favourable ratings of the book, BUS272 students have doubled my energy.

Canadian Organizational Behaviour, 2nd ed., was very much a team effort. Two people who deserve a special note of thanks are Lenard Reid and Waivah Clement. Lenard Reid was an outstanding research assistant on the first edition, but he exceeded his previous superb performance in this second edition. Lenard graduated from SFU last year and is nicely launched into his career, yet he wanted to participate in this project. He worked nights and early mornings to gather research materials, photographs, cartoons—almost everything that you see in this book. Waivah Clement was project editor on the first edition and rearranged her busy schedule to serve as project editor on the second edition. I was very touched by Waivah's request to work with me again, because she is a genuinely wonderful person who maintains the highest standards in book publishing quality. It has been a privilege to work with both Waivah and Lenard on this project.

Evelyn Veitch was an excellent sponsoring editor for this second edition. She kept me on schedule (well, I almost kept on schedule!) and was always there to support the project. I would also like to extend my continued thanks to Rod Banister for planting the original seed that resulted in the first edition of *Canadian Organizational Behaviour,* and to Michelle Berner, Anne Courtney, Tammi Mason, Henrick Jorgennsen, and Karim Karmali for their valuable research assistance on this or the first edition.

Finally, I am forever indebted to my wife and best friend, Donna Mc-Clement, and to our wonderful daughters, Bryton and Madison. Their love and support give special meaning to my life. I dedicate this book to them.

Steven L. McShane

Contents in Brief

Contents

Canadian
Organizational
Behaviour

PART

Introduction

Chapter 1
Introduction to the Field of Organizational Behaviour

Introduction to the Field of Organizational Behaviour

Courtesy of Marine Atlantic.

Marine Atlantic Inc., the Moncton-based Crown corporation that runs ferry services in Atlantic Canada, is at the forefront of customer service and productivity improvement in Canada's public sector. This is a sharp contrast to the complacent, bureaucratic, and authoritarian transportation company that Terry Ivany inherited in 1989 when he was hired as Marine Atlantic's chief executive officer.

Ivany realized that Marine Atlantic had to adapt quickly. Passenger loads were dropping due to the recession. The company's monopoly across Northumberland Strait was threatened by plans to build a bridge linking New Brunswick to Prince Edward Island. Government cost cutting raised concerns that Marine Atlantic's subsidy from Transport Canada would be reduced. Finally, a survey reported that only 72 percent of Marine Atlantic's passengers in 1989 were satisfied with the company's service. "That was just awful," says Ivany. "Any commercial enterprise dealing with the public that doesn't have an 85 percent approval rate is in deep trouble."

Productivity measurement has been the main driver behind Marine Atlantic's transformation. Important information about each department's past performance is posted so that employees can discover ways to become more efficient and effective. For example, with the aid of charts showing how much it costs to run the cafeteria, kitchen staff members aboard each ferry can learn how to reduce those costs. This feedback is further supported by a new service excellence program that teaches supervisors how to create measurement and feedback systems, give positive reinforcement, facilitate consensus decision making, and deal with conflict.

Marine Atlantic's continuous journey toward productivity improvement and service quality is paying off in many ways.

Customer satisfaction ratings have soared to 97 percent. Significant cost reductions have been found in most areas of the organization, saving Canadian taxpayers millions of dollars in annual operating subsidies. But perhaps the biggest difference is the renewed pride that employees now feel in their jobs and recognition for working at Marine Atlantic.[1]

Marine Atlantic's recent experience provides an appropriate beginning to this book about organizational behaviour. It is about a Canadian company that applied organizational behaviour concepts to increase its effectiveness in a rapidly changing environment. Canadian businesses—whether in the private or public sector—must be prepared for the challenges of increased competition and customer expectations that lie ahead. Organizational effectiveness is mentioned throughout this book because we want to improve organizations, not just understand them. We will discuss organizational effectiveness and the related concepts of productivity and total quality management later in this chapter.

The Marine Atlantic story highlights many topics in the exciting field of organizational behaviour. The company applied several OB concepts (e.g., feedback, employee involvement, and organizational behaviour modification) to become more effective. Terry Ivany's leadership was put to the test throughout the organizational change process. For example, several hundred employees left the organization because they wouldn't or couldn't adapt to Marine Atlantic's revolutionary transformation.

This book is about people working within organizations. Its main objective is to help you understand behaviour in organizations and work more effectively in organizational settings. Organizational behaviour knowledge is not only for managers and leaders; anyone who works in and around organizations should understand and apply these concepts. In this chapter, we introduce you to the field of organizational behaviour, outline the main reasons why you should know more about it, describe the fundamental perspectives behind the study of organizations, and discuss perspectives of organizational effectiveness. We conclude with a summary of the contents of this book.

The Field of Organizational Behaviour

Organizational behaviour
The study of what people think, feel, and do in and around organizations.

Organizational behaviour (OB) is the study of what people think, feel, and do in and around organizations. OB researchers systematically study individual, team, and structural characteristics that influence behaviour within organizations. Through their research, OB scholars try to predict and understand how these behaviours influence organizational effectiveness.

By saying that organizational behaviour is a field of study, we mean that experts have been accumulating a distinct knowledge about behaviour within organizations—a knowledge base that becomes the foundation of this book. Most OB texts discuss similar topics, providing evidence that OB has evolved into a reasonably well-defined field of inquiry. This is really quite remarkable considering that OB is still in its infancy. It emerged as a distinct field in the 1930s or 1940s, and continues to evolve as new perspectives and theories emerge or are imported from other disciplines.

What are organizations?

Organizations are as old as the human race. Archaeologists have discovered massive temples dating back to 3500 B.C. that were constructed through the organized actions of many people. The fact that these impressive monuments were built suggests not only that complex organizations existed, but that they were reasonably well managed.[2]

Organizations are social entities in which two or more people work interdependently through deliberately structured patterns of interaction to accomplish a set of goals.[3] Organizations are not buildings or other physical structures; they are social structures—groups of two or more individuals interacting toward some purpose. Why do people join organizations? Basically, they believe that their personal goals can be achieved more effectively by working in concert with others than by acting alone.

Organizations consist of deliberately structured patterns of interaction— repeated routines of behaviour—that presumably help to achieve organizational objectives. At Marine Atlantic, for instance, dock workers daily direct thousands of people and automobiles onto and off the ferries. They coordinate with each other to ensure passenger safety and complete their tasks promptly. These patterned interactions help the Crown corporation to survive and prosper by serving its clients, suppliers, and other stakeholders.

Finally, organizations have goals. **Organizational goals** are a desired state of affairs that the social entity is trying to achieve.[4] Organizations typically have several goals, some of which may be (and often are) in conflict with others. Goals represent the main reason why organizations exist. Who establishes these goals? Certainly top management and the board of directors play an important role, but goals are ultimately formed by the influence and actions of everyone associated with the organization (employees, customers, etc.).[5]

At this point we should distinguish stated goals from actual goals.[6] Most formal organizations have mission statements saying why they exist and what they hope to accomplish. Top managers also introduce new strategies and directions for the organization that seem to represent organizational goals. But these are only stated goals—they may distort, rationalize, or even conceal some essential aspects of the organization's true aims. Thus, the goals that organizational members actually strive for may be different from the organization's publicly stated goals.

Organizational goals also differ from individual goals.[7] People want to achieve organizational goals primarily because they believe these actions will also fulfill their personal objectives. These personal goals are based on individual needs, which we will discuss in Chapter 3.

Organizations
Social entities in which two or more people work interdependently through patterned behaviours to accomplish a set of goals.

Organizational goals
A desired state of affairs that organizations try to achieve.

Why Study Organizational Behaviour?

In all likelihood, you are reading this book as part of a required course in organizational behaviour. Apart from degree or diploma requirements, why should you learn the ideas and practices discussed in this book? There are three main reasons, namely, that organizational behaviour knowledge helps you to (1) predict and understand organizational events, (2) adopt more accurate theories of reality, and (3) control organizational events more effectively.

Satisfying the need to predict and understand

We have an inherent need to know about the world in which we live. We want to predict and understand events to satisfy our curiosity and to map out life's events more accurately. Organizations affect almost every part of our lives, so it makes sense that we should be interested in knowing when, how, and why organizational events occur.[8] The field of organizational behaviour uses scientific research to discover systematic relationships. And by learning about these discoveries, you will gain a better understanding of organizational life.

Adopting more accurate theories of reality

Through personal observation and learning from others, you have already formed numerous personal theories about the way people behave. Some of these may be quite accurate and predict behaviour in many situations. Even so, the theories and concepts presented in this book will further clarify or crystalize these personal views of the world.

Of course, not all of your personal theories of organizational life are accurate, even though many appear to be common sense. Consider the following popular beliefs about behaviour in organizations:

- A happy worker is a productive worker.
- Individuals are unlikely to repeat bad decisions.
- Conflict undermines effective decision making.
- It is better to negotiate alone than as a team.

Most people would say that these statements are obviously true. After all, they make a lot of sense, don't they? Yet systematic research suggests that these statements are incorrect or, at best, correct under very limited circumstances. Unfortunately, people who continue to rely on false beliefs may eventually make bad decisions. The field of organizational behaviour uses scientific methods and applied logic to test the accuracy of personal theories in organizational settings. The knowledge you will gain by reading this book should help you to confirm and challenge your personal theories, and give you new perspectives of reality.

Controlling organizational events

Perhaps the most practical reason for learning about organizational behaviour is that it has direct implications for controlling organizational events. Through OB research, we now understand how to make better decisions, structure organizations to fit the surrounding environment, improve individual performance, build employee commitment, and help work teams operate more effectively. At a more interpersonal level, OB theories prescribe ways to persuade and negotiate, manage conflict, and communicate with others in organizational settings. Although these practices may seem most appropriate for senior and middle managers, they are relevant to everyone who works in and around organizations. Indeed, as organizations reduce entire layers of management and delegate more responsibilities to nonmanagement employees, the concepts described in this book will become increasingly important to all employees. Everyone needs to master the knowledge and skills required to work more effectively with people in organizational settings.

Scientific Research Foundation of Organizational Behaviour   **Exhibit 1–1**

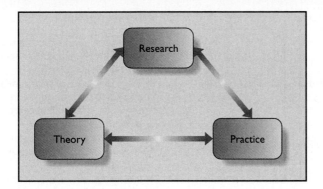

Although organizational behaviour takes a prescriptive view, it does so in the context of theory and research. OB scholars use scientific research to build strong theory that, in turn, provides the foundation for effective management practice (see Exhibit 1–1). In other words, the best organizational practices are those built on sound organizational behaviour theory and research.[9]

Fundamental Perspectives of Organizational Behaviour

Over the years, the field of organizational behaviour has adopted several fundamental beliefs and assumptions about how organizations operate and how organizational research should be conducted. These perspectives are not necessarily unique to this field—some are found in other behavioural sciences—but you should understand them to gain a better appreciation of OB knowledge. Now, let's examine these perspectives in more detail.

OB as a multidisciplinary field

Organizational behaviour is known as a multidisciplinary field because many of its theories, concepts, and methods are adopted from other disciplines. Psychology and sociology have made the largest contributions to OB knowledge, as we see in Exhibit 1–2. Psychological research has aided our understanding of motivation, stress, perceptions, attitudes, and other individual and interpersonal behaviour. Indeed, psychologists have been applying these organizational behaviour concepts at Ontario Hydro and other Canadian firms since the Second World War.[10] Sociologists generally study organizations as social systems, so their research is found mainly in the areas of team dynamics, organizational socialization, work/nonwork roles, communication, organizational power, leadership, and organizational structure.

Anthropologists investigate how societies develop norms, values, rituals, and practices that have useful functions. This knowledge has recently been applied to the OB field to improve our understanding of organizational culture as well as cross-cultural relations. Political science research has aided OB knowledge primarily in the areas of intergroup conflict, power, political behaviour, and decision making.[11] Economic theory has influenced our knowledge of organizational power, negotiations, and decision making. Finally, the field of engineer-

Exhibit 1–2		Multidisciplinary Perspective of Organizational Behaviour
Discipline	**Research Emphasis**	**Relevant Topics**
Psychology	Individual behaviour	• Motivation, perception, attitudes, personality, job stress, job enrichment, performance appraisals, leadership
Sociology	Interpersonal relations and social systems	• Team dynamics, work/nonwork roles, organizational socialization, communication patterns, organizational power, status systems, organizational structure
Anthropology	Relationship between social units and their environments	• Corporate culture, organizational rituals, cross-cultural aspects of OB, organizational adaptation
Political science	Individual and group behaviours within political systems	• Intergroup conflict, coalition formation, organizational power and politics, decision making, organizational environments
Economics	Rational behaviour in the allocation of scarce resources	• Decision making, negotiation, organizational power
Industrial engineering	Efficient operation of physical human behaviour	• Job design, productivity, work measurement

ing has contributed to organizational behaviour in the areas of work efficiency, productivity, and work measurement. Some of Canada's leading management consulting firms, including Woods Gordon and Stevenson Kellogg, were initially in the industrial engineering business, focussing their attention on work efficiency principles such as time and motion study (see Chapter 4).

The field of organizational behaviour is showing signs of maturity as OB scholars develop their own models and theories. However, there is also a risk that as the OB field matures, scholars will take too much of an inward focus by fine-tuning existing models rather than continuing to scan other disciplines for new concepts, models, and perspectives.[12] It would be unfortunate if we overlooked the new ideas generated from information science, communication, and other fields, because this knowledge would benefit our understanding, prediction, and management of people in and around organizations.

Organizations as open systems

Open systems
Organizations and other entities with interdependent parts that work together to continually monitor and transact with the external environment.

Organizations are viewed as **open systems.** This means that organizations consist of interdependent parts that work together to continually monitor and transact with the external environment.[13]

Exhibit 1–3 presents a simplified perspective of organizations as open systems. An organizational system acquires resources from its external environment, including raw materials, employees, information, financial support, and equipment. Technology (such as equipment, work methods, and information) transforms these inputs into various outputs that are exported back to the external environment. The organization receives feedback from the external environment regarding the use of these outputs and the availability of future inputs. It also receives more resources in return for its outputs. This process is cyclical and, ideally, self-sustaining, so that the organization may continue to survive and prosper.

Open Systems Perspective of Organizational Behaviour   Exhibit 1–3

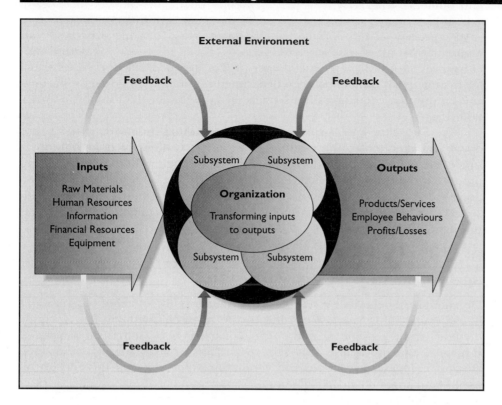

One way to understand the open systems perspective is to consider its opposite: closed systems. A closed system exists independently of anything beyond its boundaries. It has all the resources needed to survive indefinitely. Organizations are never completely closed systems, but those operating in very stable environments tend to become relatively closed by ignoring their surroundings for long periods of time.

For example, up to the early 1970s, telephone companies in North America were relatively closed systems. As regulated monopolies in a stable and predictable business, they were able to string new wires and manufacture telephones without any serious threat of competition or loss of customers.[14] Telephone companies did adapt somewhat to new technology and national requirements (such as World War II), but their response was lethargic. They reacted slowly to customer demand rather than anticipate changes. Indeed, customers did most of the adapting by tolerating multiparty telephone lines and the telephone company's standard black telephones.

The open systems perspective emphasizes that organizations survive by adapting to changes in their environments. Thus, organizational leaders must continually watch for shifting customer needs, financial markets, labour force, competition, and so on. For example, Terry Ivany forced Marine Atlantic to change because he knew the company had to adapt to reduced passenger loads, higher customer expectations, and dwindling government subsidies.

Systems Approach:

So far, we have described organizational systems in terms of their external environments. But the systems perspective also highlights the fact that organizations have many parts (called *subsystems*) that must coordinate with each other in the process of transforming inputs to outputs. To achieve its goals, an organization must monitor the relationships among these subsystems and take corrective actions whenever friction occurs. For instance, managers must watch for dysfunctional conflict between departments, monitor employee satisfaction, and ensure that communication systems facilitate rather than inhibit information flow.

The idea that organizations have many interdependent subsystems also draws our attention to the multiple cause–effect realities of organizations. A single event in one department may ripple through other subsystems and produce a variety of unintended outcomes. This point is illustrated in Perspective 1–1, which describes how a small productivity program in one department at the City of Calgary turned into a Pandora's box of unexpected problems throughout the organization.

Applying the scientific method

Scientific method
A set of principles and procedures that help researchers to systematically understand previously unexplained events and conditions.

Organizational behaviour researchers test their hypotheses about organizations by collecting information according to the **scientific method.** The scientific method is not a single procedure for collecting data; rather, it is a set of principles and procedures that help researchers to systematically understand previously unexplained events and conditions. Appendix A at the end of this book summarizes the main elements of the scientific method, as well as various ways to conduct research.

It would be convenient to have one theory predicting everything that goes on in organizations, but human behaviour is too complex. Consequently, the field of organizational behaviour uses the scientific method to test several theories.[15] Some theories explain employee motivation, others explain leadership, and still others explain team dynamics. To make matters more complex, OB theories usually take a contingency approach, which we discuss next.

The contingency approach

Contingency approach
The idea that a particular action may have different consequences in different situations; that no single solution is best in all circumstances.

"It depends" is a phrase that OB scholars often use to answer a question about the best solution to an organizational problem. The statement may frustrate some people, yet it reflects an important way of understanding and predicting organizational events, called the **contingency approach.** This perspective states that a particular action may have different consequences in different situations. In other words, no single solution is best in all circumstances.

Many early OB theorists tried to develop universal rules to predict and explain organizational life, but there were too many exceptions to make these "one best way" theories useful. For example, in Chapter 14 we will learn that leaders should use one style (e.g., participation) in some situations and another style (e.g., direction) in other situations. Thus, when faced with a particular problem or opportunity, we need to understand and diagnose the situation, and select the strategy most appropriate *under those conditions.*[16]

Perspective 1–1

Unintended Consequences of a Productivity Improvement Program at the City of Calgary

The City of Calgary's Transmission and Distribution Section (TDS) employs several hundred people and plays a vital role in constructing and maintaining water lines throughout the city. When a few dozen TDS employees were invited by senior management to suggest productivity improvement ideas, their solutions produced substantial savings within the first year. For example, the cost of repairing the City of Calgary's water mains declined by 25 percent, repair costs to underground service connections declined by 17 percent, expenditures for overtime dropped by 72 percent, and equipment costs were brought down by over 20 percent.

Managers were initially delighted with the results of this employee involvement program, until they realized that it opened a Pandora's box of unanticipated problems. One concern was that supervisors and middle managers within TDS felt threatened by the apparent loss of authority. These apprehensions were partly supported as employees—now equipped with productivity improvement skills—began confronting their immediate supervisors with evidence of their shortcomings. As the productivity program coordinator recalls: "Like the sorcerer's apprentice, we had unleashed powers that we neither completely understood or controlled, and first-line supervisors and middle managers were paying the price."

In its eagerness to embrace employee involvement, management did not restrict the TDS study groups to their own department in search of cost savings. With such loose marching orders, the teams boldly crossed departmental boundaries and areas of management discretion in search of improved productivity. Other Calgary municipal employees were bruised and buffeted as the TDS groups trespassed onto their turf.

Finally, the TDS productivity program demonstrated the complexity of a billion-dollar corporation like the City of Calgary. Changes in one area sent ripples throughout the organization and caused difficulties in other areas. A productivity improvement that saved a dollar in one section may have cost the organization two dollars in another area. Unless management thought through the initiative and saw the big picture, some ideas would end up costing more rather than saving money.

The TDS productivity improvement program achieved significant cost savings, yet it also taught the City of Calgary's senior management that even the best-laid plans are paved with unintended consequences. These misunderstandings and unexpected developments are a sign of effort, not a symptom of failure. They are milestones along the road to success, although at the time they may look more like headstones than milestones.

Source: Adapted from B. Sheehy, "A Near-Run Thing: An Inside Look at a Public-Sector Productivity Program," *National Productivity Review*, Spring 1985, pp. 139–45.

Although contingency-oriented theories are necessary in most areas of organizational behaviour, we should also be wary about carrying this perspective to an extreme. Some contingency models add more confusion than value over universal ones. Consequently, we need to balance the sensitivity of contingency factors with the simplicity of universal theories. Moreover, we should welcome universal theories when contingency models offer little advantage.

Multiple levels of analysis

Organizational events can be studied from three levels of analysis: individual, team, and organization (see Exhibit 1–4). The individual level includes the characteristics and behaviours of employees as well as the thought processes that

Exhibit 1-4   **Three Levels of Analysis in Organizational Behaviour**

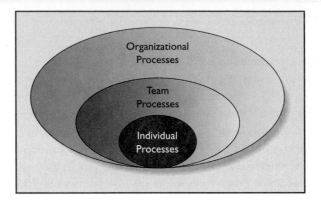

are attributed to them, such as motivation, perceptions, personalities, attitudes, and decision processes. The team level of analysis looks at the way people interact. This includes team dynamics, power, organizational politics, and leadership. At the organizational level, we focus on how people structure their working relationships and on how organizations interact with their environments. Although an OB topic is typically pegged into one level of analysis, it likely relates to all three levels. For instance, communication is an interpersonal (or team) process, yet it includes individual behaviours and relates to the organization's structure. Therefore, you should try to think about each OB topic at the individual, team, *and* organizational levels, not just at one of these levels.

Organizational Effectiveness: Doing the Right Things

Organizational effectiveness
A multifaceted concept in which the organization "does the right things." This includes achieving organizational goals, adapting as an open system to the external environment, and addressing stakeholder needs.

Throughout this book, we will discuss how various employee behaviours and management strategies can improve or undermine **organizational effectiveness.** It seems rather obvious that organizations should be effective and that managerial practices should be evaluated in terms of their contribution to organizational effectiveness. But what do we mean by the phrase *organizational effectiveness*?

Generally speaking, an organization is effective when it "does the right things." But what *are* the right things? Unfortunately, there is no simple answer.[17] Consider Marine Atlantic, described at the beginning of this chapter. The company is close to reaching its goal of total customer satisfaction. It also has dramatically improved productivity, renewed employee commitment, and lowered costs to Canadian taxpayers. Yet, the construction of a bridge between New Brunswick and Prince Edward Island could still threaten Marine Atlantic's future, even though the company has been effective in these other ways. Clearly, organizational effectiveness is a broad concept with many interpretations.[18]

Organizational effectiveness is an important concept because it is inherently tied to every theory in organizational behaviour and serves as the ultimate dependent variable in organizational research.[19] In this section, we review the three dominant perspectives of organizational effectiveness—goal attainment, systems, and stakeholder—as well as three related concepts: productivity, ethics, and quality. Although each concept has its merits, none stands alone as the definitive perspective of organizational effectiveness. Instead, we need to consider all of them to gain a clearer understanding of what we mean by this otherwise elusive concept.

Goal attainment approach

The **goal attainment approach,** which measures effectiveness by progress toward the organization's goals, is the oldest and most widely held perspective of an organization's effectiveness.[20] The most common goals include market share, profit levels, asset growth, and customer satisfaction. For example, if Marine Atlantic strives for customer satisfaction, its effectiveness will depend on the extent to which customers are happy with the company's products and services.

Goal attainment approach
Measuring organizational effectiveness in terms of progress toward organizational goals.

Limitations of the goal attainment approach

The goal attainment approach is intuitively appealing and has been the dominant perspective of organizational effectiveness for many years, but it has a number of limitations.[21] One problem is that many goals (such as customer satisfaction) are abstract and, therefore, cannot be easily or accurately measured. Companies may strive for abstract goals but never know with sufficient certainty that they are achieving them. In this respect, the goal attainment approach often fails to fulfill our need to measure organizational effectiveness.

Second, organizations usually have several goals, some of which are in conflict with others. Consider the goals of Du Pont Canada Ltd. The company wants to create a safe and nurturing work environment for employees, protect the environment, maintain a favourable community image, and be relatively competitive and profitable. In fact, Du Pont's profitability goal is to "rank among the top 25 percent of major Canadian companies."[22] These are noble objectives, but at some point they may work against each other. The company must spend large sums of money to reduce pollution and improve employee safety, but these expenditures cut into profits, at least in the short term.

Another limitation of this perspective is that organizational goals are subjective decisions by senior management. It would be easy for a company to be effective simply by having modest goals. Company A might have a goal of 10 percent return on equity, whereas Company B might have a 15 percent return objective. If both report a 12 percent return this year, can we conclude that Company A is effective and Company B is not? This may be the conclusion based on the goal attainment model, whereas most of us would say that both are equally effective in this respect. Clearly, we need an external anchor to establish the reasonableness of organizational goals.

Systems approach

The systems model, described earlier in this chapter, was introduced as an alternative to the goal attainment approach to organizational effectiveness.[23] By viewing organizations as open systems, effectiveness takes on a much broader meaning. Although the goal attainment model emphasizes organizational outputs such as profitability and market share, the systems model also emphasizes the inputs and processes or means of reaching these objectives. In particular, it considers the organization's capacity to acquire valued resources, adapt to changes in the external environment, and coordinate its subsystems efficiently in the transformation of inputs to outputs.[24]

The systems model also places more emphasis on employee well-being—job satisfaction, job stress, employee commitment, and the like—because employees represent the most important input to the organizational system. In general, the systems approach uses the concepts of survival, flexibility, and maintenance as measures of organizational effectiveness.

Limitations of the systems approach

One concern with the systems approach is that some of its concepts to define effectiveness—including organizational health, survival, flexibility, and adaptability—are ambiguous and difficult to measure. It is difficult to know when an organization has improved its organizational health or is more adaptable. A second concern is that although this approach emphasizes the need to balance inputs, outputs, and internal dynamics of the system, it neither defines this optimal balance nor specifies how this balance is achieved. For example, the systems perspective doesn't help Marine Atlantic's management know how to reconcile conflicts that invariably occur between cost reduction and customer service. Finally, many writers adopting the systems approach tend to ignore organizational outputs in their discussion of effectiveness. Consequently, they might judge an organization as effective because it acquires and efficiently transforms resources even though the final output has little societal value.[25]

Stakeholder (multiple constituency) approach

Margot Franssen, president of The Body Shop Canada, warns that companies must consider "not only the shareholders' desire for profits, but also the needs of the employees, the customers, the suppliers, the communities where the businesses reside and, in fact, society at large."[26] Franssen's statement reflects the **stakeholder or multiple constituency approach,** in which effectiveness is assessed by the organization's ability to satisfy stakeholder preferences.[27] Stakeholders are the numerous groups that have a vested interest in the organization and its activities. Exhibit 1–5 identifies several prominent stakeholders and the criteria that each typically uses to determine organizational effectiveness.

The stakeholder approach to organizational effectiveness emerged in the late 1970s as organizations faced increasing pressure to become socially responsible. Today more than ever senior executives face vocal coalitions that attempt to redirect organizational activities toward their objectives. The stakeholder approach helps decision makers map out the organization's constituents and establish strategic objectives that consider their diverse interests.[28]

Limitations of the stakeholder approach

Stakeholders have competing interests, so organizations need to decide which stakeholder groups to favour. Unfortunately, the stakeholder approach does not provide any clear guidelines.[29] Some writers claim that the relative priority of

Stakeholder or multiple constituency approach Measuring organizational effectiveness in terms of how well the organization addresses the preferences of its stakeholders—groups with a vested interest in the organization.

Examples of Stakeholders and Their Effectiveness Criteria	Exhibit 1–5

Stakeholder	Effectiveness Criteria
Owners/shareholders	Dividends, share price
Employees	Pay, interesting work, promotion opportunities
Customers	Quality, service, price
Suppliers	Timely payments, future sales potential
Government	Adhering to laws, paying taxes, creating employment
Charities	Reliable source of funds, volunteers
Special interest groups	Environmentally friendly, adhere to trading sanctions

stakeholders is an arbitrary decision and that organizational effectiveness can only be examined separately for each constituent.[30] Others believe that organizations have a social contract with society and, consequently, we must discard the archaic notion that they exist only to maximize profits. Instead, organizations are obliged to serve the needs of all society and must try to restore social inequalities when they exist.[31]

A third view is that organizations are most effective when their activities satisfy the most powerful stakeholders.[32] For example, Rogers Cablesystems and other television cable companies undoubtedly pay attention to the interests of the Canadian Radio–Television Commission because this government body regulates the cable industry. However, there is evidence that stakeholder power changes at different times in the organization's life cycle.[33] Banks and venture capital firms may be dominant stakeholders to new enterprises, but lose some power as firms gain financial stability. Thus, it is not always easy to determine which stakeholder has the greatest claim on the organization. Overall, the stakeholder perspective does not provide easy answers to difficult questions about how to allocate scarce resources.

Productivity: Doing Things Right

Productivity refers to organizational efficiency and is ordinarily measured as an input–output ratio in some aspect of the productive process.[34] An organization increases its productivity when the level of output produced increases relative to the level of inputs received by the system. For example, the housekeeping department at the Banff Springs Hotel cut one-third of its supervisory staff by letting housekeepers do their own inspections and training.[35] Productivity increased because the hotel maintained the same level of outputs with fewer employees.

Productivity is not the same as organizational effectiveness, although the two concepts are related. A productive organization does things right, but it might not do the right things. For example, a Saskatchewan manufacturer might produce furniture very efficiently, yet it would be ineffective if its products did not keep pace with changing consumer tastes. Productivity is most clearly related to the systems model of organizational effectiveness, because it emphasizes the transformation of inputs into outputs. The stakeholder approach also considers productivity, because increased efficiency benefits customers, shareholders, and other vested interests. Thus, productivity is an

Productivity
The organization's efficiency in transforming inputs to outputs.

important element in some effectiveness models, but it alone does not indicate an organization's success.

Companies typically use a few *partial productivity* indicators that compare a specific output to an input in a particular work unit or department. For example, Garrett Manufacturing Ltd., a Toronto-based electronics firm, calculates production department efficiency by a ratio of shipments to direct labour costs.[36] Organizationwide productivity is more difficult to measure because the partial indicators must be correctly weighted to form a composite measure of *total factor productivity*.[37] One of the leaders of productivity measurement is London Life Insurance Company in London, Ontario. As Perspective 1–2 describes, the company calculates total factor productivity from its 90 partial productivity measures and is now searching for increased efficiencies in business processes that cross departmental boundaries.

Canadian productivity and organizational behaviour

Productivity applies to individuals, work teams, organizations, and societies. For example, we often hear about Canada's productivity compared to other countries'. As Exhibit 1–6 reveals, Canada has the second highest labour productivity in the world, higher than Germany or Japan but somewhat lower than the United States. However, Canada has one of the lowest levels of productivity *growth* among industrialized nations. Between 1979 and 1991, output per employee in the business sector increased by 3.0 percent in Japan and 2.3 percent in France, but only 1.1 percent in Canada.[38] As you can see, our competitive edge is quickly dulling as other nations improve their efficiency faster than we do.

Canada's productivity affects our standard of living and global trade competitiveness. But what does organizational behaviour have to do with national productivity growth? The answer is that a country's productivity is determined by the efficiency of its organizations. And, in our opinion, virtually every aspect of an organization's productivity can be traced back to employee behaviours. Apart from extraneous currency fluctuations and bad weather, the people working in those organizations directly or indirectly make the difference in a country's standard of living.

Technology is quite properly credited with some productivity improvement. For example, employees at Raymond Industrial Equipment near Toronto can now weld one forklift tractor body in 35 minutes rather than the six hours required before robotic welders were introduced.[39] But we must remember that the robotic welders were ultimately invented and produced by people working in organizations. Moreover, this technology boosts productivity only if Raymond's managers and employees effectively select and implement this technology into the production process. Says a senior manager at E. B. Eddy's pulp and paper mill in Espanola, Ontario: "You can invest as much as you want in modern equipment and new technology, but the reality is that machines are still run by people."[40]

Thus, the essence of productivity improvement is effective employees. This idea has been recognized for many years in Japan and other countries that are not blessed with Canada's abundant natural resources. Instead, they have

Perspective 1–2

Service Sector Productivity Improvement at London Life

For more than a decade, London Life Insurance Company has been the service sector leader in productivity measurement and improvement. In the early 1980s, a special task force developed over 90 productivity indicators throughout the organization. For example, one department looks at the number of health claim cheques issued per person-hour while another measures the correct number of pages typed per person-hour.

A total factor productivity index was also created to track productivity improvements for the entire organization from one year to the next. This composite index required difficult decisions regarding the relative importance of the 90 partial indicators. As one vice-president recalls: "It was amazing to find out what some directors thought might be an appropriate index."

London Life's productivity measurement system soon became the model for other service sector firms. In 1986, the company won the cherished Canada Award for Excellence with a gold medal for productivity. Since then,

productivity improvement has climbed an average of 7.1 percent *per year!*

Although most of London Life's earlier productivity advances were made through improved efficiencies *within* departments, the company shifted its focus in 1990 by looking for productivity improvements in major business processes *across* departments. At the heart of this strategy is a value-added chain analysis that examines the relative value of each work activity for each business process. The company realizes that resources are limited, so it wants to be sure that resources are allocated to the most important activities.

In the value-added chain analysis, a task force carefully prioritizes business processes in terms of the company's strategic objectives, and identifies work activities that could be eliminated with minimal disruption to the organization's stakeholders. By focussing on key business processes and the value-added chain concept, London Life will continue to lead the service sector in productivity and organizational effectiveness breakthroughs.

Sources: Based on S. Warren and T. Weizer, "Beyond Functional Excellence: Organizing for Results at London Life," *National Productivity Review* 11 (Summer 1992), pp. 371–79; P. E. Larson, "Achieving Corporate Excellence," *Canadian Business Review,* Winter 1987, pp. 38–40; and J. Fleming, *Merchants of Fear: An Investigation of Canada's Insurance Industry* (Markham, Ont.: Penguin, 1986), pp. 197–98.

improved productivity by relying on various organizational behaviour concepts and practices that we will learn throughout this book.

Ethics and Organizational Effectiveness

Any discussion of organizational effectiveness ultimately brings in the issue of business ethics. **Business ethics** refers to societal judgments about whether the consequences of organizational actions are good or bad.[41] Ethical dilemmas exist whenever decisions involve personal and social values rather than purely logical reasoning. Indeed, one might argue that all business decisions are influenced by the decision maker's values and, therefore, have moral consequences.

We will discuss the conceptual foundations of business ethics in Chapter 9. At this point, you should understand that ethics relates to all three perspectives of organizational effectiveness.[42] In the goal perspective, the ethical question is

Exhibit 1–6   **Relative Labour Productivity of Selected Nations: 1961 to 1991**

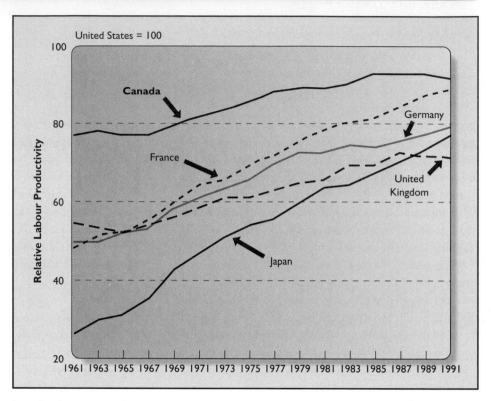

Source: Based on data from U.S. Department of Labor, Bureau of Labor Statistics, Office of Productivity and Technology, *Comparative Real Gross Domestic Product per Capita and per Employed Person, Fourteen Countries: 1960–1991* (unpublished mimeo, February 1993). Data shown here are real gross domestic product per employed person using 1985 purchasing power parities.

whose values should become the foundation of organizational goals. Some would argue that organizational goals should be based on senior management's values, whereas others believe that these goals must be established around societal values. Thus, deciding which goals to assign to the organization becomes an ethical issue.

Some organizational theorists believe that the systems approach to organizational effectiveness is *value free*, because organizational adaptation is logical, objective, and deterministic. They argue that the systems approach seems to avoid ethical debate because there are no moral choices to be made when an organization simply responds to its environment. In reality, there are different ways to adapt to environmental changes, so the systems approach invariably includes values and moral dilemmas. Even deciding whether to compete for market share or drop a product line becomes an ethical decision because the options are not logically precise.

The stakeholder approach is most readily identified with the ethical dilemmas of organizational effectiveness because it inherently recognizes that stakeholders have *multiple values*. Organizational leaders must understand the divergent values of shareholders, employees, suppliers, customers, and other vested interests when deciding how to allocate resources most appropriately.

Courtesy of E. B. Eddy

At the E. B. Eddy mill in Espanola, Ontario, senior management maintains its focus on productivity through employees. "You can invest as much as you want in modern equipment and new technology, but the reality is that machines are still run by people."

Consider the ethical dilemma that Imperial Oil recently faced when it decided to introduce drug testing in the workplace. As we see in Perspective 1–3, senior management had to weigh the privacy rights of employees with the safety and financial rights of other stakeholders.

Total Quality Management

"Quality is Job 1!" "Quality Means the World to Us!" "Leadership Through Quality!" These are just some of the slogans that Canadian companies have been proclaiming to highlight their dedication to the quality movement.[43] Two decades ago, quality was rarely mentioned and almost never studied in organizational behaviour.[44] Today, it is the single most important management practice directed toward improving organizational effectiveness.

Quality is the value that the end user perceives from the product or service. The quest for quality is a journey rather than a fixed goal, and the challenge is for the organization to provide products or services that meet (or preferably exceed) customer needs and expectations at the lowest possible cost, the first time and every time. **Total quality management** (TQM) is a philosophy and a set of guiding principles to continuously improve the organization's product or service quality.[45]

TQM includes several organizational behaviour concepts, such as employee involvement, goal setting, training, and feedback. TQM nicely binds these concepts together, making it a useful vehicle for transforming organizations. TQM has become such an important philosophy of organizational effectiveness that both the Canadian and United States governments have introduced national quality awards for companies that have satisfied several rigorous quality criteria.[46] Many firms throughout the world are also pursuing a set of international standards—called the ISO 9000 series—to demonstrate to clients that they have achieved a high level of product or service quality. For example,

Total quality management
A philosophy and a set of guiding principles to continuously improve the organization's product or service quality.

Perspective 1–3

Drug Testing at Imperial Oil: Whose Rights Take Priority?

Marty Entrop hasn't had a drink since he got over his alcohol problem in 1984. Now the Sarnia, Ontario, refinery operator is caught in a no-win situation with his employer, Imperial Oil.

In 1992, Imperial Oil introduced a tough substance abuse policy in which employees in safety-sensitive jobs must reveal past drinking problems and other forms of substance abuse. They are also subject to random tests and may be fired if they test positive for illicit drugs or excessive levels of alcohol.

To comply with this policy, Entrop disclosed his past alcohol experience. Imperial Oil immediately sent him to an addiction treatment centre in Chicago for two months to be sure that he hadn't relapsed into alcoholism. Entrop was reinstated to his job, but the damage was done. "I have been discriminated against, and this drug testing is an invasion of my privacy," he says. "It makes me feel like a criminal. It's pretty demoralizing."

The Canadian Civil Liberties Association agrees. "This is a form of urinary witch-hunt," argues the association's general counsel. "This issue is basically that the requirement for urine samples on a universal or random basis represents a gratuitous invasion on an employee's personal privacy."

But not everyone thinks that employee rights have the highest priority on the matter of drug testing. "We have a huge public responsibility and we think drug testing is the best way to address it," explains a spokesperson for the Ontario Trucking Association. In recent years, substance abuse has been linked to 20 percent of driving-related deaths among commercial drivers. Other research estimates that 10 percent of Canadians are problem drinkers and that they have three times the accident rates of nondrinkers.

One reason Imperial Oil says it adopted the policy was the number of serious industrial accidents linked to alcohol and drug abuse. One such incident was the Exxon *Valdez* tanker disaster in 1989 that resulted in a massive spill of crude oil off the Alaska coast. It was reported that the *Valdez* captain had been drinking alcohol when the tanker ran aground, although he was later acquitted of negligence. Exxon is Imperial Oil's parent company.

A recent Gallup poll found that 53 percent of Canadians believe employers should have the right to test everyone they employ for the illegal use of drugs. Another 41 percent disagree, and 6 percent are unsure. An earlier study for Transport Canada also concluded that Canadians are split on the right of employers to administer drug tests. Several Canadian companies—including Toronto Dominion Bank and the Winnipeg Police Force—have administered drug tests to employees or job applicants since the mid-1980s. Others are looking at Imperial Oil's policy as a model for the future.

Meanwhile, Marty Entrop continues to face a no-win situation at Imperial Oil. "As part of my reinstatement, I've got to tell the company if I ever feel like drinking and they will remove me from my job. And if I ever do drink, I have to tell the company and they won't guarantee my job."

Sources: W. Gerard, "Fighting Back against 'A Urinary Witch-Hunt,'" *Toronto Star,* January 30, 1993, pp. D1, D4; "Taking the Pulse," *Toronto Star,* November 30, 1992, p. A23; K. Cox, "Mandatory Drug Tests Irk Crews," *Globe & Mail,* May 6, 1992, pp. A1, A2; J. Armstrong, "Drug Testing Angers Workers," *Toronto Star,* November 18, 1991, p. A4; and "Canadians Cool to Plan for Drug Tests, Poll Finds," *Montreal Gazette,* April 23, 1990, p. E8.

Digital Canada's plant in Kanata, Ontario, successfully registered for one of the ISO 9000 standards by applying the total quality management principles described next.[47]

Total quality management principles

There are almost as many principles of total quality management as there are books written on the subject. Moreover, some well-known writers (e.g., Deming,

Total Quality Management Principles   Exhibit 1–7

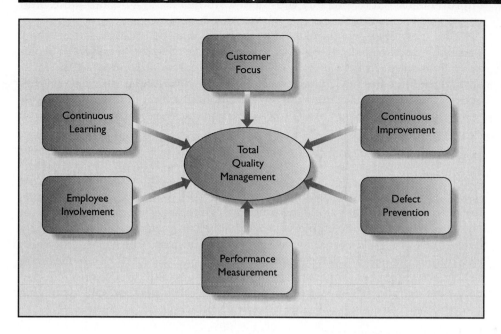

Juran, Crosby) have conflicting views on how quality should be achieved. Nevertheless, most quality "gurus" agree on the six principles shown in Exhibit 1–7.

Customer focus

Quality is always defined in terms of customers—anyone outside or inside the organization to whom the employee supplies products, services, or information.[48] Consider the experience of Standard Aero Ltd., described in Perspective 1–4. The Winnipeg-based aircraft engine repair company began the TQM process with a survey to better understand its external customers' needs. Employees then redesigned work processes and structures to match those needs.

Internal customers—other employees who receive your work—are also important. For instance, employees at Toyota Canada's Cambridge plant identify the next person on the assembly line as their customer. Similarly, all employees in Campbell Soup's production plants now have their own internal supplier and customer for which they are responsible.[49] By being close to internal and external customers, employees feel a stronger sense of responsibility to ensure that the product or service is defect-free.

Continuous improvement of operational efficiency

TQM recognizes that organizations consist of several work processes—such as production, billing, and repairing—and that the efficiency of these processes can be continually improved. But rather than expensive quantum breakthroughs, TQM relies mostly on employee ideas to continuously reduce errors, time, distance, space, and waste in work processes. This continuous improvement process, known as *kaizen*, requires relatively more investment in employees compared to the traditional "scrap and rebuild" approach to organizational improvements.[50] It is also more consistent with the idea that organizations must continuously adapt to changing customer needs.

The results of continuous improvement can be dramatic over time. Winnipeg-based Standard Aero was able to reduce the time required to repair an engine from 75 days to just 15 days. When Standard Aero bid to repair aircraft engines for the United States military, government officials couldn't believe the company's efficiency. They telephoned several times and eventually visited Standard Aero's plant to directly learn about the company's success with continuous improvement.

Defect prevention

TQM is built on the adage that "a stitch in time saves nine." A defect or error should stop at its source, because the cost of repair increases exponentially as the defect moves further along the process.[51] The only way to prevent defects or errors is to make every employee responsible for quality rather than letting defects persist until detected by inspectors or customers. The TQM philosophy also pushes toward zero defects, because even the smallest defect rate may have sizable consequences. For instance, American Express Travel Services discovered that reducing billing errors by one-tenth of 1 percent will mean that 100,000 fewer customers will have to contact the company *each month!*[52]

Performance measurement

Performance measurement is the main driver for continuous improvement and defect prevention. By measuring the efficiency of work processes and organizational outcomes, quality problems become apparent and employees can see how their efforts are reducing these problems.[53] Marine Atlantic, described at the beginning of this chapter, regularly measures customer satisfaction, charts performance in each work unit, and teaches employees about statistical tools to help them find ways to reduce costs and improve quality service.

Performance measures are only meaningful when compared to specific goals (as we shall see in Chapter 3). In TQM, these goals are established through *competitive benchmarking*, the practice of finding and observing companies that have mastered a specific organizational system or practice.[54] For example, Standard Aero set its goal to improve repair time based on information about the best competitor. Similarly, several companies visit L. L. Bean, Inc., to benchmark their inventory control process, because the mail-order company has the best practice in this work process.

Employee involvement

The word *total* in total quality management means that quality is the responsibility of all employees in everything they do. Employee involvement is important because employees have the best information about how to reduce waste and improve product or service quality. Moreover, they are able to identify quality problems and take corrective actions long before anyone else.[55] TQM is also a process of continual change, so employee involvement becomes an important factor in minimizing resistance to that change. Standard Aero's application of employee involvement through special task forces and permanent self-managing teams (described in Perspective 1–4 on page 25) is typical of TQM organizations.

Perspective 1–4

Standard Aero Ltd. Flies Higher with Total Quality Management

Total quality management (TQM) has transformed Winnipeg-based Standard Aero Ltd. from a sleepy 50-year-old collection of machine shops into one of the top three aircraft-engine repair companies in the world. At the heart of Standard Aero's TQM philosophy is an intense focus on customers. "Being close to customers and knowing their needs has been vital," says Standard Aero president Bob Hamaberg.

Standard Aero began TQM in 1990 when an employee task force visited customers and potential customers in five countries. The survey results gave the company the information needed to set some tough goals for itself and begin the process of continuous improvement. One competitor claimed that it could repair the T56 Allison turboprop engine (the major repair line at Standard Aero) in 30 days, far below the industry average of 75 days. So Standard Aero aimed for (and eventually achieved) the impossible: It would repair the T56 engine in 15 days.

To reach this goal, employees reviewed every activity involved with repairing the T56 engine and produced some very impressive ways to redesign the process. For example, a T56 gearbox previously travelled 4,200 metres and changed hands 97 times within the plant. The gearbox now travels less than 900 metres and changes hands fewer than 20 times. This saves considerable time and over $150,000 annually in paper costs alone.

To support the TQM process, employees are now grouped into small teams responsible for a natural cluster of tasks. They have completed dozens of hours of team-building sessions, as well as training in technical skills and TQM statistics. Charts are posted around every work area to give teams feedback on their performance against a variety of productivity indicators.

TQM is not cheap. Hamaberg estimates that the transformation has cost the company $13 million in its first two years, including nearly $2 million in training. It has also required some painful decisions, including dismissal of several senior managers who couldn't or wouldn't change. However, Hamaberg believes these costs were necessary and ultimately beneficial. In fact, he now spends much of his time talking at TQM seminars across Canada and sitting on a provincial group dedicated to promoting the TQM philosophy. Hamaberg also encourages people to visit his redesigned plant. Over 2,500 have done so since 1991. Most come away believing that TQM principles may be the most effective prescription for what ails Canadian industry.

Sources: Based on T. Wakefield, "No Pain, No Gain," *Canadian Business* 66 (January 1993), pp. 50–54; J. Cook, "Standard Aero Intensifies Quality Commitment," *Canadian Machinery & Metalworking* 86 (November 1991), pp. 15, 18; and P. A. Sharman, "World-Class Productivity at Standard Aero," *CMA Magazine* 65 (April 1991), pp. 7–12.

Continuous learning

Employee involvement requires knowledgeable employees who are able to work in teams and adapt to new work environments. Thus, TQM companies invest heavily in employee training and ensure that everyone has continuous learning. Standard Aero's employees receive training to help them understand the TQM philosophy, develop and maintain their team-building skills, and develop technical skills in different jobs.[56]

Total quality management and organizational effectiveness

Total quality management is associated with both the goal attainment and systems perspectives of organizational effectiveness. TQM clearly advocates that organizations have a single overarching goal: to meet or exceed customer needs and expectations. According to many TQM experts, organizations that don't pay attention to customer needs will not survive in the long term. TQM incorporates the systems perspective by recognizing that organizational systems need to adapt to their environment, particularly to changing consumer expectations. TQM writers also devote considerable attention to the idea that organizations transform inputs to outputs and that these transformation processes should be made more efficient through continuous improvement. In this respect, quality is directly linked to productivity.[57]

TQM does not embrace the stakeholder perspective. The interests and values of all other constituents are ignored or, at best, secondary to customers. For example, one is hard-pressed to find any discussion of the interests of environmental groups, local communities, or governments in TQM writing. Although suppliers and employees are discussed, it is only in terms of their contribution to customer values and needs. This oversight is important because it may be the Achilles heel of companies that blindly follow TQM without recognizing the need to pay attention to the interests of other organizational stakeholders.

Total quality management principles will likely dominate our perceptions of organizational effectiveness for quite some time. They have redirected our attention to customer needs and continuous improvement of work processes through employee involvement and training. Yet, there is growing evidence that TQM is not the complete solution to an organization's quest for effectiveness.[58] It is an expensive practice that does not sufficiently help companies in every situation. For example, Wallace Company, the Texas-based industrial distributor, recently came perilously close to bankruptcy even though it won the top quality award in the United States just a couple of years earlier.[59] The cost and time required to maintain TQM may have been partly responsible for the company's near demise. The lesson here is that TQM offers useful ideas for improvement, but it is not a perfect recipe for organizational effectiveness.

Organization of This Book

This concludes our opening discussion of the organizational behaviour field. Now let's introduce you to the rest of this book. *Canadian Organizational Behaviour,* 2nd ed., is organized into five parts, including this introduc- tion. As Exhibit 1–8 illustrates, the remaining four parts conform to the three levels of organizational behaviour: individual, team, and organization.

Part 2 examines the dynamics of individual behaviour, with particular emphasis on motivation concepts. Chapter 2 describes different types of work-related behaviour, presents a general model of employee behaviour, and introduces the learning concepts of organizational behaviour modification and social learning theory. Chapter 3 presents the main content and process theories of motivation. Chapter 4 discusses three applied motivation practices in organizational settings: rewards, discipline, and job design. The dynamics of stress and stress management practices are found in Chapter 5.

Part 3 looks at other individual and interpersonal processes within organizational settings. Chapter 6 describes the dynamics and practices of interpersonal and organizational communication. Several perception and personality

Organization of This Book   **Exhibit 1–8**

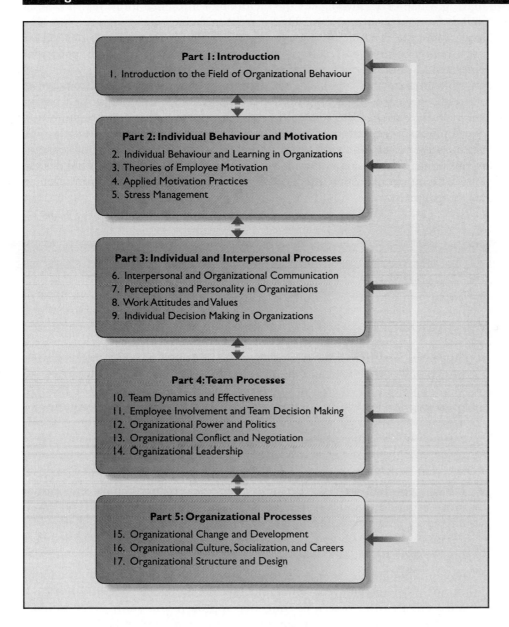

concepts in organizational settings are discussed in Chapter 7. Chapter 8 introduces the general model of work attitudes, two important work attitudes (job satisfaction and organizational commitment), and work-related values. Chapter 9 describes individual perspectives on organizational decision making and highlights three decision-making topics of particular importance: intuition, creativity, and ethics.

Part 4 examines team processes in organizations. In Chapter 10, we look at the dynamics and effectiveness of work teams. Chapter 11 looks at the forms and levels of employee involvement, as well as ways to improve team decision making. Chapter 12 investigates the factors that influence individual power, as well as the sources of and remedies for political behaviour in organizations. We learn about the dynamics of organizational conflict and negotiation in Chapter 13. Chapter 14 presents several perspectives of leadership, with particular emphasis on the emerging model of transformation leadership.

The final section of this book, Part 5, focusses on organizational level activities. We learn about organizational change and development in Chapter 15, including strategies to reduce resistance to change and recent organization development interventions. Chapter 16 introduces three organizational topics: organizational culture, socialization, and career management. The final chapter of this book, Chapter 17, examines the different forms of organizational design, and the contingencies that affect the best structural configuration in a particular environment.

Chapter Summary

- Organizational behaviour is a relatively young field of inquiry that studies what people think, feel, and do in and around organizations. It includes the behaviours of individuals working alone and in teams as well as the thought processes and structural contexts surrounding these actions. Organizations are social entities in which two or more people work interdependently through deliberately structured interaction patterns to accomplish a set of goals. Organizational goals are a desired state of affairs that the social entity is trying to achieve.

- OB concepts help us to predict and understand organizational events, adopt more accurate theories of reality, and control organizational events more effectively. They let us make sense of the work world, test and challenge our personal theories of human behaviour, and understand ways to manage organization activities.

- Organizational behaviour is a multidisciplinary field that views organizations as open systems and tests emerging theories using the scientific method. Most OB theories take a contingency approach and study organizational events from an individual, team, or organizational level of analysis.

- Organizational effectiveness is an elusive concept that is best understood through three perspectives. Goal attainment measures effectiveness by progress toward the organization's goals. The systems approach emphasizes inputs and transformation processes more than outputs. The stakeholder approach assesses organizational effectiveness by the firm's ability to satisfy stakeholder preferences.

- Three concepts related to organizational effectiveness are productivity, ethics, and quality. Productivity is the input–output ratio in some aspect of the production process. Business ethics—the extent to which the consequences of organizational actions are good or bad—relate to all three effectiveness approaches because they ultimately require decision makers to make value judgments. Quality is the value that the end user perceives from the product or service. Total quality management is a philosophy and a set of guiding principles to continuously improve the organization's product or service quality. It emphasizes the goal attainment and systems approaches to organizational effectiveness, but is not a perfect recipe for organizational success.

Discussion Questions

1. A friend suggests that organizational behaviour courses are only useful to people who will take senior executive jobs. Discuss the accuracy of your friend's statement.

2. Describe and diagram your college or university in terms of an open system. Your answer should indicate the main inputs, transformation processes, outputs, and forms of feedback.

3. "Organizational theories should follow the contingency approach." Comment on the accuracy of this statement.

4. Senior executives at Canadian Soup Co., a subsidiary of American Soup Co., believe that their organization is effective because they exceed the sales volume targets set by the U.S. parent company every year. Referring to the three main perspectives of organizational effectiveness, explain why the company might not be as effective as these senior managers believe.

5. How does productivity differ from organizational effectiveness?

6. How is Canada's labour productivity affected by the application of organizational behaviour concepts?

7. How does ethics relate to organizational effectiveness?

8. Senior management at a New Brunswick hospital wants to implement total quality management. Describe the six key principles that would be considered here, and give an example of each in the context of the hospital setting.

Notes

1. J. Schilder, "White Water, Safe Passage," *Human Resource Professional,* June 1993, pp. 13–16; K. Cox, "A Drifting Crew Finds an Anchor," *Globe & Mail,* March 23, 1993, p. B22; and "Smooth Sailing," *Commercial News,* September 1992, pp. 22–23.

2. L. E. Greiner, "A Recent History of Organizational Behavior," in *Organizational Behavior,* ed. S. Kerr (Columbus, Ohio: Grid, 1979), pp. 3–14.

3. D. Katz and R. L. Kahn, *The Social Psychology of Organizations* (New York: Wiley, 1966), Chapter 2.

4. A. Etzioni, *Modern Organizations* (Englewood Cliffs, N.J.: Prentice Hall, 1964), Chapter 2.

5. R. Cyert and J. G. March, *A Behavioral Theory of the Firm* (New York: Wiley, 1963); and C. Hardy, *Strategies for Retrenchment and Turnaround: The Politics of Survival* (Berlin: Walter de Gruyter, 1990), Chapter 14.

6. Katz and Kahn, *The Social Psychology of Organizations,* Chapter 2.

7. J. G. P. Paolillo, J. H. Jackson, and P. Lorenzi, "Fusing Goal Integration," *Human Relations* 39 (1986), pp. 385–98.

8. Etzioni, *Modern Organizations,* p. 1.

9. P. R. Lawrence, "Historical Development of Organizational Behavior," in *Handbook of Organizational Behavior,* ed. L. W. Lorsch (Englewood Cliffs, N.J.: Prentice Hall, 1987), pp. 1–9; and D. S. Pugh, "Modern Organizational Theory: A Psychological and Sociological Study," *Psychological Bulletin* 66 (1966), pp. 235–51. For a contrary view of the role of practicality on OB research, see A. P. Brief and J. M. Dukerich, "Theory in Organizational Behaviour: Can It Be Useful?" *Research in Organizational Behaviour* 13 (1991), pp. 327–52.

10. E. C. Webster, "I/O Psychology in Canada from Birth to Couchiching," *Canadian Psychology* 29 (1988), pp. 4–10; and J. P. Meyer, "Organizational Psychology in the 1980s: A Canadian Perspective," *Canadian Psychology* 29 (1988), pp. 18–29.

11. C. Hardy, "The Contribution of Political Science to Organizational Behavior," in *Handbook of Organizational Behavior,* ed. J. W. Lorsch (Englewood Cliffs, N.J.: Prentice Hall, 1987), pp. 96–108.

12. T. S. Kuhn, *The Structure of Scientific Revolutions* (Chicago: University of Chicago Press, 1970).

13. P. M. Senge, *The Fifth Discipline: The Art and Practice of the Learning Organization* (New York: Doubleday Currency, 1990), Chapter 4; and F. E. Kast and J. E. Rosenzweig, "General Systems Theory: Applications for Organization and Management," *Academy of Management Journal,* 1972, pp. 447–65.

14. L. A. Schlesinger, D. Dyer, T. N. Clough, and D. Landau, *Chronicles of Corporate Change* (Lexington, Mass.: Lexington Books, 1987), pp. 11–13.

15. C. C. Pinder and L. F. Moore, *Middle Range Theory and the Study of Organizations* (Boston: Martinus Nijoff, 1980).

16. H. L. Tosi and J. W. Slocum, Jr., "Contingency Theory: Some Suggested Directions," *Journal of Management* 10 (1984), pp. 9–26.

17. K. S. Cameron and D. A. Whetton, *Organizational Effectiveness: A Comparison of Multiple Models* (New York: Academic Press, 1983); R. M. Steers, *Organizational Effectiveness: A Behavioral View* (Santa Monica, Calif.: Goodyear, 1977); and P. S. Goodman and J. M. Pennings (eds.), *New Perspectives on Organizational Effectiveness* (San Francisco: Jossey-Bass, 1977).

18. J. L. Brown and R. E. Schneck, "Determinants of Organizational Effectiveness," *Canadian Journal of Administrative Sciences* 1 (1984), pp. 29–49.

19. K. S. Cameron, "Effectiveness as Paradox: Consensus and Conflict in Conceptions of Organizational Effectiveness," *Management Science* 32 (1986), pp. 539–53.

20. J. L. Price, "The Study of Organizational Effectiveness," *Sociological Quarterly* 13 (1972), pp. 3–15.

21. R. H. Hall, "Effectiveness Theory and Organizational Effectiveness," *Journal of Applied Behavioral Science* 16 (1980); and W. C. Birdsall, "When Benefits Are Difficult to Measure," *Evaluation and Program Planning* 10 (1987), pp. 109–18.

22. J. M. Stewart, "Less Is More," *Canadian Business Review* 16 (Summer 1989), pp. 46–49.

23. B. S. Georgopoulos and A. S. Tannenbaum, "A Study of Organizational Effectiveness," *American Sociological Review* 22 (1957), pp. 535–40.

24. E. Yuchtman and S. Seashore, "A System Resource Approach to Organizational Effectiveness," *American Sociological Review* 32 (1967), pp. 891–903.

25. A. G. Bedeian and R. F. Zammuto, *Organizations: Theory and Design* (Hinsdale, Ill.: Dryden, 1991), Chapter 2.

26. M. Franssen, "Beyond Profits," *Business Quarterly* 58 (Autumn 1993), pp. 15–20.

27. R. M. Kanter and D. Brinkerhoff, "Organizational Performance: Recent Developments in Measurement," *Annual Review of Sociology* 7 (1981), pp. 321–49; T. Connolly, E. M. Conlon, and S. J. Deutsch, "Organizational Effectiveness: A Multiple Constituency Approach," *Academy of Management Review* 5 (1980), pp. 211–18; and R. F. Zammuto, "A Comparison of Multiple Constituency Models of Organizational Effectiveness," *Academy of Management Review* 9 (1984), pp. 606–16.

28. G. T. Savage, T. W. Nix, C. J. Whitehead, and J. D. Blair, "Strategies for Assessing and Managing Organizational Stakeholders," *Academy of Management Executive* 5 (May 1991), pp. 61–75; and R. E. Freeman, *Strategic Management: A Stakeholder Approach* (Marshfield, Mass.: Pitman Publishing, 1984).

29. J. Ehreth, "Hospital Survival in a Competitive Environment: The Competitive Constituency Model," *Hospital & Health Services Administration* 38 (Spring 1993), pp. 23–44; and M. Keeley, "Impartiality and Participant-Interest Theories of Organizational Effectiveness," *Administrative Science Quarterly* 29 (1984), pp. 1–20.

30. J. P. Campbell, "On the Nature of Organizational Effectiveness," in *New Perspectives in Organizational Effectiveness,* ed. P. S. Goodman & J. M. Pennings (San Francisco: Jossey-Bass, 1977), p. 52.

31. M. Keeley, *A Social Contract Theory of Organization* (Notre Dame, Ind.: University of Notre Dame Press, 1989); E. Freeman and D. Gilbert, Jr., *Corporate Strategy and the Search for Ethics* (Englewood Cliffs, N.J.: Prentice Hall, 1988); and K. L. Kraft, "The Relative Importance of Social Responsibility in Determining Organizational Effectiveness: Managers from Two Service Industries," *Journal of Business Ethics* 10 (1991), pp. 485–91.

32. R. F. Zammuto, *Assessing Organizational Effectiveness: Systems Change, Adaptation, and Strategy* (Albany, N.Y.: State University of New York Press, 1982), pp. 42–44.

33. K. S. Cameron and D. A. Whetton, "Perceptions of Organizational Effectiveness over Organizational Life Cycles," *Administrative Science Quarterly* 26 (1981), pp. 525–44.

34. R. O. Brinkerhoff and D. E. Dressler, *Productivity Measurement: A Guide for Managers and Evaluators* (Newbury Park, Calif.: Sage, 1990); T. Mahoney, "Productivity Defined: The Relativity of Efficiency, Effectiveness, and Change," in *Productivity in Organizations,* ed. J. P. Campbell, R. J. Campbell and Associates (San Francisco: Jossey-Bass, 1988), pp. 13–39; and Etzioni, *Modern Organizations,* pp. 8–10.

35. K. Foss, "A Better Kind of Keeping House in Banff," *Foodservice and Hospitality,* May 1992, pp. 36–37; and B. Van-Lane, "Quality on Track," *Plant Engineering and Maintenance,* February 1992, pp. 22–25.

36. W. C. Tate, "Measuring Our Productivity Improvements," *Business Quarterly,* Winter 1984, pp. 87–91.

37. R. D. Pritchard, S. D. Jones, P. J. Roth, K. K. Stuebing, and S. E. Ekeberg, "The Evaluation of an Integrated Approach to Measuring Organizational Productivity," *Personnel Psychology* 42 (1989), pp. 69–115.

38. Organization for Economic Cooperation and Development, *OECD Economic Outlook* 53 (June 1993), p. 149.

39. J. Southerst, "The Next Industrial Revolution," *Canadian Business,* June 1992, p. 97.

40. "Mills Invest in Their People," *Northern Ontario Business,* April 1992, pp. 1, 3.

41. R. E. Freeman, "Ethics in the Workplace: Recent Scholarship," *International Review of Industrial and Organizational Psychology* 5 (1990), pp. 149–67; and T. M. Jones, "Ethical Decision Making by Individuals in Organizations: An Issue-Contingent Perspective," *Academy of Management Review* 16 (1991), pp. 366–95.

42. Zammuto, *Assessing Organizational Effectiveness,* pp. 29–41.

43. E. Trapunski, "Quality Is the Magic Word for Corporate Slogans," *Globe & Mail,* October 26, 1993, p. B26. The slogans belong to Ford of Canada, Motorola Canada, and Xerox Canada, respectively.

44. For example, see R. M. Steers, "Problems in the Measurement of Organizational Effectiveness," *Administrative Science Quarterly* 20 (1975), pp. 546–58.

45. For discussions on the meaning of quality and total quality management, see W. H. Schmidt and J. P. Finnigan, *The Race without a Finish Line* (San Francisco: Jossey-Bass, 1992); B. Brocka and M. S. Brocka, *Quality Management: Implementing the Best Ideas of the Masters* (Homewood, Ill.: Business One-Irwin, 1992), Chapter 1; and C. R. Farquhar and C. G. Johnston, *Total Quality Management: A Competitive Imperative* (Ottawa: Conference Board of Canada, 1990), Chapter 1.

46. The Canada Awards for Business Excellence was created by the Canadian government in 1984 and includes a "Total Quality" category. The United States government introduced the Malcolm Baldrige National Quality Award in 1987.

47. A. French and J. Nicholas, "Closing the Quality Loop," *Automation Systems* 7 (September–October 1992), pp. 18–19.

48. R. L. Flood, *Beyond TQM* (Chichester, UK: Wiley, 1993).

49. K. Romain, "Toeing the Quality Line," *Globe & Mail,* September 9, 1991, pp. B1, B6; and P. Bristol, "Campbell Changes Corporate Culture," *Food in Canada* 51, no. 6 (June 1991), pp. 22–23.

50. M. Imai, *Kaizen* (New York: Random House, 1986). For a more critical view of *kaizen,* see D. Robertson, J. Rinehart, C. Huxley, and CAW Research Group on CAMI, "Team Concept and Kaizen: Japanese Production Management in a Unionized Canadian Auto Plant," *Studies in Political Economy* 39 (Autumn 1992), pp. 77–107.

51. P. B. Crosby, *The Eternally Successful Organization* (New York: McGraw-Hill, 1988); and P. B. Crosby, *Quality Is Free* (New York: McGraw-Hill, 1979).

52. M. E. Rasmussen, "Measuring Bottom-Line Impact of Customer Satisfaction," in *Making Total Quality Happen,* ed. F. Caropreso (New York: Conference Board, 1990), pp. 55–59.

53. K. Ishikawa, *What Is Total Quality Control? The Japanese Way* (Englewood Cliffs, N.J.: Prentice Hall, 1985).

54. B. Geber, "Benchmarking: Measuring Yourself Against the Best," *Training,* November 1990, pp. 36–44; and E. F. Glanz and L. K. Dailey, "Benchmarking," *Human Resource Management* 31 (Spring/Summer 1992), pp. 9–20.

55. C. G. Johnston and C. R. Farquhar, *Empowered People Satisfy Customers* (Ottawa: Conference Board of Canada, 1992).

56. T. Cothran, "Pioneering Quality Training," *Quality,* April 1992, pp. 13–18; and J. Clemmer, *Firing on All Cylinders* (Homewood, Ill.: Business One-Irwin, 1992), Chapters 8 and 11.

57. Brinkerhoff and Dressler, *Productivity Measurement,* pp. 46–48; and Clemmer, *Firing on All Cylinders,* pp. 18–19.

58. R. Krishnan, A. B. Shani, R. M. Grant, and R. Baer, "In Search of Quality Improvement: Problems of Design and Implementation," *Academy of Management Executive* 7 (November 1993), pp. 7–20.

59. R. C. Hill, "When the Going Gets Rough: A Baldrige Winner on the Line," *Academy of Management Executive* 7 (August 1993), pp. 75–79; and M. M. Steeples, *The Corporate Guide to the Malcolm Baldrige National Quality Award,* 2nd ed. (Homewood, Ill.: Business One-Irwin, 1993), pp. 293–99.

Chapter Case

Jersey Dairies Ltd. *

Jersey Dairies Ltd. faced increasing competition that threatened its dominant market share in Eastern Ontario's "Golden Triangle." Senior management at the 300-employee dairy food processing company decided that the best way to maintain or increase market share was to take the plunge into total quality management (TQM). Jersey hired consultants to educate management and employees about the TQM process, and sent several managers to TQM seminars. A steering team of managers and a few employees visited other TQM companies throughout North America.

To strengthen the company's TQM focus, Jersey president Tina Stavros created a new position called vice-president of quality, and hired James Alder into that position. Alder, who previously worked as a TQM consultant at a major consulting firm, was enthusiastic about implementing a complete TQM program. One of Alder's first accomplishments was convincing management to give every employee in the organization several days of training in quality measurement (e.g., Pareto diagrams), structured problem solving, and related TQM practices. Jersey's largely unskilled work force had difficulty learning this material, so the training took longer than expected and another round was required one year later.

Alder worked with production managers to form continuous improvement (CI) teams—groups of employees who looked for ways to cut costs, time, and space throughout the work process. Although Alder was enthusiastic about CI teams, most supervisors and employees were reluctant to get involved. Supervisors complained that the CI teams were "asking too many questions" about activities in their department. Less than one-quarter of the production areas formed CI teams because employees thought TQM was a fancy way for management to speed up the work. This view was reinforced by some of management's subsequent actions, such as setting higher production targets and requiring employees to complete the tasks of those who were absent from work.

To gain more support for TQM, Jersey president Tina Stavros spoke regularly to employees and supervisors about how TQM was their answer to beating the competition and saving jobs. Although these talks took her away from other duties, she wanted every employee to know that their primary objective was to improve customer service and production efficiency in the company. To encourage more involvement in the CI teams, Stavros and Alder warned employees that they must support the TQM program to save their jobs. To further emphasize this message, the company placed large signs throughout the company's production facilities that said, "Our Jobs Depend on Satisfied Customers" and "Total Quality: Our Competitive Advantage."

Alder and Stavros agreed that Jersey's suppliers must have a strong commitment toward the TQM philosophy, so Jersey's purchasing manager was told to get suppliers "on board" or find alternative sources. Unfortunately, the purchasing manager preferred a more collegial and passive involvement with suppliers, so he was replaced a few months later. The new purchasing manager informed suppliers that they should begin a TQM program immediately because Jersey would negotiate for lower prices in the next contracts and would evaluate their bids partly based on their TQM programs.

Twenty months after Jersey Dairies began its TQM journey, Tina Stavros accepted a lucrative job offer from a large food products company in the United States. Jersey Dairies promoted its vice-president of finance, Thomas Cheun, to the president's job. The board of directors was concerned about Jersey's falling profits over the previous couple of years and wanted Cheun to strengthen the bottom line. Although some CI teams did find cost savings, these were mostly offset by higher expenses. The company had nearly tripled its training budget and had significantly higher paid-time-off costs as employees took these courses. A considerable sum was spent on customer surveys and focus groups. Employee turnover was higher, mainly due to dissatisfaction with the TQM program. Just before Stavros left the company, she received word that several employees had contacted the Commercial Food Workers Union about organizing Jersey's nonunion production work force.

A group of suppliers asked for a confidential meeting in which they told Cheun to reconsider the TQM demands on them. They complained that their long-term relationships with Jersey were being damaged and that other dairies were being more realistic about price, quality, and delivery requirements. Two major suppliers bluntly stated that they might decide to end their contracts with Jersey rather than agree to Jersey's demands.

Almost two years after Jersey Dairies began TQM, Thomas Cheun announced that James Alder was leaving Jersey Dairies, that the position of vice-president of quality would no longer exist, and that the company would end several TQM initiatives begun over the previous two years. Instead, Jersey Dairies Ltd. would use better marketing strategies and introduce new technologies to improve its competitive position in the marketplace.

Discussion Questions

1. **Use your understanding of organizational effectiveness to explain the problems Jersey Dairies Ltd. experienced in its TQM program.**

2. **What alternative approaches to organizational effectiveness would you recommend that Jersey Dairies Ltd. consider next?**

Source © Copyright 1995. Steven L. McShane. This case is a fictionalized composite of experiences in several Canadian companies.

Experiential Exercise

Organizational Effectiveness Analysis

Purpose: To help students learn how to apply organizational effectiveness and productivity concepts to a specific organization.

Instructions: In this exercise, student teams must think of ways to measure and improve organizational effectiveness and productivity in a specific organization and/or specific areas within that organization. The instructor will decide which organizations students will study. This exercise is intended as a classroom "think tank" and discussion activity. However, it can also be a take-home assignment or field study, in which students either collect information directly from people in the organization or indirectly through annual reports and newspaper articles. Whichever approach is used, the following steps apply:

1. Students are divided into small teams (four or five people).

2. Each team is given the name of a specific organization to analyze and possibly a specific area (e.g., teller services in a bank). In class, each team has 20–30 minutes (or the time allotted for the take-home assignment) to answer the questions below.

3. Each team presents its results to the class. These results are critiqued by students from other teams, particularly those analyzing the same organization.

Questions

1. *Goal attainment approach*—Identify the two most important goals of this organization (or area of the organization). How would these goals be realistically measured?

2. *Systems approach*—Identify two strategic resources that this organization and/or subunit depends on to achieve its objectives. What outputs (either deliberate or unintentional) does it return to the environment? Develop one partial productivity measure for this area of this organization.

3. *Stakeholder approach*—List the two most important stakeholders for this organization. Describe each stakeholder's primary needs or expectations from the organization. Describe specific actions that the organization takes to satisfy these stakeholder needs. Identify any conflicts between the needs of these stakeholders.

PART

Individual Behaviour and Motivation

Individual Behaviour and Learning in Organizations

Learning Objectives

After reading this chapter, you should be able to:

Identify five major types of work-related behaviour.

Describe the four factors that influence individual behaviour and performance.

Explain why employee learning is important for organizational effectiveness.

Discuss three strategies to match employee abilities with job requirements.

Describe the A-B-C model of organizational behaviour modification.

Discuss four limitations of organizational behaviour modification.

Outline the three features of social learning theory.

Chapter Outline

Types of Work-Related Behaviour.

A Model of Individual Behaviour and Performance.

Learning in Organizations.

Organizational Behaviour Modification.

Social Learning Theory.

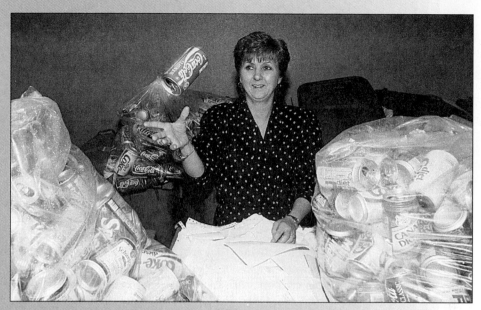

Peter Tym. Used with permission of The Globe & Mail.

*U*ntil recently, Bell Canada employees in Etobicoke, Ontario, were throwing out 800 kilograms of garbage every day—enough to fill their 12-story Fieldway building in two years. Now, under the company's innovative Zero Waste program, they dispose of just 10 kilograms of nonrecyclable material daily.

Bell Canada's Zero Waste program was successful because it altered the causes of wasteful behaviour. Fieldway employees were shown how to reduce paper waste by using both sides of paper, using scrap paper as memo pads, reusing office envelopes, and relying more on e-mail and voice mail than written memos. In the cafeteria, they learned to separate leftover food and deposit it into the appropriate compost bin. The company also installed a special telephone hotline to answer questions about recycling.

The Zero Waste program created barriers to wasteful behaviour. Paper towels were replaced with electric hand dryers in the washrooms. Styrofoam cups were replaced with reusable mugs at each employee's desk. Metal garbage cans at each workstation were replaced with plastic recycling bins. Employees were left with tiny reusable bags to carry nonrecyclables to specially marked bins located elsewhere in the building.

A volunteer task force of respected employees with representatives from each floor steered the Zero Waste program and served as role models. Bell Canada employees were also motivated by feedback about their progress toward the waste reduction goal. The task force weighed the garbage twice each week and publicly displayed these results on charts. The garbage was occasionally "audited" for incorrect behaviours, such as throwing apple cores in the paper recycling bin. Offending employees were politely encouraged to use the compost bin instead.

Behaviour change has not come easily to Bell Canada's Fieldway employees. One employee explains: "It's hard to get people to change the way they've done things; to think about, when they're going to put something in the pail: 'Oh, can this be recycled?'" A Fieldway manager recalls the first week of the Zero Waste program: "It was different, unusual. You're walking around with garbage in your hands, not sure where to put it."

Nevertheless, employees have broken old habits and the daily garbage levels have dropped by 98 percent. Zero Waste is now in place at other Bell Canada buildings and, using the same behaviour change principles, the company is launching a program to improve energy conservation.[1]

Bell Canada's Zero Waste program illustrates how important it is to understand the causes of employee behaviour. The program helped employees understand their role in waste reduction and motivated them to change long-held habits. It taught them activities that are less wasteful and altered the work environment so that it was easier to act in environmentally friendly ways.

This chapter introduces the dynamics of individual behaviour in organizations and employee learning. We begin by describing different types of work-related behaviour. Next, a general model of individual behaviour is presented, followed by a more detailed overview of the four elements of this model. The latter part of this chapter describes the two prominent perspectives of learning: organizational behaviour modification and social learning theory.

Types of Work-Related Behaviour

When studying organizational behaviour, we want to understand why employees act the way they do so that the organization's stakeholders (customers, government, environmentalists, other employees, etc.) are served more effectively. The number of work-related behaviours is limitless, but organizational behaviour research tends to emphasize the five types shown in Exhibit 2–1.

Exhibit 2–1	Types of Individual Behaviour in Organizations
Type of Behaviour	**Examples**
Joining the organization	• Submitting a job application • Accepting employment offer
Remaining with the organization	• Rejecting job offers from other firms
Maintaining work attendance	• Attending work at scheduled times • Showing up for work on time
Performing required job duties	• Completing tasks quickly • Completing tasks without error
Exhibiting organizational citizenship	• Helping co-workers with their work • Participating in organizational decisions • Learning beyond job requirements

Sources: Based on T. S. Bateman and C. P. Zeithaml, *Management: Function and Strategy* (Homewood, Ill.: Irwin, 1990), pp. 516–17; and D. Katz and R. L. Kahn, *The Social Psychology of Organizations* (New York: Wiley, 1966), pp. 337–40.

Joining the organization

Organizations need to attract qualified people to accomplish their goals and serve stakeholders. Recruitment advertising increases the number of qualified people by announcing what positions are available. Some companies try to motivate qualified applicants to accept employment offers through signing bonuses or larger paycheques.[2] For instance, during a recent nursing shortage in Alberta, a few hospitals offered $2,000 cash incentives to nurses working elsewhere so that they would accept jobs in their organization. Many Canadian firms wine and dine university and college students in the hope that they will develop a positive impression of the organization.[3] Each of these strategies tries to influence the behaviour of job applicants.

Remaining with the organization

After hiring qualified people, organizations usually try to keep them. Low turnover translates into better-qualified employees with a more thorough understanding of the organization. For example, Digital Equipment Corp. recently moved some of its computer manufacturing work from the United States to Kanata, Ontario, because the Canadian plant has a turnover rate of just 1 percent per year. Digital depends on this stable work force to maintain on-time delivery and low defect rates.[4] Digital's low turnover also reduces training costs and avoids the expense of recruiting, selecting, and training replacements. Moreover, it minimizes work disruptions and makes it easier to maintain a strong organizational culture.

Of course, companies don't want everyone to stay. They actively encourage marginal performers to find employment elsewhere by freezing their salaries and threatening dismissal if job transfers or demotions are not feasible. Companies with very low quit rates also rely on retirements to create vacancies. This provides hiring and promotion opportunities for new people with fresh ideas and new perspectives. Finally, many firms offer incentives for employees to voluntarily quit during economic downturns, thus avoiding forced layoffs.

There are many causes of employee turnover.[5] Some people are motivated to join another organization from which they expect better financial rewards or more interesting work. Others may be motivated to quit but stay because they cannot find alternate employment. Employees occasionally leave for reasons

©Graham Harrop. Used with permission.

largely beyond their control, such as when their spouse is transferred to another location. One study reported that this is the main cause of turnover among female RCMP officers. Even when their husbands are also RCMP officers, female RCMP officers quit because the organization often does not accept marriage as a justification for transferring both employees.[6]

Maintaining work attendance

Organizations need employees to show up for work at scheduled times, but absenteeism and lateness are persistent concerns to some firms. High absenteeism rates are very costly.[7] As Perspective 2–1 explains, absenteeism at Cape Breton Development Corp. is apparently so bad that it threatens the company's survival.

On average, Canadians are absent from scheduled work 9.4 days per year.[8] Research suggests that most of this is caused by the lack of motivation to attend work. Employees are more likely to miss work when they dislike their job and organizational policies such as generous sick leave reduce the financial penalty of absenteeism.[9] Of course, even with a strong attendance motivation, employees might be absent due to poor weather, illness, family responsibilities, or transportation problems.[10] Lateness is mainly affected by circumstances beyond the employee's control, such as a transit system that is behind schedule.[11] However, motivation also explains why some people are persistently late for work.

Some employers offer financial incentives to motivate good work attendance, whereas others have instituted strict absence control measures to prevent employees from abusing sick leave privileges.[12] To improve the opportunity to attend work, a few firms provide emergency transportation so that employees can attend work during snowstorms. Others have introduced workplace daycare facilities so that employees don't miss work due to lack of a babysitter.

Performing required job duties

Performance standard
A minimum acceptable level of job performance.

Organizational effectiveness is directly related to employees completing their assigned tasks above performance standards. A **performance standard** is a minimum acceptable level of performance. Some employees have specific standards, such as completing 15 production units per hour. Others are evaluated against subjective standards, such as providing satisfactory customer service. These standards may be based on organizational goals, rigorous industrial engineering analyses, or casual supervisory expectations.[13]

In most jobs, employees are evaluated on several performance dimensions. Foreign exchange traders at the Bank of Montreal must be able to identify profitable trades, work cooperatively with clients and co-workers in a stressful environment, assist in training new staff, and work on special telecommunications equipment without error. Each of these performance dimensions requires specific skills and knowledge. Some are more important than others, but only by considering all performance dimensions can we fully evaluate an employee's contribution to organizational effectiveness.

Exhibiting organizational citizenship

Many employees routinely help co-workers complete their tasks and generally contribute to a positive work environment. These activities, known as **organiza-**

Perspective 2–1

Chronic Absenteeism at Cape Breton Development Corp.

Ernest Boutilier, president of Cape Breton Development Corp. (Devco), recently told employees that unless attendance levels improve, the company won't reach its production goals and it could be forced to cut jobs. "That definitely means layoffs. We will have no money," Boutilier warned.

Devco estimates that the equivalent of 300 employees in its 2,300-person work force is absent at any given time. This works out to a 15 percent absenteeism rate at Devco's Phalen mine near New Waterford and a stunning 18 percent rate at its Prince mine in Point Aconi. Absenteeism costs the company $3 million per year, excluding the value of lost production.

Boutilier says that absenteeism is "seriously jeopardizing the whole corporate plan and our entire future. No company can stand these numbers of absentees and stay competitive." He also explains that the Canadian government, which subsidizes Devco's operations, expects absenteeism rates closer to the mining industry average of 8 percent.

The United Mine Workers of America, which represents Devco employees, dismisses the company's absenteeism figures. Although admitting that a small number of workers may skip work without just cause, the district union president suggests that most are off the job due to injuries, union business, and other legitimate reasons.

Devco's president seems to agree that most absenteeism is related to sick leave. However, he questions the legitimacy of some of these absences, arguing that the medical program and worker's compensation system make it too easy to get benefits.

Source: Based on "Devco Warns of Layoffs Over Absenteeism," *Globe & Mail,* July 14, 1993, p. B10.

---

tional citizenship behaviours, extend beyond the usual job duties.[14] They are rarely written in job descriptions. Yet, for most of this century, management writers have known that an organization's effectiveness depends on these citizenship behaviours.[15] Recent studies have also found that organizational citizenship behaviours are important when managers evaluate employee performance.[16]

> **Organizational citizenship behaviours**
> Employee behaviours that extend beyond the usual job duties, including altruism, courtesy, sportsmanship, civic duty, and conscientiousness.

Exhibit 2–2 lists the five general categories of organizational citizenship behaviour.[17] These include avoiding unnecessary conflicts, helping others without selfish intent, gracefully tolerating occasional impositions, being involved in organizational activities, and performing tasks that extend beyond normal role requirements.

Employees are more likely to engage in organizational citizenship behaviours when they feel a strong sense of fairness in the employment relationship.[18] Thus, organizations could promote organizational citizenship by correcting perceptions of injustice in the workplace. Organizational citizenship behaviours are also more common among those who hold strong ethical values, particularly a sense of social responsibility.[19] The social responsibility norm exists when employees are willing to assist others, even when they are aware that this assistance will never be repaid. It is a value learned through lifelong socialization, so organizations might try to hire people with this value.

Finally, some organizations have tried to encourage more organizational citizenship behaviours through training and public recognition. British Airways introduced a training program that teaches employees how to "walk the extra mile" for co-workers and customers.[20] Scandinavian Airlines System (SAS)

Exhibit 2–2		Types of Organizational Citizenship Behaviour
Type of Behaviour	**Definition**	**Example**
Altruism	• Helping others without regard to one's own interests	• Explaining company procedures to a new employee even though this takes time from your own work
Courtesy	• Preventing work-related problems with others	• Informing co-workers when you intend to use the lab tomorrow
Sportsmanship	• Gracefully tolerating the occasional impositions and nuisances of organizational life	• Not complaining about the noise while nearby offices are being remodelled
Civic duty	• Maintaining responsible and constructive involvement in organizational activities	• Participating in potentially important meetings even though your attendance isn't mandatory
Conscientiousness	• Working beyond strict minimum role requirements	• Purchasing coffee out of petty cash for stranded passengers even though this is not normal procedure

Sources: Based on P. M. Podsakoff, S. B. MacKenzie, and C. Hui, "Organizational Citizenship Behaviours and Managerial Evaluations of Employee Performance: A Review and Suggestions for Future Research," *Research in Personnel and Human Resources Management* 11 (1993), pp. 1–40; and D. W. Organ, "The Motivational Basis of Organizational Citizenship Behavior," *Research in Organizational Behavior* 12 (1990), pp. 43–72.

publicly recognizes exceptional "moments of truth" (interactions with customers) so that employees become more conscientious toward customers and other organizational stakeholders. A now-legendary example is the SAS employee who served coffee and biscuits to passengers waiting for a flight that was delayed by bad weather. The SAS catering supervisor refused to provide these refreshments because it wasn't standard procedure, so the SAS employee used petty cash to buy the coffee and biscuits from another airline.[21] SAS publicly celebrated the employee's actions because they went beyond normal role job requirements, yet benefited both passengers and the airline.

A Model of Individual Behaviour and Performance

Individual behaviour and performance are caused by the four factors shown in Exhibit 2–3 and listed below:

- *Motivation*—Internal forces that affect the direction, intensity, and persistence of a person's voluntary choice of behaviour.
- *Ability*—The learned capability and natural aptitude to perform the behaviour.
- *Role perceptions*—Beliefs about what behaviour is required to achieve the desired results.
- *Situational contingencies*—Environmental factors beyond the employee's control (at least, in the short run) that either constrain or facilitate his or her behaviour.

Model of Individual Behaviour and Performance   **Exhibit 2–3**

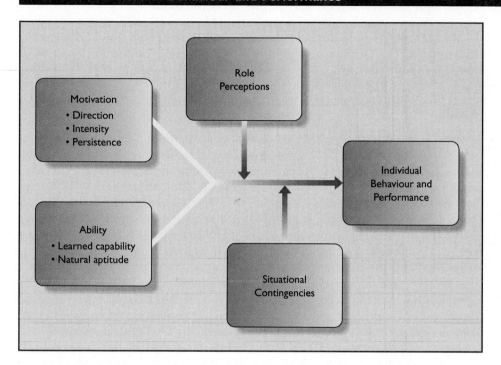

If any of these four factors weakens, employee performance will decrease. For example, highly qualified salespeople who understand their job duties and have sufficient resources will not perform their jobs as well if they aren't motivated to market the company's products or services. Similarly, those who are highly motivated to close a sale probably won't be successful if they lack sufficient knowledge about the product.

We need to understand all four factors to correctly diagnose and change individual behaviour in organizations. Too often, managers assume that poor performers are lazy or that the reward system does not provide enough incentive for them to work harder. This diagnosis is sometimes true, but other possible causes—such as the lack of proper training, inadequate resources, or unclear work objectives—are frequently ignored. If the diagnosis is incorrect, subsequent attempts to improve employee performance may be a waste of time. Let's take a closer look at these four components of individual performance.

Employee motivation

Motivation is defined as the internal forces that affect the direction, intensity, and persistence of a person's voluntary choice of behaviour.[22] *Direction* refers to the fact that motivation is goal-oriented, not random. People are motivated to reach some target, such as arriving at work early today, or finishing a project a few hours early. *Intensity* is the amount of effort allocated to the goal. For example, two employees might be motivated to finish their project a few hours early (direction), but only one of them puts forth enough effort (intensity) to achieve this goal. Finally, motivation involves varying levels of *persistence*, that is,

Motivation
The internal forces that affect the direction, intensity, and persistence of a person's voluntary choice of behaviour.

continuing the effort for a certain amount of time. Employees sustain their effort until they reach their goal or give up beforehand.

Motivation is an important organizational behaviour topic that is explained by several theories presented in Chapter 3. At this point, you should understand the meaning of motivation and note that it is one of four influences on individual behaviour.

Ability

Ability
The learned capability and innate aptitude required to successfully complete a task.

Tacit skills and knowledge
Abilities that are so subtle that they can only be learned by observing others and modelling their behaviours.

Aptitudes
Natural talents that help people learn specific tasks more quickly and perform them better.

Ability includes both the learned capability and innate aptitude required to successfully complete a task. *Learned capabilities* refer to skills and knowledge. Some abilities are learned through formal instruction in the classroom. Other abilities, called **tacit skills and knowledge,** can only be learned by observing others and modelling their behaviours.[23] For example, employees cannot effectively operate a spooling machine in a textile plant simply by being told how to do it. They can only master this skill by watching the fine details as others perform the tasks, and by directly experiencing this complex interaction of behaviour with the machine's response.

People have natural talents, called **aptitudes,** that help them to learn specific tasks more quickly and perform them better. Experts have described dozens of aptitudes relating to sensory capacity, motor functions, mechanical and clerical potential, intellectual abilities, creativity, and other facets of human activity; a few of these are described in Exhibit 2–4. Specific aptitudes contribute to performance only when they are matched with corresponding job requirements. For instance, finger dexterity—the ability to handle small objects with the fingers—is more important for employees working with microsized precision parts at Litton Systems Canada Ltd. than for warehouse workers in the same firm who typically grasp large objects.

As you might imagine, organizations are more effective when jobs are filled by employees who possess the necessary skills, knowledge, and aptitudes. Along with improved job performance, this matching process leads to better work attendance and lower turnover rates.[24] Person–job matching is a two-way process. The employee brings abilities required for the job, whereas the job brings tasks and working conditions of value to the employee.[25] Organizations apply three basic strategies to properly match people to jobs: selection, job redesign, and training.

Selecting qualified people

The most common person–job matching strategy is to select job applicants whose existing abilities best fit the required tasks. Supervisors, human resource staff, and sometimes co-workers assess job candidates through application forms, employment interviews, ability tests, and a variety of other selection methods.[26] Current employees may go through a similar process when being considered for promotion or transfer.

Redesign the job to fit existing abilities

If an employee cannot perform a particular task in the original job description, it may be possible to assign this duty to someone else until the employee

Aptitude	Description	Job Requiring Aptitude
Selected Mental and Physical Aptitudes		**Exhibit 2–4**
Finger dexterity	• Ability to make skillful and controlled manipulations of small objects, involving primarily finger movements	Precision instrument technician
Numerical aptitude	• Ability to perform mathematical operations quickly and accurately	Bookkeeper
Manual dexterity	• Ability to move arms and hands easily and skillfully in handling fairly large objects under speeded conditions	Shipping labourer
Verbal aptitude	• Ability to understand the meaning of words and to use them effectively	Supervisor
Spatial reasoning	• Ability to mentally visualize or assemble two- or three-dimensional figures or objects	Architect

develops the required knowledge and skills. This job-matching strategy is applied at Pratt & Whitney Canada and Shell Canada Resources. Production employees work in teams and are assigned tasks that match their skills. New staff members are initially given a few basic tasks. When these tasks are mastered, they are given more challenging assignments. Eventually, team members develop skills for most tasks in the work unit.

Develop abilities through training

Training programs help employees improve job performance by learning job-related skills and knowledge. Some programs also try to improve employee motivation and role perceptions. Training programs cannot change natural aptitudes, but they may help people acquire skills and knowledge more efficiently.

Training is one of the most effective interventions for improving employee performance and productivity.[27] Yet fewer than one-third of Canadian firms provide formal training to their employees. Among those with training, spending per employee is only one-half the amount spent by companies in the United States. In fact, Canada ranks only 16th out of 23 industrialized countries in corporate training expenditures.[28] On a more positive note, some companies have developed a strong focus on training to improve employee performance and organizational effectiveness. As Perspective 2–2 describes, training has helped Kao Infosystems Canada become one of the world's most productive manufacturers of computer disks.

Role perceptions

Role perceptions are a person's beliefs about what behaviours are appropriate or necessary in a particular situation. In terms of job performance, employees have accurate role perceptions when they understand the specific tasks assigned to the job, the relative importance of those tasks, and the preferred behaviours to accomplish those tasks. Employees have poor role perceptions if they identify the wrong goals or put the wrong amount of effort toward a particular goal.[29]

Inaccurate role perceptions can have a significant effect on customer service and other aspects of organizational effectiveness. For instance, many

Role perceptions
A person's beliefs about what behaviours are appropriate or necessary in a particular situation, including the specific tasks that make up the job, their relative importance, and the preferred behaviours to accomplish those tasks.

Perspective 2–2

Kao Infosystems Canada Boosts Productivity through Skill Development

Brian Dyer can operate a dozen different types of production equipment at computer diskette manufacturer, Kao Infosystems Canada Inc. The 24-year-old senior manufacturing technician also understands magnetic theory, digital electronics, and computer-aided design. It's hard to believe that Kao hired Dyer just four years ago as a machine operator with a high school education and a little experience in sheet metal work.

Bryan Dyer is not unique. Every one of Kao's 155 employees at the Arnprior, Ontario, plant must take three to five hours of company-sponsored courses each week on topics ranging from machine shop to corporate finance. Dyer completed 35 of these courses to get to his current position. The training system is so effective that Kao Canada is now helping its much larger division in the United States develop a similar training regimen.

"Training is not an option here," says Kao's Canadian president. "If you want a salary increase, you have to study." In fact, up to 25 percent of the employees' pay is tied to their ability to pass training courses and demonstrate higher productivity on the job.

Kao Corp., the Japanese soap-making giant that owns Kao Canada, isn't complaining about the cost of training at its Arnprior facility. Partly as a result of this training, Kao has boosted output per employee by 60 percent. "We're competing with companies in South East Asia and we're beating them on quality and price right here in Arnprior," says Kao Canada's president. "We can manufacture and compete with the best of them."

Sources: Based on J. Bagnall, "Kao Now: Why This Diskette Maker Is a Training Success," *Financial Times of Canada,* November 28, 1992, pp. 1, 4, 6; and "Canadian Disk Maker Expands," *Winnipeg Free Press,* November 24, 1992, p. B10.

catering employees at Vancouver's Trade and Convention Centre received European training, in which they were taught that convention delegates enjoy leisurely coffee breaks at neatly skirted tables with flowers. Yet, a survey eventually discovered that the Convention Centre's clients didn't care about fancy tables; they just wanted faster service with coffee dispensed near telephones and washrooms. Convention Centre staff members had inaccurate role perceptions about how they should direct their effort to satisfy delegates during their coffee breaks.[30]

People develop inaccurate role perceptions if they receive inconsistent information from different sources about the relative importance of their job duties. Your supervisor may say that customer service is most important, but co-workers convince you that controlling inventory is the top priority. Personal needs, values, and previous training also affect your perception of the relative importance of job duties, as well as the best way to accomplish those duties.

Employees develop more accurate role perceptions when their assigned tasks are described clearly, they are trained in the most appropriate way to accomplish those tasks, and they receive frequent and meaningful performance feedback. They also need to understand the dominant values in the organization's culture (see Chapter 16) so that their efforts are prioritized around tasks that achieve the most important values. For example, new drivers at Reimer Express Lines attend an orientation session describing the company's emphasis on customer service. The Winnipeg-based trucking company wants employees to realize that their job is not only to drive or repair trucks, but also to support other parts of the organization in the overall goal of serving customers.[31]

Courtesy of Reimer Express.

Situational contingencies

The likelihood of performing a job well partly depends on **situational contingencies.** These are the environmental conditions—time, people, budget, and physical work facilities—that may constrain or facilitate employee behaviour and performance.[32] They are beyond the individual's control, at least in the short term.

There are many types of situational contingencies. New technology dramatically increases employee productivity. Redesigned workstations reduce the amount of physical movement required to complete the job. Each of these facilitators may result in better performance even though employee abilities, motivation, and role perceptions are unaltered.

Although situational contingencies are beyond the employee's control, they may be within the control of managers, co-workers, and other people. Consider Bell Canada's Zero Waste program, described at the beginning of this chapter. By removing the nonrecyclable garbage cans from each office and workstation, the company made it more difficult for employees to casually throw things away. At the same time, by providing recycling bins, washable coffee mugs, and other resources, the company made it easier to engage in behaviours that reduce waste. To the extent that managers have control over situational contingencies, they can help their employees work more effectively on projects, attend work on time, and engage in other behaviours that improve organizational effectiveness.

Situational contingencies
Environmental conditions beyond the employee's immediate control that constrain or facilitate employee behaviour and performance.

Learning in Organizations

Employees need to learn skills and accurate role perceptions to perform effectively. **Learning** is an inferred process, manifested by a relatively permanent change in behaviour (or behaviour tendency) that occurs as a result of study, practice, or any other form of experience.[33] Behaviour change is our only evidence of learning, because learning can't be observed directly. Thus, we say

Learning
A relatively permanent change in behaviour (or behaviour tendency) that occurs as a result of study, practice, or any other form of experience.

that people have learned something when they engage in a new behaviour, such as operating a machine that they couldn't handle previously, or exhibit a previously learned behaviour at a higher or lower level of frequency. Learning occurs when the behaviour change is due to experience. This means that it results from our interaction with the environment and is not due to instinct. Finally, learning results in relatively permanent behaviour change. This distinguishes learning from situational contingencies that cause short-term behaviour changes.

Learning is an essential human process. It allows us to survive and succeed in our environment by effectively adapting to changing conditions. Learning is also important for organizations. Because an organization is a collection of people working together, its survival and success depend on employees learning about the organization's environment and adapting to changing conditions. This is reflected in recent writing about the **learning organization,** the notion that an organization will excel if it is able to tap the commitment and capacity of all employees to continuously monitor and learn about the organization's environment.[34] The learning organization concept directly relates back to the systems perspective of organizational effectiveness described in Chapter 1. Organizations "learn" through their employees, so organizational behaviour scholars are very interested in both how employees learn and how they apply what they have learned to organizational activities.

The field of organizational behaviour relies primarily on two conceptual foundations of learning: organizational behaviour modification and social learning theory. The remainder of this chapter describes these concepts and their applications for behaviour in organizational settings.

Learning organization
The notion that an organization will excel if it is able to tap the commitment and capacity of all employees to continuously monitor and learn about the organization's environment.

Organizational Behaviour Modification

Organizational behaviour modification (OB Mod) is a theory of learning and behaviour change that explains organizational behaviour in terms of the events preceding and following the behaviour. This approach involves identifying and managing environmental conditions that maintain, strengthen, or weaken observable behaviour. OB Mod is an organizational variation of B. F. Skinner's theory of operant conditioning (also known as reinforcement theory, Skinnerian theory, and behaviour modification).

OB Mod is derived from two important concepts: the law of effect and behaviourism. According to the **law of effect,** the likelihood that a behaviour will be repeated depends on its consequences. If a behaviour is followed by a pleasant experience, then the person will probably repeat the behaviour. If the behaviour is followed by an unpleasant experience or by no response at all, then the person is less likely to repeat it. The law of effect explains how people learn to associate behaviours with specific outcomes. These learned responses then become the basis for future behaviour.

OB Mod is also a theory of **behaviourism.** It focusses entirely on behaviour and observable events, rather than on a person's thoughts. This does not mean that OB Mod rejects the existence of human thoughts; rather, they are viewed as unimportant intermediate stages between behaviour and the environment. With a behaviourist perspective, OB Mod does not directly attempt to alter

Organizational behaviour modification
A theory of learning and behaviour change that explains organizational behaviour in terms of the events preceding and following the behaviour.

Law of effect
A theory stating that the likelihood a behaviour will be repeated depends on its consequences.

Behaviourism
A perspective that focusses entirely on behaviour and observable events, rather than a person's thoughts.

A-B-Cs of OB Modification   Exhibit 2–5

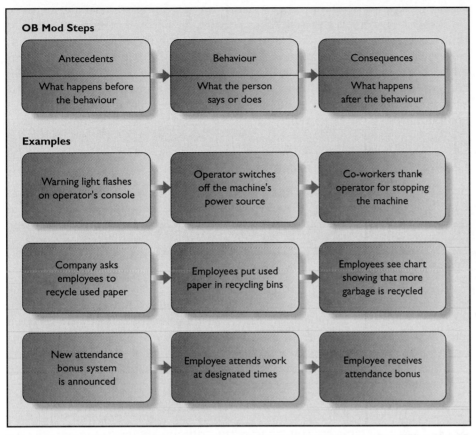

Sources: Adapted from T. K. Connellan, *How to Improve Human Performance* (New York: Harper & Row, 1978), p. 30; and F. Luthans and R. Kreitner, *Organizational Behavior Modification and Beyond* (Glenview, Ill.: Scott, Foresman, 1985), pp. 85–88.

behaviour by changing attitudes; instead, it emphasizes the environment as the source of all learning.

A-B-Cs of OB modification

The OB Mod process is easy to remember with the help of the A-B-C model shown in Exhibit 2–5. The central objective of OB Mod is to change behaviour (B) by managing its antecedents (A) and consequences (C).[35]

Antecedents are environmental cues informing employees that certain behaviours will have particular consequences. An antecedent may take the form of a posted notice about a new incentive program, or it may be a supervisor's request to complete a task. Effective organizational behaviour management alters these antecedents so that the frequency of behaviour changes.[36] At one of Procter & Gamble's plants in Ontario, for example, management noticed that few employees were wearing the protective eyewear required in the area. After consulting with employees, management placed a large sign with the words "Eye Protection Required in This Area" in full view of everyone working in the area. Managers were also required to wear safety glasses during their visits through the designated area. By changing these antecedents, employees increased their compliance to the point where they almost always wear protective eyeglasses today.[37]

Consequences are events following a particular behaviour that influence its future occurrence. Consequences follow behaviour, but they are not necessarily caused by it. Because the law of effect is a dominant OB Mod concept, it is only appropriate that much of our discussion of this theory is directed toward consequences. We now examine the four types of consequences—called the *contingencies of reinforcement*—and the five schedules used to administer these consequences.

Contingencies of reinforcement

According to OB Mod, behaviour can be strengthened, maintained, or weakened by its consequences.[38] Four types of consequences, collectively known as the **contingencies of reinforcement,** have been identified and are summarized in Exhibit 2–6.

Positive reinforcement

Contingencies of reinforcement
The four types of events following a behaviour that increase or decrease the likelihood that the behaviour will be repeated.

Positive reinforcement
Occurs when the introduction of a consequence increases or maintains the frequency or future probability of the behaviour preceding that event.

Positive reinforcement occurs when the *introduction* of a consequence *increases or maintains* the frequency or future probability of a behaviour. Let's say that you decide to call some customers to ensure that their recent orders were received and their expectations were met. Soon after, you learn that customer satisfaction ratings in your territory have increased, so you do more follow-up calls. The customer satisfaction information is positive reinforcement because it increases the frequency of follow-up sales calls.

Positive reinforcers are not the same as rewards. By definition, positive reinforcers increase behaviour, whereas rewards are something that employees desire. In fact, rewards are sometimes given without connection to any specific behaviour. You might be given the rest of the day off with pay simply because the boss is in a good mood. When this happens, the reward might not reinforce anything in particular.

Extinction

Extinction
Occurs when the removal or withholding of a consequence decreases the frequency or future probability of the behaviour preceding that event.

Extinction occurs when a consequence is *removed or withheld* and this *decreases* the frequency or future probability of a behaviour. For example, outstanding employees might stop receiving bonuses if their performance slips. Removing the performance bonus is intended to decrease the behaviours that have led to poor performance. Behaviour that is no longer reinforced tends to disappear or be extinguished. In this respect, extinction is a do-nothing strategy.[39]

Punishment

Punishment
Occurs when the introduction of a consequence decreases the frequency or future probability of the behaviour preceding that event.

Punishment occurs when the *introduction* of a consequence *decreases* the frequency or future probability of a behaviour. The president of Tabufile Atlantic Ltd. in St. John, New Brunswick, uses punishment to maintain productivity. Employees who fall below acceptable performance are warned that they will be dismissed if performance does not improve. Tabufile's president claims that this "tough love" management philosophy is effective enough to get productivity

Contingencies of Reinforcement   **Exhibit 2–6**

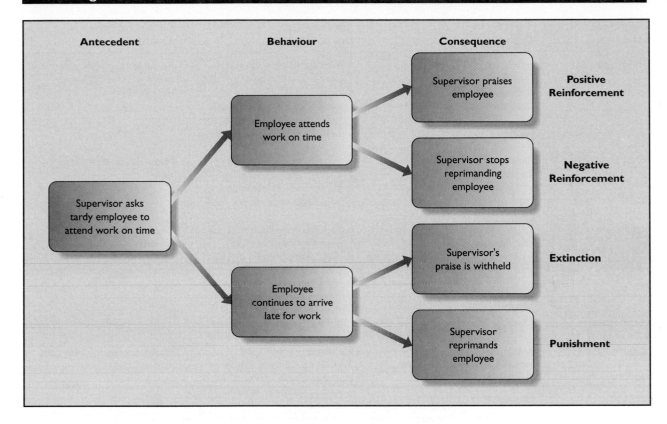

back on track, although several employees have also been fired.[40] The threat of dismissal is a form of punishment because its introduction apparently decreases the frequency of poor performance behaviours.

Negative reinforcement

Negative reinforcement occurs when the *removal or termination* of a consequence *increases or maintains* the frequency or future probability of a behaviour. Supervisors apply negative reinforcement when they stop criticizing employees whose substandard performance has improved. By withholding the criticism, employees are more likely to repeat behaviours that improve their performance.[41]

Negative reinforcement is often confused with punishment, but the two concepts are quite different. Negative reinforcement removes negative consequences, whereas punishment introduces negative consequences. Moreover, punishment reduces the frequency of a behaviour, whereas negative reinforcement increases its frequency. Consider the irritating (and embarrassing!) alarm that an air traffic controller hears when two passenger jets are too close to each other. The alarm's activation is punishment because the air traffic controller is less likely to repeat the behaviour that activated it (e.g., giving wrong directions). The alarm stops only when the air traffic controller takes corrective action to avoid a mid-air collision, thus reinforcing the corrective behaviour.

Negative reinforcement
Occurs when the removal or termination of a consequence increases or maintains the frequency or future probability of the behaviour preceding that event.

Exhibit 2–7			OB Modification Schedules of Reinforcement
Reinforcement Schedule	**Description**	**Effect on Behaviour**	**Organizational Example**
Continuous	Reinforcer follows every occurrence of desired behaviour	• Establishes or extinguishes new behaviour quickly	Praise immediately after every desired behaviour
Fixed interval	Reinforcer occurs after a fixed time period during which desired behaviour occurs	• Inconsistent effect on frequency of behaviour; relatively quick extinction of behaviour when reinforcer removed	Weekly paycheque
Variable interval	Reinforcer occurs after a variable time period during which desired behaviour occurs	• Produces a high rate of steady behaviour and a slower rate of extinction when reinforcer is removed	Promotions; safety inspections
Fixed ratio	Reinforcer occurs after a specific number of desired behaviours	• Same as continuous schedule when reinforcer follows every behaviour. Less frequent reinforcement tends to result in steady rate of behaviour; relatively quick extinction of behaviour when reinforcer removed	Piece rate; attendance rewards
Variable ratio	Reinforcer occurs after a variable number of desired behaviours	• Produces a high rate of steady behaviour; highly resistant to extinction when reinforcer is removed	Praise; successful sales calls

Source: Adapted from: F. Luthans and R. Kreitner, *Organizational Behaviour Modification and Beyond* (Glenview, Ill.: Scott, Foresman, 1985), pp. 56–59; and O. Behling, C. Schriesheim, and J. Tolliver, "Present Theories and New Directions in Theories of Work Effort," *Journal of Supplement Abstract Service of the American Psychological Association,* 1974, p. 57.

The alarm's termination is negative reinforcement because the employee is more likely to repeat that behaviour in the future.

Comparing reinforcement strategies

All four reinforcement contingencies are found in organizations, but which tends to be the best? Conventional wisdom suggests that the most effective strategy is to follow desired behaviours with positive reinforcement and follow undesirable behaviours with extinction (removing or withholding the positive reinforcer). Punishment and negative reinforcement can also influence behaviour, but there are risks involved with these approaches, as we will see in Chapter 4.[42]

Schedules of reinforcement

Besides the contingencies of reinforcement, OB Mod emphasizes the timetable or schedule that should be followed to maximize the reinforcement effect. Some research suggests that learning may be affected more by the reinforcement schedule than by the size of the reinforcer.[43] The five schedules of reinforcement are summarized in Exhibit 2–7.

Continuous reinforcement

In a **continuous reinforcement schedule,** employees are reinforced every time they complete the required behaviour. Continuous reinforcement produces more rapid learning than do intermittent schedules (the other four types listed in Exhibit 2–7). It also results in faster extinction of the behaviour when the reinforcer is removed. For this reason, continuous reinforcement is most effective for employees learning new behaviours. When practising new skills, trainees might receive immediate computer feedback whenever they perform the correct action.

    To reinforce established behaviours, an intermittent schedule should be applied. Employee activities that are supported by intermittent reinforcement schedules are more resistant to extinction if the reinforcer is unexpectedly removed. Intermittent reinforcement is also more practical because it is usually difficult or inconvenient to reward someone every time he or she completes a task well.

Fixed interval

The **fixed interval schedule** occurs when behaviour is reinforced after a fixed time. Most people receive paycheques on a fixed interval schedule because their pay period is weekly, biweekly, or some other fixed time span. As long as the job is performed satisfactorily, a paycheque is received on the appointed day.

Variable interval

The **variable interval schedule** involves administering the reinforcer after a varying length of time. Promotions typically follow this schedule because they occur at uneven time intervals. The first promotion might be received after two years of good performance, the next after four years, and the third after 18 months, and so on. Promotions are interval-based because they are typically received after a period of time rather than after a desired number of behaviours.

Fixed ratio

The **fixed ratio schedule** reinforces behaviour after it has occurred a fixed number of times. Continuous reinforcement is really a variation of this schedule because the reinforcer is applied after every occurrence of the desired behaviour. More often, fixed ratio reinforcers are applied after every 10, 100, or other number of occurrences of the behaviour. Attendance incentive systems often use a fixed ratio schedule by offering a bonus or paid day off after, say, 100 days of perfect attendance. Piece rate systems sometimes follow this schedule by paying employees after a fixed number of production units have been completed.

Variable ratio

The **variable ratio schedule** reinforces behaviour after it occurs a varying number of times. Salespeople experience variable ratio reinforcement because they make a successful sale after a varying number of client calls. They might make four unsuccessful calls before receiving an order on the fifth one. This is followed by 15 unsuccessful sales calls before another sale is made. One successful sale might be made after 10 calls, on average, but this does not mean that every 10th call will be successful.

Continuous reinforcement schedule
A schedule that reinforces behaviour every time it occurs.

Fixed interval schedule
A schedule that reinforces behaviour after it has occurred for a fixed period of time.

Variable interval schedule
A schedule that reinforces behaviour after it has occurred for a variable period of time around some average.

Fixed ratio schedule
A schedule that reinforces behaviour after it has occurred a fixed number of times.

Variable ratio schedule
A schedule that reinforces behaviour after it has occurred a varying number of times around some average.

Employee behaviour is highly resistant to extinction after it has been reinforced using a variable ratio schedule. This schedule is also cost effective because employees are rewarded infrequently using a random timetable.[44] Variable ratio schedules are difficult to fit into standard compensation practices, but many companies have successfully used variable ratio schedules for special incentives. Stroh Brewery Co. dramatically improved safety at a North Carolina plant by offering employees a lottery ticket toward a $125 cash prize for every week that they worked without a lost-time accident.[45] Knott's Berry Farm in California has had similar success with a bingo game, as shown in Perspective 2–3.

Shaping complex behaviour

Ideally, people are reinforced only when they exhibit desired behaviour, but many tasks are very complex or difficult to master. Without some early reinforcement, employees become frustrated as they continually fail to produce the ideal behaviour.

Shaping
The strategy of initially reinforcing crude approximations of the ideal behaviour, then increasing reinforcement standards until only the ideal behaviour is rewarded.

The solution to this dilemma is to initially reinforce crude approximations of the ideal behaviour, then increase the reinforcement standard until only the ideal behaviour is rewarded. This process, called **shaping**, directs employee behaviour from crude approximations up to the ideal form through continuous reinforcement.[46] For instance, a trainee might be praised initially for backing a dump truck anywhere near the desired dump location. As the trainee improves, the supervisor would provide praise only as the truck is placed close to the dump location and eventually only when the vehicle is driven to the ideal location.

Organizational behaviour modification in practice

We informally apply OB Mod concepts every day to help employees learn new tasks and alter their behaviour, but some organizations also apply OB Mod more systematically. They carefully identify critical job-related behaviours and measure baseline data. The A-B-C analysis described earlier is conducted to identify the antecedents and consequences that reinforce the existing frequency of behaviour. These environmental conditions are then altered to reinforce the desired frequency of behaviour. The target behaviour is measured throughout the intervention and the results are compared to the baseline data to determine the OB Mod program's effectiveness.[47]

Marine Atlantic, described at the beginning of Chapter 1, recently introduced a formal OB Mod program to help employees learn more productive behaviours. Terry Ivany, president of the Moncton-based ferry service, explains how the program works in his company: "The idea is for each supervisor and employee or team of employees to identify what is important, to put in place a data system to measure performance, to provide detailed feedback in graph form, to positively reinforce success, and to celebrate the achievement of measurable results."[48]

Other companies have reported that OB Mod programs have improved employee productivity, work attendance, safety, and various sales effectiveness behaviours.[49] This organizational behaviour model also seems to work well in other parts of the world. Kalinin Cotton Mill in Russia recently introduced an OB Mod program with significant improvement in employee productivity.[50]

Perspective 2–3

Bingo! Reinforcing Safe Behaviour at Knott's Berry Farm

With more than 165 amusement rides and 3.6 million visitors annually, Knott's Berry Farm takes safety very seriously. The Buena Park, California, company conducts quarterly safety audits that require an entire day to complete and provide detailed feedback to each department. Prospective ride operators are carefully trained and must successfully pass special tests to ensure that they have learned safe working procedures.

Knott's Berry Farm has also maintained a high safety record through a variable ratio reinforcement system involving a bingo game. Each department receives a bingo card and two bingo squares for each day without a lost-time injury in that department. "If there is a lost-time injury, the cards are torn up and they can start the game again two weeks later," explains Knott's health and safety manager.

When the squares win a bingo game, each employee in that department receives a $5 gift certificate. This reinforcer increases by $5 for every game won up to a $50 maximum. During the first two and one-half years of the incentive program, the company has paid out $40,000 in winnings. This is about the cost of a serious back injury.

Together with the other safety management practices, the bingo reinforcement program has significantly reduced the incidence of unsafe behaviour at the amusement park. Employee lost-time injuries have decreased by 50 percent since the program was introduced. Knott's management has also noticed a marked increase in employee commitment to safety.

Sources: Based on L. S. Howard, "Bingo! Safety at Knott's Berry Farm," *National Underwriter* 92 (December 12, 1988), pp. 17–18; and "Knott's Expresses Park Safety," *Business Insurance,* November 7, 1988, p. 26.

Limitations of organizational behaviour modification

Although many OB Mod programs are successful, some have not been as cost-effective as originally claimed.[51] Moreover, they are difficult to implement according to the theory.[52] Variable ratio schedules do not fit neatly into existing compensation systems, so they are often combined with fixed interval schedules. Antecedents and consequences that are not completely within management's control may offset the effects of the company's formal reinforcement system. For instance, co-workers may reinforce behaviours that the company is trying to extinguish.

OB Mod works best with routine and easily observed behaviours, such as work attendance, sales calls, and seat belt use. In contrast, it is difficult to use OB Mod to improve decision making and other conceptual activities because it isn't easy to see when the reinforcer should be applied. OB Mod is also difficult to apply to infrequent behaviours because the reinforcement effect takes too long.[53]

Another limitation of OB Mod programs is that the reinforcer might eventually wear off. Caterpillar of Canada Ltd. experienced this problem a few years ago when it offered employees one-half hour of paid time off for every week of perfect attendance. When these half-hour credits had accumulated to eight hours, employees could take a day off with pay. Unfortunately, the novelty of the attendance bonus soon wore off and absenteeism rose from 8.3 percent to over 9 percent the following year.[54] Part of the problem here is that OB Mod makes no attempt to explain which consequences are reinforcing or who would be reinforced by a particular consequence. Although we are tempted to say that people value a particular reinforcer and this value depends on one's needs, OB Mod avoids thought processes. In this respect, the model doesn't sufficiently explain all the dynamics of learning and behaviour change.

Ethical problems with OB modification

OB Mod has also been criticized on ethical grounds. One problem is that the variable ratio schedule is similar to a lottery. Employees are essentially betting that they will receive a reinforcer after the next behaviour. Most people don't mind this (in fact, some find it very addicting!), but a few are uncomfortable with any form of gambling. One forest products firm discovered this while experimenting with a variable ratio schedule incentive for tree planters. The incentive gave employees a $4 bonus after planting a certain number of trees, but only if they correctly guessed the outcome of a coin toss. Most employees planted more trees under this payment system than when they were guaranteed $2 for each bag of trees planted. However, productivity dropped significantly for one particular employee group because they considered the coin toss a form of gambling that was incompatible with their religious orientation.[55]

Another ethical concern, according to some critics, is that OB Mod overtly attempts to manipulate or control employee behaviour and treat people as animals with low intelligence.[56] As a counterargument, OB Mod experts point out that any attempt to change employee behaviour is a form of manipulation. This boils down to the long-standing debate of whether human behaviour is freely determined by the individual or is fatalistically determined by the environment.[57] We will not enter this debate here, but continued concerns over the manipulative perspective of OB Mod will cast a shadow over the theory for some time to come.

Social Learning Theory

Social learning theory
A theory stating that learning mainly occurs by observing others and then modelling the behaviours that lead to favourable outcomes.

Although organizational behaviour modification explains how we learn through direct reinforcement, it fails to account for the fact that we also learn by observing the behaviours and consequences of other people. Thus, OB scholars have adopted a broader perspective of learning called **social learning theory.**[58] Social learning theory states that much learning occurs by observing others and then modelling the behaviours that lead to favourable outcomes and avoiding behaviours that lead to punishing consequences. There are three related features of social learning theory: behavioural modelling, learning behaviour consequences, and self-reinforcement.

Behavioural modelling

Perhaps the most important feature of social learning theory is that we learn through behavioural modelling. We observe the model's behaviour on the critical task, then we retain the important elements of the model's actions for future recollection. Finally, we try to reproduce the model's behaviours.[59] This involves practising or role playing the model's actions many times. The behavioural modelling process is most effective when we are motivated to observe, retain, and repeat the model's actions. This motivation is strongest when the model is respected and the model's actions are followed by favourable consequences. In a training program, for example, the model should be someone that trainees respect (such as a senior co-worker), and they should see the model receive positive reinforcement for desirable behaviours.

Behavioural modelling is an effective learning process because it transfers tacit knowledge and skills, such as the baker's subtle actions when kneading dough or the salesperson's proper mix of words and actions when confronting a difficult customer. As we learned earlier in this chapter, tacit knowledge is the subtle information about required behaviours, the correct sequence of those actions, and the environmental consequences (such as a machine response or customer reply) that should occur after each action. The adage that a picture is worth a thousand words applies here. We can see much more detail by observation than from reading a procedure manual. Observation helps us develop a more precise mental model of the required behaviours and the expected responses.

Another reason why behavioural modelling is effective is that it enhances the observer's **self-efficacy**.[60] This means that people gain more self-confidence performing the task after seeing someone else do it than if they are simply told what to do. Observers develop a stronger self-efficacy when they identify with the model, such as someone who is similar in age, experience, gender, and related features. They form a "can-do" attitude when it becomes apparent that others who are similar to them are able to perform the task.

Self-efficacy
A person's beliefs and expectancies that he or she is able to perform a task effectively.

Self-efficacy is also affected by initial experiences when practising the previously modelled behaviour. Observers gain confidence when the environmental cues follow a predictable pattern and there are no unexpected surprises when practising the behaviour.[61] For example, computer trainees develop a stronger self-efficacy when they click the mouse and get the same computer response as the model did when performing the same behaviour. The expected response gives trainees a greater sense of control over the computer because they can predict what will happen following a particular behaviour.

Learning behaviour consequences

Along with explaining how people learn through behaviour modelling, social learning theory explains how we learn by observing the *consequences* that other people experience following their behaviour. Whereas OB Mod suggests that we only react to the consequences of our actions, social learning theory states that we learn to anticipate the consequences of future actions both from direct experience and observing the experiences of others. It is our anticipation of behavioural consequences, rather than actual experience of them, that directs our future behaviour.

Consider the employee who observes a co-worker receiving a stern warning from the supervisor (a form of punishment) for operating a piece of equipment in an unsafe manner. According to social learning theory, this experience would reduce the observer's likelihood of engaging in the unsafe acts that the reprimanded co-worker had performed. Even though the observer was not directly reprimanded, he or she formed an expectation about the consequences of the unsafe behaviour, and this expectation guides the observer's future behaviour.[62] The learned consequences principle has been applied for many centuries in public displays of criminal punishment. Public hangings in the Old West and the guillotine during the French Revolution applied social learning theory to deter all citizens from engaging in criminal or otherwise undesirable behaviour.

Self-reinforcement

As with OB Mod, social learning theory recognizes the importance of consequences to reinforce the desired behaviours. This may include encouraging words from a supervisor or a reward for improved performance. But social learning theory also recognizes that we often engage in *self-reinforcement.* Self-reinforcement occurs whenever an employee has control over a reinforcer but doesn't "take" the reinforcer until completing a self-set goal.[63] You might have authority to take a break from work at any time, but you don't use this privilege until a certain amount of work is completed. The work break is a form of positive reinforcement that is self-induced. You use the work break to reinforce completion of a task. Numerous consequences may be applied in self-reinforcement, including congratulating yourself for completing the task.[64]

Social learning theory is an important concept of learning in organizational settings. Behavioural modelling helps new employees learn a wide variety of behaviours. It is also an inherent part of competitive benchmarking (see Chapter 1) because representatives from one company observe people and processes in companies that have mastered a specific organizational system or practice. Finally, self-reinforcement will become increasingly important as employees are given more control over their working lives and as companies rely less on supervisors to dole out positive reinforcement and punishment.

Chapter Summary

- The field of organizational behaviour tends to emphasize five types of work-related behaviour: joining the organization, remaining with the organization, maintaining work attendance, performing required job duties, and exhibiting organizational citizenship.

- Organizational citizenship behaviours extend beyond the employee's required job duties, such as helping others and promoting a positive work environment. They are most common among individuals who possess a strong sense of social responsibility and feel a sense of fairness in the employment relationship.

- Individual behaviour is influenced by motivation, ability, role perceptions, and situational contingencies. Motivation consists of internal forces that affect the direction, intensity, and persistence of a person's voluntary choice of behaviour. Ability includes both the learned capability and innate aptitude to engage in a task. Role perceptions are a person's beliefs about what behaviours are appropriate or necessary in a particular situation. Situational contingencies are environmental conditions surrounding the job that may constrain or facilitate employee behaviour and performance.

- Learning is an inferred process, manifested by a relatively permanent change in behaviour (or behaviour tendency), that occurs as a result of experience. It allows us to survive and succeed in our environment by effectively adapting to changing conditions.

- OB Mod is based on the law of effect—the likelihood that behaviour will be repeated depends on its consequences. It also applies the concept of behaviourism because it focusses on behaviours rather than unobservable attitudes and perceptions.

- OB Mod attempts to redirect behaviour by managing its antecedents and consequences. Antecedents are environmental stimuli that provoke (not necessarily cause) behaviour. Consequences are events following behaviour that influence its future occurrence. Consequences include positive reinforcement, negative reinforcement, punishment, and extinction. The schedules of reinforcement also influence behaviour.

- OB Mod is applied informally every day to manage employees, but it is best suited to routine, observable behaviours. Other limitations with OB Mod are that reinforcers may have a diminishing effect, the ideal reinforcement schedules are often difficult to implement, the theory does not explain which consequences are reinforcing, and the theory is subject to ethical criticisms.

- Social learning theory states that much learning occurs by observing others and then modelling those behaviours that seem to lead to favourable outcomes and avoiding behaviours that lead to punishing consequences. It also recognizes that we often engage in self-reinforcement. Behavioural modelling is effective because observation communicates information clearly and enhances the observer's self-efficacy.

Discussion Questions

1. Should organizations try to minimize employee turnover?
2. Describe five types of organizational citizenship behaviour.
3. You notice that the sales representative for Eastern Ontario made 20 percent fewer sales to new clients over the past quarter than salespeople located elsewhere in Canada. Use the model of individual behaviour to explain why his or her performance was lower than others' performances.
4. Your organization wants Jack, a new employee in the shipping department, to develop accurate role perceptions about how the customers' products must be shipped and how customer service should normally take priority over cost savings. Describe three strategies that you might use to ensure that Jack develops accurate role perceptions in his shipping duties.
5. What are the A-B-Cs of OB modification?
6. Which reinforcement schedule is most effective for new employees? Which is most effective for experienced employees? Explain why.
7. Explain why behaviour modelling is often more effective than direct reinforcement for helping employees learn new behaviours.

8. **Describe the process of self-reinforcement. Compare and contrast this process with reinforcement in OB modification.**

Notes

1. J. Mills, "Bell Sets Example with 'Zero Waste' Program," *Montreal Gazette,* February 14, 1993, p. C3; C. Mahood, "Bell Zeros in on Waste," *Globe & Mail,* May 4, 1992, pp. B1, B2; "Bell Canada," *Inside Guide,* January 1993, pp. 46–48; and D. Hogarth, "Firms Reap Green Harvest," *Financial Post,* June 15–17, 1991, p. 18.

2. S. L. Rynes, "Applicant Attraction Strategies: An Organizational Perspective," *Academy of Management Review* 15 (1990), pp. 286–310.

3. P. Gammal, "Fancy Lunch and a Job Offer," *Financial Times of Canada,* March 26–April 1, 1990, p. 12.; S. Arnott, "Recruiting Bonus Wins Mixed Support." *Financial Post,* March 27, 1989, p. 9; and R. Walker, "Hospitals Offering Bounties for Nurses," *Calgary Herald,* March 18, 1989, p. A1.

4. J. Zeidenberg, "Chalk One Up for Quality," *Globe & Mail,* October 12, 1993, pp. C1, C8.

5. H. J. Arnold and D. C. Feldman, "A Multivariate Analysis of the Determinants of Job Turnover," *Journal of Applied Psychology* 67 (1982), pp. 350–60; and M. A. Abelson, "Examination of Avoidable and Unavoidable Turnover," *Journal of Applied Psychology* 72 (1987), pp. 382–86.

6. R. Linden, "Attrition Among Male and Female Members of the RCMP," *Canadian Police College Journal* 9 (1985), pp. 86–97.

7. J. J. Martocchio, "The Financial Cost of Absence Decisions," *Journal of Management* 18 (1992), pp. 133–52.

8. E. B. Akyeampong, "Absence from Work Revisited," *Perspectives on Labour and Income,* Spring 1992, pp. 44–54. This rate refers to the absense rate of full-time paid workers in Canada in 1990.

9. D. R. Dalton and D. J. Mesch, "On the Extent and Reduction of Avoidable Absenteeism: An Assessment of Absence Policy Provisions," *Journal of Applied Psychology* 76 (1991), pp. 810–17; R. G. Ehrenberg, R. A. Ehrenberg, D. I. Rees, and E. L. Ehrenberg, "School District Leave Policies, Teacher Absenteeism, and Student Achievement," *Journal of Human Resources* 26 (Winter 1991), pp. 72–105; and I. Ng, "The Effect of Vacation and Sick Leave Policies on Absenteeism," *Canadian Journal of Administrative Sciences* 6 (December 1989), pp. 18–27.

10. D. F. Colemen and N. V. Schaefer, "Weather and Absenteeism," *Canadian Journal of Administrative Sciences* 7, no. 4 (1990), pp. 35–42; S. R. Rhodes and R. M. Steers, *Managing Employee Absenteeism* (Reading, Mass.: Addison-Welsey, 1990); and J. K. Chadwick-Jones, *Absenteeism in the Canadian Context* (Ottawa: Labour Canada, July 1980).

11. J. Wolpin, R. J. Burke, M. Krausz, and N. Freibach, "Lateness and Absenteeism: An Examination of the Progression Hypothesis," *Canadian Journal of Administrative Sciences* 5 (September 1988), pp. 49–54; and A. Mikalachki and J. Gandz, *Managing Absenteeism* (London, Ont.: University of Western Ontario, 1982).

12. P. L. Booth, *Employee Absenteeism: Strategies for Promoting an Attendance-Oriented Corporate Culture* (Ottawa: Conference Board of Canada, 1993).

13. K. R. Murphy and J. N. Cleveland, *Performance Appraisal: An Organizational Perspective* (Boston: Allyn & Bacon, 1991), Chapter 6; and R. A. Guzzo and B. A. Gannett, "The Nature of Facilitators and Inhibitors of Effective Task Performance," in *Facilitating Work Effectiveness,* ed. F. D. Schoorman and B. Schneider (Lexington, Mass.: Lexington, 1988), pp. 21–41.

14. D. W. Organ, "The Motivational Basis of Organizational Citizenship Behavior," *Research in Organizational Behavior* 12 (1990), pp. 43–72.

15. C. I. Barnard, *The Functions of the Executive* (Cambridge, Mass.: Harvard University Press, 1938), pp. 83–84; and D. Katz and R. L. Kahn, *The Social Psychology of Organizations* (New York: Wiley, 1966), pp. 337–40.

16. S. B. MacKenzie, P. M. Podsakoff, and R. Fetter, "Organizational Citizenship Behavior and Objective Productivity as Determinants of Managerial Evaluations of Salespersons' Performance," *Organizational Behavior & Human Decision Processes* 50 (1991), pp. 123–50; and R. Karambayya, "Good Organizational Citizens Do Make a Difference," *Proceedings of the 1990 ASAC Conference, Organizational Behaviour Division* 11, no. 5, (1990), pp. 110–19.

17. P. M. Podsakoff, S. B. MacKenzie, and C. Hui, "Organizational Citizenship Behaviors and Managerial Evaluations of Employee Performance: A Review and Suggestions for Future Research," *Research in Personnel and Human Resources Management* 11 (1993), pp. 1–40. The discussion of altruism is also based on R. N. Kanungo and J. A. Conger, "Promoting Altruism as a Corporate Goal," *Academy of Management Executive* 7, no. 3 (1993), pp. 37–48.

18. Organ, "The Motivational Basis of Organizational Citizenship Behavior," pp. 60–63.

19. Kanungo and Conger, "Promoting Altruism as a Corporate Goal," p. 42.

20. T. A. Stewart, "Do You Push Your People Too Hard?" *Fortune,* October 22, 1990, pp. 121–22, 128.

21. J. Carlson, *Moments of Truth* (New York: Harper & Row, 1987), p. 67.

22. C. C. Pinder, *Work Motivation* (Glenview, Ill.: Scott, Foresman, 1984), pp. 7–10; and E. E. Lawler III, *Motivation in Work Organizations* (Monterey, Calif.: Brooks/Cole, 1973), pp. 2–5.

23. T. D. Wall and K. Davids, "Shopfloor Work Organization and Advanced Manufacturing Technology," *International Review of Industrial and Organizational Psychology* 7 (1992), pp. 363–98; I. Nonaka, "The Knowledge-Creating Company," *Harvard Business Review,* November–December 1991, pp. 96–104; and R. K. Wagner and R. J. Sternberg, "Practical Intelligence in Real-World Pursuits: The Role of Tacit Knowledge," *Journal of Personality and Social Psychology* 49 (1985), pp. 436–58.

24. J. E. Hunter and R. F. Hunter, "Validity and Utility of Alternative Predictors of Job Performance," *Psychological Bulletin* 96 (1984), pp. 72–98.

25. J. R. Edwards, "Person–Job Fit: A Conceptual Integration, Literature Review, and Methodological Critique," *International Review of Industrial and Organizational Psychology* 6 (1991), pp. 283–57.

26. For more detail on employee selection, see R. D. Gatewood and H. S. Feild, *Human Resource Selection,* 3rd ed. (Orlando, Fla.: Dryden, 1994).

27. R. A. Guzzo, R. D. Jette, and R. A. Katzell, "The Effects of Psychologically Based Intervention Programs on Worker Productivity: A Meta-Analysis," *Personnel Psychology* 38 (1985), pp. 275–91.

28. S. Crompton, "Studying on the Job," *Perspectives on Labour and Income* 4 (Summer 1992), pp. 30–38.

29. L. W. Porter and E. E. Lawler III, *Managerial Attitudes and Performance* (Homewood, Ill.: Richard D. Irwin, 1968).

30. B. Marson, "Building Customer-Focussed Organizations in British Columbia," *Public Administration Quarterly* (Spring 1993), pp. 30–41.

31. C. R. Farquhar and C. G. Johnston, *Total Quality Management: A Competitive Imperative* (Ottawa: Conference Board of Canada, 1990), p. 11.

32. See K. F. Kane (ed.), "Special Issue: Situational Constraints and Work Performance," *Human Resource Management Review* 3 (Summer 1993), pp. 83–175; and L. H. Peters, E. J. O'Connor, and J. R. Eulberg, "Situational Constraints: Sources, Consequences, and Future Considerations," *Research in Personnel and Human Resources Management* 3 (1985), pp. 79–115.

33. W. McGehee and P. W. Thayer, *Training in Business and Industry* (New York: Wiley, 1961), pp. 131–34; and B. Bass and J. Vaughn, *Training in Industry: The Management of Learning* (Belmont, Calif.: Wadsworth, 1966), p. 8.

34. P. M. Senge, *The Fifth Discipline: The Art and Practice of the Learning Organization* (New York: Doubleday Currency, 1990), pp. 3–5; and C. Argyris, *On Organizational Learning* (Cambridge, Mass.: Blackwell, 1992).

35. F. Luthans and R. Kreitner, *Organizational Behavior Modification and Beyond* (Glenview, Ill.: Scott, Foresman, 1985); pp. 85–88; and T. K. Connellan, *How to Improve Human Performance* (New York: Harper & Row, 1978), pp. 48–57.

36. Luthans and Kreitner, *Organizational Behavior Modification and Beyond,* Chapter 5; and Connellan, *How to Improve Human Performance,* p. 51.

37. G. Goldberg, "Matter over Mind," *Occupational Health & Safety Canada* 7 (March–April 1991), pp. 56–63.

38. Luthans and Kreitner, *Organizational Behavior Modification and Beyond,* pp. 49–56.

39. Ibid., pp. 53–54.

40. R. Wright, "Motivation Magic Made Simple," *Small Business,* March 1990, p. 80.

41. T. C. Mawhinney and R. R. Mawhinney, "Operant Terms and Concepts Applied to Industry," in *Industrial Behavior Modification: A Management Handbook,* ed. R. M. O'Brien, A. M. Dickinson, and M. P. Rosow (New York: Pergamon Press, 1982), p. 117; and R. Kreitner, "Controversy in OBM: History, Misconceptions, and Ethics," in *Handbook of Organizational Behavior Management,* ed. L. W. Frederiksen (New York: Wiley, 1982), pp. 76–79.

42. Luthans and Kreitner, *Organizational Behavior Modification and Beyond,* pp. 139–44; and W. R. Nord, "Beyond the Teaching Machine: The Neglected Area of Operant Conditioning in the Theory and Practice of Management," *Organizational Behavior and Human Performance* 4 (1969), pp. 375–401.

43. G. P. Latham and V. L. Huber, "Schedules of Reinforcement: Lessons from the Past and Issues for the Future," *Journal of Organizational Behavior Management* 13 (1992), pp. 125–49.

44. K. Evans, "On the Job Lotteries: A Low Cost Incentive that Sparks Higher Productivity," *Personnel,* April 1988, pp. 22–42.

45. P. J. Sheridan, "Rewarding Safe Performance," *Occupational Hazards* 54 (May 1992), pp. 74–76.

46. Pinder, *Work Motivation,* p. 198; Luthans and Kreitner, *Organizational Behavior Modification and Beyond,* pp. 63–64.

47. Luthans and Kreitner, *Organizational Behavior Modification and Beyond,* pp. 75–92.

48. "Smooth Sailing," *Commercial News,* September 1992, pp. 22–23.

49. E. S. Geller, "Performance Management and Occupational Safety: Start with a Safety Belt Program," *Journal of Organizational Behavior Management* 11 (1990), pp. 149–74; R. Nordstrom, R. V. Hall, P. Lorenzi, and J. Delquadri, "Organizational Behavior Modification in the Public Sector: Three Field Experiments," *Journal of Organizational Behavior Management* 9 no. 2 (1988), pp. 91–112; and W. C. Hamner and E. P. Hamner, "Behavior Modification on the Bottom Line," *Organizational Dynamics* 4 (Spring 1976), pp. 8–21.

50. D. H. B. Welsh, F. Luthans, and S. M. Sommer, "Managing Russian Factory Workers: The Impact of U.S.-based Behavioral and Participative Techniques," *Academy of Management Journal* 36 (February 1993), pp. 58–79.

51. L. M. Schmitz and H. G. Heneman III, "Do Positive Reinforcement Programs Reduce Employee Absenteeism?" *Personnel Administrator* 25 (September 1980), pp. 87–93; and G. A. Merwin, J. A. Thomason, and E. E. Sanford, "A Methodological and Content Review of Organizational Behavior Management in the Private Sector: 1978–1986," *Journal of Organizational Behavior Management* 10 (1989), pp. 39–57.

52. Latham and Huber, "Schedules of Reinforcement," pp. 132–40.

53. Pinder, *Work Motivation*, pp. 223–27; and K. O'Hara, C. M. Johnson, and T. A. Beehr, "Organizational Behavior Management in the Private Sector: A Review of Empirical Research and Recommendations for Further Investigation," *Academy of Management Review* 10 (1985), pp. 848–64.

54. C. Sinclair, "Absenteeism's Plague Has No Simple Cure," *Financial Times of Canada,* June 11, 1990, p. 7.

55. Latham and Huber, "Schedules of Reinforcement," pp. 132–33.

56. Pinder, *Work Motivation*, pp. 230–32; T. C. Mawhinney, "Philosophical and Ethical Aspects of Organizational Behavior Management: Some Evaluative Feedback," *Journal of Organizational Behavior Management* 6 (Spring 1984), pp. 5–31; and F. L. Fry, "Operant Conditioning in Organizational Settings: Of Mice or Men?" *Personnel* 51 (July–August 1974), pp. 17–24.

57. B. F. Skinner, *Beyond Freedom and Dignity* (New York: Knopf, 1971).

58. A. Bandura, *Social Foundations of Thought and Action: A Social Cognitive Theory* (Englewood Cliffs, N.J.: Prentice Hall, 1986).

59. H. P. Sims, Jr., and C. C. Manz, "Modeling Influences on Employee Behavior," *Personnel Journal,* January 1982, pp. 58–65.

60. M. E. Gist and T. R. Mitchell, "Self-Efficacy: A Theoretical Analysis of Its Determinants and Malleability," *Academy of Management Review* 17 (1992), pp. 183–211; and R. F. Mager, "No Self-Efficacy, No Performance," *Training* 29 (April 1992), pp. 32–36.

61. A. Bandura, "Self-Efficacy Mechanism in Human Agency," *American Psychologist* 37 (1982), pp. 122–47.

62. L. K. Trevino, "The Social Effects of Punishment in Organizations: A Justice Perspective," *Academy of Management Review* 17 (1992), pp. 647–76; and M. E. Schnake, "Vicarious Punishment in a Work Setting," *Journal of Applied Psychology* 71 (1986), pp. 343–45.

63. A. Bandura, "Self-Reinforcement: Theoretical and Methodological Considerations," *Behaviorism* 4 (1976), pp. 135–55.

64. C. A. Frayne, "Improving Employee Performance Through Self-Management Training," *Business Quarterly* 54 (Summer 1989), pp. 46–50.

Chapter Case

Pushing Paper Can Be Fun

A large metropolitan city government was putting on a number of seminars for managers of various departments throughout the city. At one of these sessions the topic to be discussed was motivation—how we can get public servants motivated to do a good job. The plight of a police captain became the central focus of the discussion:

> I've got a real problem with my officers. They come on the force as young, inexperienced rookies, and we send them out on the street, either in cars or on a beat. They seem to like the contact they have with the public, the action involved in crime prevention, and the apprehension of criminals. They also like helping people out at fires, accidents, and other emergencies.
>
> The problem occurs when they get back to the station. They hate to do the paperwork, and because they dislike it, the job is frequently put off or done inadequately. This lack of attention hurts us later on when we get to court. We need clear, factual reports. They must be highly detailed and unambiguous. As soon as one

part of a report is shown to be inadequate or incorrect, the rest of the report is suspect. Poor reporting probably causes us to lose more cases than any other factor.

I just don't know how to motivate them to do a better job. We're in a budget crunch and I have absolutely no financial rewards at my disposal. In fact, we'll probably have to lay some people off in the near future. It's hard for me to make the job interesting and challenging because it isn't—it's boring, routine paperwork, and there isn't much you can do about it.

Finally, I can't say to them that their promotions will hinge on the excellence of their paperwork. First of all, they know it's not true. If their performance is adequate, most are more likely to get promoted just by staying on the force a certain number of years than for some specific outstanding act. Second, they were trained to do the job they do out in the streets, not to fill out forms. All through their career it is the arrests and interventions that get noticed.

Some people have suggested a number of things, like using conviction records as a performance criterion. However, we know that's not fair—too many other things are involved. Bad paperwork increases the chance that you lose in court, but good paperwork doesn't necessarily mean you'll win. We tried setting up team competitions based upon the excellence of the reports, but the officers caught on to that pretty quickly. No one was getting any type of reward for winning the competition, and they figured why should they bust a gut when there was no payoff.

I just don't know what to do.

Discussion Questions

1. **What performance problems is the captain trying to correct?**

2. **Use the performance model to diagnose the possible causes of this unacceptable performance.**

3. **Has the captain considered all possible solutions to the problem? If not, what else might he do?**

Source: T. R. Mitchell and J. R. Larson, Jr., *People in Organizations,* 3rd ed. (New York: McGraw-Hill, 1987), p. 184.

Experiential Exercise

Performance Standards Exercise

Purpose: This exercise is designed to help you understand how specific behaviours are associated with job performance and how people may have different standards or expectations about which behaviours constitute good performance.

Instructions: The instructor will identify a job that all students know about, such as a bank teller or a professor. Students will focus on one performance dimension, such as service skills among cafeteria cashiers, technical skills of computer lab technicians, or lecture skills of professors. Whichever performance dimension or job is chosen for your team, the following steps apply:

Step 1: Students are placed into teams (preferably four or five people).

Step 2: Working alone, each student writes down five specific examples of effective or ineffective behaviour for the selected job and performance dimension. Each incident should clearly state the critical behaviour that made it effective or ineffective (e.g., "Instructor sat at desk during entire lecture;" "Bank teller chewed gum while talking to client"). The statements should describe behaviours, not attitudes or evaluations.

Step 3: Members of each team jointly number each statement and delete duplicates. Each behaviour statement is read aloud to the team and, without any discussion, each team member privately rates the statement using the 7-point behaviourally anchored rating scale accompanying this exercise. When all statements have been rated, the ratings for each statement are compared. Discard statements about which team members significantly disagree (such as when ratings are 2 or 3 points apart).

Step 4: Average the ratings of the remaining statements and write them at the appropriate location on the accompanying 7-point behaviourally anchored rating scale. An arrow or line should point to the exact place on the scale where the statement's average score is located. (You may want to put the 7-point rating scale and your results on an overhead transparency or flip chart if your results will be shown to the class.)

Step 5: Each team presents its results to the class and describes areas of disagreement. Other class members will discuss their agreement or disagreement with each team's results, including the quality of the statements (e.g., behaviour-oriented) and their location on the performance scale.

Performance Rating Scale

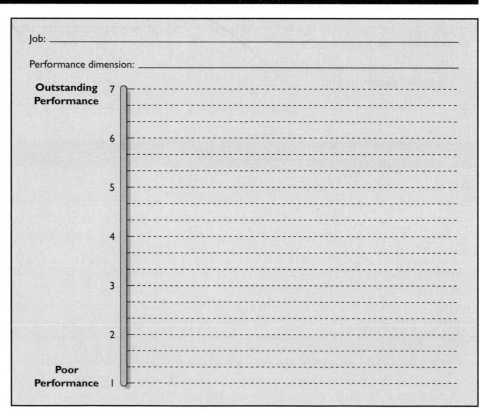

Theories of Employee Motivation

Learning Objectives

After reading this chapter, you should be able to:

Discuss the practical implications of content motivation theories.

Explain how each component of expectancy theory influences work effort.

Discuss the management implications of expectancy theory.

Describe the five characteristics of effective goal setting.

Describe the five characteristics of effective feedback.

Explain how employees react to inequity.

Chapter Outline

The Motivation Process: A Basic Framework.

Content Theories of Motivation.

Expectancy Theory of Motivation.

Goal Setting.

Providing Effective Feedback.

Equity Theory.

Are Motivation Theories Culture Bound?

Employee Motivation: A Final Word.

Darren Pittman, Clark Photographic, Halifax. Used with permission.

With more than 100 stores and $100 million annual sales, The Body Shop Canada thrives on a vision that businesses should maintain ethical standards while earning profits. According to Margot Franssen, president of The Body Shop Canada, this means linking business enterprise with customer needs, community interests, and environmental concerns.

To translate this vision into practice, The Body Shop relies on employees who are motivated to serve customers and the larger community. The retailer pays team-based performance bonuses rather than individual commissions "to avoid the cruising-shark sales approach." This provides better customer service and ensures that people entering the store aren't pressured into making purchases they don't want. But Franssen believes that employees must be motivated by more than just financial incentives: "As an employer, it is up to me to offer my employees the chance to have a meaningful job—a job that will not only support their families and themselves, but a job that will support their soul and their spirit."

Employees experience this meaningfulness through The Body Shop's many worldwide social activities, such as trading fairly with Third World countries and using environmentally correct corporate practices. Closer to home, each Body Shop Canada store initiates a community project on environmental or social causes and sets aside at least four hours per week for staff members to work on the project. Lisa Crowe and other Body Shop employees in Halifax work at soup kitchens and help out at shelters for homeless youth in the community. In Montreal, employees work with Comité SIDA Aide Montréal, the city's oldest AIDS organization, to distribute information about the disease or serve as buddies for people with AIDS.

The environmental campaigns, fair trading practices, and community projects have a powerful effect on employee motivation at The Body Shop Canada. As Franssen explains: "We want [employees] to believe that they are doing something important.... It is a way for people to bond to the company, and what it produces is a sense of passion you simply will not find in a normal business."[1]

The Body Shop is a vanguard organization for its corporate philosophy and ability to motivate employees. It is able to build an enthusiastic work force through more than just financial rewards. This chapter introduces the prominent theories of motivation in organizational settings. Some theories help us understand the basic needs that motivate employees; others explain how people are motivated to choose different courses of action. We need to understand and apply all of them to maximize employee motivation and performance.

The Motivation Process: A Basic Framework

Needs
Deficiencies that energize or trigger behaviours to satisfy those needs.

Exhibit 3–1 provides a useful framework for understanding the key elements of employee motivation. In most contemporary theories, the process of employee motivation begins with individual needs. **Needs** are deficiencies that energize or trigger behaviours to satisfy those needs. Some needs are physiological, such as the need for shelter, whereas others are psychological or sociological, such as the need for friendship. Unfulfilled needs create a tension that triggers a search for ways to reduce or satisfy those needs. The stronger a person's needs, the more motivated he or she will be to satisfy those needs. Conversely, a satisfied need does not motivate.

Employees identify relevant goals for need gratification and engage in behaviours they hope will satisfy those needs. Goal accomplishment might result in immediate need gratification, such as the feeling of achievement. Other needs are fulfilled indirectly, such as the greater financial security someone feels after receiving a pay increase for consistently good performance. Finally, employees assess the extent to which their dominant need has been satisfied. If a need deficiency still exists, then the motivation cycle is repeated using other goals and behaviours that might fulfill the deficient need more effectively. If the particular need is satisfied, then employees redirect their attention to other needs that are deficient.

Content theories of motivation
Theories that attempt to explain how people have different needs at different times.

Process theories of motivation
Theories that describe the processes through which needs are translated into behaviour.

There are essentially two types of motivation theories. **Content theories of motivation** attempt to explain why people have different needs at different times. **Process theories of motivation** describe the processes through which needs are translated into behaviour. These models explain how people choose goal-directed behaviours to satisfy their needs, but they do not directly explain how need deficiencies emerge.

Content Theories of Motivation

The earliest motivation research tried to understand how people develop need deficiencies. Dozens of different needs have been identified over the years, and

The Employee Motivation Process   **Exhibit 3–1**

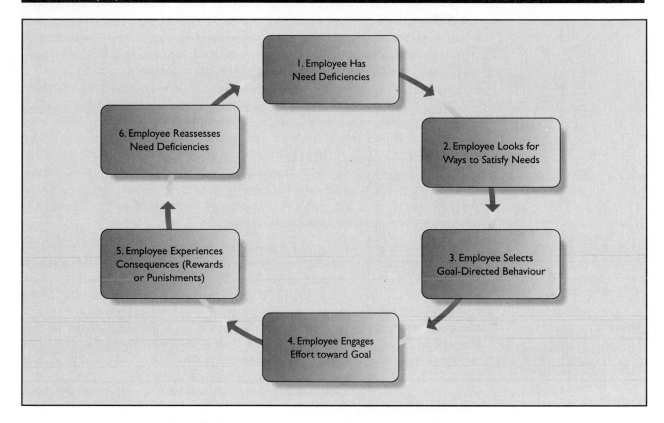

several theories have emerged to explain why people have different needs at different times. The four best-known content motivation theories are Maslow's needs hierarchy, Alderfer's ERG theory, Herzberg's hygiene-motivator theory, and McClelland's theory of learned needs. The first three view needs as instinctive characteristics of the person that may be arranged in a hierarchy of importance. In contrast, McClelland's research has looked at how people develop secondary needs or drives through learning.

Maslow's needs hierarchy theory

Abraham Maslow's **needs hierarchy theory** consists of five basic human needs placed in a hierarchy. The lowest three needs—physiological, safety, and belongingness—are known as *deficiency needs* because they are necessary for the person's basic comfort. Esteem and self-actualization needs are *growth needs* because they deal with personal growth and development.[2]

- *Physiological needs*—People need to satisfy their biological needs for food, air, water, and shelter. Organizations help fulfill these needs by providing comfortable working conditions, adequate wages, and reasonable work hours.

- *Safety needs*—These include the need for a secure and stable environment and the absence of pain, threat, or illness. Employers may help satisfy safety

Needs hierarchy theory
Maslow's content theory of motivation, stating that people have a hierarchy of five basic needs—physiological, safety, belongingness, esteem, and self-actualization—and that as a lower need becomes gratified, individuals become motivated to fulfill the next higher need.

needs by providing healthier and safer working conditions, avoiding the threat of layoffs, and providing pensions and other income protection plans.

- *Belongingness needs*—The needs for love, affection, and interaction with other people all fall into the belongingness category. Employees fulfill these needs through their daily interactions with co-workers, customers, and others.

- *Esteem needs*—Esteem needs include self-esteem through personal achievement as well as social esteem through recognition and respect from others. Many companies motivate employees through this need by publicly recognizing high performers through newsletters and award ceremonies.

- *Self-actualization needs*—The highest need level, according to Maslow, is the need for self-fulfillment—a sense that the person's potential has been realized. Several motivational strategies described in this book, including goal setting and job redesign, are based on this objective of helping employees experience self-actualization.

Satisfaction-progression process
A basic premise in Maslow's needs hierarchy theory that people become increasingly motivated to fulfill a higher need as a lower need is gratified.

Maslow recognized that an employee's behaviour is motivated simultaneously by several need levels, but one need level dominates over the others at any given time. As the person begins to satisfy the dominant need, the next higher need in the hierarchy slowly becomes the most important. This is known as the **satisfaction-progression process.** Physiological needs are initially the most important, and people are motivated to satisfy them first. As they become gratified, safety needs emerge as the strongest motivator. As safety needs are satisfied, belongingness needs become most important, and so forth. The exception to the satisfaction-progression process is self-actualization; as people experience self-actualization, they desire more rather than less of this need.

Maslow's needs hierarchy is one of the best-known organizational behaviour theories, but the model is much too rigid to explain the dynamic and unstable characteristics of employee needs.[3] Researchers have found that individual needs do not cluster neatly around the five categories described in the model. Moreover, gratification of one need level does not necessarily lead to increased motivation to satisfy the next higher need level. Overall, Maslow's model provides an important introduction to employee needs and has laid an important foundation for other need theories, but its value for predicting employee needs is questionable.

Alderfer's ERG theory

ERG theory
Alderfer's content theory of motivation, stating that there are three broad human needs: existence, relatedness, and growth.

ERG theory was developed by Clayton Alderfer to overcome the problems with Maslow's needs hierarchy theory. ERG theory groups human needs into three broad categories: existence, relatedness, and growth. (Notice that the theory's name is based on the first letter of each need.) As we can see in Exhibit 3–2, existence needs correspond to Maslow's physiological and physically related safety needs. Relatedness needs refer to Maslow's interpersonal safety, belongingness, and social esteem needs. Growth needs correspond to Maslow's self-esteem and self-actualization needs.[4]

ERG theory also applies the satisfaction-progression process. As existence needs are satisfied, relatedness needs become more important. Unlike Maslow's

Comparison of Maslow's, Alderfer's, and Herzberg's Content Theories   **Exhibit 3–2**

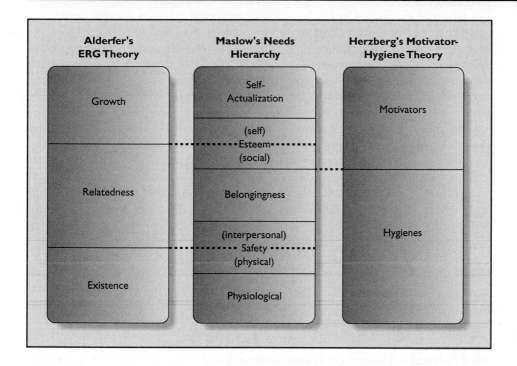

model, however, ERG theory includes a **frustration-regression process,** whereby those who are unable to satisfy a higher need become frustrated and regress back to the next lower need level. For example, if existence and relatedness needs have been satisfied but growth need fulfillment has been blocked, the individual will become frustrated and relatedness needs will again emerge as the dominant source of motivation.

Frustration-regression process
A basic premise in ERG theory that people who are unable to satisfy a higher need become frustrated and regress back to the next lower need level.

Human needs cluster more neatly around the three ERG categories than Maslow's five categories. The combined processes of satisfaction-progression and frustration-regression also provide a more accurate explanation of why employee needs change over time. Although relatively few studies have tested ERG theory, the available evidence suggests that the model reflects the dynamics of employee needs.

Herzberg's motivator-hygiene theory

Frederick Herzberg's **motivator-hygiene theory** differs from Maslow's and Alderfer's needs hierarchy models because it does not suggest that people change their needs over time. Instead, Herzberg proposes that employees are primarily motivated by characteristics of the work itself, such as recognition, responsibility, advancement, achievement, and personal growth. These factors are called *motivators,* because employees experience job satisfaction when they are received and are therefore motivated to obtain them. In contrast, factors extrinsic to the work, called *hygienes,* affect the extent to which employees feel job dissatisfaction. Hygienes include job security, working conditions, company policies,

Motivator-hygiene theory
Herzberg's content theory of motivation, stating that employees are motivated by characteristics of the work itself (called *motivators*) rather than the work context (called *hygienes*).

co-worker relations, and supervisor relations. Improving hygienes will reduce job dissatisfaction, but they will have almost no effect on job satisfaction or employee motivation.[5]

The two categories in motivator-hygiene theory parallel the deficiency and growth need categories that Maslow identified (see Exhibit 3–2). However, Herzberg's theory does not view job satisfaction and dissatisfaction as opposites. Improving motivators increases job satisfaction, but it does not decrease job dissatisfaction. Improving hygienes reduces job dissatisfaction, but it does not increase job satisfaction. Moreover, job satisfaction is produced by work content, whereas job dissatisfaction is produced by the work context. Thus, Herzberg's theory differs from the previous two hierarchy models by suggesting that a person's growth needs represent the only source of motivation.

Motivator-hygiene theory provides a unique perspective of employee motivation, but it suffers from several methodological and conceptual problems. More important, research does not support the notion that work content is the only source of employee motivation.[6] Nevertheless, Herzberg's theory is worth mentioning because it casts a spotlight on job content as a dominant source of employee motivation. Before motivator-hygiene theory was introduced, many researchers were preoccupied with the physical and social contexts of work. Few writers had addressed the idea that employees may be motivated by the work itself. Motivator-hygiene theory changed this trend and has led to considerable study into the motivational potential of jobs.[7] We will look more closely at motivational aspects of job design in Chapter 4.

McClelland's theory of learned needs

The content motivation models described so far look at the individual's primary needs and their relative importance in life. However, people also have secondary needs or drives that are learned and reinforced rather than instinctive. These drives are nurtured early in life through children's books, parental styles, and social norms. David McClelland has devoted his career to studying three secondary needs that he considers particularly important sources of motivation:[8]

- *Need for achievement*—A desire to accomplish moderately challenging performance goals, be successful in competitive situations, assume personal responsibility for work (rather than delegating it to others), and receive immediate feedback.

- *Need for power*—A desire to control one's environment, including people and material resources. Some people have a high *socialized power* need in which they seek power to help others, such as improving society or increasing organizational effectiveness. Those with a strong *personal power* need seek power so that they can revel in their power and use it to advance their career and other personal interests.

- *Need for affiliation*—A desire to seek approval from others, conform to their wishes and expectations, and avoid conflict and confrontation. People with a strong affiliation need want to form positive relationships with others, even if this results in lower job performance.

McClelland's research suggests that people with a high need for achievement make better entrepreneurs because they are able to work alone toward the challenging goal of establishing a new business. However, they tend to perform less well as senior executives because these posts require incumbents to delegate work. The best managers are those with a moderately high need for socialized power because they use power to achieve organizational objectives. Effective managers must also have a fairly low need for affiliation so that their decisions and actions are influenced more by the need to accomplish organizational objectives than by a personal need for approval.[9]

Learning needs

Because achievement, power, and affiliation needs are learned rather than instinctive, McClelland has developed training programs that strengthen these needs. In his achievement motivation program, trainees review imaginative stories written by high-achievement-need people and then practise writing their own achievement-oriented stories. They practise achievement-oriented behaviours in business games and examine whether being a high achiever is consistent with their self-image and career plans. Finally, trainees complete a detailed achievement plan for the next two years and form a reference group with other trainees to maintain their new-found achievement motive style.[10]

McClelland's program seems to work. For example, course participants in several small cities in India subsequently started more new businesses, had greater community involvement, invested more in expanding their businesses, and employed twice as many people as nonparticipants. Research on similar achievement-motive courses for North American small business owners reported dramatic increases in the profitability of the participants' businesses.

Practical implications of content theories

Content theories of motivation suggest that different people have different needs at different times. Therefore, to increase work motivation, we must look carefully at the variety of jobs and rewards that employees desire. As a senior manager at Toronto-based Telemedia Inc. explains: "Managers who can identify the particular needs that employees have and reward them accordingly . . . get the most out of their people."[11] Job assignments should be matched with employees' needs. For example, those with strong affiliation needs might be more effective in jobs that involve working directly with clients or other people.

Most organizations distribute the same reward, such as a salary increase or paid time off, to all employees with good performance. But rewards that motivate some people will have little effect on those with different needs.[12] Thus, content motivation theories advise organizations to offer employees their choice of rewards. Those who perform well might trade part of the bonus for extra time off. The result of a flexible reward system is that employees can create a reward package with the greatest value to them. This principle is also found in flexible benefits systems, in which employees select benefits that match their particular needs.

Another important lesson from the content theories is that organizations should not rely too heavily on financial rewards as a source of employee motivation. The reason is that financial rewards correspond to lower level needs, whereas growth needs eventually (or always, according to Herzberg) represent the main source of employee motivation. The Body Shop Canada, described at the beginning of this chapter, downplays the motivational potential of money for this reason. "The amount of time and effort put into thinking up new schemes to attract, motivate, and keep employees through money and things would be laughable if it were not so very sad," says Margot Franssen, The Body Shop Canada's president. Instead, the company primarily motivates employees through the esteem of working for an environmentally sensitive organization and through the self-actualization experienced from community work.

Content theories of motivation explain why people have different needs, but they don't tell us why people direct or maintain their effort toward certain goals rather than others. Instead, we must look at process theories to understand the remaining phases of the motivation process. The best-known process theories of motivation include expectancy theory, goal setting and feedback, and equity theory.

Expectancy Theory of Motivation

Expectancy theory
A process theory of motivation, stating that employees will direct their work effort toward behaviours that they believe will lead to desired outcomes.

Expectancy theory is a process motivation theory based on the idea that work effort is directed toward behaviours that people believe will lead to desired outcomes.[13] Through experience, people develop expectations of whether they can achieve various levels of job performance. They also develop expectations of whether job performance and work behaviours lead to particular outcomes. Finally, people direct their effort toward outcomes that directly or indirectly satisfy basic needs.

Expectancy theory emerged from the writings of Kurt Lewin and other social psychologists in the 1930s.[14] Victor Vroom is generally credited with introducing expectancy theory to organizational settings in 1964, although his version of the model is unnecessarily complex and often described incorrectly. The version of expectancy theory presented in this book was developed by Edward E. Lawler and is easier to understand, yet equally effective at explaining employee motivation.[15]

Graham Harrop. Used with permission.

Expectancy Theory of Motivation   Exhibit 3–3

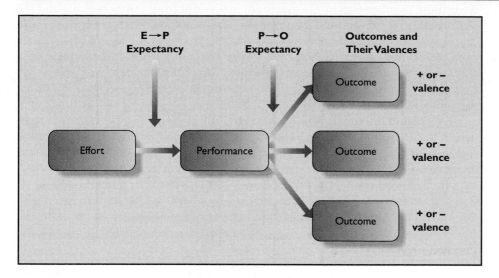

Lawler's expectancy theory model is presented in Exhibit 3–3. The key variable of interest in expectancy theory is *effort*—the individual's actual exertion of energy. An individual's effort level depends on three factors: effort-to-performance (E→P) expectancy, (2) performance-to-outcome (P→O) expectancy, and (3) outcome valences (V). Employee motivation is influenced by all three components of the expectancy theory model. If any component weakens, motivation weakens.

E→P expectancy

The **effort-to-performance (E→P) expectancy** is the individual's perception that his or her effort will result in a particular level of performance. Expectancy is defined as a *probability,* and therefore ranges from 0.0 to 1.0. In some situations, employees may believe that they can unquestionably accomplish the task (a probability of 1.0). In other situations, they expect that even their highest level of effort will not result in the desired performance level (a probability of 0.0). In most cases, the E→P expectancy falls somewhere between these two extremes.[16]

Effort-to-performance (E→P) expectancy
An individual's perceived probability that a particular level of effort will result in a particular level of performance.

P→O expectancy

The **performance-to-outcome (P→O) expectancy** is the perceived probability that a specific behaviour or performance level will lead to specific outcomes. In extreme cases, employees may believe that accomplishing a particular task (performance) will definitely result in a particular outcome (a probability of 1.0), or they may believe that this outcome definitely will not result from successful performance (a probability of 0.0). More often, the P→O expectancy falls somewhere between these two extremes.

Performance-to-outcome (P→O) expectancy
An individual's perceived probability that a specific behaviour or performance level will lead to specific outcomes.

Outcome valences

An infinite number of possible outcomes may result from our behaviour and job performance, but we tend to consider P→O expectancies only for those outcomes that are of interest to us at the time. Some outcomes are basic needs, such as feelings of self-actualization. Other outcomes are indirectly associated with basic needs. For example, a recently hired employee's satisfactory job performance might lead to permanent job status, thereby indirectly fulfilling the individual's security needs.

Valence
The anticipated satisfaction or dissatisfaction that an individual feels toward an outcome.

Expectancy theory is less concerned with the specific performance outcomes than with the **valences** of those outcomes to the employee. *Valence* refers to the anticipated satisfaction or dissatisfaction that an individual feels toward an outcome. It ranges from negative to positive. (The actual range doesn't matter; it may be from −1 to +1, or from −100 to +100.) An outcome valence is determined by the strength of the person's basic needs that are associated with the outcome. Outcomes have a positive valence when they directly or indirectly satisfy the person's needs, and a negative valence when they aggravate the person's need fulfillment.

Predicting work effort: An organizational example

The amount of work effort that an individual will exert toward a task depends on all three components of the expectancy model. Let's see how these expectancy theory components explain why Jack Wong redirected his work effort so that he would work slowly (rather than quickly) at the City of Saskatoon's Parks and Recreation Department (see Perspective 3–1). The three work performance outcomes that Jack mentions are being scolded by co-workers, getting laid off early, and trying to look busy. Jack dislikes (negative valances) all three outcomes, so he tries to avoid them.

Regarding his P→O expectancies, Jack clearly believes that he will get scolded by co-workers, get laid off early, and have to look busy if he gets his work done quickly. In other words, he has high P→O expectancies that each of these outcomes would occur if he reached a high level of job performance. If he works slowly, on the other hand, Jack probably would not get scolded or laid off early, and would not have to pretend that he is busy. By multiplying these P→O expectancies with the valences of the three outcomes, we can see that Jack prefers completing his work slowly. Jack knows that he can get the job done quickly, and he is quite confident that he can work slowly. In expectancy theory language, he has high E→P expectancies for both performance levels. Thus, Jack is more motivated to work slowly than quickly for Saskatoon's Parks and Recreation Department.

Practical implications of expectancy theory

One of the appealing characteristics of expectancy theory is that it provides clear guidelines for increasing employee motivation by altering the person's E→P expectancies, P→O expectancies, and/or outcome valences.[17] Several practical implications of expectancy theory are listed in Exhibit 3–4 and described below.

Perspective 3–1

Pacing Yourself at Saskatoon's Department of Parks and Relaxation

It didn't take long for Jack Wong to work more slowly for the City of Saskatoon's Parks and Recreation Department. Soon after he was hired as a seasonal employee, Wong heard a co-worker jokingly refer to the work unit as the department of "Parks and Relaxation." The title was quite appropriate. A few days later, while working at a pace normal to most human beings, Wong was scolded by a "lifer" (a lifetime city employee) for going too fast. Wong was told to pace himself so that the job wasn't completed so quickly.

Jack Wong soon learned that this was useful advice. There were no rewards in finishing a job early. If the work crew got the job done faster than expected, the foreman would often have nothing else for them to do. This frustrated the foreman and left employees with the painful duty of trying to look busy for the rest of the day.

"Unfortunately, I was a bad actor," admits Wong. "I couldn't look busy even if my life depended on it. Every year during my year-end evaluation, my foreman told me: 'You stand around and wait too much to be told what to do.'" So to avoid warnings from lifers and poor evaluations from his supervisor, Wong tried his best to adopt a more leisurely pace of work.

Another deterrent to working hard was that Wong and other seasonal employees would be laid off each summer after their assigned projects were completed or the department's budget for summer help was spent. The employees didn't want to get laid off early, and the department managers didn't want a budget surplus because city hall might cut the extra money from next year's budget. So everyone was quite happy to see Wong and others working slowly and taking longer coffee breaks until the budget was spent.

Eventually, Jack Wong managed to slow down his work effort. But now that he no longer works summers at the City of Saskatoon's Parks and Recreation department, he has trouble getting motivated for jobs that require real work effort. "I work at a slower pace than the living dead," he complains. "And I can't dig a hole unless five guys are watching me. Who should I blame for this sorry state?"

Source: Based on J. Wong, "Nice Work if You Can Get It (And You Can Get It if You Don't Try)," *The Globe & Mail*, December 31, 1993, p. A18.

Increasing E→P expectancies

E→P expectancies are based on self-esteem and previous experience in that situation.[18] Consequently, employees should be given the necessary abilities, clear role perceptions, and favourable situational contingencies to reach the desired levels of performance so that they form higher E→P expectancies.

Employee abilities must be matched with job requirements, or the job should be changed to fit the incumbent's existing abilities. For example, the Insurance Corporation of British Columbia assigns relatively simple automobile accident cases to newly hired adjusters. After a few months, when the adjuster feels confident with these files, more challenging cases are assigned. Even with the requisite abilities, some employees may have low E→P expectancies because they lack self-confidence. Counselling and coaching may be advisable so that employees develop confidence that they already possess the skills and knowledge to perform the job.

Finally, E→P expectancies are learned, so several reinforcement and social learning strategies described in Chapter 2 should be applied. For instance, feedback will help employees perceive that they are capable of performing the

Exhibit 3–4		Practical Applications of Expectancy Theory
Expectancy Theory Component	**Managerial Objective**	**Management Applications**
E→P expectancies	To increase the belief that employees are capable of performing the job successfully	• Select people with the required skills and knowledge • Provide required training and clarify job requirements • Provide sufficient time and resources • Assign simpler or fewer tasks until employees can master them (shaping) • Provide examples of similar employees who have successfully performed the task • Provide counselling and coaching to employees who lack self-confidence
P→O expectancies	To increase the belief that good performance will result in certain (valued) outcomes	• Measure job performance accurately • Clearly explain the outcomes that will result from successful performance • Describe how the employee's rewards were based on past performance • Provide examples of other employees whose good performance has resulted in higher rewards
Valences of outcomes	To increase the expected value of outcomes resulting from desired performance	• Distribute rewards that employees value • Individualize rewards • Minimize the presence of countervalent outcomes

effort-to-performance

performance-to-outcome

assigned tasks effectively.[19] Shaping and behavioural modelling also tend to increase E→P expectancies in many situations.

Increasing P→O expectancies

The most obvious ways to improve P→O expectancies are to measure job performance accurately and distribute more valued rewards to those with higher job performance. This is not as easy as it may sound. As we shall see in Chapter 4, reward systems sometimes have little effect on employee motivation or, worse, may inadvertently motivate undesirable behaviours.

P→O expectancies are perceptions, so employees should *believe* that higher performance will result in higher rewards. Having a performance-based reward system is important, but this fact must be communicated. When rewards are distributed, employees should understand how their rewards have been based on past performance. More generally, companies need to regularly communicate the existence of a performance-based reward system through examples, anecdotes, and public ceremonies. Exhibit 3–5 shows how the Royal Bank uses advertisements in its employee magazine to let everyone know that their valuable ideas are rewarded. Also notice how this message increases E→P expectancies by illustrating that average employees can make above-average contributions to the organization.

Increasing outcome valences

Performance outcomes influence work effort only when they are valued by employees.[20] This repeats our earlier discussion that companies must pay

Communicating Performance–Reward Linkages at the Royal Bank of Canada   Exhibit 3–5

Two heads can be better than one

June Cousineau and Ann Glasford of the savings department in Calgary's Main branch proved that old adage when their idea submitted jointly to the Staff Suggestion Program got accepted.

After each had looked into separate inquiries from customers regarding service charges on statements, the pair compared notes and noticed a pattern. A number of debit memos posted to Calculator Accounts were getting through the bank's system without being assessed the appropriate service charge.

They identified the problem as a lack of something special to distinguish chargeable debit memos in the savings activity register from those that had no service charge.

Their solution was equally straightforward: Create a code to identify the chargeable debit memos. Branch operations, the referral area which evaluated the idea, accepted it and plan to put the suggestion into practice by next year.

For branch operations the cost of implementing the idea is minimal. For the bank, revenue will be realized that might otherwise be lost. And for June and Ann? Calculations are underway to determine the cash award the two women will share under the guidelines of the Staff Suggestion program.

June and Ann provide just one example of the kind of team effort that Royal bankers display every day – teamwork that pays dividends not only for the bank, but for employees themselves.

Thinking smart, working smart

Source: Royal Bank.

attention to the needs and reward preferences of individual employees. They should develop more individualized reward systems in which employees who perform well are offered a choice of rewards to maximize the effectiveness of the reward system.[21]

Finally, expectancy theory emphasizes the need to discover and neutralize countervalent outcomes. This refers to the situation in which some outcomes of good job performance have negative valences, thereby reducing the effectiveness of existing reward systems. Earlier in Perspective 3–1 we saw how Jack Wong's work effort was curtailed by pressures from co-workers and immediate supervisors. Although the City of Saskatoon may want motivated employees, the countervalent forces in its Parks and Recreation department easily offset any outcomes that encourage higher work effort.

Does expectancy theory fit reality?

Expectancy theory has been a difficult model to test because it must recognize almost every possible performance level and outcome that employees could imagine. Most of the early studies also suffered from measurement and research design problems.[22] One criticism of expectancy theory is that it suggests that people tend to assess the costs and benefits of alternative courses of action and select the option with the highest payoff.[23] This is not a true representation of human motivation, because people are not perfectly efficient decision makers.

In spite of these limitations, it appears that the process of employee motivation is explained reasonably well by the expectancy theory model. All three components of the model have received some research support. There is particularly good evidence that P→O expectancies influence employee motivation.[24]

Goal Setting

Goals
The immediate or ultimate objectives that employees are trying to achieve from their work effort.

The general motivation process, presented at the beginning of this chapter, states that employees consider relevant goals for need gratification and engage in behaviours that are believed to accomplish those goals. **Goals** are the immediate or ultimate objectives that employees are trying to accomplish from their work effort. There are many types of goals, as the following examples illustrate:

- Finish the meeting with this client by 11:15 A.M. (deadline goal).
- Keep product rejects below 1.5 percent (performance standard goal).
- Make 10 calls to new customers each week (quota goal).
- Keep the marketing cost of widgets under $50,000 this year (budget goal).

Goal setting enhances employee motivation by fulfilling growth needs when the goal is achieved. It also improves role perceptions by focussing employee efforts on the required task. Many Canadian organizations are dedicated to goal setting. For example, Toronto's SkyDome establishes quality and service goals for all full-time employees. If corporate and individual goals are met, employees can earn bonuses up to 7.5 percent of their base salary.[25]

Characteristics of effective goals

Goal setting may seem rather straightforward, but the four conditions diagrammed in Exhibit 3–6 are necessary to maximize task effort and performance.[26]

Specific goals

Employees put more effort into a task when they work toward specific performance goals rather than "do your best" targets. A specific goal would typically

Characteristics of Effective Goal Setting   **Exhibit 3–6**

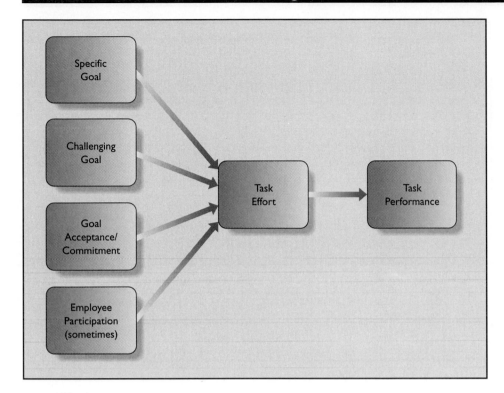

include a quantitative level of change over a specific time, such as "reduce scrap rate by 7 percent over the next six months." Specific goals communicate more precise performance expectations, resulting in a more efficient and reliable application of individual effort.

Challenging goals

Generally, the more challenging the goal, the greater the effort level and persistence. Also, the more challenging the goal, the greater the potential self-actualization.[27] But this principle is true only up to a point. Employees will reject goals that appear to be too difficult. Consequently, we need to carefully determine the level at which a goal is challenging but still acceptable, shown as the centre area in Exhibit 3–7.

Goal commitment

Goal setting will only work if employees are committed to the goal. In other words, their intention to strive toward the goal must be sufficiently strong even though obstacles are in the way.[28] Goal commitment is stronger when employees have sufficient ability and believe that they can accomplish the goal (i.e., a high E→P expectancy). It is also stronger when employees have publicly shown their support for it and co-workers also support the goal. Finally, goal commitment is stronger when it is assigned by someone who is respected, or when employees participate in the goal-setting process.[29]

Exhibit 3–7   **Effect of Goal Difficulty on Performance**

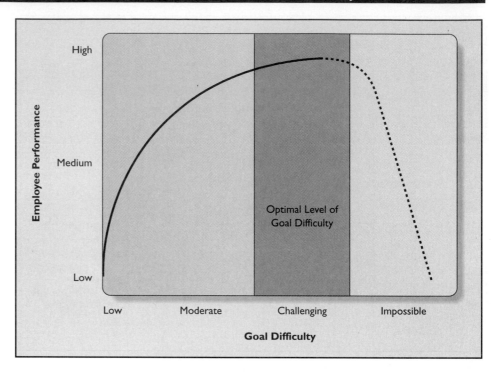

Participation in goal formation (sometimes)

Motivation sometimes increases when employees are involved in setting goals rather than having them assigned.[30] One reason, as was just mentioned, is that participation tends to increase goal commitment. Participation in the goal-setting process may also improve goal quality, because employees possess valuable information and knowledge. However, participation is not necessary when employees will be committed to assigned goals and those who decide the goals have sufficient information.

Goal feedback

Feedback is another necessary condition for effective goal setting. Without feedback, employees would not know whether they have achieved the goal or whether they are properly directing their effort toward goal accomplishment. As we discuss next, feedback has a powerful influence on employee motivation and behaviour.

Feedback
Any information that people receive about the consequences of their behaviour.

Providing Effective Feedback

Feedback is any information that people receive about the consequences of their behaviour. Feedback *motivates* people, particularly those with a strong need for achievement.[31] Employees feel a sense of accomplishment after completing a task, but only after receiving feedback that the effort was successful. Feedback is also an essential part of *learning*.[32] For example, a technician learns from an instrument dial whether the pressure valve has been opened too far. This feedback is necessary so that the employee eventually learns how far to open the valve for the best results.

Employees do not passively receive feedback; they actively seek it. Each of us has a natural need to know the consequences of our actions and how we are progressing toward our goals. Feedback fulfills this need to know and allows us to evaluate our abilities, correct errors, feel increased confidence, and experience a sense of achievement.[33]

Feedback sources

There are many sources of feedback. Some are nonsocial, such as quarterly market share reports or weekly product defect counts. With a click of the computer mouse, a marketing manager at Xerox Canada can look at the previous day's sales and compare them with the results from any other day over the previous year.[34] The job itself can be a source of feedback. Many employees see the results of their work effort by looking directly at the finished product.[35]

Feedback is often received from supervisors, clients, co-workers, and other social sources. Senior management at Dylex Corp. (Canada's leading clothing retailer) uses the company's national computer network to provide timely feedback to sales staff at individual stores. If a store in Newfoundland finishes the week with strong sales, senior management in Toronto might send the message "Well done!" and tell employees how they performed. Store employees would read the message first thing Monday morning and appreciate senior management's recognition of their efforts.[36]

Research suggests that the preferred feedback source depends on the purpose of the information. To learn about their progress toward goal accomplishment, employees usually prefer nonsocial feedback sources, such as computer printouts or self-feedback (i.e., feedback experienced directly from the work activity).[37] This is because information from nonsocial sources is considered more accurate than from social sources. Employees also prefer a nonsocial source for negative feedback because it is less damaging to their self-esteem. There is inherently more humility in learning about your failures from a person than in learning about them from a nonsocial source. Finally, nonsocial sources are often preferred because asking for feedback from other people may give them the impression that the employee requesting feedback is insecure or uncertain about his or her job performance.[38]

When employees want to improve their self-image, they seek out positive feedback from social sources. Simply put, it feels better to have co-workers say that you are performing the job well than to discover this from a computer printout.[39] Positive feedback from co-workers and other social sources is highly motivating because it fulfills two sets of needs: (1) self-actualization when you learn about the goal accomplishment, and (2) social esteem when others recognize your accomplishment.

Exhibit 3–8   **Characteristics of Effective Feedback**

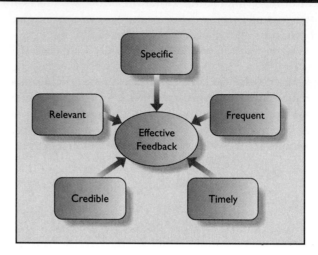

Characteristics of effective feedback

Whether it is received from a supervisor or statistical control system, feedback can greatly influence employee motivation and performance. But the value of feedback depends on the characteristics diagrammed in Exhibit 3–8.

Specific feedback

Feedback is more useful when it includes specific information such as "you exceeded your sales quota by 5 percent last month" rather than subjective and general phrases such as "your sales are going well." Specific feedback helps employees learn appropriate behaviours more easily. It also motivates employees if the details produce a greater sense of accomplishment.

Frequent feedback

Many employees seldom receive information (other than self-feedback) about their job performance, so it is safe to say that most organizations should provide more frequent feedback. This frequency varies considerably from one job to the next. Cashiers spend only a couple of minutes with each customer, so they might check their average transaction speed (calculated by the computerized cash register) several times each hour. Senior managers might receive feedback only a few times each year, because their work cycles are several months long.

The optimal feedback frequency also depends on whether the employee is working on a novel or routine task. As we learned in Chapter 2, continuous reinforcement is best for employees in new jobs, whereas variable ratio reinforcement works best for others. The same principles apply to feedback because it is a form of reinforcement. But the best strategy is to have feedback continuously available and let employees decide when they want to see it. This personal control is consistent with social learning theory (see Chapter 2) and typically results in the optimal feedback frequency.

Timely feedback

Feedback should be available as soon as possible so that employees see a clear association between their behaviour and its consequences.[40] Computers and other electronic monitoring systems can sometimes provide timely feedback, but usually only for routine behaviour. One alternative is to have those closest to the employee provide meaningful feedback when desired behaviour occurs. Perspective 3–2 describes how Delta Credit Union and other companies have introduced novel ways to provide timely feedback through co-workers.

Credible feedback

Feedback has value only when the employee accepts its content. Feedback acceptance is a complex issue that relates to the communication, perceptual bias, and persuasive communication concepts described in Chapters 6 and 7. At this point, you should know that people are more likely to accept feedback (particularly negative feedback) from trustworthy and credible sources.[41] They are also more likely to accept negative feedback from nonsocial sources (e.g., computer printouts, electronic gauges) because this does not threaten self-esteem as much as feedback from human sources.[42] When it must come from a supervisor or other human source, negative feedback should be prefaced with some positive information and then described in a nonthreatening, nonevaluative tone. As you might imagine, this isn't an easy task.

Relevant feedback

Feedback is most effective when it relates to the individual's behaviour rather than broader departmental or organizational activities. This ensures that the employee is able to connect the information to his or her own actions and control for situational contingencies.[43] Feedback is also relevant when it is linked to goals. Goals establish the benchmarks (i.e., what ought to be) against which feedback is judged. Thus, we come full circle to our earlier point that feedback is necessary for effective goal setting, just as goal setting is necessary for effective feedback.

Ethical concerns with monitoring employee performance

One of the more contentious issues in feedback management is monitoring employee performance. Employee monitoring exists in many forms, and the information is used in several ways.[44] Supervisors at the Avis call centre in Toronto randomly listen to incoming customer calls and rate employees on their telephone behaviour. At General Electric's call centre in Kentucky, some of these conversations are recorded and later played back to help employees improve their customer service skills. Managers at SwissAir, Japan Air Lines, and other commercial carriers regularly review flight recorder instrument data to check pilot performance and investigate problem flights. They also show samples of these data in training sessions.[45]

Critics view employee monitoring as a repressive management control practice and an invasion of employee privacy.[46] For instance, some physicians

Perspective 3–2

Warm-Fuzzy Feedback at Delta Credit Union

Senior managers at Delta Credit Union wanted employees to receive positive feedback on a daily basis rather than just a few times each year during formal performance reviews. Supervisors couldn't watch employees all the time, so management at the Vancouver-based financial institution had to think of another way to give meaningful, frequent feedback.

Delta's solution was to print "warm-fuzzy" cards—small, blank cards with brown, furry animals on the front. Whenever employees saw a co-worker doing a job well, they were encouraged to send the co-worker a warm-fuzzy card. Nobody sees an employee's work more than his or her co-workers, so it made sense that the person's peers should send these cards.

Ford, General Motors, and several other companies have developed a similar type of feedback to improve safe

work behaviours. For instance, General Motors prints up "safety thank you" cards (without the furry animal drawings) that supervisors and co-workers deliver to any employee who is seen performing a work behaviour safely. These thank you cards are valuable for more than their message; in many cases, employees may redeem them for prizes or use them as entries in special lotteries.

At St. Joseph's Hospital in London, Ontario, staff members send "I noticed" cards to co-workers. The pharmacy department has gone one step further by introducing a positive feedback chain letter. An employee sends a letter of thanks to a co-worker who has performed well. The receiver must then pass the letter along to another employee who deserves a note of appreciation. That person then looks for an opportunity to pass the letter on to another colleague, and so forth.

Sources: Based on J. Hurd, "Power to the People," *Inside Guide,* January 1993, pp. 33–36; P. Hassen, *Rx for Hospitals: New Hope for Medicare in the Nineties* (Toronto: Stoddart, 1993), p. 142; and E. S. Geller, "Performance Management and Occupational Safety: Start with a Safety Belt Program," *Journal of Organizational Behavior Management,* 1990, pp. 149–74.

---

were appalled when the University of Alberta Hospitals recently installed a computer system to monitor each patient's length of hospital stay and other expenses. "Some doctors were upset that we were keeping track of them to that extent," recalls the head of the surgery department.[47] A senior pilot at Delta Air Lines complains that management reviews of flight recorder data interfere with the team process in the cockpit. "It's very hard to organize a team when someone is looking over your shoulder every second."[48]

Employee monitoring also encourages companies to place too much emphasis on the measured elements of job performance and too little on the more subjective factors. Bell Canada stopped monitoring experienced operators for this reason. It realized that supervisors were evaluating their performance based on the number of calls and the amount of time per call, whereas customer service seemed to be of little importance. Now that monitoring is used only to train new staff, experienced operators say customer service has improved and their supervisors place more emphasis on the operator's service to the caller.[49]

Although monitoring raises several concerns, proponents point out that this activity helps employees perform their jobs better by providing specific and timely feedback, particularly when supervisors are otherwise unable to directly observe job performance. Recent studies report that employees see monitoring as a necessary evil, but they respond favourably when it is used by the organization to provide developmental feedback.[50]

Equity Theory

Equity theory explains how people develop perceptions of fairness in the distribution and exchange of resources. As a process theory of motivation, it explains what employees are motivated to do when they feel inequitably treated. Equity theory is also relevant to job stress, job satisfaction, and organizational conflict, so we shall refer to this concept in later chapters. Equity theory applies to any situation in which people share or exchange resources, but our discussion will focus on exchanges between the organization and its employees. There are four main elements in the equity process: outcome/input ratio, comparison other, equity evaluation, and consequences of inequity.[51]

Equity theory
A process theory of motivation that explains how people develop perceptions of fairness in the distribution and exchange of resources.

Outcome/input ratio

Inputs include skills, effort, experience, amount of time worked, performance results, and other employee contributions to the organization. Employees see their inputs as investments into the exchange relationship. Outcomes are the things employees receive from the organization in exchange for the inputs, such as pay, promotions, recognition, or an office with a window.

Both inputs and outcomes are weighted by their importance to the individual. These weights vary from one person to the next. To some people, seniority is a valuable input that deserves more organizational outcomes in return. Others consider job effort and performance the most important contributions in the exchange relationship, and give seniority relatively little weight. Similarly, equity theory recognizes that people value outcomes differently because they have different needs. For example, it accepts that some employees want time off with pay whereas others consider this a relatively insignificant reward for job performance.

Comparison other

Equity theory states that we compare our situation with a comparison other. However, the theory does not tell us who the comparison other is in a particular situation. It may be another person, group of people, or even yourself in the past. It may be someone in the same job, another job, or another organization. People tend to compare themselves with others within the same organization rather than with people in other organizations. One reason is that employees develop firm-specific skills and attachments that limit their likelihood of looking beyond the organization in which they are currently employed (i.e., the internal labour market). Another reason is that co-workers are similar to the employee and it is easier to get information about co-workers than from people working elsewhere.[52] Some research suggests that employees frequently collect information on several referents to form a "generalized" comparison other.[53] For the most part, however, the comparison other is not easily identifiable.

Equity evaluation

According to equity theory, employees form an outcome/input ratio and compare this with the ratio of the comparison other. This evaluation is shown in

Exhibit 3–9 with three different comparison situations. The first comparison illustrates the *equity condition* in which the person's outcome/input ratio is the same as the comparison other's ratio. The amount of inputs and outcomes must be proportional, but they don't necessarily have the same amount. For instance, we feel equitably treated when we work harder than the comparison other and receive proportionally higher rewards as a result.

Inequity feelings emerge when the person's ratio is significantly different from the comparison other's. People tend to ignore minimal differences, but inequity occurs when the difference in ratios exceeds a threshold level. *Underreward inequity* occurs when the person's ratio is significantly lower than the comparison other's. This may occur when two people provide the same inputs to the organization but the other person receives more outcomes, as the second comparison in Exhibit 3–9 illustrates. Underreward inequity may also occur when the outcomes are the same but the comparison other's inputs are lower, or in any other situation in which the person's ratio is lower than the comparison other's.

Overreward inequity occurs when the person's ratio is significantly higher than the comparison other's. As the third comparison in Exhibit 3–9 illustrates, overreward inequity would occur when the person receives more outcomes than the comparison other, even though the inputs are the same. Overreward inequity would also occur when the person's inputs are lower than the comparison other's but both receive the same outcomes, or in any other situation in which the person's ratio is higher than the comparison other's.

Consequences of inequity

Inequity creates an uncomfortable tension that is both stressful and dissatisfying. Employees are motivated to reduce or eliminate this tension by correcting the inequitable situation. Researchers have identified six possible ways to reduce feelings of inequity.[54]

Changing inputs

Employees who feel underrewarded tend to reduce their work effort and performance, particularly if they are on a fixed salary and lower effort does not reduce their paycheque. Those who feel overpaid sometimes (but not very often) increase their inputs by working harder and producing more.

Changing outcomes

Employees who feel underrewarded might ask for more desired outcomes, such as a pay increase. If this strategy does not work, they might become motivated to join a labour union to force these changes on management at the bargaining table.[55] Some employees who feel underrewarded increase their outcomes by using company facilities and equipment for personal use.

Changing perceptions

Feelings of equity are based on perceptions, so employees might distort inputs and outcomes to restore equity feelings. This is the most frequently used strategy for overrewarded employees. They find it more palatable to increase the perceived importance of their seniority or other inputs than to actually work harder or ask for a pay reduction![56]

Equity Theory Model   **Exhibit 3–9**

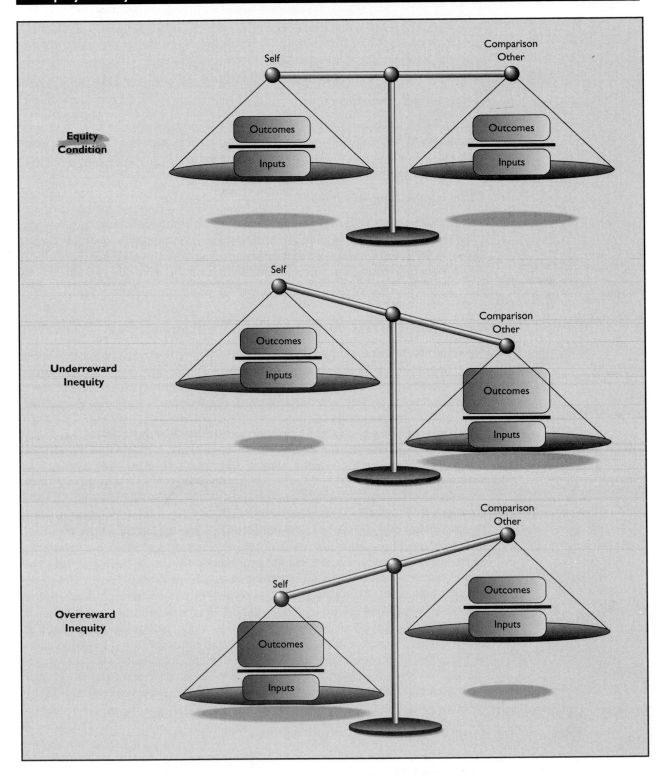

Leaving the field

In some cases, employees who believe they are treated unfairly will try to get away from the inequitable situation. In this respect, equity theory explains some instances of employee turnover and job transfer. This alternative also explains why absenteeism may be higher for employees who feel underrewarded even when they are not paid for this time off.

Acting on the comparison other

Equity is sometimes restored by changing the comparison other's inputs or outcomes. If you feel overrewarded, you might encourage the referent to work at a more leisurely pace. If you feel underrewarded, you might subtly suggest that the overpaid co-worker should be doing a larger share of the workload.

Changing the comparison other

Finally, employees who feel inequitably treated might decide to replace the comparison other with someone having a more compatible outcome/input ratio. As mentioned earlier, we sometimes form a generalized comparison other, so feelings of inequity may be reduced fairly easily by adjusting the features of this composite referent.

The equity process: An organizational example

Now that the basic components of equity theory have been described, let's apply this model to an actual business incident. Perspective 3–3 describes the experience of Jay Norris Canada Inc., a Montreal mail-order house, where some employees felt that they were unfairly paid. Equity theory can help us examine this experience more fully.

The most important input mentioned in Perspective 3–3 is employee productivity, specifically the number of orders processed per day. Employees complaining about the existing system did not accept age or seniority as acceptable inputs in the exchange process. The critical outcome in this example is employee salaries, although other rewards and perquisites might also be considered. Regarding the comparison other, disgruntled employees were clearly comparing themselves to others within the organization, particularly older workers in the same job. Finally, Perspective 3–3 describes how employees who felt inequitably rewarded reduced this tension by complaining to management and eventually receiving a compensation system that more closely reflected their perceptions of fairness. According to equity theory, these employees attempted to change their outcomes and were successful in doing so.

Nothing is said about the older employees at Jay Norris, but we know that overrewarded employees tend to change their perceptions. In our example, most of the older workers probably believed that age and seniority were important enough to justify their higher salaries. It would be equally interesting to examine their equity perceptions after the new reward system was introduced.

Equity research and implications

The Jay Norris example illustrates that equity theory can explain motivation and behaviour in the workplace. Scholarly studies also support the practical value of equity theory. Although earlier studies were based on short-term comparisons in

Perspective 3–3

Fair Pay in a Montreal Mail-Order House

Jay Norris Canada Inc., a Montreal mail-order house with annual sales of $50 million, had been experiencing declining employee morale and motivation because many of the company's 400 staff felt inequitably paid. Wages were based mainly on seniority, and the company's existing performance appraisal system was so subjective that some employees were evaluated as good performers even if they didn't do their job very well.

"People were complaining that their salaries weren't fair," explains René Schubert, vice-president of finance and administration at Jay Norris. "Long-timers were getting more salary, but they were sometimes poorer workers than others in the office. Someone processing 400 orders per day was maybe making less than the older guy doing 250 orders per day."

To restore feelings of equity, the company decided to pay employees more for their performance than their seniority. It also introduced a new performance appraisal system in which supervisors rate employees using objective standards. For example, good performance might mean that the employee typically fills 350 orders per day, whereas excellent performance might be 400 orders per day.

Schubert stresses that getting supervisors to reach a consensus on the meaning of "good" or "poor" performance has been challenging. Nevertheless, it is important that they all see performance the same way so that salaries and pay increases are decided fairly.

Source: Based on Cathy Hilborn, "Worker Incentives Can Backfire," *Small Business*, August 1989, pp. 7–8. Adapted with permission.

laboratory settings and used pay as the only outcome, more recent evidence suggests that equity theory is valid in field settings when either monetary or nonmonetary outcomes are involved.[57]

Equity theory emphasizes the social comparison process and its implications for employee motivation and behaviour. The theory clearly advises us to treat people fairly in the distribution of organizational rewards. If feelings of inequity are sufficiently strong, employees may put less effort into the job, leave the organization, steal resources or time (e.g., absenteeism), or join a labour union to force management to correct the inequities.

Maintaining feelings of equity is not an easy task, because employees have different opinions regarding which inputs should be rewarded (e.g., seniority versus performance) and which outcomes are more valuable than others.[58] Managers can try to improve equity perceptions by telling employees how rewards are distributed. They should be sensitive to employee feelings of equity, and be ready to change the factors considered in reward distribution when it becomes apparent that most employees believe the current system is unfair.

Are Motivation Theories Culture Bound?

Are the motivation theories presented throughout this chapter relevant across cultures? A few scholars don't think so. They argue that most theories of motivation were developed by American scholars and tested on Americans, so they reflect the values of Americans and don't readily apply in cultures with different values.[59]

But it isn't clear that the critics' concerns are well founded. Much of the criticism has focussed on the content theories, particularly Maslow's needs hierarchy theory. Several studies have found that Maslow's needs hierarchy is incompatible with individual needs in other cultures. But you will recall that Maslow's theory didn't work very well in North America, either. Moreover, we know that some drives (e.g., need for affiliation) are learned and, therefore, may vary with cultural values and norms. The fact that McClelland's learned drives research was successfully tested in other countries (e.g., India) lends further support to the idea that needs may vary with the person's environment.

Critics point out that Herzberg's motivator-hygiene theory doesn't hold up in other countries, but we already stated that the theory has been rejected by most North American scholars. (Herzberg recently presented evidence that his theory is valid across cultures, but problems with the theory described earlier in this chapter still remain.)[60] Overall, the cross-cultural studies do not contradict anything we have already said about content motivation theories.

Expectancy theory has also been criticized as culture bound because it assumes that people act rationally to control their environment.[61] This feeling of personal control is strong in American culture, but not in countries where people believe that the consequences of their actions are largely preordained by God or some other external force. However, expectancy theory does not assume that people feel in control; on the contrary, the E→P expectancy directly varies with the employee's perceived control over the work situation. Employees who believe that their performance is ordained by Allah will have a lower E→P expectancy. To date, there is no empirical evidence that expectancy theory is culture bound. Other process motivation theories, such as equity theory and goal setting, also allow for individual differences and, consequently, should apply equally well to other cultures.[62]

The debate over the cross-cultural relevance of motivation theories will continue for some time. Hopefully, future research will throw more light on the topic by evaluating the cross-cultural relevance of expectancy, goal setting, and other contemporary motivation theories rather than the older content theories. In the meantime, it is not clear (at least, not as clear as the critics believe) that contemporary motivation theories are culture bound.

Employee Motivation: A Final Word

Throughout this chapter, we have introduced several theories of employee motivation. While reading this material, you may have wondered why some ingenious organizational theorist didn't try to weave these ideas into a single unifying theory. The fact is that several writers *have* tried to produce integrated models of employee motivation, but they have not been very successful. At best, the unified models emphasize one perspective (typically expectancy theory) and ignore others. At worst, they confuse students with a multitude of boxes and lines.

These attempts to develop an integrated model of employee motivation are noble. However, they simply lend further support to the idea introduced in Chapter 1 that each organizational behaviour theory needs a relatively narrow focus to adequately capture the complexity of human behaviour. Although we cannot present one grand theory of employee motivation, the basic motivation process described at the beginning of the chapter links together need and process theories as well as motivation practices (discussed in Chapter 4). By understanding each motivation theory in the context of this general framework, you can begin to see how they relate to each other.

Chapter Summary

- The motivation process begins with need deficiencies that energize the person to satisfy them through goal-directed behaviour. Performance outcomes affect need fulfillment and the motivation process is repeated.

- Content motivation theories explain why people have different needs at different times. Process theories of motivation describe the processes through which needs are translated into behaviour.

- According to Maslow's need hierarchy, the lowest needs are initially most important, but higher needs become more important as the lower ones are satisfied. Alderfer's ERG theory includes three needs. Along with Maslow's satisfaction-progression process, ERG theory states that frustrated needs cause people to fall back to the next lower need level. Herzberg's motivator-hygiene theory suggests that people are only motivated by characteristics of the work itself. McClelland studied three secondary needs that are learned rather than instinctive.

- Expectancy theory states that work effort is determined by the perception that effort will result in a particular level of performance ($E \rightarrow P$ expectancy), the perception that a specific behaviour or performance level will lead to specific outcomes ($P \rightarrow O$ expectancy), and the valences that the person feels for those outcomes.

- Work effort increases through the $E \rightarrow P$ expectancy by improving the employee's ability and confidence to perform the job. The $P \rightarrow O$ expectancy increases work effort by measuring performance accurately, distributing higher rewards to better performers, and showing employees that rewards are performance based. Finally, work effort increases through outcome valences by finding out what employees want and using these resources as rewards.

- Goal setting proposes that employee motivation and performance are strongly influenced by goals. Goals are more effective when they are specific, challenging, accepted by the employee, and accompanied by meaningful feedback. Participative goal setting is important in some situations.

- Feedback is information relating to the consequences of employee behaviour. People prefer nonsocial sources of feedback to learn about their goal progress. They prefer positive feedback from social sources to improve their self-image. Effective feedback is specific, frequent, timely, credible, and relevant.

- Equity theory explains how people determine their perceptions of fairness using four elements: outcome/input ratio, comparison other, equity evaluation, and consequences of inequity. The theory also explains what people are motivated to do when they feel inequitably treated.

Discussion Questions

1. **How does McClelland's need theory differ from Maslow's needs hierarchy theory?**

2. **A neighbour who holds a management position tells you that Maslow's needs hierarchy is the best theory of motivation in the organizational sciences. Assuming that you can be candid with this manager, how would you respond to that statement?**

3. **Identify four ways that managers can increase employee motivation by altering the person's E→P expectancy.**

4. **Use all three components of expectancy theory to explain why some employees are motivated to show up for work during a snowstorm whereas others don't make any effort to leave their home.**

5. **Describe four features of effective goal setting.**

6. **When do employees prefer feedback from nonsocial rather than social sources? Explain why nonsocial sources are preferred under those conditions.**

7. **The five service representatives in your company are upset that the newly hired representative with no previous experience will be paid $1,000 per year above the usual starting salary on the pay range. The department manager explained that the new hire would not accept the entry-level rate, so the company raised the offer by $1,000. All five reps currently earn salaries near the top of the scale ($10,000 higher), although they all started at the minimum starting salary a few years earlier. Use equity theory to explain why the five service representatives feel inequity in this situation.**

8. **Why is it difficult to maintain feelings of equity among employees?**

Notes

1. M. Franssen, "Beyond Profits," *Business Quarterly* 58 (Autumn 1993), pp. 15–20; K. Tynes, "Business with Heart," *Halifax Chronicle-Herald*, September 14, 1993, p. C1; M. Lamey, "Big Hearts at Body Shop," *Montreal Gazette*, April 8, 1993, p. D9; C. Yetman, "Profits with Principles Earns Dedicated Staff," *Human Resources Professional*, May 1991, p. 12ii; and J. Deverall, "Keeping Workers Happy an Art, Bosses Say," *Toronto Star*, November 1, 1986, p. A8.

2. A. H. Maslow, "A Theory of Human Motivation," *Psychological Review* 50 (1943), pp. 370–96; and A. H. Maslow, *Motivation and Personality* (New York: Harper & Row, 1954).

3. M. A. Wahba and L. G. Bridwell, "Maslow Reconsidered: A Review of Research on the Need Hierarchy Theory," *Organizational Behavior and Human Performance* 15 (1976), pp. 212–40.

4. C. P. Alderfer, *Existence, Relatedness, and Growth* (New York: The Free Press, 1972).

5. F. Herzberg, B. Mausner, and B. B. Snyderman, *The Motivation to Work* (New York: Wiley, 1959).

6. A. K. Korman, *Industrial and Organizational Psychology* (Englewood Cliffs, N.J.: Prentice Hall, 1971), p. 149; and N. King, "Clarification and Evaluation of the Two Factor Theory of Job Satisfaction," *Psychological Bulletin* 74 (1970), pp. 18–31.

7. R. M. Steers and L. W. Porter, *Motivation and Work Behavior,* 5th ed. (New York: McGraw-Hill, 1991), p. 413.

8. D. C. McClelland, *The Achieving Society* (New York: Van Nostrand Reinhold, 1961).

9. M. J. Stahl, "Achievement, Power, and Managerial Motivation: Selecting Managerial Talent with the Job Choice Exercise," *Personnel Psychology,* 1983, pp. 775–90; D. McClelland and R. Boyatzis, "Leadership Motive Pattern and Long-Term Success in Management," *Journal of Applied Psychology* 67 (1982), pp. 737–43; and D. C. McClelland and D. H. Burnham, "Power Is the Great Motivator," *Harvard Business Review,* March–April 1976, pp. 100–110.

10. D. C. McClelland and D. G. Winter, *Motivating Economic Achievement* (New York: The Free Press, 1969); and D. Miron and D. McClelland, "The Impact of Achievement Motivation Training on Small Business," *California Management Review* 21 (1979), pp. 13–28.

11. D. Stoffman, "The Power of Positive Strokes," *Canadian Business,* October 1987, p. 94.

12. A. Brown "Today's Employees Choose Their Own Recognition Awards," *Personnel Administrator* 31 (1986), pp. 51–58.

13. D. A. Nadler and E. E. Lawler, "Motivation: A Diagnostic Approach," in *Perspectives on Behavior in Organizations,* 2nd ed., ed. J. R. Hackman, E. E. Lawler III, and L. W. Porter (New York: McGraw-Hill, 1983), pp. 67–78; and V. H. Vroom, *Work and Motivation* (New York: Wiley, 1964).

14. K. Lewin, "Psychology of Success and Failure," *Occupations* 14 (1936), pp. 926–30.

15. Lawler's version of expectancy theory is described in: J. P. Campbell, M. D. Dunnette, E. E. Lawler, and K. E. Weick, *Managerial Behavior, Performance, and Effectiveness* (New York: McGraw-Hill, 1970), pp. 343–48; E. E. Lawler, *Motivation in Work Organizations* (Monterey, Calif.: Brooks/Cole, 1973), Chapter 3; and Nadler and Lawler, "Motivation: A Diagnostic Approach," pp. 67–78.

16. H. Garland, "Relation of Effort-Performance Expectancy to Performance in Goal-Setting Experiments," *Journal of Applied Psychology* 69 (1984), pp. 79–84.

17. Nadler and Lawler, "Motivation: A Diagnostic Approach," pp. 70–73.

18. Lawler, *Motivation in Work Organizations,* pp. 53–55.

19. K. A. Karl, A. M. O'Leary-Kelly, and J. J. Martoccio, "The Impact of Feedback and Self-Efficacy on Performance in Training," *Journal of Organizational Behavior* 14 (1993), pp. 379–94; and T. Janz, "Manipulating Subjective Expectancy through Feedback: A Laboratory Study of the Expectancy-Performance Relationship," *Journal of Applied Psychology* 67 (1982), pp. 480–85.

20. J. B. Fox, K. D. Scott, and J. M. Donohoe, "An Investigation into Pay Valence and Performance in a Pay-for-Performance Field Setting," *Journal of Organizational Behavior* 14 (1993), pp. 687–93.

21. K. R. Brousseau and J. B. Prince, "Job–Person Dynamics: An Extension of Longitudinal Research," *Journal of Applied Psychology* 66 (1981), pp. 59–62.

22. M. E. Tubbs, D. M. Boehne, and J. G. Dahl, "Expectancy, Valence, and Motivational Force Functions in Goal-Setting Research: An Empirical Test," *Journal of Applied Psychology* 78 (1993), pp. 361–73; and T. R. Mitchell, "Expectancy Models of Job Satisfaction, Occupational Preference and Effort: A Theoretical, Methodological, and Empirical Appraisal," *Psychological Bulletin* 81 (1974), pp. 1053–77.

23. D. D. Baker, R. Ravichandran, and D. M. Randall, "Exploring Contrasting Formulations of Expectancy Theory," *Decision Sciences* 20 (1989), pp. 1–13; and Vroom, *Work and Motivation,* pp. 14–19.

24. C. C. Pinder, *Work Motivation: Theory, Issues, and Applications* (Glenview, Ill.: Scott, Foresman, 1984), pp. 144–47; and U. R. Larson, "Supervisor's Performance Feedback to Subordinates: The Effect of Performance Valence and Outcome Dependence," *Organizational Behavior and Human Decision Processes* 37 (1986), pp. 391–409.

25. N. Winter, "New Compensation Approaches Reap Rewards," *Canadian HR Reporter,* February 26, 1993, pp. 22, 26; and N. Winter, "No Pay, No Gain," *Globe & Mail,* January 19, 1993, p. B24.

26. E. A. Locke and G. P. Latham, *A Theory of Goal Setting and Task Performance* (Englewood Cliffs, N.J.: Prentice Hall, 1990); A. J. Mento, R. P. Steel, and R. J. Karren, "A Meta-analytic Study of the Effects of Goal Setting on Task Performance: 1966–1984," *Organizational Behavior and Human Decision Processes* 39 (1987), pp. 52–83; and M. E. Tubbs, "Goal-setting: A Meta-analytic Examination of the Empirical Evidence," *Journal of Applied Psychology* 71 (1986), pp. 474–83.

27. E. A. Locke and J. F. Bryan, "Performance Goals as Determinants of Level of Performance and Boredom," *Journal of Applied Psychology* 51 (1978), pp. 120–30.

28. M. E. Tubbs, "Commitment as a Moderator of the Goal-Performance Relation: A Case for Clearer Construct Definition," *Journal of Applied Psychology* 78 (1993), pp. 86–97.

29. Locke and Latham, *A Theory of Goal Setting and Task Performance*, Chapter 6; E. A. Locke, G. P. Latham, and M. Erez, "The Determinants of Goal Commitment," *Academy of Management Review* 13 (1988), pp. 23–39; and J. Chowdhury, "The Motivational Impact of Sales Quotas on Effort," *Journal of Marketing Research* 30 (1993), pp. 28–41.

30. Locke and Latham, *A Theory of Goal Setting and Task Performance*, Chapter 7.

31. T. Matsui, A. Okada, and T. Kakuyama, "Influence of Achievement Need on Goal Setting, Performance, and Feedback Effectiveness," *Journal of Applied Psychology* 67 (1982), pp. 645–48.

32. K. N. Wexley and G. P. Latham, *Developing and Training Human Resources in Organizations*, 2nd ed. (New York: HarperCollins, 1991), pp. 77–80; and Locke and Latham, *A Theory of Goal Setting and Task Performance*, Chapter 8.

33. S. Robinson and E. Weldon, "Feedback Seeking in Groups: A Theoretical Perspective," *British Journal of Social Psychology* 32 (1993), pp. 71–86; S. J. Ashford and L. L. Cummings, "Feedback as an Individual Resource: Personal Strategies of Creating Information," *Organizational Behavior and Human Performance* 32 (1983), pp. 370–98; and S. J. Ashford, "Feedback Seeking in Individual Adaptation: A Resource Perspective," *Academy of Management Journal* 29 (1986), pp. 465–87.

34. C. Hilborn, "Those Upwardly Mobile Machines," *Canadian Business*, October 1993, pp. 117–22.

35. M. G. Evans, "Organizational Behavior: The Central Role of Motivation," *Journal of Management* 12 (1986), pp. 203–22.

36. "Dylex Shapes MIS into Strategic Weapon," *Chain Store Age Executive*, January 1989, pp. 84–86.

37. D. M. Herold, R. C. Linden, and M. L. Leatherwood, "Using Multiple Attributes to Assess Sources of Performance Feedback," *Academy of Management Journal*, 1987, pp. 826–35.

38. S. J. Ashford and G. B. Northcraft, "Conveying More (or Less) Than We Realize: The Role of Impression Management in Feedback Seeking," *Organizational Behavior and Human Decision Processes* 53 (1992), pp. 310–34; and E. W. Morrison and R. J. Bies, "Impression Management in the Feedback-Seeking Process: A Literature Review and Research Agenda," *Academy of Management Review* 16 (1991), pp. 522–41.

39. G. B. Northcraft and S. J. Ashford, "The Preservation of Self in Everyday Life: The Effects of Performance Expectations and Feedback Context on Feedback Inquiry," *Organizational Behavior and Human Decision Processes* 47 (1990), pp. 42–64.

40. R. D. Pritchard, P. L. Roth, S. D. Jones, and P. G. Roth, "Implementing Feedback Systems to Enhance Productivity: A Practical Guide," *National Productivity Review* 10 (Winter 1990–1991), pp. 57–67.

41. P. M. Posakoff and J. Fahr, "Effects of Feedback Sign and Credibility on Goal Setting and Task Performance," *Organizational Behavior and Human Decision Processes* 44 (1989), pp. 45–67.

42. T. K. Connellan, *How to Improve Performance: Behaviorism in Business and Industry* (New York: Harper & Row, 1978), Chapter 8.

43. R. D. Guzzo and B. A. Gannett, "The Nature of Facilitators and Inhibitors of Effective Task Performance," *Facilitating Work Effectiveness*, ed. F. D. Schoorman & B. Schneider (Lexington, Mass.: Lexington Books, 1988), p. 23; and R. C. Linden and T. R. Mitchell, "Reactions to Feedback: The Role of Attributions," *Academy of Management Journal*, 1985, pp. 291–308.

44. E. Kallman, "Electronic Monitoring of Employees: Issues and Guidelines," *Journal of Systems Management* 44, no. 6 (June 1993), pp. 17–21; and R. Grant and C. Higgins, "Monitoring Service Workers via Computer: The Effect on Employees, Productivity, and Service," *National Productivity Review*, Spring 1989, pp. 101–12.

45. D. Daniel, "Making a Call Centre Work," *Computing Canada*, September 14, 1989, p. 50; G. Bylinsky, "How Companies Spy on Employees," *Fortune*, November 4, 1991, pp. 131–40; and C. P. Fotos, "Flight Safety Advances Hinge on Pilot–Management Teamwork," *Aviation Week & Space Technology*, October 9, 1989, p. 31.

46. K. A. Jenero and L. D. Mapes-Riordan, "Electronic Monitoring of Employees and the Elusive 'Right to Privacy,' " *Employee Relations Law Journal* 18 (Summer 1992), pp. 71–102.

47. A. Walmsley, "The Brain Game," *Report on Business Magazine*, April 1993, pp. 36–45.

48. Fotos, "Flight Safety Advances Hinge on Pilot–Management Teamwork," p. 31.

49. J. Coutts, "Bell Finds Morale Improved Since Monitoring Stopped," *The Globe & Mail*, February 20, 1990, p. A14; and L. Archer, "I Saw What You Did and I Know Who You Are," *Canadian Business*, November 1985, pp. 76–83.

50. B. P. Niehoff and R. H. Moorman, "Justice as a Mediator of the Relationship Between Methods of Monitoring and Organizational Citizenship Behavior," *Academy of Management Journal* 36 (June 1993), pp. 527–56; and J. Chalykoff and T. A. Kochan, "Computer-Aided Monitoring: Its Influence on Employee Job Satisfaction and Turnover," *Personnel Psychology* 42 (1989), pp. 807–34.

51. J. S. Adams, "Toward an Understanding of Inequity," *Journal of Abnormal and Social Psychology* 67 (1963), pp. 422–36; and R. T. Mowday, "Equity Theory Predictions of Behavior in Organizations," in *Motivation and Work Behavior*, 5th ed., ed. R. M. Steers & L. W. Porter (New York: McGraw-Hill, 1991), pp. 111–31.

52. C. T. Kulik and M. L. Ambrose, "Personal and Situational Determinants of Referent Choice," *Academy of Management Review* 17 (1992), pp. 212–37; J. Pfeffer, "Incentives in Organizations: The Importance of Social

Relations," in *Organization Theory: From Chester Barnard to the Present and Beyond*, ed. O. E. Williamson (New York: Oxford University Press, 1990), pp. 72–97; and A. V. Subbarao and A. deCarufel, "Pay Secrecy and Perceptions of Fairness in a University Environment," *Proceedings of the Annual ASAC Conference, Organizational Behaviour Division* 4 (Part 5) (1983), pp. 173–81.

53. T. P. Summers and A. S. DeNisi, "In Search of Adams' Other: Reexamination of Referents Used in the Evaluation of Pay," *Human Relations* 43 (1990), pp. 497–511.

54. J. S. Adams, "Inequity in Social Exchange," in *Advances in Experimental Psychology*, ed. L. Berkowitz (New York: Academic Press, 1965), pp. 157–89.

55. T. A. Kochan, *Collective Bargaining and Industrial Relations* (Homewood, Ill.: Irwin, 1980), pp. 142–45.

56. E. Hatfield and S. Sprecher, "Equity Theory and Behavior in Organizations," *Research in the Sociology of Organizations* 3 (1984), pp. 94–124.

57. J. Greenberg and S. Ornstein, "High Status Job Title as Compensation for Underpayment: A Test of Equity Theory," *Journal of Applied Psychology* 68 (1983), pp. 285–97; G. R. Oldham and H. E. Miller, "The Effect of Significant Other's Job Complexity on Employee Reactions to Work," *Human Relations* 32 (1979), pp. 247–60; R. Vecchio, "Predicting Worker Performance in Inequitable Settings," *Academy of Management Review* (1982), pp. 103–10; P. S. Goodman and A. Friedman, "An Examination of Adam's Theory of Inequity," *Administrative Science Quarterly* 16 (1971), pp. 271–88; and R. D. Pritchard, M. D. Dunnette, and D. O. Jorgenson, "Effects of Perceptions of Equity and Inequity on Worker Performance and Satisfaction," *Journal of Applied Psychology* 56 (Monograph) (1972), pp. 75–94.

58. R. P. Vecchio and J. R. Terborg, "Salary Increment Allocation and Individual Differences," *Journal of Organizational Behaviour* 8 (1987), pp. 37–43.

59. N. J. Adler, *International Dimensions of Organizational Behavior*, 2nd ed. (Boston: PWS-Kent, 1991), p. 152; and G. Hofstede, "Motivation, Leadership, and Organization: Do American Theories Apply Abroad?" *Organizational Dynamics*, Summer 1980, pp. 42–63.

60. F. Herzberg, "Worker Needs: The Same Around the World," *Industry Week*, September 21, 1987, pp. 29–32.

61. N. A. Boyacigiller and N. J. Adler, "The Parochial Dinosaur: Organizational Science in a Global Context," *Academy of Management Review* 16 (1991), pp. 262–90; and Adler, *International Dimensions of Organizational Behavior*, 2nd ed., p. 160.

62. For further discussion of the cross-cultural relevance of motivation theories, see R. S. Bhagat and S. J. McQuaid, "Role of Subjective Culture in Organizations: A Review and Directions for Future Research," *Journal of Applied Psychology* 67 (1982), pp. 653–85.

Chapter Case

Steelfab Ltd.

Jackie Ney was an enthusiastic employee when she began working in the accounting department at Steelfab Ltd. In particular, she prided herself on discovering better ways of handling invoice and requisition flows. The company had plenty of bottlenecks in the flow of paperwork throughout the organization and Jackie had made several recommendations to her boss, Mr. Johnston, that would improve the process. Mr. Johnston acknowledged these suggestions and even implemented a few, but he didn't seem to have enough time to either thank her or explain why some suggestions could not be implemented. In fact, Mr. Johnston didn't say much to any of the other employees in the department about anything they did.

At the end of the first year, Jackie received a 6 percent merit increase based on Mr. Johnston's evaluation of her performance. This increase was equal to the average merit increase among the 11 people in the accounting department and was above the inflation rate. Still, Jackie was frustrated by the fact that she didn't know how to improve her chances of a higher merit increase the next year. She was also upset by the fact that another new employee, Jim Sandu, received the highest pay increase (10 percent) even though he was not regarded by others in the finance department as a particularly outstanding performer. According to others who worked with him on some assignments, Jim lacked the skills to perform the job well enough to receive such a high reward. However, Jim Sandu had become a favoured employee to Mr. Johnston and they had even gone on a fishing trip together.

Jackie's enthusiasm toward Steelfab Ltd. fell dramatically during her second year of employment. She still enjoyed the work and made friends with some of her co-workers, but the spirit that had once carried her through the morning rush hour traffic had somehow dwindled. Eventually, Jackie stopped mentioning her productivity improvement ideas. On two occasions during her second year of employment, she took a few days of sick leave to visit friends and family in New Brunswick. She had used only two sick days during her first year and these were for a legitimate illness. Even her doctor had to urge Jackie to stay at home on one occasion. But by the end of the second year, using sick days seemed to "justify" Jackie's continued employment at Steelfab Ltd. Now, as her second annual merit increase approached, Jackie started to seriously scout around for another job.

Discussion Questions

1. **What symptom(s) exist in this case to suggest that something has gone wrong?**

2. **What are the root causes that have led to these symptoms?**

3. **What actions should the organization take to correct these problems?**

©1989 Steven L. McShane.

Experiential Exercise

Predicting Harry's Work Effort

Purpose: This exercise is designed to help you understand expectancy theory and how its elements affect a person's level of effort toward job performance.

Instructions: This exercise may be completed either individually or in small teams of four or five people. When the individuals (or teams) have completed the exercise, the results will be discussed and compared with others in the class.

Read the following interview case. Then, using the chart at the end of the case, determine whether Harry will engage in high or low performance effort under the conditions described. Valence scores range from −1.0 to +1.0. All expectancies are probabilities ranging from 0 (no chance) to 1.0 (definitely will occur). The effort level scores are calculated by multiplying each valence by the appropriate P→O expectancy, summing these results, then multiplying the sum by the E→P expectancy.

Interviewer: Hi, Harry. I have been asked to talk to you about your job. Do you mind if I ask you a few questions?

Harry: No, not at all.

Interviewer: Thanks, Harry. What are the things that you would anticipate getting satisfaction from as a result of your job?

Harry: What do you mean?

Interviewer: Well, what is important to you with regard to your job here?

Harry: I guess most important is job security. As a matter of fact, I can't think of anything that is more important to me. I think getting a raise would be nice, and a promotion would be even better.

Interviewer: Anything else that you think would be nice to get, or for that matter, that you would want to avoid?

Harry: I certainly would not want my buddies to make fun of me. We're pretty friendly, and this is really important to me.

Interviewer: Anything else?

Harry: No, not really. That seems to be it.

Interviewer: How satisfied do you think you would be with each of these?

Harry: What do you mean?

Interviewer: Well, assume that something that you would really like has a value of +1.0 and something you would really not like, that is you would want to avoid, has a value of −1.0, and something you are indifferent about has a value of 0.

Harry: OK. Getting a raise would have a value of .5; a promotion is more important, so I'd say .7; and having my buddies make fun of me, .9.

Interviewer: But, I thought you didn't want your buddies to make fun of you.

Harry: I don't.

Interviewer: But you gave it a value of .9.

Harry: Oh, I guess it should be −.9.

Interviewer: Ok, I just want to be sure I understand what you're saying. Harry, what do you think the chances are of these things happening?

Harry: That depends.

Interviewer: On what?

Harry: On whether my performance is high or just acceptable.

Interviewer: What if it is high?

Harry: I figure I stand about a 50–50 chance of getting a raise and/or a promotion, but I also think that there is a 90 percent chance that my buddies will make fun of me.

Interviewer: What about job security?

Harry: I am certain my job is secure here, whether my performance is high or just acceptable. I can't remember the last guy who was doing his job and got fired. But if my performance is just acceptable, my chances of a raise or promotion are about 10 percent. However, then the guys will not make fun of me. That I am certain about.

Interviewer: What is the likelihood of your performance level being high?

Harry: That depends. If I work very hard and put out a high degree of effort, I'd say that my chance of my performance being high is about 90 percent. But if I put out a low level of effort, you know—if I just take it easy—then I figure that the chances of my doing an acceptable job is about 80 percent.

Interviewer: Well, which would you do: put out a low level or a high level of effort?

Harry: With all the questions you asked me, you should be able to tell me.

Interviewer: You may be right!

Harry: Yeah? That's nice. Hey, if you don't have any other questions, I'd like to join the guys for coffee.

Interviewer: OK, thanks for your time.

Harry: You're welcome.

Source: Robert J. Oppenheimer, Concordia University, Montreal. Used with permission.

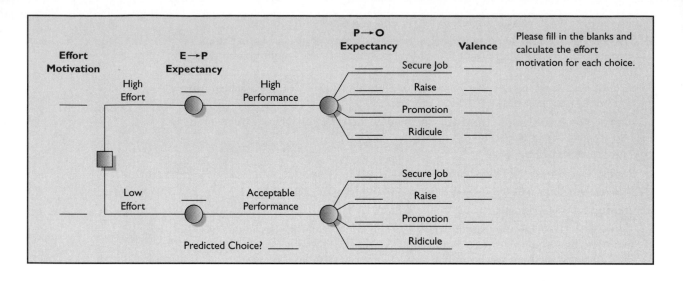

Applied Motivation Practices

Learning Objectives
After reading this chapter, you should be able to:

Identify five problems with job status-based rewards.

Explain how skill-based rewards might improve organizational effectiveness.

Give an example of an individual, team, and organizational level performance-based reward.

Critique the use of punishment in organizations.

Contrast progressive discipline and positive discipline.

Discuss the advantages and disadvantages of job specialization.

Diagram the job characteristics model of job design.

Chapter Outline

Reward Systems.

Discipline and Punishment.

Job Design.

Job Design and Work Efficiency.

Job Design and Work Motivation.

Job Design Strategies to Increase Work Motivation.

Job Design Prospects and Problems.

Northern Telecom, Canada's largest telecommunications manufacturer, sells its products through a distributor network of 1,000 sales representatives across Canada. However, Northern Telecom's main competitors use the same distributor network. "That means we must be smarter in motivating the salespeople," says Sherry Owen, a Northern Telecom sales promotion specialist in Belleville, Ontario.

But standard incentive plans have problems. Programs that distribute merchandise have a relatively low cost, but they may fall short on value. "If your target sales reps are well established in their lifestyle, it is unlikely that merchandise will motivate them," Owen advises. Travel awards are popular, but the destination's value will depend on the person's demographic group (e.g., married with children). Owen also warns that cash shouldn't be used as a reward because it is quickly forgotten.

To overcome these dilemmas, Northern Telecom introduced Meridian Plus, a national sales incentive that works like a frequent flyer program. Salespeople earn a specified number of points for selling a particular Northern Telecom product and can redeem accumulated points for any of the 800 merchandise items in Northern Telecom's special catalogue. Alternatively, points may be redeemed for travel vouchers to any destination in the world.

Each month, Northern Telecom sends the top two point earners in each sales organization a sweatshirt with the Meridian Plus logo. They also become Tour de Force members, an elite group of top point earners who receive bonus points and the opportunity to participate in special travel lotteries.

High point earners in the Meridian Plus program receive plenty of recognition along with their other rewards. They are publicly celebrated at sales meetings with Northern Telecom's management and are listed in a special insert with every salesperson's monthly incentive point statement. "Recognition is the ultimate motivator for salespeople," says Owen. "Nothing matches singling out the top sales reps in front of their peers at a sales rally."[1]

Northern Telecom is a trendsetter in the use of formal rewards. The Meridian Plus program motivates the distributor sales force by offering a variety of incentives and adding enough flexibility to match each salesperson's needs. The sales incentive program is one of many at Northern Telecom to encourage employees and distributors to work toward the organization's strategic goals and serve its prominent stakeholders.

This chapter begins by describing the four main objectives of reward systems and debating their advantages and disadvantages. Much of the discussion looks at the types of performance-based rewards and the problems that must be avoided to make them work effectively. The second part of this chapter looks at the use of discipline and punishment in organizations. As we will see, disciplining employees may be effective, but it also carries risks. Finally, this chapter explores the dynamics of job design, particularly its role in employee motivation. Several specific job design strategies are presented, and the effectiveness of recent job design interventions is discussed.

Reward Systems

Rewards are a fundamental part of the employment relationship.[2] Organizations distribute money and other benefits in exchange for the employee's availability, competence, and behaviours.[3] The importance of this economic exchange may vary somewhat across societies, but it exists in almost all employment relationships.

As we see in Exhibit 4–1, rewards serve four primary functions. Most compensation packages try to achieve more than one reward objective. However, the relative importance of each objective depends on the organization's values as well as the influences of its stakeholders. Governments influence reward system objectives through laws that regulate minimum wages, overtime premiums, paid time off, and the like. Labour unions influence wage rates, employee benefits, and seniority-based rewards.[4]

Finally, ethical values influence reward objectives as well as the types of rewards offered. As an example, 90 percent of Canadian companies provide long-term disability (LTD) insurance as income protection for disabled employees.[5] LTD does not motivate most applicants to join an organization, nor is it an incentive for other employee behaviours; instead, this insurance serves an important ethical value for the organization and its constituents by ensuring that employees do not suffer financially if they become disabled and can no longer work.

Membership and seniority-based rewards

Membership and seniority dominate reward systems in Canada. Many of us receive hourly wages or fixed salaries and have the same benefits as our co-workers. Other rewards increase with seniority, such as the amount of paid

Objectives of Organizational Reward Systems   Exhibit 4–1

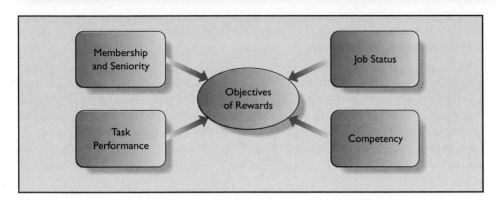

vacation time. Some employees receive seniority-based pay increases; they progress one step through the pay range for each year in the job. Even merit systems have a large seniority component because employees must spend time in the job before receiving an increase.[6] Finally, vesting arrangements in company pension plans emphasize membership and seniority, because those who leave within the first two years of employment (or longer in some provinces) forfeit the pension money that the company has contributed on their behalf.

Advantages and disadvantages

Membership-based rewards may attract job applicants, particularly when the size of the reward increases with seniority. Seniority-based rewards reduce turnover because the cost of quitting increases with the employee's length of service. Cultural values also influence the emphasis on membership-based rewards. Most French executives receive fixed pay because of their cultural aversion to the risk and uncertainty of performance-based pay.[7] One problem with membership-based rewards is that they do not directly motivate job performance. For many years, Shell Canada offered a generous pension plan and other membership-based rewards, but the company had lacklustre performance until it shifted to more performance-based pay. Another problem is that membership-based rewards discourage poor performers from leaving voluntarily because they seldom have better job offers. Instead, the good performers are lured to better-paying jobs.

Job status-based rewards

Traditional reward systems rely heavily on job status, particularly the use of job evaluation systems, to determine the size of the individual's paycheque. **Job evaluation** systematically evaluates the worth of each job within the organization by measuring its required skill, effort, responsibility, and working conditions.[8] Job evaluation results create a job hierarchy that becomes the basis for pay differentials. A senior engineer would be assigned a higher pay grade than an administrative assistant because the engineer's job has more job evaluation points. Some perquisites are also based on job status. For instance, senior

Job evaluation
Systematically evaluating the worth of jobs within the organization by measuring their required skill, effort, responsibility, and working conditions. Job evaluation results create a hierarchy of job worth.

executives at the Canadian Imperial Bank of Commerce have exclusive access to a private dining room. Procter & Gamble Canada and Amoco Canada assign larger offices with better furniture to those holding higher positions.

Advantages and disadvantages

The traditional argument for job evaluations is that they are an impersonal yardstick to maintain equity in deciding which jobs should be paid more than others. They allegedly "remove all suspicion from the employee's mind that favouritism exists."[9] They also help companies minimize pay discrimination— situations in which women are paid less than men performing work of comparable value to the organization.[10] More generally, job status-based rewards motivate employees to compete for positions further up the organizational hierarchy.

Despite these advantages, job status-based rewards have many drawbacks. Job evaluation systems have received much criticism for their subjectivity and tendency to justify the existing job hierarchy while pretending to be neutral.[11] They motivate employees to increase their job's worth by exaggerating duties in job descriptions and hoarding more organizational resources than necessary. These political behaviours may help employees move into a higher pay rate, but they undermine the organization's effectiveness.[12]

Job status-based rewards also increase resistance to change, because people fear their jobs will be re-evaluated downward. They become territorial because the resources they control largely influence the size of their paycheque. With their emphasis on job descriptions, job evaluation systems focus employee attention on narrowly defined tasks rather than the broader organizational citizenship and customer service behaviours that improve organizational effectiveness. Finally, job status-based perquisites create a psychological distance between employees and management, thereby inhibiting communication across these groups.

Many companies are responding to the problems with status-based rewards by closing their executive dining rooms and removing other status-based perquisites. Northern Telecom, Canadian General Electric, and a few other firms have gone one step further by replacing narrowly defined pay grades with *broadbanding*. Broadbanding reduces the number of pay grades in the organization, so that more people (sometimes supervisors and their subordinates) receive the same range of pay.[13] This is not always popular among managers who value their status. Nevertheless, it potentially increases the organization's flexibility to move people into different jobs, opens opportunities to pay people for their contribution or capacity rather than status, and is consistent with the trend toward hierarchically flatter organizations.

Competency-based rewards

For many years, teachers and scientists have been paid on the basis of their formal education and acquired skills. For example, a public school teacher holding a Master's degree is placed in a higher pay grade than a teacher with an undergraduate degree. Several companies have recently expanded this idea of competency- or skill-based pay to include production and office employees. In these **skill-based pay (SBP)** systems, employees earn higher pay rates with the number of skill modules they have mastered.[14] Through special training and job rotation, employees learn how to operate another machine or complete another set of tasks. When the new skill module is mastered, their pay rate increases. Employees typically perform only one skill area at a time, but their pay rate is based on the number of areas for which they are currently qualified.

Skill-based pay (SBP)
Pay structures in which employees earn higher pay rates with the number of skill modules they have mastered, even though they perform only some of the mastered tasks in a particular job.

Advantages and disadvantages

SBP plans were pioneered in the 1970s by Procter & Gamble and are applied to nonmanagement employees in team-based work units, such as at Northern Telecom, Shell Canada, Westinghouse, and Canadian General Electric. Their main objective is to develop a flexible, multiskilled work force so that employees may be moved around to fill labour shortages or satisfy immediate customer needs. Product or service quality tends to improve because multiskilled employees are more likely to know where problems originate. Moreover, employees find it easier to discover ways to improve the work process as they learn more skills and tasks in that process. For these reasons, skill-based rewards are highly compatible with total quality management (see Chapter 1) and potentially improve organizational effectiveness.[15]

One of the common complaints about skill-based rewards is that employees "top out" as they finally master all the skill modules. For example, 92 percent of the employees under Shell Canada's SBP plan have reached the top skill module. This problem is amplified when employees complete modules without any serious evaluation and are not retested later to ensure that these skills are still mastered. Another concern is that skill-based reward systems are more expensive than traditional job status-based systems. Employees spend more time learning new skills and less time performing tasks for which they are fully competent. Moreover, employees who reach the top pay rates earn more than in traditional systems.[16] Although advocates of SBP plans say that these costs are offset by productivity gains, this might not be true in every company.

Performance-based rewards

One hundred years ago, Timothy Eaton awarded bonuses to clerks with the highest monthly sales. Many years before that, the Hudson's Bay Company paid voyageurs based on distance travelled rather than a fixed rate. This motivated them to accept the arduous task of crossing the Canadian wilderness for the company.[17] Such performance-based reward systems distribute money and other economic benefits to employees based on their behaviour and consequences to the organization. Performance-based rewards are certainly not new to Canadian industry, but they now come in more varieties than ever before. Exhibit 4–2 lists the most common types of performance-based pay in each of the three levels of analysis.[18]

Individual rewards

Individual rewards have existed since Babylonian days in the 20th century B.C.[19] The oldest of these is the *piece rate,* which calculates pay by the number of units the employee produces. For instance, seamstresses at Stratton Knitting Mills in Toronto receive higher earnings if they sew more sweaters.[20] *Commissions* are

| Exhibit 4–2 | Types of Performance-Based Rewards |

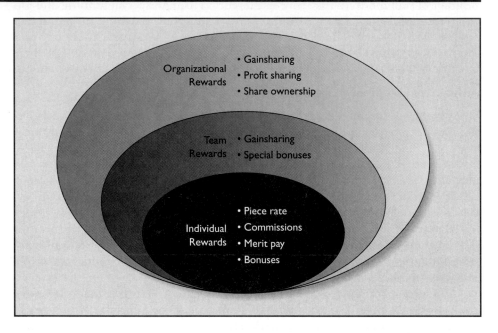

similar to piece rates, except that earnings are based on sales volume rather than units produced. Many realtors and automobile salespeople are paid straight commission. *Merit pay plans* award percentage or fixed dollar increases in the person's salary, usually based on a supervisor's appraisal of the employee's performance over the previous year.[21]

Managers often receive *bonuses* based on their achievement of specific objectives, such as increased sales volume or market share over one or two years. Some companies distribute these lump-sum payments to employees who engage in specific behaviours. Vancouver City Savings Credit Union pays a bonus to any employee who loses weight, stops smoking, or jogs 1,000 miles per year. Freightliner Canada's cab assembly plant in St. Thomas, Ontario, pays a bonus equal to an extra week's salary to any employee who shows up for work on time every day throughout the year.[22]

Team rewards

The number of team-based reward systems has soared over the past few years as more companies emphasize work teams rather than individuals as their basic building block.[23] As Perspective 4–1 describes, some of these plans distribute bonuses, paid time off, or special awards for the team's achievement of specific objectives.[24]

Gainsharing plans
A reward system usually applied to work teams that distributes bonuses to team members based on the amount of cost reductions and increased labour efficiency in the production process.

Other team-based rewards, called **gainsharing plans,** focus on cost reductions and increased labour efficiency. By identifying ways to reduce labour and/or material costs, employees share subsequent financial gains with the company using a predetermined formula. Bonuses are distributed monthly or quarterly, and some of the money is withheld in case productivity falls.[25] Magnesium Products, an auto parts manufacturer in Strathroy, Ontario, is one of many Canadian firms with a gainsharing plan for its production employees.

Perspective 4–1

The Rewards of Team Performance

Sport Mart Discount Superstores discovered a creative incentive to boost sales at its nine retail outlets across British Columbia. Management promised an entire week off with pay to employees of the store that most exceeded projected sales over a two-month period. Head office staff would operate the store while the winning sales team enjoyed the special holiday.

To keep everyone motivated throughout the two-month competition, the Kamloops-based retailer sent posters and weekly updates of the comparative standings to each store. Sales staff at one store displayed their confidence by placing coat hangers bearing the names of head office staff in their cloakroom. However, employees at another store won the prize and enjoyed their week off at a nearby ski resort. But the big winner was Sport Mart. The team-based incentive boosted sales by 8 percent over the same period the previous year and created a unique camaraderie within each of the stores.

KFC recently initiated a different type of team competition award across its Canadian operations. A senior KFC manager explains that "four-person teams from each of our units participate in an operations and service competition with regional and national awards given to the team that best reflects our operating standard." The fast-food chain hopes this competition will foster team spirit and encourage employees in each unit to focus on the company's tough quality standards.

Health Care Diaper is another company that knows how to strengthen teamwork through rewards. The Richmond, British Columbia, manufacturer of disposable baby diapers awards team bonuses based on product quality on each work shift. Quality is determined each week by a quality control technician who inspects a random case of diapers from stock. Says general manager Carolyn LeBlanc: "If everyone makes a great diaper, then everyone gets a bonus." But if any shift worker lets a defective product slip by, or if a customer complaint can be traced back to that work shift, then all members of that team forfeit their $10 bonus for that week.

Sources: Based on M. McCullough, "Who's Minding the Store?" *BC Business*, April 1993, p. 8; "Health Care Diaper," *BC Business*, October 1993, p. 38; and L. Lecours, "Creating an Effective Employee Recognition Program," *Canadian Hotel and Restaurant* 70 (September 1992), pp. 32–33.

The plan calculates improvements in the material, labour, and overhead costs that employees have control over. Monthly bonuses have ranged from $35 to $250 per employee.[26]

Organizational rewards

Some rewards are based on indicators of the organization's performance. Gainsharing plans sometimes operate at an organizational level where one plan covers all employees rather than separate plans for different work teams. **Profit sharing** is the most prominent organizational reward. This includes any arrangement in which a designated group of employees receives a share of corporate profits.[27] Although profit sharing tries to motivate employees to reduce waste and improve performance, its clearest benefit is to automatically adjust employee wages with the firm's prosperity, thereby reducing the need for layoffs or negotiated pay reductions during recessions.[28]

Employee share ownership plans (ESOPs) encourage employees to buy shares of the company. Approximately one-third of publicly traded firms in Canada have some form of ESOP.[29] Bell Canada, for example, contributes one dollar for every $3 that employees invest in BCE Inc. common shares, to a maximum of 6 percent of their salary.[30] Several Canadian provinces have

Profit sharing
A reward system in which a designated group of employees receives a share of corporate profits.

Employee share ownership plan (ESOP)
A reward system that encourages employees to buy shares of the company.

introduced tax incentives to encourage ESOPs, so their popularity over the past few years is not surprising. The employee-owned company is an extreme variation of the share ownership. In several cases, such as Saskatoon's Great Western Brewing Company, employees or managers have bought the company when it was about to fold.[31]

Problems with performance-based rewards

There is strong evidence that performance-based reward systems improve employee motivation and organizational effectiveness, particularly where employees previously received only membership-based rewards (e.g., hourly wages or straight salary).[32] However, organizational behaviour researchers have identified several problems that undermine the effectiveness of performance-based rewards.[33]

Biased performance measurement

One common problem is that many companies use inaccurate measures of employee performance, thereby weakening the P→O expectancy (see Chapter 3). In performance appraisals, some supervisors don't differentiate between good and poor performers. As one Montreal engineer laments, "Ninety-nine percent of the people here are getting the same range of salary increase. Sometimes it looks like people working very hard are not getting any more appreciation or pay than someone who isn't working at all."[34] Recent evidence further suggests that performance pay decisions are biased by organizational politics. Employees with organizational connections (e.g., friendships with senior management) tend to receive higher increases. Employees with special skills or knowledge also receive higher pay increases or bonuses, apart from their actual job performance.[35]

Difficulty adjusting for situational contingencies

Some employees perform better than others simply because situational contingencies are operating in their favour. Employees in one region may have higher sales because the economy is stronger there than elsewhere. Although management tries to control for these external factors, their adjustments are not precise. Macmillan Bloedel recently experienced this problem with its gainsharing plan. Employees enjoyed an unexpectedly large bonus because a falling Canadian dollar suddenly improved the gainsharing results. The plan was intended to reward employees for their personal productivity improvements, not for windfall gains in exchange rates.[36]

Highly interdependent jobs

The situational contingency problem is further apparent when companies implement individual rewards for jobs that are highly interdependent. Individual performance rewards are difficult to apply in chemical plants, for example, because an employee's performance is strongly influenced by the efforts of co-workers in the process.[37] Individual rewards also reduce worker cooperation, a serious problem where resources are shared and employees work interdependently. Thus, rewards based on team or organizational performance should be applied where employees have high task interdependence.

Rewards aren't motivating

Many so-called rewards don't motivate employees because they aren't valued by the people who receive them. As an example, Quality Coils recently closed its manufacturing operation in Mexico because employees wouldn't work beyond their quota under the piece rate system. In desperation, the company offered to let the Mexican employees go home early if they finished ahead of time, but that didn't work either.[38] This incident reflects the point learned in Chapter 3 that people have different needs and are therefore motivated by different rewards. Mexican employees at Quality Coil didn't want to work hard for large paycheques or extra time off. As we saw in the opening story to this chapter, Northern Telecom's Meridian Plus program tried to address this problem by letting sales staff members choose their preferred reward.

Incomplete reward coverage

Reward systems often ignore some dimensions of job performance. Employees might be rewarded for the number of clients served, but not for the quality of service provided. Based on the adage that "what gets rewarded, gets done," employees will focus their attention on the performance dimensions that get rewarded. They pay less attention to service quality while directing their effort toward processing more customers. Donnelly Mirrors, the automobile parts manufacturer, experienced this problem when it introduced a gainsharing plan that motivated employees to reduce labour but not material costs. Employees learned that they could reduce labour costs by discarding the expensive diamond grinding wheels before they wore down. The net result was that the lower labour costs were easily offset by the increased supplies costs.[39]

Wrong behaviours rewarded

Performance-based reward systems sometimes influence different behaviours than management intended. Perspective 4–2 describes two examples of this in the Canadian insurance industry. Why does this happen? Recall from our discussion of systems theory in Chapter 1 that organizations are open systems with many interdependent parts. This makes it very difficult to predict the possible consequences of organizational actions, such as the introduction of a performance-based reward system.

Discipline and Punishment

Punishment was defined in Chapter 2 as the *introduction* of a consequence that *decreases* the frequency or probability of a behaviour recurring. **Discipline** is a more ambiguous concept, but it usually refers to the act of formally punishing employees who violate an organizational rule or procedure. The objective is to regulate the behaviour of employees engaging in inappropriate activities as well as deter others from practising these behaviours.[40]

Punishment is a complex and potentially risky strategy to suppress or eliminate unwanted behaviour.[41] However, recent studies report that properly administered disciplinary actions may significantly improve work attendance, output, and quality. One explanation, based on social learning theory (see Chapter 2), is that

Discipline
The act of formally punishing employees who violate an organizational rule or procedure.

Perspective 4–2

What Gets Rewarded Gets Done

Many Canadian insurance firms pay sales agents large front-end commissions ranging from 150 to 200 percent of premiums during the year the sale was made. For example, if a customer buys a policy requiring $1,200 in first-year premium payments, the agent could immediately collect as much as $2,400 in commissions from the insurance company. One problem with this incentive system is that agents become less concerned about whether the client can afford large premium payments. If the client defaults a few years later, the agent has already earned a healthy commission.

An equally serious problem is that the large front-end commissions motivate some unscrupulous agents to engage in an illegal rebating scheme. Specifically, they offer free or discounted insurance for the first year even though the clients cannot afford the premiums in later years. The agent pays for some of the first-year premiums and still earns enough from the commission for a healthy income. Ultimately, the customer and insurance company lose while the insurance agent pockets a healthy reward.

Some insurance firms pay a higher commission rate to agents with higher annual sales. For example, an agent selling policies with $50,000 in annual premiums might earn a 120 percent commission rate, whereas someone bringing in $300,000 in premiums would receive a 200 percent rate. To maximize their income, some agents group together and submit their combined sales under one person's name. The combined sales produce a much higher commission rate and the group splits a much higher income than if each worked alone. Insurance companies end up paying much higher incentives under this poorly designed incentive scheme.

Sources: Based on J. Fleming, *Merchants of Fear: An Investigation of Canada's Insurance Industry* (Toronto: Penguin, 1986), pp. 20, 79.

---

employees who observe co-workers receiving disciplinary action are less likely to engage in inappropriate behaviours themselves. Another argument suggests that employees gain a stronger sense of fairness when wrongdoers are disciplined.[42]

Progressive discipline

Progressive discipline
An organizational discipline procedure in which the severity of punishment increases with the frequency and severity of the infraction.

Many organizations use a system of **progressive discipline** to discourage inappropriate behaviour. This process, illustrated in Exhibit 4–3, involves administering more severe forms of punishment based on the frequency and severity of the infraction. Following the first violation, the employee typically receives a verbal reprimand from the immediate supervisor. The second infraction results in a written warning. The third infraction invokes a short-term suspension from work without pay. If the behaviour is repeated, the employee may receive a longer suspension and eventually employment termination.

Progressive discipline begins with mildly aversive sanctions so that the employee has an opportunity to correct the undesirable behaviour before harsher penalties are applied. However, the severity of the offense also affects the type of discipline received. The first incidence of lateness may result in a reprimand, whereas more serious infractions (e.g., theft) often result in a suspension or immediate dismissal.[43]

Problems with punishment

Progressive discipline may be a common organizational practice, but it potentially creates several problems.[44] One concern is that punishment may evoke an

The Progressive Discipline Process   Exhibit 4–3

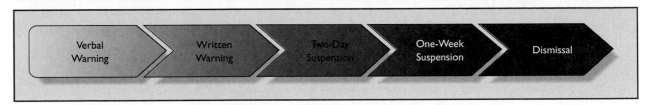

adverse emotional reaction. When supervisors engage in destructive rather than constructive criticism, employees become defensive and try to avoid the supervisor in the future.[45] In extreme cases, employees develop hostilities toward the organization that result in sabotage. This happened at a Frito-Lay plant where managers fired 58 of the 210 employees in less than one year. The remaining employees retaliated by putting obscene messages on the potato chips they packaged.[46]

Another problem is that punishment tells employees which actions are inappropriate, but it does not help them to learn appropriate behaviours. With increased hostility and interpersonal distance from the supervisor, employees also become more resistant to adaptive learning. A third concern is that punishment tends to be effective only when the source of punishment is nearby. This follows the adage that "when the cat's away, the mice will play." Some theorists suggest that employees subsequently act more immaturely on the job because punishment treats them like children.[47]

Finally, punishment can be costly. Suspending an employee without pay forces the company to hire temporary help or increase overtime. Co-workers must sometimes be bumped into other jobs to fill the vacancy. This disrupts the work flow and increases production costs.

Applying punishment effectively

Many of the problems described above can be avoided by considering a few conditions when disciplining employees. Punishment should be administered as soon as the infraction occurs so that the employee sees a clear link between the behaviour and organizational consequences. It also communicates the seriousness of the infraction. Disciplinary actions should be treated impersonally, that is, supervisors should focus on the behaviour rather than the person. This minimizes the potential emotional flare-up that people often experience when being punished.

Punishment should occur privately, because this protects the person's self-esteem and minimizes his or her hostility. The problem, of course, is that completely private discipline does not discourage others from engaging in wrongful behaviour. However, some writers note that co-workers hear about the individual's disciplinary action through the grapevine anyway.[48]

Justice literature suggests that the level of punishment should fit the crime. However, other research indicates that harsh punishment evokes an emotional response from the person receiving the discipline (usually against the punisher) that may impede adaptive learning.[49] Instead, the level of discipline should be relatively mild but symbolically clear enough to alter behaviour.

© *Graham Harrop. Used with permission.*

To maintain perceptions of equity, punishment should be applied every time the undesirable behaviour occurs, and the same sanctions should be administered to everyone who engages in the same infraction. Unfortunately, recent evidence suggests that most organizations tend to be inconsistent in their disciplinary process.[50]

An important feature of effective discipline is for the supervisor to clearly explain what behaviour is being disciplined and what consequences will follow a repetition of that behaviour. Because punishment does not direct employees to the preferred behaviour, supervisors must specifically describe and reinforce the correct behaviour (or a reasonable approximation of it). Finally, punishment is a form of persuasive communication (see Chapter 6); hence, the person administering punishment should be respected enough that the recipient accepts the legitimacy and symbolic meaning of the disciplinary action.

Mixed consequences model

Progressive discipline usually involves punishment, whereas reward systems usually (although not always) apply positive reinforcement principles. But few companies would consider using only these two strategies to control employee behaviour. Rather, they use the **mixed consequences approach,** in which all four reinforcement contingencies described in Chapter 2 are applied at appropriate performance levels.[51]

Mixed consequences approach
A behaviour change intervention that applies the four reinforcement contingencies—positive reinforcement, extinction, punishment, and negative reinforcement—at appropriate phases of employee performance.

As Exhibit 4–4 illustrates, positive reinforcement is administered following good performance or as performance improves, whereas extinction is applied when performance slips. Decreasing performance is also addressed through supportive management practices such as coaching and counselling. Persistently poor performance, however, requires the application of penalties, such as warnings of demotion or dismissal. This cannot be avoided unless the organization intends to retain poor performers.

Negative reinforcement—the removal of punishers—is administered along with positive reinforcement as marginal performance improves. For example, the supervisor would stop criticizing the marginal employee's performance and would thank him or her for improved results. An increasing number of companies have introduced mixed consequences systems to improve poor job performance and control employee absenteeism. Perspective 4–3 describes how this strategy helped improve attendance at Schneider Corp.

The Mixed Consequences Model of Discipline   Exhibit 4–4

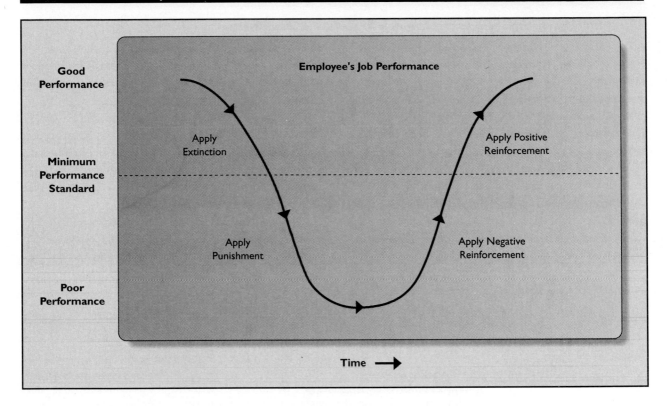

Discipline without punishment

A few organizations have introduced disciplinary procedures that try to avoid the use of punishment and its dysfunctional consequences. The concept of **discipline without punishment** (also called *positive discipline*) was introduced at a Canadian plywood mill over 30 years ago. It received little attention until an American human resource manager applied it to a Frito-Lay plant in the 1970s. Today, positive discipline has replaced traditional disciplinary procedures at New Brunswick's Department of Transport, MacMillan Bloedel, Prince George Pulp and Paper, Union Carbide Canada, and many other companies.[52]

The basic objectives of positive discipline are to counsel employees who have violated company rules, to elicit their participation in the problem-solving process, and to gain their agreement for future behaviour or to consider future career plans elsewhere. The process typically includes four steps:

- *Step 1: verbal reminder*—The supervisor verbally reminds the employee that a company rule has been violated and, without any reprimand or warnings of future disciplinary action, tries to gain the employee's agreement to solve the problem.

- *Step 2: written reminder*—The supervisor discusses (without threats) the employee's failure to abide by the original agreement, reviews why the rule or standard must be observed, reaffirms the employee's agreement to solve the problem, and summarizes this conversation in a written reminder to the employee.

Discipline without punishment
A behaviour change intervention that tries to avoid the use of punishment by counselling employees who have violated company rules and inviting them to participate in finding a solution to the problem.

Perspective 4-3

Using the Mixed Consequences Approach to Reduce Absenteeism

A few years ago, absenteeism at Schneider Corp. was hovering around 10 percent. This is close to the average rate in the Canadian manufacturing industry, but it was unacceptable to Schneider's management. To improve attendance on scheduled workdays, the Kitchener, Ontario, meat processing company introduced a mixed consequences attendance control program.

This multipronged strategy involves administering both rewards for good attendance and penalties for those with chronic attendance problems. Employees with perfect attendance receive a congratulatory letter, a token gift, and recognition in the company's newsletter. Those who are absent for justifiable health or personal reasons receive support through the company's assistance program. Based on the principle that 20 percent of the people cause 80 percent of the problem, Schneider also targets chronic leave takers. Those with poor attendance records are disciplined after one or two offences.

Schneider's mixed consequences approach has paid off handsomely. Two years after the policy was introduced, absenteeism among the company's 2,200 employees had dropped to 7.4 percent, and the meat processor has saved over $1 million in lost time. The program also sent an important message to employees.

"It's made a world of difference," says Schneider's national employee relations manager. "The employee is made to recognize his or her importance to the company."

Source: Adapted from C. Sinclair, "Absenteeism's Plague Has No Simple Cure," *Financial Times of Canada,* June 11, 1990, p. 7.

- *Step 3: decision-making leave*—This is a paid one-day leave of absence in which the employee decides to permanently change the unwanted behaviour or find employment elsewhere. The employee announces the decision the next day and, if he or she wishes to stay, then the supervisor and employee develop specific goals and an action plan for improvement.

- *Step 4: dismissal*—The next offence following decision-making leave is termination of employment.

In the spirit of positive discipline, even dismissal may be reversed in some organizations. For example, Steelcase, the office furniture manufacturer, is known for its "second chance" employees. These are people who have been dismissed and subsequently hired back on the belief that they will turn around. As a fork-lift operator with the firm explains: "They might send you out the door, and a few weeks later call you up and say, 'Have you straightened out yet?' It's a chance to come back, start fresh."[53]

Job Design

Job design
The process of assigning tasks to a job and distributing work throughout the organization.

Job design involves assigning tasks to a job and distributing work throughout the organization. Some jobs have very few tasks, each requiring limited skill or effort. Other jobs include a very complex set of tasks and can be accomplished by only a few highly trained tradespeople or professionals.

The tasks that people perform are constantly changing. Computer technology often affects job duties, although management can sometimes influence the way jobs are designed around this technology.[54] Organizational restructuring also involves job redesign, such as when the Bank of Montreal dramatically changed branch manager job duties a few years ago. Finally, the trend toward self-managing work teams has altered job duties and, in some respects, altered traditional ideas about jobs.

Job design is important because of its influence on employee attitudes, motivation, and productivity. As we shall see, job design often produces an interesting conflict between the employee's motivation and ability. To understand this issue more fully, we begin by describing early job design efforts aimed at increasing work efficiency through job specialization.

Job Design and Work Efficiency

Early management theory emphasized the notion that work efficiency increases with the subdivision of work into separate jobs assigned to different people. This division of labour leads to **job specialization,** because each job now includes a narrow subset of the tasks necessary to complete the product or service.

Work efficiency potentially increases through job specialization, because employees have fewer tasks to juggle and therefore spend less time changing activities. Training costs are reduced, because employees require fewer physical and mental skills to accomplish the assigned work. Jobs are mastered quickly, because employees practise their tasks more frequently with shorter work cycles. For example, assembly workers would typically have less than one minute to complete their task on a product before starting it again on the next product. Finally, work efficiency increases, because employees with specific aptitudes or skills can be matched more precisely to the jobs for which they are best suited.[55]

The economic benefits of job specialization were popularized over two hundred years ago by Adam Smith in his famous example of pin manufacturing.[56] According to Smith, there are several distinct operations in pin manufacturing, such as drawing out the wire, straightening it, cutting it, sharpening one end, grinding the other end, putting on the head, and whitening the head. In one factory where these tasks were divided among 10 people, Smith reported that the work team could produce almost 4,800 pins per day. But if the same 10 people made their own pins separately and independently, they would produce only 100 to 200 pins per day!

Adam Smith was mainly writing about *horizontal job specialization,* in which the basic physical behaviours required to provide a product or service are divided into different jobs (see Exhibit 4–5). *Vertical job specialization,* on the other hand, refers to separating physical tasks from the administration of these tasks (planning, organizing, scheduling, etc.). In other words, vertical job specialization divorces the "thinking" job functions from the "doing" job functions.

Scientific management

One of the strongest advocates of job specialization was Frederick Winslow Taylor, an industrial engineer who introduced the principles of **scientific management** during the early 1900s.[57] Taylor described scientific management as a revolutionary way for management and workers to view their respective roles. In practice, it involves systematically determining how work should be partitioned into its smallest possible elements and how the process of completing each task should be standardized to achieve maximum efficiency.

Job specialization
The result of division of labour in which each job now includes a narrow subset of the tasks required to complete the product or service.

Scientific management
The process of systematically determining how work should be partitioned into its smallest possible elements and how the process of completing each task should be standardized to achieve maximum efficiency.

Exhibit 4–5   **Horizontal and Vertical Job Specialization**

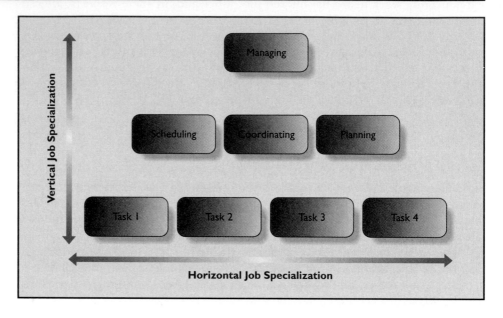

Taylor advocated vertical job specialization so that detailed procedures and work practices are developed by engineers, enforced by supervisors, and executed by employees. In Taylor's words: "All possible brain work should be removed from the shop floor and centred in the planning and laying out department."[58] Taylor paid just as much attention to horizontal job specialization. For example, he recommended specializing the supervisor's role so that one person manages operational efficiency, another manages inspection, and another is the disciplinarian.

Several practices described elsewhere in this book grew out of scientific management. Taylor was an early advocate of goal setting, employee training, and incentive systems to increase worker productivity. Frank and Lillian Gilbreth were enthusiastic followers of the scientific management philosophy and are largely credited with developing procedures known as **time and motion studies.** Time and motion studies systematically observe, measure, and time the smallest physical movements to identify more efficient work behaviours. The idea is that there is one best way to lay bricks, staple papers together, or engage in any other observable behaviour.[59] Time and motion studies are still applied in companies by industrial engineers.

There is ample evidence that scientific management has improved efficiency in many work settings. One of Taylor's earliest interventions was at a ball bearing factory where 120 women each worked 55 hours per week. Through job specialization and work efficiency analysis, Taylor increased production by two-thirds using a work force of only 35 women working fewer than 45 hours per week. Taylor also doubled the employees' previous wages. No doubt, some of the increased productivity can be credited to improved training, goal setting, and work incentives, but job specialization has also contributed to the success of scientific management.

Scientific management was just as successful in Canada. In 1927, an American industrial engineer was hired by York Knitting Mills in Toronto to increase productivity through time and motion study and wage incentives. The results were so dramatic that Douglas Woods (York's owner) and two colleagues formed their own

Time and motion study
The process of systematically observing, measuring, and timing the smallest physical movements to identify more efficient work behaviours.

Job Specialization–Job Performance Relationship   Exhibit 4–6

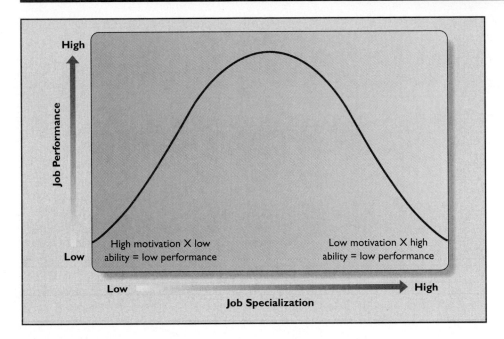

consulting firm to practise a variation of scientific management known as the "York Plan." The firm eventually expanded into other management consulting services and became Woods Gordon, one of Canada's largest consulting firms.[60]

Problems with job specialization

Job specialization tries to increase work efficiency, but this may result in lower productivity because it ignores the effects of job content on employees.[61] Highly specialized jobs are tedious, trivial, and socially isolating. These conditions lead to worker alienation, whereby employees feel powerlessness and meaninglessness in their work lives, as well as increasing removal from social norms, and a psychological separation of oneself from the activities being performed.[62]

Job specialization was supposed to let companies buy cheap, unskilled labour. Instead, many companies must offer higher wages—some call it *discontentment pay*—to compensate for the job dissatisfaction of narrowly defined work.[63] Labour unions have also been effective at organizing and negotiating higher wages for employees in specialized, short-cycle jobs. Higher turnover, absenteeism, and sabotage along with lower productivity and mental health problems have added further costs to job specialization.

Work quality has become another major concern. Employees in specialized jobs usually see only a small part of the process, so they can't identify with the customer's needs. One observer of General Motors' traditional assembly line recently reported: "Often [workers] did not know how their jobs related to the total picture. Not knowing, there was no incentive to strive for quality—what did quality even mean as it related to a bracket whose function you did not understand."[64]

Perhaps the most important reason why job specialization has not been as successful as expected is that it ignores the motivational potential of jobs. As Exhibit 4–6 illustrates, job specialization may have a curvilinear effect on job

Exhibit 4–7   **The Job Characteristics Model**

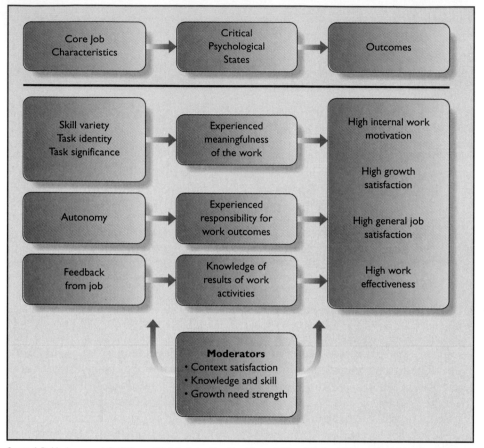

Source: J. R. Hackman and G. Oldham, *Work Redesign* (Reading, Mass.: Addison-Wesley, 1980), p. 90. Used with permission.

performance. As jobs become specialized, the work tends to become easier to perform but it is less motivating. As jobs become more complex, work motivation increases but the ability to master the job decreases. Maximum job performance occurs somewhere between these two extremes, where most people can eventually perform the job tasks efficiently, yet the work is interesting.

Job Design and Work Motivation

Industrial engineers may have overlooked the motivational effects of job characteristics, but it is now the central focus of most job design interventions.[65] Hackman and Oldham's **job characteristics model,** shown in Exhibit 4–7, details the motivational properties of jobs as well as specific personal and organizational consequences of these properties.[66] The job characteristics model identifies five core job dimensions that produce three psychological states. Employees who experience these psychological states tend to have higher levels of internal work motivation (motivation from the work itself), job satisfaction (particularly satisfaction with the work itself), and work effectiveness.

Job characteristics model
A job design model that relates five core job dimensions to three psychological states and several personal and organizational consequences.

Core job characteristics

Hackman and Oldham, along with earlier researchers, have identified five core job characteristics. Desirable work outcomes increase when jobs are redesigned such that they include more of these characteristics.

Skill variety

Skill variety refers to using different skills and talents to complete a variety of work activities. For example, sales clerks who normally only serve customers might be assigned the additional duties of stocking inventory and changing storefront displays.

Skill variety
The extent to which a job requires employees to use different skills and talents to complete a variety of work activities.

Task identity

Task identity is the degree to which a job requires completion of a whole or identifiable piece of work, such as doing something from beginning to end rather than just part of it. An employee who assembles an entire television converter rather than just solder in the power supply would develop a stronger sense of ownership or identity with the final product. Task identity also increases when there is a visible outcome of the work.

Task identity
The degree to which a job requires completion of a whole or identifiable piece of work.

Task significance

Task significance is the degree to which the job has a substantial impact on the organization and/or larger society. Jobs that noticeably affect the health, safety, and happiness of others tend to have higher levels of task significance. For instance, Canadian Coast Guard radio operators would feel a high sense of task significance because the quality of their work affects the safety of others.

Task significance
The degree to which the job has a substantial impact on the organization and/or larger society.

Autonomy

Jobs with high levels of **autonomy** provide employees with freedom, independence, and discretion in scheduling the work and determining the procedures to be used to complete the work. In autonomous jobs, employees make their own decisions rather than relying on detailed instructions from supervisors or procedure manuals.

Autonomy
The degree to which a job gives employees the freedom, independence, and discretion to schedule their work and determine the procedures to be used to complete the work.

Job feedback

Job feedback is the degree to which employees can tell how well they are doing based on direct sensory information from the job itself. Airline pilots can tell how well they land their aircraft and physicians can see whether their operations have improved the patient's health. Many jobs do not offer this type of feedback because the tasks are so simplified that job performance cannot be easily observed or there is no naturally occurring source of feedback available.

Job feedback
The degree to which employees can tell how well they are doing based on direct sensory information from the job itself.

Critical psychological states

The five core job characteristics affect employee motivation and satisfaction through three critical psychological states.[67] One of these is experienced meaningfulness—the belief that one's work is worthwhile or important. Skill variety, task identity, and task significance directly contribute to the job's meaningfulness. If the job has high levels of all three characteristics, employees are likely to feel that their job is highly meaningful. Meaningfulness drops as the job loses one or more of these characteristics.

Work motivation and performance increase when employees feel personally accountable for the outcomes of their efforts. Autonomy directly contributes to this feeling of experienced responsibility. Employees must be assigned control of their work environment to feel responsible for their successes and failures. The third critical psychological state is knowledge of results. Employees want information about the consequences of their work effort. Knowledge of results can originate from co-workers, supervisors, or clients. However, job design focusses on knowledge of results from the work itself.

Individual differences

Job redesign increases work motivation only under certain conditions. One contingency factor is the extent to which employees have the required skills and knowledge to master the more challenging work. If they lack the necessary abilities, job redesign is more likely to reduce productivity and increase worker stress. A second factor is whether employees are satisfied with their work environment (e.g., working conditions, job security, salaries.) Until the organization attends to these low level needs, changes to the work itself will have little effect on work motivation.

Finally, not everyone wants interesting or challenging work. As we learned in Chapter 3, some people are motivated mainly by social interaction or personal safety. They don't mind a boring job as long as co-workers are nearby or the paycheque meets their security needs. Consequently, job design increases the motivational value of jobs only for employees with strong growth needs.[68]

Job Design Strategies to Increase Work Motivation

Three main strategies potentially increase the motivational potential of jobs: job rotation, job enlargement, and job enrichment. As we will learn in this section, there are also several ways to implement job enrichment.

Employees at Toyota Canada's manufacturing plant in Cambridge, Ontario, participate in job rotation to relieve boredom and broaden their skills. "Job rotation is part of our philosophy," says Toyota's vice-president of manufacturing.

Ed Regan. Used with permission of The Globe & Mail.

Job Rotation and Job Enlargement   Exhibit 4–8

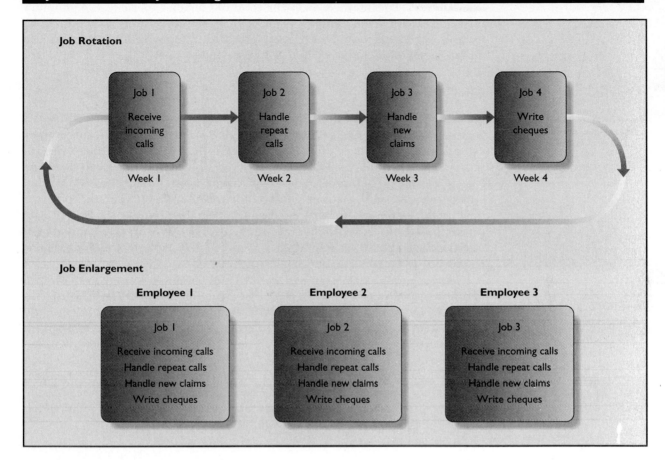

Job Rotation

| Job 1 Receive incoming calls | Job 2 Handle repeat calls | Job 3 Handle new claims | Job 4 Write cheques |
| Week 1 | Week 2 | Week 3 | Week 4 |

Job Enlargement

Employee 1

Job 1

Receive incoming calls
Handle repeat calls
Handle new claims
Write cheques

Employee 2

Job 2

Receive incoming calls
Handle repeat calls
Handle new claims
Write cheques

Employee 3

Job 3

Receive incoming calls
Handle repeat calls
Handle new claims
Write cheques

Job rotation

Job rotation is the practice of moving employees from one job to another, as shown in Exhibit 4–8. Binney and Smith, the manufacturer of Crayola Crayons, encourages job rotation at its Lindsay, Ontario, plant to reduce the boredom of repeating the same short-cycle tasks all day. Although some were initially reluctant, most employees enjoy the increased skill variety by rotating from fork lifts to hexagonal crayon mold machines.[69] Toyota also practises job rotation at its Cambridge, Ontario, assembly plant for this reason. "Job rotation is part of our philosophy," says Toyota's vice-president of manufacturing. "There's no way to get around the fact that these jobs are repetitive tasks, so you have to keep challenging yourself."[70]

But there is evidence that the current popularity of job rotation is due more to the need for employee flexibility than to its effects on employee well-being. Many years ago, Toyota engineers in Japan noted that job rotation helps employees learn other tasks and thereby increase their ability to move to jobs where they are needed. Costs are reduced because multiskilled workers can cover for each other's absences and thereby minimize downtime. Today, many companies use job rotation (along with skill-based rewards described earlier in this chapter) mainly to develop a multiskilled work force.[71]

Job rotation
Moving employees from one job to another for short periods of time.

A third objective of job rotation is to reduce the incidence of repetitive strain injuries. For instance, Snap-On Tools of Canada experienced high injury rates at its Newmarket, Ontario, plant because employees were using the same muscles in their narrowly defined jobs. Job rotation, along with better workplace design, significantly reduced these soft-tissue injury rates.[72]

Job enlargement

Job enlargement
Increasing the number of tasks employees perform within their job.

Job enlargement involves increasing the number of tasks employees perform *within* a job (see Exhibit 4–8). An assembly line worker might perform seven or eight tasks rather than just two. This lengthens the work cycle so that tasks are repeated less frequently. Job enlargement is sometimes called *horizontal job loading* because it reverses horizontal job specialization. Some critics argue that enlargement is better than job rotation for this reason. "If you ask workers if they prefer 2-minute or 24-minute work cycles, they opt for the latter," says David Robertson, a researcher at the Canadian Auto Workers union. He explains that instead of gaining a variety of skills, job rotation condemns employees to repeating several small, rigid tasks.[73]

There is evidence that job enlargement increases job satisfaction, intrinsic motivation, and possibly productivity. For example, National Cash Register in Waterloo, Ontario, and GTE Canada in Lethbridge, Alberta, introduced job enlargement in their assembly line operations and found that it increased product quality as well as employee satisfaction.[74] However, there is some evidence that job enlargement merely involves doing more tasks rather than more meaningful work. One recent study reported that job enlargement reduced job satisfaction, efficiency, and customer service. However, the opposite occurred when required job knowledge increased.[75] Increasing the required job knowledge is similar to job enrichment, which we discuss next.

Job enrichment

Job enrichment
Assigning responsibility for scheduling, coordinating, and planning work to employees who actually make the product or provide the service.

Job enrichment is based on the idea that motivation increases when the job provides opportunities for recognition, responsibility, advancement, achievement, and personal growth. The responsibility for scheduling, coordinating, and planning work is assigned to the employees who make the product or provide the service. Job enrichment is sometimes called *vertical job loading* because it reverses vertical job specialization.

Hackman and his colleagues recommend five techniques to improve the motivational potential of jobs.[76] As Exhibit 4–9 illustrates, these implementing principles alter one or more core job characteristics. Thus, the most appropriate implementing principle depends on which core job characteristics are weakest in a particular job.

Combining tasks

Combining tasks, which is essentially job enlargement, increases skill variety. For instance, Philips Electronics production employees in Toronto were given several dozen components to solder on a printed circuit board, a job requiring up to 10 minutes to complete, rather than just soldering a few components in less than 1 minute.[77] This strategy will also increase task identity when the additional job duties are related to the same product or service.

Strategies for Implementing Job Enrichment   **Exhibit 4–9**

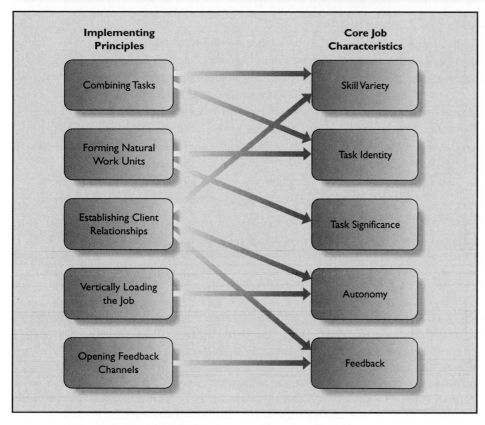

CASES use Page 122 & page 127

Source: J. R. Hackman and G. Oldham, *Work Redesign* (Reading, Mass.: Addison-Wesley, 1980), p. 135. Used with permission.

Forming natural work units

Forming natural work units combines tasks in a logical or complete grouping. A natural grouping might refer to completing an entire task, such as assembling an entire toaster rather than just some parts of it, or it might involve assignment to a specific client group, such as managing entire portfolios for specific clients rather than taking random client calls from a customer service pool. By forming natural work units, jobholders develop a sense of responsibility for an identifiable body of work. They feel a sense of ownership and, therefore, tend to increase job quality. Forming natural work units increases task identity and task significance because employees perform a complete product or service and can more readily see how their work affects others.

Establishing client relationships

As mentioned, some natural work units are employees assigned to a specific client group. Establishing client relationships takes this one step further by putting employees in *direct contact* with their client group rather than using the supervisor as a go-between. The key factor is direct communication between the employee and the client. The client submits work and provides feedback directly

Perspective 4–4

Job Enrichment at Imperial Oil

When Imperial Oil Ltd. replaced its outdated human resources information computer system, it took pains to redesign clerical jobs so that they would become more interesting and varied.

"We tried not to fracture jobs, so that people felt they weren't just a cog in the machinery," explains Maureen Donlevy, an automation consultant hired by Imperial Oil to implement the technology. "Workers need a sense of the significance of their work. They like to be able to feel that it has some impact."

Rather than centralizing the system, clerical workers in each branch now enter data directly and keep track of their own employee information databases. This provides added challenges and responsibility compared to the previous arrangement in which clerical staff simply gathered the data and shipped it off to Toronto.

"I personally welcomed the added responsibility," explains Deborah Ford, an Imperial Oil employee who worked in the Edmonton branch when the new computer system was introduced. "You have a much greater feeling of ownership of the data you worked with."

Source: Adapted from G. Blackwell, "Before Going Online, Imperial Oil Got Its Staff Onside," *Canadian Business* 61 (August 1988), p. 74.

---

to the employee rather than through a supervisor. Many companies apply variations of this implementing principle to increase customer service and product quality. One example is the James River mill at Marathon, Ontario, where production employees meet directly with clients to get feedback on their work. "We not only send supervisors, but also floor operators so that they can find out how the product is received by the clients," explains James River's human resources manager. "We find that they are coming back to the mill fully energized, and we are seeing significant change in the work force."[78]

Vertical loading

We have already described vertical loading as the most essential element in job enrichment, namely, giving employees control over scheduling, coordinating, and planning their work. In practice, vertical loading involves letting jobholders decide work methods, check quality, establish work schedules, decide how to solve problems, and even have knowledge of and control over financial budgets. In each case, the employee is given more autonomy over the work process. As described in Perspective 4–4, clerical employees at Imperial Oil experienced this form of job enrichment by gaining more responsibility and control over their data information systems.

Opening feedback channels

Employees receive some feedback from supervisors, but job design experts suggest that meaningful feedback is often generated through the job itself. This feedback may occur simply by performing an entire task and seeing the results, or it may require the assistance of gauges and other instruments to monitor production results. Some experts also include client feedback as a form of job feedback. Overall, companies need to remove barriers to existing information sources and establish new mechanisms so jobholders can check their job performance without the supervisor's assistance.

Job Design Prospects and Problems

Job design has become tremendously popular in recent years. Only 2 percent of Canadian firms had job design interventions before 1960, compared with almost 30 percent today. These interventions also have a much higher survival rate than most management interventions.[79]

But to what extent does job enrichment improve employee and organizational effectiveness? Employees with high growth needs whose jobs are enriched have higher job satisfaction, higher work motivation, lower absenteeism, and lower turnover. Productivity is also higher when task identity and job feedback are improved.[80] Work quality is the most significant improvement in job performance when jobs are enriched. Error rates, number of defects, and other quality indicators tend to improve, because job enrichment increases the jobholder's felt responsibility and sense of ownership over the product or service. Quality improvements in production and service are particularly evident when the job enrichment intervention involves completing a natural work unit or establishing client relationships.[81]

Obstacles in job design

Job design is not easy to implement. One concern is that it is difficult to accurately measure the core job characteristics.[82] Consequently, firms have trouble pinpointing which jobs require changing and how well job design interventions are working. Another problem is that many work settings require team-based job redesign because the technology is fixed or the work cycle is too complex for one person to handle alone. For example, one employee would not make an entire automobile or operate an entire petrochemical process. Although much of the job design literature has concentrated on changing individual jobs, more focus is needed on self-managing work teams and related team-based job design interventions.[83] We will discuss these practices in Chapter 11 after introducing team dynamics in Chapter 10.

Job design interventions also face resistance to change. Some employees are initially uncomfortable with more challenging work, whereas others are worried that job redesign will undermine their power base in the organization. For instance, a few highly skilled employees at Alcan's smelter in Arvida, Quebec, tried to stop the company's job enrichment program because they didn't want lesser skilled employees learning their higher status jobs.[84] Supervisors often resist job redesign interventions because they change supervising roles and may threaten job security. Consequently, job enrichment must be accompanied by the change management strategies described in Chapter 15.[85]

Labour union leaders have been bitter foes of job specialization and scientific management, yet few have been enthusiastic about job enrichment programs. They complain that job enrichment programs try to get more work out of employees for less money. At best, critics view job enrichment as a rationalized work arrangement introduced where job specialization is unprofitable. In other words, they conclude that job enrichment exists because it strengthens management's control, not because of a true interest in the employee's mental health.[86]

Finally, we need to find an appropriate balance between job enrichment and job specialization to maximize organizational effectiveness. Job specialization may improve work efficiency, but job performance may decline as employee motivation falls. Job enrichment may increase motivation, but performance may fall if employees lack the skills necessary to complete more challenging tasks. Job enrichment may increase recruiting and training costs, whereas job specialization may increase compensation costs if companies provide discontentment pay to entice people into boring jobs.[87] Finally, job enrichment improves product quality, but error rates may increase when tasks become so challenging that employees experience stress.[88] Of course, job specialization also increases stress if employees do not make effective use of their talents in narrowly defined jobs, as we will learn in Chapter 5.

Chapter Summary

- Rewards serve four primary functions. Fixed salaries and most employee benefits reward membership and seniority in the organization. Job evaluation systems and executive perquisites reward job status in the organizational hierarchy. Skill-based rewards pay higher salaries to people who have mastered more skill modules. Performance-based reward systems distribute money and other economic benefits to people based on their behaviour and consequences to the organization.

- Job status-based rewards have many drawbacks. They reinforce the existing hierarchy, encourage costly political behaviours, increase resistance to change, focus employee attention on narrowly defined tasks, and create a psychological distance between employees and management.

- Performance-based rewards significantly increase employee motivation. However, this is unlikely to happen if the performance measures are biased, inadequate adjustments are made for situational contingencies, jobs are too interdependent for individual rewards, the rewards offered aren't motivating, the rewards cover only a few performance dimensions, and the rewards influence the wrong behaviours.

- Most organizations use some form of corrective discipline to control work behaviours. Progressive discipline is most frequently applied, although the mixed consequences and discipline without punishment models are being adopted in a few companies. Discipline can be an effective practice, but it also may be risky if punishment is applied inappropriately.

- Job design involves assigning tasks to a job and distributing work throughout the organization. Job specialization reduces the number of tasks assigned to a job. This increases work efficiency because employees master the tasks quickly, spend less time changing tasks, require less training, and can be matched more closely with the jobs best suited to their skills. However, job specialization may reduce work motivation and affect workers' mental health. Production costs may increase as companies pay higher salaries to compensate for boring work and contend with higher absenteeism and turnover.

- Contemporary job design strategies reverse job specialization through job rotation, job enlargement, and job enrichment. Hackman and Oldham's job characteristics model is the most popular foundation for recent job redesign interventions because it specifies core job dimensions, psychological states, and individual differences.

- Strategies to increase work motivation include job rotation, job enlargement, and job enrichment. Hackman and his colleagues have identified five implementing principles to improve the motivational potential of jobs.

- As a form of organizational change, job enrichment is not always easy to implement, but there is evidence that morale improves and both turnover and absenteeism decrease. Work motivation increases, as does the quality of work output.

Discussion Questions

1. **Du Pont Canada was once a bureaucratic company that valued long service and promotions through a steep hierarchy. After several years of difficult change, it is now a much flatter organization that places more responsibility with self-managing work teams. Explain what changes Du Pont Canada probably made (or should have made) to align its reward system with this new corporate philosophy.**

2. **How do profit-sharing plans differ from employee share ownership plans? How are they similar?**

3. **Explain how situational contingencies interfere with the effective distribution of performance-based rewards.**

4. **A senior manager at a major trust company tells you that positive discipline is really the same as progressive discipline, except that the supervisor uses different words when addressing employees. In either method, the person eventually gets fired anyway. Comment on the accuracy of the senior manager's statement.**

5. **Describe four actions that potentially minimize the problems involved with employee discipline. Your answer should explain why the action avoids or minimizes problems with discipline.**

6. **Under what conditions would job specialization be most appropriate?**

7. **Compare and contrast job rotation with job enlargement.**

8. **The Deputy Minister of Labour in a provincial government is excited about the benefits of job enrichment and wants to apply it to the Ministry's construction inspectors located in four regional offices. Inspectors currently receive assignments from their supervisor and file their reports with the supervisor when the inspection is completed. These inspectors were construction workers in their younger years and now enjoy the easier life of a desk job. The Deputy Minister wants inspectors to perform more tasks previously assigned to their supervisor, such as receiving all work orders, scheduling inspections, and dealing directly with contractor complaints and inquiries. (Contractors don't always agree with the Ministry's inspection**

reports.) What advice would you give the Deputy Minister before this job enrichment intervention begins?

Notes

1. S. Owen, "Incentives: A Link to Employee Performance," *Marketing*, January 20, 1992, pp. 15–16.

2. S. L. McShane and B. Redekop, "Compensation Management and Canadian Wrongful Dismissal: Lessons from Litigation," *Relations Industrielles* 45 (1990), pp. 357–80.

3. R. Thériault, *Mercer Compensation Manual: Theory and Practice* (Boucherville, Que.: G. Morin Publisher, 1992), p. 3.

4. M. Gunderson, "Union Impact on Compensation, Productivity, and Management of the Organization," in *Union–Management Relations in Canada*, 2nd ed. J. C. Anderson, M. Gunderson, and A. Ponak (Don Mills, Ont.: Addison-Wesley, 1989), pp. 359–60.

5. D. Stoffman, "Good Behaviour and the Bottom Line," *Canadian Business*, May 1991, pp. 28–32. For a discussion of LTD, see R. N. Kanungo and M. Mendonca, *Compensation: Effective Reward Management* (Toronto: Butterworths, 1992), pp. 328–33.

6. L. R. Gomez-Mejia and D. B. Balkin, *Compensation, Organizational Strategy, and Firm Performance* (Cincinnati: South-Western, 1992), pp. 40–41; and E. E. Lawler III, *Strategic Pay* (San Francisco: Jossey-Bass, 1990), p. 28.

7. J. M. Pennings, "Executive Reward Systems: A Cross-National Comparison," *Journal of Management Studies* 30 (1993), pp. 261–80.

8. T. A. Mahoney, "Understanding Comparable Worth: A Societal and Political Perspective," *Research in Organizational Behavior* 9 (1987), pp. 209–45.

9. H. Moore, "Problems and Methods in Job Evaluation," *Journal of Consulting Psychology* 8 (1944), pp. 90–99.

10. M. Gunderson and R. E. Robb, "Equal Pay for Work of Equal Value: Canada's Experience," *Advances in Industrial and Labor Relations* 5 (1991), pp. 151–68; and S. L. McShane, "Two Tests of Direct Gender Bias in Job Evaluation Ratings," *Journal of Occupational Psychology* 63 (1990), pp. 129–40.

11. M. Quaid, *Job Evaluation: The Myth of Equitable Assessment* (Toronto: University of Toronto Press, 1993).

12. Lawler, *Strategic Pay*, Chapter 8.

13. D. Hofrichter, "Broadbanding: A 'Second Generation' Approach," *Compensation & Benefits Review* 25 (September–October 1993), pp. 53–58.

14. E. E. Lawler III, "From Job-Based to Competency-Based Organizations," *Jounal of Organizational Behavior* 15 (1994), pp. 3–15; R. L. Bunning, "Models for Skill-Based Pay Plans," *HR Magazine* 37 (February 1992), pp. 62–64; and G. E. Ledford, Jr., "The Design of Skill-Based Pay Plans," in *The Compensation Handbook*, ed. M. L. Rock and L. A. Berger (New York: McGraw-Hill, 1991), pp. 199–217.

15. E. E. Lawler III, G. E. Ledford, Jr., and L. Chang, "Who Uses Skill-Based Pay, and Why," *Compensation and Benefits Review* 25 (March–April 1993), pp. 22–26; and "New Ways to Pay," *The Economist*, July 13, 1991, p. 69.

16. A. Armstrong, "The Design and Implementation of Pay for Knowledge and Skill Systems: An Exploratory Investigation," *Proceedings of the Annual ASAC Conference, Personnel and Human Resources Division* 12, pt. 8 (1991), pp. 21–30; and B. Sheehy and G. Peckover, "You Get What You Pay For," *Industrial Management* 14 (September 1988), pp. 25–26.

17. G. G. Nasmith, *Timothy Eaton* (Toronto: McClelland & Stewart, 1923), p. 91; and P. C. Newman, *Caesars of the Wilderness* (Toronto: Viking, 1987), p. 121.

18. Conference Board of Canada, *Strategic Rewards Management: The Variable Approach to Pay* (Ottawa: Conference Board of Canada, 1990).

19. E. B. Peach and D. A. Wren, "Pay for Performance from Antiquity to the 1950s," *Journal of Organizational Behavior Management*, 1992, pp. 5–26.

20. J. Heinzl, "A Knack for Knit Earnings," *Globe & Mail*, September 21, 1993, p. B26.

21. G. T. Milkovich and A. K. Wigdor (eds.), *Pay for Performance: Evaluating Performance Apprasial and Merit Pay* (Washington, D.C.: National Academy Press, 1991); D. P. Schwab and C. A. Olson, "Merit Pay Practices: Implications for Pay–Performance Relationships," *Industrial and Labor Relations Review* 43 (1990), pp. 237s–55s; and R. L. Heneman, "Merit Pay Research," *Research in Personnel and Human Resources Management* 8 (1990), pp. 203–63.

22. L. Bak, "Teaming up with Flex," *Benefits Canada*, March 1992, pp. 35–37; and E. Innes, J. Lyon, and J. Harris, *The 100 Best Companies to Work for in Canada* (Toronto: HarperCollins, 1990), p. 105.

23. R. Sisco, "Put Your Money Where Your Teams Are," *Training* 29 (July 1992), pp. 41–45.

24. S. T. Johnson, "Work Teams: What's Ahead in Work Design and Rewards Management," *Compensation & Benefits Review* 25 (March–April 1993), pp. 35–41.

25. D. Nightingale and R. Long, *Gain and Equity Sharing* (Ottawa: Labour Canada, 1984); and M. Schuster, "Gain Sharing: Do It Right the First Time," *Sloan Management Review* 28 (Winter 1987), pp. 17–25.

26. J. Schilder, "Shared Pain, Shared Gain," *Human Resources Professional*, March 1993, pp. 21–23.

27. M. J. Roomkin (ed.), *Profit Sharing and Gain Sharing* (Metuchen, N.J.: IMLR Press, 1990); and M. Rashid and B. Sharma, "Optimal Sharing Ratio in Profit-Sharing Arrangement," *Canadian Journal of Administrative Science* 8 (December 1991), pp. 259–66.

28. J. Chelius and R. S. Smith, "Profit Sharing and Employment Stability," *Industrial and Labor Relations Review* 43 (1990), pp. 256s–73s.

29. R. J. Long, "The Incidence and Nature of Employee Profit Sharing and Share Ownership in Canada," *Relations Industrielles* 47 (1992), pp. 463–86.

30. R. Luuko, "Are the Boss' Shares a Good Deal?" *Financial Times of Canada,* June 24–30, 1991, p. 15.

31. D. Roberts, "The Brew Crew Takes Over," *Globe & Mail*, December 21, 1993, p. B20.

32. B. Gerhart and G. T. Milkovich, "Organizational Differences in Managerial Compensation and Financial Performance," *Academy of Management Journal* 33 (1990), pp. 663–91; C. R. Gowen III, "Gainsharing Programs: An Overview of History and Research," *Journal of Organizational Behavior Management* 11(2) (1990), pp. 77–99; K. J. Klein, "Employee Stock Ownership and Employee Attitudes: A Test of Three Models," *Journal of Applied Psychology Monograph* 72 (1987), pp. 319–32; and R. Barstow, "Stock Plan Pays Off," *Financial Times of Canada,* November 23, 1987, p. 33.

33. W. Clay Hamner, "How to Ruin Motivation with Pay," *Compensation Review,* 3rd Quarter 1975, pp. 88–98.

34. R. Maynard, "How Do You Like Your Job?" *Report on Business Magazine,* November 1987, p. 117.

35. K. M. Bartol and D. C. Martin, "When Politics Pays: Factors Influencing Managerial Compensation Decisions," *Personnel Psychology* 43 (1990), pp. 599–614.

36. M. Stevenson, "Be Nice for a Change," *Canadian Business,* November 1993, pp. 81–85.

37. Milkovich and Wigdor, *Pay for Performance,* pp. 83–84; and J. L. Pearce, "Why Merit Pay Doesn't Work: Implications from Organization Theory," in *New Perspectives on Compensation,* ed. D. B. Balkin and L. R. Gomez-Mejia (Englewood Cliffs, N.J.: Prentice Hall, 1987), pp. 169–78.

38. J. Saunders, "Cheap Labour Not Enough," *Globe & Mail,* May 10, 1993, pp. B1, B2.

39. Lawler, *Strategic Pay,* p. 120.

40. R. D. Arvey and A. P. Jones, "The Use of Discipline in Organizational Settings: A Framework for Future Research," *Research in Organizational Behavior* 7 (1985), pp. 367–408.

41. R. D. Arvey and J. M. Ivancevich, "Punishment in Organizations: A Review, Propositions, and Research Suggestions," *Academy of Management Review* 5 (1980), pp. 123–32; and H. P. Sims, Jr., "Further Thoughts on Punishment in Organizations," *Academy of Management Review* 5 (1980), pp. 133–38.

42. L. K. Trevino, "The Social Effects of Punishment in Organizations: A Justice Perspective," *Academy of Management Review* 17 (1992), pp. 647–76; M. E. Schnake & M. P. Dumler, "Some Unconventional Thoughts on the Use of Punishment in Organizations: Reward as Punishment and Punishment as Reward," *Journal of Social Behavior and Personality* 4 (1989), pp. 97–107; M. E. Schnake, "Vicarious Punishment in a Work Setting," *Journal of Applied Psychology* 71 (1986), pp. 343–45; and C. A. O'Reilly III and B. A. Weitz, "Managing Marginal Employees: The Use of Warnings and Dismissals," *Administrative Science Quarterly* 25 (1980), pp. 467–84.

43. H. A. Levitt, *The Law of Dismissal in Canada,* 2nd ed. (Aurora, Ont.: Canada Law Book, 1992).

44. G. Eden, "Progressive Discipline: An Oxymoron?" *Relations Industrielles* 47 (1992), pp. 511–27.

45. R. A. Baron, "Negative Effects of Destructive Criticism: Impact on Conflict, Self-Efficacy, and Task Performance," *Journal of Applied Psychology* 73 (1988), pp. 199–207.

46. D. N. Campbell, R. L. Fleming, and R. C. Grote, "Discipline without Punishment—at Last," *Harvard Business Review* 63 (July–August 1985), pp. 162–74; and P. Johnson, "Discipline without Punishment," *Financial Times of Canada,* April 20, 1981, pp. H16–H17.

47. C. Argyris, *Personality and Organization* (New York: Harper & Bros., 1957).

48. Trevino, "The Social Effects of Punishment in Organizations," p. 669.

49. J. M. Beyer and H. M. Trice, "A Field Study of the Use and Perceived Effects of Discipline in Controlling Work Performance," *Academy of Management Journal* 27 (1984), pp. 743–64.

50. B. S. Klaas and H. N. Wheeler, "Managerial Decision Making about Employee Discipline: A Policy-Capturing Approach," *Personnel Psychology* 43 (1990), pp. 117–34.

51. R. E. Kopelman and G. O. Schneller IV, "A Mixed-Consequence System for Reducing Overtime and Unscheduled Absences," *Journal of Organizational Behavior Management* 3(1) (1981), pp. 17–28.

52. C. A. B. Osigweh, Yg. and W. R. Hutchison, "Positive Discipline," *Human Resource Management* 28 (1989), pp. 367–83; J. Huberman, "Discipline without Punishment," *Harvard Business Review* 42 (July–August 1964), pp. 62–68; Johnson, "Discipline without Punishment;" Campbell et al., "Discipline without Punishment—at Last;" and M. Thompson, "New Brunswick's Paul Theriault," *Canadian HR Reporter,* April 4, 1988, p. 5.

53. R. H. Waterman, Jr., *The Renewal Factor* (New York: Bantam, 1987), pp. 251–52.

54. R. J. Long, *New Office Information Technology: Human and Managerial Implications* (London: Crom Helm, 1987); and J. W. Medcof, "The Effect of Extent of Use and Job of the User upon Task Characteristics," *Human Relations* 42 (1989), pp. 23–41.

55. H. Fayol, *General and Industrial Management,* trans. C. Storrs (London: Pitman, 1949); E. E. Lawler III, *Motivation in Work Organizations* (Monterey, Calif.: Brooks/Cole, 1973), Chapter 7; and M. A. Campion, "Ability Requirement Implications of Job Design: An Interdisciplinary Perspective," *Personnel Psychology* 42 (1989), pp. 1–24.

56. A. Smith, *The Wealth of Nations* (London: Dent, 1910).

57. F. W. Taylor, *The Principles of Scientific Management* (New York: Harper & Row, 1911); C. R. Littler, "Taylorism, Fordism, and Job Design," in *Job Design: Critical Perspectives on the Labour Process,* ed. D. Knights, H. Willmott, and D. Collinson (Aldershot, U.K.: Gower Publishing, 1985), pp. 10–29; and D. A. Wren, *The Evolution of Management Thought* (New York: Ronald Press, 1972).

58. Cited in H. Mintzberg, *The Structuring of Organizations* (Englewood Cliffs, N.J.: Prentice Hall, 1979), p. 74.

59. W. J. Duncan, *Great Ideas in Management* (San Francisco: Jossey-Bass, 1989), Chapter 4.

60. R. Fulford, "Firm Management," *Saturday Night,* September 1983, pp. 42–48, 52.

61. E. E. Lawler III, *High-Involvement Management* (San Francisco: Jossey-Bass, 1986), Chapter 6; and C. R. Walker and R. H. Guest, *The Man on the Assembly Line* (Cambridge, Mass.: Harvard University Press, 1952).

62. R. Kanungo, *Work Alienation: An Integrative Approach* (New York: Praeger, 1982); M. Seeman, "On the Meaning of Alienation," *American Sociological Review* 24 (1959), pp. 783–91; and R. Blauner, *Alienation and Freedom: The Factory Worker and His Industry* (Chicago: University of Chicago Press, 1964).

63. W. F. Dowling, "Job Redesign on the Assembly Line: Farewell to Blue-Collar Blues?" *Organizational Dynamics,* Autumn 1973, pp. 51–67; and Lawler, *Motivation in Work Organizations,* p. 150.

64. M. Keller, *Rude Awakening* (New York: Harper Perennial, 1989), p. 128.

65. C. S. Wong and M. A. Campion, "Development and Test of a Task Level Model of Motivational Job Design," *Journal of Applied Psychology* 76 (1991), pp. 825–37.

66. J. R. Hackman and G. Oldham, *Work Redesign* (Reading, Mass.: Addison-Wesley, 1980).

67. G. Johns, J. L. Xie, and Y. Fang, "Mediating and Moderating Effects in Job Design," *Journal of Management* 18 (1992), pp. 657–76.

68. P. E. Spector, "Higher-Order Need Strength as a Moderator of the Job Scope–Employee Outcome Relationship: A Meta Analysis," *Journal of Occupational Psychology* 58 (1985), pp. 119–27.

69. J. Wells, "Winning Colours," *Report on Business Magazine,* July 1992, pp. 26–35.

70. B. McDougall, "The Thinking Man's Assembly Line," *Canadian Business,* November 1991, pp. 40–44.

71. Y. Monden, *Toyota Production System* (Atlanta: Institute of Industrial Engineering, 1983), p. 105; and B. Van-Lane, "Jacks of All Trades," *Plant Engineering and Maintenance* 14 (March 1991), pp. 24–26.

72. W. List, "Under the Gun About Safety," *Globe & Mail,* January 4, 1994, p. B14.

73. M. Gibb-Clark, "Workplace Hard to Change," *Globe & Mail,* March 25, 1991, pp. B1, B2.

74. J. Mansell, *An Inventory of Innovative Work Arrangement in Ontario* (Toronto: Ontario Ministry of Labour, 1978), pp. 66–68; and P. P. Schoderbek and W. E. Reif, *Job Enlargement: Key to Improved Performance* (Ann Arbor, Mich.: University of Michigan, 1969).

75. M. A. Campion and C. L. McClelland, "Follow-up and Extension of the Interdisciplinary Costs and Benefits of Enlarged Jobs," *Journal of Applied Psychology* 78 (1993), pp. 339–51; and F. Herzberg, "One More Time: How Do You Motivate Employees?" *Harvard Business Review* 46 (January–February 1968), pp. 53–62.

76. J. R. Hackman, G. Oldham, R. Janson, and K. Purdy, "A New Strategy for Job Enrichment," *California Management Review* 17(4) (1975), pp. 57–71.

77. I. S. G. Meadows, "Innovative Work Arrangements—A Case Study in Job Enrichment: Philips Electronics Limited, Leaside, Ontario," unpublished paper, Ontario Ministry of Labour, Research Branch, July 1976.

78. "Mills Invest in Their People," *Northern Ontario Business* 12 (April 1992), pp. 1, 3.

79. R. J. Long, "Patterns of Workplace Innovation," *Relations Industrielles* 44 (1989), pp. 805–26.

80. Y. Fried and G. R. Ferris, "The Validity of the Job Characteristics Model: A Review and Meta-analysis," *Personnel Psychology* 40 (1987), pp. 287–322; and B. T. Loher, R. A. Noe, N. L. Moeller, and M. P. Fitzgerald, "A Meta-analysis of the Relation of Job Characteristics to Job Satisfaction," *Journal of Applied Psychology* 70 (1985), pp. 280–89.

81. D. E. Bowen and E. E. Lawler III, "The Empowerment of Service Workers: What, Why, How, and When," *Sloan Management Review,* Spring 1992, pp. 31–39; and C. A. Sales, E. Levanoni, and R. Knoop, "Employee Performance as a Function of Job Orientation and Job Design," *Relations Industrielles* 44 (1989), pp. 409–20.

82. Johns et al., "Mediating and Moderating Effects in Job Design," pp. 672–73; and R. W. Griffin, "Toward an Integrated Theory of Task Design," *Research in Organizational Behavior* 9 (1987), pp. 79–120.

83. J. B. Cunningham, "A Look at Four Approaches to Work Design," *Optimum* 20(1) (1989/90), pp. 39–55.

84. J. T. Archer, "Achieving Joint Organizational, Technical, and Personal Needs: The Case of the Sheltered Experiment of Aluminum Casting Team," in *The Quality of Working Life, Vol. 2,* ed. L. E. David, A. B. Cherns, and Associates (New York: The Free Press, 1975), pp. 253–68.

85. W. Westley, *Quality of Working Life: The Role of the Supervisor* (Ottawa: Labour Canada, 1981).

86. J. Rinehart, "Improving the Quality of Working Life Through Job Redesign: Work Humanization or Work Rationalization?" *Canadian Review of Sociology and Anthropology* 23 (1986), pp. 507–30; and C. Pinder, *Work Motivation* (Glenview, Ill.: Scott, Foresman, 1984), pp. 257–58.

87. Campion, "Ability Requirement Implications of Job Design: An Interdisciplinary Perspective," p. 20; and R. B. Dunham, "Relationships of Perceived Job Design Characteristics to Job Ability Requirements and Job Value," *Journal of Applied Psychology* 62 (1977), pp. 760–63.

88. R. Martin and T. D. Wall, "Attentional Demand and Cost Responsibility as Stressors in Shopfloor Jobs," *Academy of Management Journal* 32 (1989), pp. 69–86; and D. P. Schwab and L. L. Cummings, "Impact of Task Scope on Employee Productivity: An Evaluation Using Expectancy Theory," *Academy of Management Review* 1 (1976), pp. 23–35.

Chapter Case

VÊTEMENTS LTÉE

Vêtements Ltée is a chain of men's retail clothing stores located throughout the province of Quebec. Two years ago, the company introduced new incentive systems for both store managers and sales employees. Store managers in each store receive a salary with annual merit increases based on sales above targetted goals, store appearance, store inventory management, customer complaints, and several other performance measures. Some of this information (e.g., store appearance) is gathered during visits by senior management, while other information is based on company records (e.g., sales volume).

Sales employees are paid a fixed salary plus a commission based on the percentage of sales credited to that employee over the pay period. The commission represents about 30 percent of a typical paycheque and is intended to encourage employees to actively serve customers and to increase sales volume. Because returned merchandise is discounted from commissions, sales staff are discouraged from selling products that customers do not really want.

Soon after the new incentive systems were introduced, senior management began to receive complaints from store managers regarding the performance of their sales staff. They observed that sales employees tended to stand near the store entrance waiting for customers and would occasionally argue over "ownership" of the customer. Managers were concerned that this aggressive behaviour intimidated some customers. It also tended to leave some parts of the store unattended by staff.

Many managers were also concerned about inventory duties. Previously, sales staff would share responsibility for restocking inventory and completing inventory reorder forms. Under the new compensation system, however, few employees were willing to do these essential tasks. On several occasions, stores have faced stock shortages because merchandise was not stocked or reorder forms were not completed in a timely manner. Potential sales have suffered from empty shelves when plenty of merchandise was available in the back storeroom or at the warehouse. The company's new automatic inventory system could reduce some of these problems, but employees must still stock shelves and assist in other aspects of inventory management.

Store managers have tried to correct the inventory problem by assigning employees to inventory duty, but this has created resentment among the employees selected. Other managers have threatened sales staff with dismissals if they do not do their share of inventory management. This strategy has been somewhat effective when the manager is in the store, but staff members sneak back onto the floor when the manager is away. It has also hurt staff morale, particularly relations with the store manager.

To reduce the tendency of sales staff to hoard customers at the store entrance, some managers have assigned employees to specific areas of the store. This has also created some resentment among employees stationed in areas with less traffic or lower-priced merchandise. Some staff have openly complained of lower paycheques because they have been placed in a slow area of the store or have been given more than their share of inventory duties.

Discussion Questions

1. **What symptom(s) exist in this case to suggest that something has gone wrong?**

2. **What are the root causes that have led to these symptoms?**

3. **What actions should the organization take to correct these problems?**

© 1989 Steven L. McShane.

Experiential Exercise

Choosing the Appropriate Level of Discipline

Purpose: This exercise is designed to help you understand the difficulties in applying organizational discipline and to understand how people differ in their diagnoses of situations where some form of discipline might be applied.

Instructions: Each of the four incidents in this exercise involves a work infraction that has been brought to your attention. You are responsible for disciplinary actions in the company or this work group. Following each incident is a list of six possible actions that you have authority to apply. Read each incident, indicate your preferred disciplinary action, and explain why this alternative has been selected over others. When you have finished, the instructor may form small teams of four to five people to discuss each member's results, or the exercise may be discussed directly with the entire class.

Case of the Insulting Driver

John, a delivery driver employed by your auto parts supply firm, has apparently made insulting comments to a retail customer when delivering auto supplies. The insult occurred when the customer asked for proof that John worked for the company. You confronted John about this incident, but he denied insulting the customer. You later receive irrefutable evidence that John did make insulting comments and when told about this, John admits the misconduct and signs a written letter of apology to the customer. However, he does not seem to show any remorse about the incident. John has 18 years of full-time employment with the company with an average job performance, but was suspended a few years ago for fighting with a fellow employee in the warehouse. He has no other work infractions. John is divorced with grown children who live with their mother. Please indicate which of the following actions you would apply in this situation:

☐ No action.

☐ Verbal warning.

☐ Written warning (repetition may result in dismissal).

☐ Written final warning (repetition will result in dismissal).

☐ Dismissal with notice or severance payment. (Please state how many weeks notice or pay _____)

☐ Immediate dismissal without notice or severance payment.

Case of Discounting Sales Clerk

You have learned that Susan, a sales representative in your retail clothing company, has given price discounts over the past couple of months to members of her immediate family who have purchased the firm's products. These discounts have ranged from 10 to 40 percent of the retail price of the products family members have purchased. She knows the company's policy forbidding special discounts to customers or staff members. Susan has been employed full-time with this firm for nearly four years, which includes a three-month paid maternity leave one year ago. She is one of the best salespeople in the company, although she has been late for work a few times. Susan is married with two pre-school children. Please indicate which of the following actions you would apply in this situation:

☐ No action.

☐ Verbal warning.

☐ Written warning (repetition may result in dismissal).

☐ Written final warning (repetition will result in dismissal).

☐ Dismissal with notice or severance payment. (Please state how many weeks notice or pay _____)

☐ Immediate dismissal without notice or severance payment.

Case of the Entertaining Forklift Operator

Robert, one of the forklift operators employed by your company, has been driving the forklift in a dangerous manner in the warehouse. He has been performing fast turns and "wheelies" in an apparently successful attempt to "show off" to co-workers in the warehouse. While attempting one of his forklift tricks, Robert accidentally ran into a skid of the company's product, damaging several boxes and slightly denting the forklift. Total uninsured damages to the company resulting from this incident will be about $1,500. Robert's activities came to the company's attention when this incident occurred. A few months earlier, Robert and other employees were reminded of the company's safety rules and standards regarding operating of company vehicles. Robert was hired by the company almost two years ago, performs his job satisfactorily, and has no other disciplinary record with the company. He is young and unmarried. Please indicate which of the following actions you would apply in this situation:

☐ No action.

☐ Verbal warning.

☐ Written warning (repetition may result in dismissal).

☐ Written final warning (repetition will result in dismissal).

☐ Dismissal with notice or severance payment. (Please state how many weeks notice or pay _____)

☐ Immediate dismissal without notice or severance payment.

Case of the Side-Step Dental Technician

Rebecca is a dental technician in your company who dislikes removing garbage containers from the lab after work. Removing garbage is a very minor part of the dental technician's job, but the task is clearly stated in the job description that was revised last year. (Prior to that time, cleaning people removed the garbage each day.) Although these containers are light enough for women to carry easily, Rebecca has successfully used a variety of tactics over the past year to get other employees to perform this task. Two co-workers (out of 12 who work with Rebecca) have complained to you about Rebecca's tactics. Rebecca has admitted to you that she dislikes performing the task and has implied that she might refuse to do so if ordered. Rebecca has 10 years of continuous full-time service with the company and is married with three school-aged children. Her job performance has been satisfactory recently, although she was warned about substandard work one year ago. Please indicate which of the following actions you would apply in this situation:

☐ No action.

☐ Verbal warning.

☐ Written warning (repetition may result in dismissal).

☐ Written final warning (repetition will result in dismissal).

☐ Dismissal with notice or severance payment. (Please state how many weeks notice or pay _____)

☐ Immediate dismissal without notice or severance payment.

Stress Management

Learning Objectives

After reading this chapter, you should be able to:

Outline the stress process from stressors to consequences.

Discuss four types of role-related stressors.

Explain how work and family demands may become stressors.

Identify five ways to manage workplace stress.

Distinguish Type A from Type B employees in terms of their job performance.

Explain why social support may reduce work-related stress.

Chapter Outline

What Is Stress?

Stressors: The Causes of Stress.

Individual Differences in Stress.

Consequences of Distress.

Managing Work-Related Stress.

Fred Lum. Used with permission of The Globe & Mail.

𝒞hris McBeath knows all about deadlines. As facility manager at Vancouver's Robson Square Conference Centre, McBeath books up to 60 events each month, sometimes with no more than 12 hours' notice. It is a stressful job for even the calmest souls. To manage this stress, McBeath enrolled in a one-day sabbatical through Vancouver's Workplace Ministry on the University of British Columbia campus. The secular experience was devoted to visualization exercises and meditating strolls through the nearby gardens.

Kirsti Watson tried massages to relieve the frequent stress of her job as an air traffic controller in Toronto. They helped ease the tension at first, but it wasn't long before she felt her shoulders tighten up again. To make matters worse, Watson would stop exercising or eating right whenever her stress level rose.

To deal with the problem more effectively, Watson registered with the Relaxation Response Institute in midtown Toronto. With soothing music filling the air of a large, softly lit room adorned with hanging plants, comfortable chairs, thick carpet, and many pillows, the Relaxation Response Institute seemed like a good place to break the tension. Now Watson feels she can keep her stress under control by retreating to the Institute and practising breathing and relaxation techniques.[1]

Most Canadians experience stress at work. One-third feel constantly stressed; the same percentage has health problems caused by work-related stress. Insurance companies estimate that one-third of long-term disability claims are stress related, up from only 10 percent a decade ago. But perhaps most troubling is that people born after 1955 are up to three times as likely to experience stress-related disorders as their grandparents were.[2] In short, work-related stress has become the illness of the 1990s.

Work-related stress is costly to both the individual and the organization. Some sources estimate that work-related stress costs Canadian businesses nearly $20 billion each year in lower productivity and higher absenteeism, turnover, alcoholism, and medical attention.[3] Work-related stress can also cost employers in arbitration awards, court decisions, and occupational health and safety premiums. According to one estimate, Ontario's Workers' Compensation Board will soon be paying $178 million per year for stress-related claims.[4]

Not all stress is bad. In fact, a certain level of stress is a necessary part of life. In this chapter, we look more closely at the dynamics of work-related stress and how to manage it. The chapter begins by describing the process of experiencing stress. Next, the causes and consequences of stress are examined, along with the factors that cause some people to experience stress when others do not. The final section of this chapter looks at ways to manage work-related stress from either an organizational or individual perspective.

What Is Stress?

Stress
An individual's adaptive response to a situation that is perceived as challenging or threatening to the person's well-being.

Stress is an adaptive response to a situation that is perceived as challenging or threatening to the person's well-being.[5] Stress has both psychological and physiological dimensions. Psychologically, people perceive a situation and interpret it as challenging or threatening. This cognitive appraisal leads to a set of physiological responses, such as higher blood pressure, sweaty hands, and faster heart beat.

We often hear about stress as a negative consequence of modern living. People are stressed from overwork, job insecurity, competition, and the increasing pace of life. These events produce *distress*—people experiencing stress beyond their capacity to resist the stressful conditions. There is also a positive side of stress, called *eustress,* that refers to relatively low levels of stress over a short time. Eustress is necessary to activate and motivate people to achieve goals, change their environments, and succeed in life's challenges. However, most research focusses on distress, because it is a significant concern in organizational settings.[6] Employees frequently experience enough stress to hurt their job performance and increase their risk of mental and physical health problems. Consequently, our discussion will focus more on distress than on eustress.

General adaptation syndrome

The stress experience was first documented several years ago by Dr. Hans Selye. The Montreal-based pioneer in stress research wrote that the stress experience

Selye's General Adaptation Syndrome

Exhibit 5–1

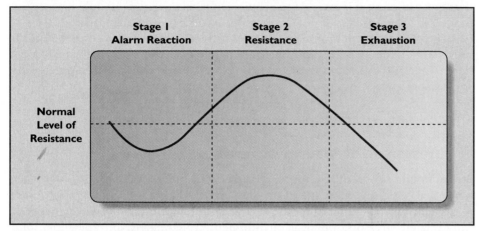

Source: J. L. Gibson, J. M. Ivancevich, and J. H. Donnelly, *Organizations: Behavior, Structure, Processes,* 8th ed. (Homewood, Ill.: Irwin, 1994), p. 265. Used with permission.

occurs in three stages: alarm, resistance, and exhaustion. This process, illustrated in Exhibit 5–1, is called the **general adaptation syndrome.**[7]

Alarm reaction

In the alarm reaction stage, the perception of a threatening or challenging situation causes the brain to send a biochemical message to various parts of the body, resulting in increased respiration rate, blood pressure, heartbeat, muscle tension, and other physiological responses. Initial exposure to the stressor reduces the person's survival capabilities and, in extreme circumstances, may cause death due to shock. In most situations, the alarm reaction alerts the person to the environmental condition and prepares the body for the resistance stage.

Resistance

Flight/Fright

The resistance stage involves introducing various biochemical, psychological, and behavioural mechanisms to deal with the stressor. For example, as adrenaline increases, the individual may try to overcome or remove the stressor. However, this resistance is directed to only one or two stressors, so that the person becomes more vulnerable to other stressors. This explains why employees are more likely to catch a cold or other illness when they have been working under pressure.

Exhaustion

People have a limited resistance capacity and, if the stressor persists, they will eventually move into the exhaustion stage as this capacity diminishes. In most work situations, the general adaptation syndrome process ends long before total exhaustion. Employees resolve tense situations before the destructive consequences of stress become manifest, or they withdraw from the stressful situation, rebuild their survival capabilities, and return later to the stressful environment

General adaptation syndrome
A model of the stress experience, consisting of three stages: alarm reaction, resistance, and exhaustion.

with renewed energy. However, people who frequently experience the exhaustion stage have increased risk of long-term physiological and psychological damage. Although it is possible to rebuild short-term energy, people have only a limited lifetime reserve of energy to resist extremely stressful situations.

The general adaptation syndrome describes the stress experience, but this is only part of the picture. To effectively manage work-related stress, we must understand its causes and consequences as well as individual differences in the stress experience.

Stressors: The Causes of Stress

Stressor
Any environmental condition that places a physical or emotional demand on the person.

Stressors, the causes of stress, include any environmental conditions that place a physical or emotional demand on the person.[8] There are numerous stressors in organizational settings and other life activities. Exhibit 5–2 lists four types of work-related stressors: physical environment, role-related, interpersonal, and organizational stressors.

Physical environment stressors

Some stressors are found in the physical work environment, such as excessive noise, poor lighting, and safety hazards. Construction workers often experience stress because they regularly face unpleasant weather and hazardous working conditions. Many logging truck drivers in Western Canada wear mouthguards because they would otherwise grind their teeth down from stress while driving the fully loaded rigs along treacherous mountain roads (particularly in winter). Office staff may also experience stress from poor lighting, stale air, and the perpetual drone of central air circulation systems (called *white noise* or *acoustic mist*).[9]

Role-related stressors

Role-related stressors include conditions under which employees have difficulty understanding, reconciling, or performing the various roles in their lives. Four particularly important role-related stressors are role conflict, role ambiguity, work overload or underload, and task characteristics.

Role conflict
A condition in which individuals face competing demands, such as when obligations of the job are incompatible with the individual's personal values (person–role conflict) or when the individual receives contradictory messages from different people (intrarole conflict).

People experience **role conflict** when they face competing demands.[10] One form of role conflict, called *person–role conflict,* occurs when obligations of the job are incompatible with personal values. Many employees experience person–role conflict when they must demonstrate emotions (e.g., compassion) toward a client even though they do not actually feel these emotions toward the person.[11] *Intrarole conflict* occurs when the individual receives contradictory messages from different people. Recent research has found that shop stewards are frequently exposed to this stressor because they must deal with competing demands from different union members and the local union executive.[12]

Role ambiguity
A condition in which employees are uncertain about their job duties, performance expectations, level of authority, and other job conditions.

Role ambiguity exists when employees are uncertain about their job duties, performance expectations, level of authority, and other job conditions. This role stressor is most apparent when people join the organization or take a foreign assignment, because they are uncertain about task and social expectations.[13] They cannot rely on past routines (e.g., how to greet people) so they

Causes and Consequences of Stress   **Exhibit 5–2**

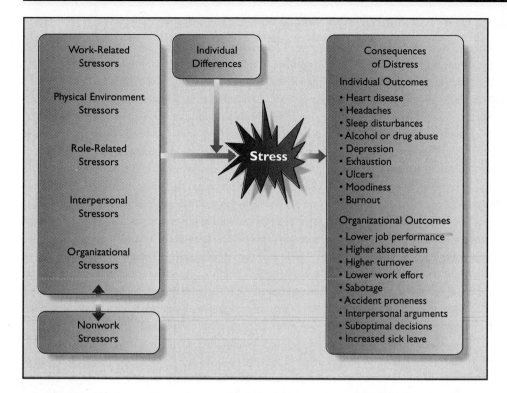

concentrate on their actions and carefully monitor responses from others. The constant vigilance and evaluation are stressful.

Work underload refers to situations in which employees receive too little work or are given tasks that do not make sufficient use of their skills or knowledge. Employees are exposed to this stressor when they are overqualified for the job and the work does not satisfy their expectations for new challenges. Work overload occurs when employees cannot keep up with deadlines or are given work that is beyond their abilities.

Task characteristics represent another type of role stressor. Tasks are most stressful when they involve decision making, monitoring equipment, or exchanging information with others.[14] Some jobs are stressful because the job incumbent lacks control over the work environment. For example, farmers must cope with the lack of control over weather, crop prices, and finances.[15] High levels of stress are also reported in companies that have adopted "lean production" practices. As Perspective 5–1 describes, lean production potentially creates a stressful work environment as task demands increase continuously.[16]

Interpersonal stressors

Interpersonal stressors include any conflicts the person may have with others. Insurance adjusters, bill collectors, and unemployment insurance agents often experience stress because they must work with clients in sensitive and difficult situations. Ineffective supervision and leadership, office politics, and sexual harassment are also interpersonal stressors.[17] In extreme cases, Canadian firms

Perspective 5–1

Lean and Mean: Work Stress in Lean Production Systems

Toyota Motor Manufacturing Canada Inc. recently increased production output by 20 percent—10,000 more Corollas each day—at its Cambridge, Ontario, plant. It hired 80 more people to cope with the increased production, but most of the adjustment was achieved through greater work efficiency of the 1,000 people already employed there. This is the world of "lean production," where *kaizen* (continuous improvement of work efficiency) and just-in-time inventory systems are applied to keep costs low and productivity high.

Lean production practices were introduced by Toyota in the 1950s and have since been copied by manufacturers in several industries. But some observers are worried about the effects of intense time deadlines, task structures, and overwork on employee stress. Everyone on the line must maintain constant attention to the work because minimizing inventory buffers lessens the room for error and the opportunity for relaxation. There is increasing regimentation as every second is devoted to a specific task element. Failure to complete a job cycle on time may shut down the entire production line.

Although some *kaizen* ideas ease work strain, most increase the employee's task demands. A common practice is double machine minding, where each employee is given responsibility for two or more machines. In Japan, some of Toyota's multiskilled operators tend more than a dozen machines at the same time. Each machine operates for a specific time before a new set-up is required, so any error on one machine will set off a chain of delays on the other equipment. The intense stress from double machine minding and other lean production activities has led to numerous accidents and an unusually high number of suicides. In fact, the Japanese have coined the word *karoshi*, meaning death by overwork, to reflect the extent of this problem.

Although lean production is relatively new in North America, there is already evidence that it is taking its toll on employee well-being. A recent survey of Mazda assembly workers in Flat Rock, Michigan, found that the lean production system resulted in such a high level of work intensity that 73 percent felt they would "be injured or worn out before I retire." An ongoing study of employees at the CAMI plant (a joint venture of General Motors Canada and Suzuki) in Ingersoll, Ontario, also reported increasing work stress. It is not surprising that the lean production system is sometimes called "management by stress."

Sources: S. Babson, "Lean or Mean: The MIT Model and Lean Production at Mazda," *Labor Studies Journal* 18 (Summer 1993), pp. 3–24; R. R. Rehder, "The Japanese Lean System vs. Volvo's Uddevalla System," *Columbia Journal of World Business* 27 (1992), pp. 56–59; D. Robertson, J. Rinehart, C. Huxley, and CAW Research Group on CAMI, "Team Concept and Kaizen: Japanese Production Management in a Unionized Auto Plant," *Studies in Political Economy* 39 (Autumn 1992), pp. 77–107; T. W. Johnson and G. H. Manoochehri, "Adopting JIT: Implications for Worker Roles and Human Resource Management," *Industrial Management* 32 (May–June 1991), pp. 2–7; K. Romain, "Teamwork at Toyota Raises Corolla Output," *Globe & Mail*, February 22, 1990, pp. B1, B4; and J. A. Klein, "The Human Costs of Manufacturing Reform," *Harvard Business Review* 67(2) (1989), pp. 60–66.

---

may be sued by employees who can demonstrate that management's actions have caused them mental distress.[18] As we shall see later, interpersonal stressors often lead to a particular stress reaction known as *job burnout*.

Organizational stressors

Various organizational actions may lead to distress. One of the most powerful of these is the threat or experience of job loss. Involuntary termination, factory closings, and unemployment all contribute to individual stress. Mergers and acquisitions are powerful stressors because they lead to organizational uncertainties and interpersonal conflicts.[19] For example, when Amoco Canada acquired Calgary-based Dome Petroleum, over 2,500 employees signed up for the company-sponsored stress management seminars to help them cope with uncertainties arising from this takeover.[20]

Work–family stressors

Invariably, our work demands and roles conflict with family, and vice versa. One recent Canadian study reports that 45 percent of employees experience high stress levels due to work–family conflicts.[21] The three types of work–family conflict include time, strain, and behaviour.[22]

Time-based conflict

Employees often experience stress due to insufficient time to adequately satisfy the demands of both work and family. Stress tends to increase with the number of hours of paid employment, because this leaves fewer hours available to fulfill family obligations.[23] Longer commuting time and extensive business travel also tend to increase stress in family relations. An inflexible work schedule can take a heavy toll on family life because it prevents employees from effectively juggling work and family duties. Shiftwork is another time-based stressor in family life; rotating shifts can disrupt routine family activities, whereas night shifts tend to increase the spouse's concern for the other's safety.[24]

The problem of balancing one's time between work and family is particularly acute for women, because they tend to perform most household chores even when holding down a full-time job.[25] Many women with children try to address this conflict by working part time.[26] However, others try to pursue a full-time career while still carrying the burden of their "second shift" performing housework. As Perspective 5–2 describes, some writers glorify this "supermom" role, whereas others suggest that women are superstressed by the impossible time-based conflicts that society expects them to overcome.

Strain-based conflict

Strain-based conflict occurs when stress from one domain spills over to the other. Death of a spouse, financial problems, and other nonwork stressors produce tension and fatigue that affect the employee's ability to fulfill work obligations. Stress from work has an even greater influence on family relations.[27] Work-related tensions make it difficult to enjoy family activities. This work stress spillover often becomes the foundation of stressful relations at home.

Role behaviour conflict

Another source of stress is the incompatible emotional roles that people must exhibit at work and home. People who act logically and impersonally at work have difficulty switching to a more compassionate role at home. For example, one study found that police officers were unable to shake off their professional role when they left the job. This was confirmed by their spouses, who reported that the officers would handle their children in the same manner as they would people in their job.[28]

Women in the work force have traditionally minimized role behaviour conflicts by holding jobs that were fairly compatible with their family roles (e.g., employee relations, public relations). This may change as they enter senior management jobs, although some writers suggest that some women are

Perspective 5–2

"Having it All": Supermoms of the 1990s

Sherry Cooper might be called one of the supermoms of the 1990s. Besides being a mother, Cooper is director of bond and money market sales at Burns Fry Ltd., a macho job in the male-dominated securities industry. In spite of the tough challenges of working in an organization unfamiliar with women at the top, Cooper is able to manage both family needs and the demands of her job.

"Having it all" describes the ideal situation for women entering the upper echelons of industry and still having the benefits of family life. But at least one critic wonders whether the supermom of the 1990s is simply a prescription for superstress. Although women are accepting increasing responsibility in business, their male counterparts are not embracing the role of homemaker quite as readily. Research indicates that when women enter the work force, they tend to keep most of their home responsibilities as well. Corporations are sometimes slow to respond to the changing family demands on its professionals and executives. Adding traditional men's work to traditional women's work inevitably results in the traditional nervous breakdown.

Many supermoms admit that it is not easy to be everything to everyone. Kathleen Christie, of Deloitte & Touche management consultants, was able to have two children and develop her career until she was made partner in charge of the Toronto consulting practice. However, her children demanded more of her time when they reached the ages of four and seven years old. "It just got to the point where the hours and the demands of the job were greater than I was prepared to give, and I give a lot." Fortunately, the firm agreed to give Christie a six-month sabbatical to catch up on family life.

Even when women can manage their time, juggling work and family responsibilities is complicated, particularly when they call for completely different roles and behaviour. "One minute you're going to a board meeting and the next you're going to a Beaver meeting," says Gail Cook-Bennett, another Toronto-based management consultant. A vice-president with Mary Kay Cosmetics Ltd. in Mississauga adds her concerns: "Sometimes I feel that I'm not doing either job marvelously. But I'm hard on myself. Nobody puts that guilt on me, but me."

Until men increase their contribution to homemaking and business learns to accommodate the new social order, many supermoms will experience frustration and stress. As comedian Lily Tomlin puts it: "If I knew what it would have been like to have it all, I would have settled for less."

Sources: A. Kingston, "Beyond the Fantasy of the Supermom," *Financial Times of Canada,* September 10, 1990, p. 13; and B. Dalglish, "Having It All," *Maclean's,* September 3, 1990, pp. 32–35.

---

minimizing role behaviour conflict by replacing traditional business attitudes (impersonal, authority based, logical) with more nurturing and supportive styles.[29]

Stress and occupations

Some jobs have more stressors than others. Among Canadian air traffic controllers, for instance, the most prominent stressors include poor equipment, the fear of causing an accident (called *collisionitis*), and work overload during peak traffic situations.[30] As a Winnipeg air traffic controller concluded: "That's the sheer terror, because you're working a lot of airplanes through a small area. . . . There's a lot of stress, and eventually it just wears you down."[31]

Several studies have attempted to identify high-stress and low-stress jobs.[32] Although the findings do not entirely agree with each other, some jobs are

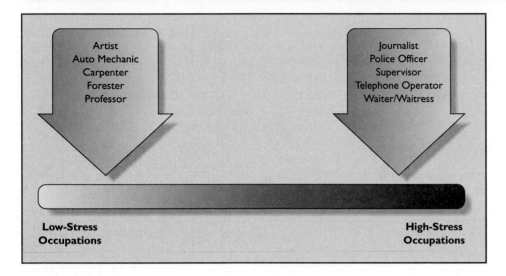

High-Stress and Low-Stress Occupations   Exhibit 5–3

consistently identified as being more stressful than others. Exhibit 5–3 lists five high-stress and five low-stress jobs. You should view this information with some caution, however. One problem with rating the stress of occupations is that task characteristics and job environments differ considerably for the same job in different organizations and societies. A police officer's job may be less stressful in a small town, for instance, than in a large city where crime rates are higher and the organizational hierarchy is more formal.

Another important point to remember when looking at Exhibit 5–3 is that a major stressor to one person is insignificant to another. In this respect, we must be careful not to conclude that people in high-stress occupations actually experience higher stress than people in other occupations. They are exposed to more serious stressors, but careful selection and training can result in stress levels no different from those experienced by people in other jobs. The next section discusses individual differences in stress.

Individual Differences in Stress

Individual differences represent another element in the relationship among stressors, stress, and stress consequences. As was illustrated earlier in Exhibit 5–2, individual characteristics moderate the extent to which different people experience stress or exhibit a specific stress outcome in a given situation. Two people may be exposed to the same stressor, such as the threat of job loss, yet they experience different stress levels or different stress symptoms.

Individual factors affect the stress experience in at least three ways. First, employees experience different stress levels because they perceive the situation differently. Those with low self-esteem are more likely to see job loss as a threat than those with higher self-esteem.[33] Second, people have different threshold levels of resistance to a stressor. Younger employees generally experience fewer

Exhibit 5-4   **Characteristics of Type A and Type B Behaviour Patterns**

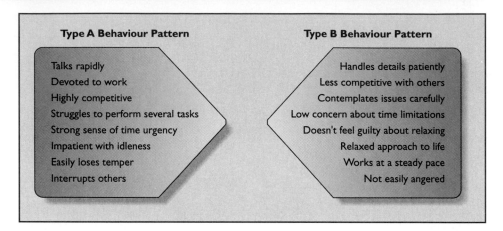

and less severe stress symptoms than older employees because they have a larger store of energy to cope with high stress levels. Finally, people may experience the same level of stress and yet exhibit different stress outcomes because they use different coping strategies. For example, there is some evidence that women are more likely to seek emotional support from others in stressful situations, whereas men try to change the stressor or use less effective coping mechanisms.[34]

Type A/Type B behaviour pattern

One of the most important individual differences is the Type A/Type B behaviour pattern. In the 1950s, two cardiologists noticed that patients with premature coronary heart disease exhibited common behaviours that were collectively labelled a **Type A behaviour pattern.** Type A people are hard-driving, competitive individuals with a strong sense of time urgency. They tend to be impatient, lose their temper, talk rapidly, and interrupt others during conversations (see Exhibit 5–4).

Type A behaviour pattern
A behaviour pattern associated with people having premature coronary heart disease; Type A people tend to be impatient, lose their temper, talk rapidly, and interrupt others.

In contrast, those with a **Type B behaviour pattern** are less competitive and less concerned about time limitations. Type B people may be just as ambitious to achieve challenging tasks, but they generally approach life more casually and systematically than do Type A people.[35] The important distinction, however, is that Type B people are less likely than Type A people to experience distress and its physiological symptoms (such as heart disease) when exposed to a stressor.[36] For example, a recent study of Montreal nurses reported that Type A nurses experienced significantly greater job stress, role ambiguity, conflict, and overload than Type B nurses.

Type B behaviour pattern
A behaviour pattern of people with low risk of coronary heart disease; Type B people tend to work steadily, take a relaxed approach to life, and are even tempered.

Regarding job performance, Type A people tend to work faster than Type B people, choose more challenging tasks, have higher self-motivation, and are more effective in jobs involving time pressure. On the other hand, Type A people are less effective than Type B people in jobs requiring patience, cooperation, and thoughtful judgment.[37] Type A people tend to be irritable and aggressive, so they generally have poorer interpersonal skills. Studies report that middle managers tend to exhibit Type A behaviours, whereas top-level executives tend to have Type B behaviours.[38] One possible explanation is that Type B people receive more promotions due to their superior human relations skills.

Consequences of Distress

At the beginning of this chapter, we learned that not all stress is bad. Eustress gives people the energy to meet the challenges of everyday life. But high degrees of stress or prolonged stress diminish the individual's resistance, resulting in detrimental consequences for both the employee and the organization. This distress often creates a vicious circle whereby stress leads to a dysfunctional consequence (such as alcoholism), which becomes a stressor leading to further dysfunctional consequences. Some of the more common outcomes of distress in organizations were listed earlier in Exhibit 5–2.

Individual consequences

High levels of stress may affect employees both emotionally and physically. Distressed employees may feel emotionally fatigued, depressed, and moody. Physiologically, they may experience such symptoms as high blood pressure, ulcers, sexual dysfunction, headaches, and coronary heart disease.

Approximately 10 percent of the Canadian work force have ulcers and other digestive system diseases. These ailments are caused by excessive secretion of gastric juices, often resulting from anxiety and worry. Coronary heart disease is one of the most disturbing effects of stress in modern society. This disease, including strokes and heart attacks, was virtually unknown a century ago but is now the leading cause of death among Canadian adults.[39] Hypertension refers to high blood pressure and is one of the major factors leading to heart disease. It is estimated that between 15 and 33 percent of Canadians have some level of hypertension. Again, stress is often identified as the primary cause.

Organizational consequences

Work-related distress undermines an organization's effectiveness. The physical symptoms of stress are felt by the organization in the form of increased absenteeism and long-term disability leave.[40] The increased moodiness of high-stress employees can result in more interpersonal conflicts. Stress undermines the quality and quantity of job performance and interferes with the employee's ability to serve clients. Employees under stress also make suboptimal decisions and are more likely to cause or be involved in workplace accidents.[41]

Job burnout

Job burnout is a commonly heard phrase in everyday conversation, yet it was coined only 25 years ago. **Burnout** refers to the process of emotional exhaustion, depersonalization, and reduced personal accomplishment resulting from prolonged exposure to stress.[42] It is a complex process that includes the dynamics of stress, coping strategies, and stress consequences. Burnout is caused by

Burnout
The process of emotional exhaustion, depersonalization, and reduced personal accomplishment resulting from prolonged exposure to stress.

Exhibit 5–5   **The Job Burnout Process**

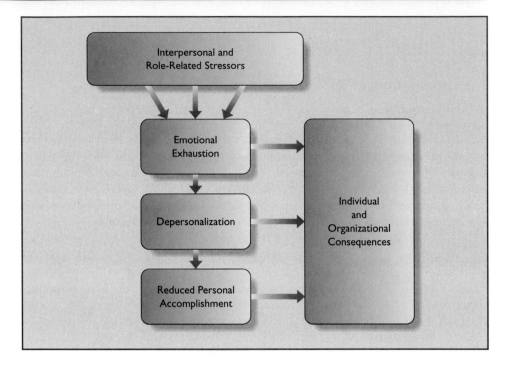

excessive demands made on people who serve or frequently interact with others. In other words, burnout is mainly due to interpersonal and role-related stressors.[43] For this reason, it is most common in helping occupations (e.g., nurses, teachers, police officers).

Exhibit 5–5 diagrams the relationship among the three components of job burnout. *Emotional exhaustion* represents the first stage and plays a central role in the burnout process.[44] It is characterized by a lack of energy and a feeling that one's emotional resources are depleted. Emotional exhaustion is sometimes called *compassion fatigue* because the employee no longer feels able to give as much support and caring to clients.

Depersonalization follows emotional exhaustion and is identified by the treatment of others as objects rather than people. Burned-out employees become emotionally detached from clients and cynical about the organization. This detachment is to the point of callousness, far beyond the level of detachment normally required in helping occupations. For example, a burned-out nurse might coldly label a patient as "the kidney in room 307." Depersonalization is also apparent when employees strictly follow rules and regulations rather than try to understand the client's needs and search for a mutually acceptable solution. *Reduced personal accomplishment*, the final component of job burnout, refers to the decline in one's feelings of competence and success and is observed by feelings of diminished competency. In other words, the person's self-efficacy declines (see Chapter 2). In these situations, employees develop a sense of learned helplessness as they no longer believe that their efforts make a difference.

Types of Stress Management Interventions   **Exhibit 5–6**

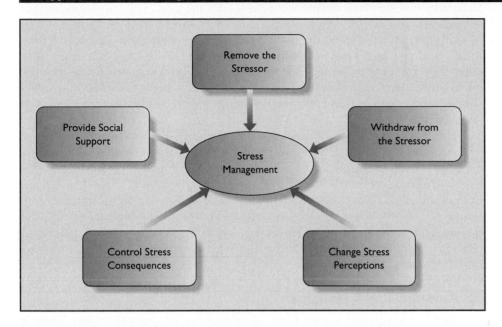

Managing Work-Related Stress

Equipped with a better understanding of the causes and consequences of stress, we can now identify several ways to effectively manage workplace stress (see Exhibit 5–6). One strategy is to directly remove unnecessary stressors or at least minimize the employee's exposure to them. Another is to temporarily remove employees from the stressful environment. A third stress management approach involves helping employees alter their interpretation of the environment so that it is not perceived as a serious stressor. Fourth, organizations can encourage employees to build better physical defenses against stress experiences. Finally, stress is often effectively managed through social support. Let's look at each of these stress management interventions in more detail.

Removing the stressor

Companies can reduce employee stress by removing unnecessary stressors or reducing exposure to them. Role ambiguity and uncertainty can be reduced by improving organizational communications. Senior managers should keep employees informed about events affecting the organization. Jobs should be redesigned to provide more reasonable workloads and time pressure. Employees should be involved in decisions affecting them.[45]

    Physical changes to the work environment can further reduce the risk of employee distress. For example, improved overhead lighting diffusers improve productivity by easing worker stress.[46] Introducing safer working conditions has the double benefit of improving the firm's occupational health and safety record and reducing the level of employee stress.

Withdrawing from the stressor

If the stressor can't be removed from the work environment, then organizations should permanently or temporarily remove employees from the stressor. The most important way to permanently remove employees from stressful jobs is through better person–job matching.[47] By carefully selecting job applicants, companies can ensure that employee skills and interests are compatible with the job requirements and work environment. Where a poor fit exists, employees should receive skill training or transfers to jobs more compatible with their skills and interests.

The Toronto Transit Commission (TTC) applied this strategy to reduce stress among its drivers. Until recently, the only factor considered when hiring TTC drivers was the applicant's ability to drive large vehicles. The result was that many drivers experienced job stress and provided poor customer service because they lacked the temperament and social skills to work continuously with transit riders. To correct the problem, the TTC now hires drivers based on their driving ability, temperament, and social skills. It also introduced passenger relations training so that drivers have the necessary skills to cope and interact with customers.[48]

Temporary withdrawal strategies

Companies are introducing a variety of options to help employees temporarily withdraw from stressful situations. Daily work breaks can reduce stress, particularly when employees are able to find quiet areas to relax without interruption. The City of Toronto and the *Toronto Sun* Publishing Corp. have introduced sabbaticals to help long-term employees restore their capacity to cope with stressful work experiences. As one *Toronto Sun* employee confirms: "Taking (a sabbatical leave) is so therapeutic, it's unbelievable. When I came back, if there was a deadline on something, I didn't let it give me anxiety attacks!"[49]

Employees typically experience role-related stressors when working in a foreign country with different values and customs. Lacking routines to guide them, they must pay constant attention to how others react to their behaviours. To manage this stress, some expatriates retreat into a **stabilization zone**—any place similar to the home country where they can rely on past routines to guide behaviour.[50] These may include attending a "Canadian night" at a club in the foreign country or having dinner with friends from the home country.

Stabilization zone
Any place where a person can rely on past routines to guide behaviour automatically; this is a stress management practice to temporarily withdraw from situations requiring constant vigilence in new surroundings.

Changing stress perceptions

People often experience different levels of stress in the same situation because they interpret it differently. Consequently, stress can be minimized by changing the individual's perception of the situation. For example, employees with higher self-esteem feel more confident that they can overcome major work challenges.

People with Type A personalities are more likely to experience stress because of their interpretation of the work environment. Fortunately, therapy and reinforcement can help Type A people reduce their sense of time urgency, have fewer meetings, and reduce the number of simultaneous work activities.[51]

Controlling the consequences of stress

Some stress management interventions help employees cope with the physiological and/or psychological consequences of stress. Thirty-six percent of large Canadian companies have stress management programs, most of them helping employees control the consequences of stress.[52]

Relaxation and meditation

Relaxation and meditation programs help employees adjust their physiological response to the stressor and stress perception. In relaxation training, employees practise muscle relaxation, breathing exercises, and visualization. The objective is to achieve a relaxation response in which heart rate, blood pressure, muscle tension, and breathing rate decrease.

Relaxation is best achieved in a quiet location, sitting in a comfortable chair, with eyes closed, using a repetitive mental device (e.g., a simple sound or chant). Meditation is a variation of relaxation involving a specific sitting position and special repetitive chant. Research suggests that relaxation and meditation programs are effective, particularly in reducing blood pressure levels and muscle tension.[53] Chris McBeath and Kirsti Watson (described in the opening story) went to relaxation centres to control their stress, but many companies have introduced in-house relaxation facilities, as we see in Perspective 5–3.

Fitness and lifestyle programs

Corporate fitness programs have probably received more financial resources from Canadian business than any other strategy to combat work-related stress. Physical exercise helps employees lower their respiration, muscle tension, heartbeat, and stomach acidity, thereby reducing the physiological consequences of stress.[54] Lifestyle programs train employees and reinforce their behaviour in better nutrition and fitness, regular sleep, and other good health habits. The fitness and lifestyle program at Maritime Telegraph & Telephone Co. Ltd. (MT&T) is typical. MT&T offers a variety of fitness facilities and activities. It also has a program to help employees stop smoking, seminars about alcohol abuse, family recreation events (swimming and skating), and funding for various in-house athletic leagues.[55]

Although research is limited, it appears that fitness and lifestyle programs may help employees control the dysfunctional consequences of stress. MT&T found a positive link between regular attendance at fitness programs and job performance ratings. A study at Canada Life Assurance Co. concluded that its exercise and lifestyle program reduced employee absenteeism, stress anxiety, and the risk of cardiovascular disease. Employees also reduced their smoking habits and developed better health attitudes.[56]

Employee counselling

Many organizations have introduced counselling services, called **employee assistance programs (EAPs)**, to help employees with stressful life experiences and to overcome ineffective coping mechanisms such as alcoholism. Most of the early EAPs in Canada started as alcoholism treatment programs, but most are now "broad-brush" programs that counsel employees on work or personal problems. Family problems often represent the largest percentage of EAP

Employee assistance programs (EAPs)
Special counselling services to help employees cope with stressful life experiences and overcome ineffective coping mechanisms, such as alcoholism.

Perspective 5–3

Shedding Work Stress through Relaxation and Meditation

Debora Foster takes off her necklace, settles herself on a padded chair, and gently leans forward. With a jazz piano tape playing softly in the background, the soothing hands of Sabina Vidunas begin to massage Foster's neck and shoulders.

"It's like an oasis in this room," purrs Foster. The room in question is the director's lounge of H. J. Heinz Co. in downtown Pittsburgh. Foster, who works in public relations at the company, enjoys the fully clothed massage for about 15 minutes every Wednesday. So does the chairman of H. J. Heinz, who swears by Vidunas's firm touch to relieve his old football injuries.

With larger workloads and lower job security, many employees hope that massages will control the consequences of work-related stress. Several U.S. companies—Emerson Electric and the Internal Revenue Service among them—have introduced in-house massage treatments for this purpose. Other relaxation and meditation activities are also offered to help employees control the consequences of stress.

Managers at British Steel were recently introduced to the stress-busting virtues of yoga as part of a course called "Management and the Use of Stress." The program taught them how to calm or energize through breathing and meditative exercises, release destructive tensions through relaxation, and improve their health through better posture. British Steel's managers were initially surprised to see yoga as part of the course, but recognized its benefits as a way to reduce the adverse effects of stress.

Meditation seems an unlikely stress management practice in business settings, but even the most conservative firms are trying it to help their battle-weary executives. McDonald's Restaurants has set aside a meditation room in its New York headquarters. Levi's corporate headquarters in San Francisco also has a quiet room, where employees chant mantras to release pent-up tension. Alcan Aluminum, Canada's largest metal producer, brought a Benedictine monk into its Montreal head office to counsel managers on the value of reflection. And, according to some sources, the most loyal practitioners of transcendental meditation are the pin-striped stockbrokers on Toronto's Bay Street.

Sources: J. Turner, "Executive Meditation," *Toronto Star,* May 24, 1993, pp. B1, B2; C. Smith, "Mind Menders," *BC Business,* March 1993, pp. 97–100; F. S. Heilbronn, "The Use of Hatha Yoga as a Strategy for Coping with Stress in Management Development," *Management Education and Development* 23 (Summer 1992), pp. 131–39; and J. S. Hirsch, "Doesn't Everyone Need to Be Kneaded Once in a While?" *The Wall Street Journal,* October 17, 1989, p. A23.

---

referrals, although this varies with industry and location. For instance, all of Canada's major banks provide post-trauma stress counselling for employees after a robbery, particularly when a weapon was visible.[57]

Social support

Social support from co-workers, supervisors, family, friends, and others is one of the more effective stress management practices.[58] Social support refers to the person's interpersonal transactions with others and involves providing either emotional or informational support to buffer the stress experience. Organizations can increase the level of social support by providing opportunities for social interaction among employees as well as their families. Managers should also adopt a supportive leadership style when employees work under stressful conditions and need this social support. Mentoring relationships with senior managers may also help junior employees cope with organizational stressors.[59]

Social support reduces stress in at least three ways.[60] First, employees improve their perception that they are valued and worthy. This, in turn, increases their self-esteem and perceived ability to cope with the stressor (e.g., "I can handle this crisis because my colleagues have confidence in me"). Second, social support provides information to help employees interpret, comprehend, and possibly remove the stressor. For instance, social support might reduce a new employee's stress because co-workers describe ways to handle difficult customers. Finally, social support can help buffer the stress experience directly when the employee perceives that he or she is not facing the stressor alone. This last point reflects the idea that "misery loves company." People seek emotional support from others when they face threatening situations.[61]

Chapter Summary

- Stress is an adaptive response to a situation that is perceived as challenging or threatening to the person's well-being. Distress represents high stress levels that have negative consequences, whereas eustress represents the moderately low stress levels needed to activate people. The stress experience, called the *general adaptation syndrome,* involves moving through three stages: alarm, resistance, and exhaustion.

- Stressors are the causes of stress and include any environmental conditions that place a physical or emotional demand on the person. Stressors are found in the physical work environment, the employee's various life roles, interpersonal relations, and organizational activities and conditions. Conflicts between work and family obligations represent a frequent source of employee stress.

- People have different reactions to stressors. Employees with Type A behaviour patterns have higher levels of distress than those exhibiting Type B behaviours.

- The emotional consequences of high or prolonged stress include fatigue, depression, and moodiness. Physiologically, people may experience such symptoms as high blood pressure, ulcers, sexual dysfunction, headaches, and coronary heart disease. Work-related stress can result in lower productivity, higher absenteeism, poorer decision making, and increased probability of accidents.

- Job burnout refers to the process of emotional exhaustion, depersonalization, and reduced personal accomplishment resulting from prolonged exposure to stress. It is mainly due to interpersonal and role-related stressors and is most common in helping occupations.

- Many interventions are available to manage work-related stress. Some directly remove unnecessary stressors or temporarily remove employees from the stressful environment. Others help employees alter their interpretation of the environment so that it is not viewed as a serious stressor. Fitness and lifestyle programs encourage employees to build better physical defenses against stress experiences. Social support provides emotional, informational, and material resource support to buffer the stress experience.

Discussion Questions

1. Two recent graduates join the same major newspaper as journalists. Both work long hours and have tight deadlines to complete their stories. They are under constant pressure to scout out new leads and be the first to report new controversies. One journalist is increasingly fatigued and despondent, and has taken several days of sick leave. The other is getting the work done and seems to enjoy the challenges. Use your knowledge of stress to explain why these two journalists are reacting differently to their jobs.

2. Describe the general adaptation syndrome process.

3. Sally works as a corporate law specialist for a leading Winnipeg law firm. She was married a few years ago and is currently pregnant with her first child. Sally expects to return to work full time a few months after the baby is born. Describe two types of work–family conflict that Sally will likely experience during the first year after her return to work.

4. Police officer and waiter are often cited as high-stress jobs, whereas professor and mechanic are low-stress jobs. Why should we be careful about describing these jobs as high or low stress?

5. Do people with Type A personalities make better managers? Why or why not?

6. A friend says that he is burned out by his job. What questions might you ask this friend to determine whether he is really experiencing job burnout?

7. How might fitness programs help employees working in stressful situations?

8. A senior official at the Canadian Auto Workers union recently stated: "All stress management does is help people cope with poor management. [Employers] should really be into stress reduction." Discuss the accuracy of this statement.

Notes

1. M. Campbell, "Freedom Another Word for Stress," *Globe & Mail,* January 3, 1994, pp. A1, A3; C. Smith, "Mind Menders," *BC Business,* March 1993, pp. 97–100; and J. Breckenridge, "Stressed Out and Sick of It," *Globe & Mail,* December 19, 1992, pp. A1, A6.

2. R. Turner, "Uptight? You're Not Alone," *Winnipeg Free Press,* April 24, 1993, p. A1; Cross-National Collaborative Group, "The Changing Rate of Major Depression: Cross-National Comparisons," *JAMA: The Journal of the American Medical Association* 268 (December 2, 1992), pp. 3098–3105; Campbell, "Freedom Another Word for Stress;" and Breckenridge, "Stressed Out and Sick of It."

3. Dr. Richard Earle, Canadian Institute of Stress, personal communication, November 1990.

4. R. Maynard, "The Pain Threshold," *Canadian Business,* February 1993, pp. 18–28; and M. T. Matteson and J. M. Ivancevich, *Controlling Work Stress* (San Francisco: Jossey-Bass, 1987).

5. R. J. Burke and T. Weir, "Coping with the Stress of Managerial Occupations," in *Current Concerns in Occupational Stress,* ed. C. L. Cooper & R. Payne (London: Wiley, 1980), pp. 299–335; M. T. Matteson and J. M. Ivancevich, *Managing Job Stress and Health* (New York: The Free Press, 1982); and J. C. Quick and J. D. Quick, *Organizational Stress and Prevention Management* (New York: McGraw-Hill, 1984).

6. M. Westman and D. Eden, "Excessive Role Demand and Subsequent Performance," *Journal of Organizational Behavior* 13 (1992), pp. 519–29; and M. Jamal, "Job Stress and Job Performance Controversy: An Empirical Assessment," *Organizational Behavior and Human Performance* 33 (1984), pp. 1–21.

7. H. Selye, *Stress without Distress* (Philadelphia: J. B. Lippincott, 1974).

8. Quick and Quick, *Organizational Stress and Prevention Management,* p. 3.

9. S. Rauchman, "What You Can't See Can Hurt You," *Canadian Occupational Health and Safety,* March–April 1989, pp. 20–21; and E. Rockett, "White Noise: Will the Hissing Have to Stop?" *Maclean's,* December 11, 1978, p. 52b.

10. R. L. Kahn, D. M. Wolfe, R. P. Quinn, J. D. Snoek, and R. A. Rosenthal, *Organizational Stress: Studies in Role Conflict and Ambiguity* (New York: Wiley, 1964); and E. K. Kelloway and J. Barling, "Job Characteristics, Role Stress and Mental Health," *Journal of Occupational Psychology* 64 (1991), pp. 291–304.

11. B. E. Ashforth and R. H. Humphrey, "Emotional Labor in Service Roles: The Influence of Identity," *Academy of Management Review* 18 (1993), pp. 88–115.

12. J. Barling, C. Fullagar, and E. K. Kelloway, *The Union and Its Members: A Psychological Approach* (Oxford, U.K.: Oxford University Press, 1992), Chapter 6; and S. D. Bluen and J. Barling, "Psychological Stressors Associated with Industrial Relations," in *Causes, Coping, and Consequences of Stress at Work,* ed. C. L. Cooper & R. Payne (Chichester, U.K.: Wiley, 1988), pp. 175–205.

13. D. L. Nelson, "Organizational Socialization: A Stress Perspective," *Journal of Occupational Behaviour* 8 (1987), pp. 311–24; and C. C. Pinder and G. A. Walter, "Personnel Transfers and Employee Development," *Research in Personnel and Human Resources Management* 2 (1984), pp. 187–218.

14. J. B. Shaw and J. H. Riskind, "Predicting Job Stress Using Data from the Position Analysis Questionnaire," *Journal of Applied Psychology* 68 (1983), pp. 253–61.

15. K. Bell, "Farm Stress Grows Deadly," *Winnipeg Free Press,* July 14, 1993 p. C5; G. S. Lowe and H. C. Northcott, *Under Pressure: A Study of Job Stress* (Toronto: Garamond Press, 1986); and R. Karasek and T. Theorell, *Healthy Work: Stress, Productivity, and the Reconstruction of Working Life* (New York: Basic Books, 1990).

16. T. D. Wall and K. Davids, "Shopfloor Work Organization and Advanced Manufacturing Technology," *International Review of Industrial and Organizational Psychology* 7 (1992), pp. 363–98; and S. M. Young, "A Framework for Successful Adoption and Performance of Japanese Manufacturing Practices in the United States," *Academy of Management Review* 17 (1992), pp. 677–700.

17. J. Seltzer and R. E. Numerof, "Supervisory Leadership and Subordinate Burnout," *Academy of Management Journal* 31 (1988), pp. 439–46; and H. C. Jain and P. Andiappan, "Sexual Harassment in Employment in Canada," *Relations Industrielles* 41 (1986), pp. 758–76.

18. For example, see *Colasurdo v. CTG Inc. et al.* (1988) 18 CCEL 264; and *Ribeiro v. Canadian Imperial Bank of Commerce* (1989) 24 CCEL 225.

19. P. H. Mirvis and M. L. Marks, *Managing the Merger: Making It Work* (Englewood Cliffs, N.J.: Prentice Hall, 1992), Chapter 5; R. J. Burke, "The Closing at Canadian Admiral: Correlates of Individual Well-Being Sixteen Months after Shutdown," *Psychological Reports* 55 (1984), pp. 91–98; and C. R. Leana and D. C. Feldman, "Individual Responses to Job Loss: Perceptions, Reactions, and Coping Behaviors," *Journal of Management* 14 (1988), pp. 375–89.

20. R. J. Burke, "Managing the Human Side of Mergers and Acquisitions," *Business Quarterly,* Winter 1987, pp. 18–23; and T. Carlisle, "Amoco Hit by Culture Shock as Dome's Spirit Lives On," *Financial Post,* March 25–27, 1989, pp. 1–2.

21. L. Duxbury, C. Higgins, and C. Lee, "The Impact of Job Type and Family Type on Work–Family Conflict and Perceived Stress: A Comparative Analysis," *Proceedings of the Annual ASAC Conference, Human Resources Division* 14(9) (1993), pp. 21–30.

22. J. H. Greenhaus and N. J. Beutall, "Sources of Conflict Between Work and Family Roles," *Academy of Management Review* 10 (1985), pp. 76–88.

23. L. Duxbury, C. Lee, C. Higgins, and S. Mills, "Time Spent in Paid Employment," *Optimum* 23 (Autumn 1992), pp. 38–45.

24. M. Jamal and V. V. Baba, "Shiftwork and Department-Type Related to Job Stress, Work Attitudes and Behavioral Intentions: A Study of Nurses," *Journal of Organizational Behavior* 13 (1992), pp. 449–64; and G. L. Staines and J. H. Pleck, "Work Schedule Flexibility and Family Life," *Journal of Occupational Behaviour* 7 (1986), pp. 147–53.

25. L. E. Duxbury and C. A. Higgins, "Gender Differences in Work–Family Conflict," *Journal of Applied Psychology* 76 (1991), pp. 60–74; and A. Hochschild, *The Second Shift* (New York: Avon, 1989).

26. D. C. Feldman, "Reconceptualizing the Nature and Consequences of Part Time Work," *Academy of Management Review* 15 (1990), pp. 103–12.

27. C. Higgins, L. Duxbury, and R. Irving, "Determinants and Consequences of Work–Family Conflict," *Organizational Behavior and Human Decision Processes* 51 (February 1992), pp. 51–75; R. J. Burke and C. A. McKeen, "Work and Family: What We Know and What We Need to Know," *Canadian Journal of Administrative Sciences* 5 (December 1988), pp. 30–40; and B. Sass, "The Centrality of Work," *Work & Stress* 2 (1988), pp. 255–60.

28. A. S. Wharton and R. J. Erickson, "Managing Emotions on the Job and at Home: Understanding the Consequences of Multiple Emotional Roles," *Academy of Management Review* 18 (1993), pp. 457–86; and S. E. Jackson and C. Maslach, "After-Effects of Job-Related Stress: Families as Victims," *Journal of Occupational Behaviour* 3 (1982), pp. 63–77.

29. J. B. Rosener, "Ways Women Lead," *Harvard Business Review,* November–December 1990, pp. 119–25; and J. Allan, "When Women Set the Rules," *Canadian Business,* April 1991, pp. 40–43.

30. A. McBride, "High Stress Occupations: The Importance of Job Components versus Job Categories," in *Current Issues in Occupational Stress: Research and Intervention,* ed. R. J. Burke (Toronto: Faculty of Administra-

tive Studies, York University, 1984), pp. 1–24; G. Shouksmith and S. Burrough, "Job Stress Factors for New Zealand and Canadian Air Traffic Controllers," *Applied Psychology: An International Review* 37 (1988), pp. 263–70; and Matteson and Ivancevich, *Managing Job Stress and Health,* p. 90.

31. B. Bird, "Jobs and Stress," *Winnipeg Free Press,* October 29, 1985, p. 27.

32. International Labour Office, *World Labour Report* (Geneva: ILO, 1993), Chapter 5; "High-Anxiety Occupations," *Globe & Mail,* March 23, 1993, p. A9; "Stress Test," *Globe & Mail,* August 11, 1992, p. B20; Karasek and Theorell, *Healthy Work;* and B. Nelson, "Bosses Face Less Risk Than Bossed," *New York Times,* April 1, 1983, p. E16.

33. R. S. Lazarus, *Psychological Stress and the Coping Process* (New York: McGraw-Hill, 1966).

34. E. R. Greenglass, R. J. Burke, and M. Ondrack, "A Gender-Role Perspective of Coping and Burnout," *Applied Psychology: An International Review* 39 (1990), pp. 5–27; and T. D. Jick and L. F. Mitz, "Sex Differences in Work Stress," *Academy of Management Review* 10 (1985), pp. 408–20.

35. M. Friedman and R. Rosenman, *Type A Behavior and Your Heart* (New York: Knopf, 1974); and J. H. Howard, D. A. Cunningham, and P. A. Rechnitzer, "Health Patterns Associated with Type A Behavior: A Managerial Population," *Journal of Human Stress* 2(1) (1976), pp. 24–31.

36. M. Jamal and V. V. Baba, "Type A Behavior, Its Prevalence and Consequences among Women Nurses: An Empirical Examination," *Human Relations* 44 (1991), pp. 1213–28; and T. Kushnir and S. Melamed, "Work-Load, Perceived Control and Psychological Distress in Type A/B Industrial Workers," *Journal of Organizational Behavior* 12 (1991), pp. 155–68.

37. M. Jamal, "Type A Behavior and Job Performance: Some Suggestive Findings," *Journal of Human Stress* 11 (Summer 1985), pp. 60–68; and C. Lee, P. C. Earley, and L. A. Hanson, "Are Type As Better Performers?" *Journal of Organizational Behavior* 9 (1988), pp. 263–69.

38. E. Greenglass, "Type A Behaviour and Occupational Demands in Managerial Women," *Canadian Journal of Administrative Sciences* 4 (1987), pp. 157–68.

39. C. Nair, F. Colburn, D. McLean, and A. Petrasovits, "Cardiovascular Disease in Canada," *Statistics Canada Health Reports* 1(1) (1989), pp. 1–22.

40. V. V. Baba and M. J. Harris, "Stress and Absence: A Cross-Cultural Perspective," *Research in Personnel and Human Resources Management, Supplement 1* (1989), pp. 317–37; and A. Arsenault and S. Dolan, "The Role of Personality, Occupation, and Organization in Understanding the Relationship between Job Stress, Performance, and Absenteeism," *Journal of Occupational Psychology* 56 (1983), pp. 227–40.

41. Jamal, "Job Stress and Job Performance Controversy: An Empirical Assessment;" S. J. Motowidlo, J. S. Packard, and M. R. Manning, "Occupational Stress: Its Causes and Consequences for Job Performance," *Journal of Applied Psychology* 71 (1986), pp. 618–29; and G. Keinan, "Decision Making under Stress: Scanning of Alternatives under Controllable and Uncontrollable Threats," *Journal of Personality and Social Psychology* 52 (1987), pp. 638–44.

42. R. J. Burke, "Toward a Phase Model of Burnout: Some Conceptual and Methodological Concerns," *Group and Organization Studies* 14 (1989), pp. 23–32; and C. Maslach, *Burnout: The Cost of Caring* (Englewood Cliffs, N.J.: Prentice Hall, 1982).

43. C. L. Cordes and T. W. Dougherty, "A Review and Integration of Research on Job Burnout," *Academy of Management Review* 18 (1993), pp. 621–56.

44. R. T. Lee and B. E. Ashforth, "A Further Examination of Managerial Burnout: Toward an Integrated Model," *Journal of Organizational Behavior* 14 (1993), pp. 3–20.

45. Karasek and Theorell, *Healthy Work;* R. A. Karasek, Jr., "Job Demands, Job Decision Latitude, and Mental Strain: Implications for Job Redesign," *Administrative Science Quarterly* 24 (1979), pp. 285–308.

46. L. G. Stulberg, "Bad Air Can Smother Productivity," *Financial Post,* August 8, 1990, p. 13.

47. R. J. Burke and G. Deszca, "Career Orientations, Satisfaction and Health among Police Officers: Some Consequences of Person–Job Fit," *Psychological Reports* 62 (1988), pp. 639–49.

48. "Transit Industry Absenteeism," *The Worklife Report,* October 1991, pp. 1, 14.

49. C. Cornell, "Loving It and Leaving It," *Human Resources Professional,* April 1991, pp. 19–22.

50. J. M. Brett, L. K. Stroh, and A. H. Reilly, "Job Transfer," *International Review of Industrial and Organizational Psychology* 7 (1992), pp. 323–62.

51. N. S. Bruning and D. R. Frew, "Can Stress Intervention Strategies Improve Self-Esteem, Manifest Anxiety, and Job Satisfaction? A Longitudinal Field Experiment," *Journal of Health and Human Resources Administration* 9 (1986), pp. 110–24; E. Roskies, *Stress Management for the Healthy Type A* (New York: Guilford Press, 1987); and J. C. Levenkron and L. G. Moore, "The Type A Behavior Pattern: Issues for Intervention Research," *Annals of Behavioral Medicine* (1988), pp. 78–83.

52. Breckenridge, "Stressed Out and Sick of It." Based on information from the Conference Board of Canada.

53. A. S. Sethi, "Meditation for Coping with Organizational Stress," in *Handbook of Organizational Stress Coping Strategies,* A. S. Sethi and R. S. Schuler (Cambridge, Mass.: Ballinger, 1984) pp. 145–65; and Matteson and Ivancevich, *Controlling Work Stress,* pp. 160–66.

54. L. E. Falkenberg, "Employee Fitness Programs: Their Impact on the Employee and the Organization," *Academy of Management Review* 12 (1987), pp. 511–22; and R. J. Shephard, M. Cox, and P. Corey, "Fitness Program Participation: Its Effect on Workers' Performance," *Journal of Occupational Medicine* 23 (1981), pp. 359–63.

55. C. Latham, "Fitness in the Workplace: Cause and Effect Relationship," *Vital Speeches* 53 (May 1, 1987), pp. 446–48.

56. P. Stulberg, "Business Finds Working Out Pays Dividends," *Financial Post*, January 26, 1990, pp. 11–13.

57. S. Day, "When the Day's Work Turns Ugly," *Globe & Mail*, November 17, 1992, p. C5; and M. P. Conlon, "Show You Care," *Canadian Business*, April 1987, pp. 64, 66, 108, 109.

58. J. M. George, T. F. Reed, K. A. Ballard, J. Colin, and J. Fielding, "Contact with AIDS Patients as a Source of Work-Related Distress: Effects of Organizational and Social Support," *Academy of Management Journal* 36 (1993), pp. 157–71; and S. L. Dolan, M. R. van Ameringen, and A. Arsenault, "Personality, Social Support and Workers' Stress," *Relations Industrielles* 47 (1992), pp. 125–39.

59. S. L. Dolan and P. Zeilig, "Occupational Stress, Emotional Exhaustion, and Propensity to Quit amongst Female Accountants: The Moderating Role of Mentoring," *Proceedings of the Annual ASAC Conference, Human Resources Division* 15(9) (1994), pp. 124–33.

60. J. S. House, *Work Stress and Social Support* (Reading, Mass.: Addison-Wesley, 1981); and S. Cohen and T. A. Wills, "Stress, Social Support, and the Buffering Hypothesis," *Psychological Bulletin* 98 (1985), pp. 310–57.

61. S. Schachter, *The Psychology of Affiliation* (Stanford, Calif.: Stanford University Press, 1959).

Chapter Case

Jim Black: Sales Representative

Jim Black impatiently drummed the steering wheel and puffed a cigarette as his car moved slowly northbound along the Don Valley Parkway. Traffic congestion was normal in the late afternoon, but it seemed much heavier today. In any event, it was another irritation that was going to make him late for his next appointment.

As a sales representative at Noram Canada Ltd., Jim could not afford to keep clients waiting. Sales of compressed oxygen and other gases were slower during this prolonged recession. Other compressed gas suppliers were eager to grab new accounts and it was becoming more common for clients to switch from one supplier to another. Jim pressed his half-finished cigarette against the ash tray and accelerated the car into another lane.

Buyers of compressed gases knew that the market was in their favour and many were demanding price discounts and shorter delivery times. Earlier in the week, for example, one of Jim's more demanding customers telephoned for another shipment of liquid oxygen to be delivered the next morning. To meet the deadline, Jim had to complete an expedited delivery form and then personally convince the shipping group to make the delivery in the morning rather than later in the day. Jim disliked making expedited delivery requests, even though this was becoming increasingly common among the reps, because it often delayed shipment of Noram's product to other clients. Discounts were even more troublesome because they reduced his commission and, except for very large orders, were frowned upon by Noram management.

Meanwhile, at Noram Canada's headquarters in nearby Brampton, senior managers were putting more pressure on sales reps to produce. They complained that the reps weren't aggressive enough and area supervisors were told to monitor each sales rep's monthly numbers more closely. Jim fumbled for another cigarette as the traffic stopped momentarily.

Two months ago, the area sales supervisor had "a little chat" (as he called it) with Jim about the stagnant sales in his district and loss of a client to the competition. It wasn't exactly a threat of being fired—other reps also received these chats—but Jim felt nervous about his work and began having sleepless nights. He began making more calls to potential clients, but was only able to find this time by completing administrative paperwork in the evenings. The evening work wasn't helping relations with his family.

To make matters worse, Noram's parent company in New York announced that it planned to sell the Canadian operations. Jim had heard rumours that a competitor was going to purchase the firm, mainly to expand its operations through Noram's Western Canadian sales force and production facilities. The competitor was well established in Ontario and probably wouldn't need a larger sales force here, so Jim's job would be in jeopardy if the acquisition took place. Jim felt another headache coming on as he stared at the endless line of red tail lights slithering along the highway ahead.

Even if Jim kept his job, any promotion into management would be a long way off if the competitor acquired Noram Canada. Jim had no particular desire to become a manager, but his wife was eager for him to receive a promotion because it would involve less travel and provide a more stable salary (less dependent on monthly sales). Business travel was a nuisance, particularly for out-of-town appointments, but Jim felt less comfortable with the idea of sitting behind a desk all day.

The loud honk of another car startled Jim as he swerved into the exit lane at Eglington Avenue. A few minutes later, he arrived at the client's parking lot. Jim rummaged through his brief case for some aspirin to relieve the headache. He heaved a deep sigh as he glanced at his watch. Jim was 15 minutes late for the appointment.

Discussion Questions

1.   **What stress symptoms is Jim experiencing?**

2.   **What stressors can you identify in this case?**

3.   **What should Jim do to minimize his stress?**

© 1991 Steven L. McShane.

Experiential Exercise

Behaviour Activity Profile—The Type A Scale

Purpose: This exercise is designed to help you estimate the extent to which you follow a Type A behaviour pattern. It also shows you specific elements of Type A patterns in various life events.

Instructions: This is a self-diagnostic exercise to be completed alone. Each of us displays certain kinds of behaviours—thought patterns of personal characteristics. For each of the 21 sets of descriptions below, circle the number that you feel best describes where you are between each pair. The best answer for each set of descriptions is the response that most nearly describes the way you feel, behave, or think. Answer these in terms of your regular or typical behaviour, thoughts, or characteristics.

1. I'm always on time for appointments.   7 6 5 4 3 2 1   I'm never quite on time.
2. When someone is talking to me, chances are   7 6 5 4 3 2 1   I listen quietly without showing any impatience.
    I'll anticipate what they are going to say, by
    nodding, interrupting, or finishing sentences
    for them.
3. I frequently try to do several things at once.   7 6 5 4 3 2 1   I tend to take things one at a time.
4. When it comes to waiting in line (at banks,   7 6 5 4 3 2 1   It simply doesn't bother me.
    theatres, etc.), I really get impatient and frus-
    trated.
5. I always feel rushed.   7 6 5 4 3 2 1   I never feel rushed.
6. When it comes to my temper, I find it hard   7 6 5 4 3 2 1   I just don't seem to have one.
    to control at times.
7. I tend to do most things like eating, walking,   7 6 5 4 3 2 1   Slowly.
    and talking rapidly.
Total score 1–7 _____= S

8. Quite honestly, the things I enjoy most are   7 6 5 4 3 2 1   Leisure-time activities.
    job-related activities.
9. At the end of a typical workday, I usually feel   7 6 5 4 3 2 1   I accomplished everything I needed to.
    like I needed to get more done than I did.
10. Someone who knows me very well would   7 6 5 4 3 2 1   I'd rather play than work.
    say that I would rather work than play.
11. When it comes to getting ahead at work   7 6 5 4 3 2 1   Many things are more important.
    nothing is more important.
12. My primary source of satisfaction comes   7 6 5 4 3 2 1   I regularly find satisfaction in nonjob pursuits,
    from my job.   such as hobbies, friends, and family.
13. Most of my friends and social acquaintances   7 6 5 4 3 2 1   Not connected with my work.
    are people I know from work.
14. I'd rather stay at work than take a vacation.   7 6 5 4 3 2 1   Nothing at work is important enough to inter-
Total score 8–14 _____= J   fere with my vacation.

15. People who know me well would describe   7 6 5 4 3 2 1   Relaxed and easygoing.
    me as hard driving and competitive.
16. In general, my behaviour is governed by a   7 6 5 4 3 2 1   What I want to do—not by trying to satisfy
    desire for recognition and achievement.   others.
17. In trying to complete a project or solve a   7 6 5 4 3 2 1   I tend to take a break or quit if I'm feeling fa-
    problem I tend to wear myself out before I'll   tigued.
    give up on it.
18. When I play a game (tennis, cards, etc.) my   7 6 5 4 3 2 1   The social interaction.
    enjoyment comes from winning.
19. I like to associate with people who are dedi-   7 6 5 4 3 2 1   Easygoing and take life as it comes.
    cated to getting ahead.
20. I'm not happy unless I'm always doing some-   7 6 5 4 3 2 1   Frequently, "doing nothing" can be quite enjoy-
    thing.   able.
21. What I enjoy doing most are competitive   7 6 5 4 3 2 1   Noncompetitive pursuits.
    activities.
Total score 15–21 _____= H

Impatience (S)	Job Involvement (J)	Hard Driving and Competitive (H)	Total Score (A) = S + J + H

The Behaviour Activity Profile attempts to assess the three Type A coronary-prone behaviour patterns, as well as provide a total score. The three a priori types of Type A coronary-prone behaviour patterns are shown:

Items	Behaviour Pattern		Characteristics
1–7	Impatience	(S)	Anxious to interrupt Fails to listen attentively Frustrated by waiting (e.g., in line, for others to complete a job)
8–14	Job involvement	(J)	Focal point of attention is the job Lives for the job Relishes being on the job Immersed by job activities
15–21	Hard driving/competitive	(H)	Hardworking, highly competitive Competitive in most aspects of life, sports, work, etc. Racing against the clock
1–21	Total score	(A)	Total of S + J + H represents your global Type A behaviour

Score ranges for total score are:

Score	Behaviour Type
122 and above	Hard-core Type A
99–121	Moderate Type A
90–98	Low Type A
80–89	Type X
70–79	Low Type B
50–69	Moderate Type B
40 and below	Hard-core Type B

Percentile Scores

Now you can compare your score to a sample of over 1,200 respondents

Percentile Score — Percentage of Individuals Scoring Lower	Raw Score	
	Males	Females
99%	_____ 140	_____ 132
95	_____ 135	_____ 126
90	_____ 130	_____ 120
85	_____ 124	_____ 112
80	_____ 118	_____ 106

Percentile Score	Raw Score	
Percentage of Individuals Scoring Lower	Males	Females
75	_____ 113	_____ 101
70	_____ 108	_____ 95
65	_____ 102	_____ 90
60	_____ 97	_____ 85
55	_____ 92	_____ 80
50	_____ 87	_____ 74
45	_____ 81	_____ 69
40	_____ 75	_____ 63
35	_____ 70	_____ 58
30	_____ 63	_____ 53
25	_____ 58	_____ 48
20	_____ 51	_____ 42
15	_____ 45	_____ 36
10	_____ 38	_____ 31
5	_____ 29	_____ 26
1	_____ 21	_____ 21

PART

Individual and Interpersonal Processes

Interpersonal and Organizational Communication

Learning Objectives

After reading this chapter, you should be able to:

Discuss the importance of communication in organizational settings.

Diagram the communication process.

Discuss two types of situations that require "rich" media.

Describe three ways that large organizations improve upward communication.

Identify three conditions that increase organizational grapevine activity.

Explain how men and women tend to differ when conversing.

List the six features of active listening.

Discuss four features of message content that increase persuasive communication.

Chapter Outline

A Model of Communication.

Communication Media.

Choosing the Best Communication Medium.

Communication in Organizational Hierarchies.

Communicating through the Grapevine.

Barriers to Effective Communication.

Cross-Cultural and Gender Communication.

Improving Interpersonal Communication.

Persuasive Communication: From Understanding to Acceptance.

Courtesy of Chrysler Canada.

Managers at Chrysler Canada's mini-van plant in Windsor, Ontario, have rediscovered the power of communication. Each day, the production and quality assurance managers hold a series of short meetings with employees throughout the manufacturing process to identify problems and hear employee solutions. The first meeting involves all employees working on the first production step and a representative from the second step. The second meeting involves everyone from the second step as well as representatives from the first and third steps of the production process.

These meetings are repeated for every production step and culminate in a 30-minute gathering of 50 managers and employees representing all areas of the plant. This session, called the Tire Kick, is an opportunity to discuss what happened on the line that day, and to encourage employees to take ownership for the manufacturing process. To further strengthen communication links with employees, the production manager has moved his desk from the executive offices to the same floor as the production facilities. "You have to show that you are part of the team," he says. "You have to find out what employees are thinking."

Chrysler has also adopted a stronger emphasis on effective communication at its Bramalea, Ontario, plant, particularly between production employees and engineers. Previously, workers who noticed problems would tell a foreman, who would tell a supervisor, who would try to find out which engineering group is responsible for this issue. More often than not, the information would get lost in the shuffle. Now, workers discuss production problems directly with engineers, resulting in a more accurate and timely transfer of information. The Bramalea plant even introduced a communications workshop designed to improve communication throughout the organization. The workshop has quickly become one of the most popular courses at Chrysler Canada.[1]

Communication
The process by which information is transmitted and understood between two or more people.

Communication refers to the process by which information is transmitted and *understood* between two or more people. We emphasize the word *understood* because transmitting the sender's intended meaning is the essence of good communication. Managers spend almost 80 percent of their day communicating, so it isn't surprising that overall managerial performance is closely related to their communication skills.[2]

Communication serves three important functions in all organizations:

- *Coordination*—Employees communicate with each other to coordinate work activities toward organizational goals. Without this communication, organizations would consist of a collection of people working independently toward their own goals.[3]

- *Decision making*—Many organizational decisions depend on accurate and timely information from employees. Without effective communication, decision makers often lack the information to identify problems and choose the best solutions.

- *Relatedness needs*—Communication helps employees fulfill relatedness needs. It maintains social bonds so that employees have a sense of connection with other organizational members. Employees identify more with the organization when they regularly receive information about it. This, in turn, increases job satisfaction and loyalty and reduces unwanted turnover and absenteeism.[4]

This chapter is about communicating in organizations—from interpersonal exchanges between two people to structured organizationwide communication programs. We begin by presenting a model of the communication process and discussing the different types of communication channels. Next, we look at the various ways that organizations promote downward, upward, and horizontal communication, and the characteristics of grapevine communication. The latter part of the chapter examines barriers to effective communication, cross-cultural and gender differences in communication, and strategies to improve interpersonal communication.

A Model of Communication

For the most part, communication is a process similar to that shown in Exhibit 6-1.[5] The sender forms a message and encodes it into words, gestures, voice intonations, and other symbols or signs. The difficulty is in finding symbols or signs with a common meaning between sender and receiver. Certain words or gestures may have different interpretations, because the sender and receiver have unique experiences and perceptions. Next, the encoded message is transmitted to the intended receiver through one or more communication media or channels. As we will discuss later in this chapter, the communication medium must be chosen carefully to ensure that it has sufficient data carrying capacity and the appropriate symbolic meaning for the intended message.[6]

Effective communication occurs when the other person receives and understands the transmitted message. This is not an easy process, because the receiver must recognize the symbols and signs through one or more senses, then decode this information by assigning the sender's intended meaning to the symbols and

The Communication Process Model   **Exhibit 6–1**

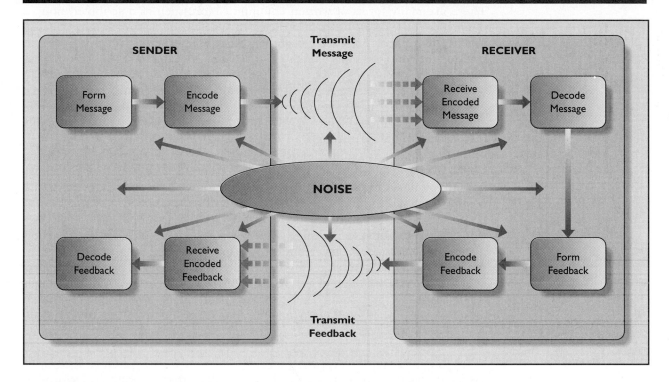

signs. If any aspect of this process fails, the sender and receiver will not have a common understanding of the message.

In most situations, the sender looks for evidence that the other person received and understood the transmitted message. This feedback may be a formal acknowledgment, such as a "Yes, I know what you mean," or indirect evidence from the receiver's subsequent actions. Notice that feedback repeats the communication process. Intended feedback is encoded, transmitted, received, and decoded from the receiver to the sender of the original message.

Communication is not a free-flowing conduit.[7] Rather, the transmission of meaning from one person to another is hampered by *noise*—the psychological, social, and structural barriers that distort and obscure the sender's intended message. Noise occurs at all stages of the communication process. For instance, noise exists when the sender and receiver have different backgrounds, resulting in different interpretations of the encoded message. It also exists when the receiver ignores the message due to his or her dominant needs or expectations. We will examine several types of communication noise later in the chapter.

Communication Media

A communication medium or channel is a conduit through which the message is transmitted. The three basic communication media are written, verbal, and nonverbal. However, these media take several forms, each with unique characteristics and advantages.

Written communication

There are many forms of written communication, such as a scribbled note, a detailed report, or an instruction manual. Written media are usually effective for recording and presenting technical details. Employees receiving written information tend to have a higher comprehension of the material than when it is received verbally.[8]

Most written messages are slow to develop and transmit, but emerging electronic media have significantly improved written communication efficiency.[9] For example, Thorn EMI's worldwide subsidiaries submit monthly financial information through an electronic data transfer system to its head office in London, England. Financial results are now available within a few days rather than several weeks after the reporting period ends.[10] Other companies are interconnecting with suppliers and customers, thereby improving the communication efficiency of just-in-time inventory systems.

Group decision support systems (groupware) represent an innovative electronic form of written communication that lets several people share information through a common server computer.[11] Five hundred employees at the Canadian Imperial Bank of Commerce are hooked up to a groupware program that lets team members keep track of databases and share information. Ault Foods and Royal Trust use groupware as a form of electronic brainstorming in which messages are posted to an electronic blackboard for others to read and debate (see Chapter 11).

Electronic mail

Electronic mail (E-mail) is a powerful technology that is rapidly transforming written communication at all organizational levels.[12] E-mail users can edit messages quickly, append information, and transmit to many people with a simple click of a mouse. E-mail reduces status differences, because the sender's and receiver's social cues are less apparent than in meetings or telephone conversations. Consequently, E-mail increases employee motivation to communicate with people at higher levels in the organization.

The efficiency of E-mail also creates problems. The number of E-mail messages tend to increase dramatically as employees become familiar with the technology and casually transmit their messages to multiple receivers. A second problem is that employees have difficulty encoding and decoding the emotional tone of E-mail messages. For instance, some writers use capital letters without realizing that many readers interpret this as a sign of anger. IBM Canada provides employees with etiquette guidelines to avoid these misunderstandings. Finally, E-mail increases the frequency of "flaming," in which an angry employee sends an emotionally charged message to others. Flaming occurs because people can post E-mail messages before their emotions subside, whereas the sender of a traditional memo or letter would have time for sober second thoughts. Presumably, flaming and other communication problems will become less common as employees learn the unique dynamics of E-mail.[13]

Verbal communication

Verbal communication ranges from a casual conversation between employees to the company president's speech transmitted to branch offices throughout the country. Face-to-face interaction is the most effective form of verbal communi-

Nonverbal Communication in a Canadian Sawmill   Exhibit 6–2

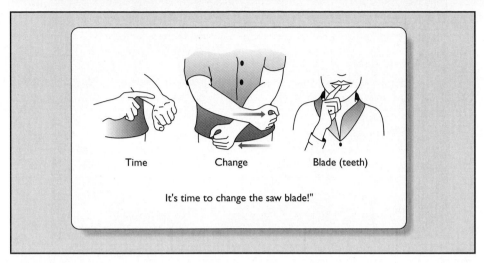

Time   Change   Blade (teeth)

It's time to change the saw blade!"

Source: M. Meissner, "The Language of Work," in *Handbook of Work, Organization, and Society,* ed. R. Dubin (Chicago: Rand McNally, 1976), p. 262.

cation when the sender wants to persuade or motivate the receiver. This may be due to the more personal nature of this channel as well as the benefit of immediate feedback, so the sender can find out whether the receiver has accepted (rather than merely received and understood) the information.

Nonverbal communication

Nonverbal communication includes actions, gestures, facial expressions, the sender's appearance, the timing of the message, the context of the message—almost anything that is not verbal or written. Nonverbal cues transmit the largest amount of information in face-to-face meetings.[14] They also influence the meaning of verbal and written symbols. Many years ago, for example, middle managers at General Electric engaged in price fixing even after being advised by senior executives not to do so. The managers ignored the verbal message because superiors typically winked their eye while giving the warning. It is still unclear whether the winks were simply a ritualistic symbol of friendship (as some GE executives claimed) or were telling managers to ignore the verbal warnings.

Nonverbal communication is necessary where physical distance or noise prevents effective verbal exchanges and the need for immediate feedback precludes written communication. One recent study reported that production employees use hand signals more than anyone else in the organization.[15] Another fascinating study identified more than 100 signals that Canadian sawmill workers use to communicate task information and maintain social relations.[16] As the distance between two workers increased, the percentage of nonverbal communication increased substantially. Exhibit 6–2 illustrates some of these nonverbal hand signals.

Some cultures place more emphasis on nonverbal than verbal communication in face-to-face interaction. To avoid offending or embarrassing the receiver (particularly outsiders), Japanese people will often say what the other person

Nonverbal communication is an important part of transmitting meaning to others, such as at this Battlefords Credit Union meeting in New Battlefords, Saskatchewan.

Courtesy of Battlefords Credit Union.

wants to hear (called *tatemae*) but send more subtle nonverbal cues indicating the sender's true feelings (called *honne*).[17] A Japanese manager might politely reject your business proposal by saying: "I will think about that" while sending nonverbal signals that he or she is not really interested. As we see in Perspective 6–1, we need to pay close attention to nonverbal communication when interacting with people from Japan and other cultures who communicate mainly through these subtle cues.

Nonverbal communication is useful in some contexts, but it tends to be extremely ambiguous. One Canadian researcher describes a plant superintendent in a concrete block plant who picked up a piece of broken brick while talking with the supervisor. This action had no particular meaning to the superintendent—just something to toy with during the conversation. Yet as soon as the senior manager had left, the supervisor ordered one half-hour of overtime for the entire crew to clean up the plant. He had mistakenly thought the superintendent was signalling him that the plant was messy.[18]

Choosing the Best Communication Medium

Employees perform better if they can quickly determine the best communication medium for the situation and are flexible enough to use different media as the occasion requires.[19] The effectiveness of a communication medium depends on whether its media richness and symbolic meaning are appropriate for the situation.

Media richness

Media richness
The data-carrying capacity of a communication medium; the volume and variety of information that it can transmit.

Communication channels can be organized into a hierarchy of **media richness,** as shown in Exhibit 6–3.[20] Media richness refers to the *data-carrying capacity* of a communication channel, that is, the volume and variety of information that it can transmit. Face-to-face interaction has the highest data-carrying capacity

Perspective 6–1

Understanding True Intentions through "Stomach Language"

Sterling Drugs was beginning to penetrate the Japanese market for over-the-counter pharmaceuticals, but the venture was not profitable enough to support the expensive advertising and sales force needed to maintain these sales. As head of Sterling's Japanese operations, Mark Zimmerman decided the answer was to approach a large Japanese pharmaceutical firm to act as Sterling's distributor outside the main cities and to supplement Sterling's sales force in Tokyo, Osaka, and other large centres.

Although Sterling Drugs had a long-established relationship with the Japanese firm, Zimmerman felt it would be best to approach top management only after an informal consensus had been obtained at the lower levels of the Japanese company. After initial inquiries, middle managers stated their willingness to discuss the distribution proposal. Several working level meetings took place between middle managers of the two companies with much discussion and a number of presentations exchanged on the distribution proposal. As discussions progressed, Sterling Drugs also set up its own task force to conduct extensive market research on the idea.

Finally, Zimmerman decided that it was time to take the proposal to top management of the Japanese company. He was confident from the middle management meetings that there would be no surprise or disagreement from top management about the distribution proposal. But when Zimmerman began to explain the idea, the president of the Japanese company pretended that this was the first time he had heard about the proposal and said that he could not comment on anything so major until his subordinates had every opportunity to discuss the proposal among themselves! After several unsuccessful attempts to get the proposal again elevated to top management of the Japanese firm, Sterling Drugs gave up on the distribution proposal.

Months later, a trusted friend in the Japanese pharmaceutical firm advised Zimmerman that senior management had told others to verbally be supportive of Sterling Drug's proposal (*tatemae*) in order not to offend Zimmerman and his colleagues, but to leave more subtle nonverbal cues that the Japanese firm was not really interested (*honne*). In hindsight, Zimmerman realized that he had pressed for the meeting with top management when middle managers of the Japanese firm would have taken that initiative if there was true interest in the project. Some of Sterling Drug's own staff had noticed other nonverbal messages indicating the Japanese firm's disinterest, but did not want to embarrass Zimmerman with this information because he had already informed Sterling Drug's head office in New York that the other firm was favourable to the distribution plan.

Source: Adapted from M. Zimmerman, *How to Do Business with the Japanese: A Strategy for Success* (New York: Random House, 1985), pp. 59–60.

---

because the sender can simultaneously transmit verbal and nonverbal signals, the receiver can provide immediate feedback, and the information exchange can be customized to suit the situation. Some electronic media are almost as rich as face-to-face interactions, but they do not allow the sender to use nonverbal cues as effectively. Next down the list are personalized written methods, such as memos and letters. Information bulletins, financial reports, and other impersonal documents are "lean" media because they allow only one form of data transmission (e.g., written), the sender does not receive timely feedback from the receiver, and the information exchange is standardized for everyone.

Nonroutine situations require rich media because the sender and receiver have little common experience and, therefore, need to transmit a large volume of information. During unexpected emergencies, for instance, you should use

Exhibit 6–3   **A Hierarchy of Media Richness**

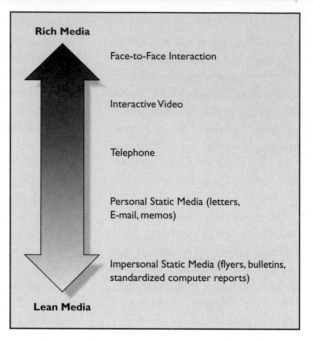

Source: Based on R. Lengel and R. Daft, "The Selection of Communication Media as an Executive Skill," *Academy of Management Executive* 2 (August 1988), p. 226.

face-to-face meetings to coordinate work efforts quickly and minimize the risk of misunderstanding and confusion. Lean media may be used in routine situations because the sender and receiver have already developed common understanding and expectations.

Ambiguous situations also require rich media because the parties must share large amounts of information to resolve multiple and conflicting interpretations of their observations and experiences.[21] The early stages of a project require rich media communication because team members need to resolve different interpretations of the project task, each member's role, and the parameters of acceptable behaviour.[22]

Symbolic meaning of the medium

Along with its data-carrying capacity, a communication medium conveys unique symbolic meaning to the receiver. Marshall McLuhan attracted attention on this point over 30 years ago with his popular phrase: "The medium is the message."[23] The University of Toronto professor was referring to the idea that the sender's choice of communication channel transmits meaning beyond the message content. For example, a personal meeting with an employee may indicate that the issue is important, whereas sending the message by memorandum may suggest less importance.

The difficulty we face when choosing a communication medium is that its symbolic meaning may vary from one person to the next. Some people view the

Communicating through Employee Magazines at Manitoba Telephone System   Exhibit 6–4

Source: Manitoba Telephone System. Used with permission.

use of E-mail as a symbol of professionalism, whereas others see it as evidence of the sender's efficiency. Still others might view an E-mail message as a low-status clerical activity because it involves typing.[24] Overall, we must be sensitive to the symbolic meaning of the selected communication medium to ensure that it amplifies rather than contradicts the meaning found in the message content.

Communication in Organizational Hierarchies

Communication flows upward, downward, and horizontally in organizations. Each direction serves different functions and requires different communication strategies.

Downward communication

Downward communication usually originates from the immediate supervisor and involves information about coordinating the subordinate's work activities. However, employees want more downward communication directly from senior management about organizational plans, productivity improvements, personnel policies, the effects of external events on their jobs, and other organizational matters of importance. Most are disappointed. One recent survey reported that less than 20 percent of firms share significant strategic information with their employees.[25]

Fortunately, some companies have introduced formal mechanisms to effectively communicate information from senior management to employees.[26] Employee magazines represent the most popular strategy. As an example, Manitoba Telephone System's magazine, shown in Exhibit 6–4, includes important information from senior management about the company's future strategy and direction. AT&T supplements its publications with daily or weekly electronic newsletters distributed to all employees through E-mail. A few firms publish employee annual reports that present a simplified version of corporate financial statements found in shareholder annual reports.

Bell Canada, B.C. Tel, and other large firms have introduced telephone hotlines to answer specific employee questions about organizational policies and practices. Corporate video programs are also gaining popularity, particularly among organizations with widely dispersed operations. As Perspective 6–2 describes, Canada Trust produces a quarterly video program that helps employees across the country feel that they are getting their information directly from senior management.

Upward communication

Formal upward communication improves the quality of corporate decision making by providing decision makers with valuable information and feedback from employees further down the hierarchy. Upward communication also serves a socioemotional function by building employee loyalty and career development opportunities through participation in organizational decisions. In spite of these benefits, upward communication is underdeveloped in most firms.[27] Employees are reluctant to send information to people at higher organizational levels, and managers usually have a poor understanding of employee concerns. To combat these upward communication problems, organizations have introduced employee surveys, upward communication coordinators, and visible management practices.

Employee surveys

Companies survey employees to gauge their general satisfaction and attitudes toward specific organizational issues. This provides feedback about the quality of corporate decisions and is sometimes an early warning system for emerging problems. James MacLaren Industries in Buckingham, Quebec, surveys its 1,800 employees every two or three years about the company's reward and promotion practices, management style, and corporate strategies. The pulp and paper company communicates the survey results back to employees and establishes a representative task force to formulate corporate priorities and action plans.

New company presidents sometimes commission employee surveys before making any corporate changes. For example, when Maurice Strong was hired as the chairman of Ontario Hydro, he distributed a 45-page survey that asked employees about their opinions on everything from solar power to cost overruns.[28] Federal Express Canada administers a special survey so that employees can provide supervisors with anonymous feedback about their performance. "The first survey is always an experience for new managers," explains a Federal Express executive. "But they soon realize they need it. Good communication increases the morale—and the productivity—of the group."[29]

Upward communication coordinators

Royal Bank, Bank of Nova Scotia, and other large Canadian firms employ special coordinators to help employees confidentially voice their complaints or opinions to senior management. The coordinator receives employee complaints in writing or through a toll-free telephone hotline. The questions and concerns

Perspective 6–2

Canada Trust Keeps Employees Tuned In

Senior management at Canada Trust knew that employees wanted more information about the financial institution's activities, but it also wanted a more personal and active presentation than newsletters and other written documents. "Executives wanted all employees to feel that they were getting their information directly from the top of the company," explains Canada Trust's manager of communication services.

The solution was a 15-minute video news magazine, called *8-to-8 Communicate,* that is distributed to every branch every three months. Named after the company's extended working hours, the video program became a great success among employees and recently won Canada Trust an international award for excellence in business communication. Employees can view the videos, along with supplemental written materials, either at their branch or at home. Past videos have discussed Canada Trust's strategic direction, progress on environmental programs, and details about how specific branches operate across Canada.

Since the release of the first *8-to-8 Communicate*

video, Canada Trust's communications department has been inundated with ideas from employees about future segments. Many have responded to the company's invitation for employees to submit video material. Although the communications department was worried about the "home movie syndrome," most employee-prepared video submissions have been right on the mark in terms of quality and subject matter. For example, one employee-prepared video detailed the challenges staff members faced when their branch office building was being renovated and they had to deliver banking services from makeshift trailers.

Canada Trust has realized many benefits of communicating through video programs. Video has mass appeal and time-saving advantages. It lets executives communicate simultaneously and consistently with the company's 18,000 employees across Canada to update them on the bank's latest developments. Finally, the video programs add a personal touch to downward communication.

Source: Adapted from R. Bonanno, "Canada Trust's Video News Program Keeps Employees Tuned-In," *Canadian HR Reporter,* October 8, 1993, p. 16.

---

are then sent anonymously to the appropriate manager and the reply is mailed by the coordinator to the employee.[30]

Visible management

Many executives are discovering that the best way to promote upward communication is through visible management. One visible management practice is **management by wandering around** (MBWA). This phrase, coined several years ago at Hewlett-Packard, refers to getting executives out of their offices to meet face to face with employees further down the organizational hierarchy.[31] Samuel Bronfman, founder of Montreal-based Seagram Co., practised MBWA many years ago by talking directly to employees throughout the organization rather than writing memos to them or their superiors. Today, many Canadian executives are routinely sighted among the troops. When Bill McCourt became Executive Vice-President of Operations at B.C. Tel, he rode around in installers' trucks to hear their concerns and ideas. McCourt is now president of the Insurance Corporation of British Columbia, where he continues this brand of visible management.[32]

Management by wandering around
A management practice of having frequent face-to-face communication with employees so that managers are better informed about employee concerns and organizational activities.

Another form of visible management involves senior executives meeting with small groups of employees to hear their views on organizational issues.[33] Toronto's Hospital for Sick Children holds open forums in which randomly selected employees discuss their concerns with the president. Hyatt Hotels has institutionalized monthly focus groups, called "Hyattalks," in which each general manager meets with a random selection of 15 employees to discuss any topics that employees want to address. Following each Hyattalk, the manager files a report and follows up on the issues identified during the session.

Horizontal communication

Horizontal communication coordinates work among employees, solves mutual problems, and maintains team cohesiveness. As we saw in the opening vignette, Chrysler Canada encourages its production employees to speak directly to engineers rather than communicate through their respective supervisors. Similarly, many Canadian firms encourage their employees to communicate directly with clients and suppliers rather than send and receive information indirectly through management. Unfortunately, these direct horizontal communication activities may threaten the manager's position power because they cut across formal lines of authority. Some supervisors try to regain their power by intervening along the communication channel, even though this produces less efficient information transfer to the intended receiver.

Communicating through the Grapevine

Grapevine
The organization's informal communication network that is formed and maintained by social relationships rather than the formal reporting relationships.

So far, our discussion has focussed mainly on the formal communication network—the communication paths explicitly sanctioned by the organization. But employees receive a considerable amount of information through the informal communication network, known as the **grapevine.** The grapevine is an unstructured network founded on social relationships rather than organizational charts or job descriptions. Employees often receive news from the grapevine before they hear about it through formal channels. For example, one recent survey reported that 45 percent of Canadian employees first hear about layoffs through the grapevine.[34]

Grapevine characteristics

The grapevine has several unique features.[35] It transmits information very rapidly in all directions throughout the organization. According to one estimate, over 75 percent of grapevine news is relatively accurate, possibly because the parties tend to use media-rich communication channels (e.g., face to face) and are motivated to communicate effectively. Nevertheless, the grapevine also distorts information by deleting fine details and exaggerating key points of the story. It transmits kernels of truth with several embellishments and, consequently, should not be viewed as the definitive source of organizational news.

The grapevine typically transmits information through the *cluster chain* pattern illustrated in Exhibit 6–5. Senders transmit grapevine information only to people they know and believe are interested. Some employees rarely receive

Transmission Pattern of Grapevine Communication   **Exhibit 6–5**

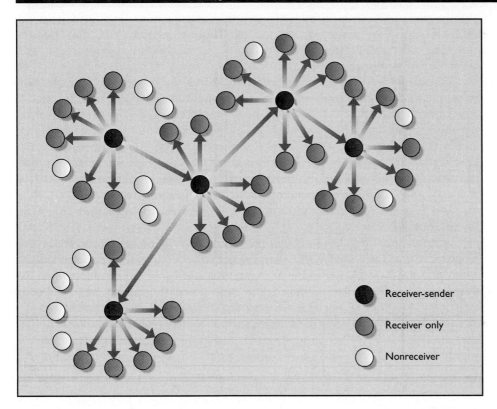

Receiver-sender

Receiver only

Nonreceiver

grapevine information because they are not integrated with the organization's social network.

The grapevine relies on social relations, so it is more active where employees have homogeneous backgrounds and are able to communicate easily with each other. It is most active when employees are anxious and information from formal channels does not satisfy their need to know.[36] Even when the formal network provides some information about a particular situation, employees will participate in the grapevine because social interaction relieves some of their anxiety. The Royal Bank of Scotland recently discovered this when it conducted a full-scale review of its branch banking system. Senior management knew that the review would increase employee anxiety, so it used newsletters and other formal communications to describe the project. Yet a company survey revealed that employee reliance on the grapevine *increased* rather than decreased during the review period.[37]

Grapevine advantages and disadvantages

Should the grapevine be encouraged, tolerated, or quashed? The difficulty in answering this question is that the grapevine has both advantages and disadvantages. One benefit is that the grapevine helps employees make sense of their workplace when the information is not available through formal channels.[38] It is also the main conduit through which organizational stories and other symbols of the organization's culture are communicated (see Chapter 16).

Along with its informational value, the grapevine is an important social process that bonds people together and fulfills their need for affiliation.[39] Finally, because it is most active when employees are worried, the grapevine is a valuable signal for managers to take appropriate action. This may include resolving the problems behind the rumours, or communicating more fully through formal networks.

The grapevine is not always beneficial. Morale tumbles when management is slower than the grapevine in communicating information, because it suggests a lack of sincerity and concern for employees. Moreover, grapevine information may become sufficiently distorted that it escalates rather than reduces employee anxieties. For example, when Dominion Insurance was put up for sale a few years ago, rumours about potential purchasers ran through the grapevine with disturbing regularity. Some of these rumours increased employee stress, such as the story that a Vancouver construction group was about to buy the Waterloo, Ontario, insurance company and intended to use it as a money-laundering front for the Mafia![40]

What should companies do about the grapevine? Some managers try in vain to stop the grapevine, but it will always exist. Others try to send messages down to employees through the grapevine, but this overlooks the problem that the grapevine has a selective audience and may distort important facts. A better strategy, as mentioned earlier, is for managers to listen to the grapevine as a signal of employee anxiety, then correct the root cause of this anxiety. B.C. Tel and the Royal Bank of Scotland also treat the grapevine as a competitor against which their newsletters and other formal communication programs are judged.

Barriers to Effective Communication

In spite of the best intentions of sender and receiver to communicate, several types of "noise" inhibit the effective exchange of information. Five of the most common barriers to effective communication include language, filtering, perceptual errors, information overload, and physical settings (see Exhibit 6–6).

Language

People must assign meaning to words and other written symbols because they carry no inherent meaning with them. Unfortunately, a symbol used by the sender might have no meaning to the receiver, or it might convey a different meaning than is intended.

Jargon

Jargon
Technical language understood by members of a particular occupational group, or recognized words with specialized meaning in specific organizations or social groups.

Jargon can be technical language of a particular occupational group (such as medical or legal terms) or recognized words with specialized meaning in specific organizations or social groups. Jargon increases communication efficiency when both sender and receiver understand this specialized language, and it improves team dynamics by distinguishing members (who understand the jargon) from outsiders. Jargon is also a powerful element in shaping and maintaining an organization's cultural values.[41]

Barriers to Effective Communication   Exhibit 6-6

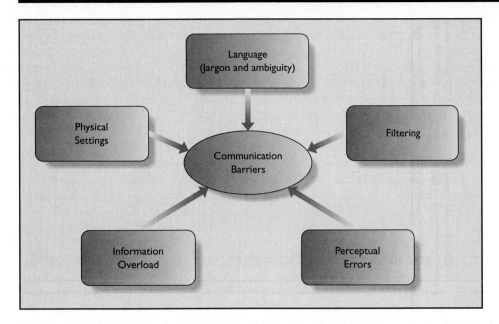

Unfortunately, jargon becomes noise in the communication process when the receiver doesn't understand this specialized language. For example, employees at Wacker Siltronic Corp. were breaking saw blades and causing a high rate of product defects after new machinery was introduced. Management eventually discovered that the manuals were written for engineers, and that employees were guessing (often incorrectly) at the meaning of the jargon. Productivity improved and machine costs dropped after the manuals were rewritten with the jargon removed.[42]

Ambiguity

Language is ambiguous when it has many meanings, and this becomes a communication barrier when the receiver assigns a different meaning than the sender intended. An example of this occurred when a supervisor asked one of his employees to "go out back and pull a stack of buckets apart." Separating the stacked buckets should have taken 20 minutes, but the employee had not returned after two hours. The supervisor went to investigate, only to find the employee literally ripping the buckets apart. The supervisor and the employee had no difficulty assigning meaning to the phrase "pull apart." Unfortunately, they used different meanings for this ambiguous phrase.[43]

Ambiguous language is sometimes used intentionally to obscure bad news. Executives talk about "rightsizing" rather than reducing their work force, and they label people as "excessed" or "organizationally displaced" rather than laid off.[44] Ambiguity is also used to communicate events in a more favourable light. One annual report by Montreal-based Provigo Inc. boasted the creation of "an operating entity [to establish] home improvement centres." Most of us would recognize these as hardware stores. A B.C. Ministry of Education official spoke glowingly of "on-site facilitators of pupil learning," known to most of us as teachers![45]

Although ambiguous language often undermines communication effectiveness, it is sometimes necessary when the situation is ill-defined or lacks agreement.[46] Effective leaders use metaphors such as "laying pipe" or "wild geese" to describe complex organizational values so that they are interpreted broadly enough to apply to diverse situations. Scholars also rely on metaphors because they convey rich meaning about complex ideas. For example, some organizational behaviour scholars label organizations as "machines" or "organisms" to reflect their complex nature.[47]

Filtering

Some messages are filtered or stopped altogether on their way up or down the organizational hierarchy. Employees and supervisors might filter upward communication so that they look more favourable to their superiors. This is most common in organizations that emphasize status differences and tolerate high levels of political behaviour, as well as among employees with strong career mobility aspirations.[48]

Filtering can be minimized through direct upward and downward communication practices described earlier (e.g., visible management, employee surveys). Another strategy is for the sender to transmit the message through more than one communication channel. By using multiple media, any filtering of one message may be different from another, so the receiver can piece together more accurate meaning. Because filtering is often a form of organizational politics, another solution is to apply the strategies described in Chapter 12 to reduce this political behaviour.

Perceptual errors

Marshall McLuhan once explained that senders and receivers wear their own set of idiosyncratic goggles. He was referring to the fact that people have unique perceptual frames of reference that represent another form of noise in the communication process. We will learn about perceptual problems in Chapter 7. At this point, you should know that perceptual differences cause the receiver to screen out parts of the message that the sender wants heard, and to emphasize different parts of the message than was intended by the sender.

Information overload

Information overload
A condition in which the volume of information received by an employee exceeds that person's ability to process it effectively.

Every job includes a varying *information load,* that is, the amount of information that must be processed per unit of time.[49] Each person in that job has a certain *information processing capacity,* that is, the amount of information that he or she is able to process in a fixed unit of time. Unfortunately, as we see in Exhibit 6–7, this information load sometimes exceeds the employee's information processing capacity, resulting in **information overload.**

Information overload is stressful for employees and, if not corrected, may result in lost information and poor decisions. Although traditionally prevalent among executives, information overload has become common among lower-level staff members as they handle increasing workloads and face the "infoglut" produced by more efficient electronic communication systems. Fortunately,

Dynamics of Information Overload   Exhibit 6–7

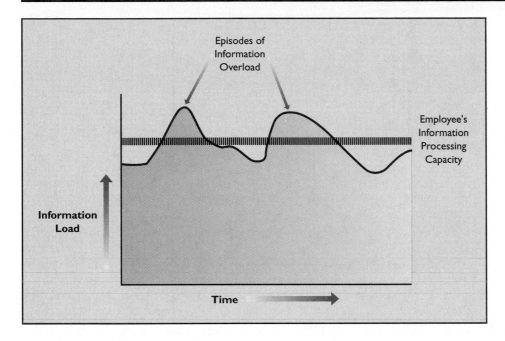

several strategies are available to minimize the frequency of information overload. One set of solutions reduces the job's information load, whereas the other increases the employee's information processing capacity.[50]

Reducing information load

We can reduce information overload by omitting, summarizing, or buffering the information. The omitting approach includes discarding junk mail unopened or deleting E-mail after reading only its title or source. Federal Express encourages omitting through "Operation Namedropper," in which employees can get their names deleted from distribution lists for computer printouts that they never read. Managers often rely on the summarizing strategy by reading executive summaries rather than entire reports. Finally, information load is kept at a reasonable level through buffering, where assistants screen the person's messages and forward only those considered essential reading.

Increasing information processing capacity

We can increase our information processing capacity either by learning to digest data more efficiently or by finding more time. People learn to digest information more quickly through speedreading, scanning, or removing distractions that slow information processing speed. Many companies try to increase the employee's information processing capacity by improving their time management skills. When information overload is temporary, some people process the excess load by working longer hours. Others develop a waiting queue and process less important messages when the information load has subsided. In situations where information overload is permanent, more people should be added to process the information.

Physical settings

The amount of communication between employees and managers decreases as their distance and physical barriers increase.[51] Because executives are often found in separate offices or buildings from other employees, it is little wonder that vertical communication is so poor in many organizations. With this in mind, Canada Packers transferred 70 executives from its Toronto headquarters out to the company's plants. "We want to shorten the lines of communication and make managers more involved," explains Canada Packers's president. "We want them back 'living over the shop.' "[52]

Many French and Japanese companies encourage vertical communication by placing executives in the centre of an open office with their subordinates. This occurs at Toyota's Cambridge, Ontario, plant, where executives sit in the same large room as the other office staff. "The fact that there are no barriers is a tangible example of how Japanese look at communication," explains a company spokesperson. "If I want to see the vice-president of administration, I just look up and see if he's at his desk. I don't have to phone his secretary and make an appointment to see him."[53]

This line-of-sight principle is also applied on the plant floor. Toyota production areas typically consist of U-shaped subassembly lines so that everyone on the line can coordinate their work and solve problems more quickly through direct communication. This contrasts with the traditional I-shaped or L-shaped lines at General Motors of Canada, which make it difficult for employees to communicate with each other.[54]

Companies are discovering that employee creativity increases when the building's physical design allows spontaneous, horizontal communication.[55] When Corning Glass learned that its engineers got 80 percent of their ideas from face-to-face discussions with colleagues, it moved employees into a low-rise building with informal meeting places and easy access to all areas. Engineering productivity increased by more than 10 percent in the new building. 3M's new building in Austin, Texas, also has several interaction areas, with blackboards, couches, and coffee machines, where employees can hold spontaneous gatherings to share knowledge.

Office arrangement

Office design influences communication between managers and their subordinates in two ways. First, office size, furniture quality, and building location convey nonverbal messages regarding the incumbent's status. These status differences may discourage effective information exchange between sender and receiver.

Second, seating arrangements and desk location during the communication episode affect the degree to which employees feel comfortable and welcome in the manager's office.[56] Exhibit 6–8 illustrates two office arrangements with different effects on the receiver. In the closed arrangement, the manager's desk is both a physical and communication barrier between the sender and receiver because it faces the door and separates the employee from the manager. In the open arrangement, the desk faces a side wall and the employee sits to one side of the manager so that the desk is not between them. This setting encourages open communication because it symbolizes the manager as a peer and helper to the employee.

Closed and Open Communication Office Arrangements   **Exhibit 6-8**

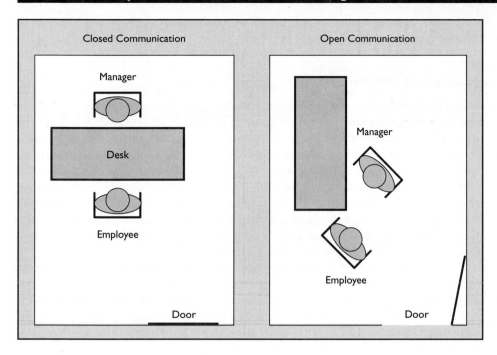

Cross-Cultural and Gender Communication

A culturally diverse work force potentially improves organizational effectiveness through better decision making, greater creativity and innovation, and more successful marketing to different types of consumers.[57] However, it also requires additional sensitivity and competence in the communication process. Employees must deal with different languages, nonverbal cues, and behavioural norms. They must overcome their reluctance to communicate with co-workers from another cultural group. Cross-cultural competence is also essential when we do business with people from other countries.

Language and verbal differences

Language differences impede communication among employees in many Canadian organizations. One study of cultural diversity in Toronto's major hotels reported that language barriers made it difficult for managers to give non-English employees meaningful feedback to help them improve their jobs. As one Toronto hotel manager explained: "If communication is difficult because of a language barrier, many supervisors don't bother to try. Messages go uncommunicated, and staff members do not get the feedback or the praise."[58]

Even when people from different cultures have mastered the same language, communication problems may occur when interpreting voice intonation.[59] A deep voice symbolizes masculinity in Canada, but African men often express their emotions using a high-pitched voice. Middle Easterners sometimes speak loudly to show sincerity and interest in the discussion, whereas Japanese people are often soft-spoken to communicate politeness or humility. These different cultural norms regarding voice loudness may cause one person to misinterpret the other.

Nonverbal differences

Most nonverbal cues are specific to a particular culture and may have a completely different meaning to people raised in different cultures.[60] For example, Canadians shake their head from side to side to say "No," but this means "Yes" to many Yugoslavians and "I understand" to some people from India. Filipinos raise their eyebrows to give an affirmative answer, yet Arabs interpret this expression (along with clicking one's tongue) as a negative response. Canadians are taught to maintain eye contact with the speaker to show interest and respect, yet this is considered rude to some Asian and Middle Eastern people, who are taught to show respect by looking down when a supervisor or older person is talking to them.

Even the common handshake communicates different meaning across cultures. Canadians tend to appreciate a firm handshake as a sign of strength and warmth in a friendship or business relationship. In contrast, many Asians and Middle Easterners favour a loose grip and regard a firm clench as aggressive. Germans prefer one good handshake stroke, whereas anything less than five or six strokes may symbolize a lack of trust in Spain. If this isn't confusing enough, people from some cultures view any touching in public—including handshakes—as a sign of rudeness.

Silence and conversational overlaps

People from different cultures must also learn to correctly interpret and tolerate different amounts of silence and conversational overlap. Japanese people tend to remain silent for a few seconds after someone has spoken, to contemplate what has just been said as a sign of respect.[61] To them, silence is an important part of communication (called *haragei*) because it preserves harmony and is more reliable than talk. In contrast, Canadians view silence as a lack of communication and often interpret long breaks as a sign of disagreement.

Conversational overlaps—when two or more people speak at the same time—are considered quite rude in Canada, but are the cultural norm in Brazil and other Latin American countries. Canadians usually stop talking when they are interrupted, whereas Brazilians typically continue talking over the other's speech. Perspective 6–3 describes how one Coca-Cola executive discovered cultural differences in conversational overlap during his assignment in Puerto Rico.

Gender differences in communication

When Monica McCandless became a vice-president at Campbell Soup Co. Ltd. in Toronto, she noticed that male colleagues were asserting their power and status in the executive meetings. Campbell Soup's CEO called it "normal male rutting behaviour," but McCandless pointed out that this behaviour wasn't helping social relations or teamwork among executive members.[62]

Perspective 6–3

Coca-Cola Executive Learns that Noise to Some Is Music to Others

George Gourlay, a senior executive at the Coca-Cola Company, recalls a meeting in Puerto Rico, attended mostly by Puerto Ricans, in which everyone seemed to be speaking at once. This seemingly incoherent babble made Gourlay uncomfortable and confused, so he used his managerial prerogative to force order in the meeting. Gourlay thought the meeting was now going well, until he noticed that the others appeared uncomfortable.

By coincidence, Gourlay took a course over the next three days in Puerto Rican culture. During the training program, the Coca-Cola manager learned that the noisy exchange with conversational overlaps in the earlier meeting was the natural way for Puerto Ricans and other Hispanics to communicate. It is normal for them to start talking while the other person is still speaking. Sometimes, three or four people would talk at the same time, thereby creating a noisy discourse to the uninitiated. By contrast, people from Germany, Canada, and a few other countries prefer a more orderly communication exchange, in which it is impolite to speak until the other person has finished.

With this knowledge in hand, Gourlay decided to adapt his style during his meetings in Puerto Rico. "I am still uncomfortable, but meetings are more productive," he admits.

Source: Based on G. Gourlay, "Quality's Cultural Foundation," in *Making Total Quality Happen*, ed. F. Caropreso (New York: Conference Board, 1990), pp. 71–74.

McCandless's observations reflect important communication differences between men and women in organizational settings. According to recent writing on this subject, men tend to view conversations as negotiations of relative status and independence.[63] They assert their status by giving advice to others' problems and using direct statements such as "You should do the following." At the same time, men are reluctant to seek advice from others because this threatens their status and power. For example, some men will drive around for nearly an hour looking for a location rather than stop to ask for directions. At best, men communicate to gather and transmit information. They engage in "report talk," in which the primary function of the conversation is impersonal and efficient information exchange.

Women also engage in "report talk," particularly when conversing with men. But they place a much higher priority than men on "rapport talk," the relatedness needs function of communication that we described at the beginning of this chapter. Rather than communicating to gather information, women will often communicate mainly to build or maintain social bonds. Women's preference for building rapport rather than asserting status is also apparent when giving advice. Women might say, "Have you considered . . . ?" or some other indirect approach that doesn't assert their superiority. Similarly, women apologize more often and seek advice from others more quickly than do men. Finally, women are more sensitive than men to nonverbal cues in face-to-face meetings.[64]

Given these differences, it isn't surprising that men and women are often frustrated with each other in conversations. Women sometimes discuss their personal experiences and problems to develop closeness with the receiver. They look for expressions of understanding, such as "That's the way I felt when it happened to me." But when men hear problems, they quickly suggest solutions because this asserts their control over the situation. Not only does this frustrate a woman's need for common understanding, but the advice actually says: "You and I are different; you have the problem and I have the answer." Meanwhile, men become frustrated because they can't understand why women don't appreciate their advice.

Improving Interpersonal Communication

Effective interpersonal communication depends on the sender's ability to get the message across and the receiver's performance as an active listener. In this section, we outline these two essential features of effective interpersonal communication.

Getting your message across

Earlier in this chapter, we mentioned that effective communication occurs when the other person receives and understands the message. To accomplish this difficult task, the sender must learn to empathize with the receiver, repeat the message, choose an appropriate time for the conversation, and be descriptive rather than evaluative.

- *Empathize*—Imagine yourself as the other person and think about how that person will decode the message. Which words are ambiguous or might trigger the wrong emotional response? By considering the receiver's background and current situation, these potential barriers will be recognized and minimized.

- *Repeat the message*—Repeat the message in a different way and explain some points more fully so that the listener will hear information that was missed the first time. The saying "Tell them what you're going to tell them; tell them; then tell them what you've told them" reflects this need for redundancy.

- *Use timing effectively*—Your message competes with other messages and noise, so find a time when the receiver is less likely to be distracted by these other matters.

- *Be descriptive*—People stop listening when the information attacks their self-esteem. Therefore, focus on the problem, not the person, if you have negative information to convey. Describe the events factually rather than label the employee. Describe your reaction to the event rather than accuse the employee. Finally, rather than pointing to the employee as the problem, suggest things he or she can do to improve.

Active listening

Listening is at least as important as talking. As one sage wisely wrote: "Nature gave people two ears but only one tongue, which is a gentle hint that they should listen more than they talk."[65] But listening is more than just being quiet; it is an active process that requires more effort than most people realize. The main elements of active listening are illustrated in Exhibit 6–9 and described below. Please remember that these guidelines apply to Canadian society and might be contrary to the norms of some other cultures.[66]

Elements of Active Listening   **Exhibit 6–9**

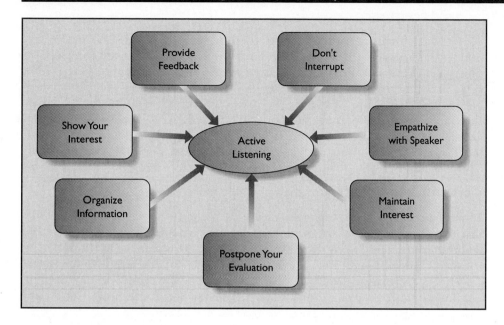

One of the most important features of active listening is to avoid interrupting the speaker. Give the other person an opportunity to complete the message, and allow a brief pause before responding. While listening, try to empathize with the speaker so that you decode the verbal and nonverbal cues from the other person's point of view.

As with any behaviour, active listening requires motivation. Too often, we close our minds soon after a conversation begins because the subject is boring. Instead, try to be interested by taking the view—probably an accurate one—that there is always something of value in a conversation; it's just a matter of actively looking for it. It is also natural to want to label a message as right–wrong or good–bad. However, early evaluation may cause the listener to screen out important points later in the conversation. Therefore, postpone your evaluation of the message until the speaker has finished.

Listeners easily become impatient and distracted because they can process information three times faster than the average rate of speech (450 words per minute versus 125 words per minute). To maintain interest, the active listener should concentrate on what the speaker is saying and regularly organize the information received so far into key points.

Along with being interested, you should motivate the speaker by showing your interest in the conversation. Eye contact and other nonverbal cues tell the speaker that you are paying attention and value the person's time. Also, send back-channel signals such as "Oh, really!" and "I see" during appropriate breaks in the conversation.

Finally, active listeners provide feedback by rephrasing the speaker's ideas at appropriate breaks ("So you're saying that . . . ?"). This further demonstrates your interest in the conversation and helps the speaker determine whether you understand the message.

Persuasive Communication: From Understanding to Acceptance

So far, our discussion has focussed on how to get people to receive and understand messages. However, we often want others to *accept* this information, not just *understand* it. People understand your message when they perceive the same meaning that you intended. People accept information when it becomes part of their structure of beliefs about the world and, consequently, changes their opinions about events and people. The elements of **persuasive communication** include characteristics of the communicator, message content, communication medium, and the audience being persuaded.[67]

Persuasive communication
The process of having receivers accept rather than just understand the sender's message.

Communicator characteristics

What makes one person more persuasive than another, even though they utter the same words under the same conditions? One important factor is the communicator's perceived expertise on the topic. Listeners mainly consider the speaker's credentials and experience, but speech pattern also influences perceived expertise. Specifically, people seem to have expertise when they talk confidently and relatively quickly, use some technical language, and avoid pauses ("umm," "uh") and hedges ("you know," "I guess").[68]

Communicators are more persuasive if they are trustworthy. Thus, employees are more likely to accept a new policy if it is communicated and supported by a respected peer. Trustworthiness also exists when communicators do not seem to profit from the persuasion attempt and state a few points against their position. For example, the effective persuader will acknowledge that an opposing position has one or two positive elements. Finally, people who are physically attractive or similar to us tend to be more persuasive because we tend to think they have expertise and trustworthiness.[69]

Message content

We are persuaded more by the communicator's characteristics when we don't consider the issue extremely important. When the issue is important, however, the message content becomes the critical feature of persuasive communication. The best strategy is to present all sides of the argument. Begin by introducing facts sympathetic to the audience's viewpoint, then shift into the theme of your position. Discussing only one point of view reduces your perceived trustworthiness and gives listeners the feeling of being cornered. When this happens, they react by rejecting your information.[70]

Your message should be limited to a few strong arguments, because listeners are more likely to remember these points.[71] These arguments should be repeated a couple of times, but not to the extent that listeners feel cornered.[72]

There has been a lot of debate about whether to use logic or emotion when communicating information. The general conclusion is that people are more strongly persuaded by emotional appeals if they are accompanied by specific recommendations to overcome the threat. In a safety campaign, for example, employees are more persuaded by graphic pictures of accident victims than by a lecture on recent accident statistics, but only if they are given explicit steps to avoid the danger.[73]

Finally, persuasive communicators use the **inoculation effect** to ensure that listeners are not influenced by other points of view.[74] This involves warning listeners that others will try to influence them in the future and that they should be wary about the opponent's arguments. This inoculation causes listeners to generate counterarguments to the anticipated persuasion attempts. For instance, a coalition that wants the company to purchase new production equipment might warn senior management about arguments the finance department will use to try to convince them otherwise. This tends to make the finance department's subsequent persuasion attempts less effective.

Inoculation effect
A persuasive communication strategy of warning listeners that others will try to influence them in the future and that they should be wary about the opponent's arguments.

Communication medium

Earlier in this chapter we recommended using two-way verbal communication to persuade or motivate the listener. The personal nature of this medium seems to increase the credibility of the information. Furthermore, it is easier for the sender to determine whether the persuasive message is having the desired effect. Two-way communication also increases the receiver's active participation in the process. As long as this participation does not involve presenting defensive statements, the receiver is more likely to be involved in the conversation and internalize some of the information presented.

Persuasion may require written documentation, however, when dealing with technical issues. Whenever written communication is necessary for this purpose, it should be combined with direct discussions for the greatest persuasive effect. The verbal exchange could repeat highlights of the report and provide graphic images for the listener, thereby adding emotional appeal to an otherwise logical message.

Audience characteristics

Not everyone is equally persuaded by the strategies and conditions we have described. For example, it is more difficult to persuade people who have high self-esteem.[75] And, as we mentioned above, it is very difficult to persuade those who have been inoculated against your persuasive intent.

Chapter Summary

- Communication is essential in organizations because it coordinates work activities, gives information to decision makers, and helps employees fulfill their relatedness needs. The communication process consists of forming, encoding, and transmitting the intended message to a receiver, who then decodes the message and provides feedback to the sender. Effective communication occurs when the sender's thoughts are transmitted to and understood by the intended receiver.

- Communication channels include written, verbal, and nonverbal, each of which has several methods of transmitting information. E-mail has become a powerful form of written communication, but it often produces information overload, misinterpretation of emotional meaning, and flaming. Nonverbal cues are important in face-to-face conversations, but they can also be ambiguous. Many cultures emphasize nonverbal more than verbal communication.

- The best communication medium depends on its data-carrying capacity (media richness) and its symbolic meaning to the receiver. Nonroutine and ambiguous situations require rich media.

- Companies try to improve downward communication through newsmagazines, employee annual reports, telephone hotlines, and video programs. Upward communication is assisted by employee surveys, special coordinators, and visible management practices. The grapevine transmits information very rapidly through a cluster chain pattern. It has both advantages and disadvantages for organizations and employees.

- Five of the most common barriers to effective communication include language (particularly jargon and ambiguity), filtering, perceptual errors, information overload, and physical settings. Communication problems also occur when we exchange information with people from different cultures.

- Effective interpersonal communication depends on the sender's ability to get the message across and the receiver's performance as an active listener.

- Persuasive communication attempts to have listeners accept rather than just understand the message. The most important conditions in persuasion deal with the characteristics of the communicator, the message content, the communication medium, and the people being persuaded.

Discussion Questions

1. A Canadian city intends to introduce electronic mail for office staff at its three buildings located throughout the city. Describe two benefits that the city will likely experience from this medium as well as two potential problems that they may face.

2. Marshall McLuhan coined the popular phrase: "The medium is the message." What does this phrase mean, and why should we be aware of it when communicating in organizations?

3. Should companies try to eliminate grapevine communication? Explain your answer.

4. Under what conditions is ambiguity good in the communications process? Under what conditions is it bad?

5. The Bank of Western Ontario (BWO) has just moved into one of the tallest skyscrapers in downtown Toronto. Senior management is proud of its decision, because each department is neatly located on its own floor with plenty of closed offices. BWO executives have a breathtaking view from their offices on the top floor. There is even a large BWO branch at street level. Unfortunately, other tenants occupy some floors between those leased by BWO. Discuss the potential effects of this physical structure on communication at BWO.

6. **Explain why men and women are sometimes frustrated with each other's communication behaviours.**

7. **Is motivation important in active listening? Explain your answer.**

8. **What type of people are generally more persuasive communicators? Under what conditions do these communicators have little persuasive effect?**

Notes

1. A. Vido, "Chrysler and Minivans: Are We There Yet?" *CMA Magazine* 67 (November 1993), pp. 11–16; C. G. Johnston and C. R. Farquhar, *Empowered People Satisfy Customers* (Ottawa: Conference Board of Canada, 1992), p. 12; and G. Brockhouse, "Can This Marriage Succeed?" *Canadian Business,* October 1992, pp. 128–36.

2. L. E. Penley, E. R. Alexander, I. E. Jernigan, and C. L. Henwood, "Communication Abilities of Managers: The Relationship to Performance," *Journal of Management* 17 (1991), pp. 57–76; H. Mintzberg, *The Nature of Managerial Work* (New York: Harper & Row, 1973); and E. T. Klemmer and F. W. Snyder, "Measurement of Time Spent Communicating," *Journal of Communication* 22 (June 1972), pp. 142–58.

3. C. Downs, P. Clampitt, and A. L. Pfeiffer, "Communication and Organizational Outcomes," in *Handbook of Organizational Communication,* ed. G. Goldhaber & G. Barnett (Norwood, N.J.: Ablex, 1988), pp. 171–211; and H. C. Jain, "Supervisory Communication and Performance in Urban Hospitals," *Journal of Communication* 23 (1973), pp. 103–17.

4. R. J. Burke and D. S. Wilcox, "Effects of Different Patterns and Degrees of Openness in Superior–Subordinate Communication on Subordinate Satisfaction," *Academy of Management Journal* 12 (1969), pp. 319–26; and R. T. Mowday, L. W. Porter, and R. M. Steers, *Employee–Organization Linkages* (New York: Academic Press, 1982).

5. K. J. Krone, F. M. Jablin, and L. L. Putnam, "Communication Theory and Organizational Communication: Multiple Perspectives," in *Handbook of Organizational Communication: An Interdisciplinary Perspective,* ed. F. M. Jablin, L. L. Putnam, K. H. Roberts, and L. W. Porter (Newbury Park, Calif.: Sage, 1987), pp. 18–40.

6. S. B. Sitkin, K. M. Sutcliffe, and J. R. Barrios-Choplin, "A Dual-Capacity Model of Communication Media Choice in Organizations," *Human Communication Research* 18 (June 1992), pp. 563–98; and R. Daft and R. Lengel, "Information Richness: A New Approach to Managerial Behavior and Organization Design," *Research in Organizational Behavior* 6 (1984), pp. 191–233.

7. S. Axley, "Managerial and Organizational Communication in Terms of the Conduit Metaphor," *Academy of Management Review* 9 (1984), pp. 428–37.

8. L. Porter and K. Roberts, "Communication in Organizations," in *Handbook of Industrial and Organizational Psychology,* ed. M. Dunnette (Chicago: Rand McNally, 1976), pp. 1553–89.

9. J. H. E. Andriessen, "Mediated Communication and New Organizational Forms," *International Review of Industrial and Organizational Psychology* 6 (1991), pp. 17–70.

10. N. J. Muller, "How E-Mail Boosts Productivity of Thorne EMI," *Chief Information Officer* 5 (Fall 1992), pp. 52–54.

11. J. Chevreau, "Lotus Notes 'Bring Competitors Together,'" *Financial Post,* March 12, 1994, p. 5; G. Blackwell, "You, Too, Can Be an Einstein," *Canadian Business,* May 1993, pp. 66–69; C. Leitch, "Big Blue Staff Let It All Hang Out—On-Line," *Globe & Mail,* February 26, 1992, p. B18; and G. DeSanctis and R. B. Gallupe, "A Foundation for the Study of Group Decision Support Systems," *Management Science* 33 (1987), pp. 589–609.

12. J. Hunter and M. Allen, "Adaptation to Electronic Mail," *Journal of Applied Communication Research,* August 1992, pp. 254–74; M. Culnan and M. L. Markus, "Information Technologies," in *Handbook of Organizational Communication: An Interdisciplinary Perspective,* ed. Jablin et al., pp. 420–43; and J. Siegel, V. Dubrowski, S. Kiesler, and T. W. McGuire, "Group Processes in Computer-Mediated Communication," *Organizational Behavior and Human Decision Processes* 37 (1986), pp. 157–87.

13. D. Asbrand, "E-mail 'Flame' Messages Can Ignite Office Angst," *InfoWorld,* December 6, 1993, p. 74; J. Scott, "The Etiquette of Email," *Vancouver Sun,* October 2, 1993, p. B3; and J. Goode and M. Johnson, "Putting Out the Flames: The Etiquette of Email," *Online,* November 1991, pp. 61–65.

14. A. Mehrabian, *Silent Messages,* 2nd ed. (Belmont, Calif.: Wadsworth, 1981).

15. R. E. Rice and D. E. Shook, "Relationships of Job Categories and Organizational Levels to Use of Communication Channels, Including Electronic Mail: A Meta-Analysis and Extension," *Journal of Management Studies* 27 (1990), pp. 195–229; Sitkin et al., "A Dual-Capacity Model of Communication Media Choice in Organizations," p. 584.

16. M. Meissner, "The Language of Work," in *Handbook of Work, Organization, and Society*, ed. R. Dubin (Chicago: Rand McNally, 1976), pp. 205–79.

17. H. Yamada, *American and Japanese Business Discourse: A Comparison of Interaction Styles* (Norwood, N.J.: Ablex, 1992), p. 34.

18. Meissner, "The Language of Work," p. 244.

19. R. L. Daft, R. H. Lengel, and L. K. Tevino, "Message Equivocality, Media Selection, and Manager Performance: Implications for Information Systems," *MIS Quarterly* 11 (1987), pp. 355–66.

20. Daft and Lengel, "Information Richness: A New Approach to Managerial Behavior and Organization Design;" R. Lengel and R. Daft, "The Selection of Communication Media as an Executive Skill," *Academy of Management Executive* 2 (1988), pp. 225–32; and G. Huber and R. Daft, "The Information Environments of Organizations," in *Handbook of Organizational Communication: An Interdisciplinary Perspective*, ed. Jablin et al., pp. 130–64.

21. R. E. Rice, "Task Analyzability, Use of New Media, and Effectiveness: A Multi-Site Exploration of Media Richness," *Organization Science* 3 (1992) pp. 475–500; and J. Fulk, C. W. Steinfield, J. Schmitz, and J. G. Power, "A Social Information Processing Model of Media Use in Organizations," *Communication Research* 14 (1987), pp. 529–52.

22. D. Stork and A. Sapienza, "Task and Human Messages over the Project Life Cycle: Matching Media to Messages," *Project Management Journal* 22 (December 1992), pp. 44–49.

23. M. McLuhan, *Understanding Media: The Extensions of Man* (New York: McGraw-Hill, 1964).

24. Sitkin et al., "A Dual-Capacity Model of Communication Media Choice in Organizations," p. 570; and J. Schmitz and J. Fulk, "Organizational Colleagues, Media Richness, and Electronic Mail: A Test of the Social Influence Model of Technology Use," *Communication Research* 18 (1991), pp. 487–523.

25. R. M. Kanter, "Transcending Business Boundaries: 12,000 World Managers View Change," *Harvard Business Review*, May–June 1991, pp. 151–64; M. Young and J. E. Post, "Managing to Communicate, Communicating to Change: How Leading Companies Communicate with Employees," *Organizational Dynamics* 22 (Summer 1993), pp. 31–43; and R. Foltz, "Communication in Contemporary Organizations," in *Inside Organizational Communication*, ed. C. Reuss and D. Silvis (New York: Longman, 1985), pp. 8–9.

26. R. Bonanno, "Bell Canada: Answering Its Employees' Calls," *Canadian HR Reporter*, June 25, 1993, p. 16; C. McGoon, "Putting the Employee Newsletter On-Line," *IABC Communication World* 9 (March 1992), pp. 16–18; P. C. Jackson, *Corporate Communications for Managers* (London: Pitman, 1987); C. Emig, "Matching Media with Audience and Message," in *Inside Organizational Communication*, ed. Reuss and Silvis, pp. 115–28; and J. C. C. Macintosh, "Reporting to Employees: Identifying the Areas of Interest to Employees," *Accounting and Finance* 27 (November 1987), pp. 41–52.

27. D. M. Saunders and J. D. Leck, "Formal Upward Communication Procedures: Organizational and Employee Perspectives," *Canadian Journal of Administrative Sciences* 10 (1993), pp. 255–68; and F. Luthans and J. K. Larson, "How Managers Really Communicate," *Human Relations* 39 (1986), pp. 161–78.

28. B. W. Little, "Employee Surveys: An Effective Agenda for Change," *Canadian Forest Industries* (August–September 1992), pp. 32–34.

29. "Changing Power Structure: A New Surge of Energy at Ontario Hydro," *Toronto Life* (April 1993), p. 10; and S. Haggett, "Motivating Employees a Leader's Greatest Challenge," *Financial Post*, May 8, 1993, p. 23.

30. S. L. McShane, "Conflict Resolution Practices for Nonunion Employees," *Human Resources Management in Canada* (January 1991), pp. 35527–36.

31. T. Peters and R. Waterman, *In Search of Excellence* (New York: Harper & Row, 1982), p. 122; and W. Ouchi, *Theory Z* (New York: Avon Books, 1981), pp. 176–77.

32. K. Kidd, "The Art of the Healer," *Report on Business Magazine* (July 1993), p. 19; C. Farquhar and C. G. Johnston, *Total Quality Management: A Competitive Imperative* (Ottawa: Conference Board of Canada, 1990), p. 50; and P. C. Newman, *Bronfman Dynasty* (Toronto: McClelland and Stewart, 1978), pp. 36–37.

33. Young and Post, "Managing to Communicate, Communicating to Manage," pp. 31–43; C. Kapel, "Look Who's Talking," *Human Resources Professional*, October 1991, pp. 9–11; and E. Watkins, "Hyatt Stays in Touch," *Lodging Hospitality*, September 1990, pp. 43–48.

34. M. Gibb-Clark, "Most Job Losers Find Out Second-Hand," *Globe & Mail*, April 14, 1993, pp. B1, B4; and J. Mishra, "Managing the Grapevine," *Public Personnel Management* 19 (Summer 1990), pp. 213–28.

35. G. Kreps, *Organizational Communication* (White Plains, N.Y.: Longman, 1986), pp. 202–6; W. L. Davis and J. R. O'Connor, "Serial Transmission of Information: A Study of the Grapevine," *Journal of Applied Communication Research* 5 (1977), pp. 61–72; and K. Davis, "Management Communication and the Grapevine," *Harvard Business Review* 31 (September–October 1953), pp. 43–49.

36. R. L. Rosnow, "Inside Rumor: A Personal Journey," *American Psychologist* 46 (May 1991), pp. 484–96; and C. J. Walker and C. A. Beckerle, "The Effect of State Anxiety on Rumor Transmission," *Journal of Social Behavior & Personality* 2 (August 1987), pp. 353–60.

37. N. Fitzgerald, "Spread the Word," *The Accountant's Magazine* 97 (February 1993), pp. 32–33.

38. D. Krackhardt and J. R. Hanson, "Informal Networks: The Company Behind the Chart," *Harvard Business Review* 71 (July–August 1993), pp. 104–11; and H. Mintzberg, *The Structuring of Organizations* (Englewood Cliffs, N.J.: Prentice Hall, 1979), pp. 46–53.

39. M. Noon and R. Delbridge, "News from Behind My Hand: Gossip in Organizations," *Organization Studies* 14 (1993), pp. 23–36.

40. E. Innes and L. Southwick-Trask, *Turning It Around* (Toronto: Fawcett Crest, 1990), p. 124.

41. L. Larwood, "Don't Struggle to Scope Those Metaphors Yet," *Group and Organization Management* 17 (1992), pp. 249–54; and L. R. Pondy, P. J. Frost, G. Morgan, and T. C. Dandridge (eds.), *Organizational Symbolism* (Greenwich, Conn.: JAI Press, 1983).

42. M. Kaeter, "Quality through Clarity," *Quality*, May 1993, pp. 19–22.

43. J. T. Miller, "Communication . . . Or Getting Ideas Across," *S.A.M. Advanced Management Journal*, Summer 1980, p. 34.

44. "By Any Other Name," *Maclean's*, November 23, 1992, p. 10.

45. "Doublespeak Award in the Mail," *Sunday News* (Coquitlam, B.C.), September 4, 1988, p. A8; and H. Bruce, "Perfectly Unclear," *Canadian Business*, March 1987, pp. 84–85, 114.

46. Larwood, "Don't Struggle to Scope Those Metaphors Yet;" R. Mead, *Cross-Cultural Management Communication* (Chichester, U.K.: Wiley, 1990), pp. 130–37; E. M. Eisenberg, "Ambiguity as a Strategy in Organizational Communication," *Communication Monographs* 51 (1984), pp. 227–42; and R. Daft and J. Wiginton, "Language and Organization," *Academy of Management Review* 4 (1979), pp. 179–91.

47. G. Morgan, *Images of Organizations* (Beverly Hills, Calif.: Sage, 1986).

48. M. J. Glauser, "Upward Information Flow in Organizations: Review and Conceptual Analysis," *Human Relations* 37 (1984), pp. 613–43.

49. A. G. Schick, L. A. Gordon, and S. Haka, "Information Overload: A Temporal Approach," *Accounting, Organizations & Society* 15 (1990), pp. 199–220; and K. Alesandrini, *Survive Information Overload* (Homewood, Ill.: Business One-Irwin, 1993).

50. Schick et al., "Information Overload," pp. 209–14; and C. Stohl and W. C. Redding, "Messages and Message Exchange Processes," in *Handbook of Organizational Communication: An Interdisciplinary Perspective*, ed. Jablin et al., pp. 451–502.

51. T. Davis, "The Influence of the Physical Environment in Offices," *Academy of Management Review* 9(2) (1984), pp. 271–83; and S. B. Bacharach and M. Aitken, "Communications in Administrative Bureaucracies," *Academy of Management Journal* 20 (1977), pp. 365–77.

52. O. Bertin, "130 Jobs Cut at Canada Packers," *Globe & Mail*, August 22, 1990, p. B7; and R. Litchfield, "The '90s Way to Tackle the Recession," *Canadian Business*, November 1990, p. 86.

53. Johnston and Farquhar, *Empowered People Satisfy Customers* p. 12; and "Top-Level Togetherness Speeds Communication," *Financial Post*, July 11, 1988, p. 15.

54. A. Goldman, "Implications of Japanese Total Quality Control for Western Organizations: Dimensions of an Intercultural Hybrid," *Journal of Business Communication* 30 (1993), pp. 29–47; and J. P. Womack, D. T. Jones, and D. Roos, *The Machine That Changed the World* (New York: Rawson, 1990), p. 79.

55. J. Kroho, Jr., "What Makes an Office Work?" *Across the Board*, May 1993, pp. 16–23; T. Peters, *Liberation Management: Necessary Disorganization for the Nanosecond Nineties* (New York: Knopf, 1992), pp. 379–80; T. H. Walker, "Designing Work Environments that Promote Corporate Productivity," *Site Selection and Industrial Development*, April 1992, pp. 8–10; and E. Sundstrom, *Work Places: The Psychology of the Physical Environment in Offices and Factories* (New York: Cambridge University Press, 1986).

56. P. C. Morrow and J. C. McElroy, "Interior Office Design and Visitor Response: A Constructive Replication," *Journal of Applied Psychology* 66 (1981), pp. 646–50; and D. E. Campbell, "Interior Office Design and Visitor Response," *Journal of Applied Psychology* 64 (1979), pp. 648–53.

57. For a review of the main issues on cultural diversity in Canadian organizations, see the series of articles edited by R. J. Burke, "Managing an Increasingly Diverse Workforce," *Canadian Journal of Administrative Sciences* 8 (1991). Also see C. M. Solomon, "Managing Today's Immigrants," *Personnel Journal*, February 1993, pp. 57–65; and T. Cox, Jr., "The Multicultural Organization," *Academy of Management Executive* 5 (May 1991), pp. 34–47.

58. J. Christensen-Hughes, "Cultural Diversity: The Lesson of Toronto's Hotels," *Cornell H. R. A. Quarterly*, April 1992, pp. 78–87.

59. Mead, *Cross-Cultural Management Communication*, pp. 161–62; and J. V. Hill and C. L. Bovée, *Excellence in Business Communication* (New York: McGraw-Hill, 1993), Chapter 17.

60. R. Axtell, *Gestures: The Do's and Taboos of Body Language around the World* (New York: Wiley, 1991); P. Harris and R. Moran, *Managing Cultural Differences* (Houston: Gulf, 1987); and P. Ekman, W. V. Friesen, and J. Bear, "The International Language of Gestures," *Psychology Today*, May 1984, pp. 64–69.

61. H. Yamada, *American and Japanese Business Discourse,* Chapter 2; and D. C. Barnlund, *Communication Styles of Japanese and Americans: Images and Realities* (Belmont, Calif.: Wadsworth, 1988).

62. J. Allan, "When Women Set the Rules," *Canadian Business,* April 1991, pp. 40–43.

63. D. Tannen, *You Just Don't Understand: Men and Women in Conversation* (New York: Ballentine Books, 1990); and S. Helgesen, *The Female Advantage: Women's Ways of Leadership* (New York: Doubleday, 1990).

64. G. H. Graham, J. Unruh, and P. Jennings, "The Impact of Nonverbal Communication in Organizations: A Survey of Perceptions," *Journal of Business Communication* 28 (1991), pp. 45–61; and J. Hall, "Gender Effects in Decoding Nonverbal Cues," *Psychological Bulletin* 68 (1978), pp. 845–57.

65. Cited in K. Davis and J. W. Newstrom, *Human Behavior at Work: Organizational Behavior,* 7th ed. (New York: McGraw-Hill, 1985), p. 438.

66. J. Brownell, *Building Active Learning Skills* (Englewood Cliffs, N.J.: Prentice Hall, 1986); and A. Mikalachki, "Does Anyone Listen to the Boss?" *Business Horizons,* March–April 1982, pp. 34–39.

67. S. Trenholm, *Persuasion and Social Influence* (Englewood Cliffs, N.J.: Prentice Hall, 1989); W. J. McGuire, "Attitudes and Attitude Change," in *Handbook of Social Psychology,* 3rd ed., vol. 2, ed. G. Lindzey and E. Aronson (New York: Random House, 1985), pp. 233–346; and P. Zimbardo and E. B. Ebbeson, *Influencing Attitudes and Changing Behavior* (Reading, Mass.: Addison-Wesley, 1969).

68. J. Cooper and R. T. Coyle, "Attitudes and Attitude Change," *Annual Review of Psychology* 35 (1984), pp. 395–426; and N. MacLachlan, "What People Really Think About Fast Talkers," *Psychology Today* 113 (November 1979), pp. 112–17.

69. D. B. Freeland, "Turning Communication into Influence," *HR Magazine* 38 (September 1993), pp. 93–96; and M. Snyder and M. Rothbart, "Communicator Attractiveness and Opinion Change," *Canadian Journal of Behavioural Science* 3 (1971), pp. 377–87.

70. E. Aronson, *The Social Animal* (San Francisco: W. H. Freeman, 1976), pp. 67–68; and R. A. Jones and J. W. Brehm, "Persuasiveness of One- and Two-Sided Communications as a Function of Awareness that There Are Two Sides," *Journal of Experimental Social Psychology* 6 (1970), pp. 47–56.

71. D. G. Linz and S. Penrod, "Increasing Attorney Persuasiveness in the Courtroom," *Law and Psychology Review* 8 (1984), pp. 1–47.

72. R. B. Zajonc, "Attitudinal Effects of Mere Exposure," *Journal of Personality and Social Psychology Monograph* 9 (1968), pp. 1–27; and R. Petty and J. Cacioppo, *Attitudes and Persuasion: Classic and Contemporary Approaches* (Dubuque, Iowa: W. C. Brown, 1981).

73. Zimbardo and Ebbeson, *Influencing Attitudes and Changing Behavior.*

74. Ibid.

75. M. Zellner, "Self-Esteem, Reception, and Influenceability," *Journal of Personality and Social Psychology* 15 (1970), pp. 87–93.

Chapter Case

Sea Pines

In the spring of 1992, the coastal town of Sea Pines, Nova Scotia, retained a Toronto consulting engineer to study the effect of greatly expanding the town's sewage system and discharging the treated waste into the harbour. At that time, fishermen in the town were experiencing massive lobster kills in the harbour and were concerned that the kills were caused by the effluent from the present Sea Pines sewage treatment plant. They were convinced that any expansion of the plant would further aggravate the problem. The fishermen invited Tom Stone, the engineer, to the monthly meeting of the local fishermen's organization to discuss their concerns. On the night of the meeting, the Legion Hall was filled with men in blue jeans and work jackets, many of whom were drinking beer. An account of this meeting follows, with Fred Mitchell, a local fisherman, speaking first.

Mitchell: Well, as you all know, Mr. Stone has been kind enough to meet with us tonight to explain his recommendations concerning the town's sewage disposal problem. We're all concerned about the lobster kills, like the one last summer, and I for one don't want to see any more sewage dumped into that harbour. [Murmurs of assent are heard throughout the hall.] So, Mr. Stone, we'd like to hear from you on what it is you want to do.

Stone: Thank you. I'm glad to get this opportunity to hear your concerns on the lobster situation. Let me say from the outset that we are still studying the problem closely and expect to make our formal recommendation to the town about a month from now. I am not prepared to discuss specific conclusions of our study, but I am prepared to incorporate any relevant comments into our study. As most of you are probably aware, we are attempting to model mathematically, or simulate, conditions in the harbour to help us predict the effects of sewage effluent in the harbour. We . . .

Mitchell: Now wait a minute. I don't know anything about models except the kind I used to make as a kid. [Laughter.] I can tell you that we never had lobster kills like we have now until they started dumping that sewage into the harbour a few years back. I don't need any model to tell me that. It seems to me that common sense tells you that if we've got troubles now in the summer with the lobster, that increasing the amount of sewage by 10 times the present amount is going to cause 10 times the problem.

A Fisherman: Yeah, you don't need to be an engineer to see that.

Stone: Although it's true that we're proposing to extend the sewage system in town, and that the resulting sewage flow will be about 10 times the present flow, the area of the sewage discharge will be moved to a larger area of the harbour, where it will be diluted with much more sea water than is the present area. In addition, if the harbour is selected for the new discharge, we will design a special diffuser to mix the treated sewage effluent quickly with ocean water. As I indicated, we are attempting to use data on currents and water quality that we collected in the harbour and combine it with some mathematical equations in our computer to help us predict what the quality in the harbour will be.

Mitchell: I don't understand what you need a computer to tell you that for. I've been fishing in this area for over 35 years now, and I don't need any computer to tell me that my lobsters are going to die if that sewage goes into the harbour.

Stone: Let me say before this goes too far that we're not talking about discharging raw sewage into the harbour. The sewage is treated and disinfected before it is discharged.

Mitchell: Isn't the sewage that's being dumped into the harbour right now being treated and disinfected, Mr. Stone?

Stone: Yes, it is, but . . .

Mitchell: The lobsters still die, so it's clear to me that "treated and disinfected" doesn't solve the problem.

Stone: Our model will predict whether the treatment provided will be sufficient to maintain the water quality in the harbour at the province's standard for the harbour.

Mitchell: I don't give a damn about any provincial standard. I just care about my lobsters and how I'm going to put bread on the table for my kids! You engineers from Toronto can come out here spouting all kinds of things about models, data, standards, and your concern for lobsters, but what it really comes down to is that it's just another job. You can collect your fees for your study, go back to your office, and leave us holding the bag.

Stone: Now wait a minute, Mr. Mitchell. My firm is well established in Canada, and we didn't get that way by giving our clients that fast shuffle and making a quick exit out of town. We have no intention of leaving you with an unworkable solution to your sewage problems. We also will not solve your sewage problem and leave you with a lobster kill problem. Perhaps I have given you the wrong impression about this modelling. We regard this as one method of analysis that may be helpful in predicting future harbour conditions, but not the only method. We have over 40 years' experience in these harbour studies, and we fully intend to use this experience, *in addition to* whatever the model tells us, to come up with a reasonable solution.

Mitchell: Well, that's all well and good, but I can tell you, and I think I speak for all the lobstermen here, that if you recommend dumping that sewage into the harbour, we'll fight you all the way down the line! [Shouts of agreement.] Why can't you pipe the sewage out to the ocean if you're so concerned about dilution? I'm sure that your model will tell you there's enough dilution out there.

Stone: I agree that the ocean will certainly provide sufficient dilution, but the whole purpose of this study is to see if we can avoid a deep ocean outfall.

Mitchell: Why?

Stone: Because the cost of constructing a deep ocean outfall in this area is very expensive—say about $500 per metre. Now, if the length of the outfall is 2,000 metres, don't you think that it makes good sense to spend a few thousand dollars studying the harbour area if we can save you millions?

Mitchell: All that money that you're going to save the town doesn't do much for the lobstermen who'll be put out of business if that sewage goes into the harbour.

Stone: As I said, we wouldn't recommend that if we thought, based on our modelling and our experience in this area, that the quality of water in the harbour would kill any lobster or any other aquatic life.

Mitchell: Well, I'm telling you again, if you try to put that stuff in our harbour, we'll fight you all the way. I think we've made our position clear on this thing, so if there are no further comments, I vote that we adjourn the meeting. [Seconded.]

When the meeting ended, the fishermen filed out, talking heatedly among themselves, leaving Mr. Stone standing on the platform.

Discussion Questions

1. **What symptom(s) exist in this case to suggest that something has gone wrong?**

2. **What are the root causes that have led to these symptoms?**

3. **What actions should Stone and his firm take to correct these problems?**

Source: This case was written by Terence P. Driscoll.

Experiential Exercise

Cross-Cultural Communication: A Not-so-Trivial Trivia Game

Purpose: This exercise is designed to develop and test your knowledge of cross-cultural differences in communication and etiquette.

Instructions: Each student chooses or is assigned a partner. Each pair is then matched with another pair of students. The instructor will hand each group of four people a stack of cards with the multiple choice questions face down. These cards have questions and answers about cross-cultural differences in communication and etiquette. No books or other aids are allowed.

The exercise begins with a member of Team 1 picking up one card from the top of the pile and asking the question on that card to both people on Team 2. The information given to Team 2 includes the question and all alternatives listed on the card. Team 2 has 30 seconds to give an answer and earns one point if the correct answer is given. If Team 2's answer is incorrect, however, Team 1 earns that point. (Correct answers to each question are indicated on the card and, of course, should not be revealed until the question is correctly answered or time is up.)

Next, one member from Team 2 picks up the next card on the pile and asks it to both members of Team 1. This procedure is repeated until all of the cards have been read or time has elapsed. The team receiving the most points wins the experiential exercise.

Important note: The textbook provides very little information pertaining to the questions in this exercise. Rather, you must rely on past learning, logic, and luck to win.

Perception and Personality in Organizations

Learning Objectives

After reading this chapter, you should be able to:

Describe the perceptual process.

Discuss the ethical problems of stereotyping.

Describe actor–observer error.

Explain how self-fulfilling prophecy influences employee performance.

Define the halo effect.

Explain how the Johari Window can help improve our perceptual accuracy.

Identify two problems associated with using personality traits in organizations.

Chapter Outline

Selective Perception.

Perceptual Organization and Interpretation.

Stereotyping.

Attribution Theory.

Self-Fulfilling Prophecy.

Other Perceptual Errors.

Improving Perceptual Accuracy.

Personality.

Selected Personality Dimensions.

Courtesy of Imperial Oil Ltd.

While recruiting new employees for Imperial Oil's information technology area, Al Chan noticed that Asians were receiving fewer job offers than Caucasians, even though many were interviewed. Chan, a chemical engineer with 20 years of service at Imperial Oil, presented his concerns to management and was asked to investigate.

"I think one of the reasons [for the discrepancy] is a significant difference in the way Westerners and Asians view authority," explains Chan. "Westerners are assertive and will challenge the leader. Generally, Asians do not—they perceive that it is their role to listen to the experienced, more senior person. In the workplace this can be misinterpreted as passiveness."

The solution, says Chan, is greater awareness of our perceptual biases. "Encouraging greater awareness is vital because the essential issue is how to get people to be more tolerant of differences. I say, 'Don't judge me on who I am; please look at the results of my work.'"

Along with Chan's observations, a group of Asian employees told senior management that they believed they were being negatively stereotyped and missing out on promotions. To explore these perceptual problems further, several dozen Imperial Oil executives attended workshops on the importance of valuing diversity. Among other things, they learned that stereotyping people and making superficial judgments about them is harmful to organizations and individuals alike. The work shops were so enlightening that managers throughout Imperial Oil now participate in them.

Imperial Oil president Ron Brenneman believes that his company's journey toward a truly multicultural work force demands changing perceptions. "We must deepen our understanding of our own biases," says Brenneman. "Shouting from the top isn't what will change things—learning and awareness will."[1]

The Greek philosopher Plato wrote long ago that we see reality only as shadows reflecting against the rough wall of a cave.[2] In other words, reality is filtered through an imperfect perceptual process. **Perception** is the process of receiving information about and making sense of the world around us. It involves deciding which information to notice, how to categorize this information, and how to interpret it within the framework of our existing knowledge.

Perception
The process of selecting, organizing, and interpreting information in order to make sense of the world around us.

As Exhibit 7–1 illustrates, the perceptual process begins when environmental stimuli are received through our senses. Most of this information is screened out through selective perception. The stimuli that get recognized are organized and interpreted based on various information processing activities. The resulting perceptions influence our attitudes and behaviour toward those objects, people, and events.[3]

This chapter begins by examining the factors that influence our selection, organization, and interpretation of sensory stimuli in organizations. Next, we look at three perceptual processes—stereotyping, attribution, and self-fulfilling prophecy—as well as four persistent perceptual errors (halo, primacy, recency, and projection). This is followed by a discussion of various strategies to improve perceptual accuracy in organizational settings. The final sections of this chapter introduce the concept of personality and its relevance to organizational behaviour.

Selective Perception

Our five senses are constantly bombarded with stimuli. Some get noticed, but most are screened out. A nurse working in post-operative care might ignore the smell of recently disinfected instruments or the sound of co-workers talking nearby, yet a small flashing red light on the nurse station console is immediately noticed because it signals that a patient's vital signs are failing. This process of filtering information received by our senses is called **selective perception.** The information we select or screen out depends on the characteristics of the object, perceiver, and situation.

Selective perception
The process of filtering (selecting and screening out) information received by our senses.

Characteristics of the object

The extent to which objects are noticed depends on their size, intensity, motion, repetition, and novelty. The red light on the nurse station console receives attention because it is bright (intensity), flashing (motion), and a rare event (novelty). It also has symbolic importance to nurses and other medical staff members. The safety poster shown in Exhibit 7–2 has a higher probability of

Model of the Perceptual Process　　　　　　　　　**Exhibit 7–1**

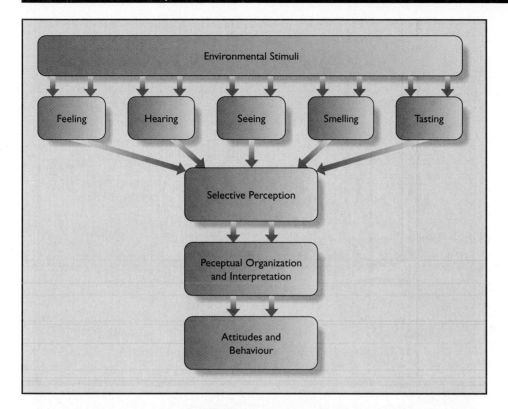

being noticed by employees if it is large (size), has high contrast (intensity), and is placed throughout the office or factory (repetition).

Size, intensity, motion, repetition, and novelty also explain why our awareness of other people depends on what they wear, the way they behave, and the way they talk. An argument in the hallway may stand out because it is loud (intensity) and is an unusual event (novelty). Organizational status also affects whether certain people and their actions are noticed. We are more likely to concentrate on the statements and actions of top management than those of peers and subordinates.

Characteristics of the perceiver

Selective perception is also influenced by characteristics of the perceiver. We tend to remember information that is consistent with our attitudes and ignore information that is inconsistent. For example, research indicates that interviewers who develop positive feelings toward the job applicant early in the interview tend to subsequently screen out negative information about that candidate.[4]

The perceiver's expectations also influence selective perception.[5] Through life experiences, we develop beliefs that condition us to be "ready" to expect certain events and to ignore others.[6] When we form a belief that a co-worker is stingy, for instance, we look for further confirming evidence and are less aware of contradictory evidence.

Exhibit 7–2   **Large, High-Contrast Safety Posters Attract Attention**

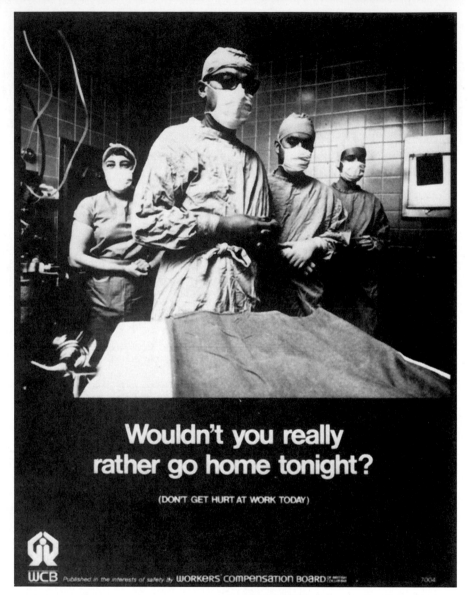

Source: Workers Compensation Board of British Columbia. Used with permission.

Cultural conditioning influences our attention to events by establishing the norms and patterns against which behaviour is judged.[7] In a conversation between a Canadian and an Egyptian, the Canadian may notice and even feel uncomfortable by the close physical distance between them, whereas the Egyptian, who is accustomed to smaller personal space in social interactions, does not notice the physical distance. But when the Canadian steps back to a more comfortable distance, the Egyptian suddenly feels that they are too far apart.

Finally, information that threatens our beliefs and values can trigger a phenomenon called **perceptual defense.** Perceptual defense screens out large blocks of stimuli, particularly from the information source.[8] A Xerox sales representative discovered this when he tried to tell a potential client how Xerox products could improve the company's paperwork flow. The manager got increasingly irritated with the sales pitch and couldn't remember most of the salesperson's explanations. The Xerox employee later learned that the manager felt strongly about moving toward a paperless office and was bothered by the word *paperwork*. On the next visit, the salesperson talked about "product documentation" and how Xerox products would help the company's productivity. Without the word *paper* to trigger a perceptual defense, the client paid attention to the salesperson's explanations and eventually placed a large order with the document management company.[9]

Perceptual defense
A defensive psychological process that involves subconsciously screening out large blocks of information that threaten the person's beliefs and values.

Characteristics of the situation

The extent to which we notice an event or person also depends on the context in which it is sensed. In particular, things that *contrast* against the background have a higher probability of being noticed. You might be aware that a client has an Australian accent if the meeting takes place in Fredericton, but not if the conversation took place in Melbourne, Australia, particularly if you had been living there for some time. On the contrary, it would be your Canadian accent that others would notice!

Perceptual Organization and Interpretation

Even after screening out most environmental stimuli, we still need to organize and interpret the selected information to make sense of people and events. Two principles—figure/ground and perceptual grouping—shape our organization and interpretation of incoming information.

Figure/ground principle

Figure/ground principle states that our perceptions of objects (figures) depend on the contexts (ground) in which they are perceived. We subconsciously use figure/ground principle to interpret the identities and behaviour of others. For example, we quickly conclude that a person working near a filing cabinet is a secretary and that someone filling a duffel bag with paper is a mailroom clerk. Figure/ground principle also applies to less observable situations, such as evaluating employees in performance appraisals. Supervisors view an average performer (figure) as marginal against a background of outstanding co-workers (ground). Yet the same person will be evaluated very favourably when co-workers in the department have marginal performance.[10]

Figure/ground principle
A principle of organizing information whereby our perceptions of objects (figures) depend on the contexts (ground) in which they are perceived.

Perceptual grouping

Perceptual grouping is the process of linking people and objects into recognizable and manageable patterns or categories. Some things are grouped based on their physical proximity, such as assuming that an employee is inefficient because he or she works in an inefficient department. Others are grouped based on their

Perceptual grouping
The perceptual organization process of linking people and objects into recognizable and manageable patterns or categories.

similarity. Honda of Canada applies this idea at its Alliston, Ontario, manufacturing plant by having everyone (including management) wear the same uniform—a white coat, white trousers, and white and green baseball caps. This symbolizes the team concept that everyone is working for the same corporate objectives.[11]

Perceptual grouping also occurs because we have a need to organize seemingly random events into continuous patterns. Managers frequently "see" a trend in market share information only to learn later that this continuous pattern did not exist. A similar grouping phenomenon is called *closure*—filling in missing information so that the object or event fits into existing categories. If you are told that the president held a meeting while you were on vacation, you would likely make assumptions about who attended, what was said, and where the meeting was held. These assumptions fill in the missing information so that you can minimize ambiguity and categorize the meeting more easily with previous meetings.

Perceptual grouping helps us to make sense of the workplace, but it can also inhibit creativity and open-mindedness. For instance, the similarity principle might cause us to assume incorrect information about a job applicant because his or her physical appearance (unkempt hair, leather jacket, etc.) is similar to someone who was recently dismissed from the organization. Perceptual grouping also leads to stereotyping, a process that is described next.

Stereotyping

Stereotyping
The process of using a few observable characteristics to assign someone to a preconceived social category and then assuming that the person also possesses other (usually less observable) characteristics of the group.

Stereotyping occurs when traits are attributed to people because of their membership in a social category.[12] Exhibit 7–3 illustrates the three steps in the stereotyping process. First, we develop social categories and assign traits that are difficult to observe (e.g., conservatism, intelligence) to each category. These unobservable traits are based on public images and personal experiences. Second, people are identified with one or more social categories based on easily observable information about them (e.g., gender, occupation).

Finally, the cluster of traits that we have formed around the social category is attributed to people identified as members of that group. For example, we develop a generalized set of beliefs about professors (e.g., absent-minded). When we enter college or university, these traits are subconsciously assigned to the professors we meet, at least until we know them better.

Stereotyping is a form of perceptual grouping that helps us to make sense of the world more quickly, but it frequently results in incorrect perceptions. One problem is that most stereotyped traits do not accurately describe every person in that social category. Although it may be true that some professors are absent-minded, many are not. Another problem is that many widely held stereotypes include factually incorrect traits. For example, a common stereotype is that athletes have lower intelligence even though there is no such relationship. A third problem is that we tend to screen out or misinterpret information that is inconsistent with the stereotype. In other words, we subconsciously try to keep our perceptions of reality simple by maintaining existing stereotypes.[13]

Ethical problems of stereotyping

Although many stereotypes are false or distorted, they remain deeply embedded in society. This raises important ethical concerns, because stereotypes are known

The Process of Stereotyping   Exhibit 7–3

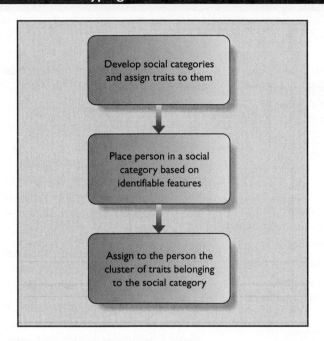

to adversely affect the employment opportunities of people assigned to certain social categories. In the opening vignette, we learned how negative stereotypes of Asians may have hurt their chances for employment and promotion at Imperial Oil. Similarly, society persistently underestimates the employment potential of people with physical and mental disabilities. As well, a recent study found that Canadian employers continue to hold traditional stereotypes of older job applicants that prevent them from gaining re-employment.[14]

Another tenacious stereotype is of women in managerial jobs. Research indicates that people increasingly accept the idea of women in management, but they still perceive women as being less suited than men in these jobs.[15] In particular, male managers hold the same masculine stereotypical view of the successful middle manager as did their male counterparts 15 years earlier. Fortunately, female managers in North America no longer stereotype the managerial position. Instead, they perceive women as more likely to hold some traits necessary for managerial success while men hold others; neither has a competitive advantage.[16]

Traditional stereotypes of women in managerial jobs are subtle, yet they create a strong, invisible barrier—known as the "glass ceiling"—into top management jobs.[17] To break the glass ceiling, the Bank of Montreal recently launched a task force to test traditional perceptions about the suitability of women for senior management positions. Their results, described in Perspective 7–1, debunk the myths behind traditional stereotypes of women.

Stereotypes influence our beliefs about identifiable groups of people, and these beliefs shape our feelings toward them. **Prejudice** refers to negative attitudes toward people belonging to a particular demographic group based on unfounded or blatantly incorrect beliefs. Canadians view themselves as fairly tolerant people living in a multicultural society, but discriminatory attitudes do exist in this country.

Prejudice
Negative feelings toward people belonging to a particular demographic group based on unfounded or blatantly incorrect beliefs.

Perspective 7–1

Breaking the Glass Ceiling by Dispelling Stereotypic Myths about Women in Management

A senior executive at one of Canada's largest banks likes to tell what happened the day she took her four-year-old daughter to work with her. When they stepped out of the elevator into the executive suite of the bank's Toronto headquarters, the child looked around for a moment, then asked, "Mommy, don't any girls work here?"

Until recently, very few women held senior management jobs in the Canadian banking industry. As with other financial institutions, the Bank of Montreal was trying to correct this imbalance through special recruiting and employment programs. But senior management knew that structural changes were not enough—it had to break the "glass ceiling" by dispelling traditional stereotypes.

After analyzing demographic data and surveying employees, a special Bank of Montreal task force published a report challenging four common myths that prevent women from rising through the corporate hierarchy:

1. *Myth:* Women at the bank are either too young or too old to compete with men for promotions.
   Reality: Male and female employees at the Bank of Montreal have the same average age. Age differences do not explain underrepresentation of women in senior management. Besides, age must no deter-mine eligibility for promotion.

2. *Myth:* Women are less committed to their careers because they have babies and leave the bank while their children are young.
   Reality: Yes, women do have babies, but they also have longer service records than men at every level up to senior management at the Bank of Montreal. Being a woman does not mean reduced commitment.

3. *Myth:* More women need to be better educated to compete in significant numbers with men for senior management jobs.
   Reality: At the nonmanagement and junior management levels—the main feeder routes to more senior jobs—more women than men have postsecondary education. Lack of education is not a barrier to women's advancement at the bank.

4. *Myth:* Women don't have the "right stuff" to compete effectively with men for more senior jobs.
   Reality: At all levels, women are more likely than men to receive the top two ratings in the company's performance appraisal system. These performance appraisal results clearly indicate that women can compete successfully for more senior jobs.

Sources: Based on Bank of Montreal, The Task Force on the Advancement of Women in the Bank, *Report to Employees* (Toronto: Bank of Montreal, November 1991); K. Gay, "Smashing the Glass Ceiling," *The Bottom Line,* May 1992, p. 37; and S. Fife, "No, Susie, There Are Still No Girl Bosses at the Banks," *Financial Times of Canada,* March 20, 1989, pp. 7–8.

One revealing study of prejudice in Canada involved four pairs of white and black subjects who were instructed to appear individually as applicants in job interviews around Toronto. Of the 201 in-person job applications, 36 job offers were received. White applicants received 27 of these offers, whereas black applicants received only nine offers. Moreover, black applicants were treated discourteously or rudely in nearly 20 percent of the job postings, whereas the white applicants were invariably treated well. A few particularly blatant examples of racial prejudice occurred in which the white applicant was given an application form, an interview, or was immediately offered a position, even though the black applicant had been told earlier the same day that the job was filled.[18]

Attribution Theory

Perceptual interpretations mainly involve drawing conclusions about why things happen. These causal inferences about people and events are derived from the **attribution process.**[19] Attributions help us to predict events and thereby reduce the stress of uncertainty. Moreover, by developing a causal map of our work environment, we are better able to achieve our goals.

The attribution process involves deciding whether the behaviour or event is largely due to internal or external causes. Internal causes refer to conditions under the person's control, such as ability and motivation. We make an internal attribution by believing that an employee is late for work because he or she is lazy. External causes refer to conditions beyond the individual's control, such as luck and other situational contingencies. An external attribution would occur if we believe that the employee is late because the public transit system broke down.

Deciding whether a person's behaviour is due mainly to internal or external causes is derived from information about whether the behaviour is:

- Similar to the person's past behaviour in that situation (consistency).
- Similar to the behaviour of others in that situation (consensus).
- Similar to the person's behaviour in other situations (distinctiveness).

Suppose that an employee is making poor-quality products one day on a particular machine. We would probably conclude that there is something wrong with the machine (an external attribution) if the employee has made good-quality products on this machine in the past (low consistency), other employees have recently had quality problems on this machine (high consensus), and the employee makes good-quality products on other machines (high distinctiveness). An internal attribution, on the other hand, would be made if the employee usually makes poor-quality products on this machine (high consistency), other employees make good-quality products on this machine (low consensus), and the employee also makes poor-quality products on other machines (low distinctiveness).[20]

Attributing behaviour to internal versus external factors affects our subsequent reactions to that event.[21] One recent study reported that grievance arbitration outcomes are largely dependent on the arbitrator's attribution of causality or responsibility for the wrongdoing. In particular, arbitration decisions favour the employee when other employees have committed the same error (high consensus) and the employee has not been guilty of the wrongdoing before (low consistency).[22]

Attribution decisions also play a major role in performance appraisal ratings and reward allocation. Employees receive more credit and higher rewards for good performance when their supervisor attributes this outcome more to internal causes (employee's ability or motivation) than to external factors.[23] We also make attributions about our own behaviour. If we perform a task well but attribute it to luck or favourable conditions, the external attribution prevents us from feeling a sense of accomplishment. It also limits our motivation to perform the task in the future.[24]

Attribution errors

Although we look at the consensus, consistency, and distinctiveness of behaviour to make attributions, this process is subject to at least two systematic errors, known as the actor–observer error and self-serving bias.[25]

Attribution process
A perceptual process whereby we interpret the causes of behaviour in terms of the person (internal attributions) or the situation (external attributions).

Actor–observer error
An attribution error whereby people tend to attribute their own actions more to external factors and the behaviour of others more to internal factors.

Actor–observer error is the tendency to make external attributions about our own behaviour and internal attributions about the behaviour of other people. We conclude that employees arrive late for work due to their lack of effort because the situational factors influencing this behaviour are not easily seen. In contrast, we see that our own lateness is due to road construction delays or other external causes because we are more aware of them. In organizational settings, this can lead to conflict between supervisors and employees over the degree to which employees should be held responsible for their poor performance or absenteeism.[26]

Self-serving bias
A perceptual error whereby people tend to attribute their own success to internal factors and their failures to external factors.

Self-serving bias is the tendency to attribute our favourable outcomes to internal factors and our failures to external factors. Simply put, we take credit for our successes and blame others or the situation for our mistakes. The existence of self-serving bias in corporate life has been well documented. In a unique study of corporate annual reports, researchers discovered that organizational successes were typically explained by internal attributions such as management strategy, work force qualities, and research/development efforts. But when explaining corporate problems, the annual reports relied more on external attributions such as bad weather, strong competition, and inflationary pressures.[27]

Self-Fulfilling Prophecy

Self-fulfilling prophecy
A phenomenon in which an observer's expectations of someone causes that person to act in a way consistent with the observer's expectation.

Self-fulfilling prophecy occurs when our expectations about another person cause that person to act in a way that is consistent with those expectations.[28] In other words, our perceptions can influence reality. If a supervisor quickly concludes that a new employee will be a poor performer, this expectation influences the supervisor's behaviour toward the employee. Without realizing it, the supervisor's actions may cause the recruit to perform the job poorly. Consequently, the supervisor's perception, even if originally incorrect, is confirmed. Overall, the self-fulfilling prophecy process may be broken into the four steps outlined in Exhibit 7–4.[29]

Expectations formed

First, the supervisor forms expectations about the employee's future behaviour and performance. These expectations are sometimes inaccurate, because first impressions are usually formed from limited information.

Behaviour toward employee

The supervisor's expectations influence his or her treatment of employees.[30] Specifically, high-expectancy employees (those expected to do well) receive more emotional support through nonverbal cues (e.g., more smiling and eye contact), more frequent and valuable feedback and reinforcement, more challenging goals, better training, and more opportunities to demonstrate their performance.

Effect on employee

Employees react to the supervisor's actions in two ways. First, high-expectancy employees learn more skills and knowledge than low-expectancy employees, because the supervisor offers higher quality training and more opportunities to practise skills. Second, the supervisor's subtle cues cause high-expectancy

The Self-Fulfilling Prophecy Cycle   **Exhibit 7–4**

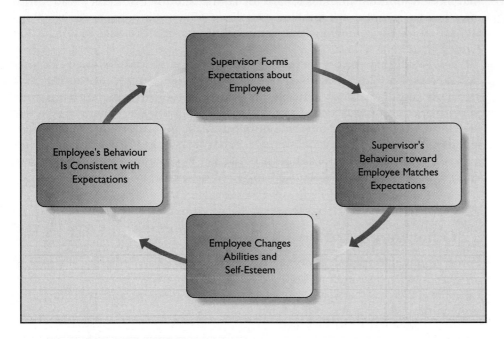

employees to increase their self-esteem in line with the supervisor's expectations. This results in higher motivation because people with high self-esteem tend to develop a higher effort-to-performance expectancy and set a higher level of achievement for themselves.

Employee behaviour and performance

With better skills and higher motivation, high-expectancy employees are more likely to demonstrate desired behaviours and better performance. This is observed by the supervisor and reinforces the original perception.

Although our discussion has centred around supervisor–subordinate relationships, self-fulfilling prophecy exists in a variety of situations. Some of the earliest work on self-fulfilling prophecy studied the influence of teacher expectancies on the subsequent behaviour and performance of elementary school children.[31] Self-fulfilling prophecy is also well known among finance experts because the stability of a bank or entire financial market depends on the public's expectation that it will be stable. As soon as people begin to doubt this belief, financial markets collapse and institutions have a "run on the bank" that threatens their survival.[32]

Self-fulfilling prophecies in practice

Expectations can have some effect on employee performance, particularly in training situations. In one study, four Israeli Defense Force combat command course instructors were told that one-third of the incoming trainees had high command potential, one-third had normal potential, and the rest had unknown potential. The trainees had been randomly placed into these categories by the researchers, but the instructors were led to believe that this was accurate information. As predicted, high-expectancy soldiers performed significantly better by the end of the course than did trainees in the other groups. They also had more favourable attitudes toward the course and the instructor's leadership effectiveness. Similar self-fulfilling prophecy effects have been reported in studies on hard-core unemployed trainees and poor-performance sailors in the United States Navy.[33]

Self-fulfilling prophecy is typically described as a perceptual error because the observer's initial expectations are usually incorrect. Yet this process can also be viewed as a potentially valuable management tool to maximize employee performance and satisfaction. Organizations can tap into the potential benefits of self-fulfilling prophecy by giving employees an opportunity to stretch their abilities in a culture of trust and support. Supervisors must learn to exhibit more contagious enthusiasm and, although providing accurate feedback, continue to express hope and optimism in each employee's potential.[34]

Other Perceptual Errors

Perception is an imperfect process. This is already apparent from our discussion of stereotyping, attribution, and self-fulfilling prophecy. Some of the other troublesome errors that distort our ability to perceive people and events include projection, halo, primacy, and recency.

Projection

Projection
A perceptual error in which we tend to believe that other people hold the same beliefs and attitudes that we do.

Projection bias occurs when we attribute to other people the same beliefs and attitudes that we hold.[35] If you are eager for a promotion, you might think that others in your position are similarly motivated. If you are thinking of quitting your job, you start to believe that other people are also thinking of quitting.

Projection bias is usually a defense mechanism to protect our self-esteem. If we break a work rule, projection justifies this infraction by claiming that "everyone does it." We feel more comfortable with the thought that our negative traits exist in others, so we are quick to believe that others also have these traits. Similarly, projection maintains the credibility of our goals and objectives. When we want an organizational policy changed, we tend to believe that others also have this goal.

Assigning your own attitudes and beliefs to other people may be harmless in some situations, but it has disastrous consequences in other situations. One of the most costly incidents of projection occurred several years ago at Calgary-based Dome Petroleum. As Perspective 7–2 describes, Dome's senior managers wanted to believe that an executive from another company would support their plan, and they were quick to assume that the other person's silence was tacit evidence of this support.

The halo effect

Halo effect
A perceptual error whereby our general impression of a person, usually based on one prominent characteristic, biases our perception of other characteristics of that person.

Halo effect occurs when our general impression of a person, usually based on one prominent characteristic, colours our perception of other characteristics of that person.[36] If we meet a client who speaks in a friendly manner, we tend to infer a host of other favourable qualities about that person. If a colleague doesn't complete tasks on time, we tend to view his or her other traits unfavourably. In

Perspective 7–2

The Costs of Projecting Silence at Dome Petroleum

Dome Petroleum was once a dazzling star in Alberta's oil patch, serving as a role model of Canadian initiative in oil exploration. In the early 1980s, chairman Jack Gallagher and president Bill Richards wanted to purchase another Canadian oil exploration company, Hudson's Bay Oil and Gas (HBOG), from its American owner, Conoco Inc. of Stamford, Connecticut. However, a direct purchase of HBOG stock in Canada would have unfavourable tax implications, so Gallagher and Richards planned to buy Conoco stock in New York and later swap it for HBOG stock.

Before buying Conoco shares on the New York Stock Exchange, Gallagher and Richards visited Conoco chairman Ralph Bailey to be sure that the American company did not view Dome's actions as a hostile takeover. Conoco was previously unaware of Dome's plans and, as the meeting began, Bailey warned that he was there merely to listen. Gallagher and Richards were certain that Conoco wanted to sell HBOG because Canada's energy legislation at the time made HBOG a poor investment for the American firm. They perceived Bailey's silence as an implied agreement to proceed with their offer and thought the Conoco chairman was trying to be discreet on this sensitive issue. However, Bailey later claimed that he was unimpressed with Dome's plan and was trying to give the Calgary oilmen the cold shoulder.

Based on their perceptions of that meeting, Gallagher and Richards launched the largest takeover that the world had ever seen by offering to purchase Conoco shares on the New York Stock Exchange. Surprised and outraged by this move, Conoco's chairman tried to block Dome's takeover plans. Dome was ultimately successful, but the heavy debt incurred from the hostile purchase (nearly $2 billion), together with rising interest rates and falling oil prices, nearly bankrupted the Calgary firm. Gallagher and Richards were eventually forced out of Dome Petroleum, and the firm was sold to Amoco Petroleum, an American oil firm, a few years later.

Source: Based on J. Lyon, *Dome: The Rise and Fall of the House that Jack Built* (Toronto: Macmillan of Canada, 1983).

each case, one trait important to the perceiver forms a general impression, and this impression becomes the basis for judgments about other traits. Halo effect is most prevalent when concrete information about the perceived person or object is missing or we are not sufficiently motivated to search for it.[37] Instead, we use our general impression of the person to fill in the missing information.

Halo effect has received considerable attention in research on performance appraisal ratings.[38] Consider the situation in which two employees have the same level of work quality, quantity of work, and customer relations performance, but one tends to be late for work. Tardiness might not be an important factor in work performance, but the supervisor has a negative impression of employees who are late for work. Halo effect would cause the supervisor to rate the tardy employee lower on *all* performance dimensions because the tardiness created a negative general impression of that employee. The punctual employee would tend to receive higher ratings on *all* performance dimensions even though his or her performance level is really the same as that of the tardy employee. Consequently, halo effect distorts our judgments and can result in poor decision making.

Primacy effect

Primacy effect relates to the saying that "first impressions are lasting impressions." It is our tendency to quickly form an opinion of people based on the first information we receive about them. This rapid perceptual organization fulfills our need to "make sense" of others and provides a convenient anchor to integrate subsequent information. For example, if we meet a new employee who avoids eye contact and speaks softly, we quickly conclude that the person is bashful. It is easier to remember the person as bashful than to recall the specific behaviours exhibited during the first encounter.

Unfortunately, first impressions tend to result in perceptual errors because they are formed with little information. Moreover, subsequent information about the person is given less attention and contradictory information is ignored. In fact, if the contradictory information is ambiguous, we often believe that it is consistent with the first impression.[39] Thus, the person we think is bashful will have difficulty shaking this first impression.

Recency effect

The **recency effect** occurs when the most recent information dominates our perception of others.[40] This effect is stronger than the primacy effect when there is a long delay between the time when the first impression is formed and the person is evaluated. In other words, the most recent information has the greater influence on our perception of someone when the first impression has worn off with the passage of time.[41]

The recency effect is found in performance appraisals, for which supervisors must recall every employee's performance over the previous year. Recent performance information dominates the evaluation because it is the most easily recalled. Some employees are well aware of the recency effect and use it to their advantage by getting their best work on the manager's desk just before the performance appraisal is conducted.

Improving Perceptual Accuracy

We may not be able to bypass the perceptual process, but we can try to minimize our distortion of reality. Five ways to improve perceptual accuracy are identified in Exhibit 7–5 and described below.

Increase awareness of perceptual biases

The journey toward greater perceptual accuracy begins by increasing our awareness of perceptual biases and how they operate. Research on performance appraisal training has found that increased awareness can minimize rating bias.[42] It may also minimize conflicts resulting from stereotypes among people working in multicultural settings.[43] McDonald's, Colgate Palmolive, Digital, and other Canadian companies have introduced diversity sessions that try to increase participants' awareness of their perceptual limitations. Imperial Oil's diversity awareness workshop, described in the chapter-opening vignette, helps managers realize that their stereotypic assumptions are often incorrect. It also makes them aware of the fact that their norms may differ from norms of employees raised in other cultures.

Improving Perceptual Accuracy   **Exhibit 7–5**

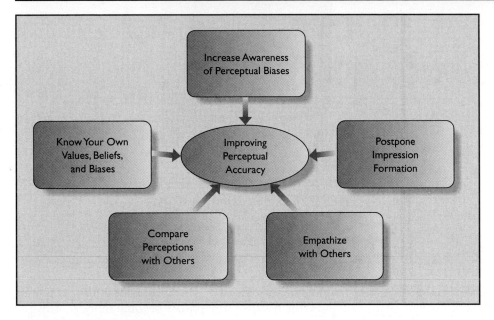

Another unique approach is to have employees take turns reading aloud to each other a short story or excerpt with cultural themes. Participants then discuss their reactions to the literary passage. Two excellent choices are recent novels by Montreal writer Neil Bissoondath: *The Innocence of Age* raises issues about racial tensions in Toronto, whereas *On the Eve of Uncertain Tomorrows* is a story of one person's experiences in Trinidad and Canada. Such read-aloud sessions encourage employees to share their beliefs and feelings about the cultural issues mentioned in the readings. This enables participants to gain a better understanding of co-workers from different cultures. It also strengthens social bonds as the diverse group shares common stories and language emerging from the reading sessions.[44]

Postpone impression formation

We have learned that people try to quickly make sense of their environment by forming first impressions from limited information and relying on existing stereotypes. Yet, more often than not, these activities lead to inaccurate perceptions. It is much better to postpone forming impressions and avoid making stereotyped inferences until more information is received. When working with people from different cultural backgrounds, for instance, you should constantly challenge your stereotypic expectations and actively seek out information that contradicts those expectations. By blocking the effects of stereotypes, first impressions, and other perceptual blinders, you are better able to engage in a developmental learning process that forms a more accurate understanding of others.[45]

Empathize with others

One of the most powerful ways to reduce several perceptual biases is to increase empathy. **Empathy** refers to a person's ability to understand and be sensitive to

Empathy
A person's ability to understand and be sensitive to the feelings, thoughts, and situation of others.

Digital Canada's "Valuing Differences" philosophy includes sessions in which employees learn to appreciate the perspectives that co-workers from different cultures bring to the workplace.

Courtesy of Digital Canada.

the feelings, thoughts, and situation of others. Empathy is useful for reducing actor–observer attribution errors because supervisors become more sensitive to external causes of the employee's performance and behaviour.[46]

The best way to increase empathy is to place yourself in the other person's shoes. Pearson Hospital, a long-term care facility in Vancouver, follows this strategy by having new employees tour the premises in a wheelchair (as most patients travel) and drink coffee from a straw (as most patients must do) during the orientation program. This experience helps them understand how their actions affect patients. As Perspective 7–3 describes, several executives are also increasing their empathy of employees and clients by "walking in their shoes."

Compare perceptions with others

Another useful approach is to compare your perceptions with the perceptions other people have about the same object or event. By sharing perceptions, you learn different points of view and potentially gain a better understanding of the situation. If your colleagues have different backgrounds but similar perceptions of the situation, then there is reason to be more confident in your interpretation. Of course, there is no way to know for sure that your perceptions are correct, but they are less likely to be wrong if people with different backgrounds have the same general interpretation of the situation.

Know yourself: Applying the Johari Window

Perceptual errors are minimized as we become more aware of and sensitive to our own values, beliefs, and prejudices. By understanding ourselves, a particular perception can be scrutinized to ensure that it is based on the information received and not distorted by personal biases.[47] Similarly, our colleagues are less likely to misunderstand our statements or actions when they know about our attitudes and experiences.

For example, suppose that you dislike a particular client who treated you badly a few years ago. If the client meets with you to re-establish the relation-

Perspective 7-3

Increasing Empathy by Being There

Holger Kluge, president of the Canadian Imperial Bank of Commerce's retail division, began working for the bank 33 years ago as a teller. He still spends a few days each year behind the counter at CIBC branches, learning firsthand from the bank's customers and frontline employees about their needs and concerns. According to Kluge, working as a teller helps him maintain more accurate perceptions of the work and relations with clients. "You can really only understand a job if you do it," says Kluge. "You have to feel it."

The CIBC chief is among a growing number of executives who are bringing their perceptions back into focus by working alongside frontline employees. Hyatt Hotels Corp. recently introduced "In Touch Day" to ensure that its executives throughout North America take on frontline employee jobs for a day. Hyatt's president worked as a doorman at the Hyatt Regency Chicago. In Vancouver, a vice-president of Hyatt's Canadian operations took over the desk clerk job in which he started 20 years earlier. Meanwhile, the desk clerk moved into the vice-president's job to gain a better perception of what it's like to work at the top.

One the most enthusiastic supporters of having executives working in frontline jobs is William Malec, chief financial officer of the Tennessee Valley Authority. Malec devotes one day each month performing a nonmanagement job and hearing the concerns of employees who work in that department. His tasks may include scrubbing toilets, punching data into the computer, or sorting mail in the middle of the night. This practice was initially intended to increase employee morale by reducing status differences, but Malec soon discovered that he would learn new perspectives and valuable information from these temporary roles.

A vivid illustration of his perceptual awakening came one day when Malec delivered mail to a manager who was always sugary sweet when Malec was in his chief financial officer job. But the manager didn't recognize Malec in his temporary role as mailroom employee, and rudely snubbed him. The incident helped Malec realize that it isn't easy to see reality when you're looking from the top of the corporate ladder. The abrupt manager also learned in his next performance review how to improve his behaviour toward employees.

Sources: Based on T. Gutner, "Meeting the Boss," *Forbes*, March 1, 1993, p. 126; "The Common Touch," *Macleans*, October 19, 1992, p. 11; D. M. Brennan, "The Hyatt Commitment," *Restaurant Business*, February 10, 1991, pp. 90, 94, 100; and J. Bermingham, "Hyatt Swap Eye-Opener," *Vancouver Province*, September 27, 1990, p. 50.

---

ship, you might be more open-minded about this business opportunity if you are conscious of your negative feelings. If you act harshly to the client, your colleagues are likely to understand the reason for your behaviour and draw this to your attention. Recognizing and acknowledging your weaknesses to others also reduces your likelihood of projecting those traits onto others.[48]

The idea that mutual understanding improves perceptual accuracy and communication is represented in a useful model called the **Johari Window**.[49] Developed by Joseph Luft and Harry Ingram (hence the name *Johari*), this model divides information about yourself into four "windows"—open, blind, hidden, and unknown—based on whether your own values, beliefs, and experiences are known to you and to others.

As we see in Exhibit 7-6, the *open area* includes information about you that is known both to you and others. For example, both you and your co-workers may be aware that you don't like to be near people who smoke cigarettes. The *blind area* refers to information that is known to others but not to yourself. For example, your colleagues might notice that you are embarrassed and awkward when meeting someone confined to a wheelchair, but you are unaware of this

Johari Window
A model of personal and interpersonal understanding that encourages disclosure and feedback to increase the open area and reduce the blind, hidden, and unknown areas of oneself.

Exhibit 7–6   **Johari Window**

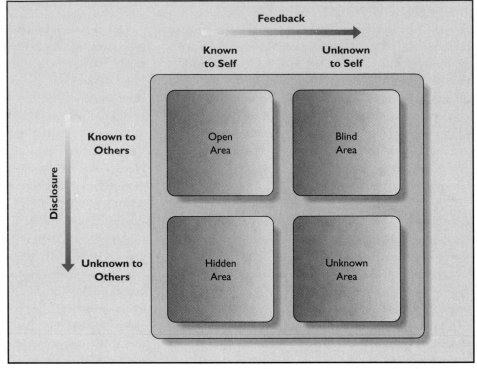

Source: Based on J. Luft, *Group Processes* (Palo Alto, Calif.: Mayfield, 1984).

fact. Information known to you but unknown to others is found in the *hidden area*. We all have personal secrets about our likes, dislikes, and personal experiences. Finally, the *unknown area* includes your values, beliefs, and experiences that aren't known to you or others.

The main objective of the Johari Window is to increase the size of the open area so that both you and colleagues are aware of your perceptual limitations. This is partly accomplished by reducing the hidden area through *disclosure*—informing others of your beliefs, feelings, and experiences that may influence the working relationship. Disclosure must be reciprocal among team members. Fortunately, self-disclosure by one person tends to cause others to make a self-disclosure.[50] The open area also increases through *feedback* from others about your behaviours. This information helps you to reduce your blind area, because co-workers often see things in you that you are unaware of. Finally, the combination of disclosure and feedback occasionally produces revelations about information in the unknown area. Thus, you and your co-workers must work together to reduce perceptual biases and improve interpersonal communication.

Johari Window in practice

Concepts behind the Johari Window have been applied in many interpersonal and diversity awareness training programs. One example is a session held by the Montreal transit authority in which bus drivers and riders from different cultural backgrounds shared their perceptions of each other. Realism was added to the program by having drivers describe to riders their experiences during role-play exercises. After the session, the Montreal bus drivers reflected on the experience and developed personal action plans to improve their customer service skills.[51]

Federal Express created a day-long program in which managers teamed up with blind people to complete a series of tasks. At the end of the day, the blind participants gave feedback about their partner's management style. The Federal Express managers also discovered their perceptual limitations throughout the day. Said one manager: "It was easy to see how I made bad assumptions about the people I work with and I grossly underestimate their abilities."[52]

Personality

Garrett Herman may not be a household name, but the CEO of brokerage firm Loewen Ondaatje has a personality to be reckoned with in Canada's investment industry. Herman has been called a "Robobroker" for his single-minded determination, overpowering need for achievement, and strong belief that he is in control of his destiny. In the 1970s, he aggressively built up his client list by following Rolls-Royces home to get the owner's address and telephone number. Herman's distinctive personality also prevails outside the office, where he races his Porsche at training tracks in Belleville, Ontario, and Daytona Beach, Florida. Says a longtime friend: "Garrett is the ultimate bull terrier—he's very tenacious, very competitive."[53]

It is difficult to describe Garrett Herman—or anyone else—without referring to the concept of personality. **Personality** refers to people's relatively stable and consistent internal states that help to explain their behavioural tendencies.[54] There are four important features of this definition. First, personality refers to internal states—characteristics of the person that we cannot see. Second, an individual's personality traits are identified by their behaviours. For example, Garrett Herman's acquaintances describe him as "aggressive" because they have observed how he drives cars and finds new clients. Third, people have relatively stable personality traits.[55] Our personality may change somewhat over time, but this usually takes many years.

Finally, personality traits represent behavioural tendencies, because our behaviour is also influenced by the situation. Talkative people spend much of their time in conversations when free to do so, but not in situations in which they are explicitly told to keep quiet. Thus, personality mainly affects behaviour in "weak" situations—environments that do not constrain the person's natural dispositions and tendencies. In "strong" situations (in which social norms and reward systems constrain or direct our behaviour), people with different personalities act very much the same.[56]

Personality
The relatively stable and consistent internal states of people that help to explain their behavioural tendencies.

How do personalities form?

An individual's personality originates from many sources. An extreme school of thought suggests that personality is mainly inherited genetically from our parents. If this is true, then our temperament is ascribed at conception and cannot be altered by life experiences. A more common view is that our personality is shaped by both heredity and environment. Personality is developed and changed by a variety of social experiences, such as early interactions with our parents, long-term friendships and affiliations, and traumatic events. Garrett Herman's aggressiveness, for instance, may have been formed by the way his parents rewarded him as a child or by his relations with school friends years ago.

Personality and organizational behaviour

To some extent, we can use personality traits to make sense of people in organizational settings, anticipate their future behaviour, and possibly increase their satisfaction and performance through better person–job matching. The effectiveness of some job design strategies and leadership styles is contingent on employee personalities. Champions of organizational change (people who effectively gain support for new organizational systems and practices) seem to possess certain personality characteristics, including high self-confidence, persistence, energy, and risk taking. Finally, personality traits affect the types of jobs in which people are interested. In fact, some vocational interest tools are based on personality concepts.[57]

Unfortunately, we still don't know how strongly personality traits relate to employee performance. Some studies indicate that we should measure a person's personality to make employment selection decisions. There is also evidence that professional interviewers often compare the applicant's personality with job requirements when deciding who should be hired.[58] Others argue that personality variables are relatively poor predictors of job performance for most jobs.[59] They cite problems with measuring personality traits and explain that any evidence of a connection between personality and performance exists only under very narrowly defined conditions. Until personality traits can be measured more accurately and appropriate traits are linked to specific tasks, we should rely on other selection methods (e.g., aptitude tests, structured behavioural interviews) to choose job applicants.

More generally, we must be careful about using personality traits to oversimplify a more complex world. These labels can become perceptual blinders that pigeonhole people even after their personal dispositions have changed.[60] Too often, we see problems as "personality clashes" rather than diagnosing the situation to discover the underlying causes. Nobel prize-winning scholar Herbert Simon warns that the concept of personality is unfortunately abused as "a magical slogan to charm away the problems that our intellectual tools don't handle."[61]

Selected Personality Dimensions

Scholars have labelled hundreds of personality traits, but a few stand out as important influences on organizational behaviour. In Chapter 3, we described three deeply embedded motive-based personality traits: need for achievement (nAch), need for affiliation (nAff), and need for power (nPow). Type A and Type B behaviour patterns, described in Chapter 5, represent another set of personality traits. Let us briefly review a few other personality traits commonly mentioned in organizational settings.

Locus of control

Locus of control refers to a generalized belief about the amount of control people have over their own lives. Individuals who feel that they are very much in charge of their own destiny have an *internal locus of control;* those who think that events in their life are due mainly to fate or luck have an *external locus of control.* Of course, externals believe that they control many specific events in their lives—such as opening a door or serving a customer—but they have a general belief that outside forces guide their fate. This is particularly apparent in new situations in which the person's control over events is uncertain.

People perform better in most employment situations when they have moderately strong internal locus of control. They tend to be more successful in their careers and earn more money than their external counterparts. Internals are also more satisfied with their jobs, cope better in stressful situations, and are more motivated by performance-based reward systems.[62]

Internals are particularly well suited to leadership positions and other jobs requiring initiative, independent action, complex thinking, and high motivation. Two studies reported that Canadian firms led by internals pursued more innovative strategies than firms led by executives with a more external locus of control. The internals invested more in research and development, introduced new products more quickly than the competition, and made more drastic product line changes. They also pursued more aggressive strategies and planned further into the future.[63]

Locus of control
A personality trait referring to the extent that people believe what happens to them is within their control; those who feel in control of their destiny have an internal locus, whereas those who believe that life events are due mainly to fate or luck have an external locus of control.

Authoritarianism and dogmatism

Authoritarianism is defined as a blind acceptance of authority. Leaders with high authoritarian personalities demand respect from subordinates and try to suppress any independence that subordinates try to gain. As followers, authoritarians are more likely to obey orders and support the power held by those in higher positions.[64]

The concept of **dogmatism** emerged from earlier research on authoritarianism and refers to a person's belief in absolute authority and intolerance of different perspectives. Highly dogmatic employees have considerable difficulty accepting information that is contrary to their beliefs. They are intolerant of those who do not abide by organizational authority. They also tend to make decisions quickly and are confident in their choices.[65] As you can imagine, people who are either dogmatic or authoritarian have difficulty working in organizations that promote employee involvement and cultural diversity!

Authoritarianism
A personality trait referring to people who blindly accept authority and expect followers to do the same.

Dogmatism
A personality trait referring to the extent that the person is open- or closed-minded about information contrary to his or her beliefs, and will tolerate others who deviate from organizational authority.

Self-monitoring

Self-monitoring refers to an individual's level of sensitivity and ability to adapt to situational cues. High self-monitors can adjust their behaviour quite easily and, therefore, show little stability in other underlying personality traits. In contrast, the social behaviour of low self-monitors is dominated by personal characteristics, so it is relatively easy to predict their behaviour from one situation to the next.[66]

The self-monitoring personality trait has been identified as a significant factor in many organizational activities. Employees who are high self-monitors tend to be better conversationalists, better organizational leaders, and better in boundary-spanning positions (in which incumbents work with people in differ-

Self-monitoring
A personality trait referring to the extent that people are sensitive to situational cues and can readily adapt their own behaviour appropriately.

ent departments or organizations). One study of Canadian business students also reported that high self-monitors experienced better job interview success and higher starting salary levels.[67]

Chapter Summary

- Perception is the process of selecting, organizing, and interpreting information to make sense of the world around us. Selective perception is influenced by characteristics of the person or object being perceived, the perceiver, and the situation. Figure/ground and perceptual grouping principles are used to organize and interpret the selected information.

- Stereotyping is a form of perceptual grouping whereby traits are attributed to people because of their membership in a social category. It frequently results in incorrect perceptions about others and may adversely affect the employment opportunities of women, people with disabilities, and older members of the labour force.

- Perceptual interpretation mainly involves making attributions about whether an employee's actions are due to the situation (external attributions) or personal characteristics (internal attributions). Two attribution errors are actor–observer error and self-serving bias.

- Self-fulfilling prophecy occurs when our expectations about another person cause that person to act in a way that is consistent with those expectations. Other perceptual errors include projection, halo, primacy, and recency effects.

- Employees can minimize perceptual errors by increasing their awareness of these errors, postponing their impression of others, learning to empathize with others, comparing their perceptions with others, and becoming more aware of their own values, beliefs, and prejudices.

- Personality refers to the relatively stable and consistent attributes of people that help to explain their behavioural tendencies. It is shaped by both heredity and environmental factors. Personality traits are important for some job design activities, championing organizational change, and matching people to jobs based on interests. We still don't know how strongly personality traits relate to employee performance.

- Along with the personal motives and Type A/B personalities described in earlier chapters, some commonly mentioned traits include locus of control, authoritarianism, dogmatism, and self-monitoring.

Discussion Questions

1. **You are part of a task force to increase worker responsiveness to emergencies on the production floor. Identify four factors that should be considered**

when installing a device that will get every employee's attention when there is an emergency.

2. During a diversity awareness session, a manager suggests that stereotypes are a necessary part of working with others. "I have to make assumptions about what's in the other person's head, and stereotypes help me do that," he explains. "It's better to rely on stereotypes than to enter a working relationship with someone from another culture without any idea of what they believe in!" Discuss the merits and problems of the manager's statement.

3. What are the potential organizational consequences when your supervisor makes an internal or external attribution about your job performance?

4. At the end of an NHL hockey game, the coach of the losing team is asked what happened. "I dunno," he begins. "We've done well in this rink over the past few years. Our busy schedule over the past two weeks has pushed the guys too hard, I guess. They're worn out. You probably noticed that we also got some bad breaks on penalties tonight. We should have done well here, but things just went against us." Use attribution theory to explain the coach's perceptions of the team's loss.

5. Explain how self-fulfilling prophecies affect employee performance.

6. Give two reasons why we sometimes project our own beliefs and values onto other people.

7. You are the leader of a newly formed project team that will work closely together over the next three months. The seven team members are drawn from as many worldwide offices. They do not know each other and come from different professional specializations. Describe the activities of a one-day retreat that would minimize perceptual errors and potential communication problems among the team members.

8. Contrast self-monitoring personality with dogmatism.

Notes

1. Adapted from J. Finlayson, "Balancing Act," *Imperial Oil Review* 77 (Summer 1993), pp. 20–23.

2. Plato, *The Republic,* trans. D. Lee (Harmondsworth, England: Penguin, 1955), Part VII, Section 7.

3. S. F. Cronshaw and R. G. Lord, "Effects of Categorization, Attribution, and Encoding Processes on Leadership Perceptions," *Journal of Applied Psychology* 72 (1987), pp. 97–106.

4. S. J. Motowidlo, "Information Processing in Personnel Decisions," *Research in the Personnel and Human Resources Management* 4 (1986), pp. 1–44.

5. F. J. Barrett and D. L. Cooperrider, "Generative Metaphor Intervention: A New Approach for Working with Systems Divided by Conflict and Caught in Defensive Perception," *Journal of Applied Behavioral Science* 26 (1990), pp. 219–39.

6. J. P. Walsh, "Selectivity and Selective Perception: An Investigation of Managers' Belief Structures and Information Processing," *Academy of Management Journal* 31 (1988), pp. 873–96; and D. C. Dearborn and H. A. Simon, "Selective Perception: A Note on the Departmental Identification of Executives," *Sociometry* 21 (1958), pp. 140–44.

7. R. Mead, *Cross-Cultural Management Communication* (Chichester, U.K.: Wiley, 1992), Chapter 8.

8. D. Goleman, *Vital Lies, Simple Truths: The Psychology of Deception* (New York: Touchstone, 1985); and M. Haire and W. F. Grunes, "Perceptual Defenses: Processes Protecting an Organized Perception of Another Personality," *Human Relations* 3 (1950), pp. 403–12.

9. R. Howard, "The CEO as Organizational Architect: An Interview with Xerox's Paul Allaire," *Harvard Business Review,* September–October 1992, pp. 107–21.

10. J. M. Ivancevich, "Contrast Effects in Performance Evaluation and Reward Practices," *Academy of Management Journal* 26 (1983), pp. 465–76.

11. B. English, "Orientation," *Canadian Business,* March 1988, pp. 58–72.

12. L. Falkenberg, "Improving the Accuracy of Stereotypes within the Workplace," *Journal of Management* 16 (1990), pp. 107–18; and D. L. Hamilton, S. J. Sherman, and C. M. Ruvolo, "Stereotype-Based Expectancies: Effects on Information Processing and Social Behavior," *Journal of Social Issues* 46 (1990), pp. 35–60.

13. C. Stangor and L. Lynch, "Memory for Expectancy-Congruent and Expectancy-Incongruent Information: A Review of the Social and Social Development Literatures," *Psychological Bulletin* 111 (1992), pp. 42–61; and C. Stangor, L. Lynch, C. Duan, and B. Glass, "Categorization of Individuals on the Basis of Multiple Social Features," *Journal of Personality and Social Psychology* 62 (1992), pp. 207–18.

14. K. J. Gibson, W. J. Zerbe, and R. E. Franken, "Employers' Perceptions of the Re-employment Barriers Faced by Older Job Hunters," *Relations Industrielles* 48 (1993), pp. 321–34; and "Defying the Stereotypes," *Globe & Mail,* October 16, 1992, p. C7.

15. S. Coate and G. C. Loury, "Will Affirmative-Action Policies Eliminate Negative Stereotypes?" *American Economic Review* 83 (1993), pp. 1220–40; and C. L. Owen and W. D. Todor, "Attitudes Toward Women as Managers: Still the Same," *Business Horizons* 36 (March–April 1993), pp. 12–16.

16. O. C. Bremmer, J. Tomkiewicz, and V. E. Schein, "The Relationship Between Sex Role Stereotypes and Requisite Management Characteristics Revisited," *Academy of Management Journal* 32 (1989), pp. 662–69; and V. E. Schein and R. Mueller, "Sex Role Stereotyping and Requisite Management Characteristics: A Cross Cultural Look," *Journal of Organizational Behavior* 13 (1992), pp. 439–47.

17. A. M. Morrison, R. P. White, E. Van Velsor, and the Center for Creative Leadership, *Breaking the Glass Ceiling: Can Women Reach the Top of America's Largest Corporations?* (Reading, Mass.: Addison-Wesley, 1987).

18. F. Henry and E. Ginzberg, *Who Gets the Work? A Test of Racial Discrimination in Employment* (Toronto: Social Planning Council of Metropolitan Toronto and Urban Alliance on Race Relations, 1985).

19. H. H. Kelley, *Attribution in Social Interaction* (Morristown, N.J.: General Learning Press, 1971).

20. H. H. Kelley, "The Processes of Causal Attribution," *American Psychologist* 28 (1973), pp. 107–28; and J. M. Feldman, "Beyond Attribution Theory: Cognitive Processes in Performance Appraisal," *Journal of Applied Psychology* 66 (1981), pp. 127–48.

21. J. D. Ford, "The Effects of Causal Attributions on Decision Makers' Responses to Performance Downturns," *Academy of Management Review* 10 (1985), pp. 770–86; and M. J. Martinko and W. L. Gardner, "The Leader/Member Attribution Process," *Academy of Management Review* 12 (1987), pp. 235–49.

22. B. Bemmels, "Attribution Theory and Discipline Arbitration," *Industrial and Labor Relations Review* 44 (April 1991), pp. 548–62. The distinctiveness factor did not significantly influence arbitration decisions.

23. J. M. Crant and T. S. Bateman, "Assignment of Credit and Blame for Performance Outcomes," *Academy of Management Journal* 36 (1993), pp. 7–27; M. G. Evans and L. T. Brown, "The Role of Attributions in the Performance Evaluation Process," *Proceedings of the Annual ASAC Conference, Organizational Behaviour Division* 10, pt. 7 (1989), pp. 31–38; A. de Carufel and J. Jabes, "Intuitive Prediction and Judgment on a Personnel Task by Naive and Experienced Judges," *Canadian Journal of Administrative Sciences* 1 (June 1984), pp. 78–94; and T. R. Mitchell and R. E. Wood, "Supervisor's Responses to Subordinate Poor Performance: A Test of an Attribution Model," *Organizational Behavior and Human Performance* 25 (1980), pp. 123–38.

24. D. R. Norris and R. E. Niebuhr, "Attributional Influences on the Job Performance–Job Satisfaction Relationship," *Academy of Management Journal* 27 (1984), pp. 424–31.

25. D. R. Ilgen and J. M. Feldman, "Performance Appraisal: A Process Focus," *Research in Organizational Behavior* 5 (1983), pp. 141–97; and E. E. Jones and R. E. Nisbett, *The Actor and Observer: Perceptions of the Causes of Behavior* (New York: General Learning Press, 1971). To simplify the discussion, the actor–observer error description also includes fundamental attribution error.

26. H. J. Bernardin and P. Villanova, "Performance Appraisal," in *Generalizing from Laboratory to Field Settings,* ed. E. A. Locke (Lexington, Mass.: Lexington Books, 1986), pp. 43–62; and S. G. Green and T. R. Mitchell, "Attributional Processes of Leader–Member Interactions," *Organizational Behavior and Human Performance* 23 (1979), pp. 429–58.

27. J. R. Bettman and B. A. Weitz, "Attributions in the Board Room: Causal Reasoning in Corporate Annual Reports," *Administrative Science Quarterly* 28 (1983), pp. 165–83.

28. R. H. G. Field, "The Self-Fulfilling Prophecy Leader: Achieving the Metherme Effect," *Journal of Management Studies* 26 (March 1989), pp. 151–75; D. Eden, *Pygmalion in Management* (Lexington, Mass.: Lexington, 1990); and L. Jussim, "Self-Fulfilling Prophecies: A Theoretical and Integrative Review," *Psychological Review* 93 (1986), pp. 429–45.

29. Similar models are presented in R. H. G. Field and M. G. Evans, "Pygmalion at Work: Manager Expectation Effects on Travel Agency Outcomes," *Proceedings of the Annual ASAC Conference, Organizational Behaviour Division* 14(5) (1993), pp. 102–11; R. H. G. Field and D. A. Van Seters, "Management by Expectations (MBE): The Power of Positive Prophecy," *Journal of General Management* 14 (Winter 1988), pp. 19–33; and D. Eden, "Self-Fulfilling Prophecy as a Management Tool: Harnessing Pygmalion," *Academy of Management Review* 9 (1984), pp. 64–73.

30. M. J. Harris and R. Rosenthal, "Mediation of Interpersonal Expectancy Effects: 31 Meta-Analyses," *Psychological Bulletin* 97 (1985), pp. 363–86.

31. R. Rosenthal and L. Jacobson, *Pygmalion in the Classroom: Teacher Expectation and Student Intellectual Development* (New York: Holt, Rinehart, & Winston, 1968); and J. B. Dusek (ed.), *Teacher Expectancies* (Hillsdale, N.J.: Erlbaum, 1985).

32. J. B. Rosser, Jr., "Belief: Its Role in Economic Thought and Action," *American Journal of Economics & Sociology* 52 (1993), pp. 355–68.

33. D. Eden and A. B. Shani, "Pygmalion Goes to Boot Camp: Expectancy, Leadership, and Trainee Performance," *Journal of Applied Psychology* 67 (1982), pp. 194–99; A. S. King, "Self-Fulfilling Prophecies in Training the Hard-Core: Supervisors' Expectations and the Underprivileged Workers' Performance," *Social Science Quarterly* 52 (1971), pp. 369–78; and K. S. Crawford, E. D. Thomas, and J. J. Fink, "Pygmalion at Sea: Improving the Work Effectiveness of Low Performers," *Journal of Applied Behavioral Science* 16 (1980), pp. 482–505.

34. D. Eden, "OD and Self-Fulfilling Prophecy: Boosting Productivity by Raising Expectations," *Journal of Applied Behavioral Science* 22 (1986), pp. 1–13.

35. T. W. Costello and S. S. Zalkind, *Psychology in Administration: A Research Orientation* (Englewood Cliffs, N.J.: Prentice Hall, 1963), pp. 36–37; and G. G. Sherwood, "Self-Serving Biases in Person Perception: A Re-examination of Projection as a Mechanism of Defense," *Psychological Bulletin* 90 (1981), pp. 445–59.

36. W. H. Cooper, "Ubiquitous Halo," *Psychological Bulletin* 90 (1981), pp. 218–44; and K. R. Murphy, R. A. Jako, and R. L. Anhalt, "Nature and Consequences of Halo Error: A Critical Analysis," *Journal of Applied Psychology* 78 (1993), pp. 218–25.

37. S. Kozlowski, M. Kirsch, and G. Chao, "Job Knowledge, Ratee Familiarity, Conceptual Similarity, and Halo Error: An Exploration," *Journal of Applied Psychology* 71 (1986), pp. 45–49; and H. C. Min, "Country Image: Halo or Summary Construct?" *Journal of Marketing Research* 26 (1989), pp. 222–29.

38. W. K. Balzer, and L. M. Sulsky, "Halo and Performance Appraisal Research: A Critical Examination," *Journal of Applied Psychology* 77 (1992), pp. 975–85; and H. J. Bernardin and R. W. Beatty, *Performance Appraisal: Assessing Human Behavior at Work* (Boston: Kent, 1984).

39. T. Hill, P. Lewicki, M. Czyzewska, and A. Boss, "Self-Perpetuating Development of Encoding Biases in Person Perception," *Journal of Personality and Social Psychology* 57 (1989), pp. 373–87; and C. L. Kleinke, *First Impressions: The Psychology of Encountering Others* (Englewood Cliffs, N.J.: Prentice Hall, 1975).

40. D. D. Steiner and J. S. Rain, "Immediate and Delayed Primacy and Recency Effects in Performance Evaluation," *Journal of Applied Psychology* 74 (1989), pp. 136–42; and R. L. Heneman and K. N. Wexley, "The Effects of Time Delay in Rating and Amount of Information Observed in Performance Rating Accuracy," *Academy of Management Journal* 26 (1983), pp. 677–86.

41. D. G. Linz and S. Penrod, "Increasing Attorney Persuasiveness in the Courtroom," *Law and Psychology Review* 8 (1984), pp. 1–47.

42. D. E. Smith, "Training Programs for Performance Appraisal: A Review," *Academy of Management Review* 11 (1986), pp. 22–40.

43. A. Rossett and T. Bickham, "Diversity Training: Hope, Faith, and Cynicism," *Training*, January 1994, pp. 40–46; and K. Foss, "Keeping Harmony in Race Relations," *Financial Times of Canada*, July 6–12, 1992, p. 17.

44. C. F. Barnum, "A Novel Approach to Diversity," *HR Magazine*, May 1992, pp. 69–73.

45. L. Beamer, "Learning Intercultural Communication Competence," *Journal of Business Communication* 29 (1992), pp. 285–303; and D. Landis and R. W. Brislin (eds.), *Handbook of Intercultural Training* (New York: Pergamon, 1983).

46. G. Egan, *The Skilled Helper: A Model for Systematic Helping and Interpersonal Relating* (Belmont, Calif.: Brooks/Cole, 1975); and D. B. Fedor and K. M. Rowland, "Investigating Supervisor Attributions of Subordinate Performance," *Journal of Management* 15 (1989), pp. 405–16.

47. Costello and Zalkind, *Psychology in Administration*, pp. 45–46.

48. Ibid., p. 36.

49. J. Luft, *Group Processes* (Palo Alto, Calif.: Mayfield Publishing, 1984). For a variation of this model, see J. Hall, "Communication Revisited," *California Management Review* 15 (Spring 1973), pp. 56–67.

50. L. C. Miller and D. A. Kenny, "Reciprocity of Self-Disclosure at the Individual and Dyadic Levels: A Social Relations Analysis," *Journal of Personality and Social Psychology* 50 (1986), pp. 713–19.

51. H. D. Stolovitch and M. Lane, "Multicultural Training: Designing for Affective Results," *Performance and Instruction* 28 (July 1989), pp. 10–15.

52. M. M. Starcevich, S. J. Stowell, and R. S. Yamahiro, "An Unusual Day of Development," *Training and Development Journal* 40 (March 1986), pp. 45–48.

53. "Ondaatje Spins Off Brokerage," *Financial Post Daily*, December 31, 1992, p. 5; A. Kingston, "Trading Up," *Financial Times of Canada*, February 26, 1990, pp. 8–10; and D. McMurdy, "A Pushy Powerhouse at Merrill Lynch," *Financial Post*, March 8, 1989, p. 16.

54. W. Mischell, *Introduction to Personality* (New York: Holt, Rinehart, & Winston, 1971); and S. R. Maddi, *Personality Theories: A Comparative Analysis* (Homewood, Ill.: Dorsey Press, 1980).

55. S. Epstein, "The Stability of Behavior: I. On Predicting Most of the People Much of the Time," *Journal of Personality and Social Psychology* 37 (1979), pp. 1097–1126.

56. H. M. Weiss and S. Adler, "Personality and Organizational Behavior," *Research in Organizational Behavior* 6 (1984), pp. 1–50.

57. J. M. Howell and C. A. Higgins, "Champions of Change: Identifying, Understanding, and Supporting Champions of Technological Innovations," *Organizational Dynamics*, Summer 1990, pp. 40–55; B. M. Bass, *Stogdill's Handbook of Leadership: A Survey of Theory and Research*, 3rd ed. (New York: Free Press, 1990); J. T. Barnowe and P. J. Frost, "Person–Thing Specialization, University Experiences, and Students' Choice of Business Specialty," *Canadian Journal of Administrative Sciences* 4 (December, 1987), pp. 469–78; and J. L. Holland, *Making Vocation Choices: A Theory of Careers* (Englewood Cliffs, N.J.: Prentice Hall, 1973).

58. P. G. Irving, "On the Use of Personality Measures in Personnel Selection," *Canadian Psychology* 34 (April 1993), pp. 208–14; R. P. Tett, D. N. Jackson, and M. Rothstein, "Personality Measures as Predictors of Job Performance: A Meta-Analytic Review," *Personnel Psychology* 44 (1991), pp. 703–42; D. N. Jackson, A. C. Peacock, and J. P. Smith, "Impressions of Personality in the Employment Interview," *Journal of Personality and Social Psychology* 39 (1980), pp. 294–307; and D. N. Jackson, A. C. Peacock, and R. R. Holden, "Professional Interviewers' Trait Inferential Structures for Diverse Occupational Groups," *Organizational Behavior and Human Performance* 29 (1982), pp. 1–20.

59. C. Fletcher et al., "Personality Tests: The Great Debate," *Personnel Management* 23 (September 1991), pp. 38–42; and N. Schmitt, R. Z. Gooding, R. D. Noe, and M. Kirsch, "Meta-Analyses of Validity Studies Published Between 1964 and 1982 and the Investigation of Study Characteristics," *Personnel Psychology* 37 (1984), pp. 407–22.

60. R. Zemke, "Second Thoughts about the MBTI," *Training*, April 1992, pp. 42–47.

61. H. A. Simon, *Administrative Behavior* (New York: The Free Press, 1957), p. xv.

62. J. M. Howell and B. J. Avolio, "Transformational Leadership, Transactional Leadership, Locus of Control, and Support for Innovation: Key Predictors of Consolidated-Business-Unit Performance," *Journal of Applied Psychology* 78 (1993), pp. 891–902; S. D. Saleh and K. Desai, "An Empirical Analysis of Job Stress and Job Satisfaction of Engineers," *Journal of Engineering & Technology Management* 7 (July 1990), pp. 37–48; P. E. Spector, "Behavior in Organizations as a Function of Employee's Locus of Control," *Psychological Bulletin* 91 (1982), pp. 482–97; and P. J. Andrisani and C. Nestel, "Internal–External Control as a Contributor to and Outcome of Work Experience," *Journal of Applied Psychology* 61 (1976), pp. 156–65.

63. D. Miller and J.-M. Toulouse, "Chief Executive Personality and Corporate Strategy and Structure in Small Firms," *Management Science* 32 (1986), pp. 1389–1409; and D. Miller, M. F. R. Ket de Vries, and J.-M. Toulouse, "Top Executive Locus of Control and Its Relationship to Strategy-Making, Structure, and Environment," *Academy of Management Journal* 25 (1982), pp. 237–53.

64. T. W. Adorno, E. Frenkle-Brunswik, D. J. Levinson, and R. N. Sanford, *The Authoritarian Personality* (New York: Harper & Row, 1950).

65. M. Rokeach, *The Open and Closed Mind* (New York: Basic Books, 1960); and R. N. Taylor and M. D. Dunnette, "Influence of Dogmatism, Risk-Taking Propensity, and Intelligence on Decision-Making Strategies for a Sample of Industrial Managers," *Journal of Applied Psychology* 59 (1974), pp. 420–23.

66. M. Snyder, *Public Appearances/Private Realities: The Psychology of Self-Monitoring* (New York: W. H. Freeman, 1987); and R. S. Adamson, R. J. Ellis, G. Deszca, and T. F. Cawsey, "Self-Monitoring and Leadership Emergence," *Proceedings of the Annual ASAC Conference, Organizational Behaviour Division* 5, pt. 5 (1984), pp. 9–15.

67. S. J. Zaccaro, R. J. Foti, and D. A. Kenny, "Self-Monitoring and Trait-Based Variance in Leadership: An Investigation of Leader Flexibility Across Multiple Group Situations," *Journal of Applied Psychology* 76 (1991), pp. 308–15; and T. F. Cawsey, G. Deszca, R. J. Ellis, and R. S. Adamson, "Self-Monitoring and Interview Success," *Proceedings of the Annual ASAC Conference, Organizational Behaviour Division* 7, pt. 5 (1986), pp. 29–37.

Chapter Case

Nupath Foods Ltd.

James Ornath read the latest sales figures with a great deal of satisfaction. The vice-president of marketing at Nupath Foods Ltd. was pleased to see that the marketing campaign to improve sagging sales of Prowess cat food was working.

Sales volume of the product had increased 20 percent in the past quarter compared with the previous year, and market share was up.

The improved sales of Prowess could be credited to Denise Roberge, the brand manager responsible for cat foods at Nupath. Roberge had joined Nupath less than two years ago as an assistant brand manager after leaving a similar job at a consumer products firm. She was one of the few women in marketing management at Nupath and had a promising career with the company. Ornath was pleased with Roberge's work and tried to let her know this in the annual performance reviews. He now had an excellent opportunity to reward her by offering the recently vacated position of market research coordinator. Although technically only a lateral transfer with a modest salary increase, the marketing research coordinator job would give Roberge broader experience in some high-profile work, which would enhance her career with Nupath. Few people were aware that Ornath's own career had been boosted by working as marketing research coordinator at Nupath several years before.

Denise Roberge had also seen the latest sales figures on Prowess cat food and was expecting Ornath's call to meet with her that morning. Ornath began the conversation by briefly mentioning the favourable sales figures, and then explained that he wanted Roberge to take the marketing research coordinator job. Roberge was shocked by the news. She enjoyed brand management and particularly the challenge involved with controlling a product that directly affected the company's profitability. Marketing research coordinator was a technical support position—a "backroom" job—far removed from the company's bottom-line activities. Marketing research was not the route to top management in most organizations, Roberge thought. She had been sidelined.

After a long silence, Roberge managed a weak "Thank you, Mr. Ornath." She was too bewildered to protest. She wanted to collect her thoughts and reflect on what she had done wrong. Also, she did not know her boss well enough to be openly critical. Ornath recognized Roberge's surprise, which he naturally assumed was her positive response to hearing of this wonderful career opportunity. He, too, had been delighted several years earlier about his temporary transfer to marketing research to round out his marketing experience. "This move will be good for both you and Nupath," said Ornath as he escorted Roberge from his office.

Roberge had several tasks to complete that afternoon, but was able to consider the day's events that evening. She was one of the top women in brand management at Nupath and feared that she was being sidelined because the company didn't want women in top management. Her previous employer had made it quite clear that women "couldn't take the heat" in marketing management and tended to place women in technical support positions after a brief term in lower brand management jobs. Obviously Nupath was following the same game plan. Ornath's comments that the coordinator job would be good for her was just a nice way of saying that Roberge couldn't go any further in brand management at Nupath. Roberge was now faced with the difficult decision of confronting Ornath and trying to change Nupath's sexist practices or submitting her resignation.

Discussion Questions

1. **What symptom(s) exist in this case to suggest that something has gone wrong?**

2. **What are the root causes that have led to these symptoms?**

3. **What actions should the organization take to correct these problems?**

© 1989 Steven L. McShane.

Experiential Exercise

Toward Consensus on Occupational Stereotypes

Purpose: This exercise is designed to help you determine the extent to which common occupational stereotypes are held among students, and to identify the implications of these stereotypes on your attitudes and behaviour toward people in these occupations.

Instructions: Four occupations in Canadian society are presented below. Each of us holds beliefs about the characteristics of people working in these occupations. Using the bipolar rating scales, please indicate *your own general beliefs* regarding the extent that people in each occupation are modest, greedy, honest, gloomy, and risk takers. You should complete these ratings alone.

After completing the ratings, the class results will be tallied on an overhead display, flip chart, or blackboard. The extent to which students hold common beliefs about people in these occupations will be apparent by the distribution of ratings. Specifically, adjectives that identify common stereotypes have extreme ratings with most students giving the same ratings.

The results having been tallied, the entire class or small groups will discuss the effects of stereotypes on behaviour and debate the relevance of these beliefs. General perceptions about people in an occupation influence your behaviour toward them, at least until you get to know individuals in that occupation. For each occupation, students should list the behaviours that they might exhibit resulting from their beliefs. For example, those who believe that people in an occupation are "greedy" might say that they are cautious about hiring or sharing financial resources with them.

Students should then discuss the relevance and implications of occupational stereotypes. Are they useful? Is there any truth to these beliefs? Should we consciously try to ignore stereotypes when meeting people in these occupations?

Accountants

Modest	I	2	3	4	5	6	7	Boastful
Greedy	I	2	3	4	5	6	7	Generous
Honest	I	2	3	4	5	6	7	Dishonest
Gloomy	I	2	3	4	5	6	7	Cheerful
Risk takers	I	2	3	4	5	6	7	Risk averse

Lawyers

Modest	I	2	3	4	5	6	7	Boastful
Greedy	I	2	3	4	5	6	7	Generous
Honest	I	2	3	4	5	6	7	Dishonest
Gloomy	I	2	3	4	5	6	7	Cheerful
Risk takers	I	2	3	4	5	6	7	Risk averse

Union Leaders

Modest	1	2	3	4	5	6	7	Boastful
Greedy	1	2	3	4	5	6	7	Generous
Honest	1	2	3	4	5	6	7	Dishonest
Gloomy	1	2	3	4	5	6	7	Cheerful
Risk takers	1	2	3	4	5	6	7	Risk averse

Canadian Government Politicians

Modest	1	2	3	4	5	6	7	Boastful
Greedy	1	2	3	4	5	6	7	Generous
Honest	1	2	3	4	5	6	7	Dishonest
Gloomy	1	2	3	4	5	6	7	Cheerful
Risk takers	1	2	3	4	5	6	7	Risk averse

Work Attitudes and Values

Learning Objectives

After reading this chapter, you should be able to:

Identify four reasons why work attitudes are important.

Discuss the linkages between beliefs and behaviour.

Explain the weak relationship between job satisfaction and performance.

Describe five strategies to increase organizational commitment.

Distinguish attitudinal commitment from continuance commitment.

Identify four values that vary across cultures.

Chapter Outline

What Are Attitudes?

Importance of Work Attitudes.

Linking Work Attitudes to Behaviour.

Job Satisfaction.

Organizational Commitment.

Work-Related Values.

Tri-City News. *Used with permission.*

$\mathcal{N}$ancy More glows as she describes her work as head brewmaster at Labatt's brewery in New Westminster, B.C. She particularly enjoys the challenges of her current task as project leader for the production of Labatt's Genuine Draft. "There's a real feeling of pride," she says. "There's an end purpose to it."

More became head brewmaster a few years ago at Labatt's plant in St. John, New Brunswick. This marked the first time a female had held such a position with a major brewery in North America. Her route to this prestigious position included working in virtually every job in the brewery, from running kettles to cleaning equipment.

When she first entered the traditionally male job, More faced co-workers with negative attitudes toward women. One co-worker warned her that women "don't usually make it in this company." After becoming a supervisor, More listened to another male colleague quip that she was "a heretic" to believe that men should work for her. The cynical co-worker is now a strong supporter of More's managerial skills.

In spite of these archaic attitudes, More is an enthusiastic supporter of working at Labatt's. "It's never boring," she says proudly. "We're really allowed to make anything we want out of our jobs. We're encouraged to take risks."[1]

Work attitudes are an everyday part of organizational life. A supervisor complains about completing the monthly payroll forms; a co-worker comments favourably about recent pay increases; a client tells an employee that she enjoys doing business with this organization. These statements reflect people's attitudes toward a variety of objects or events.

This chapter begins by explaining the three components of attitudes and identifying reasons why we should be interested in work attitudes. Next, the relationship between attitudes and behaviour is presented. We then look at two work attitudes—job satisfaction and organizational commitment—with particular emphasis on their implications for organizational behaviour. The final section of this chapter examines the topic of work-related values, particularly their importance in cross-cultural settings.

What Are Attitudes?

Attitudes
Relatively enduring emotional tendencies to respond consistently toward an attitude object.

Attitudes are relatively enduring emotional tendencies to respond consistently toward an attitude object.[2] Attitudes are attached to specific attitude objects, such as a person, idea, or place. We cannot see attitudes, although they may be inferred from the person's behaviour. They are relatively enduring, meaning that they do not appear and disappear quickly. Some scholars suggest that attitudes are strongly influenced by our personality and genetic configuration and, consequently, are very stable over time.[3] Although this view is gaining support, there is also evidence that attitudes tend to change as the situation changes.[4] For example, we might be more satisfied working in one job than in another.

Three components of attitudes

Attitudes have three major components: beliefs, feelings, and intentions (see Exhibit 8–1). *Beliefs* result from our perceptions about the attitude object. The statement "Management doesn't involve employees in decisions" is a belief because it describes a perceived characteristic of management (the attitude object). This belief might develop over time through direct experience. However, beliefs are strongly influenced by our social context. In other words, our construction of reality may be based more on what others tell us than on objective experience.[5] You are more likely to adopt the belief that management doesn't involve employees in decisions if co-workers believe this.

Feelings represent pleasant or unpleasant emotions toward the attitude object. They are judgments about where things fall along a good–bad or positive–negative continuum. You may have positive feelings toward clients, whereas you may have a negative emotional response to management. *Intentions* represent a motivation to engage in a particular behaviour. You might hear people say that they are willing to wear their safety glasses. Others try to avoid working with certain employees. Still others intend to complain to management about the lack of employee involvement. These are all examples of the intentions component of attitudes.

Three Components of Attitudes **Exhibit 8–1**

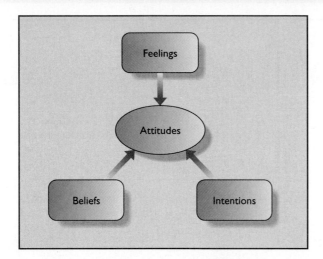

Importance of Work Attitudes

Work attitudes are an important part of organizational behaviour.[6] One reason is that some work attitudes are indicators of the organization's ethical treatment of employees. Management is rightfully proud when employee morale is strong because it demonstrates that employees are being treated well. Conversely, some managers try to hide or deny low morale because this information may tarnish the company's image as a good employer. For example, when the media reported serious morale problems in Canada's civil service a few years ago, deputy ministers were told to deny any attitude problems because this would make the Canadian government look as if it had failed its obligations as an employer.[7]

Another reason why attitudes are important is that most jobs require employees to either display or withhold evidence of their emotions. This is particularly true in service roles, such as a salesperson's interest in helping a customer or a medical professional's compassion for the patient.[8] Some employees can convincingly act out these emotions without really having them. However, most people need to feel the underlying attitude to display the corresponding behaviours. When hiring employees, many companies consider the job applicant's attitudes toward customers because they believe people with the right attitudes are more likely to display the appropriate emotions. For instance, an amusement park might hire ride operators who have a "cheery" or "fun" attitude toward life because it is easier for them to display this upbeat attitude in public for long stretches of time.

A third reason for our interest in work attitudes is that they shape and express an individual's self-identity.[9] People tend to express their attitudes not only to influence others, but also to communicate their identities to others. For example, by giving the impression that you dislike loafers on the job, you are telling others that you value the work ethic. Co-workers know more about you and tend to adjust their behaviour toward you accordingly.

Exhibit 8–2 · **Model of Attitudes and Behaviour**

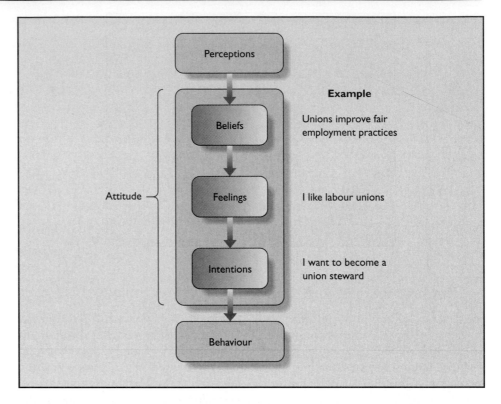

Finally, attitudes are early warning signals for future behaviour problems. Monitoring work attitudes and taking corrective action can significantly improve the organization's financial status.[10] However, the connection between an employee's work attitude and behaviour is complex, as we discuss next.

Linking Work Attitudes to Behaviour

The three attitude elements are usually linked to behaviour in the linear sequence shown in Exhibit 8–2. However, you should also be aware that the connections among beliefs, feelings, and intentions are really more complex than this.[11]

From beliefs to feelings

Beliefs form the basis of our feelings toward the attitude object. Exhibit 8–2 illustrates how a person's belief that labour unions improve fair employment practices may produce positive feelings toward labour unions. This linkage occurs because the person appreciates fair employment practices, and this positive feeling carries over to his or her feelings toward labour unions. Beliefs serve as a bridge to carry one's feelings from one attitude object to another.

It is difficult to predict behaviour from beliefs, because two people might have different feelings toward the attitude object even though they hold the same beliefs. For instance, another person might not care one way or the other about fair employment practices and, consequently, might be less likely to have positive feelings toward labour unions. Alternatively, some people might have additional beliefs about labour unions (e.g., reducing management autonomy) that offset their positive feelings relating to fair employment practices.

From feelings to intentions

Our feelings influence behaviour through our intentions to engage in that behaviour.[12] In our example, the individual has a positive feeling toward labour unions and this motivates him or her to become a union steward. However, people with the same feelings toward an attitude object can easily form different behavioural intentions. Consider two employees who are equally dissatisfied with their level of pay. One forms a strong intention to complain about this situation, whereas the other intends to quit. People form different intentions because they have different perceptions of behavioural outcomes and hold different feelings toward those outcomes. For instance, some people prefer to change jobs rather than ask for a pay raise because they may have experienced little success in the past when asking for a raise.[13]

From intentions to behaviour

As you might have guessed, a person's intentions are the best predictor of his or her actual behaviour. A person who intends to run for the position of union steward is more likely to engage in this activity than someone who does not form this intention. But intentions are not perfectly related to behaviour; the reason, as we learned in Chapter 2, is that an individual's behaviour depends on more than just his or her motivation to engage in the behaviour. You might intend to have no absenteeism during the next month, but illness or something beyond your control prevents that intention from coming true. Thus, we need to consider other elements in the performance model to understand whether a person's intentions will result in the expected behaviour.[14]

Cognitive dissonance: From behaviour to attitude

Before leaving this discussion of attitudes and behaviour, you should know that attitudes do not always lead to behaviour as we described above. Instead, our behaviours sometimes influence our attitudes. Suppose you volunteered to take a foreign assignment. You weren't particularly interested in the posting, but thought that it might be necessary for promotion into senior management. However, you later learn that most people become senior managers in this firm without spending any time on foreign assignment.

This situation creates an uncomfortable tension, called **cognitive dissonance,** because your behaviour (accepting a foreign assignment) is inconsistent with your attitude toward foreign postings. To reduce this dissonance, people tend to change their attitudes so that they are more closely aligned with their behaviours.[15] This is because it is easier to change our feelings toward

Cognitive dissonance
A state of anxiety that occurs when an individual's beliefs, attitudes, intentions, and behaviours are inconsistent with one another.

Exhibit 8–3	Some Facets of Job Satisfaction

Competence of co-workers	Pay practices
Control over pace of work	Promotion decisions
Employee benefits	Promotional opportunities
Friendliness of co-workers	Quality of work materials
Helpfulness of co-workers	Recognition of accomplishments
Hours of work	Supervisor's emotional support
Layout of work area	Supervisor's technical support
Opportunity to practise skills	Variety of work tasks
Participation in decisions	Ventilation of work area
Pay level	Workload

something than to change our past behaviour toward it, particularly when the behaviour is known to everyone, was done voluntarily, and can't be undone.

In our example, you might convince yourself that the foreign posting is not so bad after all because it will develop your management skills. Alternatively, you might downplay the features that previously made the foreign posting less desirable. Suddenly, a somewhat negative attitude toward foreign assignments has changed to a more favourable one.

Job Satisfaction

Job satisfaction
An individual's beliefs, feelings, and intentions regarding the job and the work environment.

Job satisfaction represents a person's emotional reaction toward various aspects of work. It is one of the most important and widely studied work attitudes, partly because work is the place where most people expect to receive much of their life satisfaction. In this respect, job satisfaction is closely associated with a person's self-identity.[16] Job satisfaction is often described as a single attitude, but it is really a collection of attitudes about specific facets of the job.[17] Exhibit 8–3 lists some specific facets of job satisfaction.

Employees can be satisfied with some elements of the job while simultaneously dissatisfied with others. Different types of satisfaction will lead to different intentions and behaviour. For example, you might complain to your supervisor if your pay is too low but not if you dislike your co-workers. Instead, dissatisfaction with co-workers might motivate you to ask for a transfer to another department or work team. In summary, there are many facets of job satisfaction that are associated with different aspects of the job and have different effects on employee behaviour.

If there are many types of job satisfaction, then what is an employee's overall job satisfaction? To some extent, the answer depends on the individual. Overall job satisfaction is a combination of the person's feelings toward the different job satisfaction facets. Satisfaction with the work itself is usually an important component of overall satisfaction, but this depends on how important job content is to the employee. Some people emphasize pay satisfaction when they think about their overall job satisfaction, whereas others might emphasize their physical working conditions.

A Model of Job Satisfaction   **Exhibit 8–4**

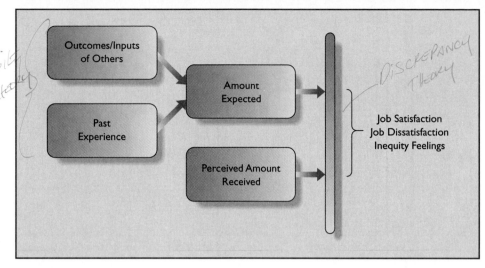

Source: Based on E. E. Lawler III, *Motivation in Work Organizations* (Monterey, Calif.: Brooks/Cole, 1973), p. 75.

A model of job satisfaction

What determines our level of job satisfaction? The best explanation is provided by a combination of **discrepancy theory** and **equity theory.**[18] Discrepancy theory states that the level of job satisfaction is determined by the discrepancy between what people expect to receive and what they experience.[19] As Exhibit 8–4 illustrates, job satisfaction or dissatisfaction results from a comparison of the amount the employee expects to receive and the perceived amount received. Job dissatisfaction occurs when the received condition is noticeably less than the expected condition. Job satisfaction improves as the person's expectations are met or exceeded (up to a point).

Equity theory is also built into Exhibit 8–4. Recall from Chapter 3 that equity occurs when the person and comparison other have similar outcome/input ratios. This is relevant to job satisfaction, because the amount we expect to receive is partly determined by our comparison with other people. For instance, the level of pay we expect to receive depends not only on how hard we work, but also on how hard other people work in this job compared to their level of pay.

Equity theory also explains why job satisfaction does not always continue to increase as the received condition exceeds expectations. As people receive much better outcomes than they expect, they typically develop feelings of guilt and a belief that management practices are unfair to others. At first, employees adjust their expectations upward when they are overrewarded. However, if the overreward is so large that it cannot be justified, then feelings of inequity persist and dissatisfaction with management practices may result.

In summary, discrepancy and equity theories predict that as reality meets and exceeds expectations, job satisfaction will increase. However, when the perceived job situation is so much better than expected that the overreward creates a feeling of guilt or unfairness, job satisfaction begins to decrease.

Discrepancy theory
A theory that partly explains job satisfaction and dissatisfaction in terms of the gap between what a person expects to receive and what is actually received.

Equity theory
A process theory of motivation that explains how people develop perceptions of fairness in the distribution and exchange of resources.

Exhibit 8–5   **Job Satisfaction in Canada**

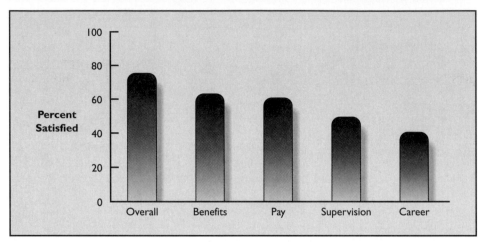

Source: Based on G. Brett, "Canadians Satisfied with Their Jobs, but Down on Bosses, Survey Finds," *Toronto Star,* September 19, 1991, pp. C1, C5.

Job satisfaction in Canada

According to one recent study, 75 percent of Canadians say they are generally satisfied with their jobs.[20] This is lower than in the mid-1980s, when the percentage of satisfied employees was above 80 percent.[21] Still, even the recent survey results suggest that most people are generally satisfied with their jobs.

The problem with these results is that the single direct question "How satisfied are you with your job?" tends to inflate estimates of general job satisfaction. Many dissatisfied employees are reluctant to reveal their feelings in a direct question because this is tantamount to admitting that they made a poor job choice and are not enjoying life. The threat to self-esteem is so great that many downplay the negative aspects of work or consciously report higher job satisfaction than they actually feel.[22]

The biasing effect of a single direct question becomes apparent when the same employees are asked whether they would choose the same kind of work if they could start all over. These surveys typically find that although most Canadians say they are reasonably happy with their jobs, almost half of them would choose another type of work if given the chance.[23] This contradiction further supports the idea that job satisfaction isn't quite as high as direct questions indicate.

Finally, surveys reporting that Canadians are *generally* satisfied with their jobs also indicate that they are less satisfied with *specific facets* of their jobs. Consider the results presented in Exhibit 8–5. Although 75 percent of Canadian employees claim to be happy with their jobs overall, only 41 percent are satisfied with career development and training and 50 percent are happy with their supervisors.

Job satisfaction and work behaviours

Job satisfaction is an important work attitude, not only because it indicates how well the company treats its employees, but also because it has been associated with a variety of important work behaviours. Some of the more prominent effects of job satisfaction are described below.

Turnover

Employees with higher levels of job satisfaction are less likely to quit their jobs.[24] However, recall that people react differently to job dissatisfaction based on their personal experiences. The satisfaction–turnover relationship is also influenced by the level of unemployment and the employee's perceived opportunity to find other employment. Specifically, dissatisfied employees tend to quit their jobs when other job opportunities exist.[25]

Absenteeism

Job dissatisfaction, particularly with the work itself, tends to be related to higher levels of absenteeism.[26] Of course, some absenteeism is due mainly to factors beyond the employee's control, such as an injury or blinding snowstorm. Yet even in these extreme events, dedicated employees have been known to battle the elements or leave their hospital beds to attend work. Others would be absent at the slight hint of rain or an oncoming head cold.[27]

Physical and mental health

Employees who are dissatisfied with their jobs are more likely to suffer mental and physical health problems.[28] Recent evidence particularly points to satisfaction with job content as a significant factor in an employee's general mental health. Others have reported that people with negative attitudes toward some aspects of their jobs may experience a loss of appetite, ulcers, difficulty in sleeping, and emotional breakdown.

Unionization and strikes

Joining a labour union and going on strike are usually associated with job dissatisfaction. However, not all forms of dissatisfaction lead to these behaviours.[29] For instance, people are more likely to go on strike because they dislike their level of pay or working conditions than if they dislike their co-workers. Nor do all dissatisfied employees choose strikes as their response to job dissatisfaction. As we explained earlier, there are several individual contingencies between a person's beliefs (e.g., management is unfair) and behaviour (going on strike). Some dissatisfied employees would rather quit than walk a picket line. Thus, the attitude–behaviour model presented earlier has important implications for managers and union leaders alike.

Deviant behaviours

Several illegal or marginal activities have been linked to job dissatisfaction. Alcoholism and drug abuse have been associated with job dissatisfaction, particularly among employees in monotonous jobs and who socialize with co-workers off the job. Dissatisfied employees have been known to deliberately sabotage company products and equipment in retaliation to management practices. In the United States, several dissatisfied employees have engaged in acts of violence against their supervisor or co-workers.[30]

A more frequent concern is that some dissatisfied employees steal from their employers, particularly to correct feelings of inequity.[31] For example, more than a dozen staff members of Canada's External Affairs department were

Perspective 8–1

No Pay-Off for Job Dissatisfaction

Kim Bertram resented the way he was treated by his employer, Canada Trust. He felt that Canada Trust scapegoated him for a mishap in the early 1980s, an incident that continued to strain his relationship with the trust company. Now he felt that his hard work as loans officer and second in command of the Don Mills branch was neither appreciated nor sufficiently rewarded.

Bertram was a workaholic who received an achievement award for bringing in over $1 million in new business to the once-sleepy Don Mills branch. He trained new staff on his own time and came in weekends to complete transactions, but the branch didn't have enough staff members to handle the volume of loans he was generating. In December 1987, Bertram received a letter from management saying that he would be fired if the operation didn't shape up. Moreover, his earlier promised pay raise was delayed as a result of the reprimand.

This situation might make many people justifiably dissatisfied with their jobs. Some might even harbour fantasies of vengeance. But Bertram, along with former Canada Trust employee Ken Wood (also disgruntled), took one step further by planning an elaborate scheme that would successfully embezzle $4.5 million of Canada Trust's funds. Bypassing Canada Trust's security system, they set up personal credit accounts using fraudulent names and started writing cheques on those accounts. Addresses of the imaginary clients were changed soon after the accounts were activated and most of the embezzled money was wired to a bank in Switzerland.

At one point Bertram and Wood were writing cheques totalling as much as $600,000 each day on phony accounts. The fraud generated such an impressive business record for the Don Mills branch that the branch manager gave Bertram and his loans department a half-day holiday in early May 1988. Ironically, Bertram's delayed pay increase finally came through, just as he and Wood were about to flee to Europe.

The scam lasted less than four months. In late May, one of Bertram's assistants noticed problems with paperwork on some of his accounts. Bertram and Wood quickly activated their prearranged escape plan by flying to Switzerland on the Victoria holiday weekend and removing their funds in cash from the Swiss bank before Canadian authorities could trace the money. The two travelled throughout Europe that summer on false American passports, but quickly grew weary of being fugitives from justice. On August 22, 1988, they were arrested in London after registering under their own names in a four-star hotel. Bertram and Wood waived their rights to the funds and did not contest extradition back to Canada. The two unhappy Canada Trust employees got back at their employer, but the price was several years in jail.

Source: S. Fife and J. Castrinos, "The Powerline Swindle," *Financial Times of Canada,* April 10, 1989, pp. 22–24.

recently caught filing bogus travel claims. Some experts explained these fraudulent activities by the fact that External Affairs employees are overworked and are suffering abysmal morale problems.[32] Perspective 8–1 provides a more extreme, but very real, example of how job dissatisfaction can lead to deviant behaviour in the workplace. If management had been more sensitive to employee attitudes in this situation, the costly outcomes and embarrassing publicity may have been avoided.

Job performance

Is a happy worker a productive worker? For many years, it seemed obvious that job performance increases when employees are more satisfied with their jobs. But quantitative studies have discovered that the relationship between job

Performance-to-Satisfaction Relationship   Exhibit 8–6

satisfaction and job performance is statistically quite low.[33] Organizational behaviour researchers have identified three reasons for this weak relationship.

One explanation, as we mentioned earlier in the chapter, is that employees often produce different intentions and behaviours from the same attitude. One person who feels unhappy about his or her job decides to put in less work effort, whereas the other maintains the same level of work effort while looking for employment elsewhere. As we noted earlier, these differences result from each person's unique values and experiences.[34]

A related argument is that employees with higher job satisfaction tend to engage in more **organizational citizenship behaviours** but not in higher levels of traditional job performance.[35] Job satisfaction has a weak association with job performance because only normal job duties are measured. Recall from Chapter 2 that organizational citizenship behaviours include working beyond required job duties, such as assisting others with their tasks and promoting a positive work environment. Satisfied employees might be more likely to help the company beyond their normal job duties because they feel a higher sense of obligation or reciprocity to the organization.

Finally, some writers argue that job performance leads to job satisfaction (rather than vice versa), but only when performance is linked to valued rewards. Higher performers receive more rewards and, consequently, are more satisfied than low-performing employees who receive fewer rewards. This idea is depicted in Exhibit 8–6. The connection between satisfaction and performance is weak because many organizations do not reward good performance.[36]

Organizational citizenship behaviours
Employee behaviours that extend beyond the usual job duties, including altruism, courtesy, sportsmanship, civic duty, and conscientiousness.

Organizational Commitment

During the mid-1800s, Samuel Cunard founded Cunard Lines, the greatest steamship line ever to cover the Atlantic ocean. The energetic Nova Scotian was able to make ship transportation dependable and safe, long before it was thought possible, by having the best ships, officers, and crew. He insisted on safety before profits and, by listening to his technical experts, was able to introduce the latest innovations. Above all, Cunard had the quaint notion that if you picked people well, paid them well, and treated them well, they would return the favour with loyalty and pride.[37]

Organizational commitment
A complex attitude pertaining to the strength of an individual's identification with and involvement in a particular organization; includes a strong belief in the organization's goals, as well as a motivation to work for and remain a member of the organization.

Nearly 150 years later, Samuel Cunard's assumptions about the benefits of **organizational commitment** have found strong support in organizational behaviour research. Organizational commitment is the strength of an individual's identification with and involvement in a particular organization.[38] This involves a strong belief in the organization's goals, a willingness to exert considerable effort on behalf of the organization, and a strong desire to remain a member of the organization.

Numerous studies have reported that loyal employees are less likely to quit their jobs, be absent from work, or show up late for work. Their willingness to exert greater effort for the organization translates into higher job performance if they have the necessary ability, role clarity, and situational contingencies. Employees with strong commitment to the organization are also more likely to engage in organizational citizenship behaviours.[39]

Negative consequences

Very high levels of organizational commitment may produce negative consequences.[40] One potential problem is that high commitment may reduce turnover to such a level that the organization stagnates. Another concern is that extreme commitment might reduce the individual's ability to accommodate family obligations and other nonwork roles.[41] Finally, highly dedicated individuals might engage in activities that benefit the organization but are illegal to society. For example, the president of a Montreal dredging company destroyed documents connected with a case that the RCMP was investigating. When asked why he had done this illegal act, the president replied: "For twenty-two years I put the company ahead of myself. I came second."[42]

The decline of organizational commitment

Given that moderately strong levels of loyalty improve organizational effectiveness, you would think that business leaders are interested in cultivating and maintaining this attitude. Some companies do take employee loyalty seriously. The Four Seasons Hotel carefully monitors this attitude through regular employee surveys. One of its hotels recently achieved an employee loyalty rating of 3.8 on the 4-point scale. A dedicated work force is also important at Sun Microsystems Canada Ltd. "The only way you grow is with committed employees," says a Sun Microsystems executive.[43]

© Graham Harrop. Used with permission.

But these companies may be exceptions. There is overwhelming evidence that organizational commitment has declined over the past couple of decades. One recent U.S. survey found that 86.7 percent of managers felt there was less loyalty between companies and their employees compared to five years earlier. The author of a recent book on loyalty says, "If you judge loyalty by the behavioural standards of 20 years ago, then it is all but dead in organizations today."[44] Another study indicates that Canadians have a much lower level of pride in their organizations than their American counterparts.[45] If corporate leaders in the United States are worried about declining organizational commitment, then Canadian leaders should perhaps be even more concerned!

Building organizational commitment

How do you build and maintain a dedicated work force? The simple answer is to practise better day-to-day management of employees. Most of the concepts and suggestions discussed in this book—from communication to organizational socialization—influence organizational commitment in some way. Some of the most important commitment-building practices are briefly described below.

Job security

Lay-off threats are frequently identified as one of the greatest blows to employee loyalty, even among those whose jobs are not immediately at risk.[46] Long-term, stable employment nurtures a sense of sharing and mutual dependence, showing employees that the organization is committed to them. They perceive employment as a relationship rather than a formal contractual exchange with the company. Employees believe their effort will be rewarded eventually and generally, not immediately and precisely as in a contractual transaction. This mutuality is undermined when the long-term relationship is threatened.[47] As Perspective 8–2 describes, Ontario Hydro will have difficulty rebuilding employee loyalty following its massive restructuring.

Trust

Trust means putting faith in the other party. It is a form of dependence that one gives voluntarily and comfortably. To build organizational commitment, executives and employees must develop trust in each other. This means monitoring employees less and giving them more flexibility in their work activities. Employees must believe that management's decisions are best for all concerned, but they must also believe that management trusts them. In other words, employees learn to trust the company when senior management shows that it trusts employees.[48] "You don't expect employee loyalty. You have to earn employee loyalty," says Mac Cosburn from the Markham, Ontario, engineering firm of Cosburn Patterson Wardman Ltd.[49]

Few companies demonstrate this trust more than Quad/Graphics. Once a year, the company's 400 managers and supervisors depart for a two-day spring retreat, leaving the printing plants entirely in the hands of production and office staff members. No manager sets foot in the plant unless an employee calls for emergency help. (No manager has ever been called in.) By bestowing trust, the company is saying that the employees are a vital part of the business.[50]

Perspective 8–2

Ontario Hydro Reorganization Threatens Employee Loyalty

Martin Scheller organized scores of going-away parties for colleagues who were part of Ontario Hydro's recent mass exodus of employees. Now Scheller has received his own "surplus notice," so he must find another job within Hydro that would match his 16 years of mechanical drafting experience.

Ontario Hydro has launched one of the most dramatic reorganizations in Canadian history to stem its huge financial losses over the past couple of years. Through generous buyouts or early retirement packages, the utility cleared out nearly 7,000 employees within a few months. The 22,000 people who chose to stay faced the unsettling experience of having to reapply for their own position—if it still existed—and compete with co-workers to get it back.

"People feel incredibly beaten up by the process of having to reapply for their jobs when there was no indication they were doing badly," says a senior manager. "You see people in their offices and you can tell all they are doing is waiting for the phone to ring. . . . It's killing people's self-esteem. Productivity is in the dumpers."

But productivity and self-esteem are not the only things suffering through Ontario Hydro's reorganization.

Employees who once had a strong sense of commitment to the Crown corporation are now feeling lost and betrayed.

Dane MacCarthy, Ontario Hydro's Vice-President of Human Resources, acknowledges that employee loyalty is at risk. "The psychological contract for many Hydro employees was: 'I will give you loyalty and you will give me security.' But that security and loyalty thing, in terms of the economic situation we are in, is no longer a viable contract." MacCarthy, who survived his own job security threat, believes that the new employment relationship will offer employees "lots of challenge and some exciting things to do," but without any guarantees of a long-lasting relationship.

Ontario Hydro employees may need a lot of healing time before they feel loyal again. In addition to watching co-workers leave and feeling the uncertainty of their own future, many still harbour the resentment of losing their jobs to others. Martin Scheller sums up the situation with a good-natured laugh: "When you have a job and you know somebody else is going to be taking it, you feel good for them—but 'to hell with them,' too!"

Sources: Based on V. Galt, "Musical Chairs a Crying Game," *Globe & Mail,* November 13, 1993, pp. B1, B2; and M. Gibb-Clark, "High-Voltage Pain at Hydro," *Globe & Mail,* July 14, 1993, pp. B1, B12.

Employee involvement

Employee involvement increases organizational commitment in two ways. First, delegating authority and responsibility to people is a demonstration of management's trust in its employees and, as mentioned above, loyalty increases with the level of mutual trust. Second, employees feel that they are part of the organization when they make decisions that guide the organization's future.[51] Through participation, employees begin to see how the organization is a reflection of their decisions. Edson Packaging Machinery Ltd. in Hamilton, Ontario, follows this strategy by having its 63 employees involved in strategic planning and major purchasing decisions. "We felt our people could do a lot more than we were allowing them to do," explains Edson's president. "You lose some predictability, but you gain a work force in which people feel part of the organization."[52]

Organizational comprehension

Commitment is stronger when employees "understand" the company. Employees make better sense of their organization when they are regularly informed about organizational activities and learn firsthand about other parts of the company. At Finning Tractor Ltd.'s Vancouver headquarters, secretaries have an opportunity to ride Caterpillar tractors to better understand the product their company sells and services. British Airways has introduced a similar program, called "Day in the Life," that introduces employees to other parts of the company they would not normally see.[53] As employees develop a fuller comprehension of their company, they are also more likely to develop a stronger sense of loyalty to it.

Social bonding

Employees tend to be more strongly attached to organizations when they form positive relationships with co-workers, particularly when work team norms are consistent with organizational goals. In other words, people who interact with others in the organization are more likely to feel loyal to the organization.[54] Companies encourage social bonding by creating more team-based work activities and reward systems, and by keeping work units small.

Continuance commitment

Our discussion has addressed only one form of organizational commitment, known as *attitudinal commitment*. Another form, called **continuance commitment,** exists when employees have an instrumental reason for continuing the employment relationship. Whereas attitudinal commitment causes employees to remain because of their psychological attachment, continuance commitment causes them to remain because of their financial or other instrumental attachment. For example, you may have met people who do not particularly enjoy working for a company but feel bound to remain there because it would be too costly to quit.[55]

Continuance commitment
An individual's willingness to remain with an organization for purely instrumental (e.g., financial) rather than emotional reasons.

Many organizations rely on continuance commitment strategies to increase job performance and minimize turnover. For example, some bank employees receive low-interest loans, but these "golden handcuffs" tie them financially to the organization.[56] Recent studies have found that employees with high levels of continuance commitment have *lower* performance ratings and are *less* likely to engage in organizational citizenship behaviours![57] The message is increasingly clear: Employers build an effective work force by winning employees' hearts (attitudinal commitment) rather than tying them financially to the organization (continuance commitment).

Work-Related Values

Values represent stable, long-lasting beliefs about what is important. They define what is right or wrong, or good or bad, in the world.[58] Some people value practicality, whereas others value the aesthetic. Some people value frugality, whereas others value generosity. Values differ from attitudes. Values are generalized conceptions of the world, whereas attitudes are directed toward specific objects, events, or people. Of course, values influence our attitudes toward those attitude objects.

Values
Stable, long-lasting beliefs about what is important to the individual.

Values are regaining the attention of managers and organizational behaviour scholars.[59] One reason for this interest is that values influence our decisions and actions. They also lay the foundation for our interpretation of what is ethical. In this respect, values are important when sorting out the actions of corporate stakeholders. A frequently cited example in the news is the ongoing conflicts between environmentalists and business leaders. Environmentalists, who value preservation of nature more than economic well-being, will view many companies as unethical. Meanwhile, corporate leaders question the ethical standards of environmentalists who spike trees and boycott customers.

Values are also important when hiring people and placing them into specific jobs. Toyota, Four Seasons Hotels, and other companies consider each job applicant's work values before making a selection decision. These companies believe that although people can learn specific skills, it is very difficult to change their values to match organizational expectations.[60] Career counsellors know that personal values are important in matching people to jobs. Some vocational interest inventories examine several work values—altruism, esthetics, security, and so on—so that people are directed toward jobs and careers that are most compatible with those values.[61]

Cultural differences in values

Another reason for the increasing interest in work-oriented values is that we need to be aware of value differences across cultures. Consider the following example. Oki Poki Designs Inc., a Montreal manufacturer of children's clothes, missed an entire shipment of spring clothes from its Mexican subcontractor. When the Montreal office called the Mexican company, they were told, "*No problema, no problema,* we'll put them on the next plane." When the shipment still didn't arrive, the Montreal office called again, only to learn that the subcontractor's owner was out of town. "We have had a very bad experience with the mentality of the people," says Oki Poki's owner, referring to his Mexican business associates. "They don't respect what they say or write."[62]

Tensions between Oki Poki and the Mexican subcontractor likely occurred because the two cultures value time differently. Time is less precise to many people in Latin America. It isn't unusual for Latin Americans to arrive half an hour late for a meeting. This contrasts with Germany, where temporal precision is highly valued. A second explanation for this conflict is that many Mexicans place a high value on saving face. In this incident, saving face meant avoiding acknowledging that production was late.

We need to understand these cultural differences in values to avoid unnecessary conflicts and subtle tensions between people from different countries. This is particularly true when a company opens operations in another culture, as we can see in Perspective 8–3.

Scholars have described over 100 personal values.[63] However, four have attracted the most attention in cross-cultural research.[64]

- *Individualism–collectivism*—The degree to which people value a loose-knit social framework in which they take care of themselves and family (individualism) or prefer a tightly knit social framework in which they depend on the clan or group in exchange for loyalty (collectivism).

- *Power distance*—The degree to which people value an unequal distribution of power (high) or a relatively equal distribution of power (low).

Perspective 8–3

Valuing Employee Cultural Values at Westin Kauai

Jim Treadway, general manager of the Westin Kauai Resort Hotel, told employees at a special meeting that the hotel was generally running smoothly, but he sensed that something was amiss. Employee morale was low and there was subtle tension between local residents and hotel management.

"I don't think what we're doing is working," said Treadway, referring to the "share the fantasy" theme that the hotel adopted when it opened during the late 1980s. Share the fantasy is based on Walt Disney customer service ideas. It includes training employees to think that the hotel is a stage and that they are performers acting out scripts. They wear formal hotel costumes with name tags bearing English titles rather than their traditional Hawaiian names.

But many aspects of the share the fantasy theme conflicted with the values held by most employees and the people of Kauai, who value free expression of their kindness and have deep respect for their heritage. When Treadway realized this, he hired George Kanahele, a management consultant and authority on Hawaiian culture, to help "Hawaiianize" the hotel.

Westin Kauai employees completed a survey about their personal values, along with the values they wanted the hotel to uphold. A volunteer committee distilled the results into a "management by values" mission statement that was later accepted by employees and unveiled in a special ceremony. Soon after, symbolic burials were held for signs and other evidence of the hotel's original Disneyesque theme.

Westin Kauai employees now wear flowing Hawaiian garb and use their own Hawaiian names. Hawaiian music permeates the hotel. A *halau* (school) offers employees and their families courses in Hawaiian language and culture. Guests see demonstrations of Hawaiian culture and crafts, and are encouraged to experience it outside the resort. Anyone can refer to the management by values statement as a guide when problems arise. Employees and managers are expected to dedicate themselves to *kakela* (excellence) and to treat each other "with fairness and respect."

By addressing the conflict with Hawaiian values, Westin Kauai hotel now has fewer grievances, higher job satisfaction, and lower turnover. Employees are much more comfortable interacting with guests. Most notably, says Westin Kauai's general manager, is that the hotel has gained "a comfortable sense of place, a stronger identity with Kauai and its people, and family-like atmosphere."

Source: Adapted from K. Seal, "Westin Kauai Values Values," *Hotel and Motel Management*, April 9, 1991, pp. 2, 68, 82.

- *Uncertainty avoidance*—The degree to which people tolerate ambiguity (low uncertainty avoidance) or feel threatened by ambiguity and uncertainty (high uncertainty avoidance).

- *Masculinity–femininity*—The degree to which people value goals and materialism (masculine) or relationships and the well-being of others (feminine).

Exhibit 8–7 shows how Canadian societal values compare to other cultures on these four dimensions. This information must be treated with some caution because it is based on a worldwide survey of employees at IBM. The values of people employed at IBM may not exactly correspond to the larger societal values, so these results may be somewhat distorted.

Our discussion has focussed on value differences among people from different countries, yet we must remember that there are several cultures *within* Canada. Cultural differences (and tensions) have existed among English, French, and aboriginal people in Canada for a few centuries. Studies have found that anglophone Canadians tend to place greater value on autonomy and

Exhibit 8–7   **Cultural Differences in Values**

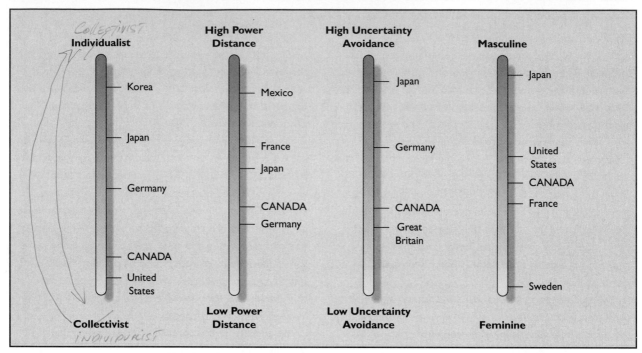

Note: Ratings are from IBM employees in these countries. Germany refers only to the former West Germany.
Source: Based on G. Hofstede, "The Cultural Relativity of Organizational Practices and Theories," *Journal of International Business Studies* 14 (Fall 1983), pp. 75–89.

achievement, whereas francophone Canadians place more emphasis on job security and status.

Cultural values in aboriginal organizations

Although there are several aboriginal cultures in Canada—such as Salish in British Columbia and Iroquois in Central Canada—they seem to be similar in terms of the four values described above. Specifically, most Native organizations have a strong collectivist value, low power distance, low uncertainty avoidance, and a relatively feminine value orientation.[65] The strong collectivist orientation is based on traditional Native ideals regarding survival of the small group. There is a strong expectation that organizational members will work toward the group's interests rather than their own.

The low power distance in aboriginal organizations is apparent by the preference for consensus-oriented decision making and selection of people based on their expertise rather than position. People in aboriginal organizations seem to have a lower uncertainty avoidance value than those in nonaboriginal Canadian companies. This is apparent by the lack of formal rules and procedures in aboriginal companies and the preference for internalized beliefs about respect, sharing, and wholeness to guide employee behaviour. Finally, there is evidence that Native firms adopt a relatively feminine value orientation. This is manifested by the emphasis on the well-being of co-workers and maintenance of positive relationships. There is decidedly less emphasis on material gain and goal accomplishment compared to non-Native organizations.

Chapter Summary

- Attitudes are relatively enduring emotional tendencies to respond consistently toward an attitude object. The three components of attitudes are beliefs, feelings, and intentions. The linkages between beliefs and behaviour are moderated by several factors, thereby weakening the relationship between attitudes and behaviour.

- We need to understand the dynamics of work attitudes, because many are early warning signals for future behaviour problems, they are an expression of an employee's self-identity, they indicate the organization's ethical treatment of employees, and most jobs require employees to either display or withhold evidence of their attitudes.

- Cognitive dissonance is an uncomfortable tension that motivates people to change their attitudes to be more consistent with past behaviours.

- Job satisfaction represents a person's emotional reaction toward various aspects of work. People tend to feel satisfied when their work expectations are realized but are not so excessive that they feel inequity. Job dissatisfaction tends to increase turnover, absenteeism, physical or mental ailments, militancy, and deviant behaviours. Satisfaction has a weak association with traditional measures of job performance.

- Organizational commitment is the strength of an individual's identification with and involvement in a particular organization. It tends to reduce turnover and absenteeism and improve job performance. Loyalty increases with job security, trust, employee involvement, organizational comprehension, and social bonding. Continuance commitment refers to an individual's commitment to remain with an organization for purely instrumental (e.g., economic) reasons.

- Values represent stable, long-lasting beliefs about what is important to us. They influence our decisions and interpretation of what is ethical. There are several cultural differences in values that may lead to conflicts and tensions unless we are aware of these differences

Discussion Questions

1. **Describe four reasons why attitudes are important in organizations.**
2. **Two students have employment interviews with two accounting firms. Both understand that firm A pays top dollar for new hires but tends to burn employees out quickly. Firm B has lower starting salaries but doesn't push**

its employees quite as hard. Use your knowledge of the belief-to-behaviour linkage to explain why these two students might end up working for different accounting firms even though they have the same beliefs.

3. Explain how an employee's attitudes might be affected by cognitive dissonance.

4. Discuss the accuracy of the statement: "Pay satisfaction increases with the size of the employee's paycheque."

5. The latest employee attitude survey in your organization indicates that employees are unhappy with some aspects of the organization. However, management tends to pay attention to the single-item question asking employees to indicate their overall satisfaction with the job. The results of this item indicate that 86 percent of staff members are very or somewhat satisfied, so management concludes that the other results refer to issues that are probably not important to employees. Explain why management's interpretation of these results may be inaccurate.

6. How does continuance commitment differ from attitudinal commitment?

7. Give two reasons why employee involvement tends to increase organizational commitment.

8. Your company is beginning to expand operations in Japan and wants you to form working relationships with Japanese suppliers. Considering only the values of individualism and uncertainty avoidance, what should you be aware of or sensitive to in your dealings with these suppliers? You may assume that your contacts hold typical Japanese values along these dimensions.

Notes

1. R. Dal Monte, "Progress Is Brewing," *Tri-City News* (Vancouver), April 5, 1992, pp. B1, B3.

2. P. Zimbardo and E. B. Ebbeson, *Influencing Attitudes and Changing Behavior* (Reading, Mass.: Addison-Wesley, 1969), p. 6; M. Fishbein and I. Ajzen, *Belief, Attitude, Intention, and Behavior* (Reading, Mass.: Addison-Wesley, 1975), p. 131; and C. C. Pinder, *Work Motivation: Theory, Issues, and Applications* (Glenview, Ill.: Scott, Foresman & Co., 1984), p. 82.

3. T. Newton, and T. Keenan, "Further Analyses of the Dispositional Argument in Organizational Behavior," *Journal of Applied Psychology* 76 (1991), pp. 781–87; R. D. Arvey, T. J. Bouchard, N. L. Segal, and J. M. Abraham, "Job Satisfaction: Environmental and Genetic Components," *Journal of Applied Psychology* 74 (1989), pp. 187–92; and B. M. Staw and J. Ross, "Stability in the Midst of Change: A Dispositional Approach to Job Attitudes," *Journal of Applied Psychology* 70 (1985), pp. 469–80.

4. U. E. Gattiker, and T. W. Nelligan, "Computerized Offices in Canada and the United States: Investigating Dispositional Similarities and Differences," *Journal of Organizational Behaviour* 9 (1988), pp. 77–96; and A. Davis-Blake and J. Pfeffer, "Just a Mirage: The Search for Dispositional Effects in Organizational Research," *Academy of Management Review* 14 (1989), pp. 385–400.

5. G. Salancik and J. Pfeffer, "A Social Information Processing Approach to Job Attitudes and Task Design," *Administrative Science Quarterly* 23 (1978), pp. 224–53; and S. E. White and T. R. Mitchell, "Job Enrichment versus Social Cues: A Comparison and Competitive Test," *Journal of Applied Psychology* 64 (1979), pp. 1–9.

6. D. Katz, "The Functional Approach to the Study of Attitudes," *Public Opinion Quarterly* 24 (1960), pp. 163–76; and P. C. Smith, L. M. Kendall, and C. L. Hulin, *The Measurement of Satisfaction in Work and Retirement* (Chicago: Rand McNally, 1969).

7. S. Cameron, "Low Morale May Not Be the Worst of It for the Federal Public Service," *Globe & Mail*, May 18, 1989, p. A2; and C. Kent, "How Low Can It Go?" *Ottawa Business Life*, April 1989, pp. 22–26, 40.

8. B. E. Ashforth and R. H. Humphrey, "Emotional Labor in Service Roles: The Influence of Identity," *Academy of Management Review* 18 (1993), pp. 88–115.

9. Katz, "The Functional Approach to the Study of Attitudes," p. 169.

10. W. F. Cascio, *Costing Human Resources: The Financial Impact of Behavior in Organizations*, 3rd ed. (Boston: PWS-Kent Pub. Co., 1991).

11. J. E. Mathieu, D. A. Hofmann, and J. L. Farr, "Job Perception–Job Satisfaction Relations: An Empirical Comparison of Three Competing Theories," *Organizational Behavior & Human Decision Processes* 56 (1993), pp. 370–87.

12. P. H. Prestholdt, I. M. Lane, and R. C. Mathews, "Nurse Turnover as Reasoned Action: Development of a Process Model," *Journal of Applied Psychology* 72 (1987), pp. 221–27.

13. M. J. Withey and W. H. Cooper, "Predicting Exit, Voice, Loyalty, and Neglect," *Administrative Science Quarterly* 34 (1989), pp. 521–39; and L. E. Parker, "When to Fix It and When to Leave: Relationships Among Perceived Control, Self-Efficacy, Dissent, and Exit," *Journal of Applied Psychology* 78 (1993), pp. 949–59.

14. Pinder, *Work Motivation*, pp. 88–89; and C. D. Fisher, "On the Dubious Wisdom of Expecting Job Satisfaction to Correlate with Performance," *Academy of Management Review* 5 (1980), pp. 607–12.

15. L. Festinger, *A Theory of Cognitive Dissonance* (Evanston, Ill.: Row, Peterson, 1957); and G. R. Salancik, "Commitment and the Control of Organizational Behavior and Belief," in *New Directions in Organizational Behavior*, ed. B. M. Staw and G. R. Salancik (Chicago: St. Clair, 1977), pp. 1–54.

16. P. C. Smith, "In Pursuit of Happiness: Why Study General Job Satisfaction?" in *Job Satisfaction*, ed. C. J. Cranny, P. C. Smith, and E. F. Stone (New York: Lexington, 1992), pp. 5–19; and M. Tait, M. Y. Padgett, and T. T. Baldwin, "Job and Life Satisfaction: A Reevaluation of the Strength of the Relationship and Gender Effects as a Function of Date of the Study," *Journal of Applied Psychology* 74 (1989), pp. 502–7.

17. E. A. Locke, "The Nature and Causes of Job Satisfaction," in *Handbook of Industrial and Organizational Psychology*, ed. M. Dunnette (Chicago: Rand McNally, 1976), pp. 1297–1350.

18. E. E. Lawler III, *Motivation in Work Organizations* (Belmont, Calif.: Wadsworth, 1973), pp. 66–69, 74–77.

19. D. B. McFarlin and R. W. Rice, "The Role of Facet Importance as a Moderator in Job Satisfaction Processes," *Journal of Organizational Behavior* 13 (1992), pp. 41–54.

20. G. Brett, "Canadians Satisfied with Their Jobs, but Down on Bosses, Survey Finds," *Toronto Star*, September 19, 1991, pp. C1, C5; and G. Brett, "Forget Japan—Canadians Happier at Their Jobs," *Toronto Star*, November 1, 1991, p. B1.

21. R. Maynard, "How Do You Like Your Job?" *Report on Business Magazine*, November 1987, pp. 112–25. A 1992 Steelcase study also reported a drop in the percentage of "very satisfied" Canadian employees to 39 percent from 45 percent two years earlier.

22. R. L. Kahn, "The Meaning of Work: Interpretations and Proposals for Measurement," in *The Human Meaning of Social Change*, ed. A. A. Campbell and P. E. Converse (New York: Basic Books, 1972).

23. Maynard, "How Do You Like Your Job?" p. 115.

24. R. P. Tett and J. P. Meyer, "Job Satisfaction, Organizational Commitment, Turnover Intention, and Turnover: Path Analyses Based on Meta-Analytical Findings," *Personnel Psychology* 46 (1993), pp. 259–93; and H. J. Arnold and D. C. Feldman, "A Multivariate Analysis of the Determinants of Job Turnover," *Journal of Applied Psychology* 67 (1982), pp. 350–60.

25. J. N. Carsten and P. E. Spector, "Unemployment, Job Satisfaction, and Employee Turnover: A Meta-Analytic Test of the Muchinsky Model," *Journal of Applied Psychology* 72 (1987), pp. 374–81; and S. L. McShane, "Perceived Employment Opportunities as a Moderator in the Turnover Decision Process: A Conceptual and Empirical Re-assessment," *Proceedings of the Annual ASAC Conference, Organizational Behaviour Division* 7, pt. 5 (1986), pp. 136–47.

26. R. D. Hackett, "Work Attitudes and Employee Absenteeism: A Synthesis of the Literature," *Journal of Occupational Psychology* 62 (1989), pp. 235–48; and S. L. McShane, "Job Satisfaction and Absenteeism: A Meta-Analytic Re-examination," *Canadian Journal of Administrative Sciences* 1 (1984), pp. 61–77.

27. D. F. Coleman and N. V. Schaefer, "Weather and Absenteeism," *Canadian Journal of Administrative Sciences* 7 (1990), pp. 35–42; G. Johns and N. Nicholson, "The Meanings of Absence: New Strategies for Theory and Research," *Research in Organizational Behavior* 4 (1982), pp. 127–72; and R. R. Haccoun and S. Dupont, "Absence Research: A Critique of Previous Approaches and an Example for a New Direction," *Canadian Journal of Administrative Sciences* 4 (1987), pp. 143–56.

28. E. K. Kelloway and J. Barling, "Job Characteristics, Role Stress and Mental Health," *Journal of Occupational Psychology* 64 (1991), pp. 291–304; and M. Jamal and V. F. Mitchell, "Work, Nonwork, and Mental Health: A Model and a Test," *Industrial Relations* 18 (1980), pp. 88–93.

29. S. D. Bluen, "The Psychology of Strikes," *International Review of Industrial and Organizational Psychology* 9 (1994), pp. 113–45; J. Barling, C. Fullagar, K. Kelloway, and K. McElvie, "Union Loyalty and Strike Propensity," *Journal of Social Psychology* 132 (1992), pp. 581–90; I. Ng, "Predictors of Strike Voting Behaviour: The Case of University Faculty," *Journal of Labor Research* 12 (1991), pp. 121–34; and S. L. McShane, "Sources of Attitudinal Union Militancy," *Relations Industrielles* 40 (1985), pp. 284–302.

30. P. Y. Chen and P. E. Spector, "Relationships of Work Stressors with Aggression, Withdrawal, Theft and Substance Use: An Exploratory Study," *Journal of Occupational & Organizational Psychology* 65 (1992), pp. 177–84; and R. C.

Hollinger, "Working Under the Influence (WUI): Correlates of Employees' Use of Alcohol and Other Drugs," *Journal of Applied Behavioral Science* 24 (1988), pp. 439–54.

31. J. Greenberg, "Employee Theft as a Reaction to Underpayment Inequity: The Hidden Cost of Pay Cuts," *Journal of Applied Psychology* 75 (1990), pp. 561–68; and R. C. Hollinger and J. P. Clark, *Theft by Employees* (Lexington, Mass.: D.C. Heath, 1983).

32. G. Allen, "Issues of Trust," *Maclean's,* November 23, 1992, pp. 16–18.

33. M. T. Iaffaldano and P. M. Muchinsky, "Job Satisfaction and Job Performance: A Meta-Analysis," *Psychological Bulletin* 97 (1985), pp. 251–73; M. M. Petty, G. W. McGee, and J. W. Cavender, "A Meta-Analysis of the Relationship Between Individual Job Satisfaction and Individual Performance," *Academy of Management Review* 9 (1984), pp. 712–21; and D. P. Schwab and L. L. Cummings, "Theories of Performance and Satisfaction: A Review," *Industrial Relations* 9 (1970), pp. 408–30.

34. B. M. Staw and S. G. Barsade, "Affect and Managerial Performance: A Test of the Sadder-but-Wiser vs. Happier-and-Smarter Hypotheses," *Administrative Science Quarterly* 38 (1993), pp. 304–31.

35. C. D. Fisher and E. A. Locke, "The New Look in Job Satisfaction Research and Theory," in *Job Satisfaction,* ed. Cranny et al., pp. 165–94; D. W. Organ, "The Motivational Basis of Organizational Citizenship Behavior," *Research in Organizational Behavior* 12 (1990), pp. 43–72; and P. M. Podsakoff, S. B. MacKenzie, and C. Hui, "Organizational Citizenship Behaviors and Managerial Evaluations of Employee Performance: A Review and Suggestions for Future Research," *Research in Personnel and Human Resources Management* 11 (1993), pp. 1–40.

36. E. E. Lawler III and L. W. Porter, "The Effect of Performance on Job Satisfaction," *Industrial Relations* 7 (1967), pp. 20–28.

37. S. Franklin, *The Heroes: A Saga of Canadian Inspiration* (Toronto: McClelland & Stewart, 1967), pp. 53–59.

38. R. T. Mowday, L. W. Porter, and R. M. Steers, *Employee Organization Linkages: The Psychology of Commitment, Absenteeism, and Turnover* (New York: Academic Press, 1982).

39. R. Karambayya, "Good Organizational Citizens Do Make a Difference," *Proceedings of the Annual ASAC Conference, Organizational Behaviour Division* 11, pt. 5 (1990), pp. 110–19; and J. P. Meyer, S. V. Paunonen, I. R. Gellatly, R. D. Goffin, and D. N. Jackson, "Organizational Commitment and Job Performance: It's the Nature of the Commitment That Counts," *Journal of Applied Psychology* 74 (1989), pp. 152–56.

40. Pinder, *Work Motivation,* pp. 105–7.

41. D. M. Randall, "Commitment and the Organization: The Organization Man Revisited," *Academy of Management Review* 12 (1987), pp. 460–71. For a contrary view, see B. S. Romzek, "Personal Consequences of Employee Commitment," *Academy of Management Journal* 32 (1989), pp. 649–61.

42. P. C. Newman, *The Canadian Establishment* (Toronto: McClelland & Stewart, 1975), p. 183.

43. D. MacArthur, "Springtime: Four Seasons Growth Goes Global," *Globe & Mail,* May 18, 1991, p. F6; and S. Haggett, "Motivating Employees a Leader's Greatest Challenge," *Financial Post,* May 8, 1993, p. 23.

44. P. Houston, "The Smartest Ways to Build Loyalty," *Working Woman* 17 (April 1992), pp. 72–74, 100, 101; and S. J. Modic, "Is Anyone Loyal Anymore?" *Industry Week,* September 7, 1987, pp. 75–82.

45. R. J. Grey and G. C. Johnson, "Trends in Employee Attitudes: Differences Between Canadian and American Workers," *Canadian Business Review* 15 (Winter 1988), pp. 24–27.

46. D. M. Noer, *Healing the Wounds* (San Francisco: Jossey-Bass, 1993); and S. Ashford, C. Lee, and P. Bobko, "Content, Causes, and Consequences of Job Insecurity: A Theory-Based Measure and Substantive Test," *Academy of Management Journal* 32 (1989), pp. 803–29.

47. L. M. Shore and S. J. Wayne, "Commitment and Employee Behavior: Comparison of Affective Commitment and Continuance Commitment with Perceived Organizational Support," *Journal of Applied Psychology* 78 (1993), pp. 774–80; D. M. Rousseau and J. M. Parks, "The Contracts of Individuals and Organizations," *Research in Organizational Behavior* 15 (1993), pp. 1–43; and D. J. Koys, "Human Resource Management and a Culture of Respect: Effects on Employees' Organizational Commitment," *Employee Responsibilities and Rights Journal* 1 (1988), pp. 57–68.

48. B. S. Frey, "Does Monitoring Increase Work Effort? The Rivalry with Trust and Loyalty," *Economic Inquiry* 31 (1993), pp. 663–70; J. M. Kouzes and B. Z. Posner, *The Leadership Challenge* (San Francisco: Jossey-Bass, 1987), pp. 146–52; P. Martin and J. Nicholls, *Creating a Committed Work Force* (London: Institute of Personnel Management, 1987), Chapter 7; and J. K. Butler, Jr., "Toward Understanding and Measuring Conditions of Trust: Evolution of a Conditions of Trust Inventory," *Journal of Management* 17 (1991), pp. 643–63.

49. J. Southerst, "The Winning Way," *Profit* 9 (November 1990), pp. 29–33.

50. R. Levering, "Can Companies Trust Their Employees?" *Business and Society Review* 81 (Spring 1992), pp. 8–12.

51. V. V. Baba and R. Knoop, "Organizational Commitment and Independence Among Canadian Managers," *Relations Industrielles* 42 (1987), pp. 325–44; and W. L. Weber, J. J. Marshall, and G. H. Haines, "Modelling Commitment and Its Antecedents: An Empirical Study," *Canadian Journal of Administrative Sciences* 6 (1989), pp. 12–23.

52. "Hamilton Firm Tries Giving Power to the Workers," *Toronto Star,* April 6, 1992, p. D1.

53. J. Aspery, "British Companies Meet the Challenge of Change," *IABC Communication World* 7 (December 1990), pp. 39–41.

54. B. Ashforth and F. Mael, "Social Identity Theory and the Organization," *Academy of Management Review* 14 (1989), pp. 20–39.

55. R. D. Hackett, P. Bycio, and P. A. Hausdorf, "Further Assessments of Meyer and Allen's (1991) Three-Component Model of Organizational Commitment," *Journal of Applied Psychology* 79 (1994), pp. 15–23; and M. Withey, "Antecedents of Value Based and Economic Organizational Commitment," *Proceedings of the Annual ASAC Conference, Organizational Behaviour Division* 9, pt. 5 (1988), pp. 124–33.

56. R. McQueen, *The Money-Spinners* (Toronto: Totem, 1983), p. 11.

57. Meyer et al., "Organizational Commitment and Job Performance: It's the Nature of the Commitment That Counts;" and Shore and Wayne, "Commitment and Employee Behavior."

58. W. H. Schmidt and B. Z. Posner, *Managerial Values in Perspective* (New York: American Management Association, 1983); and B. Z. Posner and J. M. Munson, "The Importance of Values in Understanding Organizational Behavior," *Human Resource Management* 18 (1979), pp. 9–14.

59. P. McDonald and J. Gandz, "Getting Value from Values," *Organization Dynamics,* Winter 1992, pp. 64–77.

60. G. Dessler, "Value-Based Hiring Builds Commitment," *Personnel Journal* 72 (November 1993), pp. 98–102.

61. D. E. Super, *Work Values Inventory* (New York: Houghton Mifflin, 1970); and J. L. Holland, *Making Vocational Choices: A Theory of Careers* (Englewood Cliffs, N.J.: Prentice Hall, 1973).

62. S. Day, "Mexico's Business Bottlenecks," *Financial Times of Canada,* May 8–14, 1993, p. 7.

63. M. Rokeach, *The Nature of Human Values* (New York: The Free Press, 1973); and F. Kluckhorn and F. L. Strodtbeck, *Variations in Value Orientations* (Evanston, Ill.: Row, Peterson, 1961).

64. G. Hofstede, *Culture's Consequences: International Differences in Work-Related Values* (Beverly Hills, Calif.: Sage, 1980). For a comparison of English Canadian students with their counterparts from France, see S. A. Ahmed and J. Jabes, "A Comparative Study of Job Values of Business Students in France and English Canada," *Canadian Journal of Administrative Sciences* 5 (June 1988), pp. 51–59.

65. L. Redpath and M. O. Nielson, "Crossing the Cultural Divide Between Traditional Native Values and Non-Native Management Ideology," *Proceedings of the Annual ASAC Conference, Organizational Theory Division* 15(12) (1994), pp. 70–79; I. Chapman, D. McCaskill, and D. Newhouse, *Management in Contemporary Aboriginal Organizations* (Peterborough, Ont.: Trent University, 1992), Administrative Studies Working Paper Series #92-04; and H. C. Jain, J. Normand, and R. N. Kanungo, "Job Motivation of Canadian Anglophone and Francophone Hospital Employees," *Canadian Journal of Behavioural Science* 11 (1979), pp. 160–63.

Chapter Case

*Rough Seas on the LINK650**

Professor Suzanne Baxter was preparing for her first class of the semester when Shaun O'Neill knocked lightly on the open door and announced himself: "Hi, Professor, I don't suppose you remember me?" Professor Baxter had large classes, but she did remember that Shaun was a student in her organizational behaviour class two years earlier. Shaun had decided to work in the oil industry for a couple of years before returning to school to complete his diploma.

"Welcome back!" Baxter said as she beckoned him into the office. "I heard you were on a Hibernia oil rig. How was it?"

"Well, Professor," Shaun began, "I had worked two summers in Alberta's oil fields, so I hoped to get a job on the LINK650, the new CanOil drilling rig that arrived with so much fanfare in St. John's two years ago. The LINK650 was built by LINK, Inc., in Dallas, Texas. A standard practice in this industry is for the rig manufacturer to manage its day-to-day operations, so employees on the LINK650 are managed completely by LINK managers with no involvement from CanOil. No one has forgotten the Ocean Ranger tragedy, but drilling rig jobs pay well and offer generous time off. The newspaper said that nearly one thousand people lined up to complete job applications for the 50 nontechnical positions. I was lucky enough to get one of those jobs.

"Everyone hired on the LINK650 was enthusiastic and proud. We were one of the chosen few and were really pumped up about working on a new rig that had received so much media attention. I was quite impressed—so were several other hires—with the recruiters because they really seemed to be concerned about our welfare out at sea. I later discovered that the recruiters came from a consulting firm that specializes in hiring people. Come to think of it, we didn't meet a single LINK manager during that process. Maybe things would have been different if some of those LINK supervisors had interviewed us.

"Working on LINK650 was a real shock, even though most of us had some experience working along the Newfoundland coast. I'd say that none of the 50 nontechnical people hired in St. John's was quite prepared for the brutal jobs on the oil rig. We did the dirtiest jobs in the biting cold winds of the North Atlantic. Still, during the first few months most of us wanted to show the company that we were dedicated to getting the job done. A couple of the new hires quit within a few weeks, but most of the people hired in St. John's really got along well—you know, just like the ideas you mentioned in class. We formed a special bond that helped us through the bad weather and grueling work.

"The LINK650 supervisors were another matter. They were tough SOBs who had worked for many years on oil rigs in the Gulf of Mexico or North Sea. They seemed to relish the idea of treating their employees the same way they had been treated before becoming managers. We put up with their abuse for the first few months, but things got worse when the LINK650 was brought into port twice to correct mechanical problems. These setbacks embarrassed LINK's management and they put more pressure on the supervisors to get us back on schedule.

"The supervisors started to ignore equipment problems and pushed us to get jobs done more quickly without regard to safety procedures. They routinely shouted obscenities at employees in front of others. Several of my work mates were fired and a few more quit their jobs. I almost lost my job one day just because my boss thought I could secure a fitting faster. Several people started finding ways to avoid the supervisors and get as little work done as possible. Many of my co-workers developed back problems. We jokingly called it the 'Hibernia backache' because some employees faked their ailment to leave the rig with paid sick leave.

"On top of the lousy supervisors, we were always kept in the dark about the problems on the rig. Supervisors said that they didn't know anything, which was partly true, but they said we shouldn't be so interested in things that didn't concern us. But the rig's problems, as well as its future contract work, were a major concern to crew members who weren't ready to quit. Their job security depended on the rig's production levels and whether CanOil would sign contracts to drill new holes. Given the rig's problems, most of us were concerned that we would be laid off at any time.

"Everything came to a head when Bob MacKenzie was killed because someone secured a hoist improperly. You probably read about it in the papers around this time last year. The government inquiry concluded that the person responsible wasn't properly trained and that employees were being pushed to finish jobs without safety precautions. Anyway, while the inquiry was going on, several employees decided to call the Seafarers International Union to unionize the rig. It wasn't long before most employees on LINK650 had signed union cards. That really shocked LINK's management and the entire oil industry because it was, I think, just the second time that a rig had ever been unionized in Canada.

"Since then, management has been doing everything in its power to get rid of the union. It sent a 'safety officer' to the rig, although we eventually realized that he was a consultant the company hired to undermine union support. One safety meeting with compulsory attendance of all crew members involved watching a video describing the international union president's association with organized crime. Several managers were sent to special seminars on how to manage under a union work force, although one of the topics was how to break the union. The guys who initiated the organizing drive were either fired or given undesirable jobs. LINK even paid one employee to challenge the union certification vote. The labour board rejected the decertification request because it discovered the company's union-busting tactics. Last month, the labour board ordered LINK to negotiate a first contract in good faith.

"So you see, Professor, I joined LINK as an enthusiastic employee and quit last month with no desire to lift a finger for them. It really bothers me, because I was always told to do your best, no matter how tough the situation. It's been quite an experience."

Discussion Questions

1. **Use the job satisfaction model to explain why the LINK650 employees were dissatisfied with their work.**

2. **Identify the various ways that employees expressed their job dissatisfaction on the LINK650.**

3. **Shaun O'Neill's commitment to the LINK organization dwindled over his two years of employment. Discuss the factors that affected his organizational commitment.**

© 1995 Steven L. McShane. This case is based on actual events, although names and some information have been changed.

Experiential Exercise

General Union Attitude Exercise

Purpose: This exercise is designed to help you understand the dynamics of employee attitudes toward a specific attitude object and to practise strategies of persuasion and attitude change regarding that attitude object.

Instructions: As a first step, individuals will complete the General Union Attitude Scale presented below by circling their preferred response to each item and calculating a total score.

Next, the instructor will divide the class into two parts based on whether participants fall above or below a certain point on the scale. Each part is then divided into teams of three people. Teams with members having high scores will speak in favour of labour unions, and teams with members having low scores will argue against labour unions. Students scoring in the middle of the scale will serve as observers.

Each team will be matched with a team from the other half of the class and try to convince members of the other team to change their opinion regarding labour unions. Each team first meets alone for five minutes to develop their strategy. One observer is assigned to each team to record the process. Next, the pairs of teams (one for and one against labour unions) meet for the length of time indicated by the instructor. The objective is to convince members of the opposing team that labour unions in Canada are good or bad, depending on your team's assigned position on the issue. The two observers in each debate watch the action and share notes at the end of the meeting.

At the end of the debates, the instructor draws the class together and the observers from each debate present their findings. Discussion from other participants follows the observers' presentations.

Scoring: Add up the score for all eight items. The instructor will determine the part of the class and discussion team to which you will be assigned.

		Strongly Disagree			Neutral		Strongly Agree	
1.	Unions are a positive force in this country.	1	2	3	4	5	6	7
2.	If I had to choose, I probably would not be a member of a labour union.	7	6	5	4	3	2	1
3.	I am glad that labour unions exist.	1	2	3	4	5	6	7
4.	People would be just as well off if there were no labour unions in this country.	7	6	5	4	3	2	1
5.	Unions are an embarrassment to our society.	7	6	5	4	3	2	1
6.	I am proud of the labour movement in this country.	1	2	3	4	5	6	7
7.	Most people are better off without labour unions.	7	6	5	4	3	2	1
8.	Employees are considerably better off when they belong to a labour union.	1	2	3	4	5	6	7

General Union Attitude Scale

Individual Decision Making in Organizations

Learning Objectives

After reading this chapter, you should be able to:

Diagram the basic process of decision making.

Explain why people have difficulty identifying problems.

Identify three barriers to choosing the best alternative.

Outline the causes of escalation of commitment to a poor decision.

Explain why experience is necessary for intuitive decision making.

Discuss three strategies to help employees solve problems more creatively.

Identify three basic perspectives of ethical decision making.

Chapter Outline

A General Model of Decision Making.

Barriers to Identifying Problems and Opportunities.

Barriers to Choosing the Best Solution.

Barriers to Evaluating Decision Outcomes.

Minimizing Decision Errors.

Intuitive Decision Making.

Creative Decision Making.

Ethical Decision Making.

M atthew Barrett acquired a reputation as a clean-up artist early in his career at the Bank of Montreal. Whether salvaging a mismanaged branch or defending a departmental budget, he displayed an obsession for preparation, an aptitude for analysis, and a talent for motivating others to support his decisions. "He almost feeds on tough problems," observes one long-time colleague. Now Barrett's decision-making skills are being tested in his role as the Bank of Montreal's Chief Executive Officer (CEO).

Barrett believes that good decisions depend on good information. Soon after becoming Bank of Montreal's CEO, he surveyed nearly 100 senior bank executives on the bank's major strengths and weaknesses. Barrett and his executive team then analyzed these data over several months, resulting in important decisions to refocus the bank toward customer service and retail financial services. At the same time, Barrett introduced a comprehensive system of measuring the bank's performance, thereby providing benchmarks to evaluate the success or failure of the bank's strategic decisions.

Barrett also set new ethical standards in executive decisions at the Bank of Montreal. For example, the strategic changes eliminated 3,000 positions over two years, yet the bank avoided major lay-offs by retraining and relocating employees. "I have a problem personally with proposing that people are Kleenex, people who want to work but are thrown out on the street because the company didn't invest any capital in them or train them earlier," says Barrett, referring to the massive lay-offs by other companies. His ethical values are also apparent in the bank's active promotion of women, aboriginal people, and other underrepresented groups.

Some say that Barrett's decisions are risk-averse. Explains one colleague: "He'll only take a risk if he can understand the situation better than everyone else and manage the risk out of it." But Barrett prefers to call his risk aversion "loss averse." "I will make large bets, but I won't make them uninformed," he says. "My analytical and research stuff doesn't stem from caution. It is driven by the desire for a break-out strategy. . . . I'm not going to bet it all just to impress people with what a swashbuckling guy I am."[1]

Matthew Barrett's ability to effectively solve problems and seize opportunities puts him in the minority. According to a recent survey, only 34 percent of Canadian employees believe that management makes good decisions.[2] But decision making is not the exclusive province of senior executives. As employees further down the organizational hierarchy are given more responsibility, the organization's success also depends on their decision-making skills. Decision making is a complex process of recognizing a problem or opportunity, looking for alternative ways to deal with the situation, and ensuring that the selected choice is implemented and fulfills the intended objectives. This process is fraught with the perceptual, communication, and attitude problems that were described in previous chapters.

This chapter describes the process of individual decision making in organizations, as well as the problems that people make in that process. We begin by looking at each step in the general decision-making model and exploring the barriers to identifying problems, evaluating alternatives, and evaluating decision outcomes. Potential solutions to these decision-making problems are also presented. The latter part of this chapter highlights three important decision-making topics: intuition, creativity, and ethics.

A General Model of Decision Making

Decision making
A conscious process of making choices among one or more alternatives with the intention of moving toward some desired state of affairs.

Decision making is a conscious process of making choices among one or more alternatives with the intention of moving toward some desired state of affairs.[3] It involves comparing alternatives and allocating resources toward one of those choices. People make decisions to achieve organizational or personal objectives. However, this is not an orderly process because goals are often ill-defined and not fully agreed on by others in the organization.

Exhibit 9–1 presents a general model of the decision-making process.[4] The individual becomes aware of a problem or opportunity and chooses the best way to resolve it. For most problems, alternative solutions or strategies are identified or developed and the best one is selected. The choice is implemented and its effectiveness is evaluated through feedback. Let's look at each stage more closely.

Identify problems and opportunities

Problems and opportunities do not announce themselves; rather, they are defined by the decision maker. The perceptual process plays an important role—as do the decision maker's experience and values—in deciding whether

A General Model of Decision Making   Exhibit 9–1

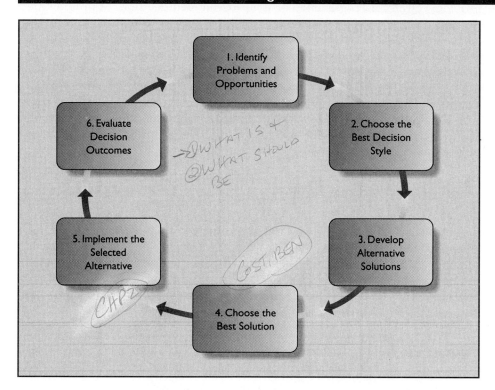

certain information signals that a problem exists. Employees, suppliers, clients, public interest groups, and other organizational stakeholders also attempt to shape the individual's perception that a problem or opportunity exists. Thus, decision making is frequently marked by politics and negotiation as vested interests try to influence decision makers in the identification and definition of the problem, as well as in other phases of the decision process.[5]

A problem is a deviation between the current and desired situation. This deviation is a symptom of more fundamental root causes in the organization. By diagnosing the problem, decision makers try to understand the link between the symptoms and their causes. The decision process is then directed toward changing the root causes so that the symptoms are reduced or eliminated.[6] Poor quality of a finished product, for instance, might be a symptom of poor machine maintenance, substandard materials, poor employee training, or a host of other factors. Identifying the correct root cause(s) helps the decision maker choose the best way to minimize this problem.

Choose the best decision style

Once the problem or opportunity has been recognized and diagnosed, we must choose the most appropriate decision style. Should other people participate in the decision? Is the best answer found in existing procedures, or is it necessary to search for new solutions? What is the best way to gather information?[7]

Programmed decision
The process whereby decision makers follow standard operating procedures to select the preferred solution without the need to identify or evaluate alternative choices.

Nonprogrammed decision
The process applied to unique, complex, or ill-defined situations whereby decision makers follow the full decision-making process, including a careful search for and/or development of unique solutions.

One of the most important questions to ask at this stage is whether the problem calls for a **programmed** or **nonprogrammed decision.**[8] A programmed decision follows standard operating procedures because the problem is routine and relevant goals are clear.[9] This process bypasses the alternative development and selection stages of decision making because the optimal solution has been identified and documented in the past. In contrast, nonprogrammed decisions require a careful search for alternatives and may include development of unique solutions. This decision style is applied to new, complex, or ill-defined problems. As problems reappear, we try to develop programmed decision routines. In this respect, programmed decisions drive out nonprogrammed decisions because we strive for predictable, routine situations.

Develop alternative solutions

The next step in the decision process is developing a list of possible solutions to the problem.[10] This usually begins by searching for ready-made solutions, such as applications that have worked well on similar problems. If an acceptable solution cannot be found, then decision makers try to design a custom-made solution or modify existing ones. Designing a custom-made solution is often a costly and risky process, because the designer usually doesn't know what the solution should look like until it is completed.

Choose the best solution

When faced with options, decision makers need to find some way to identify the choice that best meets the intended objectives. In a purely rational process, the person would identify all factors against which the alternatives are judged, assign weights reflecting the importance of those factors, rate each alternative on those factors, and calculate each alternative's total value from the ratings and factor weights. Decision makers sometimes try to evaluate alternatives in this systematic fashion. For example, operations research uses advanced statistical formulas to calculate the optimal solution to a variety of complex problems.

In many situations, however, decision makers discover that there is conflict over the selection and weighting of factors to evaluate the alternatives. Moreover, it is very difficult to predict with any accuracy the consequences of all alternatives. This lack of clarity is due to risk and uncertainty about the consequences of our actions.[11] For instance, when Matthew Barrett and the Bank of Montreal's executive team decided to emphasize retail banking, they realized that their choice was based on rough estimates of probable outcomes. It is impossible to sort out all of the effects of a decision, and there is a chance that the information is distorted by faulty perceptions and biases.

Heuristic
A rule of thumb (decision rule) used repeatedly to help decision makers evaluate alternatives under conditions of uncertainty.

Decision makers often use rules of thumb, called **heuristics,** to help them evaluate alternatives under conditions of uncertainty.[12] Heuristics may be well-tested standards ("only buy equipment with injection-molded components"), or they may represent superstitions with little basis in fact ("never visit new clients on the 13th of the month"). Heuristics simplify the decision-making process by focussing on only one or two important factors. Some highly respected business and political leaders rely on their heuristics to make important decisions. Perspective 9–1 describes how one Canadian business leader has prospered from his particular rule of thumb.

Perspective 9–1

Ted Rogers's Winning Heuristic

Ted Rogers, founder and CEO of Rogers Communications Inc., describes his favourite heuristic: "I believe in getting in on new technology in the formative stages ... to ride the wave of growth. Even if you make a lot of mistakes, growth covers them up. If you survive, you can do extraordinarily well." Using this rule of thumb of staying technologically ahead of the crowd, Rogers has built an impressive business empire:

- As a 26-year-old law student in 1960, Rogers bought a Toronto FM radio station (CHFI-FM) when only 5 percent of Canadians had FM receivers. FM radio is now a popular broadcast medium that threatens the historical dominance of AM radio.

- In the 1960s and 1970s, Rogers entered the cable television industry when few people knew what "cable TV" meant. Today, Rogers is Canada's largest cable firm.

- In the early 1980s, Rogers entered the cellular telephone market by forming Cantel Inc. Senior executives at Rogers Communications advised against this move, but Rogers followed his successful decision heuristic of leading the technological edge. Cantel has since become one of the most successful firms in the Rogers family of companies, representing half of the Canadian market in this high-growth industry.

- Now through his investment in Unitel, Ted Rogers has entered the lucrative long-distance telephone market. Again relying on his rule of thumb, Rogers plans to stay ahead of the competition by using the latest technology to compete against Bell Canada and other giants in the telephone industry.

Sources: I. McGugan, "Such Good Friends," *Canadian Business*, April 1994, pp. 54–63; M. Levin, "Mr. Rogers' Neighbourhood," *Financial Times of Canada*, February 26, 1990, p. 29; and R. Fisher, "Ted's Team," *Canadian Business* 62 (August 1989), pp. 28–34.

Implement the selected alternative

Along with making the right choices, decision makers must rally employees and mobilize sufficient resources to translate their decisions into action. Effective implementation considers all four influences on individual behaviour described in Chapter 2. Those implementing the decision must possess the necessary skills and knowledge, and they must be motivated to implement the decision. They must also understand why the decision has been made and what is expected from its implementation.

Finally, employees who implement the decision must have the skills and resources needed to fulfill their mandate. In a rather extreme example, the village council in Lakefield, Ontario, passed noise abatement by-laws permitting birds to sing for 30 minutes during the day and 15 minutes at night. The village council clerk, who was flooded with calls asking how he could get the birds to stop singing, admitted that those who passed the legislation didn't think carefully about how it could be implemented.[13]

Evaluate decision outcomes

After the preferred choice has been implemented, we need to evaluate whether the gap between "what is" and "what ought to be" has narrowed. Ideally, this information should come from systematic benchmarks, such as those intro-

Exhibit 9–2   **Barriers to Identifying Problems and Opportunities**

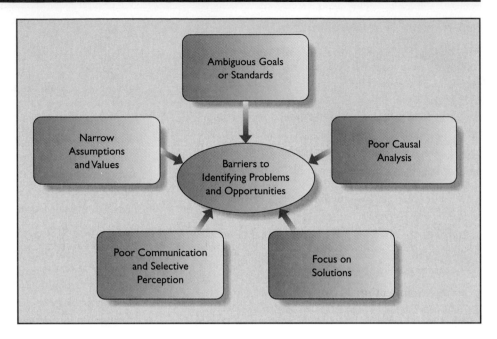

duced by Matthew Barrett at the Bank of Montreal (see the chapter-opening vignette). It is fairly easy to determine whether some decisions have been effective because relevant feedback is objective and easily observed. For example, a fairly clear indicator of a new product's success is its market share after a certain time. The success of other decisions may be more difficult to comprehend, however. The decision to invest resources in new equipment may have long-term benefits that are difficult to distinguish from the effects of other events.

Barriers to Identifying Problems and Opportunities

The decision-making process faces many perceptual, attitudinal, and communication problems. Some of the more troublesome barriers to identifying problems and opportunities are listed in Exhibit 9–2 and discussed below.

Ambiguous goals or standards

Many organizational goals are ambiguous or in conflict with each other, so it becomes more difficult to recognize problems or opportunities. In some situations, events are defined as problems only after drawn-out discussions with various organizational stakeholders.[14]

Poor causal analysis

Even if we readily see a gap between the current and desired situation, it is often difficult to figure out the causes of that gap. This is particularly true when the situation is extremely complex, the setting is emotionally charged, the decision maker faces extreme time constraints, or perceptual errors distort the situation.

Pressures from vested interests may cause the wrong problem to be identified, particularly when those groups have some degree of power over the decision maker.[15]

Focus on solutions

Another common error is to define problems in terms of their solutions. You may hear someone say: "The problem is that we need more control over our suppliers." The speaker is suggesting a solution before investigating the root causes of the apparent symptoms. The tendency to focus on solutions is based on our need to reduce uncertainty; however, it can short-circuit the problem identification stage of decision making.[16]

Some experts carry this concern one step further by suggesting that organizations are basically a collection of solutions looking for problems in the right settings. This "garbage can model" suggests that a decision occurs only when the solution, problem, and setting coexist and a decision maker is there to put the pieces together! The garbage can model may be a rather extreme view of organizations as anarchies, but it does show how some decisions are driven by solutions rather than careful diagnosis of the problem.[17]

Poor communication and selective perception

The ability to identify problems and opportunities depends on the quality of communication and the decision maker's perceptual processes. As we learned in Chapter 6, managers often don't discover problems early enough because negative information is filtered or distorted as it flows up the organizational hierarchy.[18] Even if the bad news isn't filtered out, decision makers might screen out this information through their own **perceptual defense** bias. Recall from Chapter 7 that perceptual defense occurs when people subconsciously screen out threatening information. Although it can be a useful coping device, perceptual defense also causes people to overlook important problems until the situation becomes critical.

Perceptual defense
A defensive psychological process that involves subconsciously screening out large blocks of information that threaten the person's beliefs and values.

Narrow assumptions and values

People see problems or opportunities based on their mental models of the world.[19] Mental models are images of how the world works. They are based on our experiences and values, and they produce a set of assumptions on which we base our decisions and actions. Mental models help us to make sense of our environment, but they can also blind us to changes and the problems or opportunities these changes may bring. Each of the famous missed opportunities described in Perspective 9–2 resulted from the decision maker's mental models that produced incorrect assumptions about the future or maintained values that were incompatible with emerging social trends. In each case, these assumptions and values put blinders on the decision maker's ability or motivation to perceive new problems or opportunities.

Barriers to Choosing the Best Solution

For many years, decision making in organizations was studied mainly by economic theorists who made several assumptions about how decision makers

Perspective 9–2

Famous Missed Opportunities

- In the 1970s, Thomas Bata Sr., then CEO of Toronto-based Bata Ltd., was approached by a visitor who asked for credit to finance his fledgling running shoe company. Even as head of the world's largest footwear company, Bata decided to reject the invitation because he was sceptical about extending credit to a stranger. The visitor was the founder of Reebok International Ltd., which today is one of the leading names in athletic footwear. Meanwhile, Bata Ltd. is still struggling to secure a niche in this highly profitable sector of the footwear business.

- In 1972, several Hollywood studios rejected the script for a low-budget movie called *American Graffiti* to be produced by a new film-director, George Lucas. Universal Studios initially rejected the script on the grounds that it was commercially unacceptable, but later changed its mind. *American*

Graffiti became one of the highest-grossing movies of all time. In spite of Lucas's first success, Universal and other studios rejected the director's next project, a sci-fi movie. Twentieth Century-Fox reluctantly provided some development money, but Lucas had to raise most of the money for the project himself. The project left Lucas financially broke and dispirited, but at least he kept the picture rights. His film, *Star Wars,* was a monumental success, as were its sequels.

- In 1962, Brian Epstein approached Decca Records with a demo of a new rock group he was managing. The Decca executive refused to sign the group, saying, "Groups with guitars are on their way out." Epstein's demo was rejected by three other record companies before EMI Records agreed to sign the group, known as The Beatles. The rest is history!

Sources: R. Collison, "How Bata Rules Its World," *Canadian Business,* September 1990, p. 28; L. J. Peter, *Why Things Go Wrong* (New York: Bantam, 1984), pp. 147, 148, 150; and D. Frost and M. Deakin, *I Could Have Kicked Myself* (London: André Deutsch, 1982), pp. 98, 123.

choose among alternatives. They assumed that decision makers make choices based on well-articulated and agreed-on organizational goals. Second, they assumed that decision makers are rational thinking machines who efficiently and simultaneously process facts about all alternatives and the consequences of those alternatives. Finally, these theorists assumed that decision makers always choose the alternative with the highest pay-off.

We might like to think that people are rational thinking machines, but these assumptions are far from accurate. One critic suggested that economic theory gives decision makers a "preposterously omniscient rationality [with] little discernible relation to the actual or possible behaviour of flesh-and-blood human beings."[20] In fact, organizational behaviour researchers have debunked several economic assumptions about decision making in organizations, as we see in Exhibit 9–3. Let's look at these false assumptions more closely.

Problems with goals

As we discussed in Chapter 1, many organizational goals are ambiguous, subjective, and in conflict with each other. It is difficult to decide the value of decision outcomes when goals are ambiguous and subjective. The problem is compounded when organizational members disagree over the relative importance of

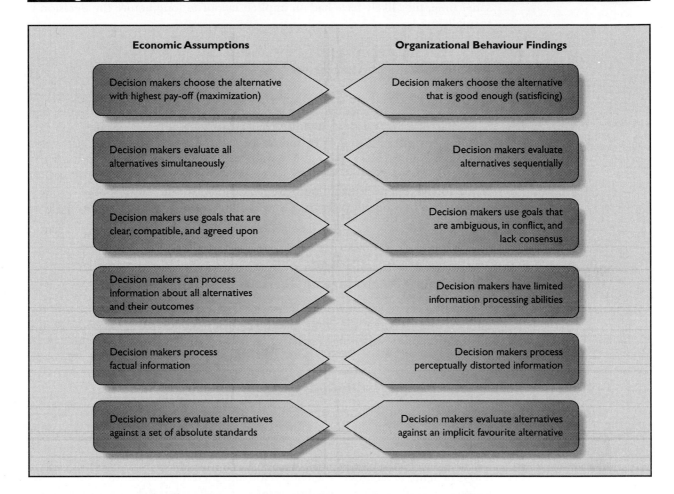

Traditional Economic Assumptions versus Organizational Behaviour Findings about Choosing Decision Alternatives   **Exhibit 9–3**

Economic Assumptions	Organizational Behaviour Findings
Decision makers choose the alternative with highest pay-off (maximization)	Decision makers choose the alternative that is good enough (satisficing)
Decision makers evaluate all alternatives simultaneously	Decision makers evaluate alternatives sequentially
Decision makers use goals that are clear, compatible, and agreed upon	Decision makers use goals that are ambiguous, in conflict, and lack consensus
Decision makers can process information about all alternatives and their outcomes	Decision makers have limited information processing abilities
Decision makers process factual information	Decision makers process perceptually distorted information
Decision makers evaluate alternatives against a set of absolute standards	Decision makers evaluate alternatives against an implicit favourite alternative

these goals. It is also doubtful that all decisions are based on organizational objectives—some decisions are made to satisfy the decision maker's personal goals even when they are incompatible with the organization's goals.

Problems with information processing

There are at least three incorrect assumptions when economic theorists say that people evaluate all facts about every alternative and their consequences. First, personal biases typically distort the selection and interpretation of information. Thus, people do not make perfectly rational decisions because they never have perfectly accurate information. Second, people have limited information processing capabilities and, therefore, engage in a limited search for and evaluation of alternatives. Their decisions are based on incomplete knowledge with only a partial comprehension of the true nature of the problem.[21]

Finally, decision makers typically look at alternatives sequentially rather than examining all alternatives at the same time. As a new alternative comes along, decision makers immediately compare it to an implicit favourite alternative that they consciously or subconsciously prefer over others evaluated earlier.[22] Even when decision makers seem to be evaluating all the choices at the same time, they likely have had an implicit favourite long before the decision is formally made.

Problems with maximization

Satisficing
The tendency to select a solution that is satisfactory or "good enough" rather than optimal or "the best."

Rather than selecting the best alternative (maximizing), decision makers generally tend to **satisfice.** In other words, they usually select the alternative that is satisfactory or "good enough." What constitutes a good enough solution depends on the availability of satisfactory alternatives. Standards rise when satisfactory alternatives are easily found and fall when few are available.[23] Satisficing fits in with the fact that decision makers tend to evaluate alternatives sequentially. They evaluate one alternative at a time against the implicit favourite and eventually select one that is good enough to satisfy their needs or preferences.

Barriers to Evaluating Decision Outcomes

Decision makers aren't completely honest with themselves when evaluating the effectiveness of their decisions. Two significant concerns are postdecisional justification and escalation of commitment.

Postdecisional justification

Postdecisional justification
A perceptual phenomenon whereby decision makers justify their choices by subconsciously inflating the quality of the selected option and deflating the quality of the discarded options.

Suppose that you are job hunting and receive several good offers. There is a good chance that you will subconsciously distort information so that the chosen offer seems more favourable while the rejected offers look less favourable. You might selectively look for more information that supports your decision. You might forget about negative attributes of the chosen job and focus on its positive features. This tendency to inflate the quality of the selected alternative and deflate the quality of the discarded alternatives is known as **postdecisional justification.**[24] It is an ego-defense mechanism that makes us more comfortable with our decisions, particularly where we must select from several favourable alternatives.

Postdecisional justification gives decision makers an excessively optimistic evaluation of their decisions, but only until they receive very clear and undeniable information to the contrary. Unfortunately, postdecisional justification inflates the decision maker's initial evaluation of the decision, so reality often comes as a painful shock when objective feedback is finally received.

Escalation of commitment

When feedback suggests that the decision was incorrect, the rational decision maker would terminate the action and reconsider the problem. Yet there is plenty of evidence that people do not react to negative feedback quite so dispassionately. Instead, decision makers often continue on the existing course of action and may even allocate more resources to the failing project. This

Courtesy of Ontario Hydro; photo #89. 0279-271.

Inside Ontario Hydro's Darlington nuclear generating station during construction. Ontario Hydro's CEO is wary of megaprojects because they encourage escalation of commitment. "Once you commit to them, there's very little you can do to reverse that commitment."

phenomenon of investing more resources into bad decisions is known as **escalation of commitment.**[25]

There are numerous examples of escalating commitment. Canadian banks have systems in place to avoid escalation of small loans, yet they seem to throw good money after bad in large transactions such as Dome Petroleum during the early 1980s and Olympia and York's Canary Wharf project a few years ago. Governments have also sunk millions of dollars into ill-fated projects ranging from cucumber greenhouses in Newfoundland to meat packing plants in Alberta.

Ontario Hydro's Darlington nuclear power plant is perhaps the most costly example of escalating commitment in Canada. With initial costs estimated at $2 billion, project expenditures are now above $14 billion. If the project had been cancelled in the early 1980s, Ontario Hydro would have saved $10 billion—one-third of its current debt load. Maurice Strong, Ontario Hydro's recent CEO, warns that Darlington and other megaprojects invite escalating commitment because they "have a very long timeline. Once you commit to them, there's very little you can do to reverse that commitment."[26] Strong urges the utility to avoid megaprojects in the future for this reason.

Escalation of commitment
Repeating an apparently bad decision or allocating more resources to a failing course of action.

Causes of escalating commitment

What leads decision makers deeper and deeper into failing projects? Experts on this topic offer four explanations (see Exhibit 9–4).[27]

Perceptual defense

Earlier in this chapter we noted that some problems are not immediately recognized or are actively denied because the decision maker ignores or explains away the negative information. The same thing occurs when information suggests that the earlier decision is producing poor results. Perceptual defense mechanisms screen out this negative information to protect the decision maker's self-esteem.

Exhibit 9–4   **Causes of Escalation of Commitment toward a Failing Course of Action**

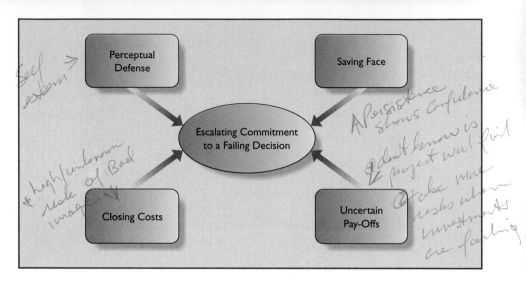

Saving face

Decision makers who are personally identified with the decision tend to persist in their course of action because it demonstrates confidence in their decision-making ability. Some cultures have a stronger emphasis on saving face than do others, so escalation of commitment is probably more common in those societies.[28]

Uncertain pay-offs

Recall that decisions are usually based on ambiguous information with uncertain risks and rewards. Consequently, decision makers hesitate to abandon a failing project because there is a chance that it will eventually be successful. Moreover, there is evidence that people are more willing to take risks when their investments are failing. This occurs because people like to think that they can beat the odds.

Closing costs

Decision makers often want to continue on the existing course of action because the costs of ending the project are high or unknown. Terminating a major project may involve large financial penalties or produce a bad image to contractors. Many government projects also have political costs. When former Ontario Premier David Peterson was asked why the Ontario government didn't stop the Darlington project in the early 1980s, he explained: "I don't think anybody can look at a situation with . . . $7 billion in the ground and just cavalierly write it off."[29] In other words, terminating the Darlington project after this large expense may have been political suicide to the Ontario government.

Minimizing Decision Errors

Human beings will never be able to completely overcome perceptual, attitudinal, or communication problems, but they can minimize some of their effects on the decision-making process. As we learned in Chapters 6 and 7, decision makers who are more aware of their perceptual biases and personal values are better able to identify problems and opportunities and avoid the pitfalls of escalating commitment and postdecisional justification. By recognizing the mental models used to understand the world, they learn to question the assumptions and values behind those models. Similarly, by discussing the situation with colleagues, decision makers can eventually discover blind spots in their problem identification and evaluation.[30]

Structural approaches to better decisions

A variety of structures and systems can help minimize some decision-making problems. Expert systems evaluate alternatives in which complex, repetitive decisions can be standardized through computer programming.[31] These systems ask users a series of questions and then calculate the optimal solution from this information using preprogrammed decision rules. American Express's expert system to identify bad credit risks among its millions of cardholders was developed from the expertise of credit authorization manager Laurel Miller. Appropriately called "Laurel's Brain," the computer program has increased productivity and reduced financial losses.[32]

Systematic evaluation of alternatives can also be accomplished without computers. Perspective 9–3 describes how a special committee at Baxter Healthcare Corporation, one of North America's largest health products firms, evaluated seven work schedules using a structured analysis of four decision factors.

Escalation of commitment can be minimized by establishing a preset level at which the decision is abandoned or reevaluated. This is similar to a stop-loss order in the stock market, whereby the stock is sold if it falls below a certain price. Another structural approach is to separate decision choosers from decision implementers. This would minimize the problem of saving face because the person responsible for implementation and evaluation would not be concerned about saving face if the project is cancelled.

Finally, there is increasing evidence that complex decisions are more effectively made by teams rather than individuals. As we will explore more fully in Chapter 11, teams can potentially identify better alternatives and select the most appropriate one because they have more information to understand the available options and their consequences. Escalation of commitment is known to exist in teams as well as individuals.[33] However, teams have the advantage that some members might warn the others about their perceptual biases when evaluating earlier decisions.

Intuitive Decision Making

Although the decision-making model is a useful template for understanding decisions, it does not explicitly address the fact that people often use their hunches or gut feelings to recognize and solve problems or opportunities. Any seasoned employee will tell you that many decisions are based more on this sixth sense than on a conscious identification of problems and evaluation of alterna-

Perspective 9–3

Deciding the Best Work Schedule at Baxter Healthcare

With increasing demand for its blood plasma products, the Hyland Therapeutics Division of Baxter Healthcare Corporation had to change production from a five-day workweek to a seven-day workweek. But when it came to choosing the best work schedule, senior management felt that several reasonable options were available and that employees were in the best position to make that decision.

A special employee advisory committee (EAC) was formed with representatives from each department. Within the first few meetings, the EAC developed and weighted four factors in choosing the best work schedule. In order of importance, they included productivity of the schedule, employee satisfaction with the schedule, experience level for each shift in the schedule, and quality of intra- and intershift communication in the schedule.

Baxter's EAC then began the complex task of identifying alternative schedules in the expanded production operation. They listened to industrial engineers about different shift rotation systems, human resource professionals about employment law issues, maintenance people about downtime issues, and security people about traffic flow during shift changes. The EAC then developed seven shift schedules and committee members polled employees in their departments to determine their acceptance level.

With this information in hand, the EAC used a multi-attribute decision process to systematically evaluate and select the best work schedule. This decision process involves rating each work schedule on each of the four factors selected earlier, and then multiplying each rating by the factor's weight. The schedule's overall score was calculated by combining the multiplied results. The EAC showed the results of the multi-attribute decision process to employees in each department, then repeated the evaluation process. The second set of calculations were very similar to the first round, and were used by the committee in its final recommendation.

The selected work schedule had the second best productivity and best level of employee satisfaction. It met the optimal level of personnel experience on each shift and had the third best rating on the communication factor. Overall, the process received considerable support because of its objective evaluation and involvement of those affected by the work schedule.

Source: Based on L. Blake, "Group Decision Making at Baxter," *Personnel Journal*, January 1991, pp. 76–82.

---

tive solutions. This is nicely phrased by the chief executive officer of Cummins Engine Company: "When the hair on the back of my neck has just given me an unpleasant sensation, either because of a recommendation or a set of facts in front of me, I know that something is wrong. We are trying to teach our managers that when you have a sixth sense that says something is screwy, pay attention to it."[34]

Intuition
The ability to know when a problem or opportunity exists and select the best course of action without the apparent use of reasoning or logic.

This sixth sense is called **intuition,** the ability to know when a problem or opportunity exists and select the best course of action without the apparent use of reasoning or logic.[35] Intuition has been romanticized by some writers (particularly training and development practitioners) as a special function of the brain's right hemisphere. This myth is based on pseudosciences of the 1800s that have been proven incorrect in scientific research.[36]

The more substantiated view is that intuition is systematic decision making burned into our subconscious by habit. It is the feeling that people experience when they perceive a familiar pattern of events or circumstances, or when circumstances do not follow the familiar pattern. Thus, intuition is based on years of training and experience in which the decision maker has learned thousands of environmental patterns.[37]

Intuition has been studied most clearly in chess masters when they play several opponents at the same time. Grand masters look at the chess board, make their move without time to systematically evaluate the situation, and proceed to another chess board. They are able to make the right choice (most of the time) because they have learned patterns of chess arrangements and are able to quickly sense a pattern that threatens their position or presents an opportunity. Intuition, therefore, involves recognizing whether the perceived situation fits a previously learned pattern and, if not, knowing how to correct the situation or take advantage of the windfall. Experienced employees and executives have this same skill. They sense when something is wrong because the situation fits—or does not fit—one of their learned patterns.

Developing more intuitive decision making

Intuition is gaining respectability in the corporate world. Konosuke Matsushita, founder of the world's largest electronics company (Matsushita), once threw out a mainframe computer because he felt that managers ought to rely more on their intuition than on quantitative analyses.[38] Some computer systems experts also believe that expert systems and data analysis should never replace the unique benefits of human intuition.[39] Compared to detailed planning and analysis, intuition identifies and solves problems more quickly and with less information. Moreover, intuition may lead to better decisions because it often considers complex and subtle variables that quantitative studies overlook.

There is a risk that decision makers may confuse their intuition with wishful thinking. To minimize this problem, we need to know how to develop intuitive abilities. Intuition requires experience and intimate knowledge of the industry and occupation so that the decision maker can develop a large dictionary of patterns. As one Canadian CEO concluded: "To run a company properly you have to understand the business very well. Otherwise you might make a decision without understanding its implications."[40]

But experience does not guarantee that employees will make intuitive decisions; they must also be able to recognize their intuitive sense and know when to act on it. A few writers believe that people with a particular personality are more likely to pay attention to their intuition while others suppress it. Some claim that people can learn to listen to their intuition by discussing intuitive experiences with co-workers and by taking relaxation breaks before acting on a decision. There is some evidence that training programs can help people become more intuitive in their decision making.[41]

Creative Decision Making

Creativity refers to developing an original product, service, or idea that makes a socially recognized contribution. A few creative ideas might come from nowhere, but most represent a unique combination of previous ideas. This ability to derive new ideas from existing ones is a core feature of creativity called *divergent thinking*. How does divergent thinking occur? Although there is no definitive answer, the available evidence suggests that the creative process has four stages (see Exhibit 9–5):[42]

Creativity
Developing an original product, service, or idea that makes a socially recognized contribution.

Exhibit 9–5   **Four Stages of Creative Decision Making**

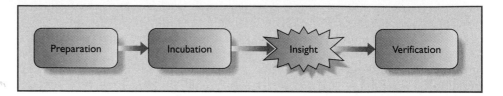

- *Preparation*—Creativity is not a passive activity; rather, we work at gathering the necessary information and learning about the elements of the problem or issue. For example, people are usually more creative when they take the problem apart and closely analyze each component.

- *Incubation*—This is the stage of reflective thought. We put the problem aside (sometimes out of frustration), but our mind is still working on it subconsciously.

- *Insight*—At some point during the incubation stage, we become aware of a unique idea. These flashes of inspiration are fleeting and can be lost quickly if not documented. In other words, creative thoughts don't keep a particular schedule; they might come to you at any time of day or night. Many great ideas have been lost because the individual did not write them down at the moment of inspiration.

- *Verification*—Insights are merely rough ideas. Their usefulness still requires verification through conscious evaluation and experimentation. This is similar to the evaluating decision outcomes stage in the decision-making model described earlier in this chapter.

Conditions for creativity

Creativity is a function of both the person and the situation. Some people are more creative than others. Creative people have strong artistic and intellectual values, tolerance of ambiguity, need for achievement, and self-confidence. People can be creative throughout their lives, although the highest level of creativity tends to occur between the ages of 30 and 40.[43]

In addition to hiring people with these features, organizations can encourage creativity by redesigning the work environment. One condition is to buffer the individual from tight deadlines and daily routines. Another important condition is to encourage risk taking by ensuring that employees aren't punished for behaving or expressing thoughts that differ from the ordinary. Third, creativity blossoms where errors are seen as learning rather than losses. Creativity results from trial and error, not from trial and rightness![44] A fourth condition is that employees have enough freedom in deciding how to accomplish the task and solve problems that arise. Finally, creativity increases with the open flow of information and ideas throughout the organization, as well as frequent interaction with people from different backgrounds.[45]

Strategies to assist creativity

A growing body of literature suggests that people can learn to be more creative.[46] Generally, creative training programs help participants in three ways. First, they make people aware that their creativity is stifled by the existing mental models that guide their thinking. Saying that something isn't logical simply means that it doesn't fit our mental model. This awareness encourages participants to question their logic and avoid closing their minds to ideas that don't fit existing mental models.

Second, creativity training programs encourage participants to spend more time understanding the problem or opportunity and, in particular, redefining it in a number of ways. In one creativity exercise, participants read a case, identify the main problem, and then compare their problem definition with others in the class. They discover that the same incident can be viewed in several ways.[47]

Finally, these programs teach people specific strategies to think differently about a problem or issue. One method is to list different dimensions of a system and the elements of each dimension, then look at each combination. This strategy encourages people to carefully examine combinations that initially seem nonsensical. For example, some Canadian fisheries executives wanted to examine new opportunities for the resource. One dimension included different uses of fish (sport, export product, etc.) and another dimension listed the benefits (employment, nutrition, etc.). The executives then looked at all combinations of the two dimensions (e.g., sport with nutrition) and were able to identify new challenges and opportunities for the industry.[48]

Another method is to use metaphors to compare the situation with something else so that the situation is seen in a different light.[49] A telephone company used this approach to find ways to reduce damage to its pay telephones. Participants were asked to think of a telephone booth as some other object that protects—such as a bank vault or medicine capsule. Then they looked at features of these other objects that might protect telephone booths. A variation of this strategy is to engage in a distinct activity (e.g., visit a museum) after learning about the facts of the situation. The stimuli experienced at the museum might spark new ways of thinking about the problem or opportunity. Notice that this is similar to the incubation stage of creativity, in which decision makers put the problem in the back of their heads for a while.

Ethical Decision Making

People are continually confronted with the need to make choices that affect the allocation of organizational resources. To varying degrees, these decisions have moral implications for the organization and the society in which it operates. As we explained in Chapter 1, **business ethics** refers to societal judgments about whether the consequences of organizational actions are good or bad. Ethical decision making involves making choices based not only on narrow problem-relevant criteria (e.g., Is there a market for this product idea?), but also on a broader set of principles used by society to judge the morality of conduct.

Canadians tend to think that they live in a society with relatively high moral standards, but it is not difficult to find unethical business practices in this

Business ethics
Societal judgments about whether the consequences of organizational actions are good or bad.

country. For example, 26 miners recently lost their lives at the Westray coal mine in Nova Scotia, apparently because senior management placed the short-term goals of investors ahead of the interests of employees and government regulators. Ironically, the poor ethical choices at Westray resulted in the company's demise and the arrest of its senior managers. Another example is Canada's financial industry, in which no fewer than 28 companies failed or suffered severe difficulties during the 1980s because of "fraud and self-dealing by the owners."[50]

Fortunately, several Canadian corporations have also led the business world toward higher standards of ethical conduct. Timothy Eaton, founder of Eaton's department stores, launched his enterprise in 1869 with a stern warning that his clerks should not deceive customers or sell them goods they did not need. Eaton also led North American industry in ethical conduct toward employees by introducing a more reasonable workweek and providing financial, medical, and other assistance to employees.[51]

Most of us would agree that Timothy Eaton's actions are morally right whereas safety violations and financial self-dealing are morally wrong, but it is very difficult to agree on the rules of ethical conduct. Three basic principles—utilitarianism, individual rights, and distributive justice—provide some guidance, but their relative priority is unclear and ethical reasoning will always be a tricky business.[52]

Utilitarianism

Utilitarianism
A moral principle stating that decision makers should seek the greatest good for the greatest number of people when choosing among alternatives.

One of the oldest moral principles, **utilitarianism,** advises us to seek the greatest good for the greatest number of people. This dictum requires a cost–benefit analysis of each decision alternative and a measure of the degree of satisfaction a decision provides to those affected. One problem is that utilitarianism judges morality by the results, but not necessarily the means to attaining those results. There are many actions, however, that people consider immoral, even though doing them would bring about the greatest good. For example, utilitarianism might indicate that stealing from a few people is acceptable as long as it benefits many others.

Another problem is that a cost–benefit analysis is difficult when decision outcomes are uncertain. We rarely know that one decision alternative will definitely benefit society more than another. This is further complicated by the fact that what is "good" for people is ambiguous and difficult to measure.

The utilitarian doctrine's drawbacks are apparent in the moral dilemma described in Perspective 9–4. Should the Sunnybrook Health Science Centre's pharmacy head buy an expensive drug for one person even though this won't leave enough money to save seven future cancer patients? In this case, utilitarianism might indicate that the greatest good is to let the patient with an expensive drug die so that seven other people might be saved a few months from now. But does this seem ethically correct while sitting at the bedside of the dying patient? Clearly, the utilitarian doctrine does not sufficiently guide moral dilemmas.

Individual rights

The morality of business decisions can also be judged by the extent that they uphold or violate individual rights. Individual rights are entitlements that let

Perspective 9–4

Tough Choices at Sunnybrook Health Science Centre

Patricia M. left Sunnybrook Health Science Centre in North York over a year ago, but head pharmacist Tom Paton remembers her well. Not her name, or her face—he didn't actually meet her. What he remembers is the $63,000 price tag for an intravenous drug that saved her life.

"The AmBisome case," says Paton, referring to the high-priced antifungal drug that Patricia received after her heart valve replacement surgery. Patricia was a Jehovah's Witness and would not authorize a blood transfusion. Fungizone, a less costly antifungal drug, would lower her blood count to the point that she would not survive open heart surgery. AmBisome was Patricia's only hope. The medicine worked, but at a whopping cost of $900 per day compared to $112 for Fungizone.

The moral dilemma that Paton faced was that Sunnybrook's $5.5 million budget for drugs must be shared by more than 17,000 inpatients each year. Now Paton was asked to spend more than 1 percent of that budget to save a single life.

The $63,000 spent on Patricia M. could have bought six courses of Neupogen—another high-priced drug—for each of seven cancer patients. The dilemma was complicated by uncertainties about the consequences of giving Neupogen to cancer patients. How many of the seven cancer patients would live? For how long? How do you perform a cost-effectiveness analysis with such imponderables?

"If I had the money available," says Paton, "I could say in those iffy cases, 'I think we should try this.' And maybe it would work." In the meantime, for Paton and pharmacists at other Canadian hospitals, scarce resources will continue to bring tough moral choices.

Source: Adapted from I. Shapiro, "Is There an Auditor in the House?" *Report on Business Magazine*, November 1993, pp. 86–102.

---

people act in a certain way. Some rights are entrenched in legal statutes and common law. For example, consumers are protected against misleading advertising, and employees are protected against unsafe working conditions. However, individual rights refer to *moral rights*, not just those entrenched in law. Most people believe in the moral rights of life and free speech. This means that we believe that everyone should have these rights even where there is no specific statute.

Business decision makers must consider the individual's moral rights when choosing alternative courses of action, but this can be a rather difficult process. Some moral rights are general values that may be difficult to translate into a specific situation. There is also the problem that some moral rights conflict with others. The shareholders' right to be informed about corporate activities may ultimately conflict with a senior manager's right to privacy. This trade-off leads us to the third moral principle of ethical conduct, distributive justice.

Distributive justice

The distributive justice principle refers to fairness. Specifically, it suggests that inequalities (other than fundamental moral rights) are acceptable if (1) everyone has equal access to the more favoured positions in society and (2) the inequalities are ultimately in the best interest of the least well off in society. The first part of this doctrine means that there should not be any barriers to the better-paying and more-valued positions in life. Employment equity programs apply this principle, because they ensure that women and visible minorities have equal opportunity to higher-paying jobs. The second part says that people can have unequal stations in society, but the differences must benefit those in the lowest stations. In other words, some people can receive greater rewards than others if this results in a greater benefit to society. Risky jobs, for example, should pay more if this ensures that people are willing to complete those necessary tasks. By filling those risky jobs, the higher-paid people are benefiting others who are less well off.

Distributive justice is consistent with equity theory (described in Chapter 3). It suggests that everyone should have the same outcome/input ratio. Some people may receive more benefits than others, but this is because they make a higher contribution to society, particularly to the least well off in that society. The problem with distributive justice, however, is that there is no agreement on what activities are the greatest benefit to the least well off. One disadvantaged person might value security, whereas another wants liberty. Moreover, the better off people in society may do things that have "trickle down" benefits to the least well off, but it is difficult to see these effects. For example, companies may claim that lower minimum wages improve employment opportunities, but it is difficult to be sure that this policy benefits unemployed people more than wealthy corporate owners.

Maintaining ethical standards in organizational decisions

Organizations are facing increasing pressure to ensure that their decisions are consistent with society's moral standards. Although this mandate will never be easily fulfilled, several safeguards can be introduced to ensure that decisions include ethical considerations. According to a recent survey, 75 percent of large organizations in Canada have implemented at least one of these ethical safeguards.[53]

Distribute a written corporate code of ethics

A corporate code of ethical conduct should be developed and distributed to all employees. Everyone who works at Imperial Oil is required to read the 20-page corporate code of ethics and sign a statement "to demonstrate your understanding of and compliance with policies contained in the booklet."[54] Recent studies indicate that most corporate ethics codes in Canada and elsewhere focus on protecting the firm rather than on broader concerns of social responsibility.[55] In particular, most codes outline conflicts of interest, such as Gulf Canada's statement in Exhibit 9–6 on accepting gifts.

Conduct ethics training seminars

Organizations should provide decision makers with basic training on ethical conduct. These seminars help employees work through ethical dilemmas by applying the corporate code of ethical conduct. The long-term objective is to help participants internalize these standards so that ethical considerations are addressed almost intuitively. Some training sessions encourage participants to conduct a "front page story" analysis before implementing their decisions. This involves imagining the public reaction to a detailed description of the decision

Gulf Canada's Ethical Conduct Guidelines Regarding Gifts and Entertainment	Exhibit 9–6

In the conduct of the company's business you may have to decide whether or not to offer or accept gifts or entertainment.

On some occasions giving or accepting gifts or entertainment is an appropriate business courtesy. On other occasions, however, such practices might compromise your ability to remain objective in making business decisions on behalf of the company, or might be perceived as using undue influence to seek business opportunities on our behalf.

The difficulty lies in defining the point where giving or receiving gifts or entertainment becomes unacceptable either in value or frequency. In extreme situations, gifts can be considered secret commissions, and are unlawful for both the giver and the receiver.

The following guidelines will help you decide the appropriateness of giving or accepting gifts or entertainment:

- You may accept advertising novelties of trivial value, which are widely distributed either by customers or vendors.
- You may both give and receive customary business amenities such as meals, provided the expenses involved are kept to a reasonable level. You should report your entertainment expenses clearly on your expense account indicating the people you entertained and the companies they represent.

Some basic principles to consider when giving or receiving gifts or entertainment are:

- the amounts and types of gifts and entertainment you receive should meet the reciprocity test; that is, you should not accept anything that you could not give within Gulf's policy guidelines,
- they should be infrequent,
- they should serve a legitimate business purpose,
- they should be appropriate to your business responsibilities.

When you have doubts about the appropriateness of your actions, consult your supervisor.

Source: Gulf Canada Resources, A Statement of Corporate Values and Ethics, 1987, pp. 9–12. Reprinted by permission.

and its consequences on the front page of a major daily newspaper. Although a front page analysis is subject to the perceptual biases that distort other aspects of decision making, it can reframe the ethical consequences of a decision in a broader light.[56]

Link ethical behaviour to the reward system

Codes of ethical conduct should be linked to the organization's reward system. This practice is found at the Royal Bank, where the company's ethical code of conduct is reviewed and discussed with employees during their performance appraisal reviews.[57] Organizational sanctions should also be linked to conscious violations of the company's moral standards. Finally, ethics should be an important factor when selecting and promoting people. This ensures that senior executives serve as exemplary role models for others to follow.[58]

Develop an ethics committee

Provigo Inc., John Labatt Ltd., and other Canadian organizations have established corporate ethics committees that give advice about moral dilemmas facing the organization and continually examine changing ethical standards in society. The ethics committee is usually a subcommittee of the board of directors that meets about six to eight times each year.

Chapter Summary

- Decision making is a conscious process of making choices among one or more alternatives with the intention of moving toward some desired state of affairs. This involves identifying problems and opportunities, choosing the best decision style, developing alternative solutions, choosing the best solution, implementing the selected alternative, and evaluating decision outcomes.

- A variety of perceptual, attitudinal, and communication problems enter the decision-making process, making it virtually impossible to reach the optimal solution. Decision makers fail to recognize problems or opportunities, they are unable to get reliable information on all possible alternatives, and they may even decide to continue on a course of action that is not working as expected.

- Some decision-making problems can be minimized by being more aware of human biases in decision making, involving others in the decision-making process, using expert systems, and separating decision choosers from those responsible for implementation and evaluation.

- People often rely on intuition to identify a problem or choose a workable solution. Intuition is systematic decision making burned into our subconscious by habit. Through experience, we learn to recognize when something is out of place or when an available solution "fits" the problem.

- There are four stages in the creative process: preparation, incubation, insight, and verification. Creativity is a function of both the person and the situation. Creativity training programs can be effective. They make people aware that their existing mental models stifle creativity and that creativity involves spending more time thinking about the problem in different ways. Finally, creativity training programs teach participants specific strategies to think differently about a problem or issue.

- Virtually every decision has moral implications because it affects various stakeholders. Three basic principles—utilitarianism, individual rights, and distributive justice—provide some guidance for decision makers when they are identifying problems and evaluating alternatives. Employees' moral conduct may increase when companies have a corporate code of ethical conduct, employees receive ethics training, ethical decisions are rewarded, and an ethics committee exists to address ethical dilemmas and evolving societal standards.

Discussion Questions

1. **How do problems or opportunities originate?**
2. **A school district is experiencing very high levels of teacher absenteeism. Describe three barriers that might prevent the administrators of that school**

district from realizing that a problem exists or from identifying the root cause(s) of the high absenteeism.

3. A management consultant is hired by a manufacturing firm to determine the best North American site for its next plant. The consultant has had several meetings with the company's senior executives regarding the factors to consider when making its recommendation. Discuss three problems that might prevent the consultant from identifying the best site location.

4. How does postdecisional justification affect the evaluation of decision outcomes?

5. In the late 1970s, the Premier of British Columbia announced that the province would host a transportation exhibition in 1986 with a modest budget of only $78 million. On at least two occasions, administrators recommended cancelling the exposition due to cost overruns and labour troubles, but the government decided to continue with the project. But by the end of Expo'86, the budget exceeded $1.5 billion with a deficit of $300 million. Using your knowledge of escalation of commitment, discuss four possible reasons why the government might have been motivated to continue with the project.

6. Senior management at Delta Canada Corp. wants employees to use their intuition more when making decisions. One executive half-joked that the company should simply hire more left-handed people because they are apparently more "right-brained." Discuss this recommendation and propose two other strategies to improve the use of intuition at Delta.

7. Describe the four stages of the creative process.

8. According to some research, most businesspeople rely on utilitarianism more than any other principle to guide their ethical conduct. Describe three problems with using utilitarianism as the only ethical principle to make organizational decisions.

Notes

1. R. Graham, "The Selling of Mr. Goodbank," *Report on Business Magazine*, April 1994, pp. 34–47; A. Ross, "BMO's Big Bang," *Canadian Business*, January 1994, pp. 58–63; and R. Collison, "Banking on the Consumer," *Canadian Business*, May 1990, pp. 46–51.

2. Wyatt Co.'s WorkCanada survey. Cited in G. Brett, "Forget Japan—Canadians Happier at Their Jobs," *Toronto Star*, November 1, 1991, p. B1.

3. F. A. Shull, Jr., A. L. Delbecq, and L. L. Cummings, *Organizational Decision Making* (New York: McGraw-Hill, 1970), p. 31.

4. This model is adapted from several sources: H. Mintzberg, D. Raisinghani, and A. Théorét, "The Structure of 'Unstructured' Decision Processes," *Administrative Science Quarterly* 21 (1976), pp. 246–75; H. A. Simon, *The New Science of Management Decision* (New York: Harper & Row, 1960); C. Kepner and B. Tregoe, *The Rational Manager* (New York: McGraw-Hill, 1965); and W. C. Wedley and R. H. G. Field, "A Predecision Support System," *Academy of Management Review* 9 (1984), pp. 696–703.

5. J. E. Dutton and S. J. Ashford, "Selling Issues to Top Management," *Academy of Management Review* 18 (1993), pp. 397–428; M. Lyles and H. Thomas, "Strategic Problem Formulation: Biases and Assumptions Embedded in Alternative Decision-Making Models," *Journal of Management Studies* 25 (1988), pp. 131–45; and D. A. Cowan, "Developing a Process Model of Problem Recognition," *Academy of Management Review* 11 (1986), pp. 763–76.

6. P. F. Drucker, *The Practice of Management* (New York: Harper & Brothers, 1954), pp. 353–57.

7. Wedley and Field, "A Predecision Support System," p. 696; Drucker, *The Practice of Management*, p. 357; and L. R. Beach and T. R. Mitchell, "A Contingency Model for the Selection of Decision Strategies," *Academy of Management Review* 3 (1978), pp. 439–49.

8. Simon, *The New Science of Management Decision,* pp. 5–6.

9. I. L. Janis, *Crucial Decisions* (New York: The Free Press, 1989), pp. 35–37.

10. Mintzberg, Raisinghani, and Théorét, "The Structure of 'Unstructured' Decision Processes," pp. 255–56.

11. J. G. March and Z. Shapira, "Managerial Perspectives on Risk and Risk Taking," *Management Science* 33 (1987), pp. 1404–18.

12. Taylor, *Behavioral Decision Making* (Glenview, Ill.: Scott, Foresman, 1984), pp. 37–39; and N. M. Agnew and J. L. Brown, "Executive Judgment: The Intuitive/Rational Ratio," *Personnel* 62 (December 1985), pp. 48–54.

13. L. J. Peter, *Why Things Go Wrong,* (New York: Morrow, 1985) pp. 35–36.

14. L. T. Pinfield, "A Field Evaluation of Perspectives on Organizational Decision Making," *Administrative Science Quarterly* 31 (1986), pp. 365–88; R. M. Cyert and J. G. March, *A Behavioral Theory of the Firm* (Englewood Cliffs, N.J.: Prentice Hall, 1963); and J. D. Thompson and A. Tuden, "Strategies, Structures, and Processes of Organizational Decision," in *Comparative Studies in Administration,* ed. J. D. Thompson, P. B. Hammond, R. W. Hawkes, B. H. Junker, and A. Tuden (Pittsburgh, Pa.: University of Pittsburgh Press, 1959).

15. I. I. Mitroff, "On Systematic Problem Solving and the Error of the Third Kind," *Behavioral Science* 9 (1974), pp. 383–93.

16. P. C. Nutt, "Preventing Decision Debacles," *Technological Forecasting and Social Change* 38 (1990), pp. 159–74.

17. M. D. Cohen, J. G. March, and J. P. Olsen, "A Garbage Can Model of Organizational Choice," *Administrative Science Quarterly* 17 (1972), pp. 1–25.

18. C. Fornell and R. Westbrook, "The Vicious Circle of Consumer Complaints," *Journal of Marketing* 48 (Summer 1984), pp. 68–78; and A. Tesser and S. Rosen, "The Reluctance to Transmit Bad News," *Advances in Experimental Social Psychology* 8 (1975), pp. 193–232.

19. P. M. Senge, *The Fifth Discipline: The Art and Practice of the Learning Organization* (New York: Doubleday Currency, 1990), Chapter 10.

20. H. A. Simon, *Administrative Behavior,* 2nd ed. (New York: The Free Press, 1957), p. xxiii.

21. Simon, *Administrative Behavior,* pp. xxv, 80–84; and March and Simon, *Organizations* (New York: Wiley, 1958), pp. 140–41.

22. P. O. Soelberg, "Unprogrammed Decision Making," *Industrial Management Review* 8 (1967), pp. 19–29; and H. A. Simon, "A Behavioral Model of Rational Choice," *Quarterly Journal of Economics* 69 (1955), pp. 99–118.

23. H. A. Simon, *Models of Man: Social and Rational* (New York: Wiley, 1957), p. 253.

24. Taylor, *Behavioral Decision Making,* pp. 163–66.

25. D. R. Bobocel and J. P. Meyer, "Escalating Commitment to a Failing Course of Action: Separating the Role of Choice and Justification," *Journal of Applied Psychology* 79 (1994), pp. 360–63; and G. Whyte, "Escalating Commitment to a Course of Action: A Reinterpretation," *Academy of Management Review* 11 (1986), pp. 311–21.

26. J. Lorinc, "The Politics of Power," *Canadian Business,* March 1993, pp. 41–42; and J. Lorinc, "Power Failure," *Canadian Business,* November 1992, pp. 50–58.

27. J. Brockner, "The Escalation of Commitment to a Failing Course of Action: Toward Theoretical Progress," *Academy of Management Review* 17 (1992), pp. 39–61; and B. M. Staw and J. Ross, "Behavior in Escalation Situations," *Research in Organizational Behavior* 9 (1987), pp. 39–78.

28. D. K. Tse, K. Lee, I. Vertinsky, and D. A. Wehrung, "Does Culture Matter? A Cross-Cultural Study of Executives' Choice, Decisiveness, and Risk Adjustment in International Marketing," *Journal of Marketing* 52 (1988), pp. 81–95.

29. S. McKay, "When Good People Make Bad Choices," *Canadian Business,* February 1994, pp. 52–55.

30. P. C. Nutt, *Making Tough Decisions* (San Francisco: Jossey-Bass, 1989).

31. C. Gower-Rees, "Automatic Pilot," *Canadian Business* 61 (October 1988), pp. 183–85.

32. F. V. Guterl, "Computers Think for Business," *Dun's Business Month,* October 1986, p. 32.

33. G. Whyte, "Escalating Commitment in Individual and Group Decision Making: A Prospect Theory Approach," *Organizational Behavior and Human Decision Processes* 54 (1993), pp. 430–55.

34. R. H. Waterman, Jr., *The Renewal Factor* (New York: Bantam, 1987), pp. 47–48.

35. Nutt, *Making Tough Decisions,* p. 54; and W. H. Agor, "The Logic of Intuition," *Organizational Dynamics,* Winter 1986, pp. 5–18.

36. T. Hines, "Left Brain/Right Brain Mythology and Implications for Management and Training," *Academy of Management Review* 12 (1987), pp. 600–606.

37. O. Behling and N. L. Eckel, "Making Sense Out of Intuition," *Academy of Management Executive* 5 (February 1991), pp. 46–54; and H. A. Simon, "Making Management Decisions: The Role of Intuition and Emotion," *Academy of Management Executive,* February 1987, pp. 57–64.

38. "Buddhist Capitalist," *Report on Business Magazine,* March 1989, p. 69.

39. H. L. Dreyfus and S. E. Dreyfus, *Mind over Machine: The Power of Human Intuition and Expertise in the Era of the Computer* (New York: The Free Press, 1986).

40. A. R. Aird, P. Nowack, and J. W. Westcott, *Road to the Top* (Toronto: Doubleday Canada, 1988), p. 88.

41. W. H. Agor, "How Top Managers Use Their Intuition to Make Important Decisions," *Business Horizons* 29 (1986), pp. 49–53.

42. B. Kabanoff and J. R. Rossiter, "Recent Developments in Applied Creativity," *International Review of Industrial and Organizational Psychology* 9 (1994), pp. 283–324.

43. J. S. Dacey, "Peak Periods of Creative Growth Across the Lifespan," *Journal of Creative Behavior* 23 (1989), pp. 224–47; and F. Barron and D. M. Harrington, "Creativity, Intelligence, and Personality," *Annual Review of Psychology* 32 (1981), pp. 439–76.

44. R. M. Burnside, "Improving Corporate Climates for Creativity," in *Innovation and Creativity at Work*, ed. M. A. West and J. L. Farr (Chichester, U.K.: Wiley, 1990), pp. 265–84; and R. Von Oech, *A Whack on the Side of the Head*, rev. ed. (New York: Warner Books, 1990), Chapter 9.

45. R. W. Woodman, J. E. Sawyer, and R. W. Griffin, "Toward a Theory of Organizational Creativity," *Academy of Management Review* 18 (1993), pp. 293–321; and T. M. Amabile, "A Model of Creativity and Innovation in Organizations," *Research in Organizational Behavior* 10 (1988), pp. 123–67.

46. B. Kabanoff and P. Bottiger, "Effectiveness of Creativity Training and Its Relation to Selected Personality Factors," *Journal of Organizational Behavior* 12 (1991), pp. 235–48; and L. H. Rose and H. T. Lin, "A Meta-Analysis of Long-Term Creativity Training Programs," *Journal of Creative Behavior* 18 (1984), pp. 11–22.

47. M. Basadur, G. B. Graen, and S. G. Green, "Training in Creative Problem Solving: Effects on Ideation and Problem Finding and Solving in an Industrial Research Organization," *Organizational Behavior and Human Performance* 30 (1982), pp. 41–70.

48. F. D. Barret, "Management by Creativity and Innovation," *Business Quarterly*, Summer 1970, pp. 64–72.

49. W. J. J. Gordon, *Synectics: The Development of Creative Capacity* (New York: Harper & Row, 1961).

50. P. Mathias, "Outstanding Ethical Issues Pose Problems for All Business People," *Financial Post*, July 24, 1989, p. 22.

51. M. E. MacPherson, *Shopkeepers to a Nation: The Eatons* (Toronto: McClelland & Stewart, 1963); and G. G. Nasmith, *Timothy Eaton* (Toronto: McClelland & Stewart, 1923).

52. W. H. Shaw and V. Barry, *Moral Issues in Business*, 5th ed. (Belmont, Calif.: Wadsworth, 1992), Chapters 1–3; and M. G. Velasquez, *Business Ethics*, 2nd ed. (Englewood Cliffs, N.J.: Prentice Hall, 1988), Chapter 2.

53. B. Irvine and L. Lindsay, "Corporate Ethics and the Controller," *CMA Magazine* 67 (December 1993), pp. 23–26; J. Gandz and F. G. Bird, "Designing Ethical Organizations," *Business Quarterly* 54 (Autumn 1989), pp. 108–12; and D. Olive, *Just Rewards: The Case for Ethical Reform in Business* (Toronto: Key Porter, 1987).

54. Olive, *Just Rewards*, p. 125.

55. B. Stevens, "An Analysis of Corporate Ethical Code Studies: 'Where Do We Go from Here?' " *Journal of Business Ethics* 13 (1994), pp. 63–69; and M. Lefebvre and J. B. Singh, "The Content and Focus of Canadian Corporate Codes of Ethics," *Journal of Business Ethics* 11 (1992), pp. 799–808.

56. B. L. Catron, "Ethical Postures and Ethical Posturing," *American Review of Public Management* 17 (1983), pp. 155–59.

57. Olive, *Just Rewards*, p. 125.

58. Gandz and Bird, "Designing Ethical Organizations," pp. 108–9.

Chapter Case

Shooting Down the Avro Arrow

The Canadian government decided in 1953 to develop an all-Canadian fighter jet as an enemy aircraft interceptor. Avro Aircraft Ltd. and Orenda Engines Ltd. of Malton, Ontario (both subsidiaries of A. V. Roe Canada Ltd.), were given the contract to design and build the Avro Arrow fighter jet and Iroquois engine. The Avro development team took the Arrow from first drawings to roll out of the prototype in only 28 months and, by March 1958, had completed the first test flight. Over the next year, test pilots took the Arrow close to record-breaking speeds even though engines on the test machines had lower power than the new Iroquois turbines. Experts later stated that the Avro Arrow was one of the most advanced fighter aircraft in the skies and would have remained so for another 20 years. Canada had become a mecca for aviation engineers and was at the forefront of aircraft technology. (A few years earlier, Avro engineers had also developed and flew the first commercial jetliner in North America!)

On February 20, 1959, the Right Honourable John Diefenbaker, Prime Minister of Canada, announced to a hushed audience in Parliament that the Arrow aircraft and Iroquois engine projects would be immediately cancelled. Several weeks later, the government ordered the destruction of all documentation and the six Arrow prototypes. (Fortunately, the front section of one Arrow was hidden for several years and is now on display in Ottawa.)

Why did Diefenbaker terminate the Arrow and Iroquois projects? Several writers have concluded that Diefenbaker disliked the arrogance of the Avro executives and the fact that the project was originated by the previous Liberal government. Indeed, a year before its final decision, the government was looking for evidence that the Arrow program should be scrapped. The government incorrectly concluded that fighter jets would lose their significance as nuclear missile technology developed. Ironically, the ill-fated nuclear missile program replacing the Arrow was partly responsible for the defeat of Diefenbaker's government in the following election.

The Arrow had a respectable flying range between refueling, but government officials were critical because they had mistakenly confused range with radius (which is one-half the distance). They were also concerned with the plane's flying time; again, the Arrow had a very good flying time, but the officials did not understand the new technology of using afterburners during combat.

The government was sincerely concerned about cost overruns at Avro, but Diefenbaker inflated the figures by including development and spare parts costs. He claimed that each aircraft would cost between $8 and $12 million when, in fact, Avro had announced a fixed price of $3.75 million per copy for the first 100 and $2.6 million for the next 100 just a few months before the cancellation.

Nearly 30,000 people lost their jobs as a result of the decision to terminate the Arrow and Iroquois projects. Hundreds of leading-edge engineers left Canada to participate in new challenges elsewhere. Several dozen joined NASA in the United States and played major roles in the Gemini and Apollo programs. Others joined Boeing or other aircraft firms to help develop new aircraft technology. Said one journalist: "The brutal termination of the Arrow was a devastating blow to our technological potential." Another wrote: "The cancellation of the Arrow project . . . put the kiss of death to one of the most advanced aeronautical research and development organizations in the world. In one fell swoop, a national asset . . . came to an abrupt end."

Discussion Questions

1. **What flaws, if any, do you see in Diefenbaker's decision process?**

2. **Did escalation of commitment occur here? Why or why not?**

Sources: G. Stewart, *Shutting Down the National Dream: A. V. Roe and the Tragedy of the Avro Arrow* (Toronto: McGraw-Hill Ryerson, 1988); M. Peden, *Fall of an Arrow* (Toronto: Stoddart, 1978); The Arrowheads, *Avro Arrow* (Erin, Ontario: Boston Mills Press, 1980); and J. Floyd, *The Avro Canada C102 Jetliner* (Erin, Ontario: Boston Mills Press, 1986).

Experiential Exercise

Ethical Dilemmas in Employment

Purpose: This exercise is designed to help you apply ethical principles to real moral dilemmas that employers and employees have faced in Canada.

Instructions: The following incidents are adapted from real events and ultimately require someone to make a decision with strong moral implications. For each incident, indicate what you would do and identify one of the three ethical principles described in this chapter to explain your decision.

When everyone is done, students will form small teams and compare their decisions and justifications for each incident. If possible, try to reach a consensus on the appropriate action for each incident, but leave enough time to discuss each incident. Finally, the class will discuss each incident, beginning by tallying the actions that each student initially wrote down as well as the group results. The subsequent discussion should look at the ethical principle that dominated over others, as well as the role of personal values in ethical decision making.

The Case of the Illegal Application Form

You want to apply for a professional job at a mid-sized manufacturing company. As part of the hiring process, you are given an application form that asks, among other things, about your age and marital status. Requesting this information is a clear violation of human rights in every Canadian jurisdiction. If you bring this fact to the employer's attention, however, there is a concern that the employer might think you won't be a loyal employee or that you aren't a team player. If you leave those sections blank, the employer might come to the same conclusion or think that you have something to hide. You don't know much about the quality of the employer, but getting this job would be important to your career. What would you do?

The Case of Questionable Objectivity

You are owner of a highly rated talk radio station in Atlantic Canada. The popular radio personality on the morning phone-in show, Judy Price, is married to John Price, a lawyer who entered provincial politics a few years ago. Last month, John Price became leader of the Official Opposition. There is increasing concern from the board of directors that the radio station's perceived objectivity would be compromised if Ms. Price remains on air as a news commentator while her husband holds such a public position in the region. Some co-workers doubt that Judy Price would publicly criticize her husband or his party's policies, although they don't know for certain. Ms. Price says that her job comes first and that any attempt to remove her would represent a form of discrimination on the basis of marital status. There are no other on-air positions available for her at this station. What would you do?

The Case of the Awkward Office Affair

As head of Human Resources, you have learned from two employees that one of the office administrators, Sandi, is having an affair with Jim, an employee in shipping and receiving. Jim is single, but Sandi is married and her husband also works in the company's shipping and receiving department. You have spoken privately to Sandi, who admits to the affair but doesn't think that her husband knows about it. Moreover, she retorted that the company has no right to snoop into her private life and that she will see a lawyer if the company does anything against her. So far, there haven't been any signs of office disruption because the handful of employees who know about the affair have not communicated it through the grapevine. However, morale problems could develop if the news spreads. The two employees who initially told you about the affair believe strongly in marriage fidelity and feel that Jim, Sandi, or both should leave the company. Finally, there is the concern that Sandi's husband might have an altercation with Jim, and that the company could be liable for the consequences. What would you do?

PART

Team Processes

Team Dynamics and Effectiveness

Learning Objectives

After reading this chapter, you should be able to:

Distinguish departmental teams from team-based organizations.

Explain why people join teams.

Discuss the effects of team size on team effectiveness.

Describe the five stages of team development.

Identify four factors that shape team norms.

Explain how team cohesiveness and norms relate to team performance.

List five ways to minimize social loafing.

Identify two team building strategies to improve the interpersonal process.

Chapter Outline

What Are Teams?

Formal Work Teams.

Informal Groups.

Why Do People Join Teams?

A Model of Team Dynamics and Effectiveness.

Team Context and Design.

Stages of Team Development.

Team Norms.

Team Cohesiveness.

Social Loafing.

Team Building.

Courtesy of GE Canada.

Teams are a way of life at GE Canada's jet engine plant in Bromont, Quebec. There is a senior management team, an A team of professionals and administrative personnel, and eight B teams of people on the plant floor. The senior management team includes the plant manager and six other executives (e.g., human resources, finance) who are responsible for the plant's overall direction. The A team has several dozen consultants and support personnel who serve the production and maintenance teams.

Most of Bromont's 600 employees are members of the eight B teams, including a maintenance team, and tooling team, a warehouse team, and five production teams. Each production team consists of approximately 80 people responsible for a specific part of the production system 24 hours per day, seven days of the week. This includes maintaining production

schedules, employee schedules, training, and product quality. Teams are also responsible for hiring new employees and coordinating with other teams. One member is selected by the others to co-ordinate the team for six months. At the end of that time, the coordinator trains the next person selected for that role.

To improve team dynamics, GE Bromont employees are trained in effective listening, conflict management, and interpersonal skill development. They learn how to become good facilitators and preside over meetings. All A team members and some B members also attend a seven-day personal development program that teaches them to manage their emotions in a group. Team members are continually mastering other tasks in their team (i.e., multiskilling) through job rotation and team training.

Bromont's emphasis on teams has paid off in higher productivity and employee satisfaction. Bromont has the lowest manufacturing costs of any plant in GE's worldwide aircraft engine division, and enjoys very low employee turnover and absenteeism.[1]

Teams are replacing individuals as the basic building block of organizations. When Asea Brown Boveri (ABB) moved its distribution switchgear division to a new building in Milton, Ontario, employees were placed into cross-functional teams responsible for different work processes in the plant. At Amoco Canada, over 1,000 task forces have been searching for superfluous assets and jobs. Vancouver City Savings, Levi Strauss, and many other businesses have formed employee committees to do everything from choosing compensation surveys to distributing charity funds.[2]

This chapter looks at the dynamics and effectiveness of formal work teams as well as informal groups in organizations. We begin by introducing the different types of teams in organizational settings and discuss the reasons why people want to belong to teams. A basic model of team dynamics and effectiveness is then outlined. Most of the chapter examines each part of this model, including team context and design, team development, norms, and cohesiveness. The chapter concludes by surveying the strategies to build more effective work teams.

What Are Teams?

Work teams and informal groups consist of two or more people who interact and mutually influence each other to achieve common goals.[3] A team may have only two people or it may have hundreds, although a large team has more difficulty maintaining meaningful interaction among its members. All groups require some form of communication so that members can coordinate and share common meaning.

All groups exist to fulfill some purpose. Members of formal work teams might share the common goal of assembling a product, providing a service, or making an important decision. An informal group might exist so that its members can enjoy each other's company. In every type of group, members are dependent on each other because their goals require collaboration with others. Finally, group members influence each other so that their effort is directed toward the group's objectives. Everyone on the team has influence, although some members are typically more powerful than others.

Formal Work Teams

Formal work team
Two or more people who interact and mutually influence each other for the purpose of achieving common goals. Formal teams are explicitly formed to serve an organizational purpose.

Formal work teams are explicitly formed to accomplish a specific set of tasks for the organization. Departments may represent formal teams, although this is not always so. Departments lack a team structure when employees work alone and report individually to the immediate supervisor, as shown in Exhibit 10–1(a).[4] Until recently, Honeywell Ltd.'s plant in Scarborough, Ontario, followed this individualistic structure. Employees were expected to take directions from the supervisor and do their work without talking to co-workers.[5]

Formal Teams in Organizations

Exhibit 10–1

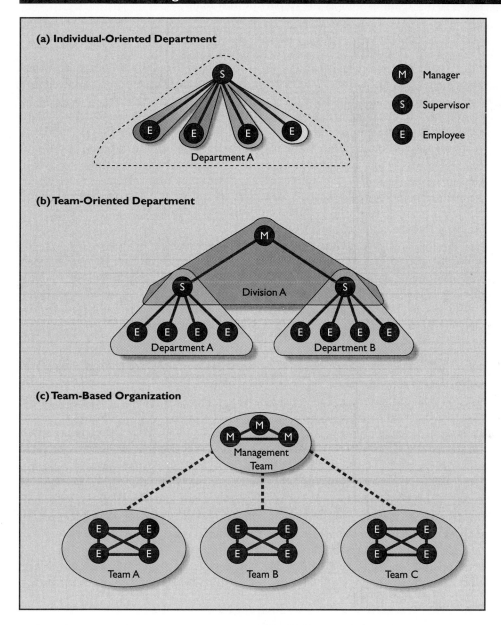

(a) Individual-Oriented Department

M   Manager

S   Supervisor

E   Employee

Department A

(b) Team-Oriented Department

Division A

Department A

Department B

(c) Team-Based Organization

Management Team

Team A

Team B

Team C

Source: Parts (a) and (b) are based on R. Likert, *New Patterns of Management* (New York: McGraw-Hill, 1961), p. 107.

A department becomes a formal work team when employees are encouraged to directly interact and coordinate work activities with each other. People feel that they are members of a team because they directly share information. As we can see in Exhibit 10–1(b), the supervisor still coordinates some work activities and serves as a "linking pin" to higher levels in the organization. This establishes a conduit for communication and maintains some degree of integration among teams. Also notice that the supervisor is a member of the supervisory team as well as the departmental team.

Team-based organizations

Team-based (or lateral) structure
A type of departmentation with a flat span of control and relatively little formalization, consisting of self-managing work teams responsible for various work processes.

GE Canada's Bromont plant and other contemporary **team-based organizational structures** (also known as *lateral* or *high involvement* organizations) resemble the form shown in Exhibit 10–1(c). This differs from traditional departmental teams in a few ways. First, team-based groups have far more autonomy than traditional departmental teams—virtually all day-to-day decisions are made by team members, rather than someone further up the organizational hierarchy. Second, most teams are formed around work processes rather than functional departments. For example, one Bromont team is responsible for an entire subassembly 24 hours per day, seven days of the week. In a traditional plant, these employees would be grouped into different functional departments (e.g., welding, electrical) and work shifts.

Finally, Bromont's teams do not have a supervisor to coordinate the work or serve as a linking pin to the next organizational level. In fact, the supervisory role is almost completely delegated to the team by having members take turns as the coordinator. The supervisor's linking pin role is replaced with longer-term directives from senior management to the entire team, as indicated by the dashed lines in Exhibit 10–1(c). We will look more closely at this emerging team-based structure in Chapter 17.

Task forces

Task forces consist of people assigned to a specific task or project. Members are often drawn from several departments so that different areas of expertise are represented. Task forces are usually short lived because they disband when the task is completed.

Concurrent engineering team
A special cross-functional task force of designers, manufacturing engineers, marketing people, and others who work together to design products and services.

Task forces have become the preferred strategy in many companies for resolving unique problems or opportunities. For instance, Toronto's Sunnybrook Health Science Centre used a task force of nurses and other professionals to develop a new chart system for medical/surgical records.[6] Many companies have introduced **concurrent engineering teams** (also called *platform teams* or *parallel processing teams*) to design products and services. As Perspective 10–1 explains, these task forces bring together design, engineering, manufacturing, and marketing people to make design decisions more quickly and effectively.

Skunkworks

Skunkwork
A task force of employees borrowed from several functional areas of the organization to develop new products, services, or procedures, usually in isolation from the organization and without the normal restrictions.

Skunkworks are task forces initiated by an innovative employee (a *champion*) who borrows people and resources (called *bootlegging*) to help the organization.[7] The term originated in the 1940s as the name of a special group that designed and built aircraft for Lockheed Corporation. Skunkworks are formed spontaneously to develop products or solve problems, and usually disband when the project is finished. They are typically isolated from the rest of the organization, and are able to ignore the more bureaucratic rules governing other organizational units. For example, Ford's popular Mustang was designed in the 1960s by a team of people that Lee Iacocca pulled together from design, marketing, and public relations. The group, called the Fairlane Committee, met regularly at a

Perspective 10–1

Concurrent Engineering Teams Improve Product Design

Pratt & Whitney Canada of Longueuil, Quebec, recently formed a concurrent engineering team to design the PW500 turbofan engine in less than 12 months. The project would have taken between 18 and 24 months with a traditional product design process, but the concurrent engineering team telescoped the time frame by working on different phases of the project simultaneously.

Concurrent engineering combines design, manufacturing, marketing, purchasing, and other people responsible for developing a product or service into a team that works in the same location. This contrasts with the traditional design process, in which a design engineer designs the product alone and then "throws it over the wall" to someone in the manufacturing department, who then passes it on to the production or purchasing department for further work. The marketing person responsible for the product might not see the result until just before production begins. These people traditionally work in separate areas of the company and, in some cases, never directly communicate with each other.

Concurrent engineering speeds up product development because team members can begin their part of the project sooner. For instance, the manufacturing engineer begins tool and assembly design as soon as he or she has tentative information about the product design. The marketing representative monitors and tests the product design with customers throughout the development process rather than afterwards. Suppliers, production line employees, and customers are often involved at various times in the design process.

Concurrent engineering teams also avoid delays by correcting design problems soon after they appear. "It's not that design engineers go out of their way to create problems for others," says Pratt & Whitney Canada's vice-president for development engineering. "They simply lack the knowledge others have. Maintenance staff and manufacturing engineers have a different perspective on the process. Their input at an earlier stage results in better designs."

Asea Brown Boveri Canada (ABB) discovered the effectiveness of concurrent engineering teams at its power transformer manufacturing plant in Guelph, Ontario. ABB's engineers had been working alone, designing transformer products that looked great on paper but had a high failure rate in the field. When ABB introduced concurrent engineering, the joint efforts of marketing, manufacturing, and design people resulted in simpler designs that were easier to manufacture. Within the first year, the product failure rate was reduced by 50 percent.

The only problem was that some ABB employees were not accustomed to working in teams. ABB Canada vice-president Lars Nilsson explains: "It was a shock for some R&D people to discuss their designs with marketing and manufacturing managers. Designers are used to working in isolation."

Sources: Based on K. Mark, "All in One Go," *Canadian Business* (Special Technology Issue), Spring 1994, pp. 39–43; W. I. Zangwill, *Lightning Strategies for Innovation: How the World's Best Firms Create New Products* (New York: Lexington, 1993); J. V. Owen, "Concurrent Engineering," *Manufacturing Engineering* 109 (November 1992), pp. 69–73; J. Zeidenberg, "New Focus for Old Strategy," *Globe & Mail,* October 1, 1991, p. B28; and L. Surtees, "A Rational View of the World," *Globe & Mail,* November 11, 1991, pp. B1, B6.

hotel of the same name rather than at Ford headquarters so that it could operate without corporate interference.[8]

Informal Groups

Along with formal teams, organizations consist of **informal groups** that exist primarily for the benefit of their members.[9] Informal groups are not specifically formed by organizational decision makers, although their structure may be influenced by the existence of formal teams. They shape communication patterns

Informal group
Two or more people who group together primarily to meet their personal (rather than organizational) needs.

This concurrent engineering team at Pratt & Whitney Canada designed the PW500 turbofan engine in less than 12 months—a process that would require more than 18 months with a traditional nonteam structure.

Laura Arsie. LA Photography. Used with permission.

in the organization, particularly the grapevine described in Chapter 6. Informal groups can also interfere with the formal team because members might resist their formal team's activities that conflict with the informal group's values.

Exhibit 10–2 illustrates how members of a formal team may belong to different informal groups. Some informal groups, such as the group you meet for lunch, might overlap with the formal team. These groups form out of convenience and the need for affiliation. Other groups are bound together for reasons other than social needs. For instance, you might belong to an informal group that shares a car pool and another group that plays together on the company's sports team.

Coalition

Two or more people who influence other people about a specific issue by banding together to increase their power.

A **coalition** is an informal group that attempts to influence people outside the group by pooling the resources and power of its members. By banding together, coalition members have more power than if each person worked alone to influence others. They also reinforce each other and further mobilize support for their position.[10] The coalition's mere existence can be a source of power by symbolizing the importance or level of support for the issue. Bill Hopper's dismissal as CEO of Petro Canada began with a coalition of some people from management and the board of directors. By aligning themselves with this informal group, coalition members convinced others that their concerns about Hopper's leadership should be taken seriously.

Informal groups and cultural diversity

The composition of informal groups is an indicator of the organization's success at integrating its culturally diverse work force. For example, most of Toronto's major hotels have a multicultural work force, but employees tend to be ethnically segregated within the organization. At one hotel, the staff cafeteria employees are mainly West Indian, whereas the executive dining room is dominated by white Canadians. Housekeeping employees at another hotel are mainly Portuguese, whereas the laundry staff members are Chinese.[11] This

Informal Groups in Organizations   **Exhibit 10–2**

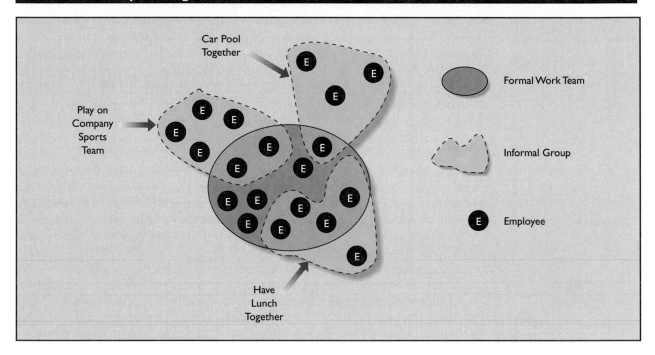

ethnic segregation is partly explained by the powerful effects of culturally based informal groups on employment patterns.

An organization's cultural diversity is indicated by the diversity of its informal groups, not just the diversity of its formal teams. Even when a formal team has a broad multicultural mixture, its members might develop informal social groups based on ethnic background. Realizing this, TRW's Space & Electronics Group assesses the effectiveness of its cultural diversity program by monitoring the ethnic and gender patterns of informal networks and relationships among employees.[12]

Why Do People Join Teams?

Why are people willing to join and maintain their membership in a group? In the case of formal work teams, employees usually must join or lose their job! But the issue is more complex than this, because people assigned to a formal team may still leave or be frequently absent. A more fundamental explanation is that people join teams because they believe their personal needs will be fulfilled better in a group than by working alone. From this perspective, we can identify three factors that attract people to teams: goal accomplishment, affiliation and status, and emotional support.

Goal accomplishment

People often join and remain members of teams to achieve goals that cannot be accomplished individually. As we learned in our discussion of job design

(Chapter 4), individuals performing specialized jobs within a team often achieve higher productivity than if each person performs all the tasks alone. For example, individual hockey players cannot win games alone, so they join forces, divide the work, assign roles, and learn to coordinate their actions. Some members play forward, others play defense, and someone serves as goal tender. As individuals learn that working together increases the probability of achieving goals, it becomes easier to attract new members who value the team's objectives, such as completing a project or winning the Stanley Cup.

Affiliation and status

People frequently join groups to fulfill their need for friendship and social interaction. As we learned in Chapter 3, most people desire friendship and approval from others. Individuals with a very high need for affiliation are particularly motivated to become team members because they want to seek approval from others, conform to those people's wishes and expectations, and avoid conflict and confrontation.

Along with receiving approval from other members, individuals may receive approval and respect from nonmembers if the team is highly regarded. A particular work team may be viewed as a high status group by outsiders. This status is then ascribed to all members of the team.[13] A related point is that we define ourselves by our group affiliations.[14] If we belong to work teams or informal groups that are viewed favourably by others, then we tend to view ourselves more favourably. We are motivated to become members of groups that are similar to ourselves because this reinforces our self-identity.

Emotional support

Under threatening circumstances, we are comforted by the physical presence of other people and are motivated to be near others, including strangers.[15] This phenomenon has been observed among soldiers under enemy fire. During the stressful conditions of battle, many soldiers tend to huddle together because it makes them feel more secure. The problem is most common among replacement soldiers—those who have recently been added to the unit—because they have not established social relations with veteran members and feel particularly insecure about battle conditions. Unfortunately, huddling together is a dangerous practice when soldiers face enemy fire. Yet even after being told repeatedly to disperse under fire, many soldiers still tend to huddle together because of the emotional support the group provides.[16]

A Model of Team Dynamics and Effectiveness

What are the characteristics of effective teams? Why do some groups have a strong team spirit while others barely survive? These questions have interested organizational theorists for some time and, as you might expect, numerous models of team effectiveness have been proposed over the years.[17]

Team effectiveness refers to how the group affects the organization in which it exists, its individual members, and the group's existence.[18] First, most groups exist to serve some purpose relating to the organization or other system in which the group operates. Production teams at GE Canada's Bromont plant try to achieve the company's objectives regarding product quality, quantity of output, efficient use of raw materials, and so forth. Many informal groups also have system-level goals, such as a coalition that wants to persuade senior management to change a corporate policy.

Second, team effectiveness includes the satisfaction and well-being of its members. People join groups to fulfill their personal needs, so it makes sense that effectiveness is partly measured by this need fulfillment. Finally, team effectiveness refers to the group's ability to survive. It must be able to maintain the commitment of its members, particularly during the turbulence of the team's development. Without this commitment, people leave and the group will quickly fall apart.

Exhibit 10–3 presents the major influences on team effectiveness that we will describe over the next several pages. First, we will look at the team's context and design, including the internal and external environment, the task that the team wants to accomplish, team size, and team composition. Next, we will examine the team's structure and processes, including the group's stage of development, its norms, and its level of cohesiveness. Generally, teams are more effective when members agree on pivotal rules to coordinate behaviour and maintain solidarity, and are motivated to maintain their membership and contribute to the accomplishment of the team's objectives.

Team effectiveness
The extent to which the team achieves its objectives, achieves the needs and objectives of its members, and sustains itself over time.

Team Context and Design

Our discussion of team dynamics and effectiveness logically begins with the contextual factors that influence group structure and processes. These inputs include the organizational environments, task characteristics, team size, and team composition.

Organizational environments

Team effectiveness varies with several features of the organizational environment. The physical layout of the worksite is important, because teams work better when their members are able to communicate easily with each other. Similarly, team effectiveness requires a favourable physical location to perform the task. This was apparent in a study of wood harvesting crews in northwestern Ontario. Harvesting crews were assigned different wood lots to cut and their performance (the amount of wood cut) clearly depended on the mix of trees in the designated harvest area. These teams could harvest more efficiently where the trees were not too large or small and the area consisted mainly of a single species.[19]

Teams are also more effective when they have supportive management and receive sufficient resources to perform the work. Two other environmental conditions are technology and external competition, both of which may

Exhibit 10–3   **A Model of Team Dynamics and Effectiveness**

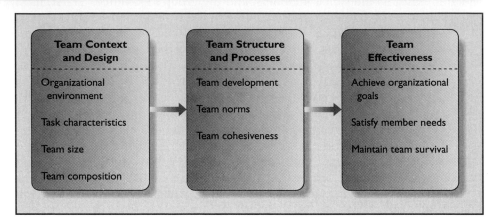

influence the team's cohesiveness. Organizational values may shape the team's norms. Finally, reward systems have a powerful influence on the team's objectives and ability to get members motivated to work together. For instance, one recent survey reported that teams most often fail because members are rewarded for individual rather than team effort.[20]

Task characteristics

The tasks that teams perform can affect their structure, process, and effectiveness.[21] Teams are generally more effective when tasks are clear and easy to implement, because team members can learn their roles more quickly.[22] In contrast, teams engaged in ill-defined tasks require more time to agree on the best division of labour and the correct way to accomplish the goal. These are typically more complex tasks requiring diverse skills and backgrounds, which further strain the team's ability to develop and form a cohesive unit.

Task interdependence
The extent to which work activities among people are interrelated.

Another important factor, called **task interdependence,** refers to the level of relationship among employees in their work activities. It exists when people share common inputs to their tasks or directly depend on others for materials, assistance, or information.[23] Teams are well suited to highly interdependent tasks because people coordinate better when working together than separately. This is why concurrent engineering teams (described earlier in Perspective 10–1) are more effective than individuals in product development. The design, marketing, and manufacturing elements of the project are highly interdependent, so a cross-functional team coordinates the work more efficiently than individuals working in separate functional departments.

Team size

What is the best size for a work team or informal group? Linimar Machine Ltd. and Magna International try to keep their plants to fewer than 200 employees so that they maintain a team spirit where everyone knows each other. Bata Footwear has taken a similar approach by shifting from large manufacturing operations that produce several different product lines to much smaller plants in which fewer employees work on a single product line. Teamwork is easier to develop in mini-plants because employees can more easily see the entire production process as well as their contribution to the plant's success.[24]

Mini-plants may engender a stronger sense of team spirit than traditional factories and offices, but the most effective teams usually have fewer than 20 members. These groups have enough people with diverse skills to accomplish their objectives, yet are small enough for members to know each other, exchange ideas, and agree on team goals. Larger teams are typically less effective because members consume more time and effort coordinating their roles and resolving differences.[25] Individuals have less opportunity to partici-pate and, consequently, are less likely to feel that they are contributing to the team's success. Larger work units tend to break into informal subgroups around common interests and work activities, leading members to form stronger commitments to their subgroup than to the larger team. For instance, although GE Canada's Bromont plant has teams of 80 people, each team would have several informal groups based on common interests or work hours.

Team composition

A team's effectiveness depends on membership composition. Members must possess the necessary abilities and role perceptions to accomplish the team's objectives, although each person may possess only some of the necessary skills.[26] Team members also must be motivated to perform the team's task, but this is more complex than motivating individuals working alone. Specifically, team members must be motivated to agree on the goal, work together rather than alone, and abide by the team's rules of conduct. Employees with a collectivist orientation—those who value group membership and mutual dependence (see Chapter 8)—tend to perform better in work teams, whereas those with a strong individualist orientation tend to perform better alone. For this reason, Shell Canada, Toyota Canada, and other companies are more carefully selecting job applicants with the motivation and ability to work in teams.[27]

Team heterogeneity

The effectiveness of a team is further influenced by the diversity of its members. **Homogeneous teams** include members with common technical expertise, ethnicity, experiences, or values, whereas **heterogeneous teams** have members with diverse personal characteristics and backgrounds. Employees experience higher satisfaction, less conflict, and better interpersonal relations when their team members have similar backgrounds. Consequently, homogeneous teams tend to be more effective on tasks requiring a high degree of cooperation and coordination, such as emergency response teams or string quartets.[28]

Heterogeneous teams experience more interpersonal conflict and take longer to develop, but they are generally more effective than homogeneous teams on complex projects and problems requiring innovative solutions.[29] This is because people from different backgrounds see a problem or opportunity from different perspectives. As we learned in Chapter 9, this ability to see things from different perspectives is important for creative decision making. Hetero-geneous team members also solve complex problems more easily because they usually have a broader knowledge base. Finally, a team's diversity may give it

Homogeneous teams
Formal or informal groups whose members have common personal characteristics, backgrounds, and values.

Heterogeneous teams
Formal or informal groups whose members have diverse personal characteristics, backgrounds, and values.

Exhibit 10–4 **Stages of Team Development**

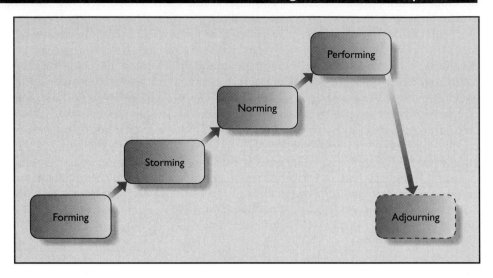

more legitimacy or allow its members to obtain a wide network of cooperation and support in the organization.

Stages of Team Development

Team members must resolve several issues and pass through several stages of development before emerging as an effective work unit. They must get to know each other, understand their respective roles, discover appropriate and inappropriate behaviours, and learn how to coordinate their work or social activities. This is an ongoing process because teams change as new members join and old members leave. Tuckman's five-stage model of team development, shown in Exhibit 10–4, provides a general outline of how teams evolve by forming, storming, norming, performing, and eventually adjourning.[30]

Forming

The first stage of team development is a period of testing and orientation in which members learn about each other and evaluate the benefits and costs of continued membership. People tend to be polite during this stage and will defer to the existing authority of a formal or informal leader who must provide an initial set of rules and structures for interaction. Members experience a form of socialization (described in Chapter 16) as they try to find out what is expected of them and how they will fit into the team.

Storming

During the storming stage of team development, individual members become more proactive by taking on specific roles and task responsibilities. This stage is marked by interpersonal conflict as members compete for leadership and other positions in the team. Coalitions may form to influence the team's goals and means of goal attainment. Members try to establish norms of appropriate behaviour and performance standards. This is a tenuous stage in the team's development, particularly when the leader is autocratic and lacks the necessary conflict-management skills.

Every formal team and informal group has two sets of roles—behaviours and expectations assigned to a particular position—that help it to survive and be more productive. One set of roles helps focus the team on its objectives, such as giving and seeking information, elaborating ideas, coordinating activities, and summarizing the discussion or past events. The other set of roles tries to maintain good working relations among team members. These socioemotional roles include resolving conflicts among team members, keeping communication channels open, reinforcing positive behaviours of other team members, and making team members aware of group process problems when they emerge.[31] During the storming stage, team members begin to sort out the specific features of these roles as well as identify the members responsible for each role.

Norming

During the norming stage, the team develops its first real sense of cohesion as roles are established and a consensus forms around group objectives. By now, members have developed a set of expectations and rules to help them interact more efficiently in the process of goal accomplishment. Through self-disclosure and feedback, members are also better able to understand and accept each other (recall the Johari Window described in Chapter 7).

Performing

The team becomes more task-oriented in the performing stage because it shifts from establishing and maintaining relations to accomplishing its objectives. Team members have learned to coordinate their actions and to resolve conflicts more efficiently. Further coordination improvements must occasionally be addressed, but the greater emphasis is on task accomplishment. In high-performance teams, members are highly cooperative, have a high level of trust in each other, are committed to group objectives, and identify with the team.[32]

Adjourning

Most work teams and informal groups eventually end. Task forces disband when their project is completed. Informal work groups may reach this stage when several members leave the organization or are reassigned elsewhere. Some teams adjourn as a result of lay-offs or plant shutdowns. Whatever the cause of team adjournment, members shift their attention away from task orientation to a socioemotional focus as they realize that their relationship is ending.

Tuckman's model provides a useful framework, but we must keep in mind that it is not a perfect representation of the dynamics of team development.[33] It does not recognize that team development is a continuous process. As membership changes and new conditions emerge, the team may cycle back to earlier stages in the developmental process. Some groups remain in a particular stage longer than others, and two stages of development may overlap.

Team Norms

Have you ever noticed how employees in some departments almost run for the exit door the minute the work day ends, whereas people performing similar work in other groups stay to finish their tasks? These differences are due to **norms**—the informal rules and expectations that groups establish to regulate the behaviour of their members. Norms apply only to behaviour, not to private thoughts or feelings. Moreover, norms exist only for behaviours that are important to the team.[34]

Norms guide many aspects of organizational life, such as the way team members deal with clients, how they share resources with other team members, and whether they are willing to work longer hours. Some norms improve team effectiveness by ensuring that members learn their roles and abide by them. This improves coordination and interaction as members know what is expected. Other norms might conflict with organizational objectives. For example, senior management at the American Cyanamid plant in Niagara Falls, Ontario, carefully selected first-level supervisors for training to develop a more participative leadership style. However, the supervisors soon returned to more autocratic ways when their colleagues scolded them for being brainwashed by the company.[35] The organization wanted more democracy in the workplace, but this conflicted with the supervisors' norm that valued a less participative management style.

Conformity to team norms

Everyone has experienced peer pressure at one time or another.[36] Co-workers grimace if we are late for a meeting or make sarcastic comments if we don't have our part of the project completed on time. In more extreme situations, the team may temporarily ostracize deviant members or threaten to terminate their membership. These actions are forms of coercive power that teams use to enforce their norms.

Norms are also directly reinforced through praise from high-status members, more access to valued resources, or other rewards available to the team.[37] But team members often conform to prevailing norms without direct reinforcement or punishment because they identify with the group and want to align their behaviour with the team's values. This effect is particularly strong in new members because they are uncertain of their status and want to demonstrate their membership in the team.

The power of conformity to team norms is revealed in the classic story of an employee assigned to work with a small group of pressers in a pajama factory.[38] The group had informally established a norm that 50 units per hour was the upper limit of acceptable output. As Exhibit 10–5 illustrates, the newcomer quickly reached this level and soon began to exceed it. By Day 12, co-workers were making sarcastic remarks about her excessive performance, so the employee reduced her output to a level acceptable to the team. On Day 20, the team had to be broken up and everyone except the new employee was transferred to other jobs. With the others gone and the team norm no longer in effect, the employee's performance in the pressing room nearly doubled within a few days. For the next 20 days, she maintained a performance level of 92 units per hour compared with 45 units in the presence of co-workers.

Influence of Team Norms on Individual Behaviour   Exhibit 10–5

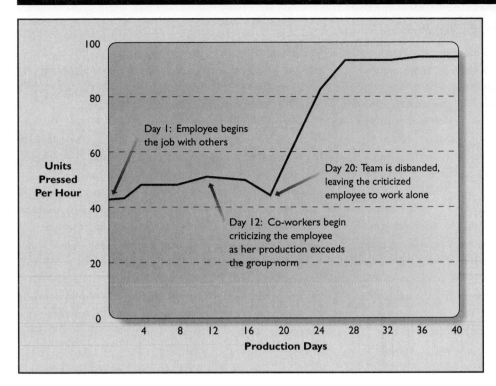

Many companies benefit from team conformity to control safety, performance, attendance, and other work behaviours. Perspective 10–2 describes how this peer pressure can improve organizational performance, but it also raises ethical questions about controlling employee behaviour through co-workers.[39]

How team norms develop

Norms develop as team members learn that certain behaviours help them function more effectively.[40] Some norms develop when team members or outsiders make explicit statements that seem to aid the team's success or survival. For example, the team leader might frequently express the importance of treating customers with respect and courtesy. A second factor triggering the development of a new norm is a critical event in the team's history. A team might develop a strong norm to keep the work area clean after a co-worker slips on metal scraps and seriously injures herself.

A third influence on team norms is the primacy effect.[41] Recall from Chapter 7 that the primacy effect is the tendency to quickly form opinions based on our initial experiences. The primacy effect causes initial team experiences to set the tone for future behaviours. Thus, the team's first meeting might establish norms about where people sit in the room or whether they address co-workers by their first or last names. Finally, norms develop from the beliefs and values that members bring to the team. For example, one recent study reported that bargaining groups form norms about appropriate bargaining behaviour based on each member's previous bargaining experience.[42]

Perspective 10–2

The Power and Politics of Peer Pressure

After a poor safety record during the mid-1980s, Dunkley Lumber introduced a safety program that put employees into small safety teams to watch each other's safety behaviour. The independently owned sawmill near Prince George, British Columbia, soon discovered that peer pressure to "do it safely or not at all" has a powerful influence on employee behaviour. Dunkley Lumber hasn't had a lost-time accident since introducing the safety team practice.

In many Japanese companies, peer pressure keeps employees at work long after the formal work day is over. Ming Ho, a graduate student at the University of Waterloo, saw how team norms had this effect when he worked at Hitachi Ltd. as part of a Canada–Japan exchange program. Working hours at Hitachi are supposed to be from 8:30 A.M. until 5:15, but everyone routinely works until 8 or 9 P.M. Many come in on weekends. "If you leave, you become very noticeable," Ho explains. "You'd be seen as slacking off if you didn't stay overtime."

Japanese auto makers have applied the power of group conformity to reduce absenteeism at their North American plants. They accomplish this by making team members carry the extra workload when a co-worker is absent. This puts incredible pressure on employees to show up for work rather than face humiliation or possibly ostracism from other team members.

Although this strategy has kept absenteeism rates low, it also raises ethical concerns in the workplace. Mumir Khalid, a union leader at McDonnell Douglas Canada, doesn't want the company to use teams for this type of conformity. "Team work leads to competition between teams, speed-up, and peer pressure within teams," he warns. "It also leads to team members reprimanding fellow workers if they are absent or can't keep up for any reason."

Many employees at CAMI Automotive Inc. in Ingersoll, Ontario, seem to agree with Khalid's statement. The joint venture of General Motors and Suzuki opened in 1989 with a strong team orientation that encourages employees to work together and solve problems. During its first year, only 19 percent of employees thought that CAMI's focus on teams was an attempt to get workers to exert pressure on one another. But in a more recent survey, 44 percent felt that teams are used as a control system to boost attendance and job performance.

Sources: Based on D. Bochove, "Culture Shock Proves a Major Component of Work-Study Tour," *Globe & Mail*, July 6, 1993, p. B16; D. Robertson, J. Rinehart, C. Huxley, and the CAW Research Group at CAMI, "Team Concept and Kaizen: Japanese Production Management in a Unionized Canadian Auto Plant," *Studies in Political Economy* 39 (Autumn 1992), pp. 77–107; R. R. Rehder, "Building Cars as if People Mattered," *Columbia Journal of World Business* 27 (Summer 1992), pp. 56–70; S. Simpson, "Dunkley Lumber Sets Itself a New Safety Standard," *Your Workplace Health and Safety*, Fall 1991, p. 1; and W. List, "CAW Rejects Concept of Work Teams as Not in Workers' Interest," *Globe & Mail*, October 23, 1989, p. B3.

Changing team norms

Although many team norms are deeply anchored, there are ways to form positive norms and change those that undermine organizational effectiveness. One approach is to apply the primacy effect by introducing performance-oriented norms as soon as the team is created. Another strategy is to select members who will bring desirable norms to the group. For example, if the organization wants team norms to emphasize safety, team members who already value this standard should be selected.

Selecting people with positive norms may be effective in new teams, but not when adding new members to existing teams with counterproductive norms. A better strategy for existing teams is to explicitly discuss the counterproductive norm with team members using persuasive communication tactics (see Chapter 6).[43]

Team-based reward systems can sometimes weaken counterproductive norms. Unfortunately, the pressure to conform to the counterproductive norm is sometimes stronger than the financial incentive.[44] For instance, employees working in the pajama factory described earlier were paid under a piece-rate system. Most individuals in the group were able to process more units and thereby earn more money, but they all chose to abide by the group norm of 50 units per hour.

Finally, a dysfunctional norm may be so deeply ingrained that the best strategy is to disband the group and replace it with people having more favourable norms. Companies should again seize the opportunity to introduce performance-oriented norms when the new team is formed, and select members who will bring desirable norms to the group.

Team Cohesiveness

An important characteristic of any work team is its level of cohesiveness. **Cohesiveness** is the degree of attraction people feel toward the team and their motivation to remain members.[45] It is the glue or *esprit de corps* that holds the group together and ensures that its members fulfill their obligations. Cohesiveness is directly connected to the three functions of teams described earlier in this chapter. Employees want to remain members because they believe the team will help them achieve their personal goals, fulfill their need for affiliation or status, or provide social support during times of crisis or trouble.[46] These fundamental motives are connected to several causes of team cohesiveness, which we discuss next.

Cohesiveness
The degree of attraction that members feel toward their team and their motivation to remain members.

Causes of team cohesiveness

The level of team cohesiveness depends on the factors listed in Exhibit 10–6. Generally, these factors influence a person's identity with the group and the group's usefulness in fulfilling the individual's basic needs.[47] Several of these factors are related to our earlier discussion of the attractiveness and development of teams. Teams become more cohesive as they reach higher stages of development and are more attractive to potential members.

Member similarity

It is easier to develop cohesiveness in a homogeneous team than a heterogeneous team. People are motivated to interact with others having similar opinions because it confirms their perspective of reality and makes them feel more comfortable with themselves.[48] People who think alike find it easier to agree on team objectives, the means to fulfill those objectives, and the rules applied to maintain group behaviour. This, in turn, leads to greater trust and less dysfunctional conflict within the group—two desirable qualities for its members.

Member interaction

Team cohesiveness increases with the amount of interaction among its members.[49] Thus, teams are cohesive when members perform highly interdependent tasks and are located in close physical proximity, and when the work space lets them interact more easily. Physical space should maximize interaction among members within

Exhibit 10–6   **Factors Contributing to Team Cohesiveness**

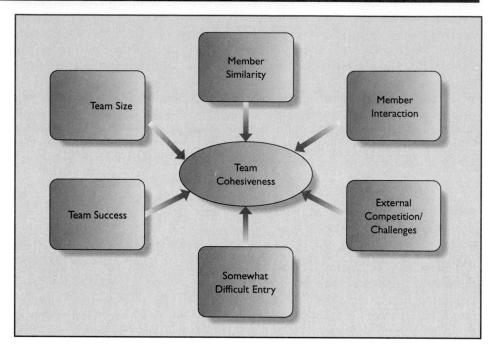

the group and avoid too much interaction with people in other groups.[50] This involves moving wall partitions and other architectural barriers so that they increase contact among team members, yet separate them from other groups.

Maintaining team cohesiveness is more of a challenge when some members work at home (i.e., telecommute) or are frequently in the field with clients. To increase interaction, team leaders will call in-person meetings so that everyone maintains a sense of commitment to the team. Calgary-based Minerva Technology has about 80 software engineers under contract at customer sites, so it maintains their cohesiveness by holding frequent social gatherings at headquarters. Minerva's president explains: "It's important to constantly bring them back for lunches and parties to keep them in touch with other employees."[51]

External competition and challenges

Team cohesiveness increases when members face external competition or a challenging, yet valued, objective. One reason is that teams serve an important socioemotional function that is particularly valuable during times of trouble. As we noted earlier, the physical presence of others in the same situation reduces the stress associated with the threatening situation. The second reason is that people feel more cohesiveness when they face an important objective that is best accomplished by the team rather than individually. Of course, teams remain cohesive only when members believe that working together is more effective than working alone to overcome the challenge. Teams quickly fall apart otherwise.

Somewhat difficult entry

Teams tend to be more cohesive when it is *somewhat* difficult to become a member. Notice the emphasis on the word *somewhat*—severe initiations result-

Strategies to Increase Team Cohesiveness	Exhibit 10–7

- Select members with similar goals, attitudes, and experiences.
- Maintain high entrance standards when selecting team members. For example, potential members should pass through several interviews and possibly complete a rigorous training schedule.
- Assign team members to the same physical area, such as a separate building or floor.
- Use open office designs within the group; use walls and partitions between groups.
- Keep the team small, without jeopardizing its ability to accomplish the task.
- Set challenging objectives that are valued by the team.
- Make the team aware of external threats, such as competition from other organizations.
- Facilitate and celebrate team successes. Provide sufficient resources for the team to complete its tasks. Personally recognize and publicize team accomplishments.

ing in humiliation or high personal expense can do more damage than good to bonding the individual to the group. Cohesiveness increases with a somewhat difficult entry because this tends to make teams more prestigious in each member's opinion. Moreover, existing team members are more willing to welcome and support new members after they have "passed the test," possibly because they have shared the same entry experience.[52]

Team success

Cohesiveness increases with the team's level of success.[53] Successful teams are more attractive to current and potential members because people like to be identified with success. Moreover, they are more likely to believe the group will achieve future goals that benefit its members.

Team size

Smaller teams tend to be more cohesive than larger teams because it is easier for a few people to agree on goals and coordinate work activities. This does not mean that the smallest teams are the most cohesive, however. Having too few members may prevent the team from accomplishing its objectives. Continued failure may undermine the cohesiveness as members begin to question the team's ability to satisfy their needs. Thus, team cohesiveness is potentially greatest when teams are as small as possible, yet large enough to accomplish the required tasks.

Team cohesiveness may be difficult to influence, but the above discussion suggests that it is possible. Exhibit 10–7 lists several actions that might increase team cohesiveness. If you want to reduce (rather than increase) cohesiveness, then the opposite recommendations should be applied.

Consequences of team cohesiveness

Every team must have some minimal level of cohesiveness to maintain its existence.[54] In high cohesion teams, members are motivated to maintain their membership and to help the team work effectively. Compared to low cohesion teams, people in high cohesion teams spend more time together, share information more frequently, and are more satisfied with each other. They are generally more sensitive to each other's needs and develop better interpersonal relationships, thereby reducing dysfunctional conflict. When conflict does arise, members of

Exhibit 10–8   **Effect of Team Cohesiveness on Task Performance**

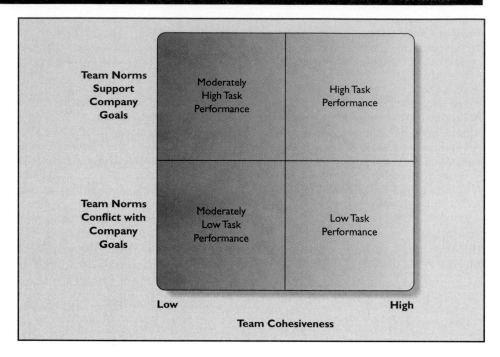

high cohesion teams seem to resolve these differences swiftly and effectively. They also provide each other with better social support in stressful situations.[55]

Cohesiveness and team performance

With better cooperation and more conformity to norms, high cohesion teams potentially perform much better than teams with low cohesiveness. However, this cooperation and conformity only improve organizational effectiveness if the team's norms are consistent with organizational objectives.[56]

As we see in Exhibit 10–8, team performance is highest when members are highly cohesive and team norms are consistent with organizational goals. But if norms conflict with organizational objectives, high cohesion teams will likely have lower task performance than less cohesive groups. This occurs because cohesiveness motivates employees to perform at a level more consistent with group norms. In our earlier example of the pajama factory, the new employee maintained low output because group norms discouraged high performance. If the group had low cohesiveness, she would have performed at a higher level because group norms would be less important to her.

Social Loafing

Social loafing
The tendency for people to perform at a lower level when working in groups than when alone.

Cohesive teams that support organizational goals might still suffer some productivity loss through **social loafing.** Social loafing is the tendency for people to perform at a lower level when working in groups than when alone.[57] Students are all too familiar with social loafers in their team projects, but social loafing affects the motivation and performance of most team members under some conditions.

Social loafing is most likely to occur in tasks with low interdependence in which individual output is not visible. It is also more prevalent in larger teams because the actions (or inaction) of individual team members are less noticeable. Social loafing is less likely to occur when the task is interesting, because individuals have a higher intrinsic motivation to perform their duties. It is less common when the group's objective is important, possibly because individuals experience more pressure from other team members to perform well. Finally, social loafing is less common among members with a strong collectivist value, because they value group membership and believe in working toward group objectives (see Chapter 8).[58]

Minimizing social loafing

By understanding the causes of social loafing, we can identify ways to minimize this problem. Some of the strategies listed below reduce social loafing by making each member's performance more visible. Others increase each member's motivation to perform his or her tasks within the group.[59]

- *Form smaller teams*—Splitting the team into several smaller groups makes each person's performance more noticeable and assigns the individual a greater obligation to the team's performance.

- *Specialize tasks*—It is easier to see everyone's contribution when each team member performs a different work activity. For example, rather than pooling their effort for all incoming customer inquiries, each customer service representative might be assigned a particular type of client.

- *Measure individual performance*—Social loafing is minimized when each member's contribution is measured, such as using cash register systems to record the number of items that each grocery store cashier has scanned over a fixed time. Of course, individual performance is difficult to measure in some team activities, such as problem-solving projects in which the team's performance depends on one person discovering the best answer.

- *Increase job enrichment*—Social loafing is minimized when team members are assigned more motivating jobs, such as requiring more skill variety or having direct contact with clients. However, this minimizes social loafing only if members have a strong growth need strength (see Chapter 4).

- *Select motivated employees*—Social loafing can be minimized by carefully selecting job applicants who are motivated by the task and have a collectivist value orientation. Those with a collectivist value are motivated to work harder for the team because they value their membership in the group.

Team Building

Standard Aero Ltd. became a more effective organization by applying total quality management principles and becoming a team-based organization. To accomplish this, employees at the Winnipeg-based aircraft engine repair company received continuous training, including dozens of hours of team building sessions.[60] **Team building** is any formal intervention directed toward improving the development and functioning of a work team. It is the most common form of organizational development and, consequently, includes some of the activities that will be discussed in Chapter 15.

Most team building activities accelerate the team development process, which, in turn, might reshape team norms or strengthen cohesiveness. Team building interventions are sometimes applied to newly established teams, but they are more common among existing teams that have regressed to earlier stages of team development. Team building is therefore most appropriate when the team experiences high membership turnover or members have lost focus of their respective roles and team objectives.[61]

Types of team building

There are four main types of team building, and most team building interventions typically include two or more of these.[62] For example, Canada Employment and Immigration held a six-day residential team building session for its managers that included most types of team building. Some parts focussed on role definition, whereas others helped team members improve their interpersonal and group problem-solving skills.[63]

Role definition

The role definition perspective examines role expectations among team members and clarifies their future role obligations to each other. Participants typically describe perceptions of their own role as well as the role expectations they have of other team members. After discussing these perceptions, team members revise their roles and present them for final acceptance.[64] This process determines whether individuals have the same role expectations that others assume of them. For example, Canada Employment and Immigration Commission's team building residential session included a "stop, start, continue" activity in which team members told each other what behaviours they can stop, start, and continue to make the team function better.

Interpersonal process

Interpersonal process interventions try to build trust and open communications among team members by resolving hidden agendas and misperceptions. One popular interpersonal process activity is Outward Bound and related programs, in which teams are placed in wilderness settings to face special challenges and threats.[65] By solving problems in unfamiliar settings, team members learn more about each other's strengths and weaknesses, and discover how interpersonal relations at work can limit each person's potential. As one participant remarked: "After four days the group had formed unbreakable bonds. . . . Underlings in the office had come to the fore and superiors had learned the wisdom of listening to new ideas, whatever their source."[66]

Another intervention, called **dialogue,** helps team members learn about the different mental models and assumptions that each person applies when working together. This process is based on the idea that a team develops a "wholeness" or sense of unity when its members continually engage in conversations to understand each other. As they gain awareness of each other's models

Perspective 10–3

Having Fun Building Better Teams

Several employees from Ortho-McNeil Pharmaceuticals Inc. in Toronto are hunched over maps of a make-believe galaxy, plotting a strategy to save the Earth. With Star Trek-style music and video images in the background, they ward off generic raiders thwarting their return to save the planet from a deadly disease. At one un-expected moment, Darth Vader bursts in and blasts away with a laser gun. As the Ortho-McNeil team members vanquish each obstacle, they are rewarded with Mars bars. And when their mission is complete, a celebratory cloud of smoke fills the air. With feet planted firmly back on Earth, the employees file into a debriefing session to learn what 90 minutes in outer space has taught them about teamwork.

Ortho-McNeil is one of many Canadian companies using experiential games to develop more effective teams in the workplace. Some games leave the teams ship-wrecked on a deserted Caribbean island; others, like *Gold of the Desert Kings,* have teams journeying across the desert for 25 days (three minutes for each day) to cash in their gold. IBM Canada, Campbell Soup, and PeopleTech have developed a six-hour game that parallels a self-managing work team.

These simulations represent an analogy of real life, but their hypothetical setting makes them less

threatening. "In an experiential (exercise), you can afford to take more risks than you would in the workplace, so the learning points become more vivid," says the training manager of Mississauga-based Janssen Pharmaceutica. Janssen uses *Gold of the Desert Kings* and other simulations to improve partnerships within the organization.

TeamPro Services, a Calgary-based management consulting firm, has been offering team building simulations for several years because they are the most convincing way to illustrate problems in team decision making. "When teamwork does not work in some cases, the facilitator can point to places where that group failed," explains TeamPro's vice-president. "For instance, one person may have dominated the whole discussion or someone else's good ideas were ignored."

But do team building games really make groups more effective? Ortho-McNeil vice-president Robert Miller thinks so: "People who never talked before are getting together for lunch and working together on problem-solving and interdepartment communication," he says. "There is a commitment to get things done and you need that if you're to be a world-class organization."

Sources: Based on R. Ray, "Playing Games for Fun and Profit: Walking on Fire Really Does Boost Sales," *Financial Times of Canada,* December 12–18, 1992, pp. 1, 17; and R. Bonanno, "Games Trainees Play," *Canadian HR Reporter,* November 19, 1992, pp. 8, 9, 14.

---

and assumptions, members eventually begin to form a common model for thinking within the team.[67]

Goal setting

As a team building strategy, goal setting involves clarifying the team's performance goals, increasing the team's motivation to accomplish these goals, and establishing a mechanism for systematic feedback on the team's goal performance. For instance, at the Canada Employment and Immigration Commission team building session mentioned earlier, teams were asked to develop vision statements as well as action plans to achieve their objectives.[68] This is very similar to individual goal setting described in Chapter 3, except that the goals are applied to teams. Consequently, team dynamics must be addressed, such as reaching agreement on goals. Recent evidence suggests goal setting is an important dimension of team building.[69]

Problem solving

This type of team building examines the team's task-related decision-making process and identifies ways to make it more effective.[70] Each decision-making stage is examined, such as how the team identifies problems and searches for alternatives (see Chapter 9). To help them improve their problem-solving skills, some teams participate in simulation games that require team decisions in hypothetical situations.[71] Some of these team building games are described in Perspective 10–3 on the previous page. Notice that these simulations also attempt to help teams improve interpersonal processes.

Is team building effective?

Team building can be costly and time consuming, so we need to know whether the time and money are well spent. So far, the answer is an equivocal "maybe." There are plenty of anecdotal accounts of satisfied customers of team building interventions. More recent empirical studies suggest that some team building interventions are successful, but just as many fail to improve team effectiveness.[72] One problem is that we don't yet know which of the four team building strategies is the most effective. This is because multiple approaches are typically used and each approach may be accomplished through different methods. For example, we don't yet know whether the team's interpersonal process is improved more through wilderness experiences or dialogue. These practices may, in fact, address different aspects of the interpersonal process.

Another concern is that team building (and other organizational change activities) works better under some conditions than others. Team building is more likely to succeed when members understand, are committed to, and fully participate in the process. The intervention must also be consistent with the existing organizational system, including rewards and corporate culture. Some experts suggest, for example, that wilderness experiences often fail because this team building process rarely includes follow-up consultation to ensure that what team members learned on site is transferred back to the workplace.[73]

One of the most popular team building games is *Gold of the Desert Kings,* developed by Eagle's Flight of Guelph, Ontario. Teams are given limited supplies to cross a desert, mine for gold in the mountains, and return within 25 days—with just 3 minutes representing each day.

Courtesy of Eagle's Flight.

Finally, there is the potential problem that team building is too effective. The intervention may create such a high level of cohesiveness and an insular perspective that members may become more loyal to the team than to the larger organization.[74] Few team building efforts seem to have had this effect, but the risk is always present. Overall, the need for team building interventions will continue to increase as more team-based organizations appear, but the effectiveness of these interventions is still unclear.

Chapter Summary

- Teams consist of two or more people who interact and mutually influence each other to achieve common goals. Formal teams are explicitly formed to accomplish specific tasks for the organization. Informal groups exist primarily for the benefit of their members and are not specifically formed by the organization. The composition of informal groups indicates the organization's success at integrating its culturally diverse work force.

- People join teams to accomplish goals that cannot be accomplished individually, to fulfill their affiliation needs, and as a source of emotional support.

- Team effectiveness includes the group's ability to survive, achieve its system-based objectives, and fulfill the needs of its members. Team effectiveness is partly affected by the team's context and design, including a supportive environment, interdependent and well-defined tasks, and optimal team size. The team's members should be motivated to work in groups and have the breadth of knowledge or skills required for the task.

- Teams develop through the stages of forming, storming, norming, performing, and eventually adjourning. They develop norms to regulate and guide the behaviours of their members. These norms may be influenced by critical events, explicit statements, initial experiences, and members' pregroup experiences.

- Cohesiveness is the degree of attraction people feel toward the team and their motivation to remain members. Cohesiveness increases with member similarity and interaction, external challenges, somewhat difficult entry, team success, and a minimal team size. Teams need some level of cohesiveness to survive, but high cohesive units have higher task performance only when their norms do not conflict with organizational objectives.

- Social loafing is the tendency for people to perform at a lower level when working in groups than when alone. It can be minimized by making each member's performance more visible and increasing each member's motivation to perform his or her tasks within the group.

- Team building is any formal intervention directed toward improving the development and functioning of a work team. Four team building strategies are role definition, interpersonal process, goal setting, and problem solving. Some team building interventions succeed, but just as many fail to accelerate team development or improve team effectiveness.

Discussion Questions

1. How do skunkworks differ from traditional task forces?

2. How does the composition of informal groups reflect the organization's success in managing cultural diversity in the work force?

3. If you were randomly assigned with four other students to complete a group project, what team-related problems might you experience? Describe the positive characteristics of student teams in this situation.

4. You have been put in charge of a concurrent engineering project that involves developing a new banking service for retail customers. The team includes representatives from marketing, information services, customer service, and accounting, all of whom will move to the same location at headquarters for three months. Describe the evidence or behaviours that you might observe during each stage of the team's development.

5. You have just been transferred from the Regina office to the Saskatoon office of your company, a Canada-wide sales organization of electrical products for developers and contractors. In Regina, you learned the importance of following up sales orders with a call to the customer to ask whether the products arrived on time and whether they are satisfied. Soon after moving to the Saskatoon office, a recently hired co-worker explained that other co-workers discouraged her from making those calls. Later, another co-worker suggested that your follow-up calls were making everyone else look lazy. The customers, products, sales commissions, and other characteristics of the workplace are almost identical between the two offices, yet co-worker attitudes toward customer follow-up calls are very different. Give three possible reasons why the norms in Saskatoon might be different from those in the Regina office.

6. Do cohesive teams improve organizational effectiveness more than teams whose members have relatively little cohesiveness? Explain your answer.

7. Describe four strategies to minimize social loafing in a work team.

8. What is a "dialogue" intervention, and how does it build more effective teams?

Notes

1. G. McKay, *Increasing the Power of Self-Managing Work Teams Through Effective Human Resource Management Strategies*. Unpublished MBA project (Burnaby, B.C.: Simon Fraser University, December 1992); S. Fife, "The Total Quality Muddle," *Report on Business Magazine*, November 1992, pp. 64–74; P. Scott, "Participative Management Means Success at GE Bromont," *CMA Magazine*, September 1989, p. 24; and "Work Innovations in Canada Multiplying," *Quality of Working Life: The Canadian Scene* 9(1) (1986), pp. 10–11.

2. J. Terrett, "New Plant Gears Up for the Future," *Modern Purchasing* 34 (March 1992), pp. 16–18; G. Boyd, "Big Oil Starts Thinking Small," *Canadian Business*, January 1992, pp. 24–29; and J. White, "Tailoring a New Workplace," *Perception* 14(1) (Winter 1990), pp. 25, 44.

3. D. Cartwright and A. Zander (eds.), *Group Dynamics: Research and Theory,* 3rd ed. (New York: Harper & Row, 1968); and M. E. Shaw, *Group Dynamics,* 3rd ed. (New York: McGraw-Hill, 1981), p. 8.

4. R. Likert, *New Patterns of Management* (New York: McGraw-Hill, 1961), pp. 106–8.

5. B. Little, "A Factory Learns to Survive," *Globe & Mail,* May 18, 1993, p. B22.

6. A. Morris and S. Thomas, "A Med/Surg Nursing Record: Convenient, Adequate—And Accepted," *Nursing Management* 23 (May 1992), pp. 68–72.

7. T. Peters, *Thriving on Chaos* (New York: Knopf, 1987), pp. 211–18; T. Kidder, *Soul of a New Machine* (Boston: Little, Brown, 1981); and T. Peters and N. Austin, *A Passion for Excellence* (New York: Random House, 1985), Chapters 9 and 10.

8. L. Iacocca and W. Novak, *Iacocca* (New York: Bantam, 1984), Chapter 6.

9. A. Savoie, "Les Groupes Informels dans les Organisations: Cadre General D'analyse," *Canadian Psychology* 34 (1993) pp. 79–97.

10. W. B. Stevenson, J. L. Pearce, and L. W. Porter, "The Concept of 'Coalition' in Organization Theory and Research," *Academy of Management Review* 10 (1985), pp. 256–68; and Shaw, *Group Dynamics,* pp. 105–10.

11. J. Christensen-Hughes, "Cultural Diversity: The Lesson of Toronto's Hotels," *Cornell H.R.A. Quarterly* 33 (April 1992), pp. 78–87.

12. K. Stephenson and V. Krebs, "A More Accurate Way to Measure Diversity," *Personnel Journal* 72 (October 1993), pp. 66–74.

13. L. N. Jewell and H. J. Reitz, *Group Effectiveness in Organizations* (Glenview, Ill.: Scott, Foresman, 1981).

14. B. E. Ashforth and F. Mael, "Social Identity Theory and the Organization," *Academy of Management Review* 14 (1989), pp. 20–39.

15. S. Schacter, *The Psychology of Affiliation* (Stanford, Calif.: Stanford University Press, 1959), pp. 12–19.

16. A. S. Tannenbaum, *Social Psychology of the Work Organization* (Belmont, Calif.: Wadsworth, 1966), p. 62.

17. For a summary of recent models, see P. S. Goodman, E. Ravlin, and M. Schminke, "Understanding Groups in Organizations," *Research in Organizational Behavior* 9 (1987), pp. 121–73.

18. J. E. McGrath, "Time Matters in Groups," in *Intellectual Teamwork: Social and Technological Foundations of Cooperative Work,* ed. J. Galegher, R. E. Kraut, and C. Egido (Hillsdale, N.J.: Erlbaum, 1990), pp. 23–61; and G. P. Shea and R. A. Guzzo, "Group Effectiveness: What Really Matters?" *Sloan Management Review* 27 (1987), pp. 33–46.

19. H. F. Kolodny and M. N. Kiggundu, "Toward the Development of a Sociotechnical Systems Model in Woodlands Mechanical Harvesting," *Human Relations* 33 (1980), pp. 623–45.

20. C. Steinburg, "The Downfall of Teams," *Training and Development,* February 1993, pp. 9–10. Also see R. Sisco, "Put Your Money Where Your Teams Are," *Training* 29 (July 1992), pp. 41–45.

21. E. Sundstrom, K. P. De Meuse, and D. Futrell, "Work Teams: Applications and Effectiveness," *American Psychologist* 45 (February 1990), pp. 120–33; and M. H. Safizadeh, "The Case of Workgroups in Manufacturing Operations," *California Management Review,* Summer 1991, pp. 61–82.

22. S. Worchel and S. L. Shackelford, "Groups Under Stress: The Influence of Group Structure and Environment on Process and Performance," *Personality & Social Psychology Bulletin* 17 (1991), pp. 640–47; and J. Kelly and J. McGrath, "Effects of Time Limits and Task Types on Task Performance and Interaction of Four Person Groups," *Journal of Personality and Social Psychology* 49 (1985), pp. 395–407.

23. M. A. Campion, G. J. Medsker, and A. C. Higgs, "Relations Between Work Group Characteristics and Effectiveness: Implications for Designing Effective Work Groups," *Personnel Psychology* 46 (1993), pp. 823–50; and M. N. Kiggundu, "Task Interdependence and the Theory of Job Design," *Academy of Management Review* 6 (1981), pp. 499–508.

24. J. Southerst, "The Next Industrial Revolution," *Canadian Business,* June 1992, pp. 92–101; and "Quick Moves Keep Bata Competitive," *Industrial Management* 10 (November 1986), p. 6.

25. J. R. Katzenbach and D. K. Smith, *The Wisdom of Teams: Creating the High-Performance Organization* (Boston: Harvard University Press, 1993), pp. 45–47; and G. Stasser, "Pooling of Unshared Information During Group Discussion," in *Group Process and Productivity,* ed. S. Worchel, W. Wood, and J. A. Simpson (Newbury Park, Calif.: Sage, 1992), pp. 48–67.

26. A. Tziner and D. Eden, "Effects of Crew Composition on Crew Performance: Does the Whole Equal the Sum of the Parts?" *Journal of Applied Psychology* 70 (1985), pp. 85–93; and A. P. Hare, *Handbook of Small Group Research,* 2nd ed. (New York: The Free Press, 1976), pp. 12–15.

27. P. C. Earley, "East Meets West Meets Mideast: Further Explorations of Collectivistic and Individualistic Work Groups," *Academy of Management Journal* 36 (1993), pp. 319–48; and J. Matthews, "Hiring: Nothing but Child's Play," *Canadian Business,* August 1991, p. 15.

28. S. M. Colarelli and A. L. Boos, "Sociometric and Ability-Based Assignment to Work Groups: Some Implications for Personnel Selection," *Journal of Organizational Behavior* 13 (1992), pp. 187–96; D. G. Ancona and D. F. Caldwell, "Demography and Design: Predictors of New Product Team Performance," *Organization Science*

executives had virtually a standing appointment at various local restaurants. Even when clients were not present, they would have several drinks before ordering their lunches. When they returned it was usually well into the afternoon and they were in no condition to make the decisions or take the actions that were often the pretext of the lunch in the first place. This practice had also spread to the subordinates of the various executives and it was not uncommon to see various groups of salespersons doing the same thing a few days each week. Jim decided that he wanted to end the practice, at least for himself and members of his group.

Jim knew this was not going to be an easy problem to solve. The drinking had become institutionalized with a great deal of psychological pressure from a central figure—in this case, the man he had replaced. He decided to plan the approach he would take and then discuss the problem and his approach for solving it with his superior, Norm Landy.

The following week Jim made an appointment with Norm to discuss the situation. Norm listened intently as Jim explained the drinking problem but did not show any surprise at learning about it. Jim then explained what he planned to do.

"Norm, I'm making two assumptions on the front end. First, I don't believe it would do any good to state strong new policies about drinking at lunch, or lecturing my people about the evils of the liquid lunch. About all I'd accomplish there would be to raise a lot of latent guilt that would only result in resentment and resistance. Second, I am assuming that the boss is often a role model for his subordinates. Unfortunately, the man I replaced made a practice of the drinking lunch. The subordinates close to him then conformed to his drinking habits and exerted pressure on other members of the group. Before you know it everyone was a drinking buddy and the practice became institutionalized, even when one member was no longer there.

"Here is what I intend to do about it. First, when I go to lunch with the other managers, I will do no drinking. More importantly, however, for the members of my group I am going to establish a new role model. For example, at least once a week we have a legitimate reason to work through lunch. In the past everyone has gone out anyway. I intend to hold a business lunch and have sandwiches and soft drinks sent in. In addition, I intend to make it a regular practice to take different groups of my people to lunch at a no-alcohol coffee shop.

"My goal, Norm, is simply to let my subordinates know that alcohol is not a necessary part of the workday, and that drinking will not win my approval. By not drinking with the other managers, I figure that sooner or later they too will get the point. As you can see, I intend to get the message across by my behaviour. There will be no words of censure. What do you think, Norm?"

Norm Landy pushed himself away from his desk and came around and seated himself beside Jim. He then looked at Jim and whispered, "Are you crazy? I guarantee you, Jim, that you are going to accomplish nothing but cause a lot of trouble. Trouble between your group and other groups if you succeed, trouble between you and your group, and trouble between you and the other managers. Believe me, Jim, I see the problem, and I agree with you that it is a problem. But the cure might kill the patient. Will all that conflict and trouble be worth it?"

Jim thought for a moment and said, "I think it will be good for the organization in the long run."

Discussion Questions

1. **What is Jim Lyons fundamentally trying to do in this case?**

2. **Do you agree with Norm Landy or Jim Lyons? Why?**

3. **What other strategies, if any, might achieve Jim's goals?**

Source: J. L. Gibson, J. M. Ivancevich, and J. H. Donnelly, Jr., *Organizations: Behavior, Structure, Processes, 8th ed.* (Burr Ridge, Ill.: Irwin, 1994), pp. 331–32.

Experiential Exercise

Team-Trust Exercise*

Purpose: This exercise is designed to help you understand the role of interpersonal trust in the development and maintenance of effective teams.

Instructions: Students are divided into teams of approximately 10 people. Each team receives 15 objects from the instructor. The same 15 objects are arranged in a specific way on a table at the front of the room (or elsewhere, as designated by the instructor). The table is behind a screened area so that the arrangements cannot be seen by participants from their work areas.

The goal of each team is to duplicate the *exact* arrangement (e.g., location, overlap, spacing) of the objects on the table, using its own matching set of objects, within 20 minutes (or other time limit given by the instructor). Participants are allowed one 30-second opportunity at the beginning of the exercise to view the screened table. They may not write, draw, or talk while viewing the screened table.

Each team will have *up to two saboteurs*. These are people who have been selected by the instructor (either before the exercise or through notes distributed to all participants). Saboteurs will use any reasonable method to prevent the team from producing an accurate configuration of objects in their work area. They are forbidden from revealing their identities.

At the end of the time limit, the instructor will evaluate each team's configuration and decide which one is the most accurate. The class members will then evaluate their experience in the exercise in terms of team development and other aspects of team dynamics.

*This exercise is based on ideas discussed in G. Thompson and P. Pearce, "The Team-Trust Game," *Training and Development*, May 1992, pp. 42–43.

Employee Involvement and Team Decision Making

Learning Objectives

After reading this chapter, you should be able to:

Describe the different forms and levels of employee involvement.

Outline the main features of self-managing work teams.

Discuss the potential benefits of employee involvement.

Identify the reasons why managers and unions resist employee involvement.

Explain how evaluation apprehension undermines team decision making.

Describe the process of group polarization.

Discuss the advantages and disadvantages of various team decision methods.

Chapter Outline

Forms and Levels of Employee Involvement.

Self-Managing Work Teams.

Potential Benefits of Employee Involvement.

Barriers to Employee Involvement.

Team Decision Making.

Improving Team Decision Making.

*M*any years ago, Sam Ault built a successful cheese factory in Winchester, Ontario, by frequently asking his employees what they needed to make the best products possible. Today, as one of Canada's largest dairy companies, Ault Foods Ltd. has returned to its roots of employee involvement. It recently formed 500 teams of employees across its plants and offices, and empowered them to do their work more effectively. At Ault's Black Diamond factory in Belleville, Ontario, some teams are in charge of work processes. Others tackle specific problems, such as creating a new product or searching for new production technology.

At corporate head office, Ault Foods' CEO Graham Freeman proudly tells how office employees are involved in corporate decisions using computer groupware. Anyone can contribute information or make comments in the 18 groupware files on the server. There is even a groupware file called "The Sherlock File" containing intelligence on competitors' frozen products. Freeman believes the computer technology is a natural fit for employee involvement. "It's group learning," he says, "so people don't have to waste time meeting."

Although some employees are still sceptical about Ault's rediscovery of employee involvement, most are pleased with the change and appreciate its value. Secretaries feel a greater sense of ownership and understanding of corporate decisions. Black Diamond production employees have better morale and feel a renewed optimism about their future. "The recession opened our eyes," admits Betty Tracze, who heads the Black Diamond Employees Independent Union. "We realized we could help Ault Foods become more competitive by using the ideas of our workers."[1]

Employee involvement
Occurs when employees take an active role in making decisions that were not previously within their mandate.

Ault Foods Ltd. is part of a growing wave of corporate interest in **employee involvement** (also called *employee participation*). Employee involvement occurs when employees have an active role in making decisions that were not previously within their mandate. In general, employees have more influence in a particular decision as their level of involvement increases.[2] Employee involvement extends beyond controlling resources for one's own job; it includes the power to influence decisions in the work unit and organization.

A generation ago, most managers viewed participation as an interesting academic theory with little practical value.[3] Today, corporate leaders believe it is an essential ingredient to the company's survival and success. For example, Placer Dome's Sigma gold mine in Val d'Or, Quebec, holds consensus meetings in which miners, supervisors, and technical staff discuss mining plans and agree on future schedules. When Manitoba Telephone System operators complained of severe stress conditions, the company involved them in a major work reorganization. And at Palliser Furniture Ltd. in Winnipeg, employees are responsible for planning budgets and establishing production quotas with their team members.[4]

This chapter builds on the team dynamics material in Chapter 10 by examining the features and contingencies of employee involvement and team decision making. We begin by describing the forms and levels of employee involvement, including a detailed discussion of self-managing work teams. This is followed by discussions of the potential benefits and limitations of employee involvement. The final sections of this chapter look at the potential problems with team decision making and strategies to minimize these concerns.

Forms and Levels of Employee Involvement

There are many forms of employee involvement (see Exhibit 11–1).[5] Formal participation activities are founded on codified policies and institutionalized practices, such as the work teams at General Electric Canada's Bromont plant. Informal participation is influenced by management style and the organization's value system, such as an employee's ability to approach a supervisor with an idea or suggestion.

Many employee involvement activities in Canada are voluntary, such as when Manitoba Telephone System invited its operators to participate in a major work reorganization. Others may be legally mandated by government statute. Several European countries have laws requiring *codetermination*—various structures that let employees participate in the organization's strategic decisions. For instance, companies operating in Germany must give employees representation on the board of directors.[6] Codetermination exists in some Canadian companies, but it is voluntary. Algoma Steel Inc. has 5 employee representatives on its 13-member board of directors because employees surrendered 15 percent of their pay to save the company. As described in Perspective 11–1, Canadian Airlines also introduced employee board representation in return for employee wage concessions.

Direct employee involvement occurs when employees personally influence the decision process, such as Placer Dome's consensus meetings in which all miners in a work area discuss mining plans with supervisors and technical staff.

Forms of Employee Involvement   Exhibit 11–1

Form of Involvement	Description	Example
Formality		
Formal	Participation is codified policy or institutionalized practice	Self-managing work teams at General Electric Canada's Bromont plant
Informal	Casual or undocumented activities at management's discretion	Employee on the shop floor makes a suggestion to the supervisor
Legal Mandate		
Statutory	Government-legislated activities	DuPont Canada employees represented on joint health and safety committees
Voluntary	Any participation activity without force of law	Manitoba Telephone System involves employees in work reorganization
Directness		
Direct	Employees are personally involved in decisions	Placer Dome's miners discuss mining plans directly with supervisors and technical specialists
Indirect	Employees participate through representation of peers	Canadian Airlines employees represented on company's board of directors

Du Pont Canada's joint health and safety committees are indirect forms of participation because employees are represented by elected peers.

Levels of employee involvement

There are different levels of employee involvement.[7] At the lowest level, employees are asked individually for specific information or opinions, but they do not necessarily recommend solutions. They might not even know details of the problem for which the information will be used.

A moderate level of employee involvement occurs when employees are consulted either individually or in a group. They are told about the problem and offer their diagnosis and recommendations, but the final decision still rests with the manager. **Quality circles** fall into this middle level of employee involvement. Quality circles are small teams of employees who meet for a few hours each week to identify quality and productivity problems, propose solutions to management, and monitor the implementation and consequences of these solutions in their work area. For example, the quality improvement teams at General Electric Canada's Camco plant consist of employees within a particular work area who voluntarily recommend ways to reduce production costs and improve product quality. These teams recommend solutions to management, but do not have the authority to implement changes unilaterally.[8]

The highest level of employee involvement occurs when employees have complete decision-making power, from problem identification to solution implementation. This is most apparent in the team-based (also called *lateral* or *high involvement*) organizations described earlier in Chapter 10 and discussed later in Chapter 17.[9] For example, teams at Ault's Black Diamond plant identify, solve, and implement many decisions without seeking authorization from a supervisor. These high-involvement groups are typically called self-managing work teams, as we discuss next.

Quality circle
A small team of employees that meets on a regular basis to identify quality and productivity problems, propose solutions to management, and monitor the implementation and consequences of these solutions in its work area.

Perspective 11–1

Codetermination at Canadian Airlines International

Canadian Airlines International has flown through turbulent economic conditions over the past few years. It lost several hundred millions of dollars during the early 1990s as a result of a recessionary economy and over-capacity in the industry. These financial difficulties led to merger talks with Air Canada, its main competitor. Canadian Airlines employees didn't want a merger, so they proposed and soon agreed to a wage concession program in return for a voice in how the company is run.

Canadian Airlines employees now participate in executive decisions through an incorporated employee organization called the Council of Canadian Airlines Employees (CCAE). The CCAE nominates are one director on the eight-member Canadian Airlines International Ltd. board and two directors on the 20-member PWA Corporation board. (PWA is the Calgary-based parent company of Canadian Airlines.) These directors regularly communicate with the CCAE to provide advice and receive feedback on major workplace issues affecting the

airline. However, they also hold a fiduciary duty to all shareholders, so the CCAE gives these directors a voice with no strings attached.

Along with board representation, a special Labour/Management Advisory Council was established that includes both senior management and union officials at Canadian Airlines. This council meets quarterly to review corporate performance and communicate business strategies.

By adopting codetermination, Canadian Airlines will require a more open management style and cooperative labour–management relations. Sidney Fattedad, CCAE's representative on the Canadian Airlines board of directors, explains: "The greatest demand will be on managers, who will find their decisions constantly challenged by employee shareholders. . . . Senior management's reaction and behaviour in dealing with challenges to their autonomy and wisdom in the coming months and years will set critical examples for middle and junior managers."

Sources: Based on S. O. Fattedad, "Behind the Scenes at Canadian Airlines," *CGA Magazine*, June 1993, pp. 30–33, 75, 76; and D. McMurdy, "A New Way of Saving Jobs," *Maclean's*, September 20, 1993, pp. 18–20.

Self-Managing Work Teams

Self-managing work team
A team of employees that completes a whole piece of work requiring several interdependent tasks and has substantial autonomy over the execution of these tasks.

In Chapter 10, we learned how General Electric Canada's Bromont plant has a team-based organizational structure in which work teams are assigned almost total responsibility for managing a specific work process. These groups, called **self-managing work teams** (SMWTs), were also mentioned in Chapter 4 as the emerging form of job enrichment where the work cycle is too complex for one person to handle alone. SMWTs complete an entire piece of work requiring several interdependent tasks (e.g., building an engine, processing chemicals) and have substantial autonomy over the execution of these tasks. Each team's work is horizontally loaded, because it includes all the tasks required to make an entire product or service. It is also vertically loaded, because the team is mostly responsible for scheduling, coordinating, and planning these tasks.[10]

SMWTs decide their own work activities as well as the pace of work. They are responsible for most support tasks—quality control, maintenance, and inventory management—along with the core production activities (manufacturing a product, serving a client). They order supplies, maintain equipment, check quality standards, and hire new co-workers with little or no outside direction.

Perspective 11-2

Self-Managing Work Teams at Pratt & Whitney

The unique geometric shape of Pratt & Whitney's Plant #41 stands out against the wilderness near the Halifax airport. The plant, which assembles over 100 varieties of expensive light-alloy casings for aircraft engines, also stands out because it is operated almost entirely by employees. There are no middle managers, no supervisors, no foremen, no executive washrooms, no executive parking spaces, and no fancy job titles. Instead, a team of eight managers sets overall plant objectives and several self-managing work teams decide how best to meet them.

Pratt & Whitney is one of many Canadian firms leading the way toward the self-managing work team concept. The Halifax plant has a "team-based" structure in which decisions are made by the work team rather than passed down from level to level. This keeps employees involved and motivated. A Pratt & Whitney executive explains: "Today's employees are better equipped to think for themselves and they don't want to defer to authority." He adds that employees who are qualified to assume highly technical jobs "just can't be expected to shove their brains into their locker with their lunchbox before they go to work."

Employees are completely responsible for their area, from programming their machines to scheduling work shifts. Plant rules and the employee benefit package are decided by a general assembly of employees. Employees even do their own hiring by working together in committees to evaluate applicants, including their ability to work in a team-based, democratic environment.

The self-managing work team approach, together with advanced computer-aided manufacturing systems, allows the plant to operate more flexibly. Retooling can sometimes be completed within a matter of hours rather than days. Employee morale is higher, as employees have more control over their work. Absenteeism is extremely low.

Introducing self-managing work teams has required a period of adjustment, particularly for those accustomed to more traditional work arrangements. Says one Pratt & Whitney veteran of 35 years: "I knew about this idea and the way this plant would be set up before I came to Halifax, but it still took some time for me to get used to it." There is also the potential dilemma of employee career development in a structure without titles or visible steps on the corporate ladder. Still, senior management is certain that Pratt & Whitney is going the right way. "Any company that doesn't take these steps," says a Pratt & Whitney executive, "will be struggling down the line."

Sources: D. Jones, "Robó-Shop," *Report on Business Magazine*, March 1994, pp. 54–62; L. Gutri, "Pratt & Whitney Employees Don't Want to Be Managed; Teams Demand Leadership," *Canadian HR Reporter*, May 2, 1988, p. 8; and J. Todd, "Firm Fashions Workplace for High-Tech Era," *Montreal Gazette*, December 12, 1987, p. B4.

Some teams are responsible for addressing problems of poor performance among team members, but many employees want management to keep this role. Perspective 11–2 describes how self-managing work teams operate at Pratt & Whitney's plant near Halifax.

Self-managing work teams were initially designed around production processes, but they are now entering administrative and service areas of the organization. GE Capital Fleet Services in Richmond Hill, Ontario, recently organized its 100 head office staff members into self-managing work teams. Banff Springs Hotel assigned housekeeping staff members to self-managing teams and gave them responsibility for supervising each other, checking their own work, and writing their own work orders. These situations are well suited to self-managing teams because members have interdependent tasks, and decisions are frequently made that require the employee's knowledge and experience.[11]

Sociotechnical design theory

Sociotechnical design
A theory stating that every work site consists of a technological system and a social system, and that organizational effectiveness is maximized when these two systems are compatible with each other.

Self-managing work teams evolved from the **sociotechnical design** theory that Eric Trist and his colleagues at Britain's Tavistock Institute introduced in the 1950s.[12] Sociotechnical design theory states that every work site consists of two interdependent parts: (1) the technological system of machines, tools, and production processes, and (2) the social system of individual skills, needs, and interpersonal relations. To maximize organizational effectiveness, both systems should be compatible with each other. Management must therefore consider the potential effects of new technology on the social structure and redesign one or both elements to improve their compatibility. A balance must be struck between production demands and employee needs to maximize the operation's productivity.[13]

An important element in the sociotechnical design concept is that the optimal situation typically occurs when employees work in teams and have sufficient autonomy to manage the work process. In other words, the technological system should encourage team dynamics, job enrichment, and employee well-being. Some self-managing work team interventions are primarily changes in the social system to fit the existing technology. For example, a company might try to develop cohesive teams and encourage employees to become multiskilled. However, sociotechnical theory says that these changes to the social system will prove ineffective if the technological system does not support a team-oriented, high-involvement environment.[14]

There is also a concern that a team-oriented technological system is not always the most efficient operation. Volvo's Kalmar and Uddevalla plants in Sweden might be two such cases.[15] Volvo's Kalmar plant was built in the early 1970s and was one of the earliest sociotechnically designed plants. The Uddevalla plant opened in the late 1980s. These plants replaced the traditional assembly line with fixed work stations at which teams of approximately 20 employees assemble and install components in an unfinished automobile chassis. This technological structure creates a strong team orientation, but productivity at the two Volvo plants is among the lowest in the automobile industry because the technological design is not sufficiently flexible. In other words, in its attempt to accommodate the social system, Volvo may have compromised technological efficiency beyond an optimal level.

Sociotechnical design at Shell Canada

Shell Canada's chemical plant in Sarnia, Ontario, is a sociotechnically designed plant that seems to work well.[16] In a traditional chemical plant, employees are assigned to specialized departments, such as polypropylene extrusion, warehousing, and quality control. In contrast, Shell Canada's chemical plant functions as a single department operated by a 20-person process team. There are six process teams working in rotating 12-hour shifts to keep the plant in continuous operation. These teams are largely self-managing as they assign work, provide or arrange for technical training, authorize overtime, schedule vacations, and help select new employees. Team members are highly flexible as they become multiskilled across several work activities.

The self-managing team structure of the Shell plant is supported by a redesigned technical structure. Traditional plants have two separate control centres for processing polypropylene and isopropyl alcohol, whereas a single control system operates both processes at Shell Canada's plant so that all team members can work together. The computer system directly provides team members with all available information, including the financial implications of operating decisions. Team members use this information to make immediate decisions without management authority.

Shell Canada's chemical plant seems to have effectively configured both the social and technological systems.[17] The plant was designed to produce 70,000 tonnes of polypropylene annually but has recently been producing more than twice that amount. Product quality has been excellent and the process teams have a good record of getting the system back to full operation following production interruptions. Very few grievances have been filed, employee turnover is low, and the plant has maintained an average safety record. The only apparent problems are that absenteeism is slightly above average for the industry and many employees have reached the top of their skill-based pay system.

Potential Benefits of Employee Involvement

For the past half century, organizational behaviour scholars have advised that self-managing work teams and other forms of employee involvement offer potential benefits for both employees and the company.[18] These benefits include improved decision quality, decision commitment, employee satisfaction/ empowerment, and employee development. These outcomes lead to higher productivity, better quality, lower absenteeism, and lower employee turnover.

Decision quality

In the 1940s, Robert Dubin explained how a Lever Brothers plant in Toronto improved production efficiency by relying on the "expert consultation" of its employees.[19] Today, many companies have discovered that employee involvement potentially results in higher-quality decisions because employees have valuable information about the work site that should be considered in the decision process.[20] They know where the company can save money, how product or service quality can be improved, and where the company can realize unused opportunities. For example, operators at one of PanCanadian Petroleum's Alberta oil and gas plants were aware that their gas field had additional reserves. They assumed that management knew about this, but didn't say anything until management decided to increase productivity through employee involvement. When given the opportunity, the employees asked management why it wasn't using the resource. Management acted on this information, resulting in a dramatic increase in gas production and profits at PanCanadian.[21]

The powerful effect of employee involvement on decision quality is dramatically illustrated in Perspective 11–3. MacMillan Bloedel's special task force, called Team 100, achieved the impossible goal of profitably harvesting a silvacultural wasteland on Vancouver Island through the advantages of team decision making.

We can see how employee involvement improves decision quality by examining three stages of the decision-making process described in Chapter 9:

Perspective 11-3

The Saga of MacMillan Bloedel's Team 100

About a century ago, fire had ravaged a plot of land on Vancouver Island called Yellow Creek 100, leaving a silvacultural wasteland. Some prime old Douglas firs remained, but the trees were scattered about and blocked by scrub brush and rough terrain. MacMillan Bloedel Ltd. had cutting rights to the Yellow Creek 100 site and wanted to replant it for a future harvest. But clearing the area would cost nearly $500,000, with little if any savings from harvestable wood.

To reduce the cost of preparing the Yellow Creek 100 site, MacMillan Bloedel's district managers decided to form a small task force called Team 100. Two riggers, two fallers, one forester, one engineer, a woods supervisor, a mechanic, a quality control person, and an employee relations coordinator were summoned into a room where one of the district managers described the task in five minutes and then walked out. After the initial shock had worn off, Team 100's newly appointed members agreed that not only would they log this mess that everyone had avoided for several decades, but they were going to make money at it!

To achieve such a daunting objective, the team had to be creative and break traditions. Normally, a forester would visit the site alone, but Team 100 decided that a more accurate analysis of the situation would result if everyone visited at the same time. The result of this unique team activity was that several areas originally considered impractical for logging were included in the cutting plan. As one team member recalls: "At first people thought we were nuts. Here we were going up to the site to check it out, or think of a new way to tackle a problem, and that was after our regular shift. But we were all having a great time."

Another innovation was to break the traditional—almost sacred—rule of having fallers on site first to cut up the virgin wood before other occupations venture in. Forestry crews, who are much lower on the status ladder, are normally brought in at the end of the job to clean up the site for replanting. Team 100's fallers suggested reversing the traditional order because the forestry crews could clear a path to allow the high-priced fallers speedier access to the harvestable wood. The idea improved work efficiency and, at one point, both fallers and forestry crews were working side by side swapping information.

Beyond everyone else's expectations, Team 100 achieved its objective. Rather than costing several hundred thousand dollars, the project netted a $30,000 profit and the Yellow Creek 100 site is now returning to a picturesque Douglas fir setting.

Sources: J. Sorenson, "MB Logging Team Kicks Convention," *Logging and Sawmilling Journal* 22(1) (January 1991), pp. 11, 15; and G. Bartosh, "A Tale of a Team" *MB Journal* 10(6) (June 1990), p. 8.

Synergy
A condition in which the interaction of two or more agents produces a greater result than if these agents had been operating independently. In employee involvement, synergy results when the quantity and/or quality of ideas generated from two or more people working together is greater than if these people had been working alone.

- *Identifying problems*—Participation may lead to a more accurate definition of the problem because employees introduce more perspectives and knowledge to understand the symptoms.

- *Developing alternative solutions*—The number of alternative solutions generated typically increases with the number of people involved. In a well-managed meeting, team members create **synergy** by pooling their knowledge to form new alternatives that no one would have designed alone. In other words, several people working together and building on each other's strengths can potentially generate more and better solutions than if these people worked alone.

- *Choosing the best alternative*—With more diverse perspectives and a better representation of values, teams are typically better than individuals at choosing the best alternative. There is less chance that a grossly inaccurate solution will be selected when knowledgeable people are involved.

Decision commitment

Surveys tell us that most Canadian employees want to be involved in decisions that affect them, although only 20 percent say their companies encourage participation.[22] Many employees resist authoritarian dictums from senior management. But when they participate in decisions, employees are more likely to identify with the decision and feel that it is part of their solution, rather than just management's directive. Consequently, they tend to exhibit less resistance to change and are more motivated to implement these decisions.[23]

Employee satisfaction and empowerment

There is strong evidence that employees are more satisfied and experience lower grievance, absenteeism, and quit rates when they are encouraged to participate in organizational decisions.[24] One of the main reasons why employee satisfaction is higher is that people feel empowered when given the opportunity to participate in decisions affecting their work lives. **Empowerment** has several meanings in the management literature, but we shall define it as a feeling of control and self-confidence that emerges when people are given power in a previously powerless situation.[25] Empowerment increases job satisfaction because employees feel less stress when they have some control over life's events. Empowerment is also a motivational experience because employees develop a strong sense of confidence in themselves.

Empowerment
A feeling of control and self-confidence that emerges when people are given power in a situation in which they previously were powerless.

Employee involvement is less likely to increase satisfaction or empowerment when this management practice is conducted superficially or when co-workers criticize those who become involved. Even when management is serious about employee involvement and co-workers support these efforts, some employees may dislike the experience because they have individualistic values that are incompatible with a participative environment.[26]

Employee development

Many forms of involvement give employees the opportunity to develop better decision-making skills and prepare themselves for higher levels of responsibility. Team decision making may offer the additional benefits of fostering teamwork and collegiality as co-workers learn more about each other and come to appreciate each other's talents.[27]

Barriers to Employee Involvement

Employee involvement is not a panacea for all organizational problems. In some situations, participation would be useful but resistance to it could threaten the company's effectiveness in other ways. Three barriers to employee involvement are cultural differences, management resistance, and labour union resistance.

Cultural differences

Employee involvement is well suited to cultures in which people value collaboration. For example, most aboriginal organizations in Canada have a consensual decision-making style in which each person's views are heard and respected.[28]

Other cultures have difficulty implementing some forms of employee involvement, however. This is particularly true in societies with high power distance and individualism values (see Chapter 8). Puerto Rico has a collectivist culture, but it also has a high power distance that discourages employees from interacting casually with their superiors. This explains why one company's attempt at participative management in Puerto Rico failed. Employees expected managers to exert their authority and viewed employee involvement activities as signs of weak leadership. Similarly, one study recently reported the failure of employee involvement in a Russian mill, probably because workers were still intimidated by memories of Soviet days when ideas were either ignored or viewed as political interference.[29]

Management resistance

Lower and middle managers resist some forms of employee involvement, particularly self-managing work teams. Their main worry is that they will necessarily lose power when employees gain power through participation.[30] Some are concerned that their jobs will lose value, whereas others believe that they will not have any jobs at all. This problem occurred at General Electric Canada's plant in Airdrie, Alberta. When production employees were put into self-managing work teams, supervisors began complaining that their days with the company were numbered. "They had to send out a vice-president promising job security before things settled down," recalls the Airdrie plant manager.[31]

Another problem is that supervisors do not know how to become "hands-off" facilitators of several work teams rather than "hands-on" supervisors of several employees.[32] Many slip back into their command-oriented supervisor styles because they are still ultimately responsible for the team's success. Litton Systems Canada Ltd. faced this problem when it introduced self-managing work teams in the late 1980s. Several supervisors at the Etobicoke, Ontario, high-technology company were reluctant to adopt the facilitator style because they felt responsible for the results in their area and believed that their experience gave them a wealth of knowledge to direct the work teams. Only after many training sessions did the supervisors begin to accept the facilitator role and allow work teams the autonomy that the company had intended.[33]

Labour union resistance

Labour unions have been strong advocates of joint health and safety committees and some quality of work life programs. A few favour team-based organizational structures. But many labour leaders are concerned about employee involvement programs that improve productivity (such as total quality management described in Chapter 1) because they may produce more intense work effort and higher stress levels without additional compensation.[34] Labour leaders are also concerned about losing control over union member rights because some employee involvement programs try to reverse work rules and remove job categories that unions have negotiated over the years. Finally, a few union leaders believe that companies use employee involvement programs as a subtle strategy to bypass the union and thereby weaken its power in the workplace.[35] The president of an International Woodworkers Union local in Vancouver sums up this concern: "There is no question the employer has done an end run around the union in going to the crews and getting their support for these things."[36]

These union fears are troublesome because employee involvement programs tend to be more successful when union leaders support them and actively participate in their implementation.[37] Union support tends to speed up the diffusion of employee involvement throughout the plant and to other operations. Union officials can influence employee reactions to these initiatives and can provide valuable ideas when deciding ways to adapt employee involvement practices to the workplace. Finally, union support can increase the chances that employee involvement will continue long after the original management champion has left the organization.

Team Decision Making

Self-managing work teams, quality circles, labour–management committees, and many other participative management practices involve team-based decisions, so it is fitting that we look at this important issue here.[38] The advantages of employee involvement described earlier apply to team decision making. When members possess the requisite skills and knowledge, the team can potentially define problems more accurately, produce a longer list of better alternatives, and select the best alternative. Team decision making increases employee commitment to the decision, increases job satisfaction, and gives employees more opportunity to improve their decision-making skills.

The advantages of team decision making are offset by several prob. as. Along with the employee involvement problems described above, teams can fall into the escalation of commitment trap that was described in Chapter 9.[39] But the most significant problems with team decision making relate to team dynamics. Five prominent problems are time constraints, evaluation apprehension, conformity, groupthink, and group polarization.

Time constraints

"Committees keep minutes and waste hours." This often-heard statement reflects the idea that teams take longer than individuals to make decisions.[40] One limitation is that groups require extra time to organize, coordinate, and socialize. Team members need time to learn about each other and build rapport. They need to manage an imperfect communication process to develop sufficient understanding of each other's ideas. They also need to coordinate roles and rules of order within the decision process. This *process loss,* as it is called, takes time away from the task of making a decision.

Another time constraint problem is that only one person typically speaks at a time.[41] The larger the group, the more time required for discussion. This problem, known as **production blocking,** causes participants to forget what they wanted to say by the time it is their turn to speak. Team members who rehearse their lines while waiting might ignore what others are saying, even though their statements could trigger more creative ideas.

Production blocking
A time constraint in meetings due to the procedural requirement that only one person may speak at a time.

Evaluation apprehension

Evaluation apprehension
An individual's tendency to withhold potentially valuable ideas that seem silly or peripheral because he or she believes that other team members are silently evaluating him or her.

Time is a precious resource in meetings, so people usually avoid mentioning thoughts that may seem silly or peripheral. They also hold back these potentially valuable ideas because they believe (often correctly) that other team members are silently evaluating them. This **evaluation apprehension** is based on the individual's desire to create a favourable self-presentation and his or her need for social esteem. It is most common when the meeting is attended by someone with higher status or expertise, or when members formally evaluate each other's performance throughout the year. Evaluation apprehension is a problem when the group wants to generate creative ideas, because these thoughts often sound bizarre or lack logic when presented. Unfortunately, many potentially valuable ideas are never presented to the group because these creative thoughts initially seem ridiculous and a waste of time.

Conformity

Chapter 10 described how cohesiveness leads individual members to conform to the team's norms. This control keeps the group organized around common goals, but it can also undermine effective team decision making. It may cause team members to suppress their dissenting opinions about discussion issues, particularly when a strong team norm is related to the issue. When someone does state a point of view that violates the majority opinion, other members might punish the violator or try to persuade him or her that the opinion is incorrect. Moreover, we partly depend on the opinions that others hold to validate our own views. If co-workers don't agree with us, then we begin to question our own opinions even without overt peer pressure. These pressures toward conformity undermine decision making because they prevent members from presenting or maintaining unique perspectives.

Groupthink

Groupthink
A situation in extremely cohesive teams in which members are so motivated to maintain harmony and conform to majority opinion that they withhold their dissenting opinions.

Groupthink is the tendency of highly cohesive groups to value consensus at the price of decision quality.[42] There are strong social pressures on individual members to maintain harmony by avoiding conflict and disagreement. They suppress doubts about decision alternatives preferred by the majority or group leader. Team members want to maintain this harmony because their self-identity is enhanced by membership in a powerful decision-making body that speaks with one voice.[43] Team harmony also helps members cope with the stress of making crucial top-level decisions.

Along with high cohesiveness, groupthink is most likely to occur when the team is isolated from outsiders, the team leader expresses an opinion (rather than remaining impartial), the team is under stress due to an external threat, the team has experienced recent failures or other decision-making problems, and the team lacks clear guidance from corporate policies or procedures.

Several symptoms of groupthink have been identified and are summarized in Exhibit 11–2. In general, teams overestimate their invulnerability and morality, become closed-minded to outside and dissenting information, and experience several pressures toward consensus.

Most research on groupthink has analyzed policy decisions that turned into fiascoes. The best-known example of groupthink is NASA's space shuttle

Symptoms of Groupthink

Exhibit 11-2

Groupthink Symptom	Description
Illusion of invulnerability	The team feels comfortable with risky decisions because possible weaknesses are suppressed or glossed over.
Assumption of morality	There is such an unquestioned belief in the inherent morality of the team's objectives that members do not feel the need to debate whether their actions are ethical.
Rationalization	Underlying assumptions, new information, and previous actions that seem inconsistent with the team's decision are discounted or explained away.
Stereotyping outgroups	The team stereotypes or oversimplifies the external threats on which the decision is based; "enemies" are viewed as purely evil or moronic.
Self-censorship	Team members suppress their doubts in order to maintain harmony.
Illusion of unanimity	Self-censorship results in harmonious behaviour, so individual members believe that they alone have doubts; silence is automatically perceived as evidence of consensus.
Mindguarding	Some members become self-appointed guardians to prevent negative or inconsistent information from reaching the team.
Pressuring dissenters	Members who happen to raise their concerns about the decision are pressured to fall into line and be more loyal to the team.

Source: Based on I. L. Janis, *Groupthink: Psychological Studies of Policy Decisions and Fiascoes,* 2nd ed. (Boston: Houghton Mifflin, 1982), p. 244.

Challenger explosion in 1986.[44] The technical cause of the explosion killing all seven crew members was a faulty O-ring seal that did not withstand the freezing temperatures the night before launch. However, a government commission pointed to a faulty decision-making process as the primary cause of the disaster. Key decision makers at NASA experienced many groupthink symptoms. They were under intense pressure to launch due to previous delays and promises of the space shuttle program's success. Information about O-ring problems was withheld to avoid conflict. Engineers raised concerns about the O-rings before the launch, but they were criticized for this.

The groupthink concept holds much promise for understanding how top-level policy teams can make defective choices. However, a few writers have suggested that other factors also account for ineffective policy decision making.[45] One such phenomenon is group polarization.

Group polarization

Group polarization refers to the tendency of teams to make more extreme decisions than individuals working alone.[46] Exhibit 11-3 shows how the group polarization process operates. Individuals form initial preferences when given several alternatives. Some of these choices are riskier than others, and the average member's opinion leans one way or the other. Through open discussion, members become comfortable with more extreme positions when they realize that their views are also held by others. Persuasive arguments favouring the dominant position convince doubtful members and help form a consensus around the extreme option. Finally, because the final decision is made by the team, individuals feel less personally responsible for the decision consequences.

Group polarization explains why groups make more *extreme* decisions than the average individual, but there is also evidence that teams usually make *riskier* decisions. Why does this occur? When given the choice between a certain

Group polarization
The tendency for teams to make more extreme decisions (either more risky or more risk averse) than the average team member would if making the decision alone.

Exhibit 11–3   **The Group Polarization Process**

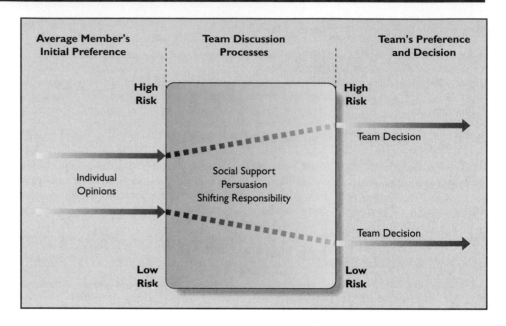

alternative and a risky one, individuals tend to initially prefer the risky option because the certain loss is viewed as more unpleasant than a more severe but less certain loss. This occurs even when the probability of success is extremely low, because people also tend to inflate the likelihood that they will beat the odds in a risky situation. For example, they tend to think, "This strategy might be unsuccessful 80 percent of the time, but it will work for me!" Thus, team members are more likely to favour the risky option.[47]

An extreme choice—whether risky or risk averse—is sometimes the correct solution to a problem or opportunity, but group polarization explains why some executive teams unwisely gamble assets and develop overoptimistic forecasts of success. Under some conditions, senior executives might support a "bet your company" solution in which most corporate assets are allocated to an investment with little probability of success. At the other extreme, teams whose members generally favour risk-averse solutions will suffer from inaction and stagnation. They will continually miss windfall opportunities and be ill-prepared for environmental changes.

Improving Team Decision Making

Teams can make better decisions than individuals in many situations, but they must first overcome time constraints, evaluation apprehension, conformity, groupthink, group polarization, and other problems. One general practice is to ensure that neither the team leader nor any other participant dominates the process. This minimizes the adverse effects of conformity and lets other team members generate more ideas.[48] Another practice is to maintain an optimal team size. The group should be large enough that members possess the collective knowledge to resolve the problem, yet small enough that the team doesn't consume too much time or restrict individual input.[49]

When it's feasible, teams should try to reach a consensus. In other words, participants should try to agree on the best alternative. Seeking a consensus requires more time, but members tend to develop a stronger commitment to the final decision and its implementation. Using majority rule or voting tends to evoke somewhat less commitment to the selected alternative, although the effect is still stronger than nonparticipation.[50]

Constructive controversy

Teams should encourage **constructive controversy** when discussing the problem and its possible solutions.[51] Constructive controversy occurs when team members openly debate their differing opinions. Debate is useful because members are more likely to re-examine their basic assumptions and consider other perspectives.

    Heterogeneous teams are more likely than homogeneous teams to engage in constructive controversy. Structured debate also encourages constructive controversy. One such approach, called **devil's advocacy,** is diagrammed in Exhibit 11–4. The process begins by describing the choice that the group prefers. The team is divided into two subgroups. One subgroup critiques the preferred alternative by looking for faulty logic, questionable assumptions, and misinterpreted information. The other subgroup listens to the critique and generates counterarguments. The critiquing subgroup forms a rebuttal to the counterarguments and the entire team then reconsiders its choice. Devil's advocacy works best when several people are critics and the team leader keeps the discussion constructive by focussing on the issues rather than people.[52]

    So far, we have been referring to traditional team decision making, known as the *interacting* approach, whereby members meet face to face to suggest solutions and debate alternatives. Discussion is usually unstructured, ideas are generated and evaluated simultaneously, and there is a tendency to search for solutions before the problem is clearly understood. Consequently, traditional interaction is usually marred by the team decision-making problems described earlier. To minimize these problems, four alternative techniques have been proposed: brainstorming, nominal group technique, Delphi technique, and electronic brainstorming.

Brainstorming

In the 1950s, advertising executive Alex Osborn wanted to find a better way for teams to generate creative ideas.[53] Osborn's solution, called **brainstorming,** separates the idea-generation stage of decision making from the idea-evaluation stage. The most important rule is that no one is allowed to evaluate or criticize ideas during the idea-generation stage. This creates a situation in which team members are less inhibited about presenting unusual solutions.

    Ideally, brainstorming rules turn the idea-generation stage into a freewheeling session in which every member generates as many alternative solutions to the problem as possible. Crazy and seemingly impossible ideas are encouraged so that evaluation apprehension is minimized. Members are also encouraged to combine or build on already presented suggestions. All ideas are recorded, usually on a flip chart, so that everyone can view them for later discussion.

    Brainstorming mainly focusses on the generation of creative ideas, but the team can later use consensus or voting to evaluate alternatives and make the

Constructive controversy
Any situation in which team members openly debate their different opinions regarding a problem or issue.

Devil's advocacy
A form of structured debate to encourage constructive controversy whereby one-half of the team looks for faulty logic, questionable assumptions, and other problems with the team's preferred choice.

Brainstorming
A freewheeling face-to-face meeting in which team members generate as many alternative solutions to the problem as possible and no one is allowed to evaluate them during the idea-generation stage.

Exhibit 11–4   **Devil's Advocacy Process**

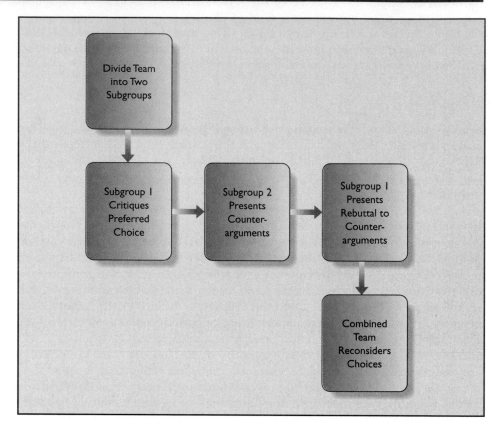

final decision. Perspective 11–4 describes how Hostess Foods uses brainstorming to generate potential solutions, then applies the consensus approach to arrive at the best solution.

Although brainstorming seems to work well at Hostess Foods, research support for this method has been mixed. Brainstorming rules tend to remove some (although not all) evaluation apprehension, but production blocking and related time constraints prevent all ideas from being presented. In fact, individuals working alone usually produce more potential solutions to a problem than if they work together using the brainstorming method. On a more positive note, brainstorming rules seem to minimize dysfunctional conflict among members and improve the team's focus on the required task. Brainstorming participants also interact and participate directly, thereby increasing decision acceptance and team cohesiveness.[54]

Nominal group technique

Nominal group technique
A structured team decision-making technique whereby members independently write down ideas, describe and clarify them to the group, and then independently rank or vote on them.

Nominal group technique tries to combine the benefits of team decision making and individual decision making by bringing people face to face without allowing them to fully interact as a team.[55] The method is called *nominal* because participants form a group *in name only* during two stages of decision making.

Perspective 11–4

Consensus Brainstorming at Hostess Foods

Hostess Foods, Canada's leading potato chip manufacturer, has discovered that team decision making provides an ideal opportunity to generate action and spark new ideas, particularly in the areas of warehousing and shipping. For example, Hostess trucks can handle a 10-foot-high load of potato chip boxes, but the cardboard packaging can withstand stacks only to 7 feet. Adding 3 more feet to each stack would allow trucks to carry more on each load and would dramatically reduce the amount of required warehouse space. An employee involvement team eventually discovered and perfected a solution to the problem.

Hostess Foods attributes much of its successful team decision making to a formal problem-solving strategy that emphasizes a consensus form of brainstorming. First, everyone is assigned a role, such as taking minutes, writing on the flip chart, keeping time, leading the discussion, and facilitating the discussion. Another role is that of gatekeeper, with the responsibility of drawing people into the discussion.

Next, team members suggest solutions to the issue, all of which are written down on the flip chart. Ideas are presented without argument. Criticism is forbidden so that people feel comfortable about making suggestions, no matter how crazy they may seem.

When the team is satisfied with the number of ideas generated, it debates each one until a consensus is reached. Doug Hughes, a Hostess Foods team leader, explains that this decision-making stage can be a powerful catalyst for effective solutions and team development. "Any group of people can generate ideas that *might* have value, but it's going through the process of convincing other team members to agree with you that often leads to the real discoveries—and helps build that essential team commitment."

Hughes has seen the results of consensus-based brainstorming and is convinced of its effectiveness. "If you let them have it out, groups will tend to come up with a better solution than any of those people would individually. It's incredible when that kind of synergy happens. It may take more effort initially, but it makes believers out of all of them and that pays dividends again and again."

Source: "Consensus Approach Gets Results," *Industrial Management* 11(8) (October 1987), p. 7.

This process, shown in Exhibit 11–5, first involves the individual, then the group, and finally the individual again.

After the problem is described to the group, team members silently and independently write down as many solutions as they can. This stage recognizes that more ideas are developed when people work alone than in open discussion. During the group stage, participants describe their solutions to the other team members, usually in a round-robin format. As with brainstorming, there is no criticism or debate, although members are encouraged to ask for clarification of the ideas presented.

The final stage returns to the individual process, in which participants silently and independently rank order or vote on each proposed solution. The results are tallied and the decision is usually determined by the pooled results of the vote. The preference for voting in nominal group technique is to avoid dysfunctional conflict that comes with debate. Voting also tends to separate the ideas from the person who made them, thereby minimizing evaluation apprehension.

Nominal group technique was used by Garrett Manufacturing Ltd., the Toronto-based high-technology and aerospace firm, when it developed a composite measure of companywide productivity. Garrett's central productivity

Exhibit 11–5   **Nominal Group Technique Process**

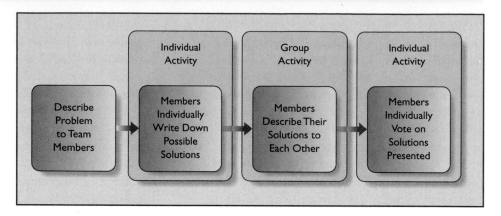

committee members individually rated the importance of each departmental indicator. The tallied results were then discussed and a composite scale was decided. St. Joseph's Hospital in London, Ontario, also applied this method when choosing demonstration projects for its total quality management program. Team members developed ideas individually, the group discussed and further developed these ideas, and then they were chosen by vote.[56]

Nominal group technique tends to produce more and better quality ideas than do traditional interacting groups.[57] Due to its high degree of structure, nominal group technique tends to maintain a high task orientation and relatively low potential for conflict within the team. However, team cohesiveness is generally lower in nominal decisions even though members still meet face to face. The problem of evaluation apprehension still exists because members still see that their ideas will be evaluated. Moreover, production blocking problems still occur during the group stage. Finally, because the nominal technique relies on voting to choose the best alternative, participants tend to have lower acceptance of the final decision compared to processes that use a consensus approach.[58]

Delphi technique

Delphi technique
A structured team decision-making method that pools the collective knowledge of experts who do not meet face to face and might not know each other's identities. The information that experts initially submit on an issue is organized and fed back to them for further comment. This cycle is repeated until a consensus or dissensus is reached.

The **Delphi technique** systematically pools the collective knowledge of experts on a particular subject to make decisions, predict the future, or identify opposing views (called *dissensus*). A unique feature of Delphi groups is that they do not meet face to face; in fact, participants are often located in different parts of the world and may not know each other's identity. Another feature is that participants do not know who "owns" the ideas submitted. This anonymity minimizes evaluation apprehension more effectively than brainstorming or nominal group technique.

The Delphi method typically includes the following steps.[59] First, a central convenor forms a panel of experts. The problem is clearly described to each panel member, who then independently and anonymously submits possible solutions or comments to the central convenor. The convenor records this information and returns the compiled results to the panel members. Each member independently and anonymously submits comments on the compiled results and adds further suggestions, thoughts, and explanations on the issue. This process may be repeated several times until some degree of consensus or dissensus is reached.

The Delphi technique was first used in the 1950s for strategic military decisions, such as choosing the optimal number of atomic bombs and target sites. More recently, British Petroleum applied this method to forecast environmental issues facing the oil and gas industry in the year 2000.[60]

The Delphi technique is effective at minimizing evaluation apprehension. Its structure and lack of interaction also ensure that participants remain focussed on the task and have minimal potential for conflict (although some may still emerge in written form). One limitation is that the Delphi method may take several months to complete using mail or other traditional forms of communication. Recent panels have used electronic mail to speed up the process, but Delphi remains the slowest approach to reaching a solution because the convenor needs time to organize and disseminate the results. A second concern is that Delphi panel members tend to have less identification with the final decision because of their remote participation in the process. Finally, the Achilles heel of the Delphi method is that the decision quality depends on the convenor's ability to select appropriate panel members.[61]

Electronic brainstorming

Sears Canada, IBM Canada, Ontario Hydro, Royal Trust, and a few other Canadian firms have built specially designed meeting rooms for small groups to participate in **electronic brainstorming.** With the aid of groupware (special computer software for groups), electronic brainstorming lets participants share ideas while minimizing the team dynamics problems inherent in traditional brainstorming sessions.[62] Individuals can enter ideas at any time on their computer terminal. These ideas are posted anonymously and randomly on the screens of all participants. A central convenor monitors the entire input to ensure that participants stay focussed on the issue.

Electronic brainstorming
Using computer software, several people enter ideas at any time on their computer terminals. Each participant can have his or her computer list a random sample of anonymous ideas generated by other people at the session to aid in thinking up new ideas.

IBM Canada's Decision Support Centre near Toronto provides the technology and setting for electronic brainstorming. The centre claims that participants can increase team decision making productivity by 50 percent.

Courtesy of IBM Canada.

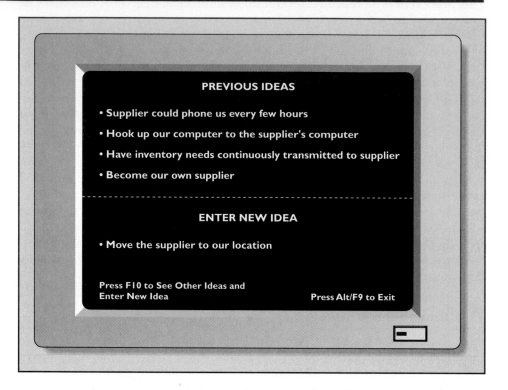

Exhibit 11–6   Computer Screen of an Electronic Brainstorming Session

Electronic brainstorming sessions typically take place in a room with up to a few dozen computer terminals. However, participants could be located in different places and attend the "meeting" at different times if the technology is available. The individual's computer screen looks similar to Exhibit 11–6. The statements shown on the upper part of the screen represent a random selection of ideas developed by the group. The individual can look at other ideas already developed by pressing the appropriate function key or mouse command. The lower part of the screen provides space for the individual to type in a new idea.

Effectiveness of electronic brainstorming

Electronic brainstorming significantly reduces the problem of production blocking because ideas are documented whenever the individual thinks of them. Creative synergy exists because participants can see the ideas generated by other people. It also minimizes the problem of evaluation apprehension because ideas are posted anonymously. "Everybody's input carries the same weight—and it's sometimes brutally honest," explains a participant at IBM Canada's decision support centre in Toronto.

Electronic brainstorming is far more efficient than traditional team decision making because there is little socializing. A study of 64 electronic brainstorming groups at aircraft manufacturer Boeing Co. found that total meeting time was reduced by 71 percent. Following an electronic brainstorming session on the company's budget, a vice-president of Royal LePage explained, "We garnered a

Effectiveness of Team Decision-Making Techniques					Exhibit 11–7

Team Decision Method	Number of Ideas Generated	Focus on Task	Time Consumption	Potential for Conflict	Commitment to Decision
Interacting teams	Low	Low	High	High	High
Brainstorming teams	Moderate	Moderate	Moderate	Low	High
Nominal group technique	Moderate	High	Moderate	Moderate	Moderate
Delphi technique	High	High	High	Low	Low
Electronic brainstorming	High	High	Low	Low	Moderate

substantial amount of information in one session that normally would have required a day or two on each of the subjects."[63]

By overcoming these team dynamics problems, electronic brainstorming generates more ideas than traditional brainstorming or nominal group technique. Electronic brainstorming group members tend to be more satisfied, motivated, and confident in the decision-making exercise compared to participants in nominal groups.[64]

Despite these advantages, electronic brainstorming isn't likely to spread quickly. Some critics have noted that the additional number of ideas generated through electronic brainstorming is not enough to justify its cost. Another concern is that managers are generally less enthusiastic about electronic brainstorming sessions than are students who participate in research samples.[65] This method feels unnatural to people accustomed to normal conversation. Moreover, some organizational leaders may feel threatened by the honesty of some statements and by their inability to control the discussion. Finally, the electronic brainstorming technology has focussed on the idea generation stage of decision making, but it has yet to find ways to effectively organize these results and provide a mechanism for participants to choose the best alternative.

Comparing team decision-making methods

Exhibit 11–7 summarizes the relative effectiveness of interacting, brainstorming, nominal, Delphi, and electronic brainstorming decision making. Electronic brainstorming and Delphi groups are most effective for their number (and quality) of ideas generated, focus on the task, and minimal potential for dysfunctional conflict. Electronic brainstorming is also valuable for its minimal time consumption, although this only applies when participants meet at the same place and at the same time. Nominal and brainstorming methods are moderately good (or bad) on most effectiveness dimensions, although nominal groups have a higher task orientation and brainstorming may be somewhat better at minimizing dysfunctional conflict. As you can see, unstructured interaction groups are more likely to produce conflict and consume valuable time than arrive at an optimal decision. Their only benefit is that participants are highly committed to the decision—if they can reach a decision.

Chapter Summary

- Employee involvement (or participation) occurs when employees have an active role in making decisions that were not previously within their mandate. It may be formal or informal, direct or indirect, and voluntary or legislated. The level of participation may range from an employee providing specific information to management without knowing the problem or issue to complete involvement in all phases of the decision process.

- Self-managing work teams are groups of employees assigned almost total responsibility for managing a specific work process, including most support tasks. They evolved from sociotechnical design theory that states that the organization's social and technical systems must be compatible with each other, and should encourage team dynamics, job enrichment, and employee well-being.

- Employee involvement may lead to higher decision quality, decision commitment, employee satisfaction and empowerment, and employee development in decision-making skills. Three barriers to some forms of employee involvement are cultural differences, management resistance, and union resistance.

- Most forms of employee involvement involve team-based decisions. Team dynamics can interfere with effective group decision making in five ways: time constraints, evaluation apprehension, conformity, groupthink, and group polarization.

- Team decision making may be improved by having a neutral team leader, maintaining optimal team size, trying to seek consensus, and encouraging constructive controversy when discussing the problem and its possible solutions. Four decision-making structures that may improve some aspects of team decision making are brainstorming, nominal group technique, Delphi method, and electronic brainstorming.

Discussion Questions

1. When Great West Life Assurance Co. decided to build a new headquarters in Winnipeg, it formed a task force of employees representing different areas of the organization. The group's mandate was to identify features of the new building that would help employees do their jobs more effectively and work more comfortably. Describe the forms and level of employee involvement in this task force.

2. Describe the characteristics of a typical self-managing work team.

3. Northern Chicken Ltd. wants to build a new chicken processing plant in Quebec that represents a sociotechnically designed operation. In a tradi-

tional chicken processing plant, employees work in separate departments—cleaning and cutting, cooking, packaging, and warehousing. The cooking and packaging processes are controlled by separate work stations in the traditional plant. Describe the general changes to the social and technical systems that may be required to ensure that Northern Chicken's plant is sociotechnically designed.

4. Discuss three ways that employee involvement potentially improves decision quality.

5. Central River Wheat Pool's management wants employees to form continuous improvement teams that recommend ways to increase productivity and product quality, but the local labour union opposes this idea. Discuss two possible reasons why the union's leadership might be against this form of employee involvement.

6. What are the conditions under which groupthink is most likely to occur?

7. What is constructive controversy? How can team leaders ensure that constructive controversy exists in their decision-making meetings?

8. Compare the advantages of electronic brainstorming with the Delphi technique.

Notes

1. A. Walmsley, "The Brain Game," *Report on Business Magazine*, April 1993, pp. 36-46; G. Pitts, "The Cheese Plant Nobody Wanted," *Globe & Mail*, February 16, 1993, p. B24; and J. Purdie, "Finding New Ways to Run a Dairy Business," *Financial Post*, April 8, 1991, p. 11.

2. V. H. Vroom and A. G. Jago, *The New Leadership: Managing Participation in Organizations* (Englewood Cliffs, N.J.: Prentice Hall, 1988), p. 15.

3. E. E. Lawler III, *High-Involvement Management* (San Francisco: Jossey-Bass, 1986), Chapter 1; and R. E. Miles, "Human Relations or Human Resources?" *Harvard Business Review*, July–August 1965, pp. 148–63.

4. D. Roberts, "A Long Way from Cambodia," *Globe & Mail*, July 5, 1994, p. B18; D. Scott, "Hard to Beat," *Canadian Mining Journal* 114 (June 1993), pp. 12–14; and B. Painter, *Good Jobs with New Technology* (Vancouver: British Columbia Research Corporation, 1991), p. 11.

5. M. N. Lam, "Forms of Participation: A Comparison of Preferences Between Chinese Americans and American Caucasians," *Canadian Journal of Administrative Sciences* 3 (June 1986), pp. 81–98; D. V. Nightingale, "The Formally Participative Organization," *Industrial Relations* 18 (1979), pp. 310–21; E. A. Locke and D. M. Schweiger, "Participation in Decision-Making: One More Look," *Research in Organizational Behavior* 1 (1979), pp. 265–339; and H. P. Dachler and B. Wilpert, "Conceptual Dimensions and Boundaries of Participation in Organizations: A Critical Evaluation," *Administrative Science Quarterly* 23 (1978), pp. 1–39.

6. J. L. Cotton, *Employee Involvement: Methods for Improving Performance and Work Attitudes* (Newbury Park, Calif.: Sage, 1993), Chapter 6; H. C. Jain (ed.), *Worker Participation: Success and Problems* (New York: Praeger, 1980); R. Long, "Recent Patterns in Swedish Industrial Democracy," in *The Organizational Practice of Democracy*, ed. R. N. Stern & S. McCarthy (New York: Wiley, 1986), pp. 375–85; and R. J. Adams and C. H. Rummel, "Workers' Participation in Management in West Germany: Impact on the Worker, the Enterprise and the Trade Union," *Industrial Relations Journal* 8 (1977), pp. 4–22.

7. B. A. Macy, M. F. Peterson, and L. W. Norton, "A Test of Participation Theory in a Work Re-Design Field Setting: Degree of Participation and Comparison Site Contrasts," *Human Relations* 42 (1989), pp. 1095–1165.

8. N. S. Bruning and P. R. Liverpool, "Membership in Quality Circles and Participation in Decision Making," *Journal of Applied Behavioral Science* 29 (March 1993), pp. 76–95; M. Brossard, "Workers' Objectives in Quality Improvement," *Employee Relations* 12(6) (1990), pp. 11–16; S. D. Saleh, Z. Guo, and T. Hull, "The Use of Quality Circles in the Automobile Parts Industry," *Proceedings of the Annual ASAC Conference, Organizational Behaviour Division* 9, pt. 5 (1988), pp. 95–104; and O. L. Crocker, J. S. L. Chiu, and C. Charney, *Quality Circles: A Guide to Participation and Productivity* (Toronto: Methuen, 1984).

9. Lawler, *High-Involvement Management*, Chapters 11 and 12; F. Shipper and C. C. Manz, "Employee Self-Management without Formally Designated Teams: An Alternative Road to Empowerment," *Organizational*

Dynamics 20 (Winter 1992), pp. 48–61; and L. C. Plunkett and R. Fournier, *Participative Management: Implementing Empowerment* (New York: Wiley, 1991).

10.   P. S. Goodman, R. Devadas, and T. L. G. Hughson, "Groups and Productivity: Analyzing the Effectiveness of Self-Managing Teams," in *Productivity in Organizations,* ed. J. P. Campbell, R. J. Campbell, and Associates (San Francisco: Jossey-Bass, 1988), pp. 295–327.

11.   D. Tjosvold, *Teamwork for Customers* (San Francisco: Jossey-Bass, 1993); J. Dibbs, "Organizing for Empowerment," *Business Quarterly* 58 (Autumn 1993), pp. 97–102; D. E. Bowen and E. E. Lawler III, "The Empowerment of Service Workers: What, Why, How, and When," *Sloan Management Review,* Spring 1992, pp. 31–39; and K. Foss, "A Better Kind of Keeping House in Banff," *Foodservice and Hospitality* 25 (May 1992), pp. 36–37.

12.   E. L. Trist, G. W. Higgin, H. Murray, and A. B. Pollock, *Organizational Choice* (London: Tavistock, 1963); and T. Cummings, "Self-Regulating Work Groups: A Socio-technical Synthesis," *Academy of Management Review* 3 (1978), pp. 625–34.

13.   H. F. Kolodny, C. P. Johnston, and W. Jeffrey, *Quality of Working Life: Job Design and Sociotechnical Systems,* rev. ed. (Ottawa: Supply and Services Canada, 1985); J. B. Cunningham, "A Look at Four Approaches to Work Design," *Optimum* 20(1) (1989–90), pp. 39–55; and W. Pasmore, C. Francis, J. Haldeman, and A. Shani, "Sociotechnical Systems: A North American Reflection on Empirical Studies of the Seventies," *Human Relations* 35 (1982), pp. 1179–1204.

14.   Goodman et al., "Groups and Productivity," p. 314.

15.   P. S. Adler and R. E. Cole, "Designed for Learning: A Tale of Two Auto Plants," *Sloan Management Review* 34 (Spring 1993), pp. 85–94; O. Hammarström and R. Lansbury, "The Art of Building a Car: The Swedish Experience Re-examined," *New Technology, Work and Employment* 2 (Autumn 1991), pp. 85–90; and J. P. Womack, D. T. Jones, and D. Roos, *The Machine that Changed the World* (New York: MacMillan, 1990). For a more favourable evaluation of Volvo's plants, see I. Magaziner and M. Patinkin, *The Silent War* (New York: Random House, 1988); and P. G. Gyllenhammar, *People at Work* (Reading, Mass.: Addison-Wesley, 1977).

16.   N. Herrick, *Joint Management and Employee Participation* (San Francisco: Jossey-Bass, 1990); T. Rankin and J. Mansell, "Integrative Collective Bargaining and New Forms of Work Organization," *National Productivity Review* 5(4) (1986), pp. 338–47; N. Halpern, "Sociotechnical System Design: The Shell Sarnia Experience," in *Quality of Working Life: Contemporary Cases,* ed. J. B. Cunningham and T. H. White (Ottawa: Supply and Services Canada, 1984), pp. 31–75; and D. A. Ondrack and M. G. Evans, "The Shell Chemical Plant at Sarnia (Canada): An Example of Union-Management Collaboration," in *Worker Participation: Success and Problems,* ed. Jain, pp. 257–73.

17.   B. Sheehy and G. Peckover, "You Get What You Pay For," *Industrial Management* 12(7), (September 1988), pp. 24–26.

18.   R. Likert, *New Patterns of Management* (New York: McGraw-Hill, 1961); D. McGregor, *The Human Side of Enterprise* (New York: McGraw-Hill, 1960); and C. Argyris, *Personality and Organization* (New York: Harper & Row, 1957).

19.   R. Dubin, "Union–Management Co-operation and Productivity," *Industrial and Labor Relations Review* 2 (1949), pp. 195–209.

20.   R. H. G. Field, W. C. Wedley, and M. W. J. Hayward, "Criteria Used in Selecting Vroom–Yetton Decision Styles," *Canadian Journal of Administrative Sciences* 6 (June 1989), pp. 18–24; L. K. Michaelson, W. E. Watson, and R. H. Black, "A Realistic Test of Individual versus Group Consensus Decision Making," *Journal of Applied Psychology* 74 (1989), pp. 834–39; R. J. Long, "Factors Affecting Managerial Desires for Various Types of Employee Participation in Decision Making," *Applied Psychology: An International Review* 37 (1988), pp. 15–34; and N. R. F. Maier, "Assets and Liabilities in Group Problem Solving: The Need for an Integrative Function," *Psychological Review* 74 (1967), pp. 239–49.

21.   C. Motherwell, "PanCanadian Uncaps the Enthusiasm of Guys Like Ed," *Globe & Mail,* August 25, 1992, p. B20.

22.   E. Innes, "Office Workers Want More Say, Poll Says," *Financial Post,* June 9, 1988, p. 16; and J. Richards, G. Mauser, and R. Holmes, "What Do Workers Want? Attitudes Towards Collective Bargaining and Participation in Management," *Relations Industrielles* 43 (1988), pp. 133–50.

23.   J. R. Hollenbeck, C. R. Williams, and H. J. Klein, "An Empirical Examination of the Antecedents of Commitment to Difficult Goals," *Journal of Applied Psychology* 74 (1989), pp. 18–23; and L. Coch and J. R. P. French, Jr., "Overcoming Resistance to Change," *Human Relations* 1 (1948), pp. 512–32.

24.   Cotton, *Employee Involvement,* Chapter 8; S. J. Havlovic, "Quality of Work Life and Human Resource Outcomes," *Industrial Relations,* 1991, pp. 469–79; K. I. Miller and P. R. Monje, "Participation, Satisfaction, and Productivity: A Meta-Analytic Review," *Academy of Management Journal* 29 (1986), pp. 727–53; and R. A. Guzzo, R. D. Jette, and R. A. Katzell, "The Effects of Psychologically Based Intervention Programs on Worker Productivity: A Meta-Analysis," *Personnel Psychology* 38 (1985), pp. 275–91.

25.   J. A. Conger and R. N. Kanungo, "The Empowerment Process: Integrating Theory and Practice," *Academy of Management Review* 13 (1988), pp. 471–82; and W. Bennis and B. Nanus, *Leaders* (New York: Harper & Row, 1985).

26.   C. C. Manz, "Self-Leading Work Teams: Moving Beyond Self-Management Myths," *Human Relations* 45 (1992), pp. 1119–40; N. Bayloff and E. M. Doherty, "Potential Pitfalls in Employee Participation," *Organizational*

Dynamics 17 (1989), pp. 51–62; and V. H. Vroom, *Some Personality Determinants of the Effects of Participation* (Englewood Cliffs, N.J.: Prentice Hall, 1960).

27. Vroom and Jago, *The New Leadership,* pp. 151–52.

28. L. Redpath and M. O. Nielson, "Crossing the Cultural Divide Between Traditional Native Values and Non-Native Management Ideology," *Proceedings of the Annual ASAC Conference, Organizational Theory Division* 15, 12 pt. (1994), pp. 70–79; and I. Chapman, D. McCaskill, and D. Newhouse, *Management in Contemporary Aboriginal Organizations* (Peterborough, Ont.: Trent University, 1992), Administrative Studies Working Paper Series #92-04.

29. D. H. B. Welsh, F. Luthans, and S. M. Sommer, "Managing Russian Factory Workers: The Impact of U.S.-Based Behavioral and Participative Programs," *Academy of Management Journal* 36 (1993), pp. 58–79; and A. J. Marrow, "The Risk and Uncertainties of Action Research," *Journal of Social Issues* 20 (1964), pp. 5–20.

30. C. C. Manz, D. E. Keating, and A. Donnellon, "Preparing for an Organizational Change to Employee Self-Management: The Managerial Transition," *Organizational Dynamics* 19 (Autumn 1990), pp. 15–26.

31. K. Mark, "Team Power," *Canadian HR Reporter,* October 18, 1989, p. 8.

32. Manz et al., "Preparing for an Organizational Change to Employee Self-Management," pp. 23–25.

33. G. McKay, *Increasing the Power of Self-Managing Work Teams Through Effective Human Resource Management Strategies.* Unpublished MBA project (Burnaby, B.C.: Simon Fraser University, December 1992).

34. P. Lush, "Unions, Middle Managers Balk at Employee Involvement Plans," *Globe & Mail,* February 24, 1990, p. B6; M. Parker and J. Slaughter, *Choosing Sides: Unions and the Team Concept* (Boston: South End Press, 1988); and T. A. Kochan, H. C. Katz, and R. B. McKersie, *The Transformation of American Industrial Relations* (New York: Basic Books, 1986), Chapters 6 and 7.

35. A. Verma and T. A. Kochan, "Two Paths to Innovations in Industrial Relations: The Case of Canada and the United States," *Labor Law Journal,* 1990, pp. 601–7; and D. Wells, *Soft Sell: Quality of Working Life Programs and the Productivity Race* (Ottawa: Canadian Centre for Policy Alternatives, 1986), Chapter 3.

36. M. Stevenson, "Be Nice for a Change," *Canadian Business,* November 1993, pp. 81–85.

37. B. Gilbert, "The Impact of Union Involvement on the Design and Introduction of Quality of Working Life," *Human Relations* 42 (1989), pp. 1057–78; and T. A. Kochan, H. C. Katz, and R. B. McKersie, *The Transformation of American Industrial Relations* (New York: Basic Books, 1986), pp. 238–45.

38. D. V. Nightingale, *Workplace Democracy: An Enquiry into Employee Participation in Canadian Work Organizations* (Toronto: University of Toronto Press, 1982).

39. G. Whyte, "Escalating Commitment in Individual and Group Decision Making: A Prospect Theory Approach," *Organizational Behavior and Human Decision Processes* 54 (1993), pp. 430–55.

40. Vroom and Jago, *The New Leadership,* pp. 28–29.

41. R. B. Gallupe, W. H. Cooper, M. L. Grisé, and L. M. Bastianutti, "Blocking Electronic Brainstorms," *Journal of Applied Psychology* 79 (1994), pp. 77–86; and M. Diehl and W. Stroebe, "Productivity Loss in Idea-Generating Groups: Tracking Down the Blocking Effects," *Journal of Personality and Social Psychology* 61 (1991), pp. 392–403.

42. I. L. Janis, *Crucial Decisions* (New York: Free Press, 1989), pp. 56–63; and I. L. Janis, *Groupthink: Psychological Studies of Policy Decisions and Fiascoes,* 2nd ed. (Boston: Houghton Mifflin, 1982).

43. M. E. Turner and A. R. Pratkanis, "Threat, Cohesion, and Group Effectiveness: Testing a Social Identity Maintenance Perspective on Groupthink," *Journal of Personality and Social Psychology* 63 (1992), pp. 781–96.

44. G. Moorhead, R. Ference, and C. P. Neck, "Group Decision Fiascoes Continue: Space Shuttle *Challenger* and a Revised Groupthink Framework," *Human Relations* 44 (1991), pp. 539–50; and Janis, *Crucial Decisions,* pp. 76–77.

45. G. Whyte, "Groupthink Reconsidered," *Academy of Management Review* 14 (1989), pp. 40–56.

46. C. McGarty, J. C. Turner, M. A. Hogg, B. David, and M. S. Wetherell, "Group Polarization as Conformity to the Prototypical Group Member," *British Journal of Social Psychology* 31 (1992), pp. 1–20; D. Isenberg, "Group Polarization: A Critical Review and Meta-analysis," *Journal of Personality and Social Psychology* 50 (1986), pp. 1141–51; and D. G. Myers and H. Lamm, "The Group Polarization Phenomenon," *Psychological Bulletin* 83 (1976), pp. 602–27.

47. D. Kahneman and A. Tversky, "Prospect Theory: An Analysis of Decision under Risk," *Econometrica* 47 (1979), pp. 263–91.

48. Janis, *Crucial Decisions,* pp. 244–49.

49. F. A. Schull, A. L. Delbecq, and L. L. Cummings, *Organizational Decision Making* (New York: McGraw-Hill, 1970), pp. 144–49.

50. D. Tjosvold and R. H. G. Field, "Effects of Social Context on Consensus and Majority Vote Decision Making," *Academy of Management Journal* 26 (1983), pp. 500–6.

51. D. Tjosvold, *Team Organization: An Enduring Competitive Edge* (Chichester, U.K.: Wiley, 1991); and D. Tjosvold, "Participation: A Close Look at Its Dynamics," *Journal of Management* 13 (1987), pp. 739–50.

52. D. M. Schweiger, W. R. Sandberg, and P. L. Rechner, "Experiential Effects of Dialectical Inquiry, Devil's Advocacy, and Consensus Approaches to Strategic Decision Making," *Academy of Management Journal* 32 (1989), pp. 745–72.

53. A. F. Osborn, *Applied Imagination* (New York: Scribner, 1957).

54. Diehl and Stroebe, "Productivity Loss in Idea-Generating Groups;" R. N. Taylor, *Behavioral Decision Making* (Glenview, Ill.: Scott, Foresman, 1984), pp. 44–47; and A. P. Hare, *Handbook of Small Group Research,* 2nd ed. (New York: Free Press, 1976), p. 319.

55. A. L. Delbecq, A. H. Van de Ven, and D. H. Gustafson, *Group Techniques for Program Planning: A Guide to Nominal Group and Delphi Processes* (Middleton, Wis.: Green Briar Press, 1986).

56. P. Hassen, *Rx for Hospitals: New Hope for Medicare in the Nineties* (Toronto: Stoddart, 1993), p. 117; and W. C. Tate, "Measuring Our Productivity Improvements," *Business Quarterly,* Winter 1984, pp. 87–91.

57. S. Frankel, "NGT + MDS: An Adaptation of the Nominal Group Technique for Ill-Structured Problems," *Journal of Applied Behavioral Science* 23 (1987), pp. 543–51; and D. M. Hegedus and R. Rasmussen, "Task Effectiveness and Interaction Process of a Modified Nominal Group Technique in Solving an Evaluation Problem," *Journal of Management* 12 (1986), pp. 545–60.

58. Tjosvold and Field, "Effects of Social Context on Consensus and Majority Vote Decision Making;" and S. G. Green and T. D. Taber, "The Effects of Three Social Decision Schemes on Decision Group Process," *Organizational Behavior and Human Performance* 25 (1980), pp. 97–106.

59. H. A. Linstone and M. Turoff (eds.), *The Delphi Method: Techniques and Applications* (Reading, Mass.: Addison–Wesley, 1975).

60. R. D. Needham and R. C. de Loë, "The Policy Delphi: Purpose, Structure, and Application," *Canadian Geographer* 34 (1990), pp. 133–42; and W. G. Rieger, "Directions in Delphi Developments: Dissertations and Their Quality," *Technological Forecasting and Social Change* 29 (1986), pp. 195–204.

61. Taylor, *Behavioral Decision Making,* p. 182.

62. Gallupe et al., "Blocking Electronic Brainstorms;" J. Blackwell, "You, Too, Can Be an Einstein," *Canadian Business,* May 1993, pp. 66–69; and C. Leitch, "Big Blue Staff Let It All Hang Out—On-Line," *Globe & Mail,* February 26, 1992, p. B18.

63. W. M. Bulkeley, " 'Computerizing' Dull Meetings Is Touted as an Antidote to the Mouth that Bored," *The Wall Street Journal,* January 28, 1992, pp. B1, B2.

64. R. B. Gallupe, A. R. Dennis, W. H. Cooper, J. S. Valacich, L. M. Bastianutti, and J. F. Nunamaker, Jr., "Electronic Brainstorming and Group Size," *Academy of Management Journal* 35 (June 1992), pp. 350–69; and R. B. Gallupe, L. M. Bastianutti, and W. H. Cooper, "Unblocking Brainstorms," *Journal of Applied Psychology* 76 (1991), pp. 137–42.

65. B. Kabanoff and J. R. Rossiter, "Recent Developments in Applied Creativity," *International Review of Industrial and Organizational Psychology* 9 (1994), pp. 283–324.

Chapter Case

Employee Involvement Cases

Case 1: New Machines Decision Problem You are a manufacturing manager in a large electronics plant. The company's management is always searching for ways of increasing efficiency. The company has recently installed new machines and put in a new simplified work system, but to the surprise of everyone, including yourself, the expected increase in productivity was not realized. In fact, production has begun to drop, quality has fallen off, and the number of employee separations has risen.

You do not believe that there is anything wrong with the machines. You have had reports from other companies using them that confirm this opinion. You have also had representatives from the firm that built the machines go over them, and they report that the machines are operating at peak efficiency.

You suspect that some parts of the new work system may be responsible for the change, but this view is not widely shared among your immediate subordinates, who are four first-level supervisors, each in charge of a section, and your supply manager. The drop in production has been variously attributed to poor training of the operators, lack of an adequate system of financial incentives, and poor morale. Clearly, this is an issue about which there is considerable depth of feeling among individuals and potential disagreement among your subordinates.

This morning you received a phone call from your division manager. He had just received your production figures for the last six months and was calling to express his concern. He indicated that the problem was yours to solve in any way that you thought best, but that he would like to know within a week what steps you plan to take.

You share your division manager's concern over the falling productivity and know that your people are also disturbed. The problem is to decide what steps to take to rectify the situation.

Case 2: Coast Guard Cutter Decision Problem   You are the captain of a 72-metre Canadian Coast Guard cutter, with a crew of 16, including officers. Your mission is general at-sea search and rescue. At 2:00 AM this morning, while en route to your home port after a routine 28-day patrol, you received word from the nearest Canadian Coast Guard station that a small plane had crashed 100 kilometres offshore. You obtained all the available information concerning the location of the crash, informed your crew of the mission, and set a new course at maximum speed for the scene to commence a search for survivors and wreckage.

You have now been searching for 20 hours. Your search operation has been increasingly impaired by rough seas, and there is evidence of a severe storm building to the southwest. The atmospherics associated with the deteriorating weather have made communications with the Coast Guard station impossible. A decision must be made shortly about whether to abandon the search and place your vessel on a northeasterly course to ride out the storm (thereby protecting the vessel and your crew, but relegating any possible survivors to almost certain death from exposure) or to continue a potentially futile search and the risks it would entail.

Before losing communications, you received an update advisory from Atmospheric Environmental Services concerning the severity and duration of the storm. Although your crew members are extremely conscientious about their responsibility, you believe that they would be divided on the decision of leaving or staying.

Discussion Questions (for both cases)

1. **To what extent should your subordinates be involved in this decision? (Note: You may assume that neither case has time constraints that would prevent the highest level of participation.) Please choose one of the following:**

   AI. You make the decision alone with no employee involvement.

   AII. Subordinates provide information that you request, but they don't offer recommendations and they might not be aware of the problem.

   CI. You describe the problem to relevant subordinates individually, getting their information and recommendations. You make the final decision, which does not necessarily reflect the advice that subordinates have provided.

CII. You describe the problem to subordinates in a meeting, in which they discuss information and recommendations. You make the final decision, which does not necessarily reflect the advice that subordinates have provided.

GII. You describe the problem to subordinates in a meeting. They discuss the problem and make a decision that you are willing to accept and implement if it has the entire team's support. You might chair this session, but you do not influence the team's decision.

2. What factors led you to choose this alternative rather than the others?

3. What problems might occur if less or more involvement occurred in this case (where possible)?

Source: Adapted from V.H. Vroom and A. G. Jago, *The New Leadership: Managing Participation in Organizations* (Englewood Cliffs, N.J.: Prentice Hall, 1988). © 1987 V. H. Vroom and A. G. Jago. Used with permission of the authors.

Experiential Exercise

Winter Survival Exercise

Purpose: This exercise is designed to help you understand the potential advantages of team decision making compared with individual decision making.

Situation: You have just crash-landed somewhere in the woods of southern Manitoba or possibly northern Minnesota. It is 11:32 A.M. in mid-January. The small plane in which you were travelling crashed on a small lake. The pilot and co-pilot were killed. Shortly after the crash, the plane sank completely into the lake with the pilot's and co-pilot's bodies inside. Everyone else on the flight escaped to land dry and without serious injury.

The crash came suddenly before the pilot had time to radio for help or inform anyone of your position. Since your pilot was trying to avoid the storm, you know the plane was considerably off course. The pilot announced shortly before the crash that you were 70 kilometres northwest of a small town that is the nearest known habitation.

You are in a wilderness area made up of thick woods broken by many lakes and rivers. The snow depth varies from above the ankles in windswept areas to more than knee-deep where it has drifted. The last weather report indicated that the temperature would reach minus 10 degrees Celsius in the daytime and minus 35 degrees at night. There are plenty of dead wood and twigs in the area around the lake. You and the other surviving passengers are dressed in winter clothing appropriate for city wear—suits, pantsuits, street shoes, and overcoats. While escaping from the plane, your group salvaged the 12 items listed in the chart below. You may assume that the number of persons in the group is the same as the number in your group, and that you have agreed to stay together.

Instructions: Your task is to rank the 12 items shown in the chart below according to their importance to your survival. In the "Individual Ranking" column, indicate the most important item with "1," going through to "12" for the least important. Keep in mind the reasons why each item is or is not important. Next, the instructor will form small teams (typically five members) and each team will rank order the items in the second column. Team rankings should be based on consensus, not simply averaging the individual rankings.

When the teams have completed their rankings, the instructor will provide the expert's ranking, which can be entered in the third column. Next, each student will compute the absolute difference (i.e., ignore minus signs) between the individual ranking and the expert's ranking, record this information in column four, and sum the absolute values at the bottom of column four. In column five, record the absolute difference between the team's ranking and the expert's ranking, and sum these absolute scores at the bottom. A class discussion of the absolute merits of individual versus team decision making will follow.

Adapted from "Winter Survival" in D. Johnson and F. Johnson, *Joining Together*, 3rd ed. (Englewood Cliffs, N.J.: Prentice Hall, 1984).

Winter Survival Tally Sheet

Items	Step 1 Your Individual Ranking	Step 2 Your Team's Ranking	Step 3 Survival Expert's Ranking	Step 4 Difference between Steps 1 and 3	Step 4 Difference between Steps 2 and 3
Ball of steel wool					
Newspapers					
Compass					
Hand axe					
Cigarette lighter					
.45-caliber pistol					
Sectional air map					
Canvas					
Shirt and pants					
Shortening					
Whiskey					
Chocolate bars					
Total				Your score	Team score

(The lower the score, the better)

Organizational Power and Politics

Learning Objectives

After reading this chapter, you should be able to:

Define the meaning of *power* **and** *counterpower.*

Outline the five bases of power in organizations.

Explain how information plays an important role in organizational power.

List five ways to increase potential power through nonsubstitutability.

Identify four strategies to increase potential power through visibility.

Discuss the advantages and disadvantages of organizational politics.

List seven types of political activity found in organizations.

Describe three ways to control organizational politics.

Chapter Outline

The Meaning of Power.

Sources of Power in Organizations.

Information and Power.

Contingencies of Power.

Consequences of Power.

Organizational Politics.

Types of Political Activity.

Conditions for Organizational Politics.

Controlling Political Behaviour.

Chris Beegen. Courtesy of Oilweek.

On a cold January afternoon, employees from Bow Valley Energy Inc. gathered in the company's computer room in downtown Calgary. In silence, they watched a man wearing a black executioner's outfit approach the company's old mainframe computer and throw the switch. The computer died, along with all the applications that ran it.

The event was a symbolic ending to Bow Valley's mainframe era. But to senior management, it was also the end—or so they hoped—to several months of organizational politics. Before that day, Bow Valley's information resided in accounting, land administration, reserves management, well administration, and other departments throughout the organization. Information was power at Bow Valley, and that information power was jealously guarded by the departments that held it.

When Bow Valley's CEO announced that the company would introduce a new computer system allowing information to flow more freely, many people feared that their power base would disappear. Tempers flared in meetings, entire departments opted out of the process, and managers were accused of grandstanding. "It was really unpleasant," winced one manager as he recalls the verbal barrages a few months earlier.

Today, information that previously resided in one department or another is now widely accessible. If someone needs a colour map, for example, he or she can retrieve it from the central server without going through the map department.

"Philosophically, you have to accept that you are not owners of the data," explains Dr. Gary Moore, the former University of Calgary business professor brought in to transform Bow Valley's information system. "You are stewards of the data on behalf of the corporation. People will buy into that—until they have to give up control."[1]

Exhibit 12–1   **Dependence in the Power Relationship**

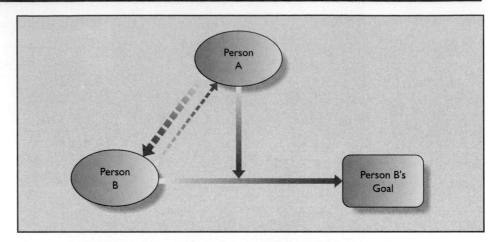

Power and politics exist in every organization. Some writers even suggest that power is the essence of organizations.[2] Power is necessary to coordinate organizational activities, but it might also serve personal objectives that threaten the organization's survival. As such, we need to be aware of the dynamics of power and learn how to control political behaviour.

We begin this chapter by defining power and presenting a basic model depicting the dynamics of power in organizational settings. We then discuss the five bases of power, as well as information as a power base. Next, we look at the contingencies necessary to translate those sources into meaningful power. The latter part of this chapter examines the dynamics of organizational politics, including the various types of political activity, the conditions that encourage organizational politics, and the ways that it can be controlled.

The Meaning of Power

Power
The capacity of a person, team, or organization to influence others.

Power is the capacity of a person, team, or organization to influence others.[3] Power is not the act of changing others' attitudes or behaviour; it is only the *potential* to do so. People frequently have power they do not use; they might not even know they have power. Using a physics analogy, power is similar to a large round rock resting at the top of a steep hill. It exerts no force and has no momentum, yet it has a tremendous capacity to change the landscape if it rolls down the hill. Just like the dormant rock, power is neither good nor bad until its potential is activated. Thus, we should be concerned not only with how power is acquired, but with how it is applied in organizational settings.

Power, dependence, and resource scarcity

Power exists when one party perceives that he or she is dependent on the other for something of value.[4] This relationship is shown in Exhibit 12–1, where Person A has power over Person B by controlling something that Person B needs to achieve his or her goals. You might have power over others by controlling a

A Model of Power within Organizations   **Exhibit 12–2**

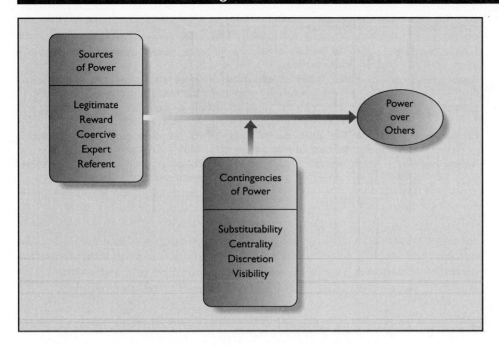

desired job assignment, useful information, or even the privilege of being associated with you! These dependency relationships are an inherent part of organizational life because work is divided into specialized tasks and the organization has limited resources with which to accomplish its goals. Power is activated when the powerholder threatens the dependent relationship, such as when a highly knowledgeable employee threatens to leave the organization. Power is ultimately a perception, so people might gain power simply by convincing others that they have something of value. Thus, power exists when you control resources that others want and they are aware that you control access to these resources.[5]

In all relationships, the dependent person or work unit also holds some power over the dominant participant. Exhibit 12–1 illustrates this by the thin line from Person B to Person A. This **counterpower**, as it is known, is strong enough to maintain Person A's participation in the exchange relationship.[6] In other words, power exists only when there is some degree of interdependence between the parties. Managers have power over subordinates by controlling their job security and promotional opportunities, but employees have counterpower by controlling the ability to work productively and thereby creating a positive impression of the supervisor to his or her boss. Counterpower motivates managers to apply their power judiciously, so that the relationship is not broken.

Counterpower
The capacity of a person, team, or organization to keep a more powerful person or group in the exchange relationship.

Power is derived from controlling something that someone else wants, but this interdependence only exists when the desired resource is scarce or is hoarded by the powerful person or department.[7] In our opening story, Bow Valley managers depended on other departments for information needed to get their job done. Before the new computer system was installed, departments

| Exhibit 12–3 | French and Raven's Five Bases of Power |

Power Base	Definition
Legitimate power	• The perceived right to influence certain behaviours of people in other positions
Reward power	• The ability to influence others by controlling the distribution of rewards valued by others and the removal of negative sanctions
Coercive power	• The ability to influence others by controlling the distribution of punishment and removal of rewards valued by others
Expert power	• The ability to influence others by possessing knowledge that is believed to help others accomplish their goals
Referent power	• The ability to influence others based on their identification with and respect for the referent's ideas and requests

carefully controlled this information, thereby creating a scarce resource. The departments lost this power under the new system because the information was plentiful—computers can make an infinite number of copies—and easily available. Thus, power exists only under conditions of resource scarcity.

A model of power in organizations

Power is the capacity to influence others under conditions of dependence and scarce resources. However, there are several sources of power and four important contingencies that moderate the level of power that these sources generate. The model shown in Exhibit 12–2 on the previous page provides a useful framework of the dynamics of power. It indicates that power is derived from five sources: legitimate, reward, coercive, expert, and referent. But tapping into one or more of these power bases only leads to increased power under certain conditions. These conditions, or contingencies of power, include the employee's or department's substitutability, centrality, discretion, and visibility. Finally, as we will discuss later, the type of power applied affects the type of influence the powerholder has over the other person or work unit.

Sources of Power in Organizations

Over 30 years ago, French and Raven listed five sources of power within organizations (see Exhibit 12–3).[8] Many researchers have studied these five power bases and searched for others. For the most part, French and Raven's list remains intact.

Legitimate power

Legitimate power
The capacity to influence others through formal authority, that is, the perceived right to direct certain behaviours of people in other positions.

Legitimate power is the perceived right to influence certain behaviours of others. It is an *agreement* among organizational members that people in certain roles can request certain behaviours of others. Managers may have the right to ask employees to stay overtime, but only if the overtime request falls within the employee's zone of acceptance. In other words, managers have this legitimate power over employees if there is mutual agreement to that right. Thus, we must be aware of the limits of our legitimate power and realize that this power is an agreement that can change unexpectedly.

Managers are not the only ones with legitimate power; employees have the right to ask supervisors and others for assistance or information that will help them perform their jobs.[9] Some aspects of legitimate power are also based on rules in the organization or society. Many organizations have formal ethics codes (see Chapter 9) that require supervisors to treat employees fairly. Canadian society has an informal rule of reciprocity ("I did that for you, so you should feel obligated to help me") that gives people legitimate power over others who owe them a favour.[10]

Legitimate power based on the powerholder's position can be very strong, because those receiving the order suspend judgment and let the powerholder guide their behaviour. Obedience to authority is strong in South Korea, where people are raised with Confucian values and military training.[11] Nevertheless, compliance is surprisingly strong in North America. This was demonstrated in a study in which an unknown doctor telephoned a request to several nurses working on their stations. The doctor asked each nurse to give a certain patient in that ward 20 milligrams of Astrogen. This drug was not on the hospital's approved list and hospital rules required a written order (rather than a telephone call) for all such requests. Moreover, the Astrogen was locked in a special cabinet and the bottle carried a label saying that the daily dose should not exceed 10 milligrams per day. Yet 59 percent of the nurses tried to comply with the unknown doctor's order! (They were stopped on their way to the patient's room.)[12] These nurses suspended judgment and placed the doctor's legitimate power above hospital rules and other warnings.

Reward power

Reward power exists for those who control the allocation of rewards valued by others and the removal of negative sanctions (i.e., negative reinforcement). Managers have formal authority that gives them power over the distribution of organizational rewards such as pay, promotions, time off, vacation schedules, and work assignments. Employees may have reward power by extolling praise and extending personal benefits within their discretion to other co-workers. As organizations delegate responsibility and authority, work teams gain reward power over their members. In some organizations, subordinates have reward power over their bosses through the use of upward performance appraisals.

Reward power
The capacity to influence others by controlling the allocation of rewards valued by them and the removal of negative sanctions.

Coercive power

Coercive power, the ability to apply punishment and remove rewards (i.e., extinction), is one of the earliest recognized sources of power. Managers have coercive power through their authority to reprimand, demote, and fire employees. Labour unions might use coercive power tactics, such as withholding services, to influence management in collective agreement negotiations. Team members sometimes apply sanctions, ranging from sarcasm to ostracism, to ensure that co-workers conform to team norms. Punishment may have undesirable consequences, as we mentioned in Chapter 4.[13] But when used appropriately, control over adverse outcomes can represent an important power base.

Coercive power
The capacity to influence others through the ability to apply punishment and remove rewards affecting these people.

Expert power

Expert power exists when an individual or subunit depends on others for valued information. Employees with unique knowledge or skills may be very powerful if the organization is dependent on this expertise to achieve organizational objectives such as operating complex equipment. Others acquire expert power by networking with co-workers to maintain a current knowledge of organizational events. These people are well known for their "inside" information that may help others.[14]

Expert power exists throughout the organizational hierarchy. Employees may depend on executives to professionally coordinate and manage the organization, whereas executives depend on employees to get the work done! A former CEO of Maple Leaf Mills acknowledges the expert power employees have over managers: "I still couldn't run a flour mill if my life depended on it, or any of the other operations we have. I am helpless without people and I tell them that all the time. I tell them how important they are and how I couldn't do their job, but together we have a job to do."[15]

Referent power

People have **referent power** when others identify with them, like them, or otherwise respect them. This form of power usually develops slowly and is largely a function of the person's interpersonal skills.[16] Referent power is related to the concept of *charisma*. Charisma is a word with many meanings, but it is often viewed as a form of interpersonal attraction whereby followers develop a respect for and trust in the charismatic individual. We will discuss charisma as a leadership characteristic in Chapter 14. Referent power is usually associated with organizational leaders, but subordinates may have referent power over their boss. Some employees also develop referent power through impression management tactics (described later in this chapter).

Information and Power

Information plays an important role in organizational power.[17] One type of information power is based on control over the flow and interpretation of data given to others. In traditional hierarchies, specific employees or departments are given legitimate power to serve as gatekeepers and selectively distribute valued information. The other type of information power refers to the individual's or subunit's ability to cope with organizational uncertainties. This is a variation of expert power that has become a central concept in the literature on organizational power. Let's look more closely at these two aspects of information power.

Control over information flow

Many employees gain power by controlling the flow of information that others need. This right to control information flow is usually accorded to certain subunits or people in specific positions and corresponds to the formal communication network. For example, the board of directors at one company was

Power through the Control of Information   **Exhibit 12–4**

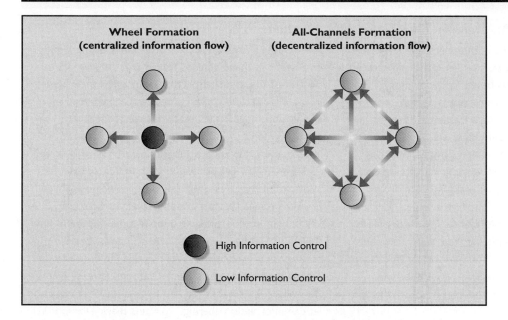

looking for a new computer system and relied on the management services department to gather and document this information. The head of management services was not directly involved in choosing the computer system, yet he influenced senior management's decision by controlling the information they received about the various computer vendors.[18] Through secrecy (withholding information) and selective dissemination of facts, gatekeepers distribute information in such a way that it shapes reality perceived by others.[19]

Exhibit 12–4 shows how information control is strongest in highly centralized organizational structures, depicted by the wheel formation. The information gatekeeper in the middle of this configuration can influence others through the amount and type of information they receive. This source of power is less likely to occur in the all-channel structure because information is freely exchanged among everyone. However, the all-channel network conflicts with the need for organizational efficiency in traditional organizational structures, so the wheel pattern tends to emerge.[20]

In the opening story to this chapter, Bow Valley's transformation to an all-channels information system created resistance, conflict, and organizational politics among those who feared their power base would disappear. Firms that introduce self-managing work teams are experiencing the same difficulties. These teams need easily accessible information to make autonomous decisions, but this threatens people whose power is based on their control of information. Perspective 12–1 describes this problem at Campbell Soup and other companies.

Coping with uncertainty

Organizations are open systems that interact with their environments by receiving inputs and transforming them into outputs (see Chapter 1). This process involves varying degrees of uncertainty, that is, a lack of information

Perspective 12–1

Information Power Shortages in Team-Based Organizations

Senior executives at Campbell Soup Company knew that information is power in corporate life, but it still created problems when the Toronto-based food processor introduced cross-functional work teams among its white-collar employees. Although Campbell Soup traditionally allowed individual employees and departments to control information flow, its emerging team-based structure required work groups to access information easily so they could make more informed decisions.

"Disrupting the flow of information is how people protected their turf," explains Joan Whitman, Campbell Soup's total quality manager. "You have to convince them that if they stop filtering information, their jobs can become more challenging because they'll have more time for other tasks."

Canadian Imperial Bank of Commerce experienced the same resistance when it introduced white-collar teams (called Project Excellence) in seven cheque processing centres across Canada. Some of the 2,400 employees in these centres feared that they would lose control of the information that maintained their power in the organization. "We recognize that information, turf, and ego are huge issues that we have to deal with," says Berkley Emmons, CIBC's director of performance improvement. "It takes a long time to break this down."

How do you get people to give up control of information that was once their source of power? Emmons hopes that participation will work at CIBC. "A key 'buy in' tool is allowing people to have a say in how their jobs will be redesigned," he contends. But this strategy didn't work when Ault Foods introduced empowered teams at its Black Diamond Cheese plant in Belleville, Ontario. "There had been a lot of secrecy and lack of information sharing," explains Black Diamond's operations manager. The company eventually replaced 5 of the 10 production supervisors because they couldn't or wouldn't share information with employees.

Sources: Based on J. Schilder, "Secret Agents," *Human Resources Professional,* January 1993, pp. 23–25; and G. Pitts, "The Cheese Plant Nobody Wanted," *Globe & Mail,* February 16, 1993, p. B24.

about future events.[21] Uncertainty interferes with the organization's ability to carry out routine activities. Consider the troubles that Canadian steel producers would face if they did not know where to find tomorrow's supply of raw materials or how much demand will exist for their products next week. They could not plan production, arrange long-term contracts with suppliers, or adjust their product lines to satisfy future customer needs. Thus, to operate more efficiently and ensure continued survival, organizations need to cope with environmental uncertainties.[22]

Individuals and subunits gain power by being able to cope with uncertainties related to important organizational goals. Coping includes any activity that effectively deals with environmental uncertainties affecting the organization. In their study of Canadian breweries and container companies, Hinings and his colleagues identified three general strategies to help organizations cope with uncertainty:[23]

- *Prevention*—The most effective strategy is to prevent environmental changes and variations from occurring. For example, financial experts acquire power by preventing the organization from experiencing a cash shortage or defaulting on loans.

- *Forecasting*—The next best strategy is to be able to predict environmental changes or variations. In this respect, marketing specialists gain power by predicting changes in consumer preferences.

| Strategies to Increase Power through Nonsubstitutability | Exhibit 12–5 |

Strategy	Example
Acquire all other sources of the critical resource	• High "union density" of a trade or industry
Become the exclusive authority over the critical resource through statute or organizational policy	• Exclusive statutory rights of medical and legal professionals to engage in certain activities
Limit distribution of unique knowledge base	• Use of jargon and limited access to specialized educational programs
Avoid written documentation of special procedures	• Verbal communication of special formulas
Customize required activities originally designed by others	• Redesign equipment outside of manufacturer's specifications
Limit entry of alternative sources	• Prevent company from hiring someone else in your area of expertise

• *Absorption*—People and subunits also gain power by absorbing or neutralizing the impact of environmental shifts as they occur. A classic example is the ability of maintenance crews to come to the rescue when machines break down and the production process stops.

Contingencies of Power

Access to one or more sources of power will influence other people or departments only under certain conditions. The four most important contingencies of power in organizations are substitutability, centrality, discretion, and visibility.[24] Keep in mind that these are not sources of power; rather, they determine whether a power base will influence others.

Substitutability

Substitutability refers to the availability of alternatives. Power is strongest when someone has a monopoly over a valued resource. Conversely, power decreases as the number of alternative sources of the critical resource increases. Substitutability refers not only to other sources that offer the resource, but also to substitutions of the resource itself. For instance, labour unions are weakened when companies introduce technologies that replace the need for their union members. At one time, a strike by telephone employees would have shut down operations, but computerized systems and other technological innovations now ensure that telephone operations continue during labour strikes and reduce the need for telephone operators during normal operations. Technology is a substitute for employees and, consequently, reduces union power.[25]

Individuals and subunits have tried numerous strategies, including those listed in Exhibit 12–5, to increase their power through nonsubstitutability. You obviously shouldn't use these approaches if they are unethical, but you should be aware that they exist and have been applied by others. Labour unions attempt to organize as many people as possible within a particular trade or industry so that employers have no other source of labour supply.[26] Lawyers, accountants, doctors and other professional groups have gained power through legislation prohibiting people outside the profession from engaging in certain

Substitutability
The extent to which those dependent on a resource have alternative sources of supply of the resource or can use other resources that would provide a reasonable substitute.

practices. They also use jargon and control educational programs to restrict access to their special knowledge base.

One study reported that maintenance workers in the French tobacco processing industry had tremendous power because they could cope with the industry's only major environmental uncertainty—machine breakdowns—and had taken several precautions to ensure that their maintenance skills were nonsubstitutable.[27] Only the dozen or so maintenance workers in each factory knew how to repair the machines because they avoided sharing their knowledge with others. They made certain that maintenance procedures were not documented and they avoided talking to production employees about their trade knowledge. Even the original manufacturer's knowledge of the machines could not weaken the maintenance workers' power because machine designs had been altered over the years and only the maintenance staff knew the details of these alterations.

Finally, information-based resources become substitutable when they are documented and routinized through standard operating procedures.[28] As expertise becomes documented, the organization can more easily transfer this knowledge to others through training. This explains why maintenance workers in the French tobacco industry trained each other verbally and avoided documenting their practices. When the industry eventually did get their knowledge in writing, it easily trained replacements and the maintenance crews became less powerful.

Centrality

Centrality
The degree and nature of interdependence between the power-holder and others.

Employees and departments have more power as their centrality increases. **Centrality** refers to the degree and nature of interdependence between the power-holder and others.[29] There are two dimensions of centrality. One dimension refers to *how many* people are affected by your actions. An organization's finance department, for instance, may have considerable power because its budget activities affect virtually every other department in the organization. In contrast, employees in a branch office may affect very few people in the organization.

The other dimension of centrality refers to *how quickly* people are affected by your actions. General Motors discovered how this aspect of centrality influences power when employees at GM's Lordstown, Ohio, parts plant walked off the job in 1992. General Motors had introduced a just-in-time (JIT) inventory system that closely linked the Lordstown plant to a dozen GM assembly plants in Canada and the United States. When the Lordstown employees went on strike, GM was forced to close down the assembly plants within a few days. Without JIT, the assembly plants would have had enough inventory stock for a few weeks of continuous operation during the strike.[30]

The just-in-time inventory system gave employees at GM's Lordstown plant more centrality which, in turn, increased their bargaining power in negotiations. As Perspective 12–2 describes, labour unions also apply this form of centrality by planning strike actions around critical times in the work process.

Discretion

The freedom to exercise judgment—to make decisions without referring to a specific rule or receiving permission from someone else—is another important

Perspective 12-2

Centrality and Power in a Major League Baseball Strike

Timing is everything in labour disputes. When a labour union needs to take strike action to put pressure on the employer, it wants to have as much power as possible so that its members are off the job for the shortest time possible. By threatening strike action at a critical time, the union increases centrality and, therefore, its power over the employer.

The major league baseball players' association knows all about centrality and power in labour disputes. In August 1993, the association made the unprecedented announcement that its members would go on strike in September unless club owners came up with an acceptable proposal to replace the existing contract. The players carefully timed the proposed strike so that the 1993 World Series would be threatened. A September strike would have cost the players only one-sixth of their salaries, whereas the owners could have lost several hundred million dollars in television revenue from the playoffs and World Series.

Paul Molitor, a Toronto Blue Jay and member of the players' association subcommittee, explains why a players' strike in late summer is better than one in December when the contract normally ends: "If we strike next spring, there's nothing stopping [the club owners] from letting us go until next June or July because they don't have that much at stake except for gate receipts. I hate to say it, but the only time you can hurt them and get them to negotiate seriously is to have the possibility of a work stoppage this fall."

The 1993 baseball strike was avoided because the baseball club owners didn't want to suffer severe financial losses. In 1994, the players repeated their strategy by going on strike in late August. Unfortunately, the owners resisted their demands and after several weeks of failed negotiations, announced that the 1994 World Series was cancelled.

Why did the power of centrality not work for the players in 1994? The answer is that the players wanted to alter the owners' financial control of the industry by removing salary caps and introducing revenue sharing with the players. The baseball club owners were willing to lose millions of dollars rather than let this happen. Although timing increases power in labour disputes, even this power has its limits.

Source: Based on J. Deacon, "No Runs, No Hits, Just Errors," *Maclean's*, September 26, 1994, p. 32; "Huge Pitch about to Come," *Calgary Herald*, August 9, 1993, p. D1.

---

contingency of power in organizations. Managers may have legitimate power over subordinates, but they don't really have this power where their discretion is limited. Even those with expert or referent power cannot exercise this power where their discretion is curtailed by organizational rules.

Consider the plight of first-line supervisors. They must administer programs developed from above and follow specific procedures in their implementation. They administer rewards and punishments, but must abide by precise rules regarding their distribution. Indeed, supervisors are often judged not on their discretionary skills, but on their ability to follow prescribed rules and regulations. This lack of discretion makes supervisors largely powerless even though they may have access to some of the power bases described earlier in this chapter.[31]

Visibility

Power does not flow to unknown people in the organization.[32] Rather, power is influenced by perceptions, so people gain power by communicating their sources of power to others. If an employee has unique knowledge to help others do their job better, the employee's knowledge will yield power only when others are aware of it.

Visibility increases with the number of people with whom you interact in the company. Thus, employees become more visible—and tend to have more successful careers—by taking people-oriented jobs that require extensive contacts rather than isolated technical positions. Similarly, visibility increases with the amount of face-to-face contact rather than less personal forms of communication. People further increase their visibility by introducing themselves to senior management and by being assigned to important task forces. Along with the valuable learning experience, these committees let you work closely with—and get noticed by—senior people in the organization.

Another way to increase visibility is through mentoring—the process of learning the ropes of organizational life from a senior person within the company. (In Chapter 16, we will discuss mentoring as a career management strategy.) However, visibility plays a significant role in this form of career management because mentors open doors to more visible work activities and make your accomplishments known to other senior people in the organization.[33]

Perhaps the most important form of visibility is to be associated with your own work rather than let your boss or someone else present or distribute the results. Paul Stern, former CEO of Northern Telecom, claims that the biggest mistake he made during the earlier part of his career was to let senior management take all the public credit for the work that he and his colleagues produced.[34]

Visibility through symbols of power

People often use public symbols as subtle (and not-so-subtle) cues to make their power sources known to others.[35] Professionals display their educational diplomas and awards on office walls to remind visitors of their expertise. Many senior executives still rely on the size of their office and related status symbols to show their legitimate power in the organization. Even the clothing we wear communicates power. Medical professionals wear white coats with a stethoscope around their neck to symbolize their legitimate and expert power in hospital settings. One recent study at the University of Manitoba reported that women who wear jackets are initially perceived as having more legitimate and expert power than women without jackets.[36]

Consequences of Power

We apply power to influence others, but the type of influence depends on the power source used. Coercive power is generally the least desirable source because it generates *resistance* by the person or department being influenced. In other words, the targeted person tends to oppose the influence attempt and actively tries to avoid carrying it out. Applying coercive power also reduces trust between the parties and increases employee dissatisfaction.[37] Resistance and distrust also occur when other power bases are used arrogantly or in a manipulative way.

Reward and legitimate power tend to produce *compliance*, whereby people are motivated to implement the powerholder's request for purely instrumental reasons. You will consciously agree to perform an extra task if your boss gives you a bonus for performing that task, but you aren't enthusiastic about it and will certainly do no more than is necessary to receive the reward. *Commitment* is the strongest form of influence, whereby people identify with the powerholder's request and are motivated to implement it even when there are no extrinsic benefits for doing so. Commitment is the most common consequence of expert and referent power. For instance, employees will follow a charismatic leader and do more than is asked because this power base evokes commitment rather than compliance or resistance.

Power also affects the powerholder. As we learned in Chapter 3, some people have a strong need for power and are motivated to acquire it for personal or organizational purposes. These individuals are more satisfied and committed to their jobs when they have increased responsibility, authority, and discretion.[38] However, you should also be warned that people who acquire too much power often abuse their position to better their personal interests and to gain more power.[39] Powerful employees tend to use their influence more often than is necessary, devalue their less powerful co-workers, and reduce their interpersonal associations with them. They also use their power to acquire more power. If unchecked, powerful employees eventually become even more powerful. In short, there appears to be some truth in Lord Acton's well-known statement that "power tends to corrupt; absolute power corrupts absolutely."[40]

Organizational Politics

Organizational politics is a concept that everyone seems to understand until they are asked to define it. Many of us believe that political behaviour is the shady side of organizational life in which people are manipulated without their consent and sometimes without their knowledge. But a more accurate view is that political behaviour sometimes makes a valuable contribution to organizational effectiveness. People need to be good politicians, particularly as they reach higher levels in the corporation.[41]

We define **organizational politics** as attempts to influence others using discretionary behaviours to promote personal objectives.[42] Organizational politics is the exercise of power to get one's own way, including the acquisition of more power, often at the expense of others. People rely on behaviours that are neither explicitly prescribed nor prohibited by the organization and are linked to one or more power bases.

Recall from this chapter's opening vignette that several departments at Bow Valley tried to scuttle the development of the new computer system because it threatened their power base. Some people tried to stall the process, whereas others questioned the competence of those who wanted the new system. A few tried to opt out of the process altogether. These actions certainly were not encouraged or sanctioned by the company, but neither were they prohibited. Rather, these informal behaviours fall somewhere between acceptable and unacceptable. As you can see, political behaviours usually occur under conditions of organizational conflict, a topic that we discuss more fully in the next chapter.[43]

Organizational politics
Attempts to influence others using discretionary behaviours for the purpose of promoting personal objectives; discretionary behaviours are neither explicitly prescribed nor prohibited by the organization and are linked to one or more power bases.

Politics and organizational effectiveness

You might think that all political activities in organizations are bad because they serve the individual's interest, but this is not necessarily so. Political tactics can help organizations achieve their objectives where traditional influence methods may fail. A manager might use politics to influence an important organizational strategy that, in the long run, may be good for the organization. Research scientists and idea champions often build coalitions and rely on other political tactics to help their ideas gain acceptance so that the company provides enough funding to bring these ideas to market.[44] Political actions are also used by individuals to acquire more power. This, again, may be good or bad for the organization, depending on the circumstances.

Although some political behaviours are beneficial, others may be very harmful to the organization. In companies in which political manoeuvres are implicitly accepted as the way to get what you want, the long-term consequences can be quite damaging. Political behaviours reduce interpersonal trust and, in the long term, can threaten organizational effectiveness through lower profitability and the loss of valuable staff.[45] This seems to be the situation that McCain Foods Ltd. has experienced since the early 1990s. As Perspective 12–3 describes, the founding brothers Harrison and Wallace McCain have used several tactics to protect their personal stake in the company, yet these activities have made day-to-day operations nearly impossible.

The ethics of organizational politics

Just as a political tactic can be helpful or harmful to the organization, so can it be either ethical or unethical to society. To determine the moral standing of a particular political behaviour, we need to ask the three questions described below. Notice that these questions correspond to the moral philosophies discussed in Chapter 9. A political behaviour is ethical only if it satisfies all three moral criteria.[46]

1. *Utilitarian rule*—Does the political tactic provide the greatest good for the greatest number of people? If it mainly benefits the individual and possibly harms the welfare of others, then the political behaviour is inappropriate. For example, if Bow Valley's new computer system is good for customers and shareholders, then employees who lose power should not try to scuttle the change effort.

2. *Individual rights rule*—Does the political tactic violate anyone's legal or moral rights? If the political activity threatens another person's privacy, free speech, due process, or other rights, then it should not be used even if the results might be beneficial to a larger audience. For example, even if an incompetent senior executive is undermining shareholder wealth and employee job satisfaction, this does not justify wiretapping his or her telephone for embarrassing evidence that would force the executive to quit.

3. *Distributive justice rule*—Does the political activity treat all parties fairly? If the political behaviour benefits those who are better off at the expense of those who are already worse off, then the activity is unethical. For example, it would be unethical for a manager to take personal credit for a subordinate's project and receive the financial benefits resulting from that performance.

Political Battles at McCain

The tranquility of Florenceville, New Brunswick, has been shattered by political infighting in the executive offices of its main employer, McCain Foods Ltd. The founding McCain brothers, Harrison and Wallace, have been accusing each other of using political tactics to strengthen their heirs' positions in the company.

A discussion paper drafted for the company's board of directors sums up the situation: "Wallace does not trust Harrison. He believes Harrison will manipulate [the board] to prevent Wallace's children from advancing in the company to the level of their competence. Harrison does not trust Wallace's business judgment and believes that, were he in control, he would advance his children beyond their level of competence to the detriment of the company."

According to Harrison, the trust was broken—and the political frenzy began—in 1990 when Wallace appointed his son Michael as chief executive officer of McCain USA. "From the day Wallace appointed Michael as CEO of the U.S. operations to this day, an atmosphere of distrust, intrigue and manoeuvring has existed," Harrison claims. Harrison further believes that Michael is a poor choice and was promoted only to give Wallace's side of the family dominance in the company.

Meanwhile, Wallace McCain accuses Harrison of spearheading a political attack against Michael. "Blocking him and undermining him is constantly on your mind," he writes. Moreover, Wallace believes that the board removed him as the company's co-chair in 1993 because Harrison has tried to dominate the board. How did Wallace lose the board's support? "Easy answer," Wallace snaps. "Your power! Your muscle! Their fear! You lined them all up in a row and cracked the whip."

Concurrently, Wallace's two sons, Michael and Scott McCain, have sued the company on the grounds that they are not receiving sufficient information to participate in the company. "[We] continue to be denied information necessary to enable us to fulfill our responsibilities," they wrote in a statement to the court. Michael and Scott believe that there is a "pattern of exclusion" against members of Wallace McCain's family while the board is hiring a new CEO for McCain Foods. Other board members deny that withholding information is another political tactic in the battle between Wallace and Harrison McCain, but no one is betting that the political infighting at McCain Foods will end soon.

Sources: B. Dalglish, "A Family Food Fight," *Maclean's*, September 19, 1994, p. 38; J. Heinzl, "McCain Sons Allege Family Freeze-Out," *Globe & Mail*, September 2, 1994, pp. B1, B2; E. Reguly, "Inside the McCain Feud," *Financial Post*, April 2, 1994, p. 8; P. Waldie, "The Battling McCains," *Financial Post*, September 18–20, 1993, p. 3; and J. Spears, "Bitter Battle over a Birthright," *Toronto Star*, September 16, 1993, pp. G1, G6.

Types of Political Activity

What political tactics are used in organizational settings? There are many, but organizational behaviour scholars have conveniently grouped most of them into the seven categories illustrated in Exhibit 12–6.[47]

Attacking or blaming others

Not long ago, senior management at the Canadian Wheat Board in Winnipeg was deciding whether to replace its mainframe with a client/server system of microcomputers. During this tense time, the mainframe and microcomputer experts in the information systems department engaged in a heated battle of political infighting by openly bad-mouthing each other.[48] The mainframe employees would tell anyone who listened that microcomputer systems were

Exhibit 12-6   **Types of Political Behaviour in Organizations**

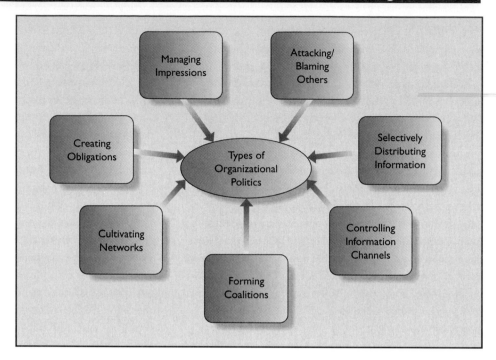

inadequate, while the microcomputer people would point to their mainframe colleagues as the source of many evils in the company.

The information systems employees at the Canadian Wheat Board were engaging in one of the most direct forms of political behaviour: attacking and blaming others. They applied the proactive strategy by attempting to give rivals a bad impression in the eyes of decision makers. A more reactive approach is for employees to dissociate themselves from undesirable situations by transferring blame to others (called *scapegoating*), distancing themselves from the event, or using excuses to form an external attribution of the cause of the problem.[49]

Selectively distributing information

Information is a political tool as well as a source of power. Departments and individuals strategically manage the distribution of information to shape perceptions, limit the potential performance of rivals, or further increase their power base. One example, described in Chapter 6, is filtering out damaging information as it is passed further up the organizational hierarchy. Another tactic is to deliberately overload someone with data so that they become dependent on you to help them screen or sort it out. Some unscrupulous division heads have deliberately withheld information from other divisions so that the others perform poorly. Perspective 12–4 traces several decades of information politics at the Canadian Imperial Bank of Commerce. As you can see, selectively distributing information rarely benefits the organization.

Perspective 12–4

Information Politics at the Canadian Imperial Bank of Commerce

For three decades, the Canadian Imperial Bank of Commerce (CIBC) was a battlefield of information politics. Until recently, the secrecy and in-fighting were so serious that one writer aptly called the bank "the Beirut of Canadian business."

In the 1960s, Neil McKinnon ruled CIBC with an effective intelligence network across Canada. He restricted access to important documents and, when away on overseas visits, would lock his door so that no one else could see them. This left senior managers dependent on McKinnon for important information about the bank's operations. CIBC's board of directors was worried that McKinnon's information politics were undermining the bank's performance, so it eventually took away some of his power. McKinnon resigned in 1973 rather than face the humiliation of being officially ousted.

CIBC's next chairman, Russell Harrison, also had a tendency to be secretive. Harrison initially shared power with president Donald Fullerton, but later demoted Fullerton because he felt that it was too difficult making decisions with two people at the top. Several talented

CIBC executives quit during Harrison's tenure, but Fullerton stayed.

In 1984, Fullerton was given the position of chief executive officer with the intention that Harrison would remain as the bank's chairman for the next three years. However, Fullerton had apparently learned the political tactics of his predecessors. He removed Harrison's name from certain circulation lists so that the chairman no longer received the information so vital to his position. Harrison had lost power, so he retired one year after Fullerton's appointment.

Fullerton immediately became CIBC's next chairman and, according to some sources, continued using information politics to secure his position. "Fullerton wants to keep everybody off guard until he builds up his power base," said one former CIBC executive. But by the time Fullerton retired in the early 1990s, CIBC's era of information politics had waned. Senior management began to share information and encouraged empowerment among employees throughout the organization. Not surprisingly, the bank's performance has improved considerably in recent years.

Sources: Based on T. Tedesco, "Unrest on the CIBC's Flagship," *Financial Times*, November 26, 1990, pp. 1, 4; S. Gittins, "Retirement No Life of Leisure for ex-CEOs," *Financial Post*, February 13, 1989, p. 17; M. Mittelstaedt, "CIBC Again Beset by Rumours; This Time over New President," *Globe & Mail*, February 1, 1985, p. B3; A. Toulin, "Bank of Commerce Chairman Steps Down as Chief Executive," *Toronto Star*, January 20, 1984, pp. E1, E3; R. McQueen, *The Money Spinners* (Toronto: Macmillan, 1983), Chapter 4; and P. C. Newman, *The Canadian Establishment* (Toronto: McClelland & Stewart, 1975), Chapter 4.

Controlling information channels

Through legitimate power, some people can control the interactions among employees as well as the topics of those discussions. Managers might discourage people in different work units from talking directly to each other because this might threaten the manager's power or reveal damaging information. Similarly, committee leaders might organize meeting agendas to suit their personal interests. If leaders want to avoid a decision on a particular topic, they might place the issue near the bottom of the agenda so that the committee either doesn't get to it or is too fatigued to make a final judgment.

Forming coalitions

In Chapter 10, we explained that a coalition is an informal group that attempts to influence other people about a specific issue. A coalition usually forms when two people agree on common objectives that they cannot achieve alone—such

Conditions for Organizational Politics

Organizational politics flourish under the right conditions.[58] One such condition is scarce resources. When budgets are slashed, people rely on political tactics to safeguard their resources and maintain the status quo. Another important condition is the existence of complex and ambiguous rules in resource allocation decisions. This occurs because decision makers are given more discretion over resource allocation, so potential recipients of those resources use political tactics to influence the factors that should be considered in the decision. Finally, political tactics are more common if they are tolerated or actually reinforced by the organization.[59] If left unchecked, organizational politics can take on a life of its own and the company becomes paralyzed. Political activity becomes self-reinforcing unless actions are taken to alter the conditions that support the political behaviour.

Personal characteristics

A person's personality and values can influence his or her likelihood of engaging in organizational politics.[60] In Chapter 3, we learned that some people have a strong personal need for power. They seek power for its own sake, and use political tactics to acquire more power. People with a high internal locus of control are more likely than those with a high external locus of control to engage in political behaviours to shape the world around them. This does not mean that internals are naturally political; rather, they are more likely to use influence tactics when political conditions are present because, unlike externals, they feel very much in charge of their own destiny.

Machiavellian value
A personal value held by some people who believe that deceit is a natural and acceptable way to influence others.

Finally, some people have strong **Machiavellian values.** They believe that deceit is a natural and acceptable way to influence others. People with strong Machiavellian values seldom trust co-workers and frequently use power to manipulate others toward their own personal goals, even when these goals are unfavourable to the organization.[61] Machiavellianism is named after Niccolo Machiavelli, the 16th-century Italian philosopher who wrote a well-known treatise about political behaviour (*The Prince*).

Controlling Political Behaviour

The conditions that fuel organizational politics also give us some clues about how to control dysfunctional political activities. When resources are necessarily scarce, companies should introduce rules and regulations to specify the use of those resources. Reward systems can be introduced that encourage information sharing. Information systems should be redesigned to avoid the wheel pattern that centralizes information power in the hands of a few people. Team norms and organizational values can eventually be restructured so they reject political tactics that interfere with organizational effectiveness. One strategy is to forewarn employees about political tactics so that people are exposed when trying to practise them. Finally, companies can try to hire people with low Machiavellianism and personal need for power.

Chapter Summary

- Power is the capacity to influence others who are in a state of dependence. It exists when one party perceives that he or she is dependent on the other for something of value. People are dependent on others when insufficient resources exist for everyone who desires them. However, the dependent person must also have counterpower to maintain the relationship.

- French and Raven have identified five power bases: legitimate (formal authority), reward (positive and negative reinforcement), coercive (punishment and extinction), expert (knowledge), and referent (charisma and attraction). Information plays an important role in organizational power. Employees gain power by controlling the flow of information that others need, and by being able to cope with uncertainties related to important organizational goals.

- Power bases are leveraged into actual power only under certain conditions. Individuals and subunits are more powerful when they are nonsubstitutable, that is, they have exclusive control over valued resources. Power increases with centrality, both in terms of the number of people affected and how quickly others are affected. Power also increases with the amount of discretion accorded to the person or work unit and its visibility to others.

- Power is applied to influence others, but the type of influence depends on the power source. Coercive power tends to produce resistance; reward and legitimate power result in compliance; expert and referent power produce commitment. People with a high need for power feel more satisfied and committed to their jobs when they have power, but many people tend to abuse their power when given too much of it.

- Organizational politics attempt to influence others using discretionary behaviours that promote personal objectives. People tend to have an unfavourable view of organizational politics, but some political activities benefit the organization. Even if political behaviour improves organizational effectiveness, it might not satisfy rules of ethical conduct.

- There are many forms of organizational politics. The most common tactics include attacking or blaming others, selectively distributing information, controlling information channels, forming coalitions, cultivating networks, creating obligations, and managing impressions.

- Organizational politics is more prevalent when scarce resources are allocated using complex and ambiguous decisions, and when the organization tolerates or rewards political behaviour. Individuals with a high need for personal power, an internal locus of control, and a Machiavellian personality have a high propensity to use political tactics.

Discussion Questions

1. **What role does counterpower play in the power relationship?**

2. **You have just been hired as a brand manager of soda biscuits for a large Canadian consumer products company. Your job mainly involves encouraging the advertising and production groups to promote and manufacture your product more effectively. These departments aren't under your direct authority, although company procedures indicate that they must complete certain tasks requested by brand managers. Describe the sources of power you can use to ensure that the advertising and production departments will help you make and sell soda biscuits more effectively.**

3. **What do we mean by "coping with uncertainty"? Describe three general strategies to help organizations cope with uncertainty.**

4. **Suppose you have formal authority to allocate performance bonuses to your employees. What contingencies must exist before this source of power will translate into actual power?**

5. **Power does not flow to unknown people in the organization. Discuss three types of activities that will increase the visibility of your power without appearing to be a disrespectful political tactic.**

6. **A co-worker suggests to you that companies would be better off if there was no organizational politics. What would you say to this person in reply?**

7. **How might employees use (or misuse) information as a political tactic?**

8. **Networking is a common political activity in organizations, yet it seems to contribute to the "glass ceiling" that prevents women from being promoted into senior management. Describe three political functions of networking and explain how networking adversely affects the promotion of women into senior management.**

Notes

1. C. Motherwell, "Bow Valley Uncaps a Well of Knowledge," *Globe & Mail*, January 18, 1994, p. B26; H. Hanley, "A Struggle for Strategic Control," *I.T. Magazine* 25 (December 1993), pp. 2–6; A. Morrall, "A Cause for Celebration," *Oilweek*, May 17, 1993, p. 8; and "Re-engineering Valley," *Economist*, May 1, 1993, p. 68.

2. R. M. Cyert and J. G. March, *A Behavioral Theory of the Firm* (Englewood Cliffs, N.J.: Prentice Hall, 1963).

3. J. Pfeffer, *Managing with Power* (Boston: Harvard Business University Press, 1992), pp. 17, 30; and H. Mintzberg, *Power In and Around Organizations* (Englewood Cliffs, N.J.: Prentice Hall, 1983), Chapter 1.

4. A. M. Pettigrew, *The Politics of Organizational Decision-Making* (London: Tavistock, 1973); R. M. Emerson, "Power-Dependence Relations," *American Sociological Review* 27 (1962), pp. 31–41; and R. A. Dahl, "The Concept of Power," *Behavioral Science* 2 (1957), pp. 201–18.

5. D. J. Brass and M. E. Burkhardt, "Potential Power and Power Use: An Investigation of Structure and Behaviour," *Academy of Management Journal* 36 (1993), pp. 441–70; and K. M. Bartol and D. C. Martin, "When Politics Pays: Factors Influencing Managerial Compensation Decisions," *Personnel Psychology* 43 (1990), pp. 599–614.

6. T. R. Mitchell and J. R. Larson, Jr., *People in Organizations* (New York: McGraw-Hill, 1988), p. 406.

7. Pfeffer, *Managing with Power*, pp. 40–41; and D. Mechanic, "Sources of Power of Lower Participants in Complex Organizations," *Administrative Science Quarterly* 7 (1962), pp. 349–64.

8. P. P. Carson and K. D. Carson, "Social Power Bases: A Meta-Analytic Examination of Interrelationships and Outcomes," *Journal of Applied Social Psychology* 23 (1993), pp. 1150–69; P. Podsakoff and C. Schreisheim, "Field Studies of French and Raven's Bases of Power: Critique, Analysis, and Suggestions for Future Research," *Psychological Bulletin* 97 (1985), pp. 387–411; and J. R. P. French and B. Raven, "The Bases of

Social Power," in *Studies in Social Power*, ed. D. Cartwright (Ann Arbor, Mich.: University of Michigan Press, 1959), pp. 150–67.

9. G. A. Yukl, *Leadership in Organizations*, 2nd ed. (Englewood Cliffs, N.J.: Prentice Hall, 1989), p. 15.

10. B. H. Raven, "The Bases of Power: Origins and Recent Developments," *Journal of Social Issues* 49 (1993), pp. 227–51.

11. R. P. Kearny, *Warrior Worker* (New York: Henry Holt & Co., 1991), pp. 69–74.

12. D. Koulack, "When It's Healthy to Doubt the Doctor," *Globe & Mail*, February 17, 1993, p. A20.

13. R. J. Burke and D. S. Wilcox, "Bases of Supervisory Power and Subordinate Job Satisfaction," *Canadian Journal of Behavioural Sciences* 3 (1971), pp. 183–93.

14. S. Finkelstein, "Power in Top Management Teams: Dimensions, Measurement, and Validation," *Academy of Management Journal* 35 (1992), pp. 505–38; and D. Krackhardt, "Assessing the Political Landscape: Structure, Cognition, and Power in Organizations," *Administrative Science Quarterly* 35 (1990), pp. 342–69.

15. A. R. Aird, P. Nowack, and J. W. Westcott, *Road to the Top* (Toronto: Doubleday Canada, 1988), p. 77.

16. Yukl, *Leadership in Organizations*, Chapter 2.

17. G. Yukl and C. M. Falbe, "Importance of Different Power Sources in Downward and Lateral Relations," *Journal of Applied Psychology* 76 (1991), pp. 416–23.

18. A. Pettigrew, "Information Control as a Power Source," *Sociology* 6 (1972), pp. 187–204.

19. S. P. Feldman, "Secrecy, Information, and Politics: An Essay on Organizational Decision Making," *Human Relations* 41 (1988), pp. 73–90; L. E. Greiner and V. E. Schein, *Power and Organization Development* (Reading, Mass.: Addison-Wesley, 1988), Chapter 3; and M. N. Wexler, "Conjectures on the Dynamics of Secrecy and the Secrets Business," *Journal of Business Ethics* 6 (1987), pp. 469–80.

20. D. J. Brass, "Being in the Right Place: A Structural Analysis of Individual Influence in an Organization," *Administrative Science Quarterly* 29 (1984), pp. 518–39; N. M. Tichy, M. L. Tuchman, and C. Frombrun, "Social Network Analysis in Organizations," *Academy of Management Review* 4 (1979), pp. 507–19; and H. Guetzkow and H. Simon, "The Impact of Certain Communication Nets upon Organization and Performance in Task-Oriented Groups," *Management Science* 1 (1955), pp. 233–50.

21. D. J. Hickson, C. R. Hinings, C. A. Lee, R. E. Schneck, and J. M. Pennings, "A Strategic Contingencies' Theory of Intraorganizational Power," *Administrative Science Quarterly* 16 (1971), pp. 216–27.

22. J. D. Thompson, *Organizations in Action* (New York: McGraw-Hill, 1967); and Cyert and March, *A Behavioral Theory of the Firm*.

23. C. R. Hinings, D. J. Hickson, J. M. Pennings, and R. E. Schneck, "Structural Conditions of Intraorganizational Power," *Administrative Science Quarterly* 19 (1974), pp. 22–44.

24. Hickson et al., "A Strategic Contingencies' Theory of Intraorganizational Power;" Hinings et al., "Structural Conditions of Intraorganizational Power;" and R. M. Kanter, "Power Failure in Management Circuits," *Harvard Business Review*, July–August 1979, pp. 65–75.

25. E. Bernard, *The Long Distance Feeling* (Vancouver: New Star Books, 1982); E. Zureik, V. Mosco, and C. Lochhead, "Telephone Workers' Reaction to the New Technology," *Relations Industrielles* 44 (1989), pp. 507–31; and S. McGovern, "Strikes Don't Stop Employers Cold Any More," *Montreal Gazette*, September 24, 1988, p. C1.

26. M. Gunderson, "Union Impact on Compensation, Productivity, and Management of the Organization," in *Union-Management Relations in Canada*, 2nd ed., ed. J. C. Anderson, M. Gunderson, and A. Ponak (Don Mills, Ont.: Addison-Wesley, 1989), pp. 347–70.

27. M. Crozier, *The Bureaucratic Phenomenon* (London: Tavistock, 1964).

28. Brass, "Being in the Right Place."

29. Brass and Burkhardt, "Potential Power and Power Use," pp. 441–70; Hickson et al., "A Strategic Contingencies' Theory of Intraorganizational Power," pp. 219–21; J. D. Hackman, "Power and Centrality in the Allocation of Resources in Colleges and Universities," *Administrative Science Quarterly* 30 (1985), pp. 61–77.

30. "Strike at GM Points Up JIT's Risks, Rewards," *Modern Materials Handling*, November 1992, pp. 14–15; and K. Kerwin, "The UAW Fires a Shot Across GM's Bow," *Business Week*, September 14, 1992, p. 28.

31. Kanter, "Power Failure in Management Circuits," p. 68; B. E. Ashforth, "The Experience of Powerlessness in Organizations," *Organizational Behavior and Human Decision Processes* 43 (1989), pp. 207–42; and J. W. Medcof, "The Power Motive and Organizational Structure: A Micro–Macro Connection," *Canadian Journal of Administrative Sciences* 2 (1985), pp. 95–113.

32. J. M. Kouzes and B. Z. Posner, *The Leadership Challenge* (San Francisco: Jossey-Bass, 1988), pp. 173–75.

33. K. Kram, *Mentoring at Work* (Glenview, Ill.: Scott, Foresman, 1985); C. A. McKeen and R. J. Burke, "Mentor Relationship in Organizations: Issues, Strategies, and Prospects for Women," *Journal of Management Development* 8 (1989), pp. 33–42; and E. A. Fagenson, "The Power of a Mentor," *Group & Organization Studies* 13 (1988), pp. 182–94.

34. P. G. Stern and T. Shachtman, *Straight to the Top* (New York: Warner Books, 1990), pp. 72–73.

35. Raven, "The Bases of Power," pp. 237–39.

36. L. E. Temple and K. R. Loewen, "Perceptions of Power: First Impressions of a Woman Wearing a Jacket," *Perceptual and Motor Skills* 76 (1993), pp. 339–48.

37. A. R. Elangovan, "Perceived Supervisor-Power Effects on Subordinate Work Attitudes and Behaviour," *Proceedings of the Annual ASAC Conference, Organizational Behaviour Division* 11, pt. 5 (1990), pp. 80–89; T. R. Hinkin and C. A. Schriesheim, "Development and Application of New Scales to Measure the French and Raven Bases of Social Power," *Journal of Applied Psychology* 74 (1989), pp. 561–67; and Raven, "The Bases of Power," p. 240.

38. J. W. Medcof, P. A. Hausdorf, and M. W. Piczak, "Opportunities to Satisfy the Need for Power in Managerial and Nonmanagerial Jobs," *Proceedings of the Annual ASAC Conference, Personnel and Human Resources Division* 12, pt. 8 (1991), pp. 80–87.

39. D. Kipnis, *The Powerholders* (Chicago: University of Chicago Press, 1976); and G. R. Salancik and J. Pfeffer, "The Bases and Use of Power in Organizational Decision Making: The Case of a University," *Administrative Science Quarterly* 19 (1974), pp. 453–73.

40. G. E. G. Catlin, *Systematic Politics* (Toronto: University of Toronto Press, 1962), p. 71.

41. T. H. Davenport, R. G. Eccles, and L. Prusak, "Information Politics," *Sloan Management Review,* Fall 1992, pp. 53–65; Pfeffer, *Managing with Power,* Chapter 17; and C. Kirchmeyer, "Organizational Politics from the Manager's Point of View: An Exploration of Beliefs, Perceptions, and Actions," *Proceedings of the Annual ASAC Conference, Organizational Behaviour Division* 9, pt. 5 (1988), pp. 57–66.

42. K. M. Kacmar and G. R. Ferris, "Politics at Work: Sharpening the Focus of Political Behavior in Organizations," *Business Horizons* 36 (July–August 1993), pp. 70–74; A. Drory and T. Romm, "The Definition of Organizational Politics: A Review," *Human Relations* 43 (1990), pp. 1133–54; and P. J. Frost and D. C. Hayes, "An Exploration in Two Cultures of a Model of Political Behavior in Organizations," in *Organizational Influence Processes,* ed. R. W. Allen and L. W. Porter (Glenview, Ill.: Scott, Foresman, 1983), pp. 369–92.

43. P. J. Frost, "Power, Politics, and Influence," in *Handbook of Organizational Communication: An Interdisciplinary Perspective,* ed. F. M. Jablin, L. L. Putnam, K. H. Roberts, and L. W. Porter (Newbury Park, Calif.: Sage, 1987), pp. 503–48.

44. P. J. Frost and C. P. Egri, "Influence of Political Action on Innovation: Part I," *Leadership and Organizational Development Journal* 11(1) (1990), pp. 17–25; and P. J. Frost and C. P. Egri, "Influence of Political Action on Innovation: Part II," *Leadership and Organizational Development Journal* 11(2) (1990), pp. 4–12.

45. P. Kumar and R. Ghadially, "Organizational Politics and Its Effects on Members of Organizations," *Human Relations* 42 (1989), pp. 305–14; and K. M. Eisenhardt and L. J. Bourgeois III, "Politics of Strategic Decision Making in High-Velocity Environments: Toward a Midrange Theory," *Academy of Management Journal* 31 (1988), pp. 737–70.

46. M. Velasquez, D. J. Moberg, and G. F. Cavanaugh, "Organizational Statesmanship and Dirty Politics: Ethical Guidelines for the Organizational Politician," *Organizational Dynamics* 11 (1983), pp. 65–79.

47. R. W. Allen, D. L. Madison, L. W. Porter, P. A. Renwick, and B. T. Mayes, "Organizational Politics: Tactics and Characteristics of Its Actors," *California Management Review* 22 (Fall 1979), pp. 77–83; and V. Murray and J. Gandz, "Games Executives Play: Politics at Work," *Business Horizons,* December 1980, pp. 11–23.

48. A. LaPlante, "Rightsizing Angst," *Forbes ASAP,* June 7, 1993, p. 100.

49. B. E. Ashforth and R. T. Lee, "Defensive Behavior in Organizations: A Preliminary Model," *Human Relations* 43 (1990), pp. 621–48.

50. E. A. Mannix, "Organizations as Resource Dilemmas: The Effects of Power Balance on Coalition Formation in Small Groups." *Organizational Behavior and Human Decision Processes* 55 (1993), pp. 1–22; A. T. Cobb, "Toward the Study of Organizational Coalitions: Participant Concerns and Activities in a Simulated Organizational Setting," *Human Relations* 44 (1991), pp. 1057–79; and W. B. Stevenson, J. L. Pearce, and L. W. Porter, "The Concept of 'Coalition' in Organization Theory and Research," *Academy of Management Review* 10 (1985), pp. 256–68.

51. D. Krackhardt and J. R. Hanson, "Informal Networks: The Company Behind the Chart," *Harvard Business Review* 71 (July–August 1993), pp. 104–11; and R. E. Kaplan, "Trade Routes: The Manager's Network of Relationships," *Organizational Dynamics,* Spring 1984, pp. 37–52.

52. R. J. Burke and C. A. McKeen, "Women in Management," *International Review of Industrial and Organizational Psychology* 7 (1992), pp. 245–83; and B. R. Ragins and E. Sundstrom, "Gender and Power in Organizations: A Longitudinal Perspective," *Psychological Bulletin* 105 (1989), pp. 51–88.

53. A. R. Cohen and D. L. Bradford, "Influence Without Authority: The Use of Alliances, Reciprocity, and Exchange to Accomplish Work," *Organizational Dynamics* 17(3) (1989), pp. 5–17.

54. R. A. Giacalone and P. Rosenfeld (eds.), *Applied Impression Management* (Newbury Park, Calif.: Sage, 1991); and J. T. Tedeschi (ed.), *Impression Management Theory and Social Psychological Research* (New York: Academic Press, 1981).

55. W. L. Gardner III, "Lessons in Organizational Dramaturgy: The Art of Impression Management," *Organizational Dynamics*, Summer 1992, pp. 33–46; R. C. Liden and T. R. Mitchell, "Ingratiatory Behaviors in Organizational Settings," *Academy of Management Review* 13 (1988), pp. 572–87; and A. MacGillivary, S. Ascroft, and M. Stebbins, "Meritless Ingratiation," *Proceedings of the Annual ASAC Conference, Organizational Behaviour Division* 7, pt. 7 (1986), pp. 127–35.

56. Stern and Shachtman, *Straight to the Top*, pp. 20–21.

57. M. Strauss, "Fur Flies at CBC," *Globe & Mail*, August 9, 1983, pp. 1–2.

58. C. Hardy, *Strategies for Retrenchment and Turnaround: The Politics of Survival* (Berlin: Walter de Gruyter, 1990), Chapter 14; S. C. Goh and A. R. Doucet, "Antecedent Situational Conditions of Organizational Politics: An Empirical Investigation," *Proceedings of the Annual ASAC Conference, Organizational Behaviour Division* 7, pt. 5 (1986), pp. 77–86; T. D. Jick and V. V. Murray, "The Management of Hard Times: Budget Cutbacks in Public Sector Organizations," *Organization Studies* 3 (1982), pp. 141–69; and J. Gandz and V. V. Murray, "The Experience of Workplace Politics," *Academy of Management Journal* 23 (1980), pp. 237–51.

59. G. R. Ferris, G. S. Russ, and P. M. Fandt, "Politics in Organizations," in *Impression Management in the Organization*, ed. R. A. Giacalone and P. Rosenfeld (Hillsdale, N.J.: Erlbaum, 1989), pp. 143–70; and H. Mintzberg, "The Organization as Political Arena," *Journal of Management Studies* 22 (1985), pp. 133–54.

60. L. W. Porter, R. W. Allen, and H. L. Angle, "The Politics of Upward Influence in Organizations," *Research in Organizational Behavior* 3 (1981), pp. 120–22; and R. J. House, "Power and Personality in Complex Organizations," *Research in Organizational Behavior* 10 (1988), pp. 305–57.

61. P. E. Mudrack, "An Investigation into the Acceptability of Workplace Behaviors of a Dubious Ethical Nature," *Journal of Business Ethics* 12 (1993), pp. 517–24; and R. Christie and F. Geis, *Studies in Machiavellianism* (New York: Academic Press, 1970).

Chapter Case

Analyzing Political Behaviour in Organizations
Incident 1: Seeking a Better Career Opportunity

Jill Pettroci, an engineering supervisor for an Ontario municipality, wanted a more challenging job in the organization. She mentioned this to her immediate supervisor a few times over the past year, but he was ambiguous and somewhat evasive about her chances of promotion. One day, a recruitment firm telephoned Jill to ask whether she was interested in a more senior management position with another Ontario municipality. Jill told the recruiter that she needed a few days before deciding to attend an interview, even though she really had no interest in leaving her current employer. During those days, Jill casually mentioned the conversation to the vice-president of human resources and explained that she hoped for a more senior job here. As Jill predicted, the VP talked to her immediate supervisor who, in turn, suddenly told Jill that she would probably receive a promotion within the next few months.

Incident 2: The Politics of Sweet Success

James Tadki's research group at Canadian Beer Ltd. identified a new sugar substitute that requires another year of laboratory work before market feasibility can be assured. Tadki believed the patent could be easily licensed to food manufacturers, but the research director felt that it deviated from the company's core business (beer) and therefore shouldn't receive more funding. Rather than watch the innovation die in the laboratory, Tadki quietly mentioned the matter to his friends throughout the company, some of whom worked with the manufacturing vice-president (the research director's boss). Tadki also "happened" to meet the company president and manufacturing VP at a golf course and briefly mentioned the issue. In reality, Tadki learned about their tee-off time from a secretary and made a point of playing golf at that time with a neighbour who belongs to the club. None of these activities were known to the research director, who was later surprised to hear the manufacturing VP suggest that Tadki's work may be valuable to the company.

Discussion Questions (for both incidents)

1. **What political tactics did Jill and James use in these incidents?**
2. **Assess the ethical justification of these political tactics using the three ethical criteria described in this chapter.**
3. **What would you have done differently than the people in these incidents?**

Experiential Exercise

Power Relations in a Loony Organization*
Purpose: This exercise is designed to help you to understand some of the power dynamics that occur across hierarchical levels in organizations.

Instructions: This exercise works best with a class of 50 people or more with a session lasting one hour or longer. It also works best when there is a secluded office, an adjoining room (with a door between them), and a large nearby hallway. Students are also asked to make a small financial sacrifice—usually contributing one dollar coin (loony) each.

After submitting their financial contribution to the instructor, students are divided into three groups by the instructor. Five people (the instructor may vary this number slightly) are put into the top group and assigned to a small closed office. They receive two-thirds of the money given to the instructor. Approximately 10 students (or twice as many as the top group) are assigned to the middle group and assigned to the adjoining office. The middle group receives the other one-third of the money. The remaining students (at least 20 people) are put into the lower group and are sent into the hallway or other moderately large space near the two closed offices. Students are given five minutes to read the rules and group tasks presented below. The exercise should take at least 30 or 40 minutes with another 20 to 30 minutes for post-exercise discussion. Representatives from each group will be asked to answer the questions below to the class during the post-exercise discussion phase.

Rules: Members of the top group are free to enter the space of either the middle or lower groups and to communicate whatever they wish, whenever they wish. Members of the middle group may enter the space of the lower group whenever they wish, but must request permission to enter the top group's space. The top group can refuse the middle group's request. Members of the lower group are not allowed to disturb the top group in any way unless specifically invited by members of the top group. The lower group does have the right to knock on the door of the middle group and request permission to communicate with them. The middle group can refuse the lower group's request.

Tasks: The top group's task is responsibility for the organization's overall effectiveness, deciding how to use its money, and learning from the exercise. The middle group's task is to assist the top group in its responsibility for the organization's overall effectiveness, and to decide how to use the middle group's money. The lower group's task is to identify its resources, decide how best to contribute to the organization's effectiveness, and how to contribute to the learning process.

Post-Exercise Discussion Questions: What can we learn from this exercise about power in organizational hierarchies? How is this exercise similar to relations in real organizations? How did students in each group feel about the amount of power they held? How did they exercise their power in relations with the other groups?

*This exercise is based on ideas in B. Oshry, *Power and Position* (Boston: Power and Systems, 1979); and L. Bolman and T. Deal, "A Simple—But Powerful—Power Simulation," *Exchange* 4 (Summer 1979), pp. 38–42.

Organizational Conflict and Negotiation

Learning Objectives

After reading this chapter, you should be able to:

Describe the conflict cycle.

Discuss the positive and negative consequences of conflict.

Identify six factors that contribute to organizational conflict.

Outline the five interpersonal styles of conflict management.

Summarize the structural approaches to managing conflict.

Outline four situational influences on negotiations.

Describe four objectives of third-party dispute resolution.

Contrast arbitration with inquisitional third-party interventions.

Chapter Outline

What Is Conflict?

Consequences of Organizational Conflict.

Sources of Conflict in Organizations.

Interpersonal Conflict Management Styles.

Structural Approaches to Conflict Management.

Stimulating Conflict.

Resolving Conflict through Negotiation.

Situational Influences on Negotiations.

Negotiator Behaviours.

Third-Party Conflict Resolution.

𝒞anadian Airlines International (CAI) is the result of five airlines that merged over six years. These airlines had energetic leaders who established distinct operating procedures and demanded absolute loyalty from their employees. When the airlines merged into CAI, employees continued their allegiance to their former airline by identifying themselves with its colour—blue for Pacific Western, orange for Canadian Pacific, yellow for Nordair, and so on. This differentiation produced a level of conflict among CAI employees that hurt morale and customer service.

Sidney Fattedad, a CAI director and former executive, describes the colour-coded conflicts that permeated the organization: "Coffee circles began to form around color codes rather than work groups, and prospective transferees were asked what colour they came from. In some areas, color heritage decided a promotion, explained a botch-up, or was offered as a reason why things couldn't change."

CAI's colour-coded conflict ended in 1992 when the company was forced by its high debt load to enter merger talks with Air Canada. CAI's employees may have come from different airlines, but they were from entrepreneurial companies that viewed Air Canada as their main rival. These common values sparked an immediate collective reaction to news of the merger talks. CAI employees formed a rescue team that developed an employee concession and investment proposal to avoid the Air Canada merger.

Even when the proposal was developed and received government support, the rescue team faced another formidable challenge—getting the six unions representing CAI's work force to set aside their past conflicts and agree on the plan. Some of the union leaders had fought with each other over past violations on picket lines and in grievances, so they were very defensive and guarded in their discussions. As one

Exhibit 13–4   **Interpersonal Conflict Management Styles**

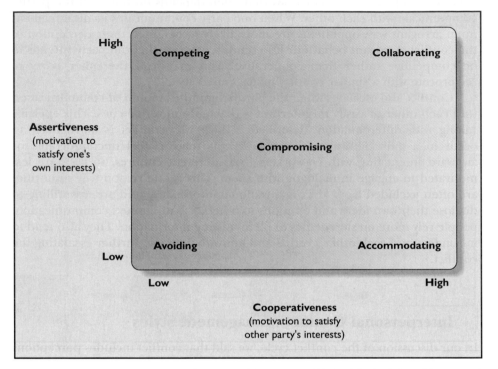

Source: Based on T. L. Ruble and K. Thomas, "Support for a Two-Dimensional Model of Conflict Behavior," *Organizational Behavior and Human Performance* 16 (1976), p. 145. Reprinted with permission.

these five conflict management styles and the conditions under which they are most effective.

- *Collaborating*—Trying to resolve the conflict through problem solving. Collaboration is best when the parties do not have perfectly opposing interests and when they have enough trust and openness to share information. Collaborating is usually desirable because organizational conflicts are rarely win–lose situations. There is usually some opportunity for mutual gain if the parties search for creative solutions.[24]

- *Avoiding*—Trying to smooth over or avoid conflict situations altogether. This may be appropriate where the issue is trivial, or as a temporary tactic to cool down heated disputes. However, conflict avoidance should not be a long-term solution because it increases the other party's frustration.

- *Competing*—Trying to win the conflict at the other's expense. This style has the strongest win–lose orientation because it has the highest level of assertiveness and lowest level of cooperativeness. Competing may be necessary where you know you are correct, the dispute requires a quick solution, and the other party would likely take advantage of more cooperative strategies. However, the competing style is usually inappropriate because organizational relationships rarely involve complete opposition.

Structural Approaches to Conflict Management   Exhibit 13-5

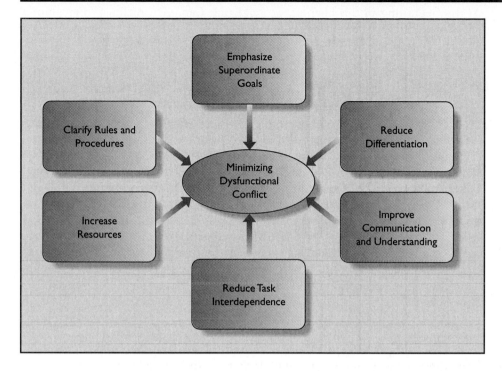

- *Accommodating*—Giving in completely to the other side's wishes, or at least cooperating with little or no attention to your own interests. This style may be appropriate when your original position is wrong, the other party has substantially more power, or the issue is not as important to you as to the other party. On the other hand, accommodating behaviours may give the other side unrealistically high expectations, thereby motivating them to seek more from you in the future. In the long run, accommodating may produce more conflict rather than resolve it.

- *Compromising*—Trying to reach a middle ground with the other party. You look for a position in which your losses are offset by equally valued gains. This style may be best when there is little hope for mutual gain through problem solving, both parties have equal power, and both are under time pressure to settle their differences. However, compromise often results in an unsettling half-way resolution for both parties. In many cases, the parties may overlook important options providing mutual gain.

Structural Approaches to Conflict Management

The conflict management styles described above focus on how to approach the other party in a conflict situation, but conflict management also involves altering the underlying structural causes of potential conflict identified in Exhibit 13-5.

Emphasizing superordinate goals

Superordinate goal
A common objective—such as an organizationwide goal—held by conflicting parties that is more important than the departmental or individual goals.

At the beginning of this chapter, we read that Canadian Airlines International employees reduced their conflict when faced with the challenge of saving the airline from financial crisis and preventing the merger with arch rival Air Canada. This illustrates how conflict can be overcome by using a **superordinate goal** to replace the antagonisms of employee differentiation or incompatible departmental goals. Superordinate goals are common interests held by conflicting parties that are more important than the departmental or individual goals on which the conflict is based. Examples of superordinate goals include warding off competing businesses or providing better customer service.

Employees often lose sight of their common goals and focus instead on incompatible departmental goals. By emphasizing superordinate goals, incompatible departmental goals become less important and conflict is reduced.[25] Until recently, this was a serious problem among Microsoft Corp.'s product groups. Each group developed its own standards and didn't care about integration or operability with other Microsoft software products. For instance, the Excel and Word programs had different-looking tool bars that weren't very compatible with each other. When customers started to complain, founder Bill Gates sent a clear message that customer needs for interoperability take priority. Now senior Microsoft people constantly remind product teams to focus on compatibility. In a few cases, a senior executive would bring product teams together and wouldn't let them leave until they agreed on some measure toward interoperability.[26] In general, programmers are learning to think more about the superordinate goal of serving customer needs than advancing the interests of their own product group.

Reducing differentiation

Some organizational conflict can be avoided by reducing differentiation among employees. Multilin, a manufacturing plant in Markham, Ontario, applied this strategy when its production and design people were moved from functional departments to cross-functional work cells. As one employee explains: "Before, we had a wall, and there was a feud going on between assemblers and technicians. Now there's respect for each other."[27]

Some companies try to reduce differentiation by developing a generalist rather than specialist career orientation within the organization. Many Japanese companies follow this strategy by moving employees around to different jobs, departments, and regions.[28] IBM and 3M rotate line personnel temporarily into staff departments (personnel, purchasing, finance, etc.) to ensure that the two groups work cooperatively and develop a better understanding of each other's needs. At Omni Hotels, each department chooses an ambassador to spend time in other departments so employees learn to empathize with their colleagues' work environments and resource constraints.[29]

Improving communication and understanding

Dysfunctional conflict can be minimized through direct communication so that people develop a better understanding of each other's work environments and resource limitations. These activities draw on the concepts described in Chapter

Perspective 13–2

Reducing Conflict through Dialogue at Nissan Canada

Soon after Ace Toyama became president of Nissan Canada Inc., he noticed that the employees were divided into two camps—the Canadians who distributed and sold vehicles, and the Japanese executives who received privileged information and devised new corporate strategy. The conflict was not obvious at first, but Toyama observed that the Canadians were reluctant to hand information over to the Japanese managers on what previously was their private fiefdom. Meanwhile, the Japanese managers kept to themselves and limited their communication with the Canadians. All around, there seemed to be a lack of trust between the two factions.

This was an unacceptable situation for Toyama, because he needed to build the Canadians and Japanese into an integrated management team. His first step was to give the Canadians the same information that was formerly for Japanese eyes only, including profitability data and new product plans. This made the Canadians feel more like their Japanese counterparts. After that it wasn't too long until the Canadians volunteered more of their information to the Japanese strategists.

Toyama's next step was to unblock perceptual differences between the Canadian and Japanese managers by introducing free-for-alls in which sacred cows were openly discussed. Members of either faction could throw out any questions they wanted to ask the others. The sessions have led to more harmony and interaction for everybody. For example, at one session a Canadian blurted out, "Why do you guys never eat lunch with us?" A Japanese director replied, "It is so hard for me to speak English all day. The only break I get is lunch." This revelation had not occurred to the Canadians. They had previously felt slighted by the fact that the Japanese managers ate together and never expressed an interest to join the Canadians for a meal. By opening the lines of communication, these misunderstandings were removed and the Canadians and Japanese managers developed a stronger working relationship.

Source: Based on W. Trueman, "CEO Isolation and How to Fight It," *Canadian Business*, July 1991, pp. 28–32.

7 concerning improving perceptions, particularly by empathizing with the other side and increasing the open area in the Johari Window. Although the parties do not become one homogeneous unit, more direct communication helps them to understand and respect each other.

One way to reduce negative stereotypes and misconceptions of others is to create opportunities for interaction, particularly through sports and other nonwork activities. For instance, senior managers at Cathay Pacific Airlines were able to overcome some of the antagonism and distorted stereotyping that employees felt toward them by joining employees in karaoke sessions. These sessions let employees see that senior managers weren't the "stuffed shirts" that they had assumed.[30]

A more direct way to improve understanding is to have a series of **dialogue** meetings so that the conflicting parties can learn about each other's underlying assumptions and beliefs. In Chapter 10 we learned that dialogue helps the two sides understand each other's mental models and fundamental assumptions so that they can create a common thinking process and mental models for the team.[31] Ace Toyama, president of Nissan Canada Inc., recently followed this strategy to overcome misunderstandings and improve relations between his Canadian and Japanese staff members. As Perspective 13–2 describes, dialogue can dissolve many misunderstandings that previously fueled organizational conflict.

Dialogue
A process of conversation among team members in which they learn about each other's personal mental models and assumptions, and eventually form a common model for thinking within the team.

Intergroup mirroring

Intergroup mirroring
A structured conflict management intervention in which the parties discuss their perceptions of each other and look for ways to improve those perceptions and relationship with each other.

When relations between two or more work teams or departments are openly hostile, it may be advisable to introduce **intergroup mirroring** with the assistance of a trained facilitator.[32] The basic objective is for the conflicting groups to express their perceptions, discuss their differences, and then work out strategies to improve the relationship. The process is unique, because both sides share their images of themselves and each other so that distortions and misunderstandings are revealed and ultimately corrected.

Intergroup mirroring is usually a multiday retreat that begins with the parties identifying and prioritizing their relationship problems. Next, the two groups separately list three sets of perceptions. One list describes the group's perception of itself. The second list describes how the group perceives the other group. The third list describes the group's beliefs about how the other group perceives it. The "mirroring" activity in intergroup mirroring occurs when the two sides meet again to exchange their perceptions of each other. After discussing these perceptions, the two sides jointly review their relationship problems, usually in small groups that combine both sides. Finally, the participants establish goals and action plans to correct their perceptual distortions and establish more favourable relationships in the future. This typically includes future meetings that review and evaluate progress.

Relations by objectives
A structured conflict management intervention designed to improve labour–management relations that includes elements of intergroup mirroring.

Intergroup mirroring interventions have resolved conflicts between headquarters and field employees, line and staff employees, and senior managers of two recently merged companies.[33] It is also a well-known part of **relations by objectives** (RBO), a conflict management process for union–management relations. RBO was first introduced in the 1970s by government mediation services in Canada and the United States to help union and management representatives overcome long-standing disputes that had escalated through perceptual distortions. According to one study of 48 RBO interventions in Canada, most union–management relationships have benefited from this process, particularly when the parties have a long-term relationship, are motivated to improve their relationship, and focus the sessions on general relationships rather than specific issues.[34] Perspective 13–3 describes how Cardinal River Coals improved labour–management relations through this intergroup mirroring process.

Reducing task interdependence

Another way to reduce dysfunctional conflict is to minimize the level of interdependence between the parties. A simple way to do this is to duplicate and divide the shared resource so that each unit has its own. Rather than increasing the size of the pool that two people or work units share, the company might be able to divide the resource so that each unit has control of its own. Cost effectiveness is a concern, but companies can apply this strategy when expanding their operations.

Combining jobs is another way to reduce task interdependence. Consider a toaster assembly line where one person inserts the heating element, another installs the power cord, and so on. By combining these tasks so that each employee assembles an entire toaster, the assembly group members now have a pooled rather than sequential form of task interdependence and the likelihood of dysfunctional conflict is reduced.

Perspective 13–3

Intergroup Mirroring at Cardinal River Coals

Cardinal River Coals Ltd. was a hotbed of conflict in the early 1980s. The Hinton, Alberta, coal mine had lost 342 days to work stoppages over the previous eight years and was plagued by an exceptionally high number of grievances and injuries. Supervisors frequently abused the four-step progressive discipline system by handing out the verbal and written warnings, suspension notice, and the pink slip all at one time! Meanwhile, the labour union representing Cardinal River's employees actively encouraged its members to file grievances by paying them $5 per grievance.

This hostility spilled over to the small community of Hinton, where people employed at Cardinal were labelled as either "company" or "union." There were incidents in which supervisors would cross the street just to avoid walking by a shop steward. A warehouse worker invited to attend a retirement party for a manager was asked to leave her shop steward husband at home.

Eventually, union and management agreed to try a more effective way to resolve their differences by inviting John Popular, an experienced mediator who introduced relations by objectives in the United States and Ontario. Popular conducted a four-day relations-by-objectives session attended by over 90 union and management representatives from Cardinal River Coals. In one session, Popular mixed key union and management people in small teams and had them watch films depicting supervisors and shop stewards. Each team was then asked to discuss supervisor–steward attitudes in these films and suggest improvements.

But the most memorable part of the retreat was the intensive intergroup mirroring activity in which union and management representatives were asked to discuss their perceptions of each other. "The first part of the meeting was pretty good because we got to tell [management] what we thought of the company," said one union leader about the intergroup mirroring experience. "But our shop stewards started to squirm a little when the company told us what they thought. It was a real soul-searching part of the program." From this activity and other elements of the retreat, participants developed a set of goals and discussed action plans to develop more harmonious relations.

The results of RBO surprised both union and management representatives. The number of grievances has fallen from 140 in 1982 to only a handful today. The union membership has endorsed three collective agreements without a strike, the latest of which was signed two months before the previous one had expired. The worldwide demand for coal dropped substantially during the late 1980s. Yet labour–management cooperation helped Cardinal River Coal become highly rated by Japanese steel producers and operate at record capacity with one-half of the previous work force. These productivity gains have extended the life of the mine and increased job security.

Sources: Personal communication with labour relations manager at Cardinal River Coals Ltd. in September 1991; and D. Burn, "They Had a Problem ... But They Fixed It," *Canadian HR Reporter*, November 14, 1988, pp. 16–17.

When task interdependencies are sequential or reciprocal, conflict can be reduced by introducing buffers between the parties. For example, subassembly groups might have sufficient inventory between each stage that a performance problem in one group will not immediately threaten the performance of others. Many companies try to save money by reducing rather than increasing inventories, yet these just-in-time practices may create higher costs by intensifying conflict. At some point, the company has to decide the optimal level of inventory so that task interdependence does not fuel costly conflict.

Finally, some companies manage task interdependence through coordinators who help the various departments complete a common task.[35] Brand managers serve this role by coordinating the efforts of the research, production, advertising, and marketing departments in launching a new product line. They are essentially human buffers that reduce the direct interaction among work units with diverse goals and perspectives.

Increasing resources

Conflict typically increases with the level of resource scarcity, so another conflict management tactic is to increase the amount of resources available. Corporate decision makers quickly dismiss this solution because of the costs involved. However, they need to carefully compare these costs with the costs of dysfunctional conflict arising out of resource scarcity. In some situations, organizational effectiveness increases when resources are shifted from one area to another, because this relieves an important source of conflict between employees and departments.

Clarifying rules and procedures

Some conflicts arise from ambiguous decision rules regarding the allocation of scarce resources. Consequently, these conflicts can be minimized by establishing rules and procedures. If two departments are fighting over the use of a new laboratory, a schedule might be established that allocates the lab exclusively to each team at certain times of the day or week. In some respects, the schedule reduces resource interdependence by dividing it up among those who need it to fulfill their goals. It also reduces the need for direct contact between the parties, thereby minimizing the likelihood of episodes that might further escalate the conflict.

Stimulating Conflict

Most of our discussion has been about ways to reduce conflict. Conflict isn't always dysfunctional, however. We have already learned how stimulating conflict can build more effective teams and can improve team decision making through constructive controversy. So how can we increase conflict? Mainly by reversing most of the strategies described in the previous section.[36] For example, suppose that an organization wants to cut costs and hopes that employees will identify areas where cutbacks will create the fewest problems. Quite often, employees will not take the time to do this until they experience conflict arising from lower budgets or arbitrary cutback decisions. The resulting conflict motivates employees to look for better solutions to the problem.

Resolving Conflict through Negotiation

Negotiation
Any attempt by two or more conflicting parties to resolve their divergent goals by redefining the terms of their interdependence.

Negotiation occurs whenever two or more conflicting parties attempt to resolve their divergent goals by redefining the terms of their interdependence.[37] In other words, people negotiate when they think that discussion can produce a more satisfactory arrangement (at least for them) in their exchange of goods or services. Negotiation is an integral part of social relations in all organizations. Employees negotiate with their supervisors over next month's work assignments,

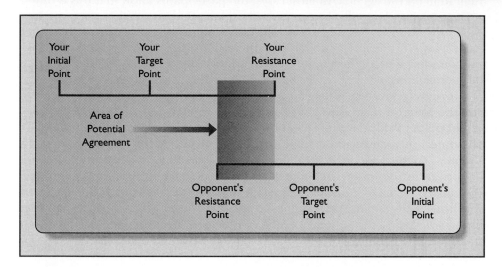

suppliers negotiate with purchasing managers over the sale and delivery schedules of their product, and union representatives negotiate with management over changes to the collective agreement.

Some writers suggest that negotiations are more successful when the parties adopt an openly collaborative style, whereas others caution that this conflict management style is sometimes costly.[38] We know that any win–lose style (competing, accommodating, etc.) is unlikely to produce the optimal solution, because the parties have not shared information necessary to discover a mutually satisfactory solution. On the other hand, people must be careful about adopting an openly collaborative style until mutual trust has been established. The concern is that information is power, so information sharing gives the other party more power to leverage a better deal if the opportunity occurs. Skilled negotiators often adopt a *cautiously* collaborative style at the outset by sharing information slowly and determining whether the other side will reciprocate. They switch to one of the win–lose styles only when it becomes apparent that a win–win solution is not possible or the other party is unwilling to share information with a cooperative orientation.

Bargaining zone model of negotiations

The negotiation process moves each party along a continuum with an area of potential overlap called the *bargaining zone*.[39] Exhibit 13–6 displays one possible bargaining zone situation. This linear diagram illustrates a purely win–lose situation—one side's gain will be the other's loss. However, the bargaining zone model can also be applied to situations in which both sides potentially gain from the negotiations. As this model illustrates, the parties typically establish three main negotiating points. The *initial offer point* is the team's opening offer to the other party. This may be its best expectation or a pie-in-the-sky starting point. The *target point* is the team's realistic goal or expectation for a final agreement. The *resistance point* is the point beyond which the team will not make further concessions.

The parties begin negotiations by describing their initial offer point for each item on the agenda. In most cases, the participants know that this is only a starting point that will change as both sides offer concessions. In win–lose situations, neither the target nor resistance points are revealed to the other party. However, people try to discover the other side's resistance point because this knowledge helps them determine how much they can gain without breaking off negotiations.

In purely win–win settings, on the other hand, the objective is to find a creative solution that keeps both parties close to their initial offer points. They can hopefully find an arrangement by which each side loses relatively little value on some issues and gains significantly more on other issues. For example, a supplier might want to delay delivery dates, whereas delivery times are not important to the business customer. If the parties share this information, they can quickly agree to a delayed delivery schedule, thereby costing the customer very little and gaining the supplier a great deal. On other items (financing, order size, etc.), the supplier might give something with minimal loss even though it is a significant benefit to the business customer.

Situational Influences on Negotiations

What makes some negotiations work more smoothly than others? What factors influence the negotiation outcomes? Exhibit 13–7 outlines four situational factors and four negotiator behaviours that provide some answers to these questions. Four of the most important situational factors are location, physical setting, time, and audience.

Location

People usually like to negotiate on their own turf because they are familiar with the negotiating environment and are able to maintain comfortable routines.[40] Members of the visiting delegation, on the other hand, must spend time and energy adjusting and familiarizing themselves with the new environment. Often, they must also cope with travel-related stress. The host team controls some aspects of the negotiating environment, such as information and administrative support, whereas visitors are dependent on their hosts for some resources and must bring the necessary information with them. The home location has some potential disadvantages because the host has certain obligations to the visitors and may be under closer scrutiny from its audience. It is also more difficult for the host to use the tactic of walking out of negotiations.

Negotiating parties are often careful to choose a neutral site so that neither side is a home team. But skilled negotiators are not averse to using location to their advantage if this tactic does not threaten the level of trust between the parties. Edgar Kaiser, Jr., former head of the Bank of British Columbia, is known for an unusual negotiating tactic during his fishing trips on Vancouver Island. One executive familiar with Kaiser's tactics explains: "We always start out in two canoes with a guide each. Then halfway up the stream Edgar switches boats, sends the two guides off on their own, and we get down to business."[41] Kaiser skillfully manages the location of his negotiations by placing the negotiator at a disadvantage in the unfamiliar waters of British Columbia!

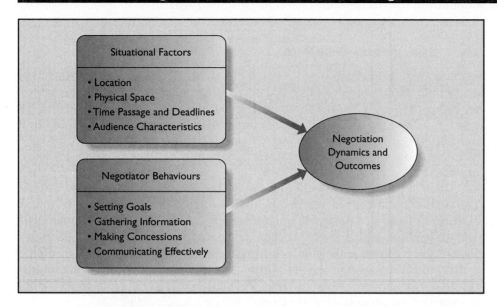

Computer technologies make it possible to conduct some parts of the negotiation without a location. The parties can instantaneously transmit new proposals and counteroffers through e-mail or facsimiles. The University of Arizona is currently experimenting with another approach to negotiations using groupware (computer software that several people access simultaneously). One of the first such negotiations took place between Sun Trans (an Arizona bus company) and its local Teamsters union. The computer facilities sped up the process of preparing and agreeing to specific contract language.[42] However, most negotiators are reluctant to use electronic communication because it lacks sufficient media richness. Electronic messages are subject to misinterpretation and conflict can easily escalate if the parties engage in flaming (see Chapter 6). Even video conferencing is seldom used in negotiations, because it does not adequately capture the subtle nonverbal cues that negotiators rely on for feedback about their offers and counteroffers.

Physical setting

In Chapter 6 we noted that the physical arrangement of tables and chairs can affect the nature and quality of communication.[43] These physical arrangements are so important that negotiations between governments have been delayed because the parties could not agree on the shape of the table! People who sit face to face are more likely to develop a win–lose orientation toward the conflict situation. When a win–win orientation is preferred, both parties should disperse their representatives around a circular table and meet in an informal setting. Labatts Breweries tried this approach a number of years ago in an attempt to keep negotiations nonadversarial. At one point, they even tried to negotiate without a table to create a single team perspective.[44] The physical distance between the parties and formality of the setting can also influence the parties' orientation toward each other and the disputed issues.

Time passage and deadlines

Time passage and deadlines are two important factors in negotiations. The more time people invest in negotiations, the stronger is their commitment to reaching an agreement. This increases the motivation to resolve the conflict, but it also results in the escalation of commitment problems described in Chapter 9. For example, the more time someone puts into negotiations, the stronger is his or her tendency to make unwarranted concessions so that the negotiations do not fail.

Time deadlines have both advantages and disadvantages in negotiations. The main advantage of having the parties agree on a deadline is that it motivates them to complete negotiations by that time. The main problem with a time deadline is that it may become a liability when exceeding deadlines is costly.[45] Negotiators make concessions and soften their demands more rapidly as the deadline approaches. Moreover, time pressure inhibits a collaborative conflict management style, because the parties have less time to exchange information or present flexible offers.

Skilled negotiators use deadlines to their advantage by keeping their own time limits flexible. For example, one Brazilian company invited a group of Americans to negotiate a contract the week before Christmas. The Brazilians knew that the Americans would want to return to the United States by Christmas, so they delayed agreement until the last minute to extract more concessions from their visitors. The final agreement definitely favoured the Brazilians.[46] When visiting foreign countries, some negotiators become victims of their own travel arrangements. They think they can complete the deal within a few days, and book their flight around that impossible schedule. The result is that they make excessive concessions to reach an agreement within that time frame rather than return empty handed or cancel their flight. Some negotiators have been known to rush through the final stages of negotiations during the taxi ride to the airport![47]

Audience characteristics

Most negotiators have audiences—anyone with a vested interest in the negotiation outcomes, such as senior management, other team members, or even the general public. Negotiators tend to act differently when their audience observes the negotiation or has detailed information about the process, compared to situations in which the audience only sees the end results.[48] When the audience has direct surveillance over the proceedings, negotiators tend to be more competitive, less willing to make concessions, and more likely to engage in political tactics against the other party.[49] The reason is that this "hard-line" behaviour shows the audience that the negotiator is working for their interests. With their audience watching, negotiators also have more interest in saving face. Sometimes, audiences are drawn into the negotiations by acting as a source of indirect appeals. The general public often takes on this role when groups negotiate with the provincial or federal governments.[50]

Negotiator Behaviours

Negotiator behaviour plays an important role in resolving conflict. Four of the most important behaviours are setting goals, gathering information, making concessions, and communicating effectively. Before deliberations begin, effective negotiators plan their strategy and establish a set of goals regarding their initial offer, target, and resistance points. One survey of business negotiations with the Japanese reported that planning was the factor most responsible for success or failure of negotiations.[51]

Many people tend to talk excessively during negotiations because they focus on persuading the other party rather than finding an optimal solution. Yet effective negotiators spend more time gathering information. Specifically, they devote more energy to listening to the other party and asking questions to probe them for details of their position.[52] Some negotiation teams collect information more efficiently by making each member responsible for listening intently to specific issues related to their expertise.[53] With more information about the opponent's interests and needs, negotiators are better able to discover low-cost concessions or proposals that will satisfy the other side.

Effective communication is a third type of negotiator behaviour that significantly influences the conflict resolution process.[54] Studies on negotiator behaviour report that negotiators are more successful when they communicate in a way that maintains effective relationships between the parties. Specifically, they tend to (1) discuss issues rather than people, (2) avoid making irritating statements such as "I think you'll agree that this is a generous offer," and (3) use effective persuasion tactics by managing the content of their messages (see Chapter 6).[55] In general, they try to avoid escalating the conflict.

Making concessions

Negotiation is a process of making offers and counteroffers in an attempt to reach a mutually acceptable settlement. Concessions are important because

"Actually, no — the negotiations aren't going at all well."

they (1) enable the parties to move toward the area of potential agreement, (2) symbolize each party's motivation to bargain in good faith, and (3) tell the other party of the relative importance of the negotiating items.[56] Negotiators need to make concessions, but how many concessions should they make? The answer partly depends on the other party's strategy, perceptions, and expectations.[57] For instance, Russian negotiators make few concessions and tend to view the opponent's concessions as a sign of weakness rather than good faith.[58]

Apart from cultural differences, it appears that the best strategy is to be moderately tough and give just enough concessions to communicate sincerity and motivation to resolve the conflict.[59] Being too tough can undermine relations between the parties, especially when they will negotiate with each other in the future. Giving too many concessions, particularly early in the proceedings, implies weakness and encourages the other party to use power and resistance. Again, we must emphasize that perceptions of toughness or weakness in concession making vary from one person to another, particularly across cultures. Overall, negotiators need to carefully read the situation and know when a new concession must be given to move the parties toward agreement.

Third-Party Conflict Resolution

Third-party conflict resolution
Any attempt by a relatively neutral person to help the parties resolve their differences.

Most of this chapter has focussed on people directly involved in a conflict, yet many disputes in organizational settings are resolved with the assistance of a third party. **Third-party conflict resolution** is any attempt by a relatively neutral person to help the parties resolve their differences. This may range from formal labour arbitration to informal managerial interventions to resolve disagreements among employees.

There are four basic objectives in third-party conflict resolution.[60] These objectives may be in conflict with each other, so those who adopt third-party roles need to decide which of these takes priority:

- *Efficient*—Trying to resolve the dispute quickly and with minimum expenditure of organizational resources.

- *Effective*—Searching for the optimal solution through rational decision making, including collecting as much relevant information as possible, so that the decision will correct the underlying causes of the conflict.

- *Outcome fairness*—Ensuring that the parties feel the solution provided by the third-party intervention is fair. Although outcome fairness is similar to effectiveness, they are not the same because people sometimes think that a solution is fair even though it does not work well in the long term.

Procedural fairness
Perceptions of fairness regarding the dispute resolution process, whether or not the outcome is favourable to the person.

- *Procedural fairness*—Ensuring that the parties feel that the dispute resolution process is fair, whether or not the outcome is favourable to them. **Procedural fairness** is particularly important when the third party makes a binding decision to resolve the dispute. In these situations, procedural fairness increases when the third party isn't biased (e.g., doesn't have a vested interest toward one party), is well informed about the facts of the situation, and has listened to all sides of the dispute. It also increases when the decision can be appealed to a higher authority and the third party applies existing policies consistently.[61]

Types of third-party intervention

There are generally three types of third-party dispute resolution activities: mediation, arbitration, and inquisition. These activities can be classified by their level of control over the process and control over the decision.[62] Mediation has high control over the intervention process but little or no control over the conflict resolution decision. Arbitration has high control over the final decision, but the process is largely determined by existing due process rules. Inquisitional interventions, which are common among managers, have a high level of control over both the process and outcomes. In this final section, we look at these three forms of third-party conflict resolution and discuss problems with the inquisitional approach that managers tend to use.

Mediation

Mediators assist in conflict resolution by managing the process and context of interaction between the disputing parties. However, the parties still make the final decision about how to resolve their differences. The Canadian Television Network recently invited a highly respected mediator of international disputes to resolve a long-standing battle among CTV's owners over control of the network. The mediator got the owners to agree to a unique bidding process that eventually decided their relative voting power.[63] The mediator at CTV was brought in to resolve a specific dispute, but mediators can help groups resolve ongoing differences. For example, earlier in this chapter we saw how mediation helped union and management representatives at Cardinal River Coals improve their working relationship.

An **ombuds officer** is someone who formally investigates complaints as well as mediates the conflict. Many governments have ombuds officers to assist disagreements involving citizens, and some postsecondary institutions have them to investigate complaints by students and staff members. MacMillan Bloedel and DuPont Canada have an ombuds officer to mediate conflicts between management and employees, such as allegations of employment discrimination. This person gathers information about the complaint and helps both the employee and manager find an acceptable solution.[64]

Ombuds officer
Someone who formally investigates complaints as well as mediates the conflict.

Arbitration

Arbitration is a form of third-party dispute resolution in which the intervenor makes a binding decision on the conflicting parties. The arbitrator has a high degree of control over the decision outcome, but the decision process rules (e.g., what information may be heard) are mainly determined by the parties or existing universal procedures.[65] Canadian labour laws give unionized employees the right to arbitration hearings in most disputes. A few Canadian companies also offer arbitration to disputes between management and nonunionized employees.

The hierarchical appeals process—such as Federal Express Canada's "guaranteed fair treatment" policy—is an arbitration type of conflict resolution in which employees can appeal a supervisor's decision to more senior management.[66] Peer tribunals represent another variation of the arbitration process in which a panel of co-workers listens to a formal complaint and makes either a recommendation to management or a binding decision. Coors Brewing Co. has used peer tribunals for more than 20 years to reduce the chances of unioniza-

Perspective 13–4

Peer Tribunals at Honda Canada and Queen's University

Any employee at Honda Canada who is about to be disciplined has the right to request a review panel of his or her peers. The panel consists of seven randomly chosen employees. The company and employee each present their side of the issue, and then the panel holds a secret ballot. Only enough ballots are opened to reveal a majority decision. This result is binding on both the company and employee.

Honda Canada has had several peer arbitration hearings since the company opened its Aliston, Ontario, plant in 1987. Most have gone in the company's favour. A senior manager at Honda explains: "I find the associates (employees) are more critical of aberrant behaviour, absenteeism, or goof-offs than the company would be."

Queen's University at Kingston, Ontario, has developed a peer tribunal process along with a peer support role to guide employees through the process. Employees who are unable to resolve problems with their supervisor can request assistance from a grievance

officer—a co-worker or administrator specially trained in conflict resolution. The grievance officer helps employees decide whether there is cause for a formal complaint and to describe the formal appeal board process.

If a complaint cannot be resolved informally, employees may request an appeal board hearing. The appeal board is a panel of three nonmanagement employees who hear the complaint. One member of the board is selected by the employee, another by the head of the department to whom the complaint is directed, and the third by the first two appointees.

The appeal board listens to the presentations from both sides of the dispute, then prepares a report with its decision. Within two weeks of the board's decision, either party may request a formal hearing before an independent external arbitrator. The person requesting the arbitration must deposit a fee of $250 with the staff liaison officer. The arbitrator's decision is final and binding on the grievor and the university.

Sources: S. L. McShane, "Conflict Resolution Practices for Nonunion Employees," *Human Resources Management in Canada,* January 1991, pp. 35527–36; and C. Woodall, "At Honda, Neckties Are Frowned Upon and Nobody Gets 'Special' Treatment," *Canadian HR Reporter,* November 1, 1989, pp. 5, 9.

---

tion.[67] As described in Perspective 13–4, Honda Canada and Queen's University also have peer tribunals for their nonunion employees.

Inquisition

Managers regularly intervene in disputes between employees and departments. Sometimes they adopt a mediator role; other times they serve as arbitrators. However, research suggests that managers usually adopt an inquisitional approach whereby they dominate the intervention process as well as make a binding decision. Specifically, inquisitional managers control all discussion about the conflict, ask questions of the disputing parties, and decide which information to select or ignore.[68]

Managers like the inquisition approach because it is consistent with the decision-oriented nature of managerial jobs, gives them control over the conflict process and outcome, and tends to resolve disputes efficiently. However, managers tend to collect limited information about the problem using this approach, so their imposed decision may produce an ineffective solution to the conflict.[69] Moreover, employees tend to think that the procedures and outcomes of inquisitions are unfair because they have little control over this approach. For everyday disputes, managers should adopt the mediation approach because this gives employees more responsibility for resolving their own disputes. When employees cannot resolve their differences, managers should serve as arbitrators using predetermined rules of evidence and other processes that seem fair to employees.

Chapter Summary

- Conflict exists when people believe that others have deliberately blocked, or are about to block, their goals. It involves a cycle of conflict episodes that begins with a conflict perception, followed by attitudes and behaviours toward the opponent that influence the opponent's perception of the relationship.

- Conflict has both positive and negative consequences. Conflict management interventions alter the level and form of conflict such that organizational effectiveness is optimized. The beneficial outcomes of conflict are found mainly in improved decision making and team dynamics. On the negative side, conflict motivates dysfunctional organizational politics, creates feelings of frustration, generates negative stereotypes toward the other party, and reduces communication necessary to resolve the conflict.

- Conflict potentially increases under conditions of goal incompatibility, differentiation, task interdependence, scarce resources, ambiguity, and communication problems. Conflict is more common in a multicultural work force because of greater differentiation and communication problems among employees.

- There are basically five interpersonal conflict management styles: avoiding, competing, accommodating, compromising, and collaborating. Collaborating is the only style that represents a purely win–win orientation—the belief that the parties will find a mutually beneficial solution to the conflict. The four other styles adopt some variation of a win–lose orientation—the belief that one party will lose if the other wins.

- Structural approaches to conflict management include emphasizing super-ordinate goals, reducing differentiation, improving communication and understanding, reducing task interdependence, increasing resources, and clarifying rules and procedures. These elements can also be altered to stimulate conflict.

- Negotiation occurs whenever two or more conflicting parties attempt to resolve their divergent goals by redefining the terms of their interdependence. Negotiations are influenced by several situational factors, including location, physical setting, time, and audience. Important negotiator behaviours include setting goals, making concessions, gathering information, and communicating effectively.

- Third-party conflict resolution is any attempt by a relatively neutral person to help the parties resolve their differences. The main objectives are to resolve the dispute efficiently and effectively, and to ensure that the parties feel that the process and outcome of dispute resolution are fair. The three main forms of third-party dispute resolution are mediation, arbitration, and inquisition. Managers tend to use an inquisition approach, although mediation is more appropriate for most everyday disputes among employees.

Discussion Questions

1. Describe the conflict cycle. When does the cycle escalate rather than defuse?

2. How does conflict benefit the decision-making process?

3. Conflict among managers emerged soon after a Swedish company was bought by a French company. The Swedes perceived the French management as hierarchical and arrogant, whereas the French thought the Swedes were naive, cautious, and lacking an achievement orientation. Describe an intergroup mirroring intervention that would reduce dysfunctional conflict in this situation. What conditions might make the intergroup mirroring process difficult here?

4. Identify three levels of interdependence and give an organizational example for each.

5. Jane has just been appointed as purchasing manager of Canadian Widget Ltd. The previous purchasing manager, who recently retired, was known for his "winner-take-all" approach to suppliers. He continually fought for more discounts and was sceptical about any special deals that suppliers would propose. A few suppliers refused to do business with Canadian Widget, but senior management was confident that the former purchasing manager's approach minimized the company's costs. Jane wants to try a more collaborative approach to working with suppliers. Will her approach work? How should she adopt a more collaborative approach in future negotiations with suppliers?

6. Suppose that Canadian Airlines International did not have a financial crisis that helped employees overcome past differences. Describe two other ways that the company could reduce employee conflict through superordinate goals.

7. Discuss two effects of time on negotiations.

8. Managers tend to use an inquisitional approach to resolving disputes between employees and departments. Describe the inquisitional approach and discuss its appropriateness in organizational settings.

Notes

1. S. O. Fattedad, "Behind the Scenes at Canadian Airlines," *CGA Magazine,* June 1993, pp. 30–33, 75, 76; D. McMurdy, "A New Way of Saving Jobs," *Maclean's,* September 20, 1993, pp. 18–20; C. Motherwell, "Loyal Employees Airline's Foundation," *Globe & Mail,* November 30, 1992, pp. B1, B7; and C. Cattaneo, "Flying to the Rescue," *Calgary Herald,* August 30, 1992, pp. B1, B2.

2. D. Tjosvold, *Working Together to Get Things Done* (Lexington, Mass.: Lexington, 1986), pp. 114–15.

3. G. Wolf, "Conflict Episodes," in *Negotiating in Organizations,* ed. M. H. Bazerman and R. J. Lewicki (Beverly Hills, Calif.: Sage, 1983), pp. 135–40.

4. This model and related discussion are based on L. R. Pondy, "Organizational Conflict: Concepts and Models," *Administrative Science Quarterly* 12 (1967), pp. 296–320.

5. H. Mintzberg, *The Nature of Managerial Work* (New York: Harper & Row, 1973); and K. W. Thomas and W. H. Schmidt, "A Survey of Managerial Interests with Respect to Conflict," *Academy of Management Journal* 19 (1976), pp. 315–18.

6. D. Nightingale, "Conflict and Conflict Resolution," in *Organizational Behavior: Research and Issues,* ed. G. Strauss, R. Miles, C. Snow, and A. Tannenbaum (Belmont, Calif.: Wadsworth, 1976), pp. 141–64; and M. P. Follett, "Constructive Conflict," in *Dynamic Administration: The Collected Papers of Mary Parker Follett,* ed. E. M. Fox and L. Ulwick (New York: Hippocrene, 1982), pp. 1–20.

7. D. Tjosvold, *The Conflict-Positive Organization* (Reading, Mass.: Addison-Wesley, 1991); and A. C. Filley, *Interpersonal Conflict Resolution* (Glenview, Ill.: Scott, Foresman, 1975), pp. 4–7.

8. C. O'Reilly, "Corporations, Culture, and Commitment: Motivation and Social Control in Organizations," *California Management Review* 31 (Summer 1989), p. 14.

9. S. P. Robbins, *Managing Organizational Conflict: A Nontraditional Approach* (Englewood Cliffs, N.J.: Prentice Hall, 1974), p. 19.

10. R. R. Blake and J. S. Mouton, *Solving Costly Organizational Conflicts* (San Francisco: Jossey-Bass, 1984).

11. H. Witteman, "Analyzing Interpersonal Conflict: Nature of Awareness, Type of Initiating Event, Situational Perceptions, and Management Styles," *Western Journal of Communications* 56 (1992), pp. 248–80; and F. J. Barrett and D. L. Cooperrider, "Generative Metaphor Intervention: A New Approach for Working with Systems Divided by Conflict and Caught in Defensive Perception," *Journal of Applied Behavioral Science* 26 (1990), pp. 219–39.

12. T. Janz and D. Tjosvold, "Costing Effective vs. Ineffective Work Relationships," *Canadian Journal of Administrative Sciences* 2 (1985), pp. 43–51.

13. R. E. Walton and J. M. Dutton, "The Management of Conflict: A Model and Review," *Administrative Science Quarterly* 14 (1969), pp. 73–84.

14. A. Weder, "Le Château Cleans House, But Its U.S. Stores Are in a Mess," *Financial Times of Canada,* March 4, 1991, p. 6.

15. M. N. Kiggundu, "Task Interdependence and the Theory of Job Design," *Academy of Management Review* 6 (1981), pp. 499–508.

16. P. C. Earley and G. B. Northcraft, "Goal Setting, Resource Interdependence, and Conflict Management," in *Managing Conflict: An Interdisciplinary Approach,* ed. M. A. Rahim (New York: Praeger, 1989), pp. 161–70.

17. J. D. Thompson, *Organizations in Action* (New York: McGraw-Hill, 1967), pp. 54–56.

18. W. W. Notz, F. A. Starke, and J. Atwell, "The Manager as Arbitrator: Conflicts over Scarce Resources," in *Negotiating in Organizations,* ed. Bazerman and Lewicki, pp. 143–64.

19. R. A. Baron, "Reducing Organizational Conflict: An Incompatible Response Approach," *Journal of Applied Psychology* 69 (1984), pp. 272–79.

20. C. Kirchmeyer and J. McLellan, "Capitalizing on Ethnic Diversity: An Approach to Managing the Diverse Workgroups of the 1990s," *Canadian Journal of Administrative Sciences* 8 (June 1991), pp. 72–79; and E. J. Mighty, "Valuing Workforce Diversity: A Model of Organizational Change," *Canadian Journal of Administrative Sciences* 8 (June 1991), pp. 64–70.

21. K. W. Thomas, "Conflict and Conflict Management," in *Handbook of Industrial and Organizational Psychology,* ed. M. D. Dunnette (Chicago: Rand McNally, 1976), pp. 889–935. For similar models see R. R. Blake and J. S. Mouton, *The Managerial Grid* (Houston: Gulf Publications, 1964); and M. A. Rahim, "A Measure of Styles of Handling Interpersonal Conflict," *Academy of Management Journal* 26 (1983), pp. 368–76.

22. R. J. Lewicki and J. A. Litterer, *Negotiation* (Homewood, Ill.: Irwin, 1985), pp. 102–6.

23. K. W. Thomas, "Toward Multi-Dimensional Values in Teaching: The Example of Conflict Behaviors," *Academy of Management Review* 2 (1977), pp. 484–90.

24. Tjosvold, *Working Together to Get Things Done,* Chapter 2; D. W. Johnson, G. Maruyama, R. T. Johnson, D. Nelson, and S. Skon, "Effects of Cooperative, Competitive, and Individualistic Goal Structures on Achievement: A Meta-Analysis," *Psychological Bulletin* 89 (1981), pp. 47–62; and R. J. Burke, "Methods of Resolving Superior–Subordinate Conflict: The Constructive Use of Subordinate Differences and Disagreements," *Organizational Behavior and Human Performance* 5 (1970), pp. 393–441.

25. M. B. Pinto, J. K. Pinto, and J. E. Prescott, "Antecedents and Consequences of Project Team Cross-Functional Cooperation," *Management Science* 39 (1993), pp. 1281–97; and M. Sherif, "Superordinate Goals in the Reduction of Intergroup Conflict," *American Journal of Sociology* 68 (1958), pp. 349–58.

26. S. Hamm, "Office Politics," *PCWeek Inside,* April 18, 1994, pp. A1, A4.

27. S. Ritchie, "Life in the Fast Lane," *Globe & Mail,* June 8, 1993, p. B24.

28. M. Zimmerman, *How to Do Business with the Japanese* (New York: Random House, 1985), pp. 170, 200; and W. G. Ouchi, *Theory Z* (New York: Avon, 1982), pp. 25–32.

29. M. Rowen, "Working Smarter," *Lodging Hospitality,* August 1989, pp. 94–101.

30. G. Alastain, "Route Masters," *Business London,* September 1990, p. 30.

31. W. N. Isaacs, "Taking Flight: Dialogue, Collective Thinking, and Organizational Learning," *Organizational Dynamics,* Autumn 1993, pp. 24–39; E. H. Schein, "On Dialogue, Culture, and Organizational Learning,"

Organizational Dynamics, Autumn 1993, pp. 40–51; and P. M. Senge, *The Fifth Discipline* (New York: Doubleday Currency, 1990), pp. 238–49.

32. Blake and Mouton, *Solving Costly Organizational Conflicts*, Chapter 6; and R. R. Blake and J. S. Mouton, "Overcoming Group Warfare," *Harvard Business Review*, November–December 1984, pp. 98–108.

33. M. L. Marks, "Merger Management HR's Way," *HRMagazine*, May 1991, pp. 61–66.

34. P. D. Bergman, *Relations by Objectives: The Ontario Experience* (Kingston, Ont.: Industrial Relations Centre, 1988).

35. P. R. Lawrence and J. W. Lorsch, *Organization and Environment* (Homewood, Ill.: Irwin, 1969).

36. E. Van de Vliert, "Escalative Intervention in Small Group Conflicts," *Journal of Applied Behavioral Science* 21 (Winter 1985), pp. 19–36.

37. D. G. Pruitt and P. J. Carnevale, *Negotiation in Social Conflict* (Buckingham, U.K.: Open University Press, 1993), p. 2; and J. A. Wall, Jr., *Negotiation: Theory and Practice* (Glenview, Ill.: Scott, Foresman, 1985), p. 4.

38. For a critical view of collaboration in negotiation, see J. M. Brett, "Managing Organizational Conflict," *Professional Psychology: Research and Practice* 15 (1984), pp. 664–78.

39. R. Stagner and H. Rosen, *Psychology of Union–Management Relations* (Belmont, Calif.: Wadsworth, 1965), pp. 95–96, 108–10; and R. E. Walton and R. B. McKersie, *A Behavioral Theory of Labor Negotiations: An Analysis of a Social Interaction System* (New York: McGraw-Hill, 1965), pp. 41–46.

40. J. W. Salacuse and J. Z. Rubin, "Your Place or Mine? Site Location and Negotiation," *Negotiation Journal* 6 (January 1990), pp. 5–10; and Lewicki and Litterer, *Negotiation*, pp. 144–46.

41. P. C. Newman, *The Acquisitors* (Toronto: Seal, 1981), p. 85.

42. B. C. Herniter, E. Carmel, and J. F. Nunamaker, Jr., "Computers Improve Efficiency of the Negotiation Process," *Personnel Journal*, April 1993, pp. 93–99.

43. Lewicki and Litterer, *Negotiation*, pp. 146–51; and B. Kniveton, *The Psychology of Bargaining* (Aldershot, Eng.: Avebury, 1989), pp. 76–79.

44. B. M. Downie, "Union–Management Co-operation in the 1980s and Beyond," in *Union–Management Relations in Canada*, ed. J. C. Anderson, M. Gunderson, and A. Ponak (Don Mills, Ont.: Addison-Wesley, 1989), pp. 261–83.

45. Pruitt and Carnevale, *Negotiation in Social Conflict*, pp. 59–61; and Lewicki and Litterer, *Negotiation*, pp. 151–54.

46. N. J. Adler, *International Dimensions of Organizational Behavior*, 2nd ed. (Belmont, Calif.: Wadsworth, 1991), p. 191.

47. Zimmerman, *How to Do Business with the Japanese*, p. 101; and H. Cohen, *You Can Negotiate Anything* (New York: Bantam, 1982), pp. 93–95.

48. B. M. Downie, "When Negotiations Fail: Causes of Breakdown and Tactics for Breaking the Stalemate," *Negotiation Journal*, April 1991, pp. 175–86.

49. Pruitt and Carnevale, *Negotiation in Social Conflict*, pp. 56–58; and Lewicki and Litterer, *Negotiation*, pp. 215–22.

50. V. V. Murray, T. D. Jick, and P. Bradshaw, "To Bargain or Not to Bargain? The Case of Hospital Budget Cuts," in *Negotiating in Organizations*, ed. Bazerman & Lewicki pp. 272–95.

51. R. Tung, *Business Negotiations with the Japanese* (Lexington, Mass.: Lexington Books, 1984).

52. M. A. Neale and M. H. Bazerman, *Cognition and Rationality in Negotiation* (New York: Free Press, 1991), pp. 29–31; and L. L. Thompson, "Information Exchange in Negotiation," *Journal of Experimental Social Psychology* 27 (1991), pp. 161–79.

53. Lewicki and Litterer, *Negotiation*, pp. 177–80; and Adler, *International Dimensions of Organizational Behavior*, 2nd ed., pp. 190–91.

54. L. L. Putnam and M. E. Roloff (eds.), *Communication and Negotiation* (Newbury Park, Calif.: Sage, 1992).

55. L. Hall (ed.), *Negotiation: Strategies for Mutual Gain* (Newbury Park, Calif.: Sage, 1993); and D. Ertel, "How to Design a Conflict Management Procedure that Fits Your Dispute." *Sloan Management Review* 32 (Summer 1991), pp. 29–42.

56. Lewicki and Litterer, *Negotiation*, pp. 89–93.

57. J. Z. Rubin, S. H. Kim, and N. M. Peretz, "Expectancy Effects and Negotiation," *Journal of Social Issues* 46 (1990), pp. 125–39; and N. J. Adler, and J. L. Graham, "Business Negotiations: Canadians Are Not Just Like Americans," *Canadian Journal of Administrative Sciences* 4 (1987), pp. 211–38.

58. Adler, *International Dimensions of Organizational Behavior*, 2nd ed., pp. 180–81.

59. Kniveton, *The Psychology of Bargaining*, pp. 100–101; J. Z. Rubin and B. R. Brown, *The Social Psychology of Bargaining and Negotiation* (New York: Academic Press, 1976), Chapter 9; and Brett, "Managing Organizational Conflict," pp. 670–71.

60. B. H. Sheppard, R. J. Lewicki, and J. W. Monton, *Organizational Justice: The Search for Fairness in the Workplace* (New York: Lexington, 1992).

61. R. Folger and J. Greenberg, "Procedural Justice: An Interpretive Analysis of Personnel Systems," *Research in Personnel and Human Resources Management* 3 (1985), pp. 141–83.

62. A. R. Elangovan, "Managerial Third-Party Intervention: Cognitive Biases and Heuristics," *Proceedings of the Annual ASAC Conference, Organizational Behaviour Division* 14, pt. 5 (1993), pp. 92–101; Sheppard et al., *Organizational Justice;* and J. W. Thibaut and L. Walker, *Procedural Justice: A Psychological Analysis* (Hillsdale, N.J.: Erlbaum, 1975).

63. J. Greenwood, "Masters of Compromise," *Financial Post Magazine,* April 1992, pp. 35–38; and R. Siklos, "High Drama as CTV Gets New Cast, Script," *Financial Post,* February 15–17, 1992, p. S20.

64. M. Crawford, "The New Office Etiquette," *Canadian Business,* May 1993, pp. 22–31; and D. M. McCabe and D. Lewin, "Employee Voice: A Human Resource Management Perspective," *California Management Review* 34 (Spring 1992), pp. 112–23.

65. M. A. Neale and M. H. Bazerman, *Cognition and Rationality in Negotiation* (New York: The Free Press, 1991), pp. 140–42.

66. D. K. Denton, "Behind the Curve," *Business Horizons* 36 (July–August 1993), pp. 1–4; Crawford, "The New Office Etiquette," p. 31; and S. L. McShane, "Conflict Resolution Practices for Nonunion Employees," *Human Resources Management in Canada,* January 1991, pp. 35527–36.

67. D. Anfuso, "Peer Review Wards Off Unions and Lawsuits," *Personnel Journal,* January 1994, p. 64.

68. B. H. Sheppard, "Managers as Inquisitors: Lessons from the Law," in *Bargaining Inside Organizations,* ed. M. Bazerman and R. J. Lewicki (Beverly Hills, Calif.: Sage, 1983), pp. 193–213.

69. Tjosvold, *The Conflict-Positive Organization,* pp. 112–13.

Chapter Case

Maelstrom Communications

Sales manager Roger Todd was fuming. Thanks to, as he put it, "those nearsighted addleheads in service," he had nearly lost one of his top accounts. When told of Todd's complaint, senior serviceperson Ned Rosen retorted, "That figures. Anytime Mr. Todd senses even the remotest possibility of a sale, he immediately promises the customer the world on a golden platter. We can't possibly provide the service they request under the time constraints they give us and do an acceptable job."

Feelings of this sort were common in the departments both Roger and Ned worked for in Maelstrom Communications. Sales and service, the two dominant functions in the company, never saw eye to eye on anything, it seemed. The problems dated well back in the history of the company, even before Roger or Ned were hired some years ago.

Maelstrom Communications is a franchised distributionship belonging to a nationwide network of communications companies that sell products such as intercom, paging, sound, and interconnect telephone systems. Maelstrom competes directly with the Bell System companies in the telephone hardware market. Equipment installation and maintenance service are an integral part of the total package Maelstrom offers.

Modern telephone system hardware is highly sophisticated and few, if any, system users have the technological know-how to do their own equipment servicing. An excellent service record is crucial to the success of any company in the field. After the direct sale of a Maelstrom system, the sales force maintains contacts with customers. There is nothing the salespeople dislike so much as hearing that a customer hasn't received the type of service promised at the time of sale. On the other hand, service technicians complain of being hounded by the salespeople whenever a preferred customer needs a wire spliced. As Ned

Rosen put it, "I can't remember the last time a service request came through that *wasn't* an emergency from a preferred customer."

Maelstrom's owner and president, Al Whitfield, has a strong sales background and views sales as the bread-and-butter department of the company. He is in on all major decisions and has final say on any matter brought to his attention. He spends most of his time working with sales and marketing personnel, and rarely concerns himself with the day-to-day activities of the service department unless a major problem of some sort crops up.

Next in line in Maelstrom's corporate hierarchy is the vice-president in charge of production, Lawrence Henderson. Henderson is responsible for the acquisition and distribution of all job-related equipment and materials and for the scheduling of all service department activities. His sympathies lie primarily with the service department.

Each week Whitfield, Henderson, and all members of the sales force hold a meeting in Maelstrom's conference room. The sales personnel present their needs to Henderson so that equipment can be ordered and jobs scheduled. Service requests reported to salespeople from customers are also relayed to Henderson at this point. Once orders for service have been placed with production, sales personnel receive no feedback on the disposition of them (unless a customer complains to them directly) other than at these weekly meetings. It is common for a salesperson to think all is well with his or her accounts when, in fact, they are receiving delayed service or none at all. When an irate customer phones the sales representative to complain, it sets in motion the machinery that leads to disputes such as the one between Roger Todd and Ned Rosen.

It has become an increasingly common occurrence at Maelstrom for sales personnel to go to Henderson to complain when their requests are not met by the service department. Henderson has exhibited an increasing tendency to side with the service department and to tell the salespeople that existing service department priorities must be adhered to and that any sales requests will have to wait for rescheduling. At this point, a salesperson's only recourse is to go to Whitfield, who invariably agrees with the salesperson and instructs Henderson to take appropriate action. All of this is time consuming and only serves to produce friction between the president and the vice-president in charge of production.

Discussion Questions

1. Use the conflict cycle to describe the events in this case.
2. What situational conditions have created the conflict in this case?
3. What actions should the organization take to manage the conflict?

Source: Written by Daniel Robey in collaboration with Todd Anthony.

Experiential Exercise

Ugli Orange Role Play
Purpose: This exercise is designed to help you understand the dynamics of interpersonal and intergroup conflict as well as the effectiveness of negotiation strategies under specific conditions.

Instructions: The instructor will divide the class into an even number of teams of three people each, with one participant left over for each team formed (e.g., six observers if there are six teams). One-half of the teams will take the role of Dr. Roland and the other half will be Dr. Jones. Teams will receive the appropriate materials from the instructor. Members within each team are given 10 minutes to learn their roles and decide negotiating strategy. After reading their roles and discussing strategy, each Dr. Jones team is matched with a Dr. Roland team to conduct negotiations.

Observers will receive observation forms from the instructor, and two observers will be assigned to watch the paired teams during prenegotiations and subsequent negotiations. At the end of the negotiations, the observers will describe the process and outcomes in their negotiating session. The instructor will then invite the negotiators to describe their experiences and the implications for conflict management.

Source: This exercise has been prepared by Robert J. House.

Organizational Leadership

Learning Objectives

After reading this chapter, you should be able to:

List the common traits found in effective leaders.

Describe the "hi–hi" leadership hypothesis.

Outline the path-goal theory of leadership.

Define transactional and transformational leadership.

Identify the four features of transformational leadership.

Explain why leaders are given too much credit or blame for organizational events.

Discuss similarities and differences in the leadership styles of women and men.

Chapter Outline

Perspectives of Leadership.

Trait Perspective of Leadership.

Behavioural Perspective of Leadership.

Contingency Perspective of Leadership.

Transformational Perspective of Leadership.

The Romance Perspective of Leadership.

Gender Issues in Leadership.

Courtesy of Newbridge Networks Corp.

$\mathcal{N}$ewbridge Networks Corp. sparks with innovative ideas in the fast-paced digital communications systems market. Much of this energy begins with the enthusiasm and direction of Newbridge's founder and chairman, Terry Matthews. Matthews has been called a visionary leader who inspires employees and builds their commitment to Newbridge's success.

Newbridge designs and manufactures multiplexers—little black boxes that bundle digital signals so that telephone conversations, computer data, and video programs can be carried on a single line. It is a market that barely existed in the mid-1980s when Matthews first saw the business opportunity. "I saw a huge change coming up," recalls Matthews. "Many people didn't, but I believed it was coming. And I believed it was coming along before most people could see it."

In 1986, Matthews invested $14 million of his own money and hired 16 people to form Newbridge Networks. The Kanata-based company now employs nearly 2,000 people and is a global leader in the multibillion dollar multiplexer market.

Matthews downplays any attention to his leadership, preferring to emphasize that Newbridge Networks depends on the contribution and leadership of every employee. Still, there is no doubt that much of Newbridge's success can be attributed to Matthews's infectious belief in the company's success. "Terry is the consummate optimist," explains one colleague. "He's got a thousand people worked up to a froth."

Some claim that Matthews is too confident, but it is his unbridled enthusiasm that ignites employees and spurs them on to achieve goals which for others would be impossible. Matthews's exuberant voice and hearty laugh thunder through the building; his sense of humour is infectious and fun. However, when a situation takes on serious overtones, Matthews speaks quietly and privately, sensitive to the feelings of others.

"Everything's got to be just right with Terry," says a Newbridge sales executive. "It's got to be perfect. That's what makes this company work."[1]

What makes Terry Matthews an effective organizational leader? One factor is certainly his ability to inspire others toward the vision of a world-class high-technology firm. Matthews challenges employees and instills hope against the odds. He keeps employees focussed on this overarching objective and provides clarity when they need direction.

Leadership
The process of influencing people and providing an environment for them to achieve team or organizational objectives.

Leadership is the process of influencing people and providing an environment for them to achieve team or organizational objectives. Effective leaders help groups of people define their objectives and find ways to achieve them.[2] They use power and persuasion to ensure that followers have the motivation and role clarity to achieve specified goals. Leaders also arrange the work environment—such as allocating resources and altering communication patterns—so that employees can achieve corporate objectives more easily.

Although we usually think of leadership in the executive suite, the concept is relevant to people at all organizational levels. Effective self-managing work teams, for example, consist of members who share leadership responsibilities or otherwise allocate this role to a responsible coordinator. Successful technology champions—employees who overcome technical and organizational obstacles to introduce technological change in their area of the organization—are effective leaders because they influence co-workers and transform the environmental conditions that have prevented the innovation from being introduced. In fact, recent Canadian studies have reported that one of the most common reasons why technology champions fail is that they lack the traits or behaviours that we associate with effective leadership.[3]

Perspectives of Leadership

Leadership has been contemplated since the days of Greek philosophers and is a popular research topic today among organizational behaviour scholars. Yet, as one respected scholar acknowledged, "leadership is one of the most observed and least understood phenomena on earth."[4] As we describe the leadership of Terry Matthews—or any other leader in the private or public sector—it becomes apparent that there are many ways to look at this topic. Although some leadership perspectives are more popular than others, each helps us to more fully understand this complex issue.

This chapter presents an overview of the different leadership perspectives outlined in Exhibit 14–1. Some researchers have studied the traits of great leaders, whereas others have looked at their behaviours. More recent studies have looked at leadership from a contingency approach by considering the appropriate leader behaviours in different settings. Currently, the most popular perspective is that leaders transform organizations through their vision, communication, and ability to build commitment. Finally, an emerging perspective suggests that leadership is mainly a perceptual bias. We distort reality and attribute events to leaders because we feel more comfortable believing that a competent individual is at the organization's helm.

Perspectives of Leadership **Exhibit 14–1**

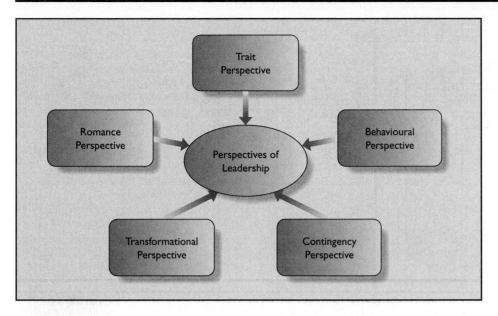

Trait Perspective of Leadership

Since the beginning of recorded civilization, people have been interested in the traits that distinguish great leaders from the rest of us. Traits include the attitudes, values, abilities, personality, appearance, and other personal characteristics that differentiate one person from the next. The ancient Egyptians demanded authority, discrimination, and justice from their leaders. The Greeks called for wisdom, justice, shrewdness, and valour. For the first half of the 20th century, researchers used scientific methods to determine whether these and other traits actually distinguish leaders from lesser souls. By identifying the traits that predict leadership effectiveness, experts hoped that they could select company presidents more scientifically.

Do great leaders have specific traits? A major review in the late 1940s concluded that no consistent list of traits could be distilled from the hundreds of studies conducted up to that time.[5] In the 1950s, another review suggested that there may be a few common traits, but they are relatively weak influences on a person's leadership. These conclusions caused many leadership scholars to give up their search for leadership traits and, instead, consider leadership behaviours and other perspectives.

Many scholars still believe that the leadership trait perspective has limited value. However, a few prominent researchers have recently returned to this theme. They argue that the earlier studies made the mistake of focussing too much on the physical appearance and abstract personality traits of leaders. Instead, the emerging view is that effective leaders have a few common values and abilities. Seven traits discussed in recent leadership literature are listed in Exhibit 14–2 and briefly described below.[6]

| Exhibit 14–2 | Seven Traits of Effective Leaders |

Leadership Trait	Description
Drive	• The leader's inner motivation to pursue goals
Leadership motivation	• The leader's need for socialized power to accomplish team or organizational goals
Integrity	• The leader's truthfulness and tendency to translate words into deeds
Self-confidence	• The leader's belief in his or her own leadership skills and ability to achieve objectives
Intelligence	• The leader's above-average cognitive ability to process enormous amounts of information
Knowledge of the business	• The leader's understanding of the company's environment to make more intuitive decisions
Self-monitoring personality	• The leader's sensitivity to situational cues and ability to adapt his or her own behaviour appropriately

Sources: Based on S. A. Kirkpatrick and E. A. Locke, "Leadership: Do Traits Matter?" *Academy of Management Executive* 5 (May 1991), pp. 48–60; and S. J. Zaccaro, R. J. Foti, and D. A. Kenny, "Self-Monitoring and Trait-Based Variance in Leadership: An Investigation of Leader Flexibility Across Multiple Group Situations," *Journal of Applied Psychology* 76 (1991), pp. 308–15.

- *Drive*—This refers to the inner motivation that leaders possess to pursue their goals. Leaders have a high need for achievement (see Chapter 3). You can see this trait in Terry Matthews, described in the chapter-opening story, through his unwavering tenacity and energy to make Newbridge Networks Corp. a global leader in its industry.

- *Leadership motivation*—This is the person's need for socialized power (described in Chapter 3). Leaders want to use their power bases to influence their team or organization and make it successful.

- *Integrity*—This refers to the leader's truthfulness and tendency to translate words into deeds. According to three large-scale studies conducted during the 1980s, followers consistently identify integrity as the most important leadership trait. Leaders will only have followers when trust is maintained through the leader's integrity.[7]

- *Self-confidence*—Leaders believe in their leadership skills and ability to achieve objectives. They also use impression management tactics (see Chapter 12) to convince followers of their confidence. Terry Matthews's confidence was apparent when he invested in Newbridge long before a market existed. In 1991, when short-sellers (investors betting the company's stock would fall) predicted the company's demise, Matthews instilled confidence in employees that Newbridge would overcome its financial obstacles.

- *Intelligence*—Leaders have above-average cognitive ability to process enormous amounts of information. Leaders aren't necessarily geniuses; rather, they have superior ability to analyze alternate scenarios and identify potential opportunities.

- *Knowledge of the business*—Leaders need to understand the environment in which they operate to make more intuitive decisions. This is consistent with our point in Chapter 9 that intuition requires experience and intimate knowledge of the industry.

- *Self-monitoring personality*—Effective leaders have a strong self-monitoring personality (see Chapter 7) so that they are sensitive to situational cues and can readily adapt their own behaviour appropriately. Recent studies have found that high self-monitors are more likely to emerge as informal leaders in small groups.[8] Moreover, the contingency leadership perspective described later in this chapter assumes that effective leaders are high self-monitors so they can adjust their behaviour to match the situation.[9]

Limitations of trait leadership perspective

These seven leadership traits have fairly strong research support, but we must be careful not to believe that people with these traits are necessarily great leaders. Leadership scholars warn that traits only indicate leadership *potential*, not leadership *performance*. People with these traits aren't necessarily effective leaders until they have mastered the necessary leadership behaviours.

A related concern is that the trait perspective implies a universal approach to leadership. It suggests that leaders must have all these traits and that they apply them in every situation. This is probably a false assumption; leadership is far too complex to have a universal list of traits that apply to every condition. Some traits might not be important all the time, although researchers have not yet explored this aspect of traits.

Finally, some traits—such as drive and self-confidence—are subjective enough that they may really be due to the follower's stereotype of leadership rather than the leader's actual characteristics. For example, we might see a successful person, call that person a leader, and then attribute to that person several unobservable traits that we consider essential for great leaders. We will discuss this perceptual distortion more fully toward the end of the chapter. At this point, you should be aware that our knowledge of leadership traits may be partly due to perceptual distortions.

Behavioural Perspective of Leadership

The leadership behaviour perspective attempts to answer the basic question: What behaviours make leaders effective? During the early days of the behavioural perspective, scholars distilled two clusters of leadership behaviours from more than 1,800 leadership behaviour items.[10] One cluster captures people-oriented behaviours, such as showing mutual trust and respect for subordinates, a genuine concern for their needs, and a desire to look out for their welfare. For example, a leader who has a strong people-oriented style would be willing to accept employee suggestions, do personal favours for employees, support their interests when required, and treat employees as equals.

The other cluster represents a task-oriented leadership style—behaviours that define and structure work roles. Leaders assign employees to specific tasks, clarify their work duties and procedures, ensure that they follow company rules, and push them to reach their performance capacity. Canadian university students apparently value task-oriented instructors because they want clear

Perspective 14–1

Task-Oriented Leadership Gets Results for IMP Group's Kenneth Rowe

Kenneth Rowe is the quintessential hard-driving business leader. Rowe founded IMP Group Ltd. in 1967 out of the ashes of two bankrupt Nova Scotia foundries. In 1970, he developed IMP's aerospace division by buying a failing Dartmouth aircraft parts maker. Since then he has purchased and turned around more than a dozen other companies. The IMP Group now boasts 1,500 employees and revenues of over $175 million.

In building IMP, Rowe has earned a reputation as a tough manager and calculating business leader. Some claim that he developed this strong task orientation while serving in the British merchant marine. Whatever the reason, Rowe is a lone-wolf operator who runs his companies with a skeleton crew of managers and takes hands-on management to an extreme. Complains one former executive: "It's annoying to work for Rowe because he's involved in everything, he's always looking over your shoulder."

Rowe is particularly finicky about keeping costs down, no matter how small the expense. He goes around turning off office lights and begrudges the expense of a water cooler. Rowe prefers soup at his desk because he doesn't like spending money in restaurants. Getting expense reports approved by Rowe is nightmarish. "He'll challenge a vice-president over spending too much on a meal," recounts a former IMP executive.

Rowe has a sense of humour and is usually approachable, but he prefers confrontation to consultation and is apt to shout at people who do things wrong. Rowe concedes that he demands much of himself and others. "I work myself hard, and that's a good example to the rest," he says. He also admits to being blunt with employees. "But I don't lose my temper often, unless someone does something very stupid," he quickly adds. "Then I'm most likely to fire him." Indeed, Rowe is renowned for firing employees who aren't up to scratch. He once fired an entire management group of a newly acquired company in a single day.

Rowe defends his strong task focus by pointing out the risk he takes in turning around failing companies. Some may criticize Rowe for not emphasizing employee interests, but no one can disagree that his leadership style has contributed to an extremely well-run organization. "We need 10 more Ken Rowes down here," says a Dartmouth-based senior executive of Moosehead Breweries Ltd. "He starts things. He's a builder." In the difficult economy of Atlantic Canada, IMP Group's financial picture is impressive. Insiders say the company enjoys low debt and superb profits. "We do very nicely," Rowe agrees.

Sources: Based on "Business Magician: Rowe Turns Halifax-Based IMP into Aerospace Giant," *Halifax Chronicle Herald,* March 16, 1993, p. B1; R. Sikos, "The Black Knight that's Hunting Leigh," *Financial Times,* March 28, 1988, pp. 10–11; M. Salter, "Canada's Toughest Bosses," *Report on Business Magazine,* December 1987, p. 79; and A. Bruce, "Rowe Mirrors Maritime Spirit," *Globe & Mail,* March 9, 1987, p. B13.

course objectives and well-prepared lectures that abide by the course objectives.[11] Terry Matthews, described at the beginning of this chapter, has a task focus because he challenges employees to push Newbridge to the forefront of technological innovation. Kenneth Rowe, the hard-driving and very successful founder of Halifax-based IMP Group, could also be labelled a task-oriented leader, as Perspective 14–1 describes.

The "hi–hi" leadership hypothesis

Scholars initially thought that people-oriented and task-oriented leadership were at opposite ends of a behaviour spectrum. In other words, they believed that a strong task-oriented leader was necessarily a weak people-oriented leader.

But scholars later concluded that these styles are independent of each other. According to this view, some people are high on both styles, others are low on both, and most are somewhere in between. Behavioural leadership scholars also hypothesized that the most effective leaders exhibit high levels of both types of behaviour.[12] This became known as the **"hi–hi" leadership hypothesis.**[13]

Several studies seem to support the hi–hi leadership hypothesis. For example, Canadian students working on a decision-making exercise performed best when their student "manager" demonstrated high levels of concern for production (task orientation) as well as personal warmth (people orientation).[14] Students with the lowest performance worked with managers who demonstrated lots of personal warmth but did not emphasize the task. Other research suggests that subordinates have higher levels of satisfaction and lower absenteeism, grievances, and turnover when their supervisors use the people-oriented style.[15] They have somewhat higher absenteeism and turnover when their supervisors are task-oriented, but this leadership style seems to increase productivity and team unity.

Hi–hi leadership hypothesis
A proposition stating that effective leaders exhibit high levels of both people-oriented and task-oriented behaviours.

Limitations of the behavioural leadership perspective

Although some research seems to support the hi–hi hypothesis, most leadership scholars now believe that effective leaders do not consistently exhibit high levels of both people-oriented and task-oriented leadership in all situations.[16] Their main concern is that studies supporting the hi–hi leadership hypothesis relied on very subjective questionnaire items, so it was easy for stereotyping and other biases to falsely link effective leaders with high levels of both styles.[17] Followers may have concluded that someone is a great leader and this positive halo caused them to rate the leader highly on the people-oriented and task-oriented items in the questionnaire.

Contemporary leadership scholars have also moved away from the behavioural perspective because it is a universal approach. It tries to find the best predictors of leadership under all conditions. The behavioural perspective ignores the possibility that the best leadership style may depend on the situation, such as employee and task characteristics.[18] This severely limits the predictive value of the behavioural perspective and explains why it has been largely set aside in favour of contingency theories of leadership, which we describe next.

Contingency Perspective of Leadership

The contingency perspective of leadership is based on the idea that the most appropriate leadership style depends on the situation. Most (although not all) contingency leadership theories assume that effective leaders must be both insightful and flexible.[19] They must be able to adapt their behaviours and styles to the immediate situation. Yet, as we see in Perspective 14–2, leaders typically have a preferred style. Thus, it takes considerable effort for leaders to learn when and how to alter their styles to match the situation. As we noted earlier, leaders must have a high self-monitoring personality so they can diagnose the circumstances and match their behaviours accordingly.

Perspective 14–2

Learning Path-Goal Leadership at Merisel Canada

Sue Miller is struggling to become a more participative leader. The president of Merisel Canada, Inc., the Toronto-based distributor of computer hardware and software, was promoted through the ranks for her ability to take charge and get things done. "I just did my job so damn well people couldn't help but notice," she says. "Now I have to learn a whole new set of skills."

Miller is not alone. One of the most difficult challenges for most managers is to learn to adapt their leadership style with the situation. Like Miller, many have been promoted for their ability to achieve difficult objectives and to use directive- or achievement-oriented styles to increase employee performance. But although the achievement-oriented style potentially works well for subordinates at all levels, the directive style is usually inappropriate when the subordinate is a skilled manager with several years of experience.

Meanwhile, Miller is still working at being a more effective leader by adjusting her style to the situation. At an executive meeting Miller started to tell the vice-president of finance to put a new credit procedure in place: "Will you designate . . . " Miller stopped in mid-sentence to change her style to a more participative tone: "Do you think it would be a good idea if we were to designate . . .?"

Source: Based on J. Allan, "When Women Set the Rules," *Canadian Business*, April 1991, pp. 40–43.

Path-goal theory of leadership

Path-goal leadership theory
A contingency theory of leadership based on expectancy theory of motivation that includes four leadership styles as well as several employee and situational contingencies.

Several contingency theories have been proposed over the years, but **path-goal leadership theory** has withstood scientific critique better than the others. As Exhibit 14–3 illustrates, path-goal theory considers four distinct leadership styles and several contingency factors leading to three indicators of leader effectiveness.[20]

Path-goal theory has its roots in the expectancy theory of motivation (see Chapter 3). First, it states that effective leaders motivate employees by making their need satisfaction contingent on effective job performance. Thus, leaders strengthen the performance-to-outcome expectancy and valences of those outcomes by ensuring that employees who perform their jobs well have a higher degree of need fulfillment than employees who perform poorly. Second, effective leaders strengthen the effort-to-performance expectancy by providing the information, support, and other resources necessary to help employees complete their tasks.[21]

Leadership styles

Path-goal theory suggests that leaders motivate and satisfy employees in a particular situation by adopting one or more of the four leadership styles described below:

- *Directive*—The leader lets subordinates know what is expected of them, describes what should be done and how it should be done, maintains clear performance standards, and ensures that procedures and practices are followed. Directive leadership is the same as task-oriented leadership described earlier and echoes our discussion in Chapter 2 on the importance of clear task perceptions in employee performance.

Path-Goal Leadership Theory   **Exhibit 14–3**

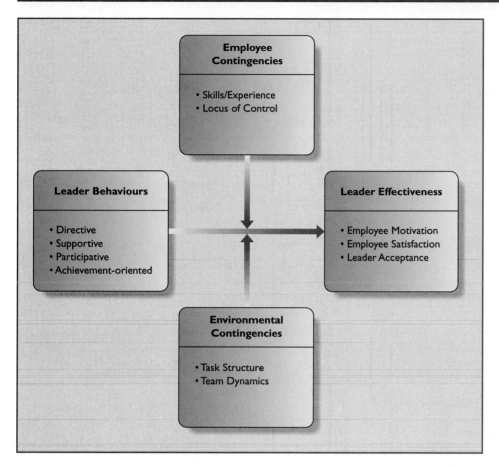

- *Supportive*—The leader is friendly and approachable; makes the work more pleasant; treats employees with equal respect; and shows concern for the status, needs, and well-being of employees. Supportive leadership is the same as people-oriented leadership described earlier and reflects the benefits of social support to help employees cope with stressful situations (see Chapter 5).

- *Participative*—The leader consults with employees, asks for their suggestions, and takes these ideas into serious consideration before making a decision. Participative leadership is connected to the employee involvement literature described in Chapter 11.

- *Achievement-oriented*—The leader sets challenging goals, expects employees to perform at their highest level, continuously seeks improvement in employee performance, and shows a high degree of confidence that employees will assume responsibility and accomplish challenging goals. Achievement-oriented leadership applies goal-setting theory (Chapter 3) as well as positive expectations in self-fulfilling prophecy (Chapter 7).

The path-goal model contends that effective leaders are capable of selecting the most appropriate behavioural style (or styles) for that situation. Leaders might

Exhibit 14–4			Selected Contingencies of Path-Goal Theory	
	Directive	**Supportive**	**Participative**	**Achievement-oriented**
Employee Contingencies				
Skill and experience	Low	Low	High	High
Locus of control	External	External	Internal	Internal
Environmental Contingencies				
Task structure	Nonroutine	Routine	Nonroutine	???
Team dynamics	Negative norms	Low cohesion	Positive norms	???

simultaneously use more than one style at a time. For example, they might be both supportive and participative in a specific situation.

Contingencies of path-goal theory

As a contingency theory, path-goal theory states that each of these four leadership styles will be effective in some situations but not in others. The path-goal leadership model specifies two sets of situational variables that moderate the relationship between a leader's style and effectiveness: (1) employee characteristics and (2) characteristics of the employee's work environment. Several contingencies have already been studied within the path-goal framework, and the model is open for more variables in the future.[22] However, we will examine only four contingencies here (see Exhibit 14–4).

Skill and experience

A combination of directive and supportive leadership is best for employees who are (or perceive themselves to be) inexperienced and unskilled. Directive leadership gives subordinates information about how to accomplish the task, whereas supportive leadership helps them cope with the uncertainties of unfamiliar work situations. Directive leadership is detrimental when employees are skilled and experienced because it introduces too much supervisory control. Instead, these employees should receive participative and achievement-oriented leadership because employees have the necessary knowledge to meet the demands of autonomy and challenging goals.

Locus of control

Locus of control
A personality trait referring to the extent that people believe what happens to them is within their control; those who feel in control of their destiny han an internal locus, whereas those who believe that life events are due mainly to fate or luck have an external locus of control.

Recall from Chapter 7 that people with an internal **locus of control** believe that they have control over their work environment. Consequently, these employees prefer participative and achievement-oriented leadership styles and may become frustrated with a directive style. In contrast, people with an external locus of control believe that their performance is due more to luck and fate, so they tend to be more satisfied with directive and supportive leadership.

Task structure

Directive leadership should be adopted when the task is complex, because this style minimizes role ambiguity that would otherwise occur in complex work situations (particularly for inexperienced employees).[23] Employees in highly routine and simple jobs may require supportive leadership to help them cope with the tedious nature of the work and lack of control over the pace of work. In contrast, the participative leadership style is desirable for employees performing nonroutine tasks because the lack of rules and procedures gives them more discretion to achieve challenging goals. The directive style is ineffective when employees have routine and simple tasks because the manager's guidance serves no purpose and may be viewed as unnecessarily close control. The participative style is also ineffective for employees in structured tasks because they lack discretion over their work.

Team dynamics

Cohesive teams with performance-oriented norms act as a substitute for most leader interventions. High team cohesiveness substitutes for supportive leadership, whereas performance-oriented team norms substitute for directive and possibly achievement-oriented leadership. Thus, when team cohesiveness is low, leaders should use the supportive style. Leaders should apply a directive style to counteract team norms that oppose the team's formal objectives. For example, the team leader may need to use legitimate power if team members have developed a norm to "take it easy" rather than get a project completed on time.

Evaluating path-goal theory

Path-goal theory is the leading contingency theory of leadership and has a number of strengths. One advantage is that most of its contingencies refer to specific conditions (e.g., employee abilities, task structure) so that it is relatively easy to identify conditions in which a specific style is preferred. Another advantage is that path-goal theory is founded on expectancy theory, which has received considerable support. A third advantage is that path-goal theory can be amended by adding more contingency variables as they are identified through research.[24] For example, the locus of control contingency was added a few years after the original model was introduced.

Recent reviews generally conclude that research supports most elements of the path-goal leadership model, but it still requires considerable work and clarification.[25] One problem is that although the theory was first introduced over 25 years ago, several contingencies and leadership styles have received relatively little scholarly investigation. For example, you probably noticed that some cells in Exhibit 14–4 have question marks. This is because we do not yet know how those leadership styles apply to those contingencies.

Another concern is that as path-goal theory adds more contingencies, the model may become too complex for practical use. Although this may provide a close representation of the complexity of leadership, it may become too cumbersome for training people in leadership styles. Few people would be able to remember all the contingencies and appropriate leadership styles for those contingencies. Overall, path-goal theory is far from perfect, but it remains the most complete and robust contingency leadership theory available.

Other contingency theories

Path-goal theory is one of several leadership theories with a contingency perspective. Some contingency theories overlap with the path-goal model in terms of leadership styles, but most use simpler and more abstract contingencies. For example, one contingency model that is popular among training consultants relies on subordinate "readiness" as the only contingency factor to determine which of four leadership styles to apply.[26] Although one contingency variable is easy to remember, it possibly explains why that contingency theory lacks empirical support.[27]

A few leadership theories emphasize contingencies that have not yet been explored by path-goal researchers. One contingency, presented by Canadian scholar Bill Reddin, is organizational climate. Specifically, he suggests that leaders need to adjust their style to the type of relations between employees and management. Another contingency factor that leaders should consider is situational control, that is, the degree of power and influence that the leader possesses in a particular situation.

Changing the situation to match the style

Most contingency leadership theories assume that leaders can change their style to match a given situation. However, at least one prominent scholar has argued that leadership style is related to the individual's personality and, consequently, is relatively stable over time.[28] Leaders might be able to alter their style temporarily, but they tend to use a preferred style in the long term. Instead of having leaders change their style, organizations should engineer the situation to fit the leader's dominant style. A directive leader might be assigned inexperienced employees who need direction rather than seasoned people who work less effectively under a directive style. Alternatively, companies might transfer supervisors to workplaces where their dominant style fits best. For instance, directive leaders might be parachuted into work teams with counterproductive norms, whereas leaders who prefer a supportive style should be sent to departments in which employees face work pressures and other stressors.

Leadership substitutes

Leadership substitutes
Characteristics of the employee, task, or organization that either limit the leader's influence or make it unnecessary.

So far, we have looked at theories that recommend using different leadership styles in various situations. But one theory, called **leadership substitutes,** identifies contingencies that either limit the leader's ability to influence subordinates or make that particular leadership style unnecessary. When substitute conditions are present, employees are effective without a specific leadership style. Some conditions substitute for task-oriented leadership, whereas others substitute for people-oriented leadership. For example, clearly defined work procedures keep employees directed toward organizational goals, so it would be redundant or impossible to provide task-oriented behaviours under these conditions. Similarly, cohesive work teams replace the need for both people- and task-oriented leadership because co-workers provide these behaviours.

Many elements of the leadership substitutes model parallel contingencies in the path-goal leadership model. As an example, the leadership substitute model states that skilled and experienced employees replace task-oriented (directive) leadership. Similarly, path-goal theory states that directive leadership is unnecessary—and possibly dysfunctional—when employees are skilled and experienced. Recent reviews indicate that many aspects of the leadership substitute model require further refinement, but there is general support for the overall notion that some conditions neutralize or substitute for leadership styles.[29]

The Leadership Grid® Figure   Exhibit 14–5

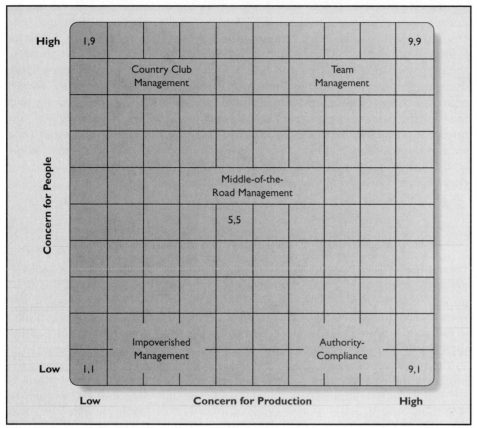

The Leadership Grid®

Robert Blake and Jane Mouton developed a popular leadership program in the 1960s called the **Leadership Grid®** (formerly known as the Managerial Grid). This model, shown in Exhibit 14–5, was born out of the behavioural perspective and initially embraced the hi–hi leadership hypothesis. It originally stated that leaders are most effective when they have both a high concern for people and a high concern for production. However, the most recent version of the Leadership Grid® takes a contingency view. It now states that effective leaders have the *capacity* for high levels of both dimensions, but they should choose appropriate levels of both dimensions for the specific situation.[30]

According to the Leadership Grid® model, *team management* (9,9) leaders rely on commitment, participation, and conflict resolution to seek results. In contrast, *authority-compliance managers* (9,1) try to maximize productivity through power and authority; *country club managers* (1,9) focus on developing good feelings among employees even when production suffers; *middle-of-the-road managers* (5,5) try to maintain the status quo by adopting a middle-of-the-road

Leadership Grid®
A model of leadership developed by Blake and Mouton that assesses an individual's leadership effectiveness in terms of his or her concern for people and production.

approach; and *impoverished managers* (1,1) do the minimum required to fulfill their leadership role and keep their job.

The Leadership Grid® was designed as an organizational development intervention to improve leadership as well as relations between managers and employees within work units. The program has been implemented in hundreds of organizations throughout Canada and the United States. The first phase of the intervention consists of a one-week seminar in which managers learn about the grid philosophy as well as their own leadership style on the Grid. Participants are involved in numerous problem-solving situations intended to help them move toward a more team management style. Later phases of the intervention include seminars to improve relations between leaders and their employees, relations between staff in different departments, and organizational goal setting. In other words, the Leadership Grid® is an organizationwide change strategy that may require several years to complete.

Transformational Perspective of Leadership

Bob Lunney wants his organization to provide good customer service by delivering the right products in the most efficient, cost-conscious way. This is an impressive goal for the leader of an organization with 1,400 employees, a 400-vehicle fleet, and a budget of $100 million. But as Chief of Peel Regional Police in Ontario, Lunney is a lightning rod of change in the way that police think about their work. "Go out and give good customer service," says Lunney when he stops by the squad room as the officers change shift. It is a radical philosophy in this industry, and one that makes Peel Regional Police a vanguard organization.[31]

Bob Lunney is a **transformational leader.** Through his vision and actions, he is helping Peel Regional Police adapt more effectively to its changing environment. Transformational leaders are agents of change. They develop a vision for the organization or work unit, inspire employees to strive for that vision, and give them a "can do" attitude that makes the vision achievable.[32]

Transformational leader
One who transforms organizations by creating, communicating, and modelling a vision for the organization or work unit, and inspiring employees to strive for that vision.

In the mid-1800s, Timothy Eaton, founder of Eaton's Department Stores, was a transformational leader who envisioned new ways to serve customers and develop employees.

Courtesy of Eaton's Department Stores.

Perspective 14–3

A Leader for All Seasons

In three short decades, Isadore Sharp has built Toronto-based Four Seasons Hotels Inc. into the largest and most successful luxury hotel chain in the world. Several Four Seasons hotels receive North America's top rankings; 10 have received the American Automobile Association's coveted Five Diamond awards. Sharp credits his impeccable staff for the company's success, but friends and associates say that his leadership has made the difference. "Sharp's personal stamp becomes corporate mythology," says Four Seasons director Benjamin Swirsky.

Sharp's vision is that the Four Seasons name will be synonymous with carefully crafted elegance and service. This was apparent in his first hotel, built in Toronto in 1961. But the company vision became clear to Sharp in the early 1970s in a strained partnership with the Sheraton chain to build a hotel across from Toronto's city hall. The project grew to over 1,400 rooms and became the antithesis of Sharp's personal vision as a hotelier, so he quickly sold his stake. "Our involvement with the Sheraton crystallized what we wanted to build—medium-sized hotels which cater to the luxury market," says Sharp. As if energized by this experience,

Sharp moved quickly to build small but classy hotels across North America.

Sharp leads by example rather than by fiat, modelling his rigorous standards of quality and elegance to more than 9,000 employees at over 25 properties around the world. In spite of his penchant for details, the "Issy Sharp" style of leadership is more like a coach than a commander. "The way he pays attention to his people makes a tremendous difference," explains the general manager of Four Seasons's New York hotel. "If I have a problem, he won't just tell me how to solve it; he will make me part of the solution. He'll ask me, how do you think we can make this better?"

Further evidence of Sharp's leadership is his persistence and optimism through the ups and downs of the hotel business, including a tragic fire at Toronto's Inn on the Park in 1981. Says Sharp: "You need that, you might call it, fanatical belief that it will work. You must at points in time overcome a lot of scepticism and the naysayers and disbelievers. And on the downside if you risk and lose, it doesn't stop you. You're able to pick up the pieces and start over again."

Sources: P. King, "Building a Team the Sharp Way," *Canadian Business*, November 1990, pp. 96–101; I. Sharp, "Quality for All Seasons," *Canadian Business Review* 17 (Spring 1990), pp. 21–23; K. Foss, "Isadore Sharp," *Foodservice and Hospitality*, December 1989, pp. 20–30; J. DeMont, "Sharp's Luxury Empire," *Maclean's*, June 5, 1989, pp. 30–33; and D. Chong, "Power Is Proprietorship," *Canadian Business*, December 1988, p. 54.

Transformational leaders such as Timothy Eaton, H. R. McMillan, Elizabeth Arden, and Samuel Cunard dot the landscape of Canadian history. Today, transformational leaders may be found in all types of organizations, and at all levels of the enterprise. At the beginning of this chapter, we described how Terry Matthews's optimism and vision leveraged a unique idea into one of the largest high-technology companies in Canada. Perspective 14–3 describes how Isadore Sharp applies these same leadership skills.

Transformational versus transactional leadership

Transformational leadership is different from **transactional leadership.** Transactional leadership is about helping organizations more efficiently achieve their current objectives, such as by linking job performance to valued rewards and ensuring that employees have the resources needed to get the job done.[33] The contingency and behavioural theories described earlier adopt the transactional perspective because they focus on leader behaviours that improve employee

Transactional leadership
Helping organizations more efficiently achieve their current objectives, such as by linking job performance to valued rewards and ensuring that employees have the resources needed to get the job done.

performance and satisfaction. In contrast, transformational leaders change organizational objectives to ones that fit better with the surrounding environment.[34] This parallels the distinction between productivity and organizational effectiveness that we described in Chapter 1. Transactional leaders improve productivity; transformational leaders improve organizational effectiveness.

Organizations need both transactional and transformational leadership. Transactional leadership improves organizational efficiency, whereas transformational leadership steers organizations onto a better course of action. Unfortunately, too many leaders get trapped in the daily managerial activities that represent transactional leadership.[35] They lose touch with the transformational aspect of effective leadership. Without transformational leaders, organizations stagnate and eventually become seriously misaligned with their environments.

Are transformational leaders charismatic? This question has been the source of much controversy and confusion among leadership experts. Some writers think charisma is referent power that helps leaders build follower commitment to their goals. Others indicate that leaders are charismatic because they use the transformational behaviours to get results.[36] In our opinion, *charisma* is an overused term that adds little value to our understanding of transformational leadership. We must be careful not to view charisma as the "gee whiz" perspective in which charisma is everything wonderful about leaders that we don't understand.[37]

Features of transformational leadership

Although research continues to explore the dynamics of transformational leadership, four features seem to emerge from the literature. As illustrated in Exhibit 14–6, these features include creating a strategic vision, communicating the vision, modelling the vision, and building commitment toward the vision.

Creating a strategic vision

Transformational leaders are the brokers of dreams.[38] They help shape a strategic vision of a realistic and attractive future that draws employees together and focusses their energy toward a superordinate organizational goal.[39] Visions represent the substance of transformational leadership. They reflect a future for the company or work unit that is ultimately accepted and valued by organizational members. Strategic visions might originate with the leader, but they are just as likely to emerge from employees, clients, suppliers, or other constituents. They typically begin as abstract ideas that become progressively clearer through critical events and discussions with staff about strategic and operational plans.[40]

Communicating the vision

If vision is the substance of transformational leadership, then communicating that vision is the process. Effective leaders are able to communicate meaning and elevate the importance of the visionary goal to employees.[41] They frame their messages around a grand purpose with emotional appeal that captivates employees and other corporate stakeholders. George Cohen, the ebullient CEO of McDonald's Canada, used framing to achieve his vision of McDonald's in Russia. Cohen views his mission not as selling hamburgers in foreign countries, but as making the world a better place through "hamburger diplomacy."[42]

Elements of Transformational Leadership   Exhibit 14–6

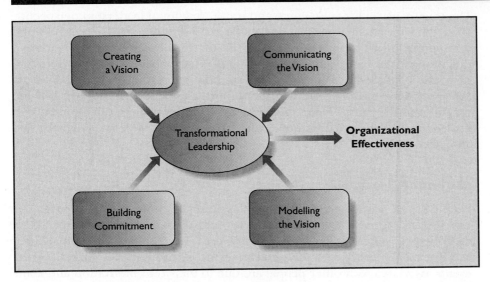

Transformational leaders also bring their visions to life through symbols, metaphors, stories, and other vehicles that transcend plain language.[43] Great business leaders have talked about "wild ducks," "laying pipe," and other phrases that symbolize their vision. Samuel Cunard built his Halifax-based Cunard Steamship Lines during the 1800s by constantly communicating his vision of an "ocean railway." This metaphor referred to his belief that ships could transport people across the Atlantic Ocean just as safely and on schedule as trains could transport people across Canada. The ocean railway metaphor reflected the values of safety and reliability that were easily accepted by employees during an age when ocean travel was a risky business.[44]

Modelling the vision

Transformational leaders not only talk about a vision, they enact it. They "walk the talk" by stepping outside the executive suite and doing things that symbolize the vision.[45] Walking the talk includes altering mundane events and decisions—meeting agendas, office locations, executive work schedules, wall hangings, and so on—so that they are consistent with the vision and its underlying values. Transformational leaders are reliable and persistent in their actions. They stay on course, thereby legitimizing the vision and providing further evidence that they can be trusted.[46] Walking the talk and staying on course are two important features of transformational leaders, because employees and other stakeholders are executive watchers who look for evidence that the leader's vision is sincere.[47]

Building commitment toward the vision

Transforming a vision into reality requires employee commitment. Transformational leaders build this commitment in several ways. Their words, symbols, and stories build a contagious enthusiasm that energizes people to adopt the vision as their own. Leaders demonstrate a "can do" attitude by enacting their vision and staying on course. Their persistence and consistency reflect an image of honesty, trust, and integrity. Finally, leaders build commitment by involving employees in the process of shaping the organization's vision.

The Romance Perspective of Leadership

The trait, behaviour, contingency, and transformational leadership perspectives make the basic assumption that leaders "make a difference." There is no doubt that people in leadership positions do influence the organization's success.[48] But as one writer has recently quipped, "it is easier to believe in leadership than to prove it."[49] Some leadership experts now suggest that three perceptual processes cause people to inflate the importance of leadership in explaining organizational events. These processes, collectively called the "romance of leadership," include attribution errors, stereotyping, and the need for situational control.

Attributing leadership

Actor-observer error
An attribution error whereby people tend to attribute their own actions more to external factors and the behaviour of others more to internal factors.

People have a strong need to attribute the causes of events around them so they can feel more confident about how to control them in the future. As we described in Chapter 7, the **actor–observer error** is a common perceptual bias in this attribution process. Actor–observer error is the tendency to believe that events associated with other people are due to their own motivation and ability rather than situational contingencies. In the context of leadership, the actor–observer error causes employees to believe that organizational events are due more to the motivation and ability of their leaders than to environmental conditions. Leaders are given credit or blame for the company's success or failure because employees do not readily see the external forces that also influence these events. Leaders reinforce this belief by taking credit for organizational successes.[50]

Stereotyping leadership

There is some evidence that people rely on leadership stereotypes to make sense of organizational events. Almost everyone has a set of shared expectations regarding what an effective leader should look and act like.[51] These preconceived ideas influence perceptions about whether someone is an effective leader. By relying on these stereotypes, employees and other stakeholders evaluate a leader's effectiveness more on his or her appearance and actions than on actual outcomes. Part of the reason why this occurs is that the outcome of a leader's actions may not be known for months or years. Consequently, employees depend on immediate information to decide whether the leader is effective. If the leader fits the mold, then employees are more confident that the leader is effective.

The need for situational control

A third perceptual distortion of leadership suggests that people want to believe leaders make a difference. There are two basic reasons for this belief.[52] First, leadership is a useful way for us to simplify life events. It is easier to explain organizational successes and failures in terms of the leader's ability than by analyzing a complex array of other forces. For example, there are usually many reasons why a company fails to change quickly enough in the marketplace, yet we tend to simplify this explanation down to the notion that the company president or some other corporate leader was ineffective. Second, there is a strong tendency in Canada and other Western societies to believe that life events are generated more from people than from uncontrollable natural forces.[53] This illusion of control is satisfied by believing that events result from the rational actions of leaders. In short, employees feel better believing that leaders make a difference, so they actively look for evidence that this is so.

The romance of leadership perspective questions the importance of leadership, but it also provides valuable advice to improve leadership effectiveness. This approach highlights the fact that leadership is a perception of followers as much as the actual behaviours and characteristics of people calling themselves leaders. Potential leaders must be sensitive to this fact, understand what followers expect, and act accordingly. Individuals who do not make an effort to fit leadership prototypes will have more difficulty bringing about necessary organizational change.[54]

Gender Issues in Leadership

Women are entering leadership positions in increasing numbers. Women represent 39 percent of all middle and upper managers in Canada, compared to just 16 percent in 1971. Some say that the 1990s is the decade of women in leadership.[55] This is certainly apparent by the appointments of female CEOs at General Motors of Canada, Xerox Canada, and the Export Development Corporation. These changes also provoke the question: Do women lead differently than men? As we see in Perspective 14–4, this is a question with many answers.

Several writers argue that women have a more interactive style that includes more people-oriented and participative leadership.[56] They suggest that women bring the "female qualities" of affiliation and attachment, cooperativeness, nurturance, and emotionality to their leadership roles. They further assert that these qualities make women particularly well suited to leadership roles at a time when companies are adopting a stronger emphasis on teams and employee involvement. These arguments are consistent with sex role stereotypes, namely that men tend to be more task oriented whereas women are more people oriented.

Are these stereotypes true? Do women adopt more people-oriented and participative leadership styles? The answer, according to recent literature reviews, is that these stereotypes of female leaders are mostly false. Although laboratory studies (in which people evaluate role plays or written cases) indicate that women are slightly more people oriented, this is probably because there is limited information about the leader, so people use sex stereotypes to fill in the missing information. In contrast, leadership studies in field settings have generally found that real male and female leaders do not differ in their levels of task-oriented or people-oriented leadership. The main explanation why men and women do not differ on these styles is that real-world jobs require similar behaviour from male and female job incumbents.[57] Cynthia Trudell, manager of the General Motors engine plant in St. Catherines, has applied both task-oriented and people-oriented styles to create a more entrepreneurial culture,

Perspective 14–4

When Women Lead

Danielle-Maude Gosselin still remembers her first job as a secretary two decades ago, seated at one of the rows of desks where she and her co-workers faced their boss. "It was grade school," recalls Gosselin. "To signal coffee break, he would rap the side of his desk with a pencil. I vowed I would never abuse a position of authority like that."

Gosselin has kept her word. Today, as president of the 45,000-member Quebec Civil Service, she applies a more participative leadership style than her predecessor. "She tends to delegate more and is always looking for a consensus," says Jean LaPorte, who works with Gosselin. "People are happy because they have an input into decisions. On the other hand, consensus takes longer."

With more women taking over positions of power in Canadian businesses and government, people are asking whether women lead differently than their male counterparts. Some female leaders claim that they are more people oriented and, like Gosselin, use a more participative decision-making style. Other female leaders claim that they are just as task oriented as men. Maureen Sabia, chairperson of the Ottawa-based Export Development Corporation, is one of them. She believes that men and women who have the same backgrounds and aspirations lead in basically the same way. "I don't think it's the job of managers to be caretakers, but to expect standards of their employees," Sabia explains. "Women will be promoted because they have spines of steel, not hearts of gold."

One thing that most women agree on about their leadership experience is that they must address the expectations and stereotypical assumptions that others have about them. Gillian Smart, who heads Beam of Canada, believes that female leaders must shrug off these stereotypes and adopt a leadership style that works best for the situation. "The challenge is not to put limitations on yourself or accept the limitations other people put on you," she advises.

Sources: K. Gay, "Female CEOs Take Hammer to the Glass Ceiling," *Financial Post,* April 16, 1994, p. S14; and M. Nemeth, "When the Boss Is a Woman," *Maclean's,* October 4, 1993, pp. 20–23.

---

one that will help the plant win more work from the parent company. She uses these styles because the situation demands it. "We have to earn our future," Trudell explains. "We have to be relevant to General Motors."[58]

One leadership style that women do adopt more readily than their male counterparts is participation. Scholars explain that women are possibly more participative because their upbringing has made them more egalitarian and less status oriented. There is also some evidence that women have somewhat better interpersonal skills than men, and this translates into their relatively greater use of the participative leadership style. Finally, women might be more participative because subordinates expect them to be so, based on their own sex stereotypes. If a female manager tries to be more autocratic, subordinates are more likely to complain (or use some other power base) because they expect the female manager to be participative.[59]

A disturbing finding in the gender and leadership research is that people evaluate female leaders slightly less favourably than equivalent male leaders, and this difference is almost completely due to sex stereotype bias. Specifically, women are evaluated negatively when they adopt a stereotypically male leadership style (i.e., autocratic) and occupy traditionally male-dominated positions. Men also tend to give female leaders lower ratings than do other women. These negative evaluations suggest that women "pay the price" for entering traditionally male leadership jobs and for adopting a male-stereotypic leadership style.[60]

As manager of General Motors' engine plant in St. Catherines, Ontario, Cynthia Trudell uses both task-oriented and people-oriented leadership styles to create a more entrepreneurial culture. "We have to be relevant to General Motors," Trudell explains.

Tibor Holley. Used with permission of The Globe & Mail.

It also lends further support to our earlier point on why women adopt a more participative style.

The debate regarding leadership differences between men and women isn't over yet. Meanwhile, we should be careful about perpetuating the apparently false assumption that women leaders are less task oriented or more people oriented. By holding these assumptions, many corporate decision makers have shifted women into staff roles—such as human resources, public relations, and customer service—and out of line management jobs that most frequently lead to senior management positions. Moreover, our implicit assumptions about how female leaders should act may lead to unfair negative evaluations of them under conditions in which the leader must adopt a stereotypically male style. This is consistent with our discussion in the previous section on the romance of leadership. Leaders must be sensitive to the fact that followers have expectations about how leaders should act, and negative evaluations may go to leaders who deviate from those expectations.

Chapter Summary

- Leadership is the process of having an incremental influence on other team members toward defined objectives. They use power and persuasion to motivate followers, and arrange the work environment so that they do the job more effectively.

- The trait perspective tries to identify the characteristics that distinguish effective leaders. Recent writing suggests that leaders have drive, leadership motivation, integrity, self-confidence, above-average intelligence, knowledge of the business, and a high self-monitoring personality. However, people with these features only have leadership potential.

- The behavioural perspective of leadership attempts to identify the behaviours used by effective leaders. Most researchers in this area distinguish people-oriented from task-oriented leadership. This perspective introduced the "hi–hi" leadership hypothesis, meaning that the most effective leaders exhibited high levels of both types of behaviours. This hypothesis has since been cast into doubt.

- The contingency perspective of leadership takes the view that effective leaders accurately diagnose the situation and adapt their style to fit that situation. The path-goal model is the prominent contingency theory that identifies four leadership styles and several contingencies relating to the characteristics of the employee and of the situation. The Leadership Grid®, a popular management training intervention, was born out of the behavioural approach, although its authors now claim more of a contingency approach.

- Transformational leaders develop a vision for the organization or work unit, inspire employees to strive for that vision, and give them a "can do" attitude that makes the vision achievable. The four basic elements of transformational leadership include creating a strategic vision, communicating the vision, modelling the vision, and building commitment toward the vision. This contrasts with transactional leadership, which involves linking job performance to valued rewards and ensuring that employees have the resources needed to get the job done. The contingency and behavioural perspectives adopt the transactional view of leadership.

- According to the romance perspective, people inflate the importance of leadership through attribution, stereotyping, and fundamental needs for human control.

- Women generally do not differ from men in the degree of people-oriented or task-oriented leadership. However, female leaders more often adopt a participative style. Recent reviews also suggest that people evaluate female leaders slightly less favourably than equivalent male leaders, but this is mainly due to sex stereotype biases.

Discussion Questions

1. **Northern Lights Industrials Ltd. is searching for a vice-president to lead the company's new products division. Describe four leadership traits that the company might want to consider when selecting job applicants for this position.**

2. **What leadership styles does the behavioural perspective identify, and what is the hypothesized relationship between these styles?**

3. **Your employees are skilled and experienced customer service representatives who perform nonroutine tasks, such as solving unique customer problems or special needs with the company's equipment. Use path-goal theory to identify the most appropriate leadership style(s) you should use in**

this situation. Be sure to fully explain your answer and discuss why other styles are inappropriate.

4. **What motivation theory is applied by path-goal theory? How?**

5. **Discuss the accuracy of the following statement: "Contingency theories don't work because they assume leaders can adjust their style to the situation. In reality, people have a preferred leadership style that they can't easily change."**

6. **What role does communication play in transformational leadership?**

7. **Why do people tend to give leaders too much credit or blame for organizational outcomes?**

8. **You hear two people debating the merits of women as leaders. One person claims that women make better leaders than do men because women are more sensitive to their employees' needs and involve them in organizational decisions. The other person counters that although these leadership styles may be increasingly important, most women have trouble gaining acceptance as leaders when they face tough situations in which a more autocratic style is required. Discuss the accuracy of the comments made in this discussion.**

Notes

1. A. Kainz, "Newbridge Touch Spans Globe," *Montreal Gazette,* June 19, 1993, pp. D1, D2; D. Girard, "High-Flying Newbridge Called a Global Success Story," *Toronto Star,* April 18, 1993, pp. H1, H5; J. Bagnall, "Smart, Scrappy, Innovative, and Profitable: Newbridge Networks Shows How It's Done," *Financial Times of Canada,* August 3, 1992, pp. 10–12; F. Misutka, "Newbridge: Choking on Its Own Success?" *Canadian Business* 63 (November 1990), pp. 90–95; and J. Stackhouse, "Second Empire," *Report on Business Magazine,* October 1990, pp. 72–77.

2. D. Miller, M. F. R. Ket de Vries, and J. M. Toulouse, "Top Executive Locus of Control and Its Relationship to Strategy-Making, Structure, and Environment," *Academy of Management Journal* 25 (1982), pp. 237–53; S. Withane, "Leadership Influence on Organizational Reorientations: A Strategic Choice Model," *Proceedings of the Annual ASAC Conference, Organizational Behaviour Division* 7, pt. 5 (1986), pp. 218–27; and P. Selznick, *Leadership in Administration* (Evanston, Ill.: Row, Peterson, 1957), p. 37.

3. C. A. Beatty, "Implementing Advanced Manufacturing Technologies: Rules of the Road," *Sloan Management Review,* Summer 1992, pp. 49–60; J. M. Howell and C. A. Higgins, "Champions of Technological Innovation," *Administrative Science Quarterly* 35 (1990), pp. 317–41; and M. N. Wexler, "Technology Champions: Complications of the Pro-Innovation Bias," *Innovating* 5 (in press).

4. J. M. Burns, *Leadership* (New York: Harper & Row, 1978), p. 2.

5. R. M. Stogdill, *Handbook of Leadership* (New York: The Free Press, 1974), Chapter 5.

6. The first six traits are described in S. A. Kirkpatrick and E. A. Locke, "Leadership: Do Traits Matter?" *Academy of Management Executive* 5 (May 1991), pp. 48–60.

7. J. M. Kouzes, and B. Z. Posner, *Credibility: How Leaders Gain and Lose It, Why People Demand It* (San Francisco: Jossey-Bass, 1993).

8. S. J. Zaccaro, R. J. Foti, and D. A. Kenny, "Self-Monitoring and Trait-Based Variance in Leadership: An Investigation of Leader Flexibility across Multiple Group Situations," *Journal of Applied Psychology* 76 (1991), pp. 308–15; G. H. Dobbins, W. S. Long, E. J. Dedrick, and T. C. Clemons, "The Role of Self-Monitoring and Gender on Leader Emergence: A Laboratory and Field Study," *Journal of Management* 16 (1990), pp. 609–18; and R. J. Ellis and R. S. Adamson, "Antecedents of Leadership Emergence," *Proceedings of the Annual ASAC Conference, Organizational Behaviour Division* 7, pt. 5 (1986), pp. 49–57.

9. R. S. Adamson, R. J. Ellis, G. Deszca, and T. F. Cawsey, "Self-Monitoring and Leadership Emergence," *Proceedings of the Annual ASAC Conference, Organizational Behaviour Division* 5, pt. 5 (1984), pp. 9–15.

10. G. A. Yukl, *Leadership in Organizations,* 2nd ed. (Englewood Cliffs, N.J.: Prentice Hall, 1989), pp. 74–80; R. Likert, *New Patterns of Management* (New York: McGraw-Hill, 1961); and E. A. Fleishman and E. F. Harris,

"Patterns of Leadership Behavior Related to Employee Grievances and Turnover," *Personnel Psychology* 15 (1962), pp. 43–56.

11. V. V. Baba, "Serendipity in Leadership: Initiating Structure and Consideration in the Classroom," *Human Relations* 42 (1989), pp. 509–25.

12. R. L. Kahn, "The Prediction of Productivity," *Journal of Social Issues* 12(2) (1956), pp. 41–49; and P. Weissenberg and M. H. Kavanagh, "The Independence of Initiating Structure and Consideration: A Review of the Evidence," *Personnel Psychology* 25 (1972), pp. 119–30.

13. Stogdill, *Handbook of Leadership,* Chapter 11.

14. D. Tjosvold, "Effects of Leader Warmth and Directiveness on Subordinate Performance on a Subsequent Task," *Journal of Applied Psychology* 69 (1984), pp. 222–32.

15. A. K. Korman, "Consideration, Initiating Structure, and Organizational Criteria—A Review," *Personnel Psychology* 19 (1966), pp 349–62; and E. A. Fleishman, "Twenty Years of Consideration and Structure," in *Current Developments in the Study of Leadership,* ed. E. A. Fleishman and J. C. Hunt (Carbondale, Ill.: Southern Illinois University Press, 1973), pp. 1–40.

16. L. L. Larson, J. G. Hunt, and R. N. Osborn, "The Great Hi–Hi Leader Behavior Myth: A Lesson from Occam's Razor," *Academy of Management Journal* 19 (1976), pp. 628–41; and A. K. Korman, "Consideration, Initiating Structure, and Organizational Criteria—A Review," *Personnel Psychology* 19 (1966), pp. 349–62.

17. G. N. Powell and D. A. Butterfield, "The 'High–High' Leader Rides Again!" *Group & Organization Studies* 9 (1984), pp. 437–50.

18. S. Kerr, C. A. Schriesheim, C. J. Murphy, and R. M. Stogdill, "Towards a Contingency Theory of Leadership Based upon the Consideration and Initiating Structure Literature," *Organizational Behavior and Human Performance* 12 (1974), pp. 62–82.

19. R. Tannenbaum and W. H. Schmidt, "How to Choose a Leadership Pattern," *Harvard Business Review,* May–June 1973, pp. 162–80.

20. M. G. Evans, "The Effects of Supervisory Behavior on the Path-Goal Relationship," *Organizational Behavior and Human Performance* 5 (1970), pp. 277–98; M. G. Evans, "Extensions of a Path-Goal Theory of Motivation," *Journal of Applied Psychology* 59 (1974), pp. 172–78; and R. J. House, "A Path-Goal Theory of Leader Effectiveness," *Administrative Science Quarterly* 16 (1971), pp. 321–38.

21. R. J. House and T. R. Mitchell, "Path-Goal Theory of Leadership," *Journal of Contemporary Business,* Autumn 1974, pp. 81–97.

22. J. C. Wofford and L. Z. Liska, "Path-Goal Theories of Leadership: A Meta-Analysis," *Journal of Management* 19 (1993), pp. 857–76; and J. Indvik, "Path-Goal Theory of Leadership: A Meta-Analysis," *Academy of Management Proceedings,* 1986, pp. 189–92.

23. R. T. Keller, "A Test of the Path-Goal Theory of Leadership with Need for Clarity as a Moderator in Research and Development Organizations," *Journal of Applied Psychology* 74 (1989), pp. 208–12.

24. R. J. House and M. L. Baetz, "Leadership: Some Empirical Generalizations and New Research Directions," *Research in Organizational Behavior* 1 (1979), pp. 341–423.

25. Wofford and Liska, "Path-Goal Theories of Leadership: A Meta-Analysis;" Yukl, *Leadership in Organizations,* pp. 102–4; and Indvik, "Path-Goal Theory of Leadership: A Meta-Analysis."

26. P. Hersey and K. H. Blanchard, *Management of Organizational Behavior: Utilizing Human Resources,* 5th ed. (Englewood Cliffs, N.J.: Prentice Hall, 1988).

27. W. Blank, J. R. Weitzel, and S. G. Green, "A Test of the Situational Leadership Theory," *Personnel Psychology* 43 (1990), pp. 579–97; and R. P. Vecchio, "Situational Leadership Theory: An Examination of a Prescriptive Theory," *Journal of Applied Psychology* 72 (1987), pp. 444–51.

28. F. E. Fiedler, *A Theory of Leadership Effectiveness* (New York: McGraw-Hill, 1967); and F. E. Fiedler and M. M. Chemers, *Leadership and Effective Management* (Glenview, Ill.: Scott, Foresman, 1974).

29. P. M. Podsakoff, B. P. Niehoff, S. B. MacKenzie, and M. L. Williams, "Do Substitutes Really Substitute for Leadership? An Empirical Examination of Kerr and Jermier's Situational Leadership Model," *Organizational Behavior and Human Decision Processes* 54 (1993), pp. 1–44.

30. R. R. Blake and A. A. McCanse, *Leadership Dilemmas—Grid Solutions* (Houston: Gulf Publishing Company, 1991); and R. R. Blake and J. S. Mouton, "Management by Grid Principles or Situationalism: Which?" *Group and Organization Studies* 7 (1982), pp. 207–10.

31. W. Trueman, "Born-Again Bureaucrats: Chief Bob Lunney," *Canadian Business* 64 (November 1991), pp. 64–71.

32. J. M. Howell and B. J. Avolio, "Transformational Leadership, Transactional Leadership, Locus of Control, and Support for Innovation: Key Predictors of Consolidated-Business-Unit Performance," *Journal of Applied Psychology* 78 (1993), pp. 891–902; J. A. Conger and R. N. Kanungo, "Perceived Behavioural Attributes of Charismatic Leadership," *Canadian Journal of Behavioural Science* 24 (1992), pp. 86–102; and J. Seltzer and B. M. Bass, "Transformational Leadership: Beyond Initiation and Consideration," *Journal of Management* 16 (1990), pp. 693–703.

33. B. J. Avolio and B. M. Bass, "Transformational Leadership, Charisma, and Beyond," in *Emerging Leadership Vistas*, ed. J. G. Hunt, H. P. Dachler, B. R. Baliga, and C. A. Schriesheim (Lexington, Mass.: Lexington Books, 1988), pp. 29–49.

34. W. Bennis and B. Nanus, *Leaders: The Strategies for Taking Charge* (New York: Harper & Row, 1985), p. 21; A. Zaleznik, *The Managerial Mystique* (New York: Harper & Row, 1989); and A. Zaleznik, "Managers and Leaders: Are They Different?" *Harvard Business Review* 55(5) (1977), pp. 67–78.

35. W. Bennis, *An Invented Life: Reflections on Leadership and Change*, (Reading, Mass.: Addison-Wesley, 1993); and D. Tjosvold and M. M. Tjosvold, *The Emerging Leader* (New York: Lexington, 1993), p. 25.

36. J. A. Conger and R. N. Kanungo, "Toward a Behavioral Theory of Charismatic Leadership in Organizational Settings," *Academy of Management Review* 12 (1987), pp. 637–47; and R. J. House, "A 1976 Theory of Charismatic Leadership," in *Leadership: The Cutting Edge*, ed. J. G. Hunt and L. L. Larson (Carbondale, Ill.: Southern Illinois University Press, 1977), pp. 189–207.

37. J. M. Burns, "Forward," in *Leadership: Multidisciplinary Perspectives*, ed. B. Kellerman (Englewood Cliffs, N.J.: Prentice Hall, 1984), p. vii.

38. L. Sooklal, "The Leader as a Broker of Dreams," 1985, Manchester Business School, Working Paper no. 108; and R. C. Hodgson, "Transformational Management," *Business Quarterly* 53(2) (Autumn 1988), pp. 17–20.

39. J. M. Stewart, "Future State Visioning—A Powerful Leadership Process," *Long Range Planning* 26 (December 1993), pp. 89–98; Bennis and Nanus, *Leaders*, pp. 27–33, 89; and J. M. Kouzes and B. Z. Posner, *The Leadership Challenge* (San Francisco: Jossey-Bass, 1987), Chapter 5.

40. T. J. Peters, "Symbols, Patterns, and Settings: An Optimistic Case for Getting Things Done," *Organizational Dynamics* 7 (Autumn 1978), pp. 2–23.

41. J. A. Conger, "Inspiring Others: The Language of Leadership," *Academy of Management Executive* 5 (February 1991), pp. 31–45.

42. L. Black, "Hamburger Diplomacy," *Report on Business Magazine* 5 (August 1988), pp. 30–36.

43. J. Pfeffer, "Management as Symbolic Action: The Creation and Maintenance of Organizational Paradigms," *Research in Organizational Behavior* 3 (1981), pp. 1–52; and Kouzes and Posner, *The Leadership Challenge*, pp. 118–21.

44. S. Franklin. *The Heroes: A Saga of Canadian Inspiration* (Toronto: McClelland and Stewart, 1967), p. 53.

45. N. H. Snyder and M. Graves, "Leadership and Vision," *Business Horizons* 37(1) (1994), pp. 1–7; P. Tommerup, "Stories About an Inspiring Leader," *American Behavioral Scientist* 33 (1990), pp. 374–85; and D. E. Berlew, "Leadership and Organizational Excitement," in *Organizational Psychology: A Book of Readings*, ed. D. A. Kolb, I. M. Rubin, and J. M. McIntyre (Englewood Cliffs, N.J.: Prentice Hall, 1974).

46. Bennis and Nanus, *Leaders*, pp. 43–55.

47. Kouzes and Posner, *Credibility: How Leaders Gain and Lose It, Why People Demand It.*

48. N. Weiner and T. A. Mahoney, "A Model of Corporate Performance as a Function of Environmental, Organizational, and Leadership Influences," *Academy of Management Journal* 24 (1981), pp. 453–70.

49. J. R. Meindl, "On Leadership: An Alternative to the Conventional Wisdom," *Research in Organizational Behavior* 12 (1990), pp. 159–203.

50. G. R. Salancik and J. R. Meindl, "Corporate Attributions as Strategic Illusions of Management Control," *Administrative Science Quarterly* 29 (1984), pp. 238–54; and J. M. Tolliver, "Leadership and Attribution of Cause: A Modification and Extension of Current Theory," *Proceedings of the Annual ASAC Conference, Organizational Behaviour Division* 4, pt. 5 (1983), pp. 182–91.

51. S. F. Cronshaw and R. G. Lord, "Effects of Categorization, Attribution, and Encoding Processes on Leadership Perceptions," *Journal of Applied Psychology* 72 (1987), pp. 97–106; J. W. Medcof and M. G. Evans, "Heroic or Competent? A Second Look," *Organizational Behavior and Human Decision Processes* 38 (1986), pp. 295–304; and A. de Carufel and S. C. Goh, "Implicit Theories of Leadership: Strategy, Outcome, and Precedent," *Proceedings of the Annual ASAC Conference, Organizational Behaviour Division* 8, pt. 5 (1987), pp. 47–55.

52. Meindl, "On Leadership: An Alternative to the Conventional Wisdom," p. 163.

53. J. Pfeffer, "The Ambiguity of Leadership," *Academy of Management Review* 2 (1977), pp. 102–12; and Yukl, *Leadership in Organizations*, pp. 265–67.

54. Cronshaw and Lord, "Effects of Categorization, Attribution, and Encoding Processes on Leadership Perceptions," pp. 104–5.

55. J. Naisbett and P. Aburdene, *Magatrends 2000* (New York: Morrow, 1990).

56. S. H. Appelbaum and B. T. Shapiro, "Why Can't Men Lead Like Women?" *Leadership and Organization Development Journal* 14 (1993), pp. 28–34; J. B. Rosener, "Ways Women Lead," *Harvard Business Review* 68 (November–December 1990), pp. 119–25; and J. Grant, "Women as Managers: What They Can Offer to Organizations," *Organization Dynamics*, Winter 1988, pp. 56–63.

57. G. N. Powell, "One More Time: Do Female and Male Managers Differ?" *Academy of Management Executive* 4 (August 1990), pp. 68–75; K. K. Lush and M. J. Withey, "Gender as a Moderator in the Path-Goal Theory of

Leadership," *Proceedings of the Annual ASAC Conference, Organizational Behaviour Division* 11, pt. 5 (1990), pp. 140–49; and G. H. Dobbins and S. J. Platts, "Sex Differences in Leadership: How Real Are They?" *Academy of Management Review* 11 (1986), pp. 118–27.

58. T. Pritchard, "Employees Try to Rev Up Threatened GM Complex," *Globe & Mail*, August 5, 1994, pp. B1, B16.

59. A. H. Eagly and B. T. Johnson, "Gender and Leadership Style: A Meta-Analysis," *Psychological Bulletin* 108 (1990), pp. 233–56.

60. A. H. Eagly, M. G. Makhijani, and B. G. Klonsky, "Gender and the Evaluation of Leaders: A Meta-Analysis," *Psychological Bulletin* 111 (1992), pp. 3–22; and R. L. Kent and S. E. Moss, "Effects of Sex and Gender Role on Leader Emergence," *Academy of Management Journal* 37 (1994), pp. 1335–46.

Chapter Case

Leadership in Whose Eyes?

Two senior managers—John Waisglass and Sammi Intar—are discussing Tegan Upton, the company president who joined the organization last year. Waisglass says: "I think Upton is great. She has given us a clearer sense of what we want to be as an organization. I feel much better about working here since she took over. Haven't you noticed the difference? Upton is visible and approachable. She's listened to everyone's ideas and pulled them into something that we can aim for. Upton also does what she says. Remember in one of our first meetings with her that we agreed to spend more time with our clients? Soon after, Upton was personally calling on clients and sending production people out with sales staff to hear about any customer complaints. I was sceptical at first, thinking that Upton's actions were temporary. But she's maintained this focus. And I now hear employees throughout the company using that buzz word of hers— "reality-based action"—meaning that our actions must be consistent with the customer's needs. She's great!"

Sammi Intar replies: "I don't know, John. I want to believe that Upton is a great leader for this company, but I can't. She doesn't look the part. Just listen to her. She sounds like Mickey Mouse with a cold. And the way she walks into a room doesn't look to me like someone who should be running a $30 million business. I've heard a few clients notice this—not many, mind you, just a few. They seem to shrug it off, pointing to some good things that our company has done for them since she took over. But my clients can go elsewhere if they have to. For me, this company is a career. Even though Upton has been doing some good things and our results have been good, I get very concerned about the future with her in charge."

Discussion Question

John Waisglass and Sammi Intar are relying on two different perspectives of leadership in their judgment of Tegan Upton. Describe these two perspectives, using specific comments to illustrate the features of each model.

Experiential Exercise

Leadership Diagnostic Analysis

Purpose: To help students learn about the different path-goal leadership styles and when to apply each style.

Instruction: The exercise begins with students individually writing down two incidents in which someone had been an effective manager or leader over them. The leader and situation might be from work, a sports team, a student work group, or any other setting where leadership might emerge. For example, students might describe how their supervisor in a summer job pushed them to reach higher performance goals than they would have done otherwise. Each incident should state the actual behaviours that the leader used, not just general statements (e.g., "My boss sat down with me and we agreed on specific targets and deadlines, then he said several times over the next few weeks that I was capable of reaching those goals.") Each incident only requires two or three sentences.

After everyone has written their two incidents, the instructor will form small groups (typically between 4 or 5 students). Each team will answer the following questions for each incident presented in that team:

1. Which path-goal theory leadership style(s) (i.e., directive, supportive, participative, or achievement-oriented) did the leader apply in this incident?

2. Ask the person who wrote the incident about the conditions that made this leadership style (or these styles, if more than one was used) appropriate in this situation? The team should list these contingency factors clearly and, where possible, connect them to the contingencies described in path-goal theory. (Note: the team might identify path-goal leadership contingencies that are not described in the book. These, too, should be noted and discussed.)

After the teams have diagnosed the incidents, each team will describe to the entire class its most interesting incident as well as its diagnosis of that incident. Other teams will critique the diagnosis. Any leadership contingencies not mentioned in the textbook should also be presented and discussed.

PART

Organizational Processes

Organizational Change and Development

Learning Objectives

After reading this chapter, you should be able to:

Identify five prominent forces for change in Canadian business.

Describe six reasons why people resist organizational change.

Diagram force field analysis.

Discuss five strategies to minimize resistance to change.

Describe how to diffuse successful organizational change projects.

Outline the action research approach to organization development.

Compare incremental with quantum organizational change.

Discuss four ethical dilemmas facing organization development.

Chapter Outline

Forces for Change.

Resistance to Change.

Managing Organizational Change.

Organization Development.

Selected Organization Development Interventions.

Effectiveness of Organization Development.

Paul Orenstein. Used with permission.

Until recently, Schneider Corp. was suffering from intense price wars, the result of a consumer trend away from red meat consumption. Profits at the Kitchener, Ontario, meat processing company were also hammered by an ill-fated corporate diversification. Cost cutting and technological change pummelled employee morale, leading to the first labour strike in the company's 100-year history. "We had to do something, fast," says Schneider CEO Douglas Dodds. "There simply wasn't the opportunity to dabble with alternatives until we found a formula that worked."

One part of Schneider's survival plan was to introduce poultry and low-fat products that fit changing consumer tastes. Another was to dramatically improve productivity through employee involvement, just-in-time, and other value-added management practices. Unfortunately, senior management failed in its first attempt to change the company.

"We fell flat on our face," Dodds recalls. "We failed because we did not recognize the difficulty in transferring the concepts from the classroom to the shop floor." Employees resisted because they saw the change effort as just another management gimmick that would increase workloads and reduce job security. Supervisors balked because they believed the change would threaten their hard-earned status and maybe their jobs.

Senior management began the second change effort with a pilot project in the and were told they would not lose their jobs due to continuous improvement. Supervisors were also told that their jobs would change, but would not be lost. Productivity shot up as smokehouse employees embraced the change effort. More important, they soon became disciples, spreading the gospel of value-added management among co-workers throughout the plant.

Eighteen months later, with the aid of training and communication, more than half of the employees at the Kitchener plant were practising value-added management. Labour and material costs at Schneider Corp. fell by $8 million. Inventory levels were down by over $6 million, customer returns fell by 45 percent, lost-time accident claims dropped by 65 percent, and worker morale increased to levels not seen in many years.[1]

Organizations live in a sea of change. Schneider Corp. transformed its traditional structure because of changing consumer tastes and increasing competition. Marine Atlantic, Standard Aero, Canadian Airlines International, and many other organizations described earlier in this book have survived and prospered by changing in the face of new environmental conditions. Unfortunately, Leigh Instruments, Massey Ferguson, AES Electronics, Lavelin Industries, and many other Canadian companies did not adapt quickly enough.

This chapter examines the effective management of change in organizations. We begin by considering some of the more significant forces for organizational change and the forces resisting change. Next, a general model is presented that considers these opposing forces and proposes ways to effectively manage the change process. The latter part of this chapter introduces the field of organization development (OD). In particular, we review the OD process, specific OD interventions, and an assessment of OD effectiveness.

Forces for Change

Organizations are open systems that need to remain compatible with their external environments. But these environments are constantly changing, so organizations must recognize these shifts and respond accordingly to survive and remain effective. Successful organizations monitor their environments and take appropriate steps to maintain a compatible fit with the new external conditions. Rather than resisting change, employees in successful companies embrace change as an integral part of organizational life.[2] Over the next few pages, we describe a few conditions (there are many others) that have had a profound influence on Canadian businesses over the past decade or will force them to change in the near future.

Population changes

Canadians are significantly different today than in 1900.[3] At the beginning of this century, one-third of the population was under 15 years of age and only 5 percent was over 65. Life expectancy ran to about 50 years. Today, more than 12

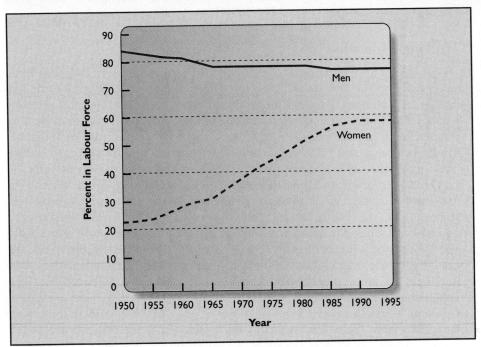

Source: Statistics Canada, The Labour Force (Ottawa: Minister of Supply and Services Canada, various years).

percent of Canadians are over 65, and this will rise to between 25 and 30 percent by the year 2040. Meanwhile, life expectancy has risen to more than 75 years.

In 1900, most Canadians lived on farms and very few advanced beyond primary school. Now, 80 percent of us live in cities and over 40 percent have received some post-secondary education. Canada is now a much more culturally diverse society. Immigrants arriving in Canada up to the 1950s came mainly from Europe. Today, they come from virtually every part of the world. Another dramatic change is the percentage of women who have entered the work force. As depicted in Exhibit 15–1, only 23 percent of working-age women participated in the labour force in 1950. This number has now risen to almost 60 percent. At the same time, the male participation rate has dropped from 84 percent in 1950 to 76 percent today.

These population and labour force changes have several implications for organizational behaviour. With a more culturally diverse work force, companies need to introduce new management practices to improve communication and minimize dysfunctional conflict. The emerging work force requires different contractual arrangements, including more flexible work hours and reward systems that fit more diverse needs. Employee involvement has become more common in response to the increasing levels of employee education. Team dynamics and perceptions of women in society have been altered as more women take on paid employment. And, as Schneider Corp. discovered, equally significant organizational changes are necessary to adapt to the changing demography and preferences of consumers.

Changing legislation

New government legislation is another source of significant organizational change. During the late 1970s, the energy industry was jolted by the Canadian government's National Energy Program. In the 1980s, the trucking industry had to adapt quickly to deregulation. In the 1990s, telephone companies have reorganized to prepare for deregulation of the telecommunications industry.[4] Other recent legislation dealing with the environment and human rights issues is forcing companies to change their production and employment practices.

The North American Free Trade Agreement (NAFTA) has perhaps had the most dramatic effect on Canadian businesses in recent years. Consider the experience of CCL Industries Inc. Before free trade, the Toronto-based company had a booming business producing labels and containers in Canada for large U.S. manufacturers of brand-name products such as Javex and Arrid. But under free trade, many of these firms are serving the Canadian market from their U.S. facilities, thereby threatening CCL's survival. Fortunately, CCL's management anticipated these environmental changes by acquiring competing firms and expanding operations worldwide. Says CCL's president and chief executive officer: "Free trade was the worst and best thing that ever happened to us. It forced us to become more focussed and much more aggressive to survive."[5]

Increasing competition

Partly as a result of recent legislation, most Canadian businesses are experiencing higher levels of competition, both at home and abroad. We are moving toward a global marketplace, so competitors are just as likely to be located in Japan, Germany, Mexico, or the United States than somewhere else in Canada.[6] Emerging trading blocs in Europe, Asia, and other areas of the world add to the intense competitive pressures Canadian firms now face. "It's a whole new, aggressive world out there," says Arthur Soler, president of Neilson-Cadbury, Canada's leading candy manufacturing company. "Change—rapid change—has become the way of life."[7]

Global competition extends to the public sector, where cities and higher levels of government enter international battles to expand their corporate tax base. Winnipeg 2000, the city's economic development team, is constantly marketing the community's advantages such as central location, low costs, and competitive tax rates. Moncton has also mounted a formidable marketing team to help the New Brunswick city survive and prosper in this changing world of economic development.[8]

Technological changes

Technology is changing offices and production facilities at a dizzying speed. Clerical, professional, and management employees have witnessed the introduction of microcomputers, electronic mail systems, facsimile (fax) machines, advanced telephone switching systems, and other electronic gadgetry.[9]

Computer-aided design and manufacturing (CAD/CAM) systems have transformed many production processes. In doing so, they have significantly reduced employment levels and changed the skill requirements of remaining employees.[10] For example, Weston Bakeries has changed its Longueuil, Quebec, operation into the most technically advanced bakery in North America. As part of this transformation, 100 of the 350 employees have been trained in computerized manufacturing methods, while the others have been transferred or laid off.[11] In effect, the new technology requires a relatively small team of highly skilled employees instead of a much larger number of low-skilled workers.

Some sociologists believe that technological change reduces employee skill requirements.[12] This is sometimes true, but recent studies suggest that job quality typically improves with technological change.[13] In fact, one government report concluded that Canadian employees will require continuous skill renewal as they experience more frequent career changes resulting from future technological change and global competition.[14]

Mergers and acquisitions

Dozens of mergers and acquisitions have been consummated in Canada over the past few years, including Rogers Communications with Maclean Hunter, Royal Bank with Royal Trust, Saint John Shipbuilding with Halifax-Dartmouth Industries Ltd., Canada Post with Purolator, and Molson Breweries with Carling O'Keefe. These corporate marriages often produce traumatic changes for employees, because they need to adjust to new corporate practices and philosophies.

Corporate mergers increase the threat of job loss or status. For instance, when Lloyds Bank Canada acquired Continental Bank, productivity in both organizations plummetted as employees spent more time talking about what might happen to them. Some employees even admitted going out of their way to make things go wrong just to prove that the deal would not work![15] Overall, mergers and acquisitions are powerful organizational stressors requiring organizational change strategies to minimize employee resistance and health problems.[16]

Resistance to Change

In the opening story to this chapter, we saw how supervisors and employees at Schneider Corp. initially resisted senior management's efforts to introduce value-added management practices. No matter how noble the cause, most organizational change efforts are resisted by employees, managers, clients, or other stakeholders.[17] Resistance to change can take many forms: passive noncompliance, complaints, absenteeism, turnover, or collective action (e.g., strikes, walkouts). Resistance is often an important symptom that problems exist, but this is even more reason to understand why resistance occurs and to prevent it wherever possible. Resistance is not an irrational act; rather, it stems from a logical motivation to maintain the status quo rather than comply with new behaviour patterns. The main reasons why people typically resist change are shown in Exhibit 15–2 and discussed in the following list:[18]

Exhibit 15–2   **Forces Resisting Organizational Change**

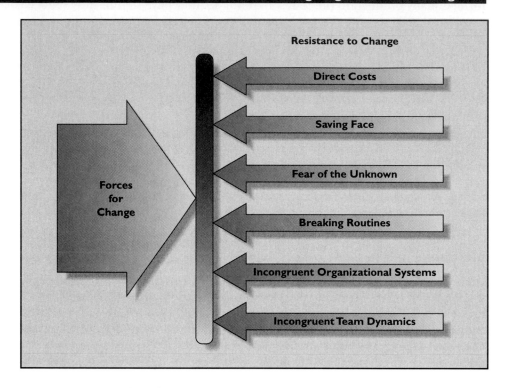

- *Direct costs*—People resist change whenever they believe the new state of affairs will have higher direct costs or lower benefits than the existing situation. At Schneider Corp., employees initially resisted change because they believed that it might increase their workload and reduce job security. At Campbell Soup Ltd. and Bow Valley Energy (both described in Chapter 12), employees resisted change because they believed that they would lose power over the information that maintained their status in the organization.

- *Saving face*—Some people resist change as a political strategy to "prove" that the decision is wrong or that the change agent is incompetent. For example, senior management in a manufacturing firm bought a computer other than the system recommended by the information systems department. Soon after the system was in place, several information systems employees let minor implementation problems escalate to demonstrate that senior management had made a poor decision.

- *Fear of the unknown*—Change is resisted because it involves facing uncertainty. Employees might worry about lacking the necessary skills or losing valued work arrangements after the transition.

- *Breaking routines*—Change necessarily involves abandoning some habits and learning new ones. Unfortunately, people are creatures of habit. They like to maintain routine role patterns that make life more predictable and less troublesome.[19] Consequently, many people resist organizational changes that force them to abandon old ways and require investing time and energy learning new role patterns.

- *Incongruent organizational systems*—Rewards, selection, training, and other control systems ensure that employees maintain desired role patterns. Yet the organizational systems that maintain stability also discourage employees from adopting new ways. The implication, of course, is that organizational systems must be altered to fit the desired change. Unfortunately, control systems can be difficult to change, particularly when they have supported role patterns that worked well in the past.[20]

- *Incongruent team dynamics*—As we learned in Chapter 10, work teams develop and enforce conformity to a set of norms that guide behaviour. However, conformity to existing team norms may discourage employees from accepting organizational change. Change agents need to recognize and alter team norms that conflict with the desired changes.

Managing Organizational Change

Now that we know why employees resist organizational change, how do change agents overcome these barriers? The answer to this question comes from Kurt Lewin, a leading behavioural scientist in the 1950s, who introduced a useful change model called **force field analysis.**

As shown in Exhibit 15–3, one side of Lewin's force field model represents the *driving forces* that push organizations toward a new state of affairs. The other side represents the *restraining forces* that try to maintain the status quo. Stability occurs when the driving and restraining forces are roughly in equilibrium, that is, they are of approximately equal strength in opposite directions. Change occurs when the driving forces are stronger than the restraining forces. This relatively simple perspective of organizational change provides a very useful way to diagnose the situation before beginning the change process.[21]

The central idea behind Lewin's model is that effective change begins by **unfreezing** the current situation and ends by **refreezing** it. Unfreezing means that the change agent produces a disequilibrium between the driving and restraining forces. Refreezing introduces systems and conditions that reinforce and maintain the new role patterns and prevent the organization from slipping back into the old way of doing things.

Unfreezing the status quo

Unfreezing occurs by strengthening the driving forces, weakening the restraining forces, or doing some combination of both. Change agents are often tempted to strengthen the driving forces alone, such as by threatening employees who do not actively support the change effort. However, this strategy tends to be ineffective, because the restraining forces often adjust to counterbalance the driving forces, rather like the coils of a mattress. The harder management pushes for new procedures without employee acceptance, the stronger employees tend to resist these changes. This antagonism threatens the change effort by producing tension and conflict within the organization.

Although change agents often need to increase driving forces (or simply make these forces better known to employees), they should mainly focus on reducing the restraining forces. This occurs by altering the four conditions for

Force field analysis
A model that helps change agents diagnose the forces that drive and restrain proposed organizational change.

Unfreezing
The first part of the change process whereby the change agent produces a disequilibrium between the driving and restraining forces. It typically includes making people aware of the need for change and providing them with the necessary skills, knowledge, and resources to execute the new role patterns.

Refreezing
The introduction of systems and conditions that reinforce and maintain the new role patterns and prevent the organization from slipping back into the old way of doing things.

Exhibit 15–3   **Lewin's Force Field Analysis**

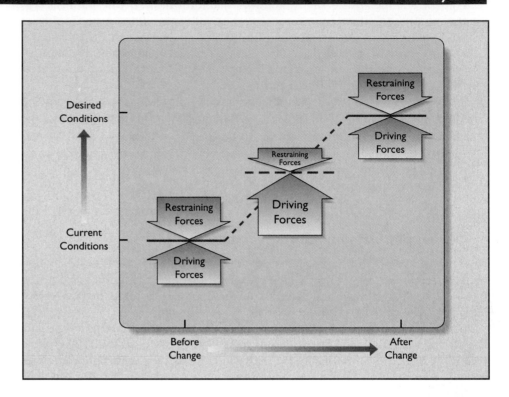

individual performance—ability, motivation, role perceptions, and situational contingencies (see Chapter 2)—in favour of the change effort. Specifically, the change agent tries to motivate people to support the change effort, make them aware of their new roles, and provide the skills, knowledge, and resources needed to execute those role patterns.

Exhibit 15–4 outlines six ways to overcome employee resistance. Communication, training, employee involvement, and stress management try to reduce the restraining forces and, if feasible, should be attempted first.[22] However, negotiation and coercion are necessary for people who will clearly lose something from the change and when the speed of change is critical.

Communication

Although time consuming and costly, communicating the change effort is an important strategy to minimize resistance. When employees are continually informed, they have less fear of the unknown and are more likely to develop team norms more consistent with the change effort.[23] MDS Laboratories relied on extensive communication to minimize employee resistance. In particular, company president Allan Torrie visited dozens of MDS locations throughout Ontario to explain the changes and listen to employee concerns. "It is essential that people feel connected to the architecture of change," explains Torrie.[24]

Methods for Dealing with Resistance to Change			Exhibit 15–4
Strategy	**Example**	**When Used**	**Problems**
Communication	Telephone "hotline" keeps employees informed of the change	• When employees don't understand the need for change and how it will affect them	• Time consuming and potentially costly
Training	Employees learn how to work in teams as company adopts a team-based structure	• When employees need to break old routines and adopt new role patterns	• Time consuming and potentially costly
Employee involvement	Company forms task force to recommend new customer service practices	• When the change effort needs more employee commitment, some employees need to save face, and/or employee ideas would improve decisions about the change strategy	• Very time consuming; might also lead to conflict and poor decisions if employees' interests are incompatible with organizational needs
Stress management	Employees attend sessions to discuss their worries about the change	• When communication, training, and involvement do not sufficiently ease employee worries	• Time consuming and potentially expensive; some methods may not reduce stress for all employees
Negotiation	Employees agree to replace strict job categories with multiskilling in return for increased job security	• When employees will clearly lose something of value from the change and would not otherwise support the new conditions; also necessary when the company must change quickly	• May be expensive, particularly if other employees want to negotiate their support; also tends to produce compliance but not commitment to the change
Coercion	Company president tells managers to "get on board" the change or leave	• When other strategies are ineffective and the company needs to change quickly	• Can lead to more subtle forms of resistance, as well as long-term antagonism with the change agent

Training

In most change efforts, employees need to learn new skills and knowledge, so training is an essential ingredient in the change management strategy. Training is time consuming, but it lets people learn new role patterns more easily and, consequently, tends to minimize resistance due to the problem of breaking routines. As Perspective 15–1 describes, Winnipeg-based Reimer Express Enterprises Ltd. has invested time and money training employees in quality management so that everyone is able to fit into the trucking firm's new approach to doing business.

Employee involvement

Employee involvement is a powerful way to reduce resistance where there are potential concerns about saving face and fear of the unknown.[25] It also helps companies make better decisions about the type of change needed. Bell Canada's Zero Waste program (described in Chapter 2) relied on employee involvement through a task force to gain employee acceptance. Similarly, the Workers Compensation Board of Ontario relied on two action planning

Perspective 15–1

Revving Up Change through Training at Reimer Express Enterprises Ltd.

With sales exceeding $250 million, Reimer Express is one of Canada's largest trucking companies. The Winnipeg-based transportation company employs 1,000 people who drive 1,400 vehicles and handle half a million shipments each year. Not many of those packages go astray. When one does and a delivery is late, Reimer refunds the shipper's money in full.

Reimer has been able to succeed in this intensely competitive business by constantly training employees throughout the organization in quality management practices. This training also enables the company to bring about meaningful change even though its employees are located in facilities across the country.

Every two months, supervisors use videotapes and written materials to teach employees about one of the company's eight work processes. This training shows employees how the quality process is relevant to their jobs, and how their jobs fit into the entire business process. Supervisors spend two days in the company's

management course to focus their roles in working with employees and learning about quality management. Reimer also measures its quality performance and regularly communicates this information to employees through newsletters.

Before Reimer introduced quality management, a new employee would have watched a long-time employee for a few days. Now, new employees sit through training videos showing exactly what needs to be done in their jobs. Each new staff member is also attached to a current employee "sponsor" who ensures that he or she understands the importance of customer service.

Employee training at Reimer Express constantly reminds employees why it is so important to give customers error-free service. It is also an important reason why the company has been able to apply quality management practices where other organizations have failed.

Sources: Based on S. Fife, "The Total Quality Muddle," *Report on Business Magazine*, November 1992, pp. 64–74; C. R. Farquhar and C. G. Johnston, *Total Quality Management: A Competitive Imperative* (Ottawa: Conference Board of Canada, 1990); and J. Lorinc, "Dr. Deming's Traveling Quality Show," *Canadian Business* 63 (September 1990), pp. 38–42.

committees to design and minimize employee resistance to a new model for managing WCB cases. Employees gained acceptance to the radical change in WCB case management because their peers were involved in the process.[26]

Stress management

Stress is a common problem in organizational change, particularly during mergers and other organizationwide transformations.[27] The stress and anxiety that result from these changes can increase employee resistance, turnover, and time required to adjust to the new conditions. Communication and employee involvement can reduce some of the tension, but companies also need to introduce stress management practices to help employees cope with the changes.

Labatt's Breweries recognized the need for stress management during a recent corporate restructuring. "[The restructuring] certainly was not an easy process for anyone," recalls the general manager of Labatt's Newfoundland operations. "However, the company had systems in place from day one to help people cope with the stress of the change." These systems included "rap sessions" in which employees shared their thoughts and concerns with Labatt's senior managers.[28] Perspective 15–2 describes how Beaty Products Ltd. applied similar practices to reduce employee stress when the Canadian office products manufacturer was sold to a Japanese conglomerate.

Perspective 15–2

Beaty Products Ltd. Minimizes the Stress of Merger-Related Change

In June 1989, employees at Beaty Products Ltd. learned that the family-owned Canadian office products manufacturer would be sold to a Japanese conglomerate. With 1,000 employees and $122 million in revenues, Beaty needed investment for new technology, and the Japanese firm was willing to inject the needed capital to help Beaty survive.

Senior management knew that employees would experience stress from the merger, so the company hired consultants to help Beaty's supervisors understand merger-related stress and how employees can cope with it.

Beaty held weekly "merger raps" in its headquarters and main plant. These voluntary sessions, held during lunch, provided a forum in which people could share

their feelings about the merger. Many employees used the sessions as an opportunity to describe the emotional impact the merger was having on them, their co-workers, and their families. Others sat and listened but felt better knowing that their emotional reactions were shared.

Beaty's senior managers realized that communication about the merger would ease some of the stress, but they were troubled by the fact that they could make few promises about the future until the merger was completed. However, the company provided listening-skills training to its supervisors. These skills were useful during the monthly departmental meetings in which employees discussed the proposed merger.

Source: Based on M. L. Marks, "Merger Management HR's Way," *HRMagazine*, May 1991, pp. 61–66.

Negotiation

Communication, training, employee involvement, and stress management won't necessarily overcome resistance among those who will clearly lose out from the change activity. It may, therefore, be necessary to negotiate certain benefits to offset some of the cost of the change. When GE Capital Fleet Services in Richmond Hill, Ontario, recently removed two levels of management, the company faced serious resistance by supervisors worried that they would lose their status. After several months, senior management negotiated with the supervisors and eventually created an intermediate manager position to overcome this resistance. "In our case, the decision to delayer was non-negotiable," recalls a GE Capital manager. "As time was subsequently to show, however, we should have been prepared to negotiate on the number of layers to be eliminated."[29]

Coercion

Occasionally, coercion may be required to overcome resistance and gain sufficient compliance to organizational change. For instance, when Standard Aero introduced total quality management during the early 1990s, president Bob Hamaberg threatened to fire senior managers who were resisting these changes. Some eventually supported the change effort; others did not and were dismissed. "You must have senior management commitment," Hamaberg says bluntly. "I had some obstacles. I removed the obstacles."[30] As a form of punishment, coercion may produce an adverse emotional reaction to management and the organization (see Chapter 4). Consequently, it should be used only when speed is essential and other tactics are ineffective.

Bell Canada's Zero Waste program cut waste paper and other garbage by more than 90 percent at many sites. Zero Waste minimized resistance to change through employee involvement, such as this task force at Bell Canada's Fieldway building in Etobicoke, Ontario.

Courtesy of Bell Canada.

Refreezing the desired conditions

After unfreezing and changing the previous conditions, we need to refreeze them so that people do not slip back into their previous work practices.[31] Refreezing creates organizational systems and team dynamics that maintain the desired changes. For example, efforts to introduce employee involvement are likely to fail unless organizational structures and procedures are made more compatible with this intervention.[32] Reward systems must be altered to reinforce the new behaviours and attitudes rather than previous practices. Information and support must be continuously transmitted to reaffirm the new practices. New feedback systems must be introduced and existing ones recalibrated to focus on the new priorities and performance goals.

Pratt & Whitney Canada replaced old performance measures to refreeze changes at its jet engine plant in Longueuil, Quebec.[33] The plant previously manufactured many units of the same engine and measured performance in terms of production efficiency, such as the number of units produced per hour. Now the plant uses a short-run synchronous process (i.e., making only a few units of many types of engines) that is more flexible to the customer's needs. This requires more emphasis on customer needs and minimizing inventory costs, so the company introduced new measures and rewards around these factors rather than the previous measures of production efficiency.

Diffusion of change

In the opening vignette to this chapter, Schneider Corp. learned how to implement change more effectively by starting with a pilot project and later diffusing this experience to other areas of the company. Recent evidence suggests that successful organizational transformations usually begin with pilot projects, because this approach is more flexible and less risky than centralized organizationwide programs.[34]

But how do we successfully diffuse the results of the pilot project? Richard Walton, who has studied the diffusion of work restructuring programs at Alcan Aluminum and other companies, offers several recommendations for the effective diffusion of change.[35] Generally, diffusion is more likely to occur when the pilot project is successful within one or two years and receives visibility (e.g., favourable news media coverage). These conditions tend to increase top management support for the change program and persuade other managers to introduce the change effort in their operations. Successful diffusion also depends on labour union support and active involvement in the diffusion process.

Another important condition is that the diffusion strategy isn't described too abstractly, because this makes the instructions too vague to introduce the change elsewhere. Neither should the strategy be stated too precisely, because it might not seem relevant to other areas of the organization. Finally, without producing excessive turnover in the pilot group, people who have worked under the new system should be moved to other areas of the organization. These employees bring their knowledge and commitment of the change effort to work units that have not yet experienced it.

Organization Development

Force field analysis and the diffusion of change explain the main dynamics of change that occur every day in organizations. However, there is an entire field of study, called **organization development (OD),** that tries to understand how to manage planned change in organizations. OD is a planned systemwide effort, managed from the top with the assistance of a change agent, that uses behavioural science knowledge to improve organizational effectiveness.[36] OD relies on many of the organizational behaviour concepts described in this book, such as team dynamics, perceptions, job design, and conflict management. OD also takes a systems perspective, because it recognizes that organizations have many interdependent parts and must adapt to their environments. Thus, OD experts try to ensure that all parts of the organization are compatible with the change effort, and that the change activities help the company fit its environment.[37]

Virtually all OD activities rely on **action research** as the primary blueprint for planned change. As depicted in Exhibit 15–5, action research is a data-based, problem-oriented process that diagnoses the need for change, introduces the OD intervention, and then evaluates and stabilizes the desired changes.[38]

Action research is a highly participative process, involving the client throughout the various stages.[39] It typically includes an action research team consisting of people both affected by the organizational change and having the power to facilitate it. This participation is a fundamental philosophy of OD, but it also increases commitment to the change process and provides valuable information to conduct organizational diagnosis and evaluation. Let's look at the main elements of the action research process.

The client–consultant relationship

Organizational change requires a **change agent**—a manager, consultant, labour union official, or anyone else who possesses enough knowledge and power to guide and facilitate the change effort. External consultants with special training in the behavioural sciences and previous experience in OD techniques are sometimes hired as change agents. A few large Canadian firms employ internal

Organization development (OD)
A planned systemwide effort, managed from the top with the assistance of a change agent, that uses behavioural science knowledge to improve organizational effectiveness.

Action research
A data-based, problem-oriented process that focusses on organizational diagnosis and action planning, implementation, and evaluation of an intervention to the system involved.

Change agent
A person who possesses enough knowledge and power to guide and facilitate the change effort. This may be a member of the organization or an external consultant.

Exhibit 15–5 The Action Research Approach to Organization Development

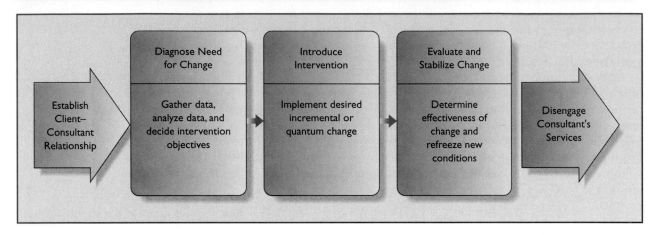

Establish Client–Consultant Relationship → Diagnose Need for Change: Gather data, analyze data, and decide intervention objectives → Introduce Intervention: Implement desired incremental or quantum change → Evaluate and Stabilize Change: Determine effectiveness of change and refreeze new conditions → Disengage Consultant's Services

OD consultants to assist change activities in the company. However, change agents are usually line managers and team leaders who serve as champions to keep the change effort on track.

Change agents first need to determine the client's readiness for change, including whether people are motivated to participate in the process, are open to meaningful change, and possess the abilities to complete the process. They watch out for people who enter the process with preconceived answers before the situation is fully diagnosed, or who intend to use the change effort to their personal advantage (e.g., closing down a department or firing a particular employee). Change agents also need to establish their power base in the client relationship.[40] Effective consultants rely on expertise and perhaps referent power to have any influence on the participants. However, they *should not* use reward, legitimate, or coercive power, because these bases may weaken trust and neutrality in the client–consultant relationship.

Change agents need to agree with their clients on the most appropriate role in the relationship. This might range from providing technical expertise on a specific change activity to facilitating the change process. Many OD experts prefer the latter role, commonly known as **process consultation.**[41] Process consultation involves helping the organization solve its own problems by making it aware of organizational processes, the consequences of those processes, and the means by which they can be changed. Rather than providing expertise about the content of the change—such as how to introduce continuous improvement teams—process consultants help participants learn how to solve their own problems by guiding them through the change process.[42]

Process consultation
A method of helping the organization solve its own problems by making it aware of organizational processes, the consequences of those processes, and the means by which they can be changed.

Diagnose the need for change

Action research is a problem-oriented activity that carefully diagnoses the problem (or opportunity) through systematic analysis of the situation. *Organizational diagnosis* involves gathering and analyzing data about an ongoing system. Various data collection methods are available, but the consultant needs to consider the advantages and disadvantages of each method.[43] Interviews are common, because OD consultants can build rapport with the client, explore specific issues spontaneously, and cover a range of subjects. However, they are susceptible to perceptual bias and are expensive in large client groups. Questionnaires allow the consultant to collect and quantify information from many people relatively easily and inexpensively, although they are more impersonal and inflexible than are interviews. Direct observation can be used when small teams are involved, but this method is too time consuming in large work units. Secondary data, such as monthly productivity records and union grievance reports, represent an unobtrusive source of diagnostic information, although they may be too politically sensitive and expensive to retrieve.

The consultant typically organizes and interprets the data, then presents it to the client to identify symptoms, problems, and possible solutions. The data analysis also motivates participants to support the change intervention, because it allows them to see the need for change. The data analysis should be neutral and descriptive to avoid perceptual defensiveness. The information should also relate to factors over which participants have control.

Along with gathering and analyzing data, the diagnostic process involves agreeing on specific prescriptions for action, including the appropriate change method and the schedule for these actions. This process, known as *joint action planning*, ensures that everyone knows what is expected of them and that standards are established to properly evaluate the process after the transition.[44]

Introduce the OD intervention

The OD process includes several interventions, including the consultant's entry into the relationship and the diagnostic process.[45] Nevertheless, the focal intervention involves altering specific system variables identified in the organizational diagnosis and planning stages. These changes might alter tasks, strategic organizational goals, system controls (e.g., rewards), or interpersonal relationships. We will outline some specific OD interventions later in this chapter.

An important issue during implementation is the degree of change that should occur. **Incremental change** is an evolutionary strategy, because the organization fine-tunes the existing organization and takes small steps towards the change effort's objectives.[46] Continuous improvement (described in Chapter 1) usually applies incremental change, because it attempts to make small improvements to existing work processes. Organizational change experts usually recommend incremental change, because it produces less resistance and involves less risk. It is less threatening and stressful to employees, because they have time to adapt to the new conditions. Moreover, any problems in the intervention can be corrected while the change process is occurring, rather than afterwards.[47]

Quantum change is a revolutionary strategy, because the organization breaks out of its existing ways and moves toward a totally different configuration of systems and structures. Quantum change is necessary when environmental shifts occur suddenly or leaders have delayed action until the situation is critical.[48] Some writers now argue that companies need more "reengineering" (quantum change) rather than incremental tinkering to survive in this rapidly changing environment.[49] Ford Motor Company initially considered incremental changes, such as automating some accounting processes, to reduce costs.

Incremental change
An evolutionary approach to change in which existing organizational conditions are fine-tuned and small steps are taken toward the change effort's objectives.

Quantum change
A revolutionary approach to change in which the organization breaks out of its existing ways and moves toward a totally different configuration of systems and structures.

Perspective 15–3

The High-Speed Transformation of Richmond Savings Credit Union

In the mid-1980s, Richmond Savings Credit Union was drowning in a sea of red ink, with loan losses exceeding the value of its capital base. The financial institution's new CEO, Don Tuline, moved quickly to change the situation by developing new services, introducing a new computer system to personalize client relations, and changing the service fee structure. Employees were slow to adapt to the new customer orientation, so special training and incentives were introduced to assist the change process. Tuline also fired the existing senior management team except for one lone survivor. "I had to have senior staff working with me who could work under pressure, who could see not just problems but solutions, and who had a strong marketing bent," explains Tuline.

Within just three years, Richmond Savings returned to profitability and a healthy balance sheet. Its computer system also won the top award from an American organization that monitors microcomputer applications in the financial industry. Still, the high-speed turnaround effort has taken its toll. As Tuline acknowledges: "We brought a number of changes in very rapidly and this added to the stress of our employees. They were nervous, always having to learn something new; there wasn't much fun in their jobs."

The change process also took its toll on Tuline. "I ended up with a heart attack," says the Richmond Savings CEO. "That forced me to realize I wasn't doing the organization any service by getting so stressed out. I've learned to pace myself better."

What would have eased this massive culture change? A slower pace, suggests Tuline—time for the organization to catch up to the changes. Rapid growth continues to be a potential Achilles heel for Richmond Savings as it opens new branches around Vancouver. It strains both employees and capital, and there is never time to evaluate the previous transformation.

"But you can never stand still," adds Tuline, reflecting the prevailing philosophy at Richmond Savings. "To sustain our competitive advantages we have to continue to look ahead to how we can offer services to our members that they can't get elsewhere. And we have to ensure the technology is always upgraded to allow us to keep the initiative."

Sources: Based on M. Zuehlke, "Bold Marketing Rescues Richmond Savings," *Small Business*, September 1990, pp. 14–17; and C. Furlong, "Saving a Credit Union," *BC Business*, January 1989, pp. 40–49.

Instead, the company reengineered the entire accounting structure by moving most payment authorization activities from the accounts payable department to the employees at the receiving dock. This quantum change eliminated most of the accounts payable department and helped Ford reduce costs more than through incremental changes.

Although reengineering and other forms of quantum change are sometimes necessary, they also present risks. One problem is that quantum change usually includes the costly task of altering organizational structures and systems. Many costs, such as getting employees to learn completely different roles, are hidden and not apparent until the change process has started. Another problem is that quantum change is usually traumatic and rapid, so change agents rely more on coercion and negotiation rather than employee involvement to build support for the change effort.[50] As we see in Perspective 15–3, quantum change at Richmond Savings Credit Union resulted in human problems that were not contemplated before the process began.

Evaluate and stabilize change

OD interventions can be very expensive, so it makes sense that we should measure their effectiveness. To evaluate an OD intervention, we need to recall its objectives that were developed during the organizational diagnosis and action planning stages. But even when these goals are clearly stated, the effectiveness of an OD intervention might not be apparent for several years. It is also difficult to separate the effects of the intervention from external factors (e.g., improving economy, introduction of new technology). Evaluating OD interventions may be difficult, but the potential value of this information makes the challenge worthwhile. If the intervention is having the desired effect, then the change agent and participants stabilize the new conditions. In other words, they alter organizational systems and team dynamics to refreeze conditions so that people do not slide back into old practices.

Selected Organization Development Interventions

Organization development includes any planned change intended to improve organizational effectiveness. As you can imagine, OD covers almost every area of organizational behaviour, as well as many aspects of strategic and human resource management. Some OD activities are discussed elsewhere in this book, such as job design (Chapter 4), team building (Chapter 10), intergroup mirror (Chapter 13), and managing culture change (Chapter 16). Although early OD work focussed on interpersonal relations and other humanistic concerns, the field has shifted its emphasis in recent years toward productivity and organizational effectiveness. For example, the most popular OD interventions in Canada today are job design, employee involvement, and team building.[51] In this section, we briefly discuss sensitivity training (one of the earliest OD activities) as well as two emerging interventions: parallel learning structures and appreciative inquiry.

Sensitivity training

Sensitivity training (also called *T-group* or *encounter group*) is an unstructured and agendaless session in which a small group of people meet face to face, often for a few days, to learn more about themselves and their relations with others. This process helps participants become more aware of how they affect others and how others affect them.[52] Learning occurs as participants disclose information about themselves and receive feedback from others during the session.

Sensitivity training can be traced back to Kurt Lewin's interracial training seminar in Connecticut during the summer of 1946. Lewin died the next year, but some of his training seminar participants formed the National Training Laboratory (NTL) in the United States, where they further developed sensitivity training.[53] Soon after, a grass-roots group from Saskatchewan began attending NTL sessions and set up a comparable summer residential sensitivity training program in that province.[54] By the mid-1950s, other Canadians who had attended NTL were bringing these processes into human service and educational settings. The Canadian YMCA experimented with a residential intergroup

Sensitivity training
An unstructured and agendaless session in which participants become more aware through their interactions of how they affect others and how others affect them.

mirroring program. Sir George Williams (now Concordia) University began a human relations training program. Toronto's Forest Hill school system used NTL methods to help teachers and administrators work with alienated youth.[55]

Steinberg's Ltd., the Quebec-based supermarket chain, was probably one of the first businesses in Canada to practise sensitivity training.[56] One of Steinberg's divisional general managers participated in an NTL seminar in 1963 and, soon after, the company invited a well-known American human relations scholar to conduct an on-site session involving Steinberg's top management. Sensitivity training was a popular business OD activity during the 1960s and 1970s, but is less common today. Two reasons are that its link to business activities is indirect and the intervention is potentially threatening to each participant's self-esteem.[57] For example, Steinberg's management used sensitivity training for only a couple of years, then switched to the Leadership Grid® program (described in Chapter 14). As one manager explained: "The Grid is less threatening and more work oriented."

Parallel learning structures

Parallel learning structure
A highly participative social structure constructed alongside (i.e., parallel to) the formal organization with the purpose of increasing the organization's learning.

Parallel learning structures are highly participative arrangements, composed of people from most levels of the organization who follow the action research model to produce meaningful organizational change. They are social structures developed alongside the formal hierarchy with the purpose of increasing the organization's learning.[58] Ideally, parallel learning structure participants are sufficiently free from the constraints of the larger organization that they may solve organizational issues more effectively.

The Canadian government used parallel learning structures during the early 1970s to transform its Canada Employment Centres.[59] More recently, Reimer Express introduced a parallel learning structure to implement its quality improvement program. This consisted of an executive steering committee and quality improvement groups at every work site that helped to implement quality improvement training and practices at those sites. By separating the intervention from the traditional hierarchy, the Winnipeg-based trucking company was able to instill new attitudes, role patterns, and work behaviours to the larger organization more effectively.

Appreciative inquiry

The action research process described earlier in this chapter is based on the traditional problem-solving model. OD participants try to discover problems with the existing organizational system and identify ways to correct those problems. Unfortunately, this deficiency model of the world—in which something is wrong that must be fixed—focusses on the negative dynamics of the group or system rather than its positive opportunities.

Appreciative inquiry
An organization development intervention that directs the group's attention away from its own problems and focusses participants on the group's potential and positive elements.

Appreciative inquiry tries to break out of the problem-solving mentality by reframing relationships around the positive and the possible. It takes the view that organizations are creative entities in which people are capable of building synergy beyond their individual capabilities. To avoid dwelling on the group's own shortcomings, the process usually directs its inquiry toward a successful organization with similar characteristics. This external focus becomes a form of behavioural modelling, but it also increases open dialogue by redirecting the

The Appreciative Inquiry Process   **Exhibit 15–6**

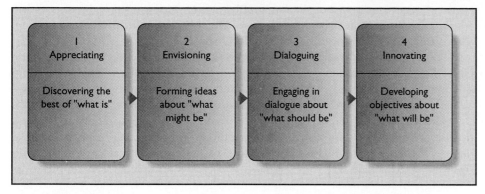

Source: Based on F. J. Barrett and D. L. Cooperrider, "Generative Metaphor Intervention: A New Approach for Working with Systems Divided by Conflict and Caught in Defensive Perception," *Journal of Applied Behavioral Science* 26 (1990), p. 229.

group's attention away from its own problems. Appreciative inquiry is especially useful when participants are aware of their "problems" or already suffer from enough negativity in their relationships. The positive orientation of appreciative inquiry enables groups to overcome these negative tensions and build a more hopeful perspective of their future by focussing on what is possible.

Exhibit 15–6 outlines the four main stages of appreciative inquiry.[60] The process begins with *appreciating*—identifying the positive elements of the observed organization. For instance, participants might interview members of the other organization to discover its fundamental strengths. As participants discuss their findings, they shift into the *envisioning* stage by considering what might be possible in an ideal organization. By directing their attention to another organization and its ideal state, participants feel safer revealing their hopes and aspirations than if they were discussing their own organization.

As participants make their private thoughts public to the group, the process shifts into the third stage, called *dialoguing*. **Dialogue,** which we introduced in Chapter 10, is a long-term process in which participants listen with selfless receptivity to each others' models and assumptions and eventually form a collective model for thinking within the team.[61] As this model takes shape, group members shift the focus back to their own organization. In the final stage of appreciative inquiry, called *innovating*, participants establish specific objectives and direction for their own organization based on their model of what should be.

Dialogue
A process of conversation among team members in which they learn about each other's personal mental models and assumptions, and eventually form a common model for thinking within the team.

Effectiveness of Organization Development

Is organization development effective? Considering the incredible range of organization development interventions, answering this question is not easy. Nevertheless, a few studies have generally reported that some OD interventions have a moderately positive effect on employee productivity and attitudes. According to some reviews, team building and intergroup mirroring produce the most favourable results when a single intervention is applied.[62] Others report that self-managing work teams are very effective.[63] One of the most consistent findings is that OD is most effective when it includes two or more types of interventions. For instance, Blake and Mouton's Leadership Grid® (described in Chapter 14) is effective because it includes team building, intergroup mirroring, and leadership development.

There is increasing evidence that many OD techniques originating from the United States do not work as well in other cultures. For instance, intergroup mirroring and sensitivity training do not work well in many Asian cultures, because saving face and nonverbal communication patterns are valued more than direct, candid discussion.[64] Overall, organization development holds much promise as a process and a set of tools to improve organizational effectiveness, but the field will gain further momentum as it develops a more contingency-oriented perspective.

The ethics of organization development

An increasingly important issue regarding the effectiveness of organization development is whether it satisfies conditions of ethical conduct in organizations.[65] One ethical problem, according to some writers, is that OD interventions increase management's power by inducing compliance and conformity in organizational members. This power shift occurs because OD initiatives create uncertainty and reestablish management's position in directing the organization. Moreover, because OD is a systemwide activity, it requires employee participation rather than allowing individuals to get involved voluntarily. Indeed, one of the challenges of OD consultants is to "bring onside" those who are reluctant to engage in the process.

Another ethical concern is that OD activities may threaten the individual's privacy rights. The action research model is built on the idea of collecting information from organizational members, yet this requires employees to provide personal information that they may not want to divulge. The scientific nature of the data collection exercise may mislead employees into believing that their information is confidential when, in reality, senior management can sometimes identify opinions of individual employees.[66] Other OD activities, such as sensitivity training, may threaten individual privacy rights because employees are asked to publicly disclose their personal beliefs and experiences.

A third ethical problem is that some OD activities may undermine the individual's self-esteem. The unfreezing process requires participants to disconfirm their existing beliefs, sometimes including their own competence at certain tasks or interpersonal relations. Sensitivity training and intergroup mirroring may involve direct exposure to personal critique by co-workers as well as public disclosure of one's personal limitations and faults. For example, one hospital recently engaged in a "fishbowl" intervention in which 70 people observed several managers in a budget meeting. When the OD consultants noticed some hostility in the meeting (the nursing director called the chief financial officer a "bean counter"), they encouraged the managers to publicly discuss their emotions and find ways to overcome this hostility.[67] With several dozen people watching, the fishbowl is certainly not an activity that lets participants save face!

The ethical problems of privacy and self-esteem in OD interventions are evident in a recent incident in which the owners of Seagull Pewter and Silversmiths Ltd. tried to engage employees in a process of personal develop-

Perspective 15-4

Seagull Pewter and the Ethics of OD Interventions

Sandra McClary attended eight company-sponsored seminars while working at Seagull Pewter and Silversmiths Ltd. in Pugwash, Nova Scotia. Some of these sessions seemed fairly innocuous; others changed her behaviour enough to provoke comment from her family and friends. "All I would do is talk about Seagull. People would say to me, 'You're acting really strange, what's wrong?' "

The breaking point came after McClary participated in a three-day "human potential" training session at a Halifax hotel, attended by a dozen other Seagull employees as well as several people in the community. It was an intense session in which participants described their personal beliefs and experiences. Near the end of the program, McClary was in the spotlight, with the facilitator encouraging her to describe her marriage and sexual relations. "I found myself standing up in front of 40 or 50 people, crying and describing the most private details of my marriage. That wasn't me. I was a totally changed person."

When McClary and some other employees learned that Seagull's owners planned to offer a similar session during working hours, they called the United Steelworkers of America about unionization. The steelworkers union lost the first certification vote, but Seagull employees voted in favour of unionization in 1994. (McClary and a few other employees have since received psychological counselling to deal with the upset caused by Seagull's organization development activities.)

Seagull's owners believe that the company-sponsored courses were intended to foster personal development

in their employees, yet many people felt uncomfortable with the personal nature of these OD sessions and some claimed they conflicted with religious beliefs. Fran Williams, who works in Seagull's sales division, was also concerned that the interventions weren't voluntary. "Even though management stated people were invited, which is their wording, the employees definitely felt intimidated. They felt their job was at stake if they didn't attend the course."

Seagull Pewter and Silversmiths is not the only company implementing OD interventions with questionable ethical implications. During the late 1980s, the California Public Utilities Commission investigated hundreds of complaints from Pacific Bell employees that the company was requiring them to take human potential training. In Canada, the company that provides some of this human potential OD intervention lists Campbell Soup and Abitibi-Price as clients.

"Ten years ago, I used to get calls from parents because their kids had joined the Hare Krishna movement or the Moonies," says Rob Tucker, director of the Council on Mind Abuse Inc. in Toronto. "Now I get calls from kids who say dad has come back from a training seminar and is acting strange." Tucker is worried that some OD interventions increase employee loyalty and performance in the short term, but may create long-term problems. "Some corporations now seem to be interested in the technology of change, which is similar to brainwashing," says Tucker. "I don't think [they] have thought through some of the implications and consequences."

Sources: Based on "Seagull Workers Sign First Contract," *Halifax Chronicle Herald*, January 10, 1994, p. A3; A. Johnson, "Mind Cults Invade the Boardroom," *Canadian Business* 65 (January 1992), pp. 38–42; and D. Jones, "Seagull Flies into Culture Clash," *Globe & Mail*, December 2, 1991, p. B3

---

ment through "human potential" seminars. As Perspective 15–4 describes, several employees felt that their individual rights were so violated by the Nova Scotia company's activities that they eventually joined a labour union to protect those rights.

Finally, OD consultants are continually faced with the ethical dilemma of their role in the client relationship. Generally, they should occupy "marginal" positions with the clients they are serving. This means that they must be sufficiently detached from the organization to maintain objectivity and avoid having the client become too dependent on them.[68] However, this can be a difficult objective to satisfy due to the politics of organizational change. OD consultants and clients have their own agendas, and these are not easily resolved without moving beyond the marginal positions that change agents should ideally attain.

Chapter Summary

- Organizations face numerous forces for change, such as changing population, changing legislation, increasing competition, technological changes, and mergers and acquisitions. Organizational change efforts are typically resisted, due to perceived higher direct costs, saving face, fear of the unknown, breaking existing routines, incongruent organizational systems, and incongruent team dynamics.

- Lewin's force field analysis proposes that change occurs when the driving forces are stronger than the restraining forces. Lewin recommended unfreezing the status quo mainly by reducing the resisting forces. Six ways to overcome resistance include communication, training, employee involvement, stress management, negotiation, and coercion. After the change, it is necessary to refreeze the desired state so that employees do not slip back into their previous role patterns. Pilot projects need to be diffused throughout the organization to ensure their success.

- Organization development (OD) is a planned systemwide effort, managed from the top with the assistance of a change agent, that uses behavioural science knowledge to improve organizational effectiveness. Planned change is based on the action research model, which calls for organizational diagnosis and action planning, implementation, and evaluation of the intervention's effect on the system involved. Change agents need to determine the readiness for change, establish their power base in the client relationship, and understand their appropriate role in the change process. An important issue in choosing an intervention is whether change should be evolutionary (incremental change) or revolutionary (quantum change).

- One of the earliest OD interventions, sensitivity training, helps participants become more aware of how they affect others and how others affect them. Two emerging OD interventions are parallel learning structures and appreciative inquiry. Parallel learning structures are social structures developed alongside the formal hierarchy with the purpose of increasing the organization's learning. Appreciative inquiry focusses participants on the positive and possible rather than on problems within the group.

- OD activities, particularly those with multiple types of interventions, have a moderately positive effect on employee productivity and attitudes. However, OD faces several ethical dilemmas, including individual rights, the consultant's role in the client relationship, and the effect of the OD intervention on management's power over employees.

Discussion Questions

1. **Use Lewin's force field analysis to describe the dynamics of organizational change at Schneider Corp.**

2. **According to Lewin, what is the best strategy to move the status quo to a desired state?**

3. **Senior management of a large multinational corporation is planning to restructure the organization. Currently, the organization is decentralized around geographical areas so that the executive responsible for each area has considerable autonomy over manufacturing and sales. The new structure will transfer power to the executives responsible for different product groups; the executives responsible for each geographic area will no longer be responsible for manufacturing in their area but will retain control over sales activities. Describe two types of resistance senior management might encounter from this organizational change.**

4. **Organizational change is closely related to the model of individual behaviour and performance that was described in Chapter 2. Read the Bell Canada "Zero Waste" story at the beginning of Chapter 2 and identify the actions that overcame specific types of resistance to organizational change.**

5. **Web Circuits Ltd. is a Montreal-based manufacturer of computer circuit boards for high-technology companies. Senior management wants to introduce value-added management practices to reduce production costs and remain competitive. A consultant has recommended that the company start with a pilot project in one department and, when successful, diffuse these practices to other areas of the organization. Discuss the merits of this recommendation and identify three conditions (other than the pilot project's success) that would make diffusion of the change effort more successful.**

6. **Outline the organization development process based on the action research model.**

7. **Describe appreciative inquiry, and explain how it differs from traditional OD interventions.**

8. **Describe three ethical problems that may arise from organization development activities.**

Notes

1. D. B. Scott, "Lean Machine," *Report on Business Magazine*, November 1992, pp. 90–98; O. Bertin, "A Slaughterhouse on the Cutting Edge," *Globe & Mail*, August 11, 1992, p. B20; and D. W. Dodds, "Making It Better . . . and Better," *CMA Magazine* 66 (February 1992), pp. 16–21.

2. P. E. Larson, *Winning Strategies* (Ottawa: Conference Board of Canada, January 1989), Report 36-89-E.

3. Economic Council of Canada, *Legacies* (26th Annual Review) (Ottawa: Supply and Services Canada, 1989), p. ix.

4. B. Crosariol, "War of the Wires," *Report on Business Magazine*, May 1994, pp. 32–46.

5. D. McMurdy, "Packaged for Growth," *Maclean's*, August 12, 1991, p. 31.

6. K. Ohmae, *The Borderless World* (New York: HarperBusiness, 1990); and Economic Council of Canada, *Transitions for the 90s* (27th Annual Review) (Ottawa: Supply and Services Canada, 1990), Chapter 1.

7. S. McKay, "The Challenge of Change," *Financial Post Magazine*, April 1992, pp. 43–46.

8. A. Walmsley, "City Lights," *Report on Business Magazine*, August 1993, pp. 49–54.

9. D. Tapscott and A. Laston, *Paradigm Shift* (New York: McGraw-Hill, 1993); W. H. Davidow and M. S. Malone, *The Virtual Corporation* (New York: HarperBusiness, 1992); and R. J. Long, *New Office Information Technology* (London: Croom Helm, 1987).

10. S. D. Saleh and B. R. Hastings, "The Impact of Integrated Automation and Robotics on Plant Activities," *Canadian Journal of Administrative Sciences* 6 (March 1989), pp. 42–50; and O. L. Crocker and R. Guelker, "The Effects of Robotics on the Workplace," *Personnel*, September 1988, pp. 26–36.

11. R. Bonanno, "Labour Relations Have Never Been Better at Weston Bakeries Quebec," *Canadian HR Reporter*, July 16, 1993, p. 16; and R. Litchfield, "Solving an Education Crisis," *Canadian Business*, February 1991, pp. 57–64.

12. J. W. Rinehart, *The Tyranny of Work* (Toronto: Harcourt Brace Jovanovich, 1987); and H. Braverman, *Labor and Monopoly Capital* (New York: Monthly Review Press, 1974).

13. R. J. Long, "New Information Technology and Employee Involvement," *Proceedings of the Annual ASAC Conference, Organizational Behaviour Division* 14, pt. 5 (1993), pp. 161–70; R. J. Long, "The Impact of New Office Information Technology on Job Quality of Female and Male Employees," *Human Relations* 46 (1993), pp. 939–61; J. W. Medcof, "The Effect of Extent of Use of Information Technology and Job of the User upon Task Characteristics," *Human Relations* 42 (1989), pp. 23–41; and K. D. Hughes, "Office Automation: A Review of the Literature," *Relations Industrielles* 44 (1989), pp. 654–79.

14. Economic Council of Canada, *Legacies*, p. 1.

15. P. McLaughlin, "Merger Doctors," *Vista* 2 (May 1989), pp. 58–61.

16. J. H. Astrachan, *Mergers, Acquisitions, and Employee Anxiety* (New York: Praeger, 1990); G. A. Walter, "Culture Collisions in Mergers and Acquisitions," in *Organizational Culture*, ed. P. Frost et al. (Beverly Hills, Calif.: Sage, 1985); and A. F. Buono and J. L. Bowditch, *The Human Side of Mergers and Acquisitions* (San Francisco: Jossey-Bass, 1989).

17. C. Hardy, *Strategies for Retrenchment and Turnaround: The Politics of Survival* (Berlin: Walter de Gruyter, 1990), Chapter 13.

18. D. A. Nadler, "The Effective Management of Organizational Change," in *Handbook of Organizational Behavior*, ed. J. W. Lorsch (Englewood Cliffs, N.J.: Prentice Hall, 1987), pp. 358–69; and D. Katz and R. L. Kahn, *The Social Psychology of Organizations*, 2nd ed. (New York: Wiley, 1978).

19. R. Katz, "Time and Work: Toward an Integrative Perspective," *Research in Organizational Behavior* 2 (1980), pp. 81–127.

20. D. Miller, "What Happens after Success: The Perils of Excellence," *Journal of Management Studies* 31 (1994), pp. 325–58.

21. K. Lewin, *Field Theory in Social Science* (New York: Harper & Row, 1951).

22. J. P. Kotter and L. A. Schlesinger, "Choosing Strategies for Change," *Harvard Business Review*, March–April 1979, pp. 106–14.

23. L. C. Caywood and R. P. Ewing, *The Handbook of Communications in Corporate Restructuring and Takeovers* (Englewood Cliffs, N.J.: Prentice Hall, 1992); and D. M. Schweiger and A. S. DeNisi, "Communication with Employees Following a Merger: A Longitudinal Field Experiment," *Academy of Management Journal* 34 (1991), pp. 110–30.

24. A. Kingston, "Power to the People," *Report on Business Magazine*, July 1992, pp. 15–24.

25. K. D. Dannemiller and R. W. Jacobs, "Changing the Way Organizations Change: A Revolution of Common Sense," *Journal of Applied Behavioral Science* 28 (1992), pp. 480–98; and M. Pollock and N. L. Colwill, "Participatory Decision Making in Review," *Leadership and Organization Development Journal* 8(2) (1987), pp. 7–10.

26. K. Mark, "Board Games," *Human Resources Professional*, July–August 1993, pp. 9–13.

27. P. H. Mirvis and M. L. Marks, *Managing the Merger* (Englewood Cliffs, N.J.: Prentice Hall, 1992); and R. J. Burke, Managing the Human Side of Mergers and Acquisitions," *Business Quarterly*, Winter 1987, pp. 18–23.

28. S. McKay, "The Challenge of Change," *Financial Post Magazine*, April 1992, pp. 43–46.

29. J. Dibbs, "Organizing for Empowerment," *Business Quarterly* 58 (Autumn 1993), pp. 97–102.

30. T. Wakefield, "No Pain, No Gain," *Canadian Business*, January 1993, pp. 50–54.

31. T. G. Cummings and E. F. Huse, *Organization Development and Change*, 4th ed. (St. Paul, Minn.: West, 1989), pp. 477–85; P. Goodman and J. Dean, "Creating Long-Term Organizational Change," in *Change in Organizations*, ed. P. Goodman and Associates (San Francisco: Jossey-Bass, 1982), pp. 226–79; and W. W. Burke, *Organization Development: A Normative View* (Reading, Mass.: Addison-Wesley, 1987), pp. 124–25.

32. G. R. Bushe, "Quality Circles in Quality of Work Life Projects: Problems and Prospects for Increasing Employee Participation," *Canadian Journal of Community Mental Health* 3 (Fall 1984), pp. 101–13.

33. W. K. Beckett and K. Dang, "Synchronous Manufacturing: New Methods, New Mind-Set," *Journal of Business Strategy,* January–February 1992, pp. 53–56.

34. M. Beer, R. A. Eisenstat, and B. Spector, *The Critical Path to Corporate Renewal* (Boston, Mass.: Harvard Business School Press, 1990).

35. R. E. Walton, *Innovating to Compete: Lessons for Diffusing and Managing Change in the Workplace* (San Francisco: Jossey-Bass, 1987); Beer et al., *The Critical Path to Corporate Renewal,* Chapter 5; and R. E. Walton, "Successful Strategies for Diffusing Work Innovations," *Journal of Contemporary Business,* Spring 1977, pp. 1–22.

36. R. Beckhard, *Organization Development: Strategies and Models* (Reading, Mass.: Addison-Wesley, 1969), Chapter 2. Also see Cummings and Huse, *Organization Development and Change,* pp. 1–3.

37. Burke, *Organization Development,* pp. 12–14.

38. W. L. French and C. H. Bell, Jr., *Organization Development: Behavioral Science Interventions for Organization Improvement,* 4th ed. (Englewood Cliffs, N.J.: Prentice Hall, 1990), Chapter 8. For a recent discussion of action research model, see J. B. Cunningham, *Action Research and Organization Development* (Westport, Conn.: Praeger, 1993).

39. A. B. Shani and G. R. Bushe, "Visionary Action Research: A Consultation Process Perspective," *Consultation: An International Journal* 6(1) (1987), pp. 3–19.

40. M. L. Brown, "Five Symbolic Roles of the Organizational Development Consultant: Integrating Power, Change, and Symbolism," *Proceedings of the Annual ASAC Conference, Organizational Behaviour Division* 14, pt. 5 (1993), pp. 71–81; D. A. Buchanan and D. Boddy, *The Expertise of the Change Agent: Public Performance and Backstage Activity* (New York: Prentice Hall, 1992); and L. E. Greiner and V. E. Schein, *Power and Organization Development: Mobilizing Power to Implement Change* (Reading, Mass.: Addison-Wesley, 1988).

41. M. Beer and E. Walton, "Developing the Competitive Organization: Interventions and Strategies," *American Psychologist* 45 (February 1990), pp. 154–61.

42. E. H. Schein, *Process Consultation: Its Role in Organization Development* (Reading, Mass.: Addison-Wesley, 1969).

43. D. Nadler, *Feedback and Organization Development: Using Data-Based Methods* (Reading, Mass.: Addison-Wesley, 1977); and J. A. Waters, P. F. Salipante, Jr., and W. W. Notz, "The Experimenting Organization: Using the Results of Behavioral Science Research," *Academy of Management Review* 3 (1978), pp. 483–92.

44. Beer, *Organization Change and Development,* pp. 101–2.

45. D. F. Harvey and D. R. Brown, *An Experiential Approach to Organization Development,* 3rd ed. (Englewood Cliffs, N.J.: Prentice Hall, 1988), pp. 93–94.

46. D. A. Nadler, "Organizational Frame Bending: Types of Change in the Complex Organization," in *Corporate Transformation: Revitalizing Organizations for a Competitive World,* ed. R. H. Kilmann, T. J. Covin, and Associates (San Francisco: Jossey-Bass, 1988), pp. 66–83.

47. J. M. Kouzes and B. Z. Posner, *The Leadership Challenge* (San Francisco: Jossey-Bass, 1988), Chapter 10; and C. Lindblom, "The Science of Muddling Through," *Public Administration Review* 19 (1959), pp. 79–88.

48. C. R. Hinings and R. Greenwood, *The Dynamics of Strategic Change* (Oxford, England: Basil Blackwell, 1988), Chapter 6; and D. Miller and P. H. Friesen, "Structural Change and Performance: Quantum versus Piecemeal-Incremental Approaches," *Academy of Management Journal* 25 (1982), pp. 867–92.

49. M. Hammer and J. Champy, *Reengineering the Corporation: A Manifesto for Business Revolution* (New York: Harper Business, 1993); and M. Hammer, "Reengineering Work: Don't Automate, Obliterate," *Harvard Business Review* 68 (July–August 1990), pp. 104–12.

50. P. A. Strassmann, "The Hocus-Pocus of Reengineering," *Across the Board* 31 (June 1994), pp. 35–38.

51. A. H. Church, W. W. Burke, and D. F. Van Eynde, "Values, Motives, and Interventions of Organization Development Practitioners," *Group and Organization Management* 19 (1994), pp. 5–50; and N. J. Adler, "The Future of Organization Development in Canada," *Canadian Journal of Administrative Sciences* 1 (1984), pp. 122–32. Also see R. J. Long, "Patterns of Workplace Innovation in Canada," *Relations Industrielles* 44 (1989), pp. 805–24.

52. Cummings and Huse, *Organization Development and Change,* pp. 158–61.

53. French and Bell, *Organization Development,* Chapter 3.

54. H. G. Dimock, "Thirty Years of Human Service Education and Training in Canada—One Perspective," *Canadian Journal of Community Mental Health* 3(2) (1984), pp. 15–41; and H. G. Dimock, "Canada's Experience with Human Relations Training," *Annual Handbook for Group Facilitators* (San Diego, Calif.: University Associates, 1975), pp. 233–37.

55. L. B. Jones and K. A. Leithwood, "Draining the Swamp: A Case Study of School System Design," *Canadian Journal of Education* 14 (1989), pp. 242–60; and M. Fullan and M. Miles, "OD in Schools: The State of the Art," in *Organization Development: Theory, Practice, and Research,* rev. ed., ed. W. L. French, C. H. Bell Jr., and R. A. Zawacki (Plano, Texas: Business Publications, 1983), pp. 493–500.

56. H. Rush, "Organization Development at Steinberg's Limited—A Case Study," in *Contemporary Issues in Canadian Personnel Administration,* ed. H. C. Jain (Scarborough, Ont.: Prentice Hall of Canada, 1974), pp. 262–69.

57. R. E. Kaplan, "Is Openness Passé?" *Human Relations* 39 (1986), pp. 229–43.

58. E. M. Van Aken, D. J. Monetta, and D. S. Sink, "Affinity Groups: The Missing Link in Employee Involvement," *Organization Dynamics* 22 (Spring 1994), pp. 38–54; and G. R. Bushe and A. B. Shani, *Parallel Learning Structures* (Reading, Mass.: Addison-Wesley, 1991).

59. W. M. A. Brooker, "Integrating Social and Technical Change: A Pilot Project," *Optimum* 3(2) (1972), pp. 55–65.

60. F. J. Barrett and D. L. Cooperrider, "Generative Metaphor Intervention: A New Approach for Working with Systems Divided by Conflict and Caught in Defensive Perception," *Journal of Applied Behavioral Science* 26 (1990), pp. 219–39.

61. G. R. Bushe and G. Coetzer, "Appreciative Inquiry as a Team Intervention," *Journal of Applied Behavioral Science* (forthcoming); and L. Levine, "Listening with Spirit and the Art of Team Dialogue," *Journal of Organizational Change Management* 7 (1994), pp. 61–73.

62. G. A. Neuman, J. E. Edwards, and N. S. Raju, "Organizational Development Interventions: A Meta-Analysis of Their Effects on Satisfaction and Other Attitudes," *Personnel Psychology* 42 (1989), pp. 461–89; and R. A. Guzzo, R. D. Jette, and R. A. Katzell, "The Effects of Psychologically Based Intervention Programs on Worker Productivity: A Meta-Analysis," *Personnel Psychology* 38 (1985), pp. 275–91.

63. R. J. Long, "The Effects of Various Workplace Innovations on Productivity: A Quasi-Experimental Study," *Proceedings of the Annual ASAC Conference, Personnel and Human Resources Division* 11, pt. 9 (1990), pp. 98–107.

64. T. C. Head and P. F. Sorenson, "Cultural Values and Organizational Development: A Seven-Country Study," *Leadership and Organization Development Journal* 14 (1993), pp. 3–7; J. M. Putti, "Organization Development Scene in Asia: The Case of Singapore," *Group and Organization Studies* 14 (1989), pp. 262–70; and A. M. Jaeger, "Organization Development and National Culture: Where's the Fit?" *Academy of Management Review* 11 (1986), pp. 178–90.

65. C. M. D. Deaner, "A Model of Organization Development Ethics," *Public Administration Quarterly* 17 (1994), pp. 435–46; and M. McKendall, "The Tyranny of Change: Organizational Development Revisited," *Journal of Business Ethics* 12 (February 1993), pp. 93–104.

66. G. A. Walter, "Organization Development and Individual Rights," *Journal of Applied Behavioral Science* 20 (1984), pp. 423–39.

67. T. N. Gilmore and C. Barnett, "Designing the Social Architecture of Participation in Large Groups to Effect Organizational Change," *Journal of Applied Behavioral Science* 28 (1992), pp. 534–48.

68. Burke, *Organization Development,* pp. 149–51; and Beer, *Organization Change and Development,* pp. 223–24.

Chapter Case

Eastern Provincial Insurance Corporation

Eastern Provincial Insurance Corporation (EPIC) is a Crown Corporation formed 10 years ago to provide all automobile insurance in the province. Last year, the provincial government (through EPIC's Board of Directors) hired a new president and gave her a mandate for organizational renewal. To fulfill this mandate, the new president replaced three vice-presidents. Jim Leon was hired as vice-president of Claims, EPIC's largest division with 600 unionized employees, 20 managers, and 4 regional directors.

Jim immediately met with all claims managers and directors, and visited the 20 claims centres throughout the province. As an outsider, this was a formidable task, but his strong interpersonal skills and uncanny ability to remember names and ideas helped him through the process. Through these visits and discussions, Jim discovered that the division had been managed in a relatively authoritarian, top-down manner. He could also see the aftermath of the month-long strike from the previous year. Morale was very low and employee—management relations were guarded. High workloads and isolation (adjusters work in tiny cubicles) were two other common complaints. Several managers acknowledged that the high turn-over among claims adjusters was partly due to these conditions.

Following discussions with EPIC's president, Jim decided to make morale and management style his top priority. He initiated a divisional newsletter with a tear-off feedback form for employees to register their comments. He announced an open-door policy in which any Claims Division employee could speak to him directly and confidentially without going first to the immediate supervisor. Jim also fought organizational and contractual barriers to initiate a flex-time program so that employees could design work schedules around their needs. This program later became a model for other areas of EPIC.

One of Jim's most pronounced symbols of change was the "Claims Management Credo" outlining the philosophy that every claims manager would follow. At his first meeting with the complete claims management team, Jim presented a list of what he thought were important philosophies and actions of effective managers. The management group was asked to select and prioritize items from this list. They were told that the resulting list would be the division's management philosophy and all managers would be held accountable for abiding by its principles. Most claims managers were uneasy about this process, but they also understood that the organization was under government pressure to change its style and that Jim was using this exercise to demonstrate his leadership.

The claims managers developed a list of 10 items, such as encouraging teamwork, fostering a trusting work environment, setting clear and reasonable goals, and so on. The list was circulated to senior management in the organization for their comment and approval, and sent back to all claims managers for their endorsement. Once this was done, a copy of the final document was sent to every claims division employee. Jim also announced plans to follow up with an annual survey to evaluate each claims manager's performance. This concerned the managers, but most of them believed that the credo exercise was a result of Jim's initial enthusiasm and that he would be too busy to introduce a survey after settling into the job.

One year after the credo had been distributed, Jim announced that the first annual survey would be conducted. All unionized employees in the claims division would complete the survey and return it confidentially to the union steward in their centre. The stewards would send the completed forms to EPIC's information systems division for processing. The survey asked the extent to which the manager had lived up to each of the 10 items in the credo. Each form also provided space for comments.

Claims managers were surprised that a survey would be conducted, but they were even more worried about Jim's statement that the results would be shared with employees. What "results" would employees see? Who would distribute these results? What happens if a manager gets poor ratings from his or her subordinates? "We'll work out the details later," said Jim in response to these questions. "Even if the survey results aren't great, the information will give us a good baseline for next year's survey."

The claims division survey had a high response rate. In some centres, every employee completed and returned a form. The information systems division processed the surveys and produced reports for each claims manager. Each manager's report showed his or her average score for each of the 10 items as well as how many employees rated the manager at each level of the five-point scale. The reports also included every comment made by employees at that centre.

No one was prepared for the results of the first survey. Most managers received moderate or poor ratings on the 10 items. Very few managers averaged above 3.0 (out of a 5-point scale) on more than a couple of items. This suggested that, at best, employees were ambivalent about whether their claims centre manager had abided by the 10 management philosophy items. The comments were even more devastating than the ratings. Comments ranged from mildly disappointed to extremely critical of their claims manager. Employees also described their long-standing frustration with EPIC, high workloads, and isolated working conditions. Several people bluntly stated that they were sceptical about the changes that Jim had promised. "We've heard the promises before, but now we've lost faith," wrote one claims adjuster.

The survey results were sent to each claims manager, the regional director, and executive members of the union representing claims centre employees. Jim instructed managers to discuss the survey data and comments with their regional manager and directly with employees. The managers went into shock when they realized that the discussion reports included personal comments. Some managers went to their regional director, complaining that revealing the personal comments would ruin their careers. Many directors sympathized, but the union executive had the results, so they were already available to employees. It would be impossible to ask the union leaders to return the reports or keep them confidential because this might look like management had something to hide and wanted to keep the union out of the process.

When Jim heard about these concerns, he agreed that the results were lower than expected and that the comments should not have been shown to employees. After discussing the situation with his directors, he decided that the discussion meetings between claims managers and their employees should proceed as planned. To delay or withdraw the reports would undermine the credibility and trust that Jim was trying to develop with unionized employees. However, each discussion meeting would be attended by the regional director to control or avoid any direct confrontations that might otherwise emerge between claims managers and their employees.

Although many of these meetings went smoothly, a few created harsh feelings between managers and their employees. The source of some comments were easily identified by their content, and this created a few delicate moments in several sessions. A few months after these meetings, two claims managers quit and three others asked for transfers back to unionized positions in EPIC. Meanwhile, Jim wondered how to manage this process more effectively, particularly since employees expected another survey the following year.

Discussion Questions

1. **What symptom(s) exist in this case to suggest that something has gone wrong?**

2. **What are the root causes that have led to these symptoms?**

3. **What actions should the company take to correct these problems?**

EXPERIENTIAL EXERCISE

Appreciative Inquiry for Team Development: A Student Exercise*

Purpose: To give students the opportunity to practise appreciative inquiry as part of a team development process.

Instructions: Ideally, this exercise uses ongoing teams for a class project or other assignment because the exercise can potentially extend to the innovating stage of appreciative inquiry. Appreciative inquiry can be a lengthy process, so teams typically engage only in the appreciating and envisioning stages during a one- or two-hour meeting. However, this exercise begins a potentially valuable process for existing teams to continue their discussion to the innovating stage on their own time.

Alternatively, this exercise can be applied to "stranger groups"—small groups of students specifically for this exercise and who will not be working together beyond this activity. Members of these groups can practise the process of appreciating, envisioning, and dialoguing, and then use this experience to improve the dynamics of their own permanent groups (innovating). Both existing and stranger groups should follow the first two steps below. The third step below should be assigned only to ongoing teams if the exercise is given two or three hours and a facilitator is involved to guide the process.

Step 1: (appreciating): Each team member is asked to recall the best team experience he or she has ever had. Even those who have seldom worked with other people tend to have had some gratifying team experience that they can recall. While the team member is describing the previous team experience, other team members should engage in dialogue with the focal person. They should explore the characteristics of the person, the situation, the task, and others that made this a "best" team experience. Team members should try to express their own perceptions of their teammate's experience (e.g., "So are you saying that. . . ?") to confirm mutual understanding. The key purpose here is for all team members to understand the individual's experience without relying on their own preconceptions.

Step 2: (envisioning and dialoguing): Based on what they have learned from their best team experiences, team members are asked to list the attributes of highly effective teams. This process includes considering what might be possible in an ideal team and what these teams look like. Team members engage in active discussion of these items to form a consensus.

Step 3: (innovating): (This step is for existing teams, preferably with the guidance of a facilitator.) While describing their mental models of an ideal team, participants are invited to publicly acknowledge anything they have seen other team members do that has helped the group move closer toward that ideal model. Team members engage in a contracting process whereby they agree on specific objectives and direction for their own group based on the items formed in Step 2 above.

*This exercise is based on an experimental intervention developed by Dr. Gervase Bushe and Graeme Coetzer, described in G. R. Bushe and G. Coetzer, "Appreciative Inquiry as a Team Intervention," Journal of Applied Behavioral Science (forthcoming).

Organizational Culture, Socialization, and Careers Types

Learning Objectives

After reading this chapter, you should be able to:

Distinguish between an organization's dominant culture and its subcultures.

List four types of artifacts through which organizational culture is communicated.

Explain how to strengthen an organization's dominant culture.

Describe the three stages of organizational socialization.

Explain how socialization agents potentially assist new employees.

Outline the stages through which people pass in their careers.

Describe the boundaryless career.

Chapter Outline

What Is Organizational Culture?

Organizational Culture and Effectiveness.

Communicating Organizational Culture.

Merging Organizational Cultures.

Strengthening Organizational Culture.

Organizational Socialization.

Stages of Socialization.

Managing the Socialization Process.

Organizational Careers.

Emerging Issues in Career Development.

Employees at Rocky Mountain Bicycle Company don't just make bikes; their lives revolve around them. At work, they produce some of the highest quality off-road bicycles made in Canada— hand-crafted, precision machines ranging from $800 to several thousand dollars. At other times, they put Rocky Mountain's bikes through the paces on the trails and in races.

A tour through Rocky Mountain's manufacturing plant in Richmond, British Columbia, quickly reveals evidence of this "cyclist culture." Most of the company's 100 employees wear cyclist shorts at work, revealing leg muscles that would make a bodybuilder proud. In the lunch room, they show off raw patches where skin had been left behind on some mountain trail. Employees swap stories about riding Rocky Mountain bikes over British Columbia's rugged terrain. A few recall close calls with steep cliffs and wild animals.

Rocky Mountain's employees also share a strong team-oriented enthusiasm and support for the company's success. This cultural value is evident from their willingness to work beyond usual job duties. For example, bike assembler Pat Fitzsimmons likes to try his hand at writing copy for the company's brochures. Everyone, from the welders who painstakingly piece together the aluminum and titanium frames to the people who pack bicycle parts, can apply for the 20 places each year on the team that designs new models.

Rocky Mountain's founder and president, Grayson Bain, points out that this corporate culture is vital to the company's success. "Most of the people here are avid cyclists," he explains. "There's a high degree of ownership and teamwork. We don't just think about it; we do it."[1]

Rocky Mountain Bicycle Company has a distinctive organizational culture that is apparent to anyone who visits the firm. This chapter begins by examining the complex meaning of organizational culture, followed by a discussion of how it is recognized and transmitted. Next, we consider specific strategies for maintaining a strong organizational culture. The second part of this chapter turns to the topic of organizational socialization. Here, we examine how newcomers adjust to the physical, social, and cultural dimensions of their work environment. The final part of this chapter looks at organizational careers, with a special emphasis on the emergence of lateral and boundaryless careers.

What Is Organizational Culture?

Organizational culture
The basic pattern of shared assumptions, values, and beliefs governing the way employees within an organization think about and act on problems and opportunities.

Organizational culture is the basic pattern of shared assumptions, values, and beliefs considered to be the correct way of thinking about and acting on problems and opportunities facing the organization.[2] Culture operates unconsciously, serving as an automatic pilot that directs employee attitudes and behaviour. Organizational culture is, therefore, a deeply embedded form of social control whereby individuals abide by cultural prescriptions shared with others within the organization.

Organizational culture is shaped by critical events in the organization's history, the organization's founder and subsequent leaders, the industry in which the organization operates, and cultural values of the larger society.[3] Employees are motivated to internalize the organization's dominant culture because it fulfills their need for social identity. By sharing common values with others in the organization, employees experience a sense of personal meaning and connection with co-workers. In other words, organizational culture is part of the "social glue" that bonds people together and makes them feel part of the organizational experience.[4]

Artifacts of organizational culture

We cannot directly see an organization's cultural assumptions and values. As depicted in Exhibit 16–1, these core elements lie beneath the surface of organizational behaviour. Values are closer to the surface because people are aware of them, whereas assumptions lie much deeper because employees take them for granted. For instance, employees at Rocky Mountain Bicycle know that they value teamwork, yet they probably don't question or even think about whether this is good for customers or the organization. They just naturally assume that this style works best for them and their company.

Artifacts
The observable symbols and signs of an organization's culture, including its physical structures, ceremonies, language, and stories.

Although we can't see the assumptions or values that represent an organization's culture, we can look for indirect evidence of them through **artifacts.** Artifacts are the observable symbols and signs of an organization's culture, such as its physical structures, ceremonies, language, and stories. They maintain and transmit shared meanings and perceptions of reality within the organization. If we visited Rocky Mountain Bicycle, we would notice artifacts that symbolize its cycling culture—employees dressed in cycling shorts, stories about jumping off a bike before it plummeted off a 30-metre cliff, and a company president who bikes to work every day of the year. It is not always easy to decipher artifacts when we are trying to identify an organization's dominant values for the first

The Visible and Hidden Elements of Organizational Culture   Exhibit 16–1

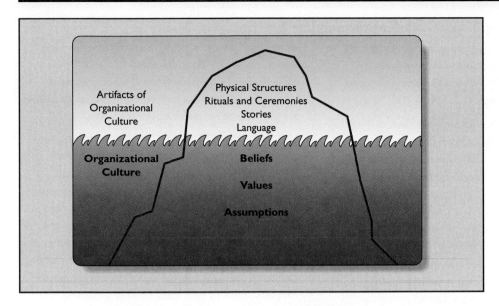

time. Artifacts are subtle and often ambiguous indicators of culture, so we need to examine many artifacts and search for common themes through these diverse pieces of evidence.[5]

Content and strength of organizational cultures

Organizations differ in terms of the content of their cultures, that is, their relative ordering of beliefs and values.[6] Rocky Mountain Bicycle Company has strong cultural beliefs in teamwork and the cycling lifestyle. Other organizational cultures might emphasize technological efficiency, customer service, employee welfare, or maximizing profits. Some writers and consultants have attempted to classify organizational cultures into a few categories with catchy labels such as "clubs" and "fortresses." Although these typologies might reflect the values of a few organizations, they oversimplify the diversity of cultural values in Canadian businesses. Worse, they tend to distort rather than clarify our attempts to diagnose corporate culture.

Perspective 16–1 briefly describes the dominant values of three Canadian companies. You should be somewhat cautious about the accuracy of these descriptions, because deciphering an organization's dominant values requires a thorough investigation of cultural artifacts, rather than a journalist's brief interview and observations. Nevertheless, these examples do illustrate the diversity of cultural values that likely exist in Canadian companies.

To understand how organizational culture influences a company's effectiveness, we need to consider the strength of its culture, not just its content. *Cultural strength* refers to how many employees in the organization accept the dominant values; how strongly, deeply, and intensely they believe in these values; and how long these values have dominated in the organization. Strong cultures are long lasting, dispersed across subunits, deeply internalized by employees, and institutionalized through well-established artifacts.[7] In contrast, companies have

Perspective 16–1

The Cultural Content of Three Canadian Companies

Some Canadian companies have strong values; others are quite weak and difficult to decipher. For those with strong cultures, the dominant values are quite diverse, as we see in the following examples:

- *Davies, Ward, and Beck:* The Toronto law firm of Davies, Ward, and Beck has a strong culture that emphasizes hard-driving performance with a focus on big-name commercial contracts. "They're all completely driven maniacs," says one observer of the Toronto legal community. "I don't know if anybody works quite as hard as the people at Davies. They've got little couches so you don't ever have to go home. They bring sandwiches around on a cart so you don't ever have to leave your office." Another observer adds: "Either you are a Davies person or you won't last two weeks there."

- *The Body Shop Canada:* With over 100 stores in Canada, The Body Shop Canada embraces the cultural values of its British parent company. This culture evolves around the deeply held belief that organizations should serve society, not just shareholders. Body Shop employees are paid to help various community groups and social causes. They use environmentally friendly products, minimize waste, and don't push customers to buy products they don't want. "Business should do more than make money," says Body Shop Canada president Margot Franssen. "We believe that companies should actually help solve major social problems."

- *Hees International Bancorp:* Canadian merchant bank Hees International Bancorp has a set of cultural values that distinguishes it from other banking organizations in Canada. Hees's culture emphasizes modest lifestyles, efficient management, and equity stakes in their work activities. Hees partners are known as the "lunch box crowd" in the banking industry because of their frugal ways and the lending decisions they make in the boardroom over lunch. Partners don't fly first class or ride around in limousines, as do executives in other Canadian banks. They are also required to take an equity stake in their decisions so that investments are prudent rather than risky. "There are certainly a lot of people who view it [Hees International's cultural values] as a religion," says a Hees managing partner. "It goes beyond work and extends to the way we live and behave."

Sources: G. McLaughlin, "Corporate Cults," *Financial Post Magazine*, November 1993, pp. 118–23; M. Franssen, "Beyond Profits," *Business Quarterly* 58 (Autumn 1993), pp. 15–20; M. Wente, "A Heady Mixture of Vision and Values," *Globe & Mail*, October 16, 1993, p. A2; and L. Holstrom and A. Dugan, "The House that Jack Built," *Euromoney*, August 1990, pp. 20–29.

weak cultures when the dominant values are short lived, poorly communicated, and held mainly by a few people at the top of the organization.

Organizational Culture and Effectiveness

Should companies have a strong culture? Several writers think so. They claim that firms with strong cultures are better managed and have superior financial performance over the long term than those with weak cultures.[8] This makes sense if we consider that culture is a form of social control guiding both decisions and behaviour. A strong culture also creates common bonds among employees, resulting in more efficient communication and higher levels of cooperation. Finally, a strong culture makes it easier for employees to make sense of organizational events and understand what is expected of them.

However, the relationship between cultural strength and organizational effectiveness is not as simple as we might initially think. In fact, recent studies have found only a modestly positive relationship between the organization's cultural strength and its economic performance. One reason for the weak relationship is that a strong culture increases organizational effectiveness only when the cultural content is appropriate for the organization's environment.[9] Companies that operate in a highly competitive environment would be better served with a culture that engenders efficiency; companies in environments that require dedicated employees will be more successful with an employee-oriented culture. When a firm's culture does not fit its environment, on the other hand, employees have difficulty anticipating and responding to the needs of the company's dominant stakeholders.

A second problem is that a company's culture might be so strong that employees blindly focus on the mental model shaped by that culture. Recall from Chapter 9 that mental models produce a set of assumptions on which we base our decisions and actions. When an organization's culture intensely emphasizes customer service, for example, employees tend to see problems as customer service problems, even though some are really problems about efficiency or technology. Thus, strong cultures might cause decision makers to overlook or incorrectly define subtle misalignments between the organization's activities and the changing environment.[10]

Finally, the stronger the culture, the more it suppresses dissenting values. In the long term, this prevents organizations from nurturing new cultural values that should become dominant values as the environment changes. For this reason, corporate leaders need to recognize that healthy organizations have subcultures with dissenting values that may produce dominant values in the future. Let's look more closely at this subcultural perspective of organizational culture.

Organizational subcultures

When discussing organizational culture, we are actually referring to the *dominant culture,* that is, the themes shared most widely by the organization's members. However, organizations are also comprised of subcultures located throughout its various subunits.[11] Some subcultures enhance the dominant culture by espousing parallel assumptions, values, and beliefs; others are countercultures because they directly oppose the organization's core values. For example, when Shell Canada's senior management decided that the company should become more aggressive as well as move its headquarters from Toronto to Calgary, employees in the computer department formed a powerful counter-culture, complete with its own underground newspaper, *Trash,* to voice their opposition to management's tactics. Interestingly, *Trash* became a popular vehicle for dissension—it was even read by senior management![12]

Countercultures may irritate some corporate leaders, but they serve two important functions. First, as mentioned earlier, companies eventually need to replace their dominant values with ones that are more appropriate for the changing environment. Subcultures are the spawning grounds for these emerging values that keep the firm aligned with the needs of its dominant stakeholders. Companies that try to subdue their subcultures may be less able to replace cultural values that no longer fit the environment.

The second reason why we should respect the existence of subcultures is that they maintain the organization's standards of performance and ethical behaviour. Employees who belong to countercultural groups are an important source of surveillance and critique over the dominant order.[13] They encourage constructive controversy and more creative thinking about how the organization should interact with its environment. Strong cultures can cause people to act blindly, whereas subcultures ensure that corporate activities do not violate wider societal values of ethical behaviour. Thus, while maintaining a reasonably strong dominant culture, leaders also need to support the organization's subcultures.

Communicating Organizational Culture

Artifacts represent an important dimension of organizational culture because they are the means by which culture is communicated.[14] Artifacts come in many forms, but they may be generally classified into four broad categories: organizational stories, rituals and ceremonies, language, and physical structures and space.

Organizational stories

Four Seasons Hotels has a strong customer service culture, partly because employees share stories about the company's past events and corporate heroes. One of the most famous stories is about a bellman at the Four Seasons Yorkville hotel in Toronto who wanted to return a briefcase that a visiting diplomat had left behind. The diplomat had left for Washington, D.C., so the bellman flew there at his own expense to personally ensure that the diplomat received the briefcase intact. Employees also like to recall the story about Four Seasons staff members receiving a call from visiting rock star Rod Stewart for someone to play the bagpipes in his suite. The employees were able to find a willing bagpipe player, even though Stewart phoned in the request at *midnight!*[15]

These anecdotes about employees at Four Seasons Hotels illustrate how organizational stories serve as powerful social prescriptions of "the way things should (or should not) be done around here." They provide human realism to individual performance standards and use role models to demonstrate that organizational objectives are attainable. Stories are most effective at communicating the organization's culture when they are told to employees throughout the company, the stories describe real people, employees believe that the stories are true, and the stories are prescriptive—they describe how things are to be done (or not to be done) in the organization.[16]

Rituals and ceremonies

Rituals
The programmed routines of daily organizational life that dramatize the organization's culture.

Ceremonies
Deliberate and usually dramatic displays of organizational culture, such as celebrations and special social gatherings.

Rituals are the programmed routines of daily organizational life that dramatize the organization's culture. They include such activities as how often senior managers visit subordinates, how meetings are conducted, how visitors are greeted, and how much time employees take for lunch. **Ceremonies** are planned activities conducted specifically for the benefit of an audience, such as publicly rewarding (or punishing) employees, or celebrating the launch of a new product or newly won contracts.[17]

Sun Microsystems Canada has numerous rituals and ceremonies that communicate its egalitarian and performance-oriented culture. "We are big on recognition, and we have our rituals for the people who have done something beyond the call of duty," explains Sun Canada's Director of Marketing. "It's an egalitarian organization without big offices, oak walls, or limited-edition prints. Anyone can talk to anyone regardless of title without protocol. It means there are fewer political games."

Organizational language

As was mentioned in Chapter 6, language is an important element in transmitting and sustaining shared values. Specifically, people adopt metaphors and other special vocabularies that represent their perspective of reality.[18] IBM employees use the phrase "wild ducks" to describe co-workers who like to deviate from traditional practices. Subcultures also develop metaphors to symbolize values that oppose the dominant culture. For instance, employees at Merrill Lynch Canada refer to themselves as the "Canadian colony" and the company's world headquarters in New York as "the palace." These metaphors communicate the tense relationship between Merrill Lynch and its Canadian subsidiary.[19]

Physical structures and space

Anyone who walks along Front and Yonge Streets in Toronto can't help but notice the relatively squat, solid-looking building with unusually rich, reflective windows. This is the Royal Bank of Canada's headquarters, and it symbolizes the company's undeniable image of financial security and strength. Indeed, the building literally glistens with 2,500 ounces of gold coating on its mirror-glass exterior, ostensibly for climate control within the building, but also conveying a deeper meaning.[20] (Some people half-jokingly suggest that if there was ever a run on the bank, Royal Bank could simply start melting its windows!)

Physical structures and spaces provide subtle images of the company's underlying values and beliefs.[21] Perspective 16–2 describes how companies are discovering the importance of building and office design to reinforce and transmit corporate culture. The size, shape, location, and age of buildings might suggest the organization's emphasis on teamwork, risk aversion, flexibility, or any other set of values.

Graham Harrop. Used with permission.

Perspective 16–2

Transmitting Cultural Values through Building Design

A few years ago, British Petroleum's (BP) new chairperson decided that the best way to get rid of the company's hierarchical and bureaucratic culture was to move from its 35-story headquarters building in London, England, to a structure that more closely represented an open, efficient, and egalitarian value system. Soon after, BP's headquarters were relocated a few hundred yards down the road to Number One, Finsbury Circus. The new building has open space and few closed offices. A few people do get their own offices at Finsbury Circus, but strictly on the basis of need rather than status.

"We were trying to reflect two aspects," explains BP's manager in charge of the relocation. "One was a flatter, less hierarchical society and, two, a more open arrangement of interchanging information and being more aware of what's going on around you inside the company. That really means that you do two things: first, you don't give everybody an office in which they can shut the door and pretend there's no one else around, and, second, you keep the place as open-plan as possible."

Nike Inc. is another company that has successfully reinforced its corporate culture through building and office design. Set on 74 sprawling acres amid Oregon's pine groves, the Nike World Campus exudes the energy, youth, and vitality that have become synonymous with Nike's products. It is a monument to the shoe manufacturer's corporate values.

Ben and Jerry's Homemade, Inc., the Vermont-based ice cream manufacturer, has a unique corporate culture that requires an equally unique building design. When founders Ben Cohen and Jerry Greenfield decided to build a new manufacturing facility for their expanding business, they wanted to maintain the company's values of individuality, having fun, and keeping close to the customer. This is reflected in the barnlike manufacturing building that has become one of Vermont's most popular sightseeing attractions. Visitors watch the manufacturing process from a glassed-in mezzanine and enjoy samples of the company's decadent delights. The fun element of Ben and Jerry's is apparent when sizing up the company's offices. One cubicle has a papier-mâché arm coming out of it; another displays a three-dimensional cow's head. The offices are painted with "interesting pastels" and the doors are all trimmed in hot pink.

Sources: G. S. Capowski, "Designing a Corporate Identity," *Management Review,* June 1993, pp. 37–39; and A. Oakley, "The Company Character Revealed in Design," *Management Today,* February 1993, p. 83.

Office design represents another relevant artifact. Organizational cultures that emphasize hierarchy tend to carefully measure offices so that higher officials have larger spaces and more expensive furniture. Procter & Gamble Canada, for instance, has a well-defined protocol for office size, furniture, and carpeting according to the person's position in the organization. In contrast, one Brazilian bank (Bradesco) has no private offices for its 137,000 employees, reflecting that organization's egalitarian and team-oriented culture. These values are also emphasized at the head office, where senior managers don't even have private desks; instead, they sit around two large tables in one room.[22]

Merging Organizational Cultures

Until recently, mergers and acquisitions were decided almost entirely from a financial or marketing perspective. Little consideration was given to differences

Perspective 16–3

Bombardier's Bicultural Audit of Potential Acquisitions

Bombardier Inc., the Montreal-based transportation vehicle manufacturer, has acquired several companies over the years, and developed a strict set of guidelines for deciding whether to proceed with new purchases. The targeted company must be in a niche of the transportation business, have sales of at least $300 million, and be in a sector in which Bombardier can play a leadership role. But even if these conditions are met, Bombardier's management will walk away from the deal if the targeted company's cultural values are out of line.

An organization's values and beliefs aren't found at the bottom of a financial statement, so a management team conducts a personal diagnosis and evaluation of the situation. "When we look at a possible acquisition, the first thing we look at in-house is whether or not we share the same values," says Bombardier president Raymond Royer. "What we are trying to do is to see if there is a common understanding of what we are trying to achieve as a company and what the firm we are looking at purchasing is trying to achieve."

Before purchasing Canadair from the Canadian government, Royer and other Bombardier managers interviewed Canadair's managers at all levels, asking them to assess their organization. Based on this process, Bombardier's management knew that a dramatic shakeout would be required to transform the aircraft maker's sluggish bureaucracy into Bombardier's entrepreneurial and aggressive culture. "We are bringing Bombardier culture to Canadair and not the opposite," Bombardier CEO Laurent Beaudoin said confidently at the time. Canadair employees have since adopted a set of beliefs and values more closely aligned with those of Bombardier.

Bombardier's management conducted a similar bicultural audit with Short Brothers PLC in Northern Ireland before it was acquired. "For Short, we went and did our investigation much more deeply," explains Royer. Bombardier's bicultural audit team met with all of Short's top executives and leaders of its seven labour unions. Employee representatives from Short Brothers were then invited to visit their counterparts at Canadair (Bombardier's aircraft division). Only after Bombardier's management was confident that a cultural connection could be made did it purchase Short Brothers from the British government.

Sources: D. Estok, "Putting a Bloom on Intangibles," *Financial Post 500*, Summer 1990, pp. 56–61; and A. Zerbisias, "How Do You Make a Turkey Soar?" *Report on Business Magazine*, October 1987, pp. 82–89.

---

in the organizational cultures of the companies involved. Yet attempting to merge two organizations with distinct values and beliefs could result in a cultural collision that threatens the success of an otherwise strategically compatible merger.[23]

The risk of a postmerger culture clash can be minimized by conducting a bicultural audit that diagnoses cultural relations between the companies.[24] A bicultural audit begins with interviews, questionnaires, focus groups, and observation of cultural artifacts to identify cultural differences between the merging companies. Next, the audit data are analyzed to determine which differences between the two firms will result in conflict and which cultural values provide common ground on which to build a cultural foundation in the merged organization. The final stage of the bicultural audit involves identifying strategies and preparing action plans to bridge the two organizations' cultures. Perspective 16–3 describes how Bombardier Inc. uses a bicultural audit before acquiring other companies.

Strategies to merge different organizational cultures

In some cases, the bicultural audit results in a decision to end merger talks because the two cultures are too different to merge effectively. However, even with vastly different cultures, two companies may form a workable union if they apply the appropriate merger strategy. The four main strategies for merging different corporate cultures are integration, deculturation, assimilation, and separation.[25]

The integration strategy involves combining the two cultures into a new composite culture that preserves the best features of the previous cultures. This is usually a slow and potentially risky strategy, because there are many forces preserving the existing cultures. Integration is most effective when the two companies have relatively weak cultures, or when their cultures include several overlapping values. Integration also works best when people realize that their existing cultures are ineffective and are, therefore, motivated to adopt a new set of dominant values.

Deculturation occurs when the acquiring organization imposes its culture and practices on the acquired organization. This is the most common strategy; it is also potentially the most destructive. It creates high levels of confusion, conflict, resentment, and stress, particularly when the acquired company has a strong and distinct set of dominant values.

A preferred situation is assimilation, in which employees at the acquired company willingly embrace the cultural values of the acquiring organization. This tends to occur when the acquired company has a weak culture that is dysfunctional, whereas the acquiring company's culture is strong and focussed on clearly defined values.

Finally, some mergers adopt a separation strategy, in which the merging companies agree to remain distinct entities with minimal exchange of culture or organizational practices. In other words, the two companies are sufficiently independent that the acquired firm can maintain its existing culture. Separation is most appropriate when the two merging companies are in unrelated industries because, as noted earlier, the most appropriate cultural values tend to differ with industry. Unfortunately, the acquiring company usually wants to control managerial decisions by imposing its own cultural values, so few mergers result in a long-lasting separation strategy.

Strengthening Organizational Culture

Whether merging two cultures or reshaping the firm's existing values, corporate leaders need to understand how to strengthen weak organizational cultures. As we warned earlier, strong cultures increase organizational effectiveness only if the cultural content fits the external environment and the culture is not so strong that it drives out dissenting views. With these concerns in mind, let's examine the five strategies in Exhibit 16–2 to strengthen organizational culture.

Actions of founders and leaders

Founders have a major effect on organizational culture because, from the very beginning, they establish the organization's purpose and lay down its basic

Strategies for Strengthening Organizational Culture   Exhibit 16–2

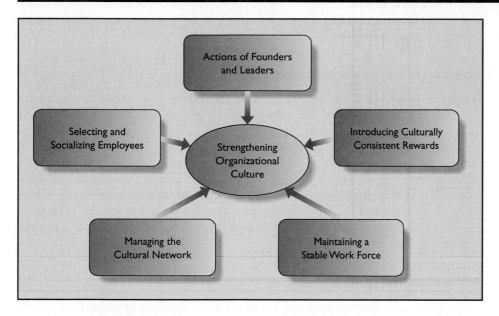

philosophy for interaction with the external environment.[26] We can certainly see the powerful influence of living founders such as Isadore Sharp at Four Seasons Hotels, Anita Roddick at The Body Shop, and Frank Stronach at Magna International. The founder's cultural imprint often remains with the organization for many years after other leaders take over the company's direction. For example, Eaton's well-known emphasis on customer satisfaction was established by Timothy Eaton soon after his first store opened in 1869.[27] He coined the company's credo of "goods satisfactory or money refunded"—a phrase that continues to reflect Eaton's core values of customer service and value.

By communicating and enacting their vision of the future, transformational leaders strengthen organizational culture.[28] Cultural values are particularly reinforced when leaders behave in ways that are consistent with the vision ("walking the talk"). Four Seasons Hotels founder Isadore Sharp maintains a strong quality service culture by ensuring that managers are consistent with this cultural standard. "Employees watch their managers and take their cues from them, so our managers have to act as role models," says Sharp. "We made changes at the very top—head-office senior executives, hotel general managers—until those whom others would imitate were setting the proper standard. The message got through and superior service became our competitive edge."[29]

Introducing culturally consistent rewards

Reward systems can strengthen corporate culture when they are consistent with cultural values.[30] For example, Microsoft Corporation uses stock options, new job opportunities, and competition between project groups to strengthen its culture, known as "The Microsoft Way." The Microsoft Way includes working late at night and on weekends to ensure that the company's products dominate the market. Another example is the Canadian federal government, in which a performance appraisal system for senior government administrators was introduced so that they would maintain a common set of cultural values across government departments.[31]

Maintaining a stable work force

An organization's culture is embedded in the minds of its employees. Organizational stories are rarely written down; rituals and celebrations do not usually exist in procedures manuals; organizational metaphors are not found in corporate directories. Thus, organizations depend on a stable work force to communicate and reinforce the dominant beliefs and values. The organization's culture can literally disintegrate during periods of high turnover or rapid expansion because employees have not sufficiently learned the ways to do things around the organization.[32] For this reason, some organizations try to keep their culture intact by moderating employment growth and correcting turnover problems.

Managing the cultural network

Organizational culture is learned, so an effective network of cultural transmission is necessary to strengthen the company's underlying assumptions, values, and beliefs. According to Max De Pree, CEO of furniture manufacturer Herman Miller Inc., every organization needs "tribal storytellers" to keep the organization's history and culture alive.[33] The cultural network exists through the organizational grapevine, but it can be further supported by providing opportunities for frequent interaction among employees so that stories may be shared and rituals reenacted. Senior executives must tap into the cultural network, sharing their own stories and creating new ceremonies and other opportunities to demonstrate shared meaning. Company magazines and other media can also strengthen organizational culture by communicating cultural values and beliefs more efficiently.

Selecting and socializing employees

Another way to strengthen an organization's culture is to hire people whose own beliefs and values are consistent with that culture. This strategy also increases employee satisfaction and organizational commitment, because new hires with values compatible to the corporate culture adjust more quickly to the organization.[34] Shell Canada Ltd. and Toyota Canada Ltd. carefully select people with a deeply ingrained team orientation, to ensure that a team-based culture is perpetuated at their new plants.[35]

Organizational socialization
The process by which individuals learn the values, expected behaviours, and social knowledge necessary to assume their organizational roles.

Organizations also maintain strong cultures through the effective socialization of new employees. **Organizational socialization** refers to the process by which individuals learn the values, expected behaviours, and social knowledge necessary to assume their roles in the organization.[36] By communicating the company's dominant values, job candidates and new hires are more likely to internalize these values quickly and deeply. Newcomers learn about the organization's culture through recruiting literature, orientation programs, and informal interactions with other employees. Companies that describe "the way things are done around here" during recruitment help applicants decide whether they identify with or reject the company's culture. This strategy also reduces employee turnover, because selected employees are less likely to experience conflict with the organization's dominant values after they are hired.[37] Let's look more closely at the process of organizational socialization.

Organizational Socialization

Organizational socialization is a process of both learning and change. It is a learning process because newcomers try to make sense of the organization, including its physical arrangements, social relationships, and cultural values. To develop a cognitive map of their new work environment, newcomers need to find reliable sources of information. Job applicants receive some objective information during the recruiting process, such as how much they are paid, where they work, and what tasks they will perform. But new employees are heavily dependent on co-workers for soft information, such as who has power, what is expected of newcomers, and how employees really get ahead in the organization.

Organizational socialization is also a process of change, because individuals need to adapt to their new work environment.[38] They develop new work roles, adopt new team norms, and practise new behaviours. To varying degrees, newcomers also acquire the values and assumptions of the organization's dominant culture as well as the local subculture. Some people quickly internalize the company's culture; a few others rebel against these attempts to change their mental models and values. Ideally, newcomers adopt a level of creative individualism in which they eventually accept the absolutely essential elements of the organization's culture and team norms, yet maintain a healthy individualism that challenges the allegedly dysfunctional elements of organizational life.

Socialization is a continuous process, beginning long before the first day of employment and continuing throughout one's career within the company. However, it is most intense when people cross organizational boundaries, such as when they first join a company, move to a new department or regional branch office, get transferred to (or back from) an international assignment, or get promoted to a higher level in the firm. For each of these transitions, employees need to learn about and adjust to an entirely new work context as well as learn role-specific behaviours.[39]

Stages of Socialization

The organizational socialization process can be divided roughly into three stages: pre-employment socialization, encounter, and role management (see Exhibit 16–3). These stages parallel the individual's transition from outsider, to newcomer, and then to insider.[40]

Stage 1: Pre-employment socialization

Think back to the weeks and days before you began working in a new job (or attending a new school). You actively searched for information about the company, formed expectations about working there, and felt some anticipation

Exhibit 16–3   **Stages of Organizational Socialization**

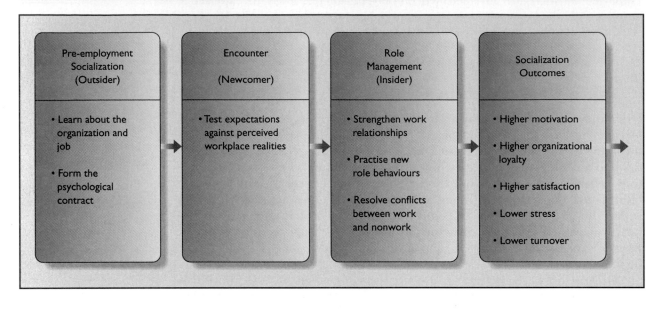

about fitting into that environment. The pre-employment socialization stage encompasses all of the learning and adjustment that occurs prior to the first day of work in a new position. Individuals are outsiders, so they must rely on friends, employment interviews, recruiting literature, and other indirect information to form expectations about what it is like to work in the organization. The employer is also forming a set of expectations about the job applicant, such as the unique skills and vitality that he or she will bring to the organization.

During the pre-employment socialization stage, both employers and job candidates form a set of perceived mutual obligations about their exchange relationship, called the **psychological contract.** The psychological contract consists mainly of implicit understandings or assumptions about what the employee should contribute to and receive from the organization. We say that these are perceived mutual obligations, because employees naturally presume that the company holds the same set of beliefs about the relationship. For example, people who believe their job may require temporary transfers to other regions of the country assume that the company has the same expectations.[41]

Psychological contract
The set of perceived mutual obligations that the employer and employee have about their exchange relationship.

Conflicts when exchanging information

Job applicants and employers need an open exchange of accurate information during pre-employment socialization to ensure that they form the same psychological contract. Unfortunately, as Exhibit 16–4 illustrates, four conflicts make it difficult for both parties to send or receive accurate information.[42]

Conflict A occurs between the employer's need to attract qualified applicants and the applicant's need for complete information to make accurate employment decisions. Many firms use a "flypaper" approach by describing only positive aspects of the job and company, causing applicants to accept job offers on the basis of incomplete or false expectations.

Conflict B occurs between the applicant's need to look attractive to employers and the organization's need for complete information to make

Information Exchange Conflicts During Pre-employment Socialization

Exhibit 16–4

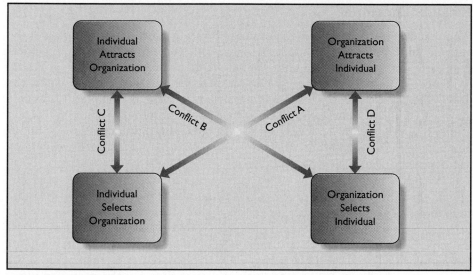

Source: L. W. Porter, E. E. Lawler III, and J. R. Hackman, *Behavior in Organizations* (New York: McGraw-Hill, 1975), p. 134. Reprinted by permission.

accurate selection decisions. The problem is that applicants sometimes emphasize favourable employment experiences and leave out less favourable events in their careers. This provides employers with inaccurate data, thereby distorting their expectations of the job candidate and weakening the quality of organizational selection decisions.

Conflict C occurs when applicants avoid asking important career decision questions because they convey an unfavourable image. For instance, applicants usually don't like to ask about starting salaries and promotion opportunities because it makes them sound greedy or overaggressive. Yet, unless the employer presents this information, applicants might fill in the missing information with false assumptions that produce an inaccurate psychological contract.

Finally, conflict D occurs when employers avoid asking certain questions or using potentially valuable selection devices because they might put the organization in a bad light. For instance, some employers refuse to use aptitude or ability tests, because they don't want to give the impression that the organization treats employees like mice running through a maze. Unfortunately, without the additional information, employers may form a less accurate opinion of the job candidate's potential as an employee.

Postdecisional justification

Both employers and job applicants further distort their perceptions of the psychological contract through the process of postdecisional justification that we discussed in Chapter 9. After the decision to accept employment has been made, new hires subconsciously increase the importance of favourable elements of the job and justify or completely forget about some negative elements. At the same time, they reduce the quality of job offers that they turned down. Employers often distort their expectations of new hires in the same way. The result is that both parties develop higher expectations of each other than they will actually experience during the encounter stage.

Stage 2: Encounter

The first day in the new work environment typically marks the beginning of the encounter stage of organizational socialization. During this stage, newcomers test their prior expectations with the perceived realities. According to recent evidence, most come to the conclusion that the employer has violated the psychological contract.[43] This sometimes occurs because the employer is unable to meet its obligations, such as failing to provide training, promotions, or job duties that were promised to job applicants. However, this perceived violation is just as likely to occur because the employee has formed a distorted psychological contract during the pre-employment socialization stage.

Reality shock
The gap between pre-employment expectations and the perceived organizational reality that employees experience as they begin work.

Whatever the cause, newcomers usually experience some degree of **reality shock** when they realize that their expectations about the employment relationship have not been met. Reality shock is the gap between what is and what ought to be. It is a specific application of discrepancy theory (described in Chapter 8) in which the perceived reality falls significantly short of the newcomer's pre-employment expectations. Some reality shocks are apparent as soon as the employee walks through the door, such as discovering that the promised office with a window is not available until next year. Other shocks are more subtle, such as eventually realizing that the company's emphasis on profits over safety are at odds with the newcomer's own values.

Reality shock can be stressful for most people, particularly when they have made a significant investment or sacrifice to join the organization (such as moving to another city or turning down other potentially good jobs). Reality shock impedes the socialization process because the newcomer's energy is directed toward managing the stress rather than learning and accepting organizational knowledge and roles.[44]

Stage 3: Role management

During the role management stage in the socialization process, employees settle in as they make the transition from newcomers to insiders. They strengthen relationships with co-workers and supervisors, practise new role behaviours, and adopt attitudes and values consistent with their new position and organization.

Role management also involves resolving the conflicts between work and nonwork activities. In particular, employees must redistribute their time and energy between work and family, reschedule recreational activities, and deal with changing perceptions and values in the context of other life roles. They must address any discrepancies between their existing values and those emphasized by the organizational culture. New self-identities are formed that are more compatible with the work environment.

Managing the Socialization Process

Organizational socialization has a profound effect on organizational effectiveness, so companies should consider various ways to guide this process. Two important strategies are realistic job previews and recognizing the importance of socialization agents.

Realistic job previews

Many companies use a flypaper approach to recruiting: They exaggerate positive features of the job and neglect to mention the undesirable elements in the hope that the best applicants will be hired and "stick" to the organization thereafter. In reality, as was described earlier, this strategy tends to produce a distorted psychological contract that eventually leads to mistrust and higher turnover.

Rather than selling the job with distorted information, companies should provide **realistic job previews** (RJPs)—giving job applicants a realistic balance of positive and negative information about the job and work context.[45] The British Columbia Transit Authority (B.C. Transit) recently adopted a realistic job preview process for people applying for bus driver positions. Job applicants are shown a video depicting angry riders, knife attacks, and other abuses that bus drivers must endure on their routes. Next, applicants meet with a union representative who explains, among other things, that new drivers are typically assigned night shifts and the poorest routes. Finally, applicants are given the opportunity to actually drive a bus. For many, it is their first experience manoeuvering a large vehicle. B.C. Transit's RJP scares away some applicants, but this minimizes hiring costs and reduces turnover of bus drivers during their first year of employment.

RJPs reduce employee turnover and increase organizational commitment because they help applicants develop more accurate pre-employment expectations that, in turn, minimize reality shock. RJPs represent a type of vaccination by preparing employees for the more challenging and troublesome aspects of work life. Moreover, applicants self-select themselves when given realistic information. For example, B.C. Transit applicants who don't like working with people tend to withdraw their job application when they realize that bus drivers frequently interact with customers. Finally, RJPs tend to build a loyal work force because they demonstrate that the company respects the psychological contract and cares about the welfare of its employees.[46]

Realistic job previews
Giving job applicants a realistic balance of positive and negative information about the job and work context.

Socialization agents

Supervisors, co-workers, and other socialization agents help newcomers learn more about and adjust to their new work setting.[47] Newcomers tend to ask supervisors for technical information as well as performance feedback and information about job duties. Supervisors also improve the socialization process by giving newcomers reasonably challenging first assignments, buffering them from excessive demands, and helping them form social ties with co-workers.[48]

Co-workers are typically the most important socialization agents, because they are easily accessible, can answer questions when problems arise, and serve as role models for appropriate behaviour. When new employees are integrated into the work team, co-workers tend to provide social support to minimize stress related to organizational socialization. Co-workers also aid the socialization process by accepting and integrating newcomers into their work roles, particularly by being flexible and tolerant in their interactions with these new hires.

Perspective 16–4

Separating the Steam from the Haze

"We need more steam mix for our hamburger buns," an experienced employee calls out to the new hire at a McDonald's Restaurant in suburban Vancouver. "Go downstairs and bring up another package of mix, please."

For the newly hired McDonald's employee, this is just another task to learn in the fast-paced and confusing world of fast-food restaurants. For seasoned employees, it is a ritual for all newcomers that usually brings hilarity to the otherwise serious work-oriented setting.

Some new employees get the joke immediately, but most scramble down the basement stairs to the food storage area in search of the elusive package of steam mix. They check among the stacks of hamburger buns and in the freezer around the boxes of french fries for any package that says "steam mix" on it. After five or ten minutes, the discouraged recruits return empty-handed and ask for further directions.

Sometimes, if it isn't too busy, co-workers might say: "It's the big bag clearly marked 'Steam Mix!'—the one with the picture of a kettle on it." Occasionally, the hazing might go one step further. With a straight face, an

employee might reply, "Oh, that's right. We're out of steam mix. Here, take this bucket and go next door to Wendy's Hamburgers. We often borrow some of their mix."

Eager to please their fellow employees, newcomers jaunt across the parking lot with a McDonald's bucket in hand and politely ask a Wendy's employee for some of their steam mix. A few Wendy's staff members have learned to play along with the game by telling the visitor that their steam mix is different than what McDonald's uses. More often, the new McDonald's worker is politely reminded that steam comes from boiled water and doesn't require any other ingredients.

Across the parking lot, co-workers watch the embarrassed (and occasionally angry) newcomer return with the empty McDonald's bucket. Somehow, the hazing ritual never loses its appeal, maybe because it provides a welcome break from the work. No one has quit over the experience, although most newcomers are cautious whenever co-workers ask them to retrieve anything from the storage area.

Source: Based on information provided to Steven L. McShane by a student who survived this hazing ritual and watched many others experience it.

Newcomers who quickly form social relations with co-workers tend to have a less traumatic socialization experience and are less likely to quit their jobs within the first year of employment.[49] However, co-workers sometimes engage in hazing—the practice of fooling or intimidating newcomers as a practical joke or initiation ritual. Perspective 16–4 describes how employees at a McDonald's restaurant in Vancouver haze new employees by asking them to look for "steam mix." This initiation seems innocent enough and certainly provides entertainment for other staff members, but it can further stress new hires and interfere with their need to form social bonds with co-workers.

Organizational Careers

Career
A sequence of work-related experiences in which people participate over the span of their working lives.

A **career** is a sequence of work-related experiences that people participate in over the span of their working lives.[50] A person's career might include lateral and downward moves, rather than just the traditional promotional climb through the organizational hierarchy. A career might cross several occupational boundaries and involve employment in several different companies over the course of the person's working life. Effective career development improves employee satisfaction and self-esteem, minimizes stress, and strengthens the employee's psychological and physical health. Effective career development benefits organizations because employees adapt more quickly to changing organizational needs.[51]

Through childhood and early work experiences, people develop a sense of their personal career interests, perceptions of personal strengths and weaknesses, and beliefs about their personal goals. This self-image, known as a **career anchor,** influences the jobs that people select as well as their personal definition of career success.[52] There are several career anchors that people might adopt to guide their career development. For example, some employees organize their careers around specific areas of technical or functional competence, such as systems engineering or commercial law; others may have a strong service anchor, so they choose jobs that involve working with clients.

Career anchor
A person's self-image of his or her abilities, motivations, and attitudes relating to a particular career orientation.

Career stages

In addition to having career anchors, people tend to pass through a series of career stages throughout their working lives.[53] There are several career stage models, but one of the most popular (shown in Exhibit 16–5) identifies the following four stages:

- *Exploration and trial:* Young adults explore different career options, receive career-related training, possibly experience one or more false starts, and begin to develop a self-image in terms of new occupational and organizational roles.

- *Establishment and advancement:* People have developed a fairly well-defined career anchor and tend to experience feelings of career progress as they receive challenging assignments, promotions, and perhaps better opportunities with other organizations. They are more motivated than at other stages to achieve career objectives and confirm their career self-identities.

- *Midcareer transition:* Beginning around age 40, this usually marks the start of a maintenance phase in which people try to hold onto their place in the organization and devote more attention to nonwork activities. Those stuck in dead-end jobs begin a psychological withdrawal from organizational life. Midcareer transition is barely noticeable for some people, because their careers continue on a growth trajectory.

- *Career disengagement:* This usually involves preparing for retirement and shifting life interests to activities outside the labour force. Some people continue their organizational roles through the later years of life and begin disengagement only when their physical and mental powers decline.

By viewing careers as a series of stages, we can better understand how they change over a person's lifetime. However, please remember that everyone has a unique career experience. You might pass through a particular stage more than once, or you might pass through a particular stage quickly or slowly. Overall, the career stages model is a general perspective, not a final statement about what your future will look like.

Exhibit 16-5   **Stages of Career Development**

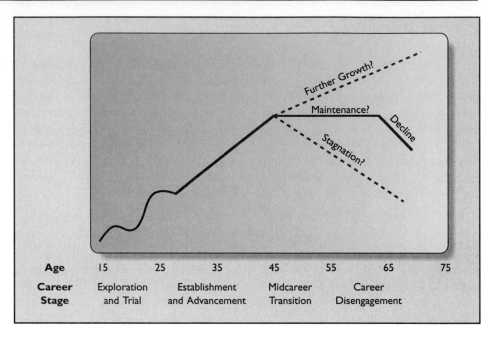

Age	15	25	35	45	55	65	75
Career Stage	Exploration and Trial		Establishment and Advancement	Midcareer Transition	Career Disengagement		

Emerging Issues in Career Development

Forty years ago, William F. Whyte wrote *Organization Man,* in which he satirically criticized how white-collar Americans defined career success in terms of secure employment with slow, steady promotions through several professional and management layers. These people devoted their entire lives to the same company, slowly working their way up the corporate ladder.[54]

Some people still follow (or believe they are following) this structured model of career development, but most do not. Increasing product competition, organizational restructuring, and flatter organizational structures have dramatically changed careers and the employment relationship. Rather than exchanging loyalty for job security and promotions, the new deal rewards people with team skills who are flexible and able to learn new tasks quickly. Rather than discussing career management, companies expect employees to practise career self-management, including finding better opportunities with other companies.[55]

Career development in lateral organizations

Traditional career paths are difficult to find today because many companies have transformed from hierarchical to team-based, lateral structures. Rather than a dozen steps on the career ladder, companies today might have four or five. The result is that career success is increasingly defined in terms of challenging work, not in the number of steps up the corporate hierarchy.

In 1979, 75 percent of middle managers were optimistic about their chances for advancement; today, less than one-third have these promotion expecta-

Du Pont Canada cut layers of management to increase its competitiveness, but this drastically reduced career advancement opportunities up the organizational heirarchy. Instead, the company now encourages lateral career development, whereby employees participate in team-based projects and develop skills across the organization.

Courtesy of DuPont Canada.

tions.[56] As a DuPont Canada manager acknowledges: [DuPont Canada employees] are suffering from the same problem every other company is: traditional movement up the corporate ladder isn't there. Downsizing and reducing layers of management have limited the opportunities. The crew ahead of me are all in their forties, and they are not going anywhere."[57]

To avoid job stagnation, DuPont and many companies now emphasize the value of **lateral career development.**[58] The idea behind lateral career development is that employees can fulfill their personal needs in different jobs across the organization rather than moving through the organizational hierarchy. DuPont and other firms have delegated more responsibility to self-managing work teams and special task forces throughout the organization, thereby making lateral job transfers more challenging and meaningful. Many career experts now encourage employees to think about their careers as a "lattice" rather than a ladder. They suggest that career success will be defined in terms of the variety of challenging work assignments a person completes across the three or four organizational levels that still remain.

Lateral career development The perspective that career success occurs when employees fulfill their personal needs in different jobs across the organization rather than by moving through the organizational hierarchy.

To encourage and assist lateral career development, many companies regularly communicate new job openings and help employees with career self-assessments. For instance, the Canadian Imperial Bank of Commerce has opened up employment development centres across the country to help employees assess their skills, see how those skills fit in the organization, and learn how they can gain the skills needed to meet their career goals. Apple Computer offers its employees a comprehensive career resource library, networking group meetings to learn about other areas of the company, and computer-based job postings.[59]

Lateral career development also requires a shift from job-status to competency-based pay systems, as was described in Chapter 4. Northern Telecom, one of the leaders in lateral career development, replaced its 21 pay grades with just 10 across the entire organization. "We wanted very much to encourage people to develop themselves through lateral moves," explains a Northern Telecom executive. "It means that there's room to give people some recognition through an increase in pay without having to get into the business of formal promotion." Bank of Montreal has applied the same strategy to reward lateral career development. "The focus is on the growth of the individual as opposed to moving up the ladder," says the Bank of Montreal's human resources vice-president. "People will be paid more on the basis of knowledge, skills, and competencies," rather than according to a job title.[60]

The boundaryless career

Jean Forrest recently left a secure position as sales and marketing director at a Canadian Pacific Hotel near Ottawa to fill the same position at the Rimrock Resort Hotel in Banff. The new job gives Forrest valuable new experience, but she mainly left because her career would be more successful by moving than by waiting a few years for better opportunities at Canadian Pacific.[61]

Boundaryless career
The idea that careers operate across company and industry boundaries rather than just within a single organizational hierarchy.

Jean Forrest is part of a growing trend toward the **boundaryless career**—the idea that careers operate across company and industry boundaries rather than just within a single organizational hierarchy. People are moving more often than ever before to different companies rather than remaining with the same employer.[62] In fact, employees currently work only five or six years for the same company. Even in Japan, where lifetime employment is supposedly the norm, employees change firms every eight years.

Although Jean Forrest changed jobs voluntarily, many career moves result from massive organizational restructuring and delayering. Downsizing— reducing the number of people on the company's payroll—has become almost fashionable among senior executives. Canadian National, IBM Canada, and other companies have announced major work force reductions in recent years. Since 1989, Labatt Breweries of Canada has chopped 25 percent of its work force. In 1993, Ontario Hydro cleared out nearly 7,000 employees within a few months.[63]

These layoffs, early retirements, and other forms of work force reduction have communicated the new message: Employees must watch out for their own career survival. An extreme version of this philosophy recently took place at Ontario Hydro, where thousands of employees had to reapply for their own jobs. Those who were replaced by co-workers had to find other employment. (At least one of Canada's major banks has also followed this massive job reapplication process.)

Outsourcing (or contracting out) is another practice that has pushed the trend toward the boundaryless career.[64] *Outsourcing* refers to spinning off work processes that are peripheral to the organization's core function. Maintenance, delivery, payroll, and information systems employees have been most affected. For example, Halifax-based Maritime Telegraph and Telephone Co. Ltd. decided to concentrate on core services and farm out its data processing activities to SHL Systemhouse Inc. of Ottawa. Pacific Press Ltd., publisher of Vancouver's two main daily newspapers, laid off 117 truck drivers and gave its bulk delivery business to a private trucking company.[65] Outsourcing forces employees to work for new employers and, by having fewer core employees, companies encourage more frequent movement across organizational boundaries.

Chapter Summary

- Organizational culture is the basic pattern of shared assumptions, values, and beliefs that govern behaviour within a particular organization. Artifacts are the observable symbols and signs of an organization's culture. They include organizational stories, rituals and ceremonies, language, and physical structures and space. Companies with strong cultures are generally more effective than those with weak cultures, but only when the cultural content is appropriate for the organization's environment and the culture is not so strong that it drives out the emergence of dissenting values.

- In addition to the dominant culture, organizations are comprised of subcultures. Some enhance the dominant culture by espousing parallel assumptions, values, and beliefs. Countercultures have values that oppose the organization's core values. Subcultures help organizations because they are the source of emerging values that replace aging core values. Moreover, countercultural group members provide a surveillance function to maintain ethical standards and promote creative thinking.

- Strengthening organizational culture is important if the cultural content "fits" the external environment. A strong culture is perpetuated through the actions of founders and leaders. Culture is also strengthened by selecting and socializing employees, introducing culturally consistent rewards, maintaining a stable work force, and managing the cultural network.

- Mergers should include a bicultural audit to diagnose the compatibility of the two organizational cultures. The four main strategies for merging different corporate cultures are integration, deculturation, assimilation, and separation.

- Organizational socialization is the process by which individuals learn the values, expected behaviours, and social knowledge necessary to assume their roles in the organization. It is a learning process in which newcomers try to make sense of their new work environment. It is also a process of change, as newcomers practise new behaviours and adopt new perspectives in line with team norms and the organizational culture.

- Organizational socialization is continuous, but it is most intense when people cross organizational boundaries. Employees typically pass through three socialization stages: pre-employment socialization, encounter, and role management. To manage the socialization process, organizations should introduce realistic job previews and recognize the value of socialization agents in the process.

- A career is a sequence of work-related experiences in which people participate over the span of their working lives. People develop career anchors that influence the jobs they select as well as their personal definition of career success. They also pass through a series of career stages throughout their working lives: exploration and trial, establishment and advancement, mid-career transition, and career disengagement.

- Career patterns have changed dramatically in recent years. Rather than the "organization man" system of working for a single organization and rising slowly through its hierarchy, people are increasingly faced with flatter organizations and corporate restructuring. The trend is now toward lateral career development and the boundaryless career.

Discussion Questions

1. Identify four types of artifacts used to communicate organizational culture. Why are artifacts used for this purpose?

2. Some people suggest that the most effective organizations have the strongest cultures. What do we mean by the "strength" of organizational culture, and what possible problems are there with a strong organizational culture?

3. Acme Ltd. is planning to acquire Beta Corp., which operates in a different industry. Acme's culture is entrepreneurial and fast paced, whereas Beta employees value slow, deliberate decision making by consensus. Which merger strategy would you recommend to minimize culture shock when Acme acquires Beta? Explain your answer.

4. Discuss what is meant by the statement, "Organizational socialization is a process of learning and change."

5. After three months on the job, you feel that the company has violated the psychological contract. The job is not as exciting as you originally expected, and your current boss is no better than the supervisor in your previous job. The people who interviewed you are concerned about your feelings, but say that they didn't misrepresent either the job or the fact that some supervisors are not as good as others here. Explain how your perceived psychological contract may have been distorted during pre-employment socialization.

6. Give three reasons why realistic job previews tend to reduce employee turnover and increase organizational commitment.

7. What types of career changes possibly occur during the midcareer transition? Which transition is most common during this stage? Why?

8. What can companies do to encourage and facilitate lateral career development?

Notes

1. Gillian Shaw, "Hard Work Takes the Skin Right Off Their Bodies, but Rocky Mountain's Bike Builders Like That," *Vancouver Sun,* July 6, 1993, pp. D1, D2; and "Rocky Mountain's Bikes Win 'Almost a Cult Following,' " *Calgary Herald,* July 27, 1992, p. C2.

2. E. H. Schein, "What Is Culture?" in *Reframing Organizational Culture,* ed. P. J. Frost, L. F. Moore, M. R. Louis, C. C. Lundberg, and J. Martin (Beverly Hills, Calif.: Sage, 1991), pp. 243–53; and A. Williams, P. Dobson, and M. Walters, *Changing Culture: New Organizational Approaches* (London, England: Institute of Personnel Management, 1989).

3. For the effect of industry on organizational culture, see J. A. Chatman and K. A. Jehn, "Assessing the Relationship Between Industry Characteristics and Organizational Culture: How Different Can You Be?" *Academy of Management Journal* 37 (1994), pp. 522–53.

4. B. Ashforth and F. Mael, "Social Identity Theory and the Organization," *Academy of Management Review* 14 (1989), pp. 20–39.

5. A. Furnham and B. Gunter, "Corporate Culture: Definition, Diagnosis, and Change," *International Review of Industrial and Organizational Psychology* 8 (1993), pp. 233–61; E. H. Schein, "Organizational Culture," *American Psychologist*, February 1990, pp. 109–19; J. S. Ott, *The Organizational Culture Perspective* (Pacific Grove, Calif.: Brooks/Cole, 1989), Chapter 2; and W. J. Duncan, "Organizational Culture: 'Getting a Fix' on an Elusive Concept," *Academy of Management Executive* 3 (1989), pp. 229–36.

6. A. de Carufel, "Changing 'Corporate Culture' in the Public Sector: Lessons from Two Canadian Case Studies," *Proceedings of the Annual ASAC Conference, Organizational Behaviour Division* 8, pt. 5 (1987), pp. 37–46; and J. P. Siegel, "Searching for Excellence: Company Communications as Reflections of Culture," *Proceedings of the Annual ASAC Conference, Organizational Behaviour Division* 5, pt. 5 (1984), pp. 1–8.

7. G. S. Saffold, III, "Culture Traits, Strength, and Organizational Performance: Moving Beyond 'Strong' Culture," *Academy of Management Review* 13 (1988), pp. 546–58; and Williams et al., *Changing Culture*, pp. 24–27.

8. C. Siehl and J. Martin, "Organizational Culture: A Key to Financial Performance?" in *Organizational Climate and Culture*, ed. B. Schneider (San Francisco, Calif.: Jossey-Bass, 1990), pp. 241–81; J. B. Barney, "Organizational Culture: Can It Be a Source of Sustained Competitive Advantage?" *Academy of Management Review* 11 (1986), pp. 656–65; V. Sathe, *Culture and Related Corporate Realities* (Homewood, Ill.: Irwin, 1985), Chapter 2; and T. E. Deal and A. A. Kennedy, *Corporate Cultures* (Reading, Mass.: Addison-Wesley, 1982), Chapter 1.

9. G. G. Gordon and N. DiTomasco, "Predicting Corporate Performance from Organizational Culture," *Journal of Management Studies* 29 (1992), pp. 783–98; and D. R. Denison, *Corporate Culture and Organizational Effectiveness* (New York: Wiley, 1990).

10. E. H. Schein, "On Dialogue, Culture, and Organizational Learning," *Organization Dynamics*, Autumn 1993, pp. 40–51.

11. S. Sackmann, "Culture and Subcultures: An Analysis of Organizational Knowledge," *Administrative Science Quarterly* 37 (1992), pp. 140–61; J. Martin and C. Siehl, "Organizational Culture and Counterculture: An Uneasy Symbiosis," *Organizational Dynamics*, Autumn 1983, pp. 52–64; Ott, *The Organizational Culture Perspective*, pp. 45–47; and Deal and Kennedy, *Corporate Cultures*, pp. 138–39.

12. C. Waddell, "Suffering from Shell Shock," *Report on Business Magazine*, March 1985, pp. 87–92.

13. A. Sinclair, "Approaches to Organizational Culture and Ethics," *Journal of Business Ethics* 12 (1993), pp. 63–73.

14. J. S. Pederson and J. S. Sorensen, *Organisational Cultures in Theory and Practice* (Aldershot, England: Gower, 1989), pp. 27–29.

15. K. Foss, "Isadore Sharp," *Foodservice and Hospitality*, December 1989, pp. 20–30; and J. DeMont, "Sharp's Luxury Empire," *Maclean's*, June 5, 1989, pp. 30–33.

16. R. Zemke, "Storytelling: Back to a Basic," *Training* 27 (March 1990), pp. 44–50; A. L. Wilkins, "Organizational Stories as Symbols Which Control the Organization," in *Organizational Symbolism*, ed. L. R. Pondy, P. J. Frost, G. Morgan, and T. C. Dandridge (Greenwich, Conn.: JAI Press, 1984), pp. 81–92; and J. Martin and M. E. Powers, "Truth or Corporate Propaganda: The Value of a Good War Story," in *Organizational Symbolism*, ed. Pondy et al. pp. 93–107.

17. J. M. Beyer and H. M. Trice, "How an Organization's Rites Reveal Its Culture," *Organizational Dynamics* 15(4) (1987), pp. 5–24; and L. Smirchich, "Organizations as Shared Meanings," in *Organizational Symbolism*, ed. Pondy et al. pp. 55–65.

18. L. A. Krefting and P. J. Frost, "Untangling Webs, Surfing Waves, and Wildcatting," in *Organizational Culture*, ed. P. J. Frost, L. F. Moore, M. R. Louis, C. C. Lundberg, and J. Martin (Beverly Hills, Calif.: Sage, 1985), pp. 155–68.

19. P. Best and J. Stackhouse, "The Palace Revolution," *Financial Times*, March 27, 1989, pp. 18, 20.

20. P. Young, "Monuments to Money," *Maclean's*, November 26, 1990, pp. 72–73.

21. J. M. Kouzes and B. Z. Posner, *The Leadership Challenge* (San Francisco: Jossey-Bass, 1988), pp. 207–8.

22. L. Schuster, "At a Bank in Brazil, Stress on Teamwork Pays Dividends," *The Wall Street Journal*, August 22, 1985.

23. G. A. Walter, "Culture Collisions in Mergers and Acquisitions," in *Organizational Culture*, ed. Frost et al. pp. 301–14; A. F. Buono and J. L. Bowditch, *The Human Side of Mergers and Acquisitions* (San Francisco, Calif.: Jossey-Bass, 1989), Chapter 6; and Schein, *Organizational Culture and Leadership*, pp. 33–36.

24. M. Raynaud and M. Teasdale, "Confusions and Acquisitions: Post-Merger Culture Shock and Some Remedies," *IABC Communication World*, May/June 1992, pp. 44–45.

25. A. R. Malekazedeh and A. Nahavandi, "Making Mergers Work by Managing Cultures," *Journal of Business Strategy*, May/June 1990, pp. 55–57.

26. E. H. Schein, "The Role of the Founder in Creating Organizational Culture," *Organizational Dynamics* 12(1) (Summer 1983), pp. 13–28.

27. G. G. Nasmith, *Timothy Eaton* (Toronto: McClelland & Stewart, 1923); and M. E. MacPherson, *Shopkeepers to a Nation: The Eatons* (Toronto: McClelland & Stewart, 1963).

28. E. H. Schein, *Organizational Culture and Leadership* (San Francisco, Calif.: Jossey-Bass, 1985), Chapter 10; and T. J. Peters, "Symbols, Patterns, and Settings: An Optimistic Case for Getting Things Done," *Organizational Dynamics* 7(2) (Autumn 1978), pp. 2–23.

29. I. Sharp, "Quality for All Seasons," *Canadian Business Review* 17(1) (Spring 1990), p. 22.

30. J. Kerr and J. W. Slocum, Jr., "Managing Corporate Culture Through Reward Systems," *Academy of Management Executive* 1 (May 1987), pp. 99–197; Williams et al., *Changing Cultures*, pp. 120–24; and K. R. Thompson and F. Luthans, "Organizational Culture: A Behavioral Perspective," in *Organizational Climate and Culture,* ed. Schneider pp. 319–44.

31. M. Meyer, "Culture Club," *Newsweek,* July 11, 1994, pp. 38–42; and J. Bourgault, S. Dion, and M. Lemay, "Creating a Corporate Culture: Lessons from the Canadian Federal Government," *Public Administration Review* 53 (1993), pp. 73–80.

32. W. G. Ouchi and A. M. Jaeger, "Type Z Organization: Stability in the Midst of Mobility," *Academy of Management Review* 3 (1978), pp. 305–14; and K. McNeil and J. D. Thompson, "The Regeneration of Social Organizations," *American Sociological Review* 36 (1971), pp. 624–37.

33. M. De Pree, *Leadership Is an Art* (East Lansing, Mich.: Michigan State University Press, 1987).

34. J. A. Chatman, "Matching People and Organizations: Selection and Socialization in Public Accounting Firms," *Administrative Science Quarterly* 36 (1991), pp. 459–84.

35. J. Matthews, "Hiring: Nothing but Child's Play," *Canadian Business,* August 1991, p. 15; and K. Romain, "Teamwork at Toyota Raises Corolla Output," *Globe & Mail,* February 22, 1990, pp. B1, B4.

36. J. Van Maanen, "Breaking In: Socialization to Work," in *Handbook of Work, Organization, and Society,* ed. R. Dubin (Chicago: Rand McNally, 1976), p. 67.

37. C. A. O'Reilly III, J. Chatman, and D. F. Caldwell, "People and Organizational Culture: A Profile Comparison Approach to Assessing Person–Organization Fit," *Academy of Management Journal* 34 (1991), pp. 487–516.

38. C. D. Fisher, "Organizational Socialization: An Integrative View," *Research in Personnel and Human Resources Management* 4 (1986), pp. 101–45; and N. Nicholson, "A Theory of Work Role Transitions," *Administrative Science Quarterly* 29 (1984), pp. 172–91.

39. C. C. Pinder and K. G. Schroeder, "Time to Proficiency Following Job Transfers," *Academy of Management, 2nd ed. Journal* 30 (1987), pp. 336–53; and N. J. Adler, *International Dimensions of Organizational Behavior* (Belmont, Calif.: Wadsworth, 1991), Chapter 8.

40. Van Maanen, "Breaking In," pp. 67–130; L. W. Porter, E. E. Lawler III, and J. R. Hackman, *Behavior in Organizations* (New York: McGraw-Hill, 1975), pp. 163–67; and D. C. Feldman, "The Multiple Socialization of Organization Members," *Academy of Management Review* 6 (1981), pp. 309–18.

41. S. L. Robinson, M. S. Kraatz, and D. M. Rousseau, "Changing Obligations and the Psychological Contract: A Longitudinal Study," *Academy of Management Journal* 37 (1994), pp. 137–52; and D. M. Rousseau and J. M. Parks, "The Contracts of Individuals and Organizations," *Research in Organizational Behavior* 15 (1993), pp. 1–43.

42. Porter et al., *Behavior in Organizations,* Chapter 5.

43. S. L. Robinson and D. M. Rousseau, "Violating the Psychological Contract: Not the Exception but the Norm," *Journal of Organizational Behavior* 15 (1994), pp. 245–59.

44. M. R. Louis, "Surprise and Sensemaking: What Newcomers Experience in Entering Unfamiliar Organizational Settings," *Administrative Science Quarterly* 25 (1980), pp. 226–51; and D. L. Nelson, "Organizational Socialization: A Stress Perspective," *Journal of Occupational Behaviour* 8 (1987), pp. 311–24.

45. J. A. Breaugh, *Recruitment: Science and Practice* (Boston: PWS-Kent, 1992), Chapter 7; J. P. Wanous, *Organizational Entry,* 2nd ed. (Reading, Mass.: Addison-Wesley, 1992), Chapter 3; and A. M. Saks and S. F. Cronshaw, "A Process Investigation of Realistic Job Previews: Mediating Variables and Channels of Communication," *Journal of Organizational Behavior* 11 (1990), pp. 221–36.

46. J. P. Wanous and A. Colella, "Organizational Entry Research: Current Status and Future Directions," *Research in Personnel and Human Resources Management* 7 (1989), pp. 59–120.

47. N. J. Allen and J. P. Meyer, "Organizational Socialization Tactics: A Longitudinal Analysis of Links to Newcomers' Commitment and Role Orientation," *Academy of Management Journal* 33 (1990), pp. 847–58; F. M. Jablin, "Organizational Entry, Assimilation, and Exit," in *Handbook of Organizational Communication,* ed. F. M. Jablin, L. L. Putnam, K. H. Roberts, and L. W. Porter (Beverly Hills, Calif.: Sage, 1987), pp. 679–740; G. R. Jones, "Socialization Tactics, Self-Efficacy, and Newcomers' Adjustments to Organizations," *Academy of Management Journal* 29 (1986), pp. 262–79; and Fisher, "Organizational Socialization," pp. 132–37.

48. E. W. Morrison, "Newcomer Information Seeking: Exploring Types, Modes, Sources, and Outcomes," *Academy of Management Journal* 36 (1993), pp. 557–89; Fisher, "Organizational Socialization," pp. 135–36; and Porter et al., *Behavior in Organizations,* pp. 184–86.

49. S. L. McShane, "Effect of Socialization Agents on the Organizational Adjustment of New Employees," Paper presented at the Annual Conference of the Western Academy of Management, Big Sky, Montana, March 1988; and W. M. Evan, "Peer-Group Interaction and Organizational Socialization: A Study of Employee Turnover," *American Sociological Review* 28 (1963), pp. 436–40.

50. M. B. Arthur, D. T. Hall, and B. S. Lawrence, "Generating New Directions in Career Theory: The Case for a Transdisciplinary Approach," in *Handbook of Career Theory*, ed. M. B. Arthur, D. T. Hall, and B. S. Lawrence (Cambridge, England: Cambridge University Press, 1989), pp. 7–25.

51. D. T. Hall, *Careers in Organizations* (Glenview, Ill.: Scott, Foresman, 1976), pp. 93–97; T. McAteer-Early, "Career Development and Health-Related Complaints: Development of a Measuring Instrument," *Proceedings of the Annual ASAC Conference, Personnel and Human Resources Division* 12, pt. 8 (1991), pp. 70–79; and R. J. Burke and E. R. Greenglass, "Career Orientations, Satisfaction and Health: A Longitudinal Study," *Canadian Journal of Administrative Sciences* 7 (September 1990), pp. 19–25.

52. E. H. Schein, "Individuals and Careers," in *Handbook of Organizational Behavior*, ed. J. W. Lorsch (Englewood Cliffs, N.J.: Prentice Hall, 1987), pp. 155–71; and R. P. Bourgeois and T. Wils, "Career Concepts, Personality and Values of Some Canadian Workers," *Relations Industrielles* 42 (1987), pp. 528–43.

53. Hall, *Careers in Organizations*, Chapter 3; and J. H. Greenhaus, *Career Management* (Chicago, Ill.: Dryden, 1987), Chapter 5.

54. W. F. Whyte, *Organization Man* (New York: Simon & Schuster, 1956).

55. B. O'Reilly, "The New Deal: What Companies and Employees Owe One Another," *Fortune*, June 13, 1994, pp. 44–52.

56. W. F. Cascio, "Downsizing: What Do We Know? What Have We Learned?" *Academy of Management Executive* 7 (February 1993), pp. 95–104.

57. E. Innes, J. Lyon, and J. Harris, *100 Best Companies to Work For in Canada* (Toronto: HarperCollins, 1990), p. 46.

58. D. T. Hall and J. Richter, "Career Gridlock: Baby Boomers Hit the Wall," *Academy of Management Executive* 4 (August 1990), pp. 7–22.

59. T. Degler, "Career Planning Joins Outplacement to Facilitate Employee Transition," *Canadian HR Reporter*, July 18, 1994, pp. 8–9; and S. Caudron, "Apple Computer Leaves No Stone Unturned in Employee Career Management," *Personnel Journal* 73 (April 1994), p. 64E.

60. D. Luckow, "Moving Up by Moving Sideways," *Financial Times of Canada*, April 10–16, 1993, pp. 19–20.

61. Luckow, "Moving Up by Moving Sideways," p. 19.

62. M. B. Arthur, "The Boundaryless Career: A New Perspective for Organizational Inquiry," *Journal of Organizational Behavior* 15 (1994), pp. 295–306.

63. V. Galt, "Musical Chairs a Crying Game," *Globe & Mail*, November 13, 1993, pp. B1, B2; and W. Cuthbert, "Corporate Life after Downsizing," *Financial Post*, March 20, 1993, p. 8.

64. R. J. Defillippi and M. B. Arthur, "The Boundaryless Career: A Competency-Based Perspective," *Journal of Organizational Behavior* 15 (1994), pp. 307–24.

65. A. Safer, "Revenge on the Nerds," *Canadian Business* 65 (October 1992), pp. 137–42; and R. Williamson, "Pacific Press Cuts Trucking Unit," *Globe & Mail*, May 12, 1993, p. B4.

Chapter Case

The Cultural Collision of Manulife Financial and Dominion Life

In 1985, Manulife Financial was Canada's second-largest life insurance company, with assets of more than $16 billion and business dealings in 15 countries. Although the company was performing well internationally, it was losing market share within Canada, so senior management decided to decentralize Manulife's Canadian division and buy another insurance firm with a well-established Canadian base.

Dominion Life of Waterloo, Ontario, was put up for sale by its principal shareholder, an American insurance company, and seemed an ideal fit for Manulife, at least from a business perspective. It was an efficiently run, medium-sized operation with a healthy group life business, and its major shareholder was willing to sell. By purchasing Dominion and moving Manulife's Canadian operations from Toronto to Waterloo, Manulife would achieve its objective of separating its Canadian and international businesses. Recalls Manulife's chief actuary: "When Dominion Life came up as a possibility, I thought it was a 'saviour,' an instant, justifiable fix."

Announcing the Acquisition   The announcement that Manulife had purchased Dominion Life and would move its Canadian operations to Waterloo sent shock waves throughout the company's luxurious Bloor Street headquarters. Employees had become accustomed to Manulife's recently completed North Tower with its new fitness centre, beautiful gardens, and view of a parklike ravine in the heart of Toronto. The stress was not eased any when Manulife's CEO called employees to a meeting and bluntly announced that he was not concerned with moving people below the senior level to Waterloo! The company later backtracked on this ill-advised statement and eventually began to actively woo employees to Waterloo.

Dominion Life staff were equally stressed, but for somewhat different reasons. They had known for the past six months that Dominion was up for sale, but no other details of prospective buyers were provided. Consequently, unreliable rumours ran through the company with disturbing regularity. One story was that a construction group from Vancouver had purchased the company and intended to use it as a money-laundering front for the Mafia! News that Manulife had purchased the company finally reached Dominion's employees through the local newspaper, not through a company announcement. Morale was low and the uncertainties that lay ahead fuelled more rumours.

Colliding Cultures   The merger process began when 10 entrepreneurial and aggressive Manulife managers moved their offices to Waterloo. They immediately began assessing duplications in personnel and set up task forces to deal with the logistics of the move. With the benefit of hindsight, one manager confided that the process was more difficult than they had anticipated. "We trivialized the whole thing," he says. "We underestimated the magnitude of just about the whole thing—the systems side, the administrative side, the new problems we had, and the culture change, too."

When a consulting firm was brought in to evaluate Dominion Life's management team, Manulife's team began to realize how much of a cultural chasm divided the two firms. Manulife's culture was aggressive, entrepreneurial, consultative, and sales oriented. Dominion, by contrast, was more bureaucratic, formal, patriarchal, and focussed on financial controls. "Dominion was operationally driven, but hadn't been very successful in a marketing or sales sense," recalls a former Dominion executive. "It was a very expense-driven company." Moreover, Dominion's culture was "top-down driven and far less participative than Manulife's."

No one was prepared for the consequences of the culture shock of merging the two groups. Within six months of the merger, 70 of Dominion's 500 staff resigned, were given early retirement, or were fired. Only two of Dominion's senior management survived the merger; the others were fired or given early retirement because of their "poor fit" with Manulife's culture. Although Manulife handled the departures fairly, resentment and bitterness against the invading company ran high in Waterloo for some time afterward.

Meanwhile, remaining Dominion employees experienced incredible stress as they tried to adjust to the cultural assumptions of their new employer. Recalls one survivor: "We saw Manulife's culture as a real opportunity, not a threat. But we also saw it as power without control or restraint. It was freedom, but we were frightened by it." Dominion employees also met arrogance on the part of some

Manulife employees. Explains one manager: "People began to feel like second-hand goods—'I've been bought.'"

Other Problems Develop As Manulife's business units moved to Waterloo, another problem emerged. Dominion Life was operated out of two different buildings and the increased pressure of added staff meant that another two office locations had to be rented. But even with four separate offices around Waterloo, conditions were cramped and uncomfortable. Some employees were squeezed into a basement originally built for storage, leaving some Manulife staff to wonder why they had agreed to transfer from their plush offices in Toronto.

One of the most serious crises during the merger occurred in the annuities business unit, where six of the seven key people at Manulife refused to move and the three annuities people at Dominion quit soon after the merger. As a result, every key person in that area had left the company within a span of two or three months. Annuity payments fell three months behind schedule before the problem was corrected.

These and other difficulties placed incredible pressure on the work force. Most employees had to work long overtime hours in cramped conditions to clear the backlog of work. New staff were hired to fill the gaps, resulting in lower productivity and a lot of unfamiliar faces. At the same time, employees from two very different organizational cultures had to learn to adjust to each other and operate as a single company.

Taking Action Realizing that the merger process was in trouble, Manulife's executives asked its organization development unit to introduce better communication systems and think of ways for staff from the two companies to become better acquainted. For example, Manulife's employees were given bus tours of Waterloo and were put up in the homes of Dominion Life workers for orientation sessions. Focus groups and counselling were provided to help both Dominion and Manulife staff to cope with the stress.

Perhaps the single most effective action to strengthen the new organizational culture came in the form of a new building in 1988, two years after the merger began. Unlike the previous cramped quarters, the new structure has bright and comfortable offices looking onto landscaped gardens and parkland. This more closely represents Manulife's tradition of quality and concern for employees. Moving to the new Waterloo headquarters has "already done a lot to consolidate culture," agrees a senior manager, "making it possible to manage by walking around, function as a team, and much easier to communicate."

Discussion Questions

1. **How are Manulife's and Dominion Life's cultures different? Explain how these cultural differences made the acquisition more difficult.**

2. **Discuss the relevance of organizational socialization in this case.**

3. **Discuss the relevance of physical structures in this case.**

4. **What could Manulife have done differently to improve the acquisition process?**

Sources: Based on L. Welsh, "Manulife Plans Move to Waterloo," *Globe & Mail*, November 17, 1984, p. B3; and E. Innes and L. Southwick-Trask, *Turning It Around* (Toronto: Fawcett Crest, 1990), pp. 122–37.

Experiential Exercise

Socialization Diagnosis

Purpose: To help students understand the socialization strategies that organizations should use for new employees, and to learn about the impediments to forming an accurate psychological contract.

Instructions: The instructor will form small teams of three or four students. Each member will describe one particularly memorable positive or negative experience encountered when entering an organization. (Students without employment experience can describe their entry into a school, volunteer group, or other organization.) For example, the person might describe how he or she was greeted during the first day of work, how the company kept him or her informed before the first day of work, how the company did (or didn't) tell the person about negative aspects of the work or job context.

Based on these experiences, the team will develop a list of strategies that companies should use to improve the socialization process. Some experiences will reflect effective management of the socialization process. Other experiences will indicate what companies have done ineffectively, so the team must identify strategies to avoid those problems.

When the list of strategies has been developed, each team describes one of the incidents its members have experienced and then describes what corporate socialization strategy was (or should have been) used to make this experience effective. This process can be repeated until the most significant anecdotes and their implications have been presented. The class will discuss common elements among experiences presented (e.g., realistic job previews, problems adjusting to new values, violations of the psychological contract) and strategies companies should follow to make the socialization process more effective.

Organizational Structure and Design

Learning Objectives

After reading this chapter, you should be able to:

Describe the two fundamental requirements of organizational structures.

Outline the advantages and disadvantages of centralization.

Compare the functional structure with the divisional structure.

Explain why multinational firms have difficulty selecting the best form of departmentation.

Describe four features of team-based organizational structures.

Identify four contingencies of organizational design.

Chapter Outline

Division of Labour and Coordination.

Elements of Organizational Structure.

Traditional Forms of Departmentation.

Emerging Forms of Departmentation.

Contingencies of Organizational Design.

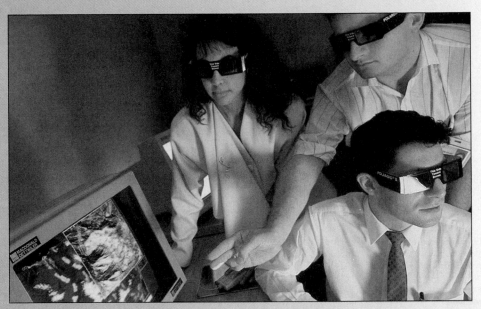

Courtesy of MacDonald Dettwiler & Associates.

*M*acDonald Dettwiler & Associates Ltd. (MDA) of Richmond, British Columbia, is a world leader in customized computer-based systems development. Its impressive list of clients includes NASA, the European Space Agency, the U.S. Air Force, and the Canadian Government. As a contract-driven company, MDA depends on a unique organizational structure that makes the most efficient and effective use of its highly skilled work force. This structure consists primarily of four business units, as well as several functional departments (engineering, finance, etc.) that report to the company president. The business units cover four product and/or client groups: meteorological systems, space and defence, geological information systems, and aviation. Each business unit has a permanent staff of marketing people as well as several temporary project teams that exist for the length of a specific contract (typically several months to a few years).

Most project team members are deployed from MDA's engineering department rather than permanent staff from the business unit. This is a type of matrix structure in which engineers have a permanent manager within the engineering department as well as a temporary project manager for the duration of the contract. When MDA is awarded a new contract, the project manager submits to the engineering department descriptions of the personnel required and, where appropriate, the names of specific employees who would suit the project's needs. The project manager coordinates work activities and reviews the performance of the people assigned to him or her throughout the project.

The eight functional engineering managers assign and assess the professionals under their command. They ensure that their employees are fully allocated to productive work activities and that these assignments provide the best possible results for the organization. The functional managers try to accommodate each project manager's request in light of competing demands for their employees. For example, when two project managers request the same employee, the engineering manager responsible for that person must use good judgment to ensure that the assignment decision is fair and ultimately in the organization's best interest. Overall, both the project and engineering managers have a healthy balance of power in the matrix structure.[1]

Organizational structure
The division of labour as well as the patterns of coordination, communication, work flow, and formal power that direct organizational activities.

Organizational design
The creation and modification of organizational structures.

This chapter introduces the different elements of organizational structure as well as the contingency factors that help determine which type of structure is best in a particular situation. You will learn, for example, why MacDonald Dettwiler & Associates uses a matrix structure to group its specialists around specific projects, whereas McDonald's Restaurants of Canada relies on a centralized functional structure to make hamburgers. **Organizational structure** refers to the division of labour as well as the patterns of coordination, communication, work flow, and formal power that direct organizational activities.[2] An organizational structure reflects the assumptions and values that are taken for granted by organizational leaders. It also reflects power relationships and ensures that certain behaviours and actions are carried out as expected.[3] Our knowledge of this subject provides the basic tools to engage in **organizational design,** that is, to create and modify organizational structures.

We begin our discussion by considering the two fundamental processes in organizational structure: division of labour and coordination. This is followed by a detailed investigation of the four main elements of organizational structure: span of control, centralization, formalization, and departmentation. The latter part of this chapter examines the contingencies of organizational design, including organizational size, technology, external environment, and strategy.

Division of Labour and Coordination

All organizational structures include two fundamental requirements: the division of labour into distinct tasks and the coordination of that labour so that employees are able to accomplish common goals.[4] Recall from Chapter 1 that organizations are social entities in which two or more people work interdependently through deliberately structured patterns of interaction to accomplish a set of goals.[5] When people gather to collectively accomplish goals, they tend to divide the work into manageable chunks, particularly when there are many different tasks to perform. They also introduce various coordinating mechanisms to ensure that everyone is working effectively toward the same objectives.

Division of labour

Job specialization
The result of division of labour, in which each job now includes a narrow subset of the tasks required to complete the product or service.

Division of labour refers to the subdivision of work into separate jobs assigned to different people. As we learned in Chapter 4, subdivided work leads to **job specialization,** because each job now includes a narrow subset of the tasks necessary to complete the product or service.

Work may be divided horizontally and vertically. Horizontal job specialization involves distributing into different jobs the tasks required to provide a product or service. Assembling a satellite at Spar Aerospace, for example, requires thousands of specific tasks that are divided among hundreds of people. Vertical job specialization separates the performance of work from its administration. In other words, it divides the thinking job functions from the doing functions. For example, secretaries might perform work processing tasks, whereas scheduling that work might be assigned to their immediate supervisor.

Organizations divide work into specialized jobs, because it increases work efficiency.[6] Job incumbents can master their tasks quickly, because work cycles are very short. Less time is wasted changing from one task to another. Training costs are reduced, because employees require fewer physical and mental skills to accomplish the assigned work. Finally, job specialization makes it easier to match people with specific aptitudes or skills to the jobs for which they are best suited.

Coordinating work activities

When work is divided among people, the organization needs to provide a coordinating mechanism to ensure that everyone works in concert.[7] Employees who work close together can coordinate directly through informal communication. Supervisors usually provide a coordinating role. Unfortunately, informal communication and direct supervision don't work well when large groups of employees are involved in complex tasks.

As organizations grow, they increasingly coordinate work activities through standardization. Some firms introduce formal instructions and job descriptions. Others use goals and product or service output indicators (e.g., customer satisfaction, production efficiency) to focus and coordinate employee work effort. When work activities are too complex to standardize through procedures or goals, companies often coordinate work effort by extensively training employees or hiring people who have learned precise role behaviours from educational programs. In hospital operating rooms, surgeons, nurses, and other operating room professionals coordinate their work more through training than goals or company rules.

Elements of Organizational Structure

There are four basic elements of organizational structure. This section introduces three of them: span of control, centralization, and formalization. The fourth element of organizational structure—departmentation—is presented in the next section.

Span of control

Span of control refers to the number of people directly reporting to a supervisor. Early management theorists prescribed a relatively narrow span of control, typically no more than 20 employees per supervisor and 6 supervisors per manager. These prescriptions were based on the assumption that managers simply cannot monitor and control any more subordinates closely enough.

More recently, scholars have concluded that the optimal span of control varies with specific circumstances.[8] One factor is the presence of other coordi-

Span of control
The number of people directly reporting to a supervisor. This element of organizational structure determines the number of hierarchical levels required in the organization.

nating mechanisms. Span of control relates to direct supervision, but the organization may also coordinate work through some form of standardization, thereby allowing a much wider span of control. For example, some senior managers have little difficulty supervising more than 40 middle managers because these managers are guided by corporate goals and extensive training.

A wider span of control may be possible when subordinates perform the same tasks, because either work processes or outputs can be standardized. When tasks are diverse, on the other hand, direct supervision becomes a more prominent coordinating mechanism. Managers simply cannot apply the same rules and practices to production staff as to the marketing staff, for example. A wider span of control might also be possible when tasks are routine, because work processes can be standardized and less time is required to discuss exceptional cases with subordinates. Finally, the optimal span of control depends on the supervisor's other duties. Someone whose main job is to supervise and coach employees may have a wider span of control than one who has many nonsupervisory tasks.

Tall and flat structures

The average span of control within the organization determines the number of hierarchical levels required. As shown in Exhibit 17–1, a tall structure has many hierarchical levels, each with a relatively narrow span of control, whereas a flat structure has few levels, each with a wide span of control.[9] Early writers recommended a relatively narrow span of control, so they necessarily prescribed many hierarchical levels. In the 1950s, Peter Drucker questioned those perspectives by saying that companies should have no more than seven hierarchical levels. In the 1980s, Tom Peters challenged management to cut the number of layers to three within a facility and to five within the entire organization.[10]

Air Canada, Domtar Inc., Labatt's Breweries, and other companies have moved toward a flatter or "delayered" organizational structure.[11] A flatter structure increases organizational productivity by cutting overhead costs. It is also consistent with the trend toward employee involvement and teamwork that we described in Chapters 10 and 11. The Toronto-Dominion (T-D) Bank, for example, has moved toward a flatter organizational structure by cutting layers of middle management and dramatically widening the average span of control. Explains a T-D manager: "[We] have developed a very flat structure to accomplish [teamwork]. Branch managers report to divisional senior vice-presidents who report to the president. That's three layers and—believe me, for a bank—that's flat!"[12]

Centralization and decentralization

Centralization
The degree that formal decision authority is held by a small group of people, typically those at the top of the organizational hierarchy.

Decentralization
The degree that decision authority is dispersed throughout the organization.

Centralization means that formal decision authority is held by a small group of people, typically those at the top of the organizational hierarchy. **Decentralization** means that decision authority is dispersed throughout the organization. With the increasing popularity of empowerment by delegating decision-making power to people further down the hierarchy, many companies have opted for more decentralized structures. However, there are pressures for both centralization and decentralization.

Span of Control Associated with Tall and Flat Structures   Exhibit 17–1

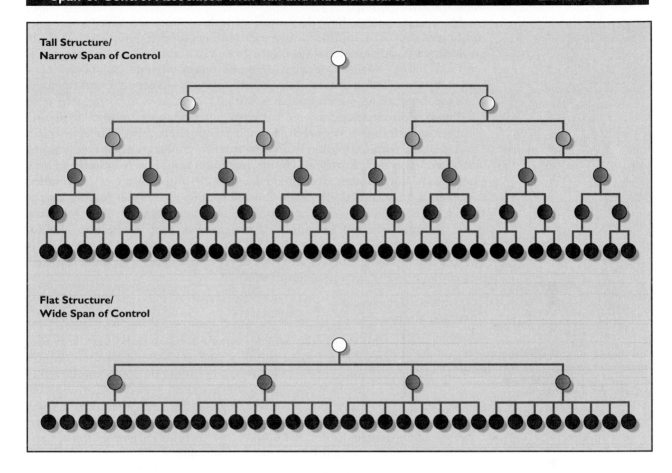

**Tall Structure/
Narrow Span of Control**

**Flat Structure/
Wide Span of Control**

Most organizations begin with centralized structures, as the founder makes most of the decisions and tries to direct the business toward his or her vision. But as organizations grow, work activities are divided into more specialized functions, a broader range of products or services is introduced, and operations expand into different regions or countries. Under these conditions, decentralization occurs because the founder and senior management lack the necessary time and expertise to process all the decisions that significantly influence the business.[13] Thus, structures become more decentralized when organizations grow and become more diverse.

Although organizational size and diversity push for decentralization, other forces push for centralization.[14] Managers try to gain decision control during times of turbulence and organizational crisis; however, when the problems are over, decision-making power does not quickly return to the lower levels. Senior executives push for centralization to increase their organizational power over organizational activities. The marketing vice-president in a chain of Canadian retail pharmacies wanted to centralize control over product displays, ostensibly because this would improve organizational efficiency. Instead, it only served to increase the senior executive's power. Sales dropped because store owners no longer had the power to put cold remedies and umbrellas in a prominent place when it started raining.

Many organizations have decentralized to be more responsive to changing conditions and to satisfy increasing expectations among lower-level staff for involvement in organizational decisions. However, there are also advantages to centralization. Centralized decisions increase uniformity and reduce the need for extensive reporting procedures. Centralization also keeps top management more informed about organizational activities.

Finally, centralization can reduce costs if, as we noted above, it doesn't reduce local flexibility too much. Compac Computers faces this issue in its European operations. The American computer manufacturer had freestanding business units in each European country so that it would be responsive to local conditions. Unfortunately, this created expensive duplication of distribution and administrative functions. When Europe formed a common trading bloc in 1992, Compac decided to centralize its distribution and administrative functions at the regional level but keep general managers in each country to monitor local conditions. The company hopes that this arrangement will keep it close to each country's market needs and yet increase operating efficiency through centralized distribution and administration.[15]

Formalization

Formalization
The degree that organizations standardize behaviour through rules, procedures, formal training, and related mechanisms.

Formalization is the degree to which organizations standardize behaviour through rules, procedures, formal training, and related mechanisms. Highly formalized organizations specify what employees should be doing and how they should be doing it. Job descriptions establish required work behaviours and performance goals. Instruction manuals describe the steps required to transform inputs to outputs. Communication patterns and interpersonal behaviours are regulated by detailed rules and procedures. Decisions are programmed and leave little room for individual initiative or discretion.[16]

Organizations formalize their structures to reduce the variability of employee behaviour so that clients receive reliable products and services. Air Canada formalizes work activities to maximize transportation safety and ensure that flight schedules are on time. As reported in Perspective 17–1, McDonald's Restaurants of Canada Ltd. has developed a highly formalized organizational structure to ensure that its hamburgers sold in St. John's, Newfoundland, look, taste, smell, and cost the same as those sold in Saanich, British Columbia.

Organizations tend to become more formalized as they age and grow in size. As firms age, roles and work activities become routinized, making them easier to document into standardized practices. Larger companies formalize as a coordinating mechanism, because direct supervision and informal communication among employees do not operate as easily. Formalization is also affected by the demands of organizational stakeholders for standardization. For instance, safety rules are introduced and strictly enforced to conform to government regulations. Specific accounting rules and procedures are followed so that the auditors will give the company a clean bill of financial health. Ethical standards of conduct are strengthened as the company faces increasing pressure from its stakeholders.

Perspective 17–1

Formalization at McDonald's Restaurants of Canada Ltd.

Formalization has been a way of life at McDonald's Restaurants of Canada Ltd. since 1968, when the company's first restaurant opened in this country. At the heart of McDonald's machine efficiency is the carefully guarded 658-page Operations and Training Manual. The book covers every activity in explicit detail, from making hamburgers in Chapter 1 to restaurant security and insurance in Chapter 26.

Every job is broken down into the smallest detail. Color photographs depict ingredients and individual products at every stage of preparation. These rules and procedures are further reinforced by videotapes to systematically train employees, three Canadian Institutes of Hamburgerology to develop McDonald's restaurant managers, and computerized machines to guide employee behaviour on the job. Says a McDonald's of Canada vice-president: "I sometimes think we invented the word system."

With clearly detailed procedures and thorough training, McDonald's 600 Canadian restaurants operate as precisely as Swiss watches. Mustard is doled out in five perfect drops. A quarter ounce of onions and two pickles—three if they're small—are used per sandwich. Drink cups are filled with ice up to a point just below the arches on their sides. Take-out bags are folded exactly twice. French fries are stacked exactly six boxes high and one inch apart, with two inches between the stacks and walls of the freezer. Cooking and bagging fries are explained in 19 steps. The strict rules even prescribe what colour of nail polish to wear.

McDonald's standards ensure that supplies are used neither too generously nor too sparsely. A jar of Big Mac sauce should produce 170 to 180 servings. Between 111 and 135 pickle slicings should be expected per pound of pickles. A pound of lettuce should dress 24 to 28 sandwiches. A gallon of milkshake mix should yield anywhere from 15.2 to 15.6 milkshakes. If a home-office field consultant discovers that a licensee is squeezing 16 shakes out of a gallon, that licensee hears about it.

The operations manual also specifies how many people it will take to open in the morning, handle the lunchtime rush, and close up the restaurant at night. McDonald's licensees have some discretion, such as whether to add more people to the order counter than stated in the operations manual, but these decisions are the result of detailed management development at the company's training centres. Explains a McDonald's of Canada senior executive: "McDonald's is not a job. It's a way of life. You have to have hamburger in your brains and ketchup in your veins."

Sources: C. Davies, "1990 Strategy Session," *Canadian Business,* January 1990, pp. 49–50; G. Morgan, *Creative Organization Theory: A Resourcebook* (Newburg Park, Calif.: Sage, 1989), pp. 271–73; and K. Deveny, "Bag Those Fries, Squirt that Ketchup, Fry that Fish," *Business Week,* October 13, 1986, p. 86.

Problems with formalization

Formalization sometimes decreases rather than increases organizational effectiveness. Rules and procedures reduce organizational flexibility, so employees follow prescribed behaviours even when the situation clearly calls for a customized response. Some work rules become so convoluted that organizational efficiency would decline if they were actually followed as prescribed. Indeed, labour unions sometimes call work-to-rule strikes, in which their members closely follow the formalized rules and procedures established by an organization. This tactic increases union power, because the company's productivity falls significantly when employees follow the rules that are supposed to guide their behaviour.

Another concern is that although employees with very strong security needs and a low tolerance for ambiguity like working in highly formalized organizations, others become alienated and feel powerless in these structures. Canada Post experiences this problem, because employees must follow the Crown corporation's rigid rules of behaviour. Finally, rules and procedures have been known to take on a life of their own in some organizations. They become the focus of attention rather than the organization's ultimate objectives of producing a product or service and serving its dominant stakeholders.

Mechanistic versus organic structures

Mechanistic structure
An organizational structure with a narrow span of control and high degrees of formalization and centralization.

Organic structure
An organizational structure with a wide span of control, very little formalization, and highly decentralized decision making.

The three elements of organizational structure described so far—span of control, centralization, and formalization—are sometimes grouped into two distinct forms known as *mechanistic* and *organic structures*.[17] A **mechanistic structure** has high degrees of formalization and centralization. It is characterized by many rules and procedures, limited decision making at lower levels, large hierarchies of people in specialized roles, and vertical rather than horizontal communication flows. Tasks are rigidly defined, and are altered only when sanctioned by higher authorities. An **organic structure** is just the opposite. It usually has very little formalization and highly decentralized decision making. Communication flows in all directions with little concern for the formal hierarchy. Tasks are fluid, adjusting to new situations and organizational needs.

Traditional Forms of Departmentation

Departmentation
An element of organizational structure specifying how employees and their activities are grouped together, such as by function, product, geographic location, or some combination.

Span of control, centralization, and formalization are important elements of organizational structure, but most people think about organizational charts when the discussion of organizational structure arises. The organizational chart represents the fourth element in the structuring of organizations, called **departmentation.** Departmentation specifies how employees and their activities are grouped together. It is a fundamental strategy for coordinating organizational activities, as it influences organizational behaviour in the following ways:[18]

- Departmentation establishes a system of common supervision among positions and units within the organization. It establishes formal work teams, as we learned in Chapter 10.

- Departmentation typically determines which positions and units must share resources. Thus, it establishes interdependencies among employees and subunits (see Chapter 13).

- Departmentation usually creates common measures of performance. Members of the same work team, for example, share common goals and budgets, giving the company standards against which to compare subunit performance.

- Departmentation encourages coordination through informal communication among people and subunits. With common supervision and resources, members within each configuration typically work near each other, so they can use frequent and informal interaction to get the work done.

There are almost as many organizational charts as there are businesses, but we can identify four pure types of departmentation: simple, functional, divisional, and matrix. Few companies fit exactly into any of these categories, but they represent a useful framework for discussing more complex hybrid forms of departmentation. This section also introduces two emerging forms of departmentation: team-based and network structures.

Simple structure

Simple structure refers to organizations that do not group employees into subunits, although a hierarchy may still exist.[19] Small businesses fall into this category, because they typically employ only a few people and offer only one distinct product or service. Del Comal Foods Ltd., the Alberta-based manufacturer of Mexican snack foods, has a simple structure, because its six employees share duties and may be assigned different tasks as the need arises. Employees are grouped in broadly defined roles, because there are insufficient economies of scale to assign them to specialized roles. For example, Ulla Meredith is usually responsible for the broad areas of marketing, purchasing, and accounting. (She is also a minority shareholder and daughter of Del Comal's founder.)[20]

Simple structures are flexible designs, yet they usually depend on the owner's direct supervision to coordinate work activities. Consequently, this structure is very difficult to operate under complex conditions. Del Comal's founder, Jorgen Rasmussen, is experiencing this problem, because expansion plans are forcing him to consider more complex forms of organizational structure.

Functional structure

A **functional structure** organizes employees around specific skills or other resources. Employees with marketing expertise are grouped into a marketing unit, those with production skills are located in manufacturing, engineers are found in product development, and so on. Exhibit 17–2 illustrates a functional structure similar to one found at B.C. Hydro. Although some departments report directly to the chief executive officer and others report to the president, all divide work activities into traditional functions.

Organizations with functional structures are typically centralized to coordinate their activities effectively. Coordination through standardization of work processes is the most common form of coordination used in a functional structure. Most organizations use functional structures at some level or at some time in their development.

Functional structure
A type of departmentation that organizes employees around specific skills or other resources.

Advantages and disadvantages

An important advantage of functional structures is that they foster professional identity and clarify career paths. They permit greater specialization so that the organization has expertise in each area. Direct supervision is easier, because managers have backgrounds in that functional area and employees approach them with common problems and issues. Finally, functional structures create common pools of talent that typically serve everyone in the organization. This creates an economy of scale that would not exist if functional specialists were spread over different parts of the organization.[21]

Functional structures also have their limitations. Because people are grouped together with common interests and backgrounds, these designs promote differentiation among functions. Dysfunctional conflict is a potential problem for this reason, as well as that functional units require high levels of interdependence. A related concern is that functional structures tend to empha-

Exhibit 17–2   Functional Organizational Structure

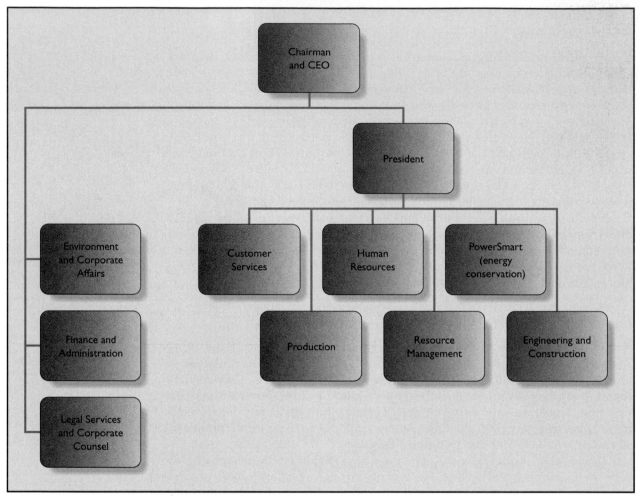

Source: Adapted from 1991 organization structure of British Columbia Hydro and Power Authority.

size subunit goals over superordinate organizational goals. Engineers, for example, tend to give lower priority to the company's product or service than to the goals of the engineering department. A third concern is that functional structures perpetuate specialization at the expense of more holistic management. Unless managers are transferred from one function to the next, they fail to develop a broader understanding of the business. Together, these problems require substantial formal controls and coordination when functional structures are used.

Divisional structure

Divisional structure
A type of departmentation that groups employees around outputs, clients, or geographic areas.

A **divisional structure** groups employees around outputs, clients, or geographic areas. Divisional structures are sometimes called *self-contained units* or *strategic business units* (SBUs), because they are normally more autonomous than functional structures and may be separate entities (e.g., subsidiaries) of the larger enterprise.

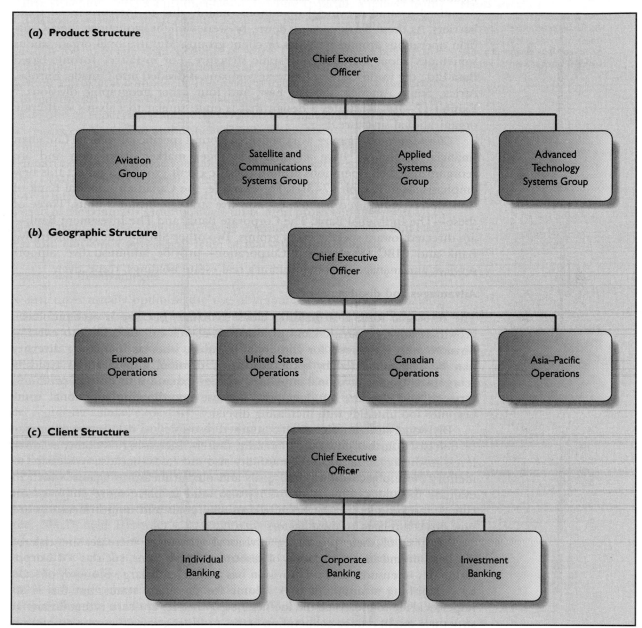

Three Types of Divisional Structure   Exhibit 17–3

(a) **Product Structure**

Chief Executive Officer

Aviation Group | Satellite and Communications Systems Group | Applied Systems Group | Advanced Technology Systems Group

(b) **Geographic Structure**

Chief Executive Officer

European Operations | United States Operations | Canadian Operations | Asia–Pacific Operations

(c) **Client Structure**

Chief Executive Officer

Individual Banking | Corporate Banking | Investment Banking

Note: Structure (*a*) is similar to Spar Aerospace Ltd.'s organizational structure; structure (*b*) is similar to the brewing businesses of Labatt's Breweries; and structure (*c*) is similar to three divisions of the Canadian Imperial Bank of Commerce.

Types of divisional structure

As we see in Exhibit 17–3, there are several types of divisional structure. *Product/service structures* organize work around distinct outputs. Exhibit 17–3(*a*) displays a simplified variation of a product structure at Spar Aerospace Ltd., with its four distinct product groups.

Exhibit 17–4   **A Simplified Matrix Structure**

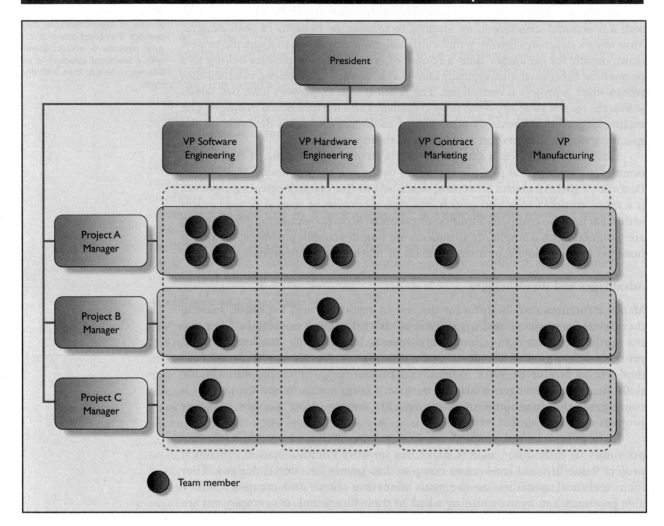

quires effective negotiation skills and a decision process based on the principles of procedural justice described in Chapter 13. It is not easy to coordinate 20 or 30 professionals, so functional managers require computer assistance to track each employee's assignment schedule, performance, and career paths. Finally, people who feel comfortable in structured bureaucracies tend to have difficulty adjusting to the relatively fluid nature of matrix structures. Stress is a common symptom of poorly managed matrix structures, because employees must cope with two managers with potentially divergent needs and expectations.

Hybrid structure

As organizations grow, they typically move from a simple to hybrid structure that combines two or more of the departmentation forms described above. Very few companies adopt a purely functional structure, because work activities become too complex to coordinate activities across functions. Moreover, this design ignores the homogeneity and significance of product and regional activities. The geographic divisionalized form enables firms in diverse markets to adopt local customs and preferences more readily. However, this tends to fragment product development and may isolate the international operations from each other. Product-based divisions are better at coordinating product development activities, but they may weaken the firm's ability to understand and adapt to unique client demands in different geographic markets. Finally, it is difficult to imagine a pure matrix structure, because finance, human resources, and other functions typically apply across the entire company rather than within specific project teams.

Multinational structures

Selecting the best hybrid structure becomes increasingly important and difficult as organizations grow into multinational corporations (MNCs).[29] As discussed in Perspective 17–2, Northern Telecom has been grappling with this problem over the past few years by trying different variations of hybrid structures. Research suggests that MNCs should develop structures and systems that maintain some balance of power and effectiveness across functional, product, and geographic groups.[30] In other words, they must ensure that functional managers do not dominate product managers, product managers do not dominate regional managers, and so forth.

Emerging Forms of Departmentation

All organizations include one or more of the forms of departmentation described in the previous section. However, due to changes in the work force and information technology, two new forms of departmentation are emerging: team-based and network structures. Although they typically exist within or in conjunction with traditional departmentation, team-based and network structures have unique features and someday may become the dominant structural design in some industries.

Team-based (lateral) structure

In 1994, Eastman Kodak Co. spun off its chemical division into a separate company called Eastman Chemical Co. Before doing so, it reorganized the operation into the shape of a pizza with pepperoni sprinkled over it. Each pepperoni represents a cross-functional team responsible for managing a business, a geographic area, or a core competence in a specific technology or area. GE Canada's plant in Bromont, Quebec (described at the beginning of Chapter 10), has a similar structure. But when Bromont's employees decided to draw their team-based design, they produced a three-dimensional shape of a large sphere with several bubbles inside.[31]

Eastman Chemical and GE Bromont are two examples of the **team-based organizational structure** that we introduced in Chapter 10. This emerging design has many names in the business press. Some writers call it a *lateral structure* because, with few organizational levels, it is very flat (like a pizza). Others refer to it as a *circle* or *dome structure* (similar to Bromont's sphere), because senior management becomes an outer casing that serves the free-

Team-based (or lateral) organizational structure
A type of departmentation with a flat span of control and relatively little formalization, consisting of self-managing work teams responsible for various work processes.

Perspective 17–2

Searching for the Perfect Hybrid Structure at Northern Telecom

Northern Telecom, the Canadian-based multinational telecommunications manufacturer, is having difficulty deciding whether to use a hybrid or geographic structure to compete effectively in the global marketplace.

During the 1980s, Northern Telecom was divided mainly into three geographic business units: Canada, the United States, and other countries (called "World Trade"). The executives heading each geographical area were responsible for marketing, manufacturing, and most product development for their region. But having each regional group develop its own products led to fragmentation. "We lacked cohesion," said Paul Stern, Northern Telecom's CEO at the time.

To increase efficiency and product consistency, Northern Telecom introduced a hybrid structure in 1991, with three product groups responsible for global product development and four geographically based subsidiaries responsible for marketing and manufacturing in their territories. The new product groups included public networks, private networks, and wireless systems,

whereas the geographic units represented Canada, United States, Europe, and the Asia–Pacific region.

All seven heads of these units reported directly to Northern Telecom's CEO. However, the hybrid structure essentially shifted some power away from the regional chiefs, because they were stripped of their control over product development and had to share decision making in the CEO's office with the four new product chiefs.

This arrangement didn't last long. In late 1993, Northern Telecom reorganized again, this time around two geographical groups—North America and World Trade. What happened to the product divisions? They now report to the head of the company's North American operations. In effect, Northern Telecom decided again to give priority to geographic divisionalization, while giving somewhat lower power to product development. As the company continues to alternate between geographic and hybrid organizational structures at the top, it also uses functional, matrix, and emerging (e.g., team-based) structures further down the hierarchy.

Sources: Based on "Nortel Splits Operating Roles," *Globe & Mail*, December 23, 1993, p. B3; and L. Surtees, "Power Shifts at Northern Telecom," *Globe & Mail*, February 14, 1991, pp. B1, B2.

---

floating team units within.[32] The team-based organization is also known as a *cluster structure,* because it is composed of a cluster of teams. Exhibit 17–5 illustrates two of these perspectives of team-based organizations.

No matter what name is used or how it is drawn, the team-based structure has a few distinguishing features from other organizational forms. First, it is based on self-managing work teams rather than individuals as the basic building block of organizations. This means that work is assigned to teams rather than to specific employees and that these teams exist throughout the organization, not just in the production area (where self-managing work teams are traditionally found).

A second feature is that the team-based structure organizes most teams around work processes, such as making a specific product or serving a specific client group. Very few employees are grouped into functional specialties (e.g., legal, human resources). The San Diego Zoo provides a good example of this. The zoo replaced most of its 50 functional departments (horticulture, maintenance, animal keeping, etc.) with teams assigned to different bioclimate exhibit areas. Thus, the team assigned to the Gorilla Tropics area takes care of the animals, plants, maintenance, construction, and several other functional activi-

Two Perspectives of a Team-Based (Lateral) Structure   Exhibit 17–5

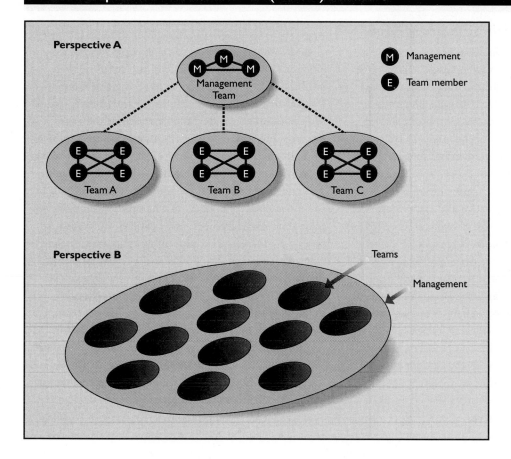

ties. Although members tend to retain their expertise, they typically work together on various tasks within the exhibit area.[33]

A third distinguishing feature of team-based organizations is that they have a very flat span of control, usually with no more than two or three management levels. As we explained in Chapter 10, team-based organizations typically have no first-line supervisors. Instead, most supervisory activities are delegated to the team by having members take turns as the coordinator.

Finally, the team-based organization has very little formalization. Virtually all day-to-day decisions are made by team members rather than someone further up the organizational hierarchy. Teams are given relatively few rules about how to organize their work. Instead, management controls focus on output goals, such as the volume and quality of product or service, or productivity improvement targets for the work process.

Team-based structures are usually found within larger divisionalized forms. For example, GE Canada's Bromont plant is organized around a team-based structure, but it is part of GE Canada's larger product divisions. However, a few innovative (and daring!) companies are experimenting with a team-based structure from the top to the bottom of the organization. One well-publicized example of the team-based structure is Semco S/A, Brazil's largest marine and

Perspective 17–3

The Circle (Team-Based) Structure of Semco S/A

Semco S/A is a fast-growing Brazilian company with 800 employees who manufacture marine pumps, digital scanners, and a variety of industrial equipment for the food processing industry. Semco's management is based on three fundamental values: democracy, profit sharing, and information. Many aspects of the company reflect these values, but perhaps the most dramatic is its circular organizational structure.

Semco has three management layers represented by three concentric circles. One tiny central circle consists of the five counsellors who integrate the company's activities. In traditional terms, this includes the president and top management team, although they prefer to be called *counsellors*. A second, larger circle is composed of the heads (called *partners*) of the eight divisions. Finally, a huge third circle holds all the other employees. Most of these people (called *associates*) perform the research, design, sales, and manufacturing work, and have no one reporting to them on a regular basis. The large circle also includes between 6 and 12 free-floating triangles for each business unit. These triangles represent coordinators who serve as temporary or permanent team leaders.

The third circle also consists of many small manufacturing cells. At the food processing equipment plant, for example, one cell of employees makes only slicers, another makes scales, and so forth. Each cell is self-contained, so the work of people in that team is unaffected by other cells. Work teams are also formed without structure. Teams appoint their own coordinators rather than having this imposed from above by the partners or counsellors.

Status and money tend to reinforce organizational hierarchy in most companies, but not at Semco. It is not uncommon for an associate to make a higher salary than the coordinator who manages his or her unit. In fact, a few earn even more than the partners, so they can increase their status and compensation without entering the other circles.

Semco replaced the formalized rules and regulations that reinforce organizational hierarchy with the "rule of common sense" and made its employees responsible for using their own judgment. For example, the company scrapped complex rules about travel expenses, such as how much to spend on hotels and whether to charge the firm for a theatre ticket. Explains Semco president Ricardo Semler: "If we can't trust people with our money and their judgment, we sure as hell shouldn't be sending them overseas to do business in our name."

The company is very, very rigorous about its financial controls—it wants the numbers ready for display by the 5th of each month. But these controls simply allow the coordinators and associates to have almost complete autonomy over the operations. They come in to work when they like, see all the company's financial figures (including how much the partners earn), and make decisions about whether the company should acquire another business or move to new facilities. As Semler points out: "They can do whatever the hell they want. It's up to them to see the connection between productivity and profit and to act on it."

Source: Based on R. Semler, *Maverick* (New York: Warner Books, 1993); and "Managing Without Managers," *Harvard Business Review*, September–October 1989, pp. 76–84.

---

food processing machinery manufacturer. As we describe in Perspective 17–3, Semco is organized into three circles and has delegated virtually complete responsibility to its employees.

Network structure

Walden Paddlers Inc. designed, produced, and marketed a technically sophisticated kayak from recycled plastic, one that significantly undercuts its competition on price and outmanoeuvers in its performance. The company accomplished this feat with few employees. Instead, it outsourced just about everything in the pursuit of eternal flexibility, low overhead, and the leading edge.[34]

Walden Paddlers is one of the many companies with a **network structure.** A network structure is an alliance of several organizations for the purpose of creating a product or serving a client.[35] In some cases, the original organization has spun off its departments into separate business units; in other cases, the network may be a consortium of smaller firms beehived around a prime contractor in a major project.[36] Increasingly, the network structure is formed by an independent core firm that buys the services of independent companies to fulfill the functions normally provided by departments within the organization.

As illustrated in Exhibit 17–6, a network structure might have an entire product or service designed, manufactured, marketed, delivered, and sold by subcontracting firms located anywhere around the world. The core company's main function is to initiate the process and coordinate the activities of the subcontracting firms.

An organization with a network structure is often called a **virtual corporation.**[37] However, it is more accurate to say that companies with a network structure tend to approach this state of existence. The virtual corporation is a pure condition in which the organization instantaneously reorganizes itself to create a product or provide a service in real time (at the moment the customer

Network structure
An alliance of several organizations for the purpose of creating a product or serving a client.

Virtual corporation
A hypothetically pure form of network structure in which the organization instantaneously reorganizes itself to create a product or provide a service at the moment the customer first wants it.

A Network Structure	Exhibit 17–6

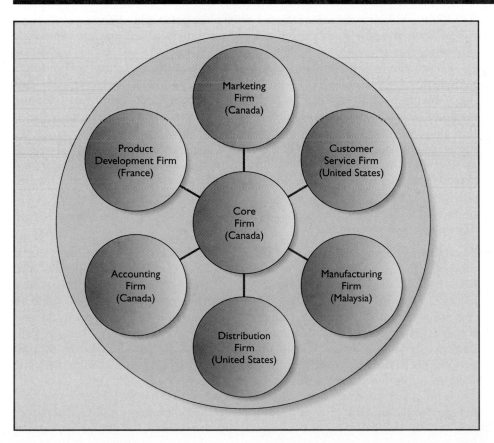

Perspective 17-4

The Network Structure of Emergex Planning Inc.

When MacMillan Bloedel's Powell River Division wanted to develop a comprehensive emergency preparedness plan, it called Emergex Planning Inc. in Vancouver for help. Tully Waisman, an emergency preparedness consultant and Emergex's only full-time employee, quickly pulled together three full-time professionals to handle the complex project.

Emergex Planning is the ultimate network organization—an alliance of companies that temporarily join forces to make a product or serve a client. Emergex is composed of 14 independent consulting firms (called *associates*) that provide resources when specific projects require their assistance. Every time Emergex takes on a new contract, Waisman and the associates name a team and project manager. They often subcontract some work to outside specialists or companies near the client's site. "You only get the people you need for the length of time you need them," explains an Emergex associate.

Why would several independent consulting firms work together through Emergex? The answer is that some of their clients need work requiring diverse expertise. Emergex serves as a contractor of emergency services. Few firms could afford to keep this depth and variety of talent in house, so Emergex's network organizational structure is a logical choice. Emergex's associates include a former Vancouver police chief who does security assessments, a public relations firm that draws up crisis management plans, an emergency training specialist, an architect, a facilities planning firm, and several others.

Source: Based on "The Un-Corporation," *BC Business*, November 1993, pp. 10-11.

first wants it). A virtual corporation's borders are permeable because communication flows as actively with suppliers and customers as among the company's internal teams and units.

Companies with network structures come close to being virtual corporations because they can usually form new alliances to fit a client's needs quickly and more effectively than can companies with other structural forms. Consider the example of Emergex Planning, described in Perspective 17-4. Emergex forms new alliances with outside companies—some of them are associates, others are independent vendors—whenever it begins a new project. The client's requirements shape the project team that, in turn, shapes Emergex's structure for that project. Although Emergex is not quite a virtual organization, its ability to change alliances to fit client needs brings it relatively close to this state.

Advantages and disadvantages

Flexibility is the main advantage of network structures. If a product or service is no longer in demand, the core firm can wind down operations as contracts end. If it wants to shift into a different type of product or service, it forms new alliances with other firms offering the appropriate resources. Because network structures depend on markets rather than hierarchies to create products and services, they potentially make better use of skills and technology. The core firm becomes globally competitive as it shops worldwide for subcontractors with the best people and the best technology at the best price. It is not saddled with the same resources used for previous products or services.

A potential disadvantage of network structures is that they expose the core firm to the same market forces used to get the best resources. Other companies may bid up the price for subcontractors in any functional area, whereas the short-term cost would be lower if the company hired its own employees to provide this function. Another problem is that although information technology makes worldwide communication much easier, it will never replace the degree of control organizations have when manufacturing, marketing, and other functions are in house. The core firm can use arm's-length incentives and contract provisions to maintain the subcontractor's quality, but these actions are relatively crude compared to those used to maintain performance of in-house employees.

Contingencies of Organizational Design

Organizational theorists and practitioners are interested not only in the elements of organizational structure, but also in the contingencies that determine or influence the optimal design. By understanding the best span of control, level of centralization and formalization, and type of departmentation in a particular situation, we can hopefully design a structure that will strengthen the organization's chances for survival. In this section, we introduce four contingencies of organizational design: size, technology, environment, and strategy.

Organizational size

As you might expect, larger organizations have considerably different structures than do smaller organizations.[38] Many studies have confirmed that organizational size—the number of people within the social entity—influences organizational structure. There is overwhelming evidence that larger organizations have greater job specialization due to a greater division of labour. The size of an organization reflects the breadth of its work activities, and it is virtually impossible for one person to comprehend everything to be done in a large business.

An increasing division of labour requires greater use of more elaborate coordinating mechanisms. Consequently, larger organizations are more likely to use standardization of work processes and outputs to coordinate work activities. These coordinating mechanisms create an administrative hierarchy and greater formalization. At the same time, informal communication among employees becomes less prevalent for coordinating work activities. Finally, there is evidence that larger organizations are more decentralized. As we noted earlier in this chapter, neither founders nor senior managers have sufficient time or expertise to process all the decisions that significantly influence the business as it grows. Therefore, decision-making authority is pushed down to lower levels, where incumbents are able to cope with the narrower range of issues under their control.[39]

Technology

In Chapter 1, we said that employees use technology (such as equipment, work methods, and information) to transform inputs into various outputs. The effectiveness of an organization's structure depends, in part, on whether it is compatible with the organization's dominant technology. However, complex organizations have different types of technology in different divisions and other work units. Therefore, our examination of technology explains why the type of

Exhibit 17–7   **Four Types of Technology**

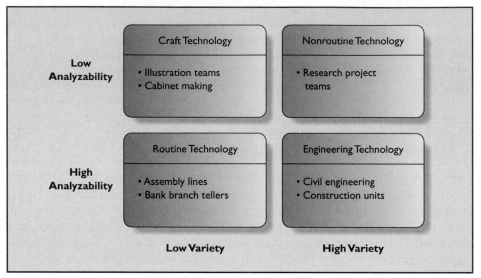

Source: Based on C. Perrow, "A Framework for the Comparative Analysis of Organizations," *American Sociological Review* 32 (1967), pp. 194–208.

departmentation, formalization, centralization, and span of control should vary in different parts of the company.

Two important technological contingencies that influence the best type of organizational structure are the variety and analyzability of work activities.[40] *Variety* refers to the number of exceptions to standard procedure that can occur in the team or work unit. *Analyzability* refers to the extent that the transformation of input resources to outputs can be reduced to a series of standardized steps. These two dimensions establish the four technological typologies shown in Exhibit 17–7.

In *routine technology* work units, employees perform tasks with low variety and high analyzability. Automobile assembly lines represent a classic example of these technological conditions. Employees install tires, bumpers, door panels, and the like with few exceptions. When problems do arise, there are usually standard operating procedures available to resolve them. Work units with routine technology usually work best with mechanistic structures. This includes a high degree of formalization and centralization as well as standardization of work processes.

In *nonroutine technology* work units, employees perform tasks with high variety and low analyzability. Research project teams operate under these conditions. They apply their skills to unique situations with little opportunity for repetition. Problems are unique, so team members must use creative thinking rather than searching for solutions in a standard procedures manual. Nonroutine technology work units operate best with an organic structure, one with low formalization, highly decentralized decision-making authority, and coordination mainly through informal communication among team members.

Engineering technology work units have high variety and high analyzability. This means that although the work involves many exceptions to the normal routine, any problems that arise can usually be resolved through standard procedures. As you might expect, engineering work units usually fit into this category. They work with complex technology involving many variables, yet few problems are unique. Work units that fall into this category should use an organic structure, but it is possible to have somewhat greater formalization and centralization due to the analyzability of problems.

Finally, *craft technology* work units have both low variety and low analyzability. Work units that include skilled tradespeople are typically in this category, because the tasks involve few exceptions but the problems that arise are difficult to resolve. The artisan's skills are necessary to find a solution to the unique problems that emerge. This situation allows more centralization and formalization than in a purely organic structure, but coordination must include informal communication among the skilled employees so that unique problems can be resolved.

External environment

Throughout this book, we have emphasized the importance of the external environment as an influence on organizational behaviour. This influence extends to the best structure an organization should adopt. The external environment includes anything outside the organization, including most stakeholders (e.g., clients, suppliers, government), resources (e.g., raw materials, human resources, information, finances), and competitors. Four relatively distinct characteristics of external environments influence the type of organizational structure best suited to a particular situation: dynamism, complexity, diversity, and hostility.[41]

Dynamic environments

Dynamic environments have a high rate of change, leading to novel situations and a lack of identifiable patterns. In contrast, stable environments are characterized by regular cycles of activity and steady changes in supply and demand for inputs and outputs. For example, the women's fashion industry faces rapidly changing consumer tastes, whereas the market for drywall building materials is quite stable.

Research findings consistently support the conclusion that organic structures are better suited to dynamic environments.[42] Organic structures have low formalization, high decentralization, and a wide span of control, enabling employees to adjust their work activities and coordinate new relationships through informal communication. Network and team-based structures seem to be most effective in dynamic environments, because they usually have these features. In stable environments, on the other hand, organizations introduce standardization as a more efficient approach to coordination. Events are more predictable, enabling the firm to apply rules and procedures.

Complex environments

Complex environments have more elements in the environment to consider than do simple environments. For instance, a multinational corporation has to take into account the interests of more stakeholders than does the corner grocery store. Decentralized structures seem to be better suited to complex environments, because it is difficult for a central authority to comprehend all the factors necessary to make effective decisions in all organizational contexts.

By passing decision powers down the hierarchy, those closest to the environmental information are able to make more informed choices.

Diverse environments

Organizations located in diverse environments have a greater variety of products or services, clients, and/or jurisdictions. In contrast, an integrated environment is one in which the firm must understand only one client, product, and geographic area. The more diversified the organization's markets are, the more it should adopt a divisionalized form aligned with that diversity. For example, if a company sells a single product around the world, it probably should organize around a geographic divisionalized form to reflect the diverse territories in which it operates. If it sells several different types of products or services in a single geographical area, then a product-based design may be preferred. As we explained earlier, multinational companies have difficult decisions to make because they have diverse products, clients, and geographic markets. Typically, they create a hybrid structure around all three dimensions, giving priority to the divisional form that best fits its corporate strategy and culture.

Hostile environments

An organization's environment may range from munificent to hostile. Firms located in a hostile environment face resource scarcity and more competition marketing their products or services. Hostile environments are typically dynamic ones because they reduce the predictability of access to resources and demand for outputs. As the availability of inputs decreases, the risk of shortages increases as suppliers gain power in the marketplace. Similarly, as competition for customers increases, the certainty that the organization's products or services will be purchased decreases.

Insofar as hostility is similar to dynamism, organic structures should be most appropriate for this environmental condition. However, experts suggest that extremely hostile environments drive organizations to temporarily centralize.[43] They explain that crises demand quick decisions, so organizations centralize, because direct supervision is the tightest and fastest form of coordination. During organizational crises, such as the loss of a major client or supplier, the leader quickly steps in to make decisions. Ironically, centralization may result in lower-quality decisions during organizational crises, because top management has less information, particularly when the environment is complex. If the hostile environment persists, the organization's survival may be at risk if centralized decision making continues.

Organizational strategy

Although size, technology, and environment influence the optimal organizational structure, these contingencies do not necessarily determine structure. Instead, there is increasing evidence that corporate leaders formulate and implement strategies that shape both the characteristics of these contingencies as well as the organization's resulting structure. **Organizational strategy** refers to the way the organization positions itself in its setting in relation to its stakeholders, given the organization's resources, capabilities, and mission.[44] The idea that an organization interacts with its environment rather than being totally deter-

Organizational strategy
The way the organization positions itself in its setting in relation to its stakeholders given the organization's resources, capabilities, and mission.

mined by it is known as **strategic choice.**[45] In other words, organizational leaders take steps to define and manipulate their environments, rather than let the organization's fate be entirely determined by external influences.

The notion of strategic choice can be traced back to the work of Alfred Chandler in the early 1960s.[46] Chandler's proposal was that structure follows strategy. He observed that organizational structures follow the growth strategy developed by the organization's decision makers. Moreover, he noted that organizational structures change only after decision makers decide to do so. This recognizes that the link between structure and the contingency factors described earlier is mediated by organizational strategy.

Chandler's thesis that structure follows strategy has become the dominant perspective of business policy and strategic management. An important aspect of this view is that organizations can choose the environments in which they want to operate. Some businesses adopt a **differentiation strategy** by bringing unique products to the market or attracting clients who want customized goods and services. They try to distinguish their outputs from those provided by other firms through marketing, providing special services, and innovation. Others adopt a **cost leadership strategy,** in which they maximize productivity and are, thereby, able to offer popular products or services at a competitive price.[47]

The type of organizational strategy selected leads to the best organizational structure to adopt.[48] Organizations with a cost leadership strategy should adopt a mechanistic, functional structure with high levels of job specialization and standardized work processes. This is similar to the routine technology category described earlier because they maximize production and service efficiency. A differentiation strategy, on the other hand, requires more customized relations with clients, so the technology would either be engineering or craft oriented. MacDonald Dettwiler has adopted a differentiation strategy because it relies on unique contracts rather than mass market products. A matrix structure with less centralization and formalization is most appropriate here so that technical specialists are able to coordinate their work activities more closely with the client's needs. Overall, it is now apparent that organizational structure is influenced by size, technology, and environment, but the organization's strategy may reshape these elements and loosen their connection to organizational structure.

Strategic choice
The idea that an organization interacts with its environment rather than being totally determined by it.

Differentiation strategy
The strategy of bringing unique products to the market or attracting clients who want customized goods and services.

Cost leadership strategy
The strategy of maximizing productivity in order to offer popular products or services at a competitive price.

Chapter Summary

- Organizational structure refers to the division of labour as well as the patterns of coordination, communication, work flow, and formal power that direct organizational activities. All organizational structures divide labour into distinct tasks and coordinate that labour to accomplish common goals. The primary means of coordination are informal communication, direct supervision, and various forms of standardization.

- The four basic elements of organizational structure include span of control, centralization, formalization, and departmentation. Span of control—the number of people directly reporting to a supervisor—determines the number of hierarchical levels in the organization. The recent trend is toward flatter structures with a wide average span of control.

- Centralization occurs when formal decision authority is held by a small group of people, typically senior management. Organizational size and diversity push for decentralization, whereas centralization increases during crises and in response to management and staff needs for power.

- Formalization refers to the degree that organizations standardize behaviour through rules, procedures, formal training, and related mechanisms. Companies tend to become more formalized over time, but this can reduce organizational flexibility and employee satisfaction.

- Departmentation specifies how employees and their activities are grouped together. Organizations usually begin as simple structures, then develop into functional, divisionalized, matrix, or hybrid forms. A functional structure organizes employees around specific skills or other resources. A divisional structure groups employees around outputs, clients, or geographic areas. A matrix structure typically overlays a product-based divisional structure with a functional structure. Most larger organizations adopt a hybrid structure that includes some combination of functional, divisionalized, and/or matrix grouping.

- Two emerging forms of departmentation are team-based and network structures. A team-based structure (also known as a lateral or circle structure) uses self-managing work teams as the basic building block. It is a very flat structure with low formalization that organizes teams around work processes rather than functional specialties. A network structure is an alliance of several organizations for the purpose of creating a product or serving a client. Companies with network structures are almost virtual corporations, because they can quickly and efficiently reorganize themselves to suit the client's requirements.

- Four factors influence the best type of organizational structure to adopt. Larger organizations need greater job specialization and elaborate coordinating mechanisms than do smaller firms. They also tend to be less centralized and more formalized. The work unit's technology—including variety of work and analyzability of problems—influences whether to adopt an organic or mechanistic structure.

- Four environmental factors influence the optimal organizational structure. Organic structures are best suited to dynamic environments. Decentralized structures seem to be better suited to complex environments. Organizations in diversified environments should adopt a divisionalized form aligned with that diversity. Firms in moderately hostile environments should adopt organic structures to maintain flexibility. In extremely hostile conditions, firms tend to centralize, although this may be an ineffective strategy in the long term.

- Although size, technology, and environment influence the optimal organizational structure, these contingencies do not necessarily determine structure. Rather, organizational leaders formulate and implement strategies to define and manipulate their environments. These strategies, rather than the other contingencies, directly shape the organization's structure.

Discussion Questions

1. Why are organizations moving toward flatter structures?

2. Canadian Widgets Ltd. makes widgets in every Canadian province, because each jurisdiction has unique regulations governing the manufacturing and selling of this product. The company makes four types of widgets, each type to be sold to different types of clients. For example, one widget design is sold exclusively to automobile repair shops, whereas another is used mainly in hospitals. Client expectations and needs are similar throughout Canada (i.e., they don't vary by province). The Canadian government has announced that it intends to break down interprovincial barriers, including the unnecessary regulatory and manufacturing restrictions on widgets. Deregulation would allow Canadian Widgets to manufacture and distribute its widgets from any Canadian location. If this occurs, how might Canadian Widget reorganize its manufacturing and distribution operations to maximize efficiency, yet keep in touch with its markets?

3. Why don't all organizations group people around product-based divisions?

4. What must top management, functional managers, and project managers do to make a matrix structure more effective?

5. Many companies claim to have a team-based organization, yet relatively few have actually adopted this form of departmentation. Describe four structural features that would suggest that a company has adopted a team-based organizational structure.

6. What is a network structure? Why do some writers believe that a network structure is an effective design for global competition?

7. Explain how environmental dynamism, complexity, diversity, and hostility influence organizational structure.

8. What do we mean by "strategy follows structure"?

Notes

1. Based on personal interviews with senior engineering management at MacDonald Dettwiler, October 1991.

2. A. G. Bedeian and R. F. Zammuto, *Organizations: Theory and Design* (Hinsdale, Ill.: Dryden, 1991), pp.117–18.

3. S. Ranson, R. Hinings, and R. Greenwood, "The Structuring of Organizational Structure," *Administrative Science Quarterly* 25 (1980), pp. 1–14.

4. H. Mintzberg, *The Structuring of Organizations* (Englewood Cliffs, N.J.: Prentice Hall, 1979), pp. 2–3.

5. D. Katz and R. L. Kahn, *The Social Psychology of Organizations* (New York: Wiley, 1966), Chapter 2.

6. H. Fayol, *General and Industrial Management*, trans. C. Storrs (London: Pitman, 1949); E. E. Lawler III, *Motivation in Work Organizations* (Monterey, Calif.: Brooks/Cole, 1973), Chapter 7; and M. A. Campion, "Ability Requirement Implications of Job Design: An Interdisciplinary Perspective," *Personnel Psychology* 42 (1989), pp. 1–24.

7. Material in this section is based on Mintzberg, *The Structuring of Organizations*, pp. 2–8.

8. D. D. Van Fleet and A. G. Bedeian, "A History of the Span of Management," *Academy of Management Review* 2 (1977), pp. 356–72; Mintzberg, *The Structuring of Organizations*, Chapter 8; and D. Robey, *Designing Organizations*, 3rd ed. (Homewood, Ill.: Irwin, 1991), pp. 255–59.

9. Mintzberg, *The Structuring of Organizations*, p. 136.

10. T. Peters, *Thriving on Chaos* (New York: Knopf, 1987), p. 359.

11. J. Lorinc, "Managing When There's No Middle," *Canadian Business,* June 1991, pp. 86–94.

12. L. Gutri, "Teamwork Puts Depth into Working," *Canadian HR Reporter,* April 18, 1988, p. 4.

13. A. Dastmalchian and M. Javidan, "Centralization and Organizational Context: An Analysis of Canadian Public Enterprises," *Canadian Journal of Administrative Sciences* 4 (1987), pp. 302–19.

14. Peters, *Thriving on Chaos,* pp. 356–57.

15. "Compaq Centralises to Cut Costs," *Business Europe* 33 (January 8, 1993), pp. 6–7.

16. Mintzberg, *The Structuring of Organizations,* Chapter 5.

17. T. Burns and G. Stalker, *The Management of Innovation* (London: Tavistock, 1961).

18. Mintzberg, *The Structuring of Organizations,* p. 106.

19. Ibid., Chapter 17.

20. C. Motherwell, "Mexican Munchies with a Danish Accent," *Globe & Mail,* February 21, 1994, p. B4.

21. Robey, *Designing Organizations,* pp. 186–89.

22. R. Collison, "How Bata Rules the World," *Canadian Business,* September 1990, pp. 28–34.

23. Robey, *Designing Organizations,* pp. 191–97; and Bedeian and Zammuto, *Organizations: Theory and Design,* pp. 162–68.

24. S. Hamm, "Office Politics," *PCWeek Inside,* April 18, 1994, pp. A1, A4.

25. H. F. Kolodny, "Managing in a Matrix," *Business Horizons,* March–April 1981, pp. 17–24; and S. M. Davis and P. R. Lawrence, *Matrix* (Reading, Mass.: Addison-Wesley, 1977).

26. K. Knight, "Matrix Organization: A Review," *Journal of Management Studies,*" May 1976, pp. 111–30.

27. G. Rifkin, "Digital Dumps Matrix Management," *Globe & Mail,* July 21, 1994, pp. B1, B4.

28. H. Denis, "Matrix Structures, Quality of Working Life, and Engineering Productivity," *IEEE Transactions on Engineering Management* EM-33 (August 1986), pp. 148–56; and J. L. Brown and N. M. Agnew, "The Balance of Power in a Matrix Structure," *Business Horizons,* November–December 1982, pp. 51–54.

29. A. M. Rugman, *Inside the Multinationals: The Economics of International Markets* (London: Croom Helm, 1981); and M. E. Porter, *Competitive Advantage* (New York: The Free Press, 1985).

30. C. A. Bartlett and S. Ghoshal, "Managing across Borders: New Organizational Responses," *Sloan Management Review,* Fall 1987, pp. 43–53.

31. J. A. Byrne, "Congratulations. You're Moving to a New Pepperoni," *Business Week,* December 20, 1993, pp. 80–81; and C. G. Johnston and C. R. Farquhar, *Empowered People Satisfy Customers* (Ottawa: Conference Board of Canada, 1992).

32. J. B. Rieley, "The Circular Organization: How Leadership Can Optimize Organizational Effectiveness," *National Productivity Review* 13 (Winter 1993/1994), pp. 11–19; J. R. Galbraith, *Competing with Flexible Lateral Organizations* (Reading, Mass.: Addison-Wesley, 1994); J. A. Byrne, "The Horizontal Corporation," *Business Week,* December 20, 1993, pp. 76–81; R. Tomasko, *Rethinking the Corporation* (New York: AMACOM, 1993); and D. Quinn Mills (with G. Bruce Friesen), *Rebirth of the Corporation* (New York: Wiley, 1991), pp. 29–30.

33. T. A. Stewart, "The Search for the Organization of Tomorrow," *Fortune,* May 18, 1992, pp. 93–98.

34. E. O. Welles, "Virtual Realities," *Inc.* 15 (August 1993), pp. 50–58.

35. R. E. Miles and C. C. Snow, "Causes of Failure in Network Organizations," *California Management Review* 34 (Summer 1992), pp. 53–72.

36. H. F. Kolodny, "Some Characteristics of Organizational Designs in New/High Technology Firms," in *Organizational Issues in High Technology Management,* ed. L. R. Gomez-Mejia and M. W. Lawless (Greenwich, Conn.: JAI Press, 1990), pp. 165–76.

37. R. Nagel and D. Allen, "Virtual Winners," *International Management* 48 (June 1993), p. 64; and W. H. Davidow and M. S. Malone, *The Virtual Corporation* (New York: HarperBusiness, 1992).

38. Mintzberg, *The Structuring of Organizations,* Chapter 13; and D. S. Pugh and C. R. Hinings (eds.), *Organizational Structure: Extensions and Replications* (Farnborough, England: Lexington Books, 1976).

39. Robey, *Designing Organizations,* p. 102.

40. C. Perrow, "A Framework for the Comparative Analysis of Organizations," *American Sociological Review* 32 (1967), pp. 194–208.

41. Mintzberg, *The Structuring of Organizations,* Chapter 15.

42. Burns and Stalker, *The Management of Innovation;* P. R. Lawrence and J. W. Lorsch, *Organization and Environment* (Homewood, Ill.: Irwin, 1967); and D. Miller and P. H. Friesen, *Organizations: A Quantum View* (Englewood Cliffs, N.J.: Prentice Hall, 1984), pp. 197–98.

43. Mintzberg, *The Structuring of Organizations,* p. 282.

44.   R. H. Kilmann, *Beyond the Quick Fix* (San Francisco: Jossey-Bass, 1984), p. 38.

45.   J. Child, "Organizational Structure, Environment, and Performance: The Role of Strategic Choice," *Sociology* 6 (1972), pp. 2–22.

46.   A. D. Chandler, *Strategy and Structure* (Cambridge, Mass.: MIT Press, 1962).

47.   M. E. Porter, *Competitive Strategy* (New York: The Free Press, 1980).

48.   D. Miller, "Configurations of Strategy and Structure," *Strategic Management Journal* 7 (1986), pp. 233–50.

Chapter Case

*Joyce Aircraft Corporation**

Joyce Aircraft Corporation undertook a reorganization of its Engineering Division to improve control of projects, the development times of engineering programs, and the motivation of the division's employees. The management's rationale was that assigning personnel to projects that overlaid their basic functional workgroups would allow them greater autonomy and facilitate identification with projects. This would in turn increase motivation, shorten development times, and improve control of projects through the new role of project manager. Prior to the reorganization, the Engineering Division was organized functionally, with separate groups for engineering design, drafting, and engineering tests and substantiation.

Nature of the Work   The Engineering Division was responsible for the design and testing of new and modified aircraft. After design prototypes had flown and passed certification tests specified by the Federal Aviation Administration (FAA), the firm's Production Division took responsibility for quantity production of the new models. Prior to this transfer of responsibility, three major groups within the Engineering Division played complementary roles. Engineering Design developed new models. Because aircraft are very complex and require the application of considerable technical expertise, departments within this group had been formed to concentrate on different components of aircraft. Some specialized in wing, fuselage, or tail assembly design, and others had responsibility for design of power plants or electrical systems. Thus, the overall task of designing a complete airplane was fragmented and the several departments constituted for this purpose were interdependent. Ultimately, the wing had to mate with the fuselage, the empennage had to provide sufficient control power to manoeuver the aircraft, and the power plant had to deliver sufficient thrust to propel it at the desired cruise speed and payload.

In order to ensure that products met these design criteria, the Tests and Substantiations Group conducted evaluations to assess each aircraft's performance and structural integrity, as marketing specifications and governmental regulations required. The group had three departments to accomplish these tasks. The Aerodynamics Department conducted performance analyses and wind tunnel tests. The Flight Test Department actually flew prototype versions of new models to determine experimentally whether or not they met their design specifications and the extent to which they satisfied FAA requirements regarding controllability and aerodynamic safety. The Structures Department determined the loads that an aircraft must sustain in flight and conducted tests to ensure that structures proposed by the Design Group could actually bear these loads in practice. When the results of aerodynamic or structural analyses or tests suggested a problem with a design, appropriate departments in the Design Group made modifications, and new tests were performed before the design became final. Although the greatest interdependence between departments occurred within the Design Group and within the Tests and Substantiations Group, there was significant interdependence between departments in different groups as well.

The Drafting Group became involved in the process as a final design for an aircraft neared completion. Draftsmen transformed design drawings that had been used for prototype construction into production drawings incorporating all the design changes necessary to produce an FAA-certifiable aircraft that met desired performance specifications. In contrast to the work performed in the engineering groups, this work, although intricate, was quite routine. When changes to design drawings were minor, as they often were, a draftsman would simply trace the designer's work, paying a bit more attention to scale and the quality of the finished drawing. Interdependence among draftsmen was relatively low even when individuals were working on highly interdependent parts of an airplane, because the design drawings from which they worked already fit together as a result of previous design and analysis.

Reorganization   The reorganization created a matrix structure by establishing a formal project management system overlaying these three major groups of the Engineering Division. The firm appointed a project manager for each of the aircraft development projects in progress. These people were responsible for overall project integration. Their task was to ensure that personnel effectively attended to the interdependencies that every project involved by providing a management perspective oriented toward whole aircraft rather than toward their subsystems and components. Project managers were assigned greater influence and formal power than the department managers. Department managers were to provide technical direction to their employees who were also assigned to project managers, but project managers actually directed these employees' activities on the projects. Project managers had the authority to overrule any of the department managers, even on technical matters, although it was expected that they would exercise this prerogative judiciously. The role of project manager was intended to resemble that of the owner of a small engineering or manufacturing firm, and incumbents were viewed as totally responsible for the success or failure of their projects.

Discussion Questions

1. **Describe the structure of the engineering division before and after the reorganization.**

2. **Why was the reorganization undertaken?**

3. **Describe the interdependence in the work of the division before reorganization.**

4. **Will the reorganization improve efficiency and effectiveness as anticipated by management?**

Source: D. Robey, *Designing Organizations* (Homewood, Ill.: Irwin, 1991), pp. 537–38; adapted from William F. Joyce, "Matrix Organization: A Social Experiment," *Academy of Management Journal* 29, no. 3 (1986), pp. 541–43.

Experiential Exercise

Purpose: To help students understand the contingencies and dynamics of organizational design, as well as the important roles of division of labour and coordination of work activities.

Instructions: The instructor will form large groups (typically between 8 and 12 people). Each group is a company in competition with the other companies, so all groups should have approximately the same number of students. Each company should be assigned to an area of the room where its employees can work together without interference from other companies. At least three people in the class will serve as members of the "Words Marketing Board." The marketing board evaluates the output of every company in the industry and calculates their success in the industry.

All students must carefully read and understand the corporate objectives, raw materials and production standards, product delivery, and quality control information below. The instructors will give the companies time (between 10 and 15 minutes) to organize themselves for the first production run. There will be at least two production runs in the exercise. Each production run uses the raw material provided by the instructor and has strict time deadlines (between 5 and 10 minutes). The marketing board will score the output from each company and post the results before the next production run begins. Each company has time (5 minutes or more) to reorganize itself while the marketing board is evaluating the product output. This process will be repeated for each production run in the exercise.

After the final production run and the winning team is announced, the class will discuss the dynamics of organizational structure and design in this exercise. Each company will be asked to diagram an organizational chart depicting its structure and to explain why that structure was used. It will identify the division of labour and coordinating mechanisms used. The class will examine the contingencies of organizational design—size, technology, environment, and strategy—that influenced the best structures in this exercise.

STUDENTS MUST CAREFULLY READ THE FOLLOWING INFORMATION

Corporate Objectives You are a small company that manufactures words and then packages them into meaningful English-language sentences. Market research indicates that sentences are saleable only if they are at least three words and no more than six words long. The words-in-sentences industry is highly competitive. Every company in the industry has the same raw materials, technology, and pricing, so your firm's ability to compete depends on (a) the number of sentences produced and (b) the quality of those sentences. You will be given time before each production run to organize employees in a way that generates the most efficient and effective organization.

Raw Materials and Production Standards For each production run, all companies will be given the same word or phrase. The letters in that word or phrase represent the company's raw material from which it forms meaningful sentences. For example, if the raw material is the word "organization," then a company might produce the sentence "Nat ran to a zoo." Here are several production rules and standards that each company must follow. The marketing board will reject any sentences that do not satisfy these standards.

1. Each word can use a particular letter only as many times as it exists in the raw material. For example, if the raw material is the word "organization," then the word "razor" would be *unacceptable* because "r" appears only once in the raw material.

2. Although the use of specific letters within a word is limited, there is no such limitation on the use of specific letters in a sentence. For instance, the sentence "Nat ran to a zoo" uses three "a" letters even though the raw material word (organization) has only two "a" letters.

3. A word can be used only once in a production run. For example, if you use the word "razor" in one sentence, it cannot be used again. Moreover, adding an "s" or other suffix will be considered the same word. For example, you cannot use the word "razors" (even if the raw material had an "s" letter) because it is considered a variation of "razor."

4. The marketing board will only accept words in the English language that are not slang. Names and places are acceptable, however.

5. Sentences and words must be meaningful, not nonsense.

6. Sentences must have no less than 3 words and no more than 6 words.

Product Delivery   All sentences produced by a company must be printed legibly on paper and submitted to the marketing board within 30 seconds after the production run has ended (as announced by the instructor). The marketing board will not accept production submitted after 30 seconds, nor will it accept any sentences that are difficult to read.

Quality Control   The marketing board is the final arbiter of production quality and quantity. It will count the number of words in the sentences that satisfy the standards set forth above. These results will be posted as a count of the number of words produced by each company. If any word does not meet the minimum acceptable standards, then the marketing board will automatically reject the entire sentence (i.e., none of the words in that sentence are counted).

*The source of this exercise is unknown.

End of Text Cases

Case 1 **Arctic Mining Consultants***

Tom Parker enjoyed working outdoors. At various times in the past, he worked as a ranch hand, high steel rigger, headstone installer, prospector, and geological field technician. Now 43, Parker is a geological field technician and field coordinator with Arctic Mining Consultants. He has specialized knowledge and experience in all nontechnical aspects of mineral exploration, including claim staking, line cutting and grid installation, soil sampling, prospecting, and trenching. He is responsible for hiring, training, and supervising field assistants for all of Arctic Mining Consultants' programs. Field assistants are paid a fairly low daily wage (no matter how long they work, which may be up to 12 hours or more) and are provided meals and accommodation. Many of the programs are operated by a project manager who reports to Parker.

Parker sometimes acts as a project manager, as he did on a job that involved staking 15 claims near Eagle Lake, British Columbia. He selected John Talbot, Greg Boyce, and Brian Millar, all of whom had previously worked with Parker, as the field assistants. To stake a claim, the project team marks a line with flagging tape and blazes along the perimeter of the claim, cutting a claim post every 500 metres (called a "length"). The 15 claims would require almost 100 kilometers of line in total. Parker had budgeted seven days (plus mobilization and demobilization) to complete the job. This meant that each of the four stakers (Parker, Talbot, Boyce, and Millar) would have to complete a little over seven "lengths" each day. The following is a chronology of the project.

Day 1   The Arctic Mining Consultants crew assembled in the morning and drove to Eagle Lake, from where they were flown by helicopter to the claim site. On arrival, they set up tents at the edge of the area to be staked, and agreed on a rota for cooking duties. After supper, they pulled out the maps and discussed the job—how long it would take, the order in which the areas were to be staked, possible helicopter landing spots, and areas that might be more difficult to stake.

Parker pointed out that with only a week to complete the job, everyone would have to average seven and a half lengths per day. "I know that is a lot," he said, "but you've all staked claims before and I'm confident that each of you is capable of it. And it's only for a week. If we get the job done in time, there's a $100 bonus for each man." Two hours later, Parker and his crew members had developed what seemed to be a workable plan.

Day 2   Millar completed six lengths, Boyce six lengths, Talbot eight, and Parker eight. Parker was not pleased with Millar's or Boyce's production. However, he didn't make an issue of it, thinking that they would develop their "rhythm" quickly.

Day 3   Millar completed five and a half lengths, Boyce four, and Talbot seven. Parker, who was nearly twice as old as the other three, completed eight lengths. He also had enough time remaining to walk over and check the quality of stakes that Millar and Boyce had completed, then walk back to his own area for helicopter pickup back to the tent site.

That night Parker exploded with anger. "I thought I told you that I wanted seven and a half lengths a day!" he shouted at Boyce and Millar. Boyce said that he was slowed down by unusually thick underbrush in his assigned area. Millar said that he had done his best and would try to pick up the pace. Parker did not mention that he had inspected their work. He explained that as far as he was concerned, the field assistants were supposed to finish their assigned area for the day, no matter what.

Talbot, who was sharing a tent with Parker, talked to him later. "I think that you're being a bit hard on them, you know. I know that it has been more by luck than anything else that I've been able to do my quota. Yesterday I only had five lengths done after the first seven hours and there was only an hour before I was supposed to be picked up. Then I hit a patch of really open bush, and was able to do three lengths in 70 minutes. Why don't I take Millar's area tomorrow and he can have mine? Maybe that will help."

"Conditions are the same in all of the areas," replied Parker, rejecting Talbot's suggestion. "Millar just has to try harder."

Day 4 Millar did seven lengths and Boyce completed six and a half. When they reported their production that evening, Parker grunted uncommunicatively. Parker and Talbot did eight lengths each.

Day 5 Millar completed six lengths, Boyce six, Talbot seven and a half, and Parker eight. Once again Parker blew up, but he concentrated his diatribe on Millar. "Why don't you do what you say you are going to do? You know that you have to do seven and a half lengths a day. We went over that when we first got here, so why don't you do it? If you aren't willing to do the job then you never should have taken it in the first place!"

Millar replied by saying that he was doing his best, that he hadn't even stopped for lunch, and that he didn't know how he could possibly do any better. Parker launched into him again: "You have got to work harder! If you put enough effort into it, you will get the area done!"

Later Millar commented to Boyce, "I hate getting dumped on all the time! I'd quit if it didn't mean that I'd have to walk 50 miles to the highway. And besides, I need the bonus money. Why doesn't he pick on you? You don't get any more done than me; in fact, you usually get less. Maybe if you did a bit more he wouldn't be so bothered about me."

"I only work as hard as I have to," Boyce replied.

Day 6 Millar raced through breakfast, was the first one to be dropped off by the helicopter, and arranged to be the last one picked up. That evening the production figures were Millar eight and a quarter lengths, Boyce seven, and Talbot and Parker eight each. Parker remained silent when the field assistants reported their performance for the day.

Day 7 Millar was again the first out and last in. That night, he collapsed in an exhausted heap at the table, too tired to eat. After a few moments, he announced in an abject tone, "Six lengths. I worked like a dog all day and I only got a lousy six lengths!" Boyce completed five lengths, Talbot seven, and Parker seven and a quarter.

Parker was furious. "That means we have to do a total of 34 lengths tomorrow if we are to finish this job on time!" With his eyes directed at Millar, he added: "Why is it that you never finish the job? Don't you realize that you are part of a team, and that you are letting the rest of the team down? I've been checking your lines and you're doing too much blazing and wasting too much time making picture-perfect claim posts! If you worked smarter, you'd get a lot more done!"

Day 8 Parker cooked breakfast in the dark. The helicopter dropoffs began as soon as morning light appeared on the horizon. Parker instructed each assistant to complete 8 lengths and, if they finished early, to help the others. Parker said that he would finish the other 10 lengths. Helicopter pickups were arranged for one hour before dark.

By noon, after working as hard as he could, Millar had only completed three lengths. "Why bother," he thought to himself, "I'll never be able to do another five lengths before the helicopter comes, and I'll catch the same amount of abuse from Parker for doing six lengths as for seven and a half." So he sat down and had lunch and a rest. "Boyce won't finish his eight lengths either, so even if I did finish mine, I still wouldn't get the bonus. At least I'll get one more day's pay this way."

That night, Parker was livid when Millar reported that he had completed five and a half lengths. Parker had done ten and a quarter lengths, and Talbot had completed eight. Boyce proudly announced that he finished seven and a half lengths, but sheepishly added that Talbot had helped him with some of it. All that remained were the two and a half lengths that Millar had not completed.

The job was finished the next morning and the crew demobilized. Millar has never worked for Arctic Mining Consultants again, despite being offered work several times by Parker. Boyce sometimes does staking for Arctic, and Talbot works full time with the company.

*© Copyright 1995 Steven L. McShane and Tim Neale. This case is based on actual events, but names and some characteristics have been changed to maintain anonymity.

Case 2 **A Window on Life***

For Gilles LaCroix, there is nothing quite as beautiful as a handcrafted wood-framed window. LaCroix's passion for windows goes back to his youth in St. Jean, Quebec, where he was taught how to make residential windows by an elderly carpenter. He learned about the characteristics of good wood, the best tools to use, and how to choose the best glass from local suppliers. LaCroix apprenticed with the carpenter in his small workshop and, when the carpenter retired, was given the opportunity to operate the business himself.

LaCroix hired his own apprentice as he built up business in the local area. His small operation soon expanded as the quality of windows built by LaCroix Industries Ltd. became better known. Within eight years, the company employed nearly 25 people and the business had moved to larger facilities to accommodate the increased demand from southern Quebec. In these early years, LaCroix spent most of his time in the production shop, teaching new apprentices the unique skills that he had mastered and applauding the journeymen for their accomplishments. He would constantly repeat the point that LaCroix products had to be of the highest quality because they gave families a "window on life."

After 15 years, LaCroix Industries employed over 200 people. A profit-sharing program was introduced to give employees a financial reward for their contribution to the organization's success. Due to the company's expansion, headquarters had to be moved to another area of town, but the founder never lost touch with the work force. Although new apprentices were now taught entirely by the master carpenters and other craftspeople, LaCroix would still chat with plant and office employees several times each week.

When a second work shift was added, LaCroix would show up during the evening break with coffee and boxes of doughnuts and discuss how the business was doing and how it became so successful through quality workmanship. Production employees enjoyed the times when he would gather them together to announce new contracts with developers from Montreal and Toronto. After each announcement, LaCroix would thank everyone for making the business a success. They knew that LaCroix quality had become a standard of excellence in window manufacturing across Canada.

It seemed that almost every time he visited, LaCroix would repeat the now well-known phrase that LaCroix products had to be of the highest quality because they provided a window on life to so many families. Employees never grew tired of hearing this from the company founder. However, it gained extra meaning when LaCroix began posting photos of families looking through LaCroix windows. At first, LaCroix would personally visit developers and homeowners with a camera in hand. Later, as the "window on life" photos became known by developers and customers, people would send in photos of their own families looking through elegant front windows made by LaCroix Industries. The company's marketing staff began using this idea, as well as LaCroix's famous phrase, in their advertising. After one such marketing campaign, hundreds of photos were sent in by satisfied customers. Production and office employees took time after work to write personal letters of thanks to those who had submitted photos.

As the company's age reached the quarter-century mark, LaCroix, now in his mid-fifties, realized that the organization's success and survival depended on expansion into the United States. After consulting with employees, LaCroix made the difficult decision to sell a majority share to Build-All Products, Inc., a conglomerate with international marketing expertise in building products. As part of the agreement, Build-All brought in a vice-president to oversee production operations while LaCroix spent more time meeting with developers around North America. LaCroix would return to the plant and office at every opportunity, but often this would be only once a month.

Rather than visiting the production plant, Jan Vlodoski, the new production vice-president, would rarely leave his office in the company's downtown headquarters. Instead, production orders were sent to supervisors by memorandum. Although product quality had been a priority throughout the company's history, less attention had been paid to inventory controls. Vlodoski introduced strict inventory guidelines and outlined procedures on using supplies for each shift. Goals were established for supervisors to meet specific inventory targets. Whereas employees previously could have tossed out several pieces of warped wood, they would now have to justify this action, usually in writing.

Vlodoski also announced new procedures for purchasing production supplies. LaCroix Industries had highly trained purchasing staff who worked closely with senior craftspeople when selecting suppliers, but Vlodoski wanted to bring in Build-All's procedures. The new purchasing methods removed production leaders from the decision process and, in some cases, resulted in trade-offs that LaCroix's employees would not have made earlier. A few employees quit during this time, saying that they did not feel comfortable about producing a window that would not stand the test of time. However, unemployment was high in St. Jean, so most staff members remained with the company.

After one year, inventory expenses decreased by approximately 10 percent, but the number of defective windows returned by developers and wholesalers had increased markedly. Plant employees knew that the number of defective windows would increase as they used somewhat lower-quality materials to reduce inventory costs. However, they heard almost no news about the seriousness of the problem until Vlodoski sent a memo to all production staff saying that quality must be maintained. During the latter part of the first year under Vlodoski, a few employees had the opportunity to personally ask LaCroix about the changes and express their concerns. LaCroix apologized, saying due to his travels to new regions, he had not heard about the problems, and that he would look into the matter.

Exactly 18 months after Build-All had become majority shareholder of LaCroix Industries, LaCroix called together five of the original staff in the plant. The company founder looked pale and shaken as he said that Build-All's actions were inconsistent with his vision of the company and, for the first time in his career, he did not know what to do. Build-All was not pleased with the arrangement either. Although LaCroix windows still enjoyed a healthy market share and were competitive for the value, the company did not quite provide the minimum 18 percent return on equity that the conglomerate expected. LaCroix asked his long-time companions for advice.

Case 3 Cantron Ltd.*

Cantron Ltd., a Canadian manufacturer of centralized vacuum systems, was facing severe cash flow problems in 1985 due to increasing demand for its products and rapid expansion of production facilities. Steve Heinrich, Cantron's founder and majority shareholder, flew to Germany to meet with management of Rohrtech Gmb to discuss the German company's willingness to become majority shareholder of Cantron in exchange for an infusion of much-needed cash. A deal was struck whereby Rohrtech would become majority shareholder while Heinrich would remain as Cantron's president and general manager. One of Rohrtech's senior executives would become the chairperson of Cantron's board of directors, and Rohrtech would appoint two other board members.

This relationship worked well until Rohrtech was acquired by a European conglomerate in 1987 and the new owner wanted more precise financial information and controls placed on its holdings, including Cantron. Heinrich resented this imposition and refused to provide the necessary information. By 1989, relations between Rohrtech and Cantron had soured to the point where Heinrich refused to let Rohrtech representatives into the Cantron plant. He also instituted legal proceedings to regain control of the company.

According to Canadian law, any party who possesses over two-thirds of a company's shares may force the others to sell their shares. Heinrich owned 29 percent of Cantron's shares, whereas Rohrtech owned 56 percent. The remaining 15 percent of Cantron shares were held by Jean Parrot, Cantron's head of operations in Quebec. Parrot was a long-time manager at Cantron and remained on the sidelines throughout most of the legal battle between Rohrtech and Heinrich. However, in late September of 1990, Parrot finally agreed to sell his shares to Rohrtech, thereby legally forcing Heinrich to give up his shares. When Heinrich's bid for control failed, Rohrtech purchased all remaining shares and Cantron's board of directors (now dominated by Rohrtech) dismissed Heinrich as president and general manager in October 1990. The board immediately appointed Parrot as Cantron's new president.

Searching for a new general manager

In the spring of 1990, while Heinrich was still president and trying to regain control of his company, the chairman of Cantron's board of directors received instructions from Rohrtech to hire a management consulting firm in Toronto to identify possible outside candidates for the position of general manager at Cantron. The successful candidate would be hired after the conflict with Heinrich had ended (presumably with Heinrich's departure). The general manager would report to the president (the person eventually replacing Heinrich) and would be responsible for day-to-day management of the company. Rohrtech's management correctly believed that most of Cantron's current managers were loyal to Heinrich and, by hiring an outsider, the German firm would gain more inside control over its Canadian subsidiary.

Over 50 candidates applied for the general manager position, and three candidates were interviewed by Cantron's chairman and another Rohrtech representative in August 1990. One of these candidates, Kurt Devine, was vice-president of sales at an industrial packaging firm in Toronto and, at 52 years old, was looking for one more career challenge before retirement. The Rohrtech representatives explained the current situation and said that they were offering stable employment after the problem with Heinrich was resolved so that the general manager could help settle Cantron's problems. When Devine expressed his concern about rivalry with internal candidates, the senior Rohrtech manager stated: "We have a bookkeeper, but he is not our choice. The sales manager is capable, but he is located in New York and doesn't want to move to Canada."

One week after Heinrich's dismissal and the appointment of Parrot as president, Cantron's chairman invited Devine to a meeting at a posh Toronto hotel attended by the chairman, another Rohrtech manager on Cantron's board of directors, and Parrot. The chairman explained the recent events at Cantron and formally invited Devine to accept the position of vice-president and general manager of the company. After discussing salary and details about job duties, Devine asked the others whether he had their support as well as the support of Cantron's employees. The two Rohrtech representatives said "Yes," while Parrot remained silent. When the chairman left the room to get a bottle of wine to toast the new general manager, Devine asked Parrot how long he had known about the decision to hire him. Parrot replied, "Just last week when I became president. I was surprised . . . I don't think I would have hired you."

Confrontation with Tom O'Grady

Devine began work at Cantron in early November and, within a few weeks, noticed that the president and two other Cantron managers were not giving him the support he needed to accomplish his work. For example, Parrot would call the salespeople almost daily, yet rarely speak with Devine unless the general manager approached him first. The vice-president of sales acted cautiously toward Devine. But it was Tom O'Grady, the vice-president of finance and administration, who seemed to resent Devine's presence the most. O'Grady had been promoted from the position of controller in October and now held the highest rank at Cantron below Devine. After Heinrich was dismissed, Cantron's board of directors had placed O'Grady in charge of day-to-day operations until Devine took over.

Devine depended on O'Grady for information because he had more knowledge than anyone else about many aspects of the business outside of Quebec. However, O'Grady provided incomplete information on many occasions and would completely refuse to educate the general manager on some matters. O'Grady was also quick to criticize many of Devine's decisions and made indirect statements to Devine about his inappropriateness as a general manager. He also mentioned how he and other Cantron managers didn't want the German company (Rohrtech) to interfere with their company.

Devine would later learn about other things O'Grady had said and done to undermine his position. For example, O'Grady actively spoke to office staff and other managers about the problems with Devine, and encouraged them to tell the president about their concerns. Devine overhead O'Grady telling another manager that Devine's memoranda were a "complete joke" and that "Devine didn't know what he was talking about." On one occasion, O'Grady let Devine send out incorrect information about the organization's structure even though O'Grady knew that it was incorrect "just to prove what an idiot Rohrtech had hired."

Just six weeks after joining Cantron, Devine confronted O'Grady with his concerns. O'Grady was quite candid with the general manager, saying that everyone felt that Devine was a "plant" by Rohrtech and was trying to turn Cantron into a branch office of the German company. He said that some employees would quit if Devine did not leave because they wanted Cantron to maintain its independence from Rohrtech. In a later meeting with Devine and Parrot, O'Grady repeated these points and added that Devine's management style was not appropriate for Cantron. Devine responded that he had not received any support from Cantron since the day he had arrived, even though Rohrtech had sent explicit directions to Parrot and other Cantron managers that he was to have complete support in managing the company's daily operations. Parrot told the two men that they should work together and that, of course, Devine was the more senior person.

Decision by Cantron's board of directors

As a member of Cantron's board of directors, Parrot ensured that the matter of Devine was discussed at the January 1991 meeting and that the board invite O'Grady to repeat his story. Based on this testimony, the board decided to remove Devine from the general manager job and give him a special project instead. O'Grady was immediately named acting general manager. The chairman and other Rohrtech representatives on Cantron's board were disappointed that events did not unfold as they had hoped, but they agreed to remove Devine rather than face the mass exodus of Cantron managers that Parrot and O'Grady had warned about.

In late April of 1991, Devine attended a morning meeting of Cantron's board of directors to present his interim report on the special project. The board agreed to give Devine until mid-June to complete the project. However, the board recalled Devine into the boardroom in the afternoon and Parrot bluntly asked Devine why he didn't turn in his resignation. Devine replied: "I can't think of a single reason why I should. I will not resign. I joined your company six months ago as a challenge. I have not been allowed to do my job. My decision to come here was based on support from Rohrtech and on a great product." The next day, Parrot came to Devine's office with a letter of dismissal signed by the chairman of Cantron's board of directors.

*© 1991 Steven L. McShane. This case is based mainly on events described in an unpublished Canadian court case. Dates, locations, and industry have been changed. All names of people and companies have also been changed and should not be identified with actual people or companies with these names.

Case 4 Eastern Province Light and Power*

I work as a systems and procedures analyst for the Eastern Province Light and Power Company. The systems and procedures department analyzes corporate policies, procedures, forms, equipment, and methods to simplify and standardize operations. We apply "organized common sense" to develop new practices and to improve old ones.

Requests for analysis of organizational problems are submitted to the systems and procedures department by persons of department head or higher status. Our manager places projects in line for consideration and assigns them to an analyst on the basis of availability; projects are accepted and assigned on the FIFO (first in–first out) method. Projects must undergo analysis, design, and implementation before a change in procedure is realized. What follows is a description of a problem assigned to me. I am in the midst of investigating it right now.

The problem

For some time, management had been concerned with the inventory carrying charges that accrue when material is stored in company warehouses. Not only is there a cost attached to carrying inventory for future use, but there are additional related costs such as labour to handle the inventory, warehouse usage in terms of square feet taken up in storage, and clerical time used to account for materials flowing into and out of inventory. One type of material stored is office supplies—pens, writing pads, forms, stationery, envelopes, and dozens of similar items. A desire to reduce the costs of storing these items prompted the head of the department of purchasing and material control to submit a request for study by systems and procedures.

The request came in the required written form. It described the current procedures, estimated their costs, and invited us to explore ways of changing the procedures to reduce costs. In brief, at the time the study request was submitted, purchases of office supplies were made through 11 vendors. The items were stored in a common warehouse area and disbursed to using departments as requested. As is customary, I convened a meeting of the requesting manager and others who seemed most directly involved in the problem.

The first meeting

I opened the meeting by summarizing the present procedures for purchasing and storing office supplies and the estimated costs associated with these problems. I explained that we were meeting to explore ways of reducing these costs. I suggested we might try to generate as many ideas as we could without being too critical of them, and then proceed to narrow the list by criticizing and eliminating the ideas with obvious weaknesses.

Just as soon as I finished my opening remarks, the head of purchasing and material control said that we should conduct a pilot study in which we would contract with one of the regular vendors to supply each involved department directly, eliminating company storage of any inventory. The vendor would continue to sell us whatever we usually purchased from it, but would sell and deliver the items to various departments instead of to our central purchasing group. A pilot study with one vendor would indicate how such a system would work with all vendors of office supplies. If it worked well we could handle all office supplies this way.

She went on to explain that she had already spoken to the vice-president to whom she (and, through intermediate levels, the rest of us) reported and that he recognized the potential savings that would result. She also said that she had gone over the idea with the supervisor of stores (who reported to her) and that he agreed. She wanted to know how long it would take me to carry out the pilot study. I looked at a few faces to see if anybody would say anything, but nobody did. I said I didn't know. She said, "Let's meet in a week when you've come up with a proposal." The meeting ended without anything else of any real substance being said.

I felt completely frustrated. She was the highest-ranking person in the meeting. She had said what she wanted and, if her stature wasn't enough, she had invoked the image of the vice-president being in agreement with her. Nobody, including me, had said anything. No idea other than hers was even mentioned, and no comments were made about it.

I decided that I would work as hard as I could to study the problem and her proposed pilot study before the next meeting and come prepared to give the whole thing a critical review.

Between meetings

I talked to my boss about my feeling that it seemed as though I was expected to rubber-stamp the pilot study idea. I said that I wished he would come to the next meeting. I also said that I wanted to talk to some people close to the problem, some clerks in stores, some vendors, and some buyers in purchasing to see if I could come up with any good ideas or find any problems in the pilot study area. He told me to learn all I could and that he would come to the next meeting.

My experience with other studies had taught me that sometimes the people closest to the work had expertise to contribute, so I found one stores clerk, two buyers, and two vendor sales representatives to talk to. Nobody had spoken to any of them about the pilot study and the general plan it was meant to test. This surprised me a little. Each one of these people had some interesting things to say about the proposed new way of handling office supplies. A buyer, for example, thought it would be chaotic to have 17 different departments ordering the same items. She thought we might also lose out on some quantity discounts, and it would mean 17 times the paperwork. A vendor said he didn't think any vendor would like the idea because it would increase the number of contacts necessary to sell the amount that could be sold now through one contact—the buyer in the purchasing department. A stores clerk said it might be risky to depend on a vendor to maintain inventories at adequate levels. He said, "What if a vendor failed to supply us with, say, enough mark-sensing tools for our meter readers one month, thereby causing them to be unable to complete their task and our company to be unable to get its monthly billings out on time?"

The second meeting

Armed with careful notes, I came to the next meeting prepared to discuss these and other criticisms. One of the stores clerks had even agreed to attend so that I could call on him for comments. But when I looked around the conference room, everyone was there except the stores clerk. The head of purchasing and material control said she had talked to the clerk and could convey any of his ideas so she had told him it wasn't necessary for him to come.

I pointed out that the stores clerk had raised a question about the company's ability to control inventory. He had said that we now have physical control of inventory, but the proposal involved making ourselves dependent on the vendor's maintaining adequate inventory. The head of purchasing and material control said, "Not to worry. It will be in the vendor's own interest to keep us well supplied." No one, including my boss, said anything.

I brought up the subject of selecting a vendor to participate in the pilot study. My boss mentioned that I had told him some vendors might object to the scheme because the additional contacts would increase their costs of sales. The head of purchasing and material control said, "Any vendor would be interested in doing business with a company as big as Eastern Province Light and Power." No further comments were made.

I mentioned that it was the practice of the systems and procedures staff to estimate independently the costs and benefits of any project before undertaking it, and also to have the internal auditing department review the proposal. I said we would need to go ahead with those steps. I asked the head of purchasing and material control to give me the name of somebody in her area I should contact to get the costs of the present system. She said that it really didn't seem necessary to go through all the usual steps in this case since she had already submitted an estimate. Besides, it was only going to be a pilot study. She said, "I think we can all agree on that and just move ahead now with the designation of a vendor." She looked around the table and nobody said anything. She said, "Fine. Let's use Moore Business Forms." Nobody said anything. She then said to me, "OK, let's get back together after you've lined things up."

*D. R. Hampton, *Contemporary Management* (New York: McGraw-Hill, 1981). Used with permission.

Case 5   Hickling Associates Ltd.*

Introduction

For almost seven years prior to June 1983, Tony Azzara had been employed by Pisces Exporters Ltd. The company, located in Vancouver, was a subsidiary of a U.S. food products conglomerate headquartered in Los Angeles. Pisces was one of the largest exporters for fresh and frozen seafood on Canada's west coast, and had generated revenues between $40 million and $60 million annually, depending on the quality of the fishing season and market demand. The company's major markets were primarily in Europe as well as several areas of Asia and Japan. Pisces also traded other food products, which, over the years, overtook seafood as the main revenue producer for the firm.

At the age of 27, Tony Azzara began his career with Pisces as a salesperson, where he learned the complexities of exporting both fresh and frozen sea products to various countries. Within two and a half years he was promoted to the position of sales manager responsible for all seafood exports to Europe. This was an exciting job and a respected position. He was given a comfortable office and a very acceptable compensation package. There was an annual bonus based on group sales, which was as high as 100 percent of Tony's base salary in the best years. Even in the poorest years, the bonus was about 20 percent of base salary. He also received a generous car allowance. The work required Tony to develop contacts with other people in the seafood industry in Canada as well as with the major customers in Europe. He was able to take several trips to Europe to expand the market there and develop better relations with Pisces's existing customers. The job was also a constant challenge, because of the increasing international competition in seafood sales and the need to closely coordinate the sales group with the buyers in Pisces. Tony learned early in his career that product quality and delivery time were just as important as price in this market, and only by keeping in touch with the company's seafood buyers could he make those guarantees to his overseas customers.

After about two years as sales manager, it became increasingly clear that Pisces's products were being priced out of the European market. The competition from Asia and Scandinavia was increasing dramatically as they improved their export marketing practices to Europe. Equally important was the appreciation of the Canadian dollar against most European currencies. This dramatically increased the price of Canadian goods in most European countries, whereas the seafood products entering from the Pacific Rim did not experience these fluctuations. By the end of 1982, European seafood sales from Pisces and all other North American exporters had dropped in both volume and market share. Only in the higher end of the market—the expensive seafood products—did the price have only a modest effect on European market share.

Unfortunately, the American parent company of Pisces Exporters Ltd. was also experiencing serious financial problems for several different reasons and, combined with the depressed export market in seafood, the entire fresh and frozen seafood export division of Pisces Exporters Ltd. was discontinued in the second week of June 1983. Consequently, the vice-president, 6 sales managers (including Tony Azzara), 10 salespeople, and 5 support staff lost their jobs. The notices of permanent layoff were given in March, and all laid-off staff were given reasonable severance payments in June in amounts that corresponded to their position and length of service. For Tony, this was equivalent to about four months' salary.

An opening at Hickling Associates Ltd.
In the weeks leading up to the final day of work at Pisces Exporters Ltd., Tony Azzara began telephoning around to the people he knew in the Vancouver area in order to let it be known that he was looking for a job in the industry. He had the right experience and had become fairly well known in the city as a good trader in the canned and frozen seafood business. The president of Pisces even approached Tony before he left to say that he would be pleased to write a letter of reference if it would help Tony's search for alternate employment. Tony was flattered by the gesture. In spite of these factors, however, Tony Azzara did not expect to find another job in the seafood exporting business in the near future.

With a depressed seafood market and high unemployment throughout British Columbia, securing alternate employment was not going to be easy. In fact, Tony entertained the possibility of changing industries and even began to look through the newspapers for sales positions in other products.

In early June, Mr. James Hickling telephoned Tony Azzara at his office and invited him to lunch the next day. Mr. Hickling owned Hickling Associates Ltd., a medium-sized trading organization in Vancouver that specialized in the import and export of several types of canned and frozen foods. In addition, the company traded a few other commodities such as grains and finishing nails. Tony had met Mr. Hickling in two joint ventures between the two companies a few years earlier. However, Tony had worked mainly with Thomas Siu, who was the export seafood trader at Hickling Associates.

Following the call from James Hickling, Tony tried to recall what else he knew about Hickling Associates Ltd. and later in the day made several inquiries regarding the firm. He knew that the company was mainly an importer of canned foods such as mushrooms and oriental foods from several Asian countries. Seafood trading was restricted mainly to the export of canned salmon and represented a very small factor in the business. As far as Tony knew, Thomas Siu was the only person responsible for this part of the operation and had been employed by Hickling Associates for about five years. Tony also learned from one of his contacts in the industry that Hickling Associates was financially very strong and well established. It was founded by James Hickling's father in 1934 and grew steadily throughout the years. When the elder Hickling retired in the late 1960s, James Hickling took over the company and had been given a lot of credit for the company's current success.

James Hickling was considered by many people in the import–export industry to be something of a maverick, and was generally respected for his business sense and solid understanding of the international merchant business. Tony had heard a rumour of a disenchanted trader in canned foods who left Hickling Associates Ltd. a few years previously. The trader joined a rival importer and took with him a few Asian accounts whose contracts with Hickling Associates Ltd. were about to expire. Nevertheless, James Hickling subsequently won back some of those customers and further expanded his business in the import of mushrooms, bamboo shoots, and other canned goods.

The meeting with James Hickling

Tony Azzara arrived early at the posh restaurant where Mr. Hickling had made reservations and ordered a glass of white wine while he waited. Precisely at 12:15, the time of the scheduled meeting, James Hickling arrived. He was conservatively dressed in a dark blue suit and looked to be in his early 50s. He introduced himself as he arrived at the table and ordered a double scotch on the rocks. After a few initial pleasantries and acknowledgements of the troubles in the European market, Mr. Hickling got right to the point.

"Tony, I'm looking for a man like you to take charge of the seafood export trading in Hickling Associates. It's been a small part of the company for too long, in my opinion. The market is down in a few areas such as Europe and that's knocked the wind out of some of the competition. I believe that you could help me to get a bigger share of the canned salmon market and even get into the export of fresh fish over the next few years as the market rebounds."

Tony took a quick sip of his wine. He had been sure that this meeting was about a possible job opening, but was surprised by the sudden offer. These jobs were rare in Vancouver in 1983, and there were a lot of good traders around.

"This sounds like the sort of challenge that I'd like," Tony replied, trying to sound calm and interested in the position at the same time. "As you know, I've been in this business for a few years now and have developed several contacts in Europe and other markets. I've also worked with Tom Siu on occasion, as you'll recall." Tony was hoping to find out how he and Tom Siu would be working together.

"Yes, indeed," Hickling continued. "Those ventures turned out very well. Siu told me that the two of you worked well together. That's why I think you can do an excellent job in this market."

"What do you have in mind, Mr. Hickling?" It was a risky question but worth asking. Tony had seen situations at Pisces Exporters where two traders clashed because the vice-president neglected to clarify their respective duties. He also wanted to avoid stepping on Tom Siu's toes by taking his job away from him.

Hickling took a final bite of his sole florentine and ordered another double scotch. "Siu's done a good job as a trader for me, but his strength is as a buyer, not as a seller," he explained. "He came to us about five years ago from [the Canadian Department of] Fisheries and really knows the quality of seafood. His knowledge of the processing industry on the West Coast has been a real plus. My intention is to bring you in as the export seller and Siu will be primarily responsible as the buyer."

Tony felt satisfied. The job looked challenging and the set-up would take advantage of both Tom Siu's and his talents.

Hickling continued. "Tony, there's a lot of opportunity in Hickling Associates if you decide to join our team. I'll start you at $40,000 per year and, depending on your contribution, you'll receive a bonus with no ceiling. That means a virtually unlimited earnings potential if you boost our export seafood business. And I know you will."

The offer was quite satisfactory to Tony, especially considering his employment alternatives. The salary was slightly lower than his current $42,000 salary, but this could be made up in bonuses. He was curious about the bonus plan, but felt that this was not diplomatically the right time to go into details on compensation matters. It was not a large company, and written employment contracts were rarely seen in the industry, even at the senior executive level.

"That sounds reasonable." Tony didn't want to sound too enthusiastic. "Of course, I'll have to give this some thought. Could you tell me more about the company's facilities for export trading?"

James Hickling explained the computer system that had recently been introduced to keep track of client accounts as well as purchase inventories. Tony would have complete access to the support staff and would have freedom to develop fresh and frozen seafood sales. In order to develop these sales, Tony would be free to travel as required. In addition, traders at Hickling Associates Ltd. were given a company car up to a certain value. This value was about $3,000 lower than Tony's car, because Pisces had a higher limit. However, Hickling agreed to raise this limit for as long as Tony had his present automobile. The limit would then be lowered for any subsequent car purchase.

The conversation wandered into the quality of recent salmon catches and the opportunities for international merchants with the rapid growth of fish farms along British Columbia's coast. Tony saw these farms as an excellent source for fresh salmon exports, particularly in competition with the Norwegians, who had been taking an increasing percentage of market share in several areas of the world.

About one and a half hours after the lunch began, Tony Azzara and James Hickling shook hands and left the restaurant. Tony promised to get back to Hickling within the next couple of days with an answer. That evening, Tony discussed the offer with his wife, and the next day he accepted Mr. Hickling's offer. Tony would start work on July 18, 1983, giving Tony and his wife a few weeks of vacation on Vancouver Island in early July.

The start of a new job

Promptly at 8 A.M. on Monday, July 18, Tony Azzara walked into the office of Hickling Associates Ltd. in downtown Vancouver eager to accept his new challenge. Mr. Hickling had not arrived yet, but the receptionist had just sat down at her desk. Tony could hear that other people were already at work behind the partition that separated the receptionist from the rest of the offices.

When Tony introduced himself to the receptionist, she answered in an apologetic way that she knew nothing of his arrival. It was evident from her awkwardness that the receptionist wasn't quite sure how to deal with this situation, so Tony let himself into the general office and wandered through the various areas (see Exhibit 1). There were five secretarial workstations directly behind the reception area and, along the hallway to the left, another larger, open section of the office where several men and a few women were working. As Tony entered this area, an oriental gentleman in his late 30s approached him. It was Thomas Siu. Tom looked genuinely pleased to meet Tony as the two men shook hands. After short introductions, Tom walked Tony over to a far corner of the room and pointed to two of the large desks butted up against each other.

"This is where you'll be working, Tony," Tom said with a smile. "Mr. Hickling likes to have the traders who work together near each other. Since I'm doing the buying and you're doing the selling, I'll be right here." Tom put his hand on the other desk.

The proximity of the work areas was something of a shock to Tony. He was accustomed to his own office and, although aware that Hickling Associates had an open office arrangement, he did not expect to be so physically close to the other traders. Tony looked around the large room. It was an older building with high ceilings and large arched windows. The offices of Hickling Associates took up half of the fourth floor of the 10-story office building. The clerical workstations he had passed earlier were very modern, whereas the trader desks were large oak pieces with wooden swivel rockers. Except for the carpeting and fixtures, the room looked much like it would have 30 years earlier. It was actually rather appealing to Tony, except for the physical arrangements. The other traders were at their desks, most of them on the telephone or just coming in to work.

At that moment James Hickling walked in from the entrance on the far side of the room and walked toward Tony and Tom. "Good morning, Tony. I see that you're getting yourself all settled in." He shook Tony's hand and then sat down at the desk at the head of the room.

Exhibit I   Office Layout of Hickling Associates Ltd.

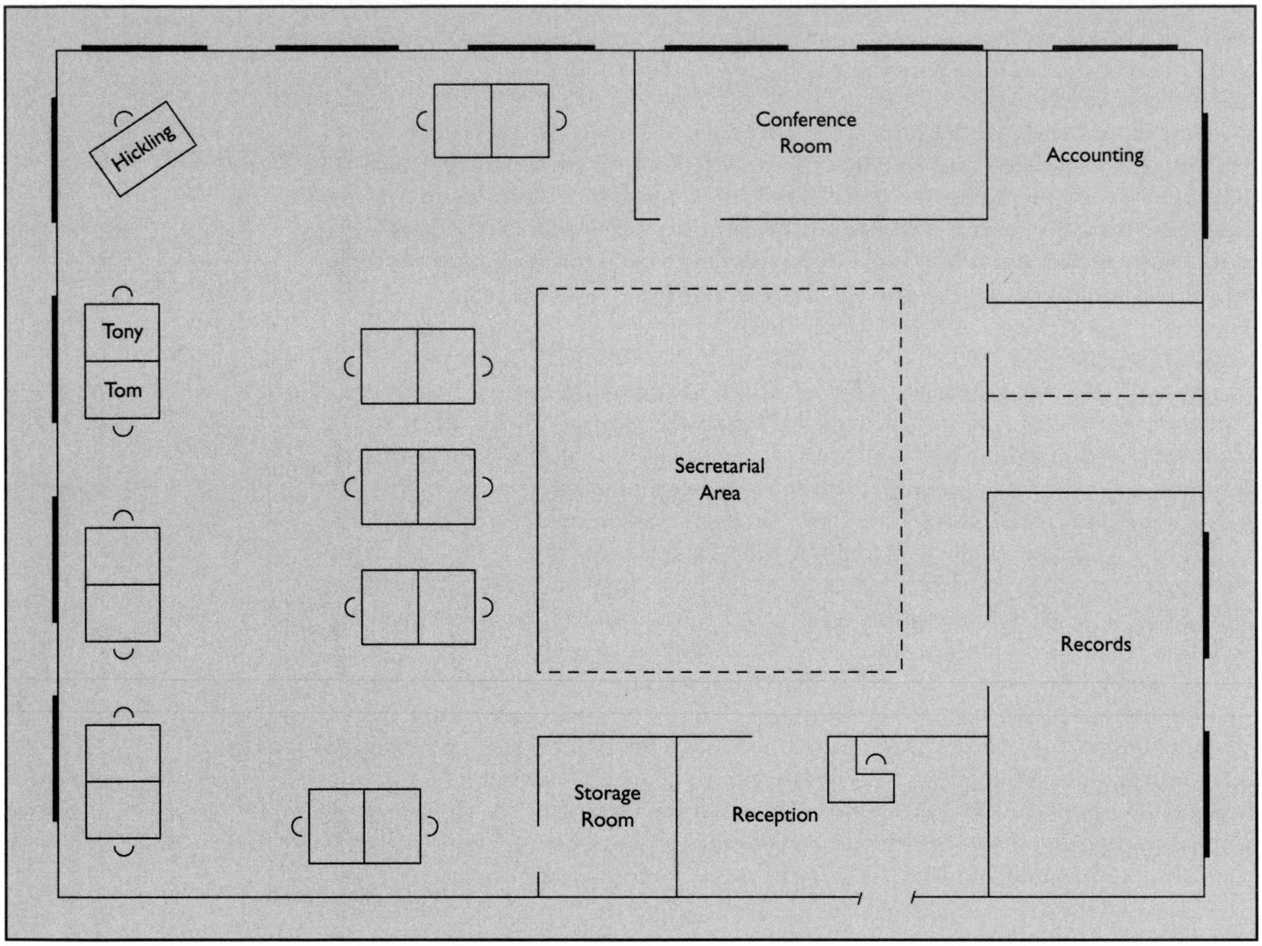

Tony's heart sank. Hickling's desk was only five feet from his, allowing Hickling to literally look over Tony's shoulder. He sat down and looked around the room again. It then dawned on him that he was the only person wearing a suit. The other traders were dressed casually in slacks and open shirts. Some were even wearing blue jeans. Tony glanced back to Hickling who was on the telephone and looking out the window. He was dressed in corduroy pants and a plaid sport shirt—a sharp contrast from Tony's three-piece dark grey pinstripe suit with white shirt and tie.

Not knowing quite what to do, Tony rummaged through his desk to discover what supplies were available. He jotted down the supplies he needed and made a short list of his goals for the next few weeks. Unfortunately, this didn't take very long, and Tony was soon left with the task of finding something else to do. It wasn't a good idea to ask Tom about work procedures yet, with Hickling just a few feet away. That wouldn't leave a good impression. Instead, Tony walked around the office, introducing himself to the other traders and staff in the firm. In a casual manner, he observed some of the forms and procedures the other traders were using while asking them about their product areas. After about half an hour, Tony returned to his desk. His watch said it was only 9:30 A.M. It was going to be an awkward morning. For the next few hours, Tony made telephone calls to some of his contacts to inform them that he was now employed at Hickling Associates Ltd.

James Hickling left the office before lunch and didn't return until late in the afternoon. This gave Tony the opportunity to talk with Tom and learn more about the firm's buy and sell procedures. Tom was very helpful as the two discussed matters over lunch. They also formed a fairly good understanding of how they could coordinate the work. Tom was quite pleased that he was now handling only the purchases of seafood, but Tony felt that Tom wasn't very enthusiastic either about his job or the possibility of expanding the product line to fresh fish exports.

Settling in

During the first month, Tony Azzara made several successful foreign sales of canned salmon and other fish products and was able to use the records and inventory system at Hickling Associates Ltd. with minimal difficulty. Having previous experience in the industry was a definite help. Much of the job could be performed in a similar manner no matter where he worked. However, there was still a lot of uncertainty about some of the more technical procedures and the extent of his authority. Hickling hadn't given Tony any idea about this. The office layout was also difficult to get used to. It was quite clear that Mr. Hickling had tried to overhear some of Tony's telephone conversations. The records people also were putting pressure on Tony to sign all correspondence with the company name rather than his own. This made him feel very uncomfortable because these were contacts and customers that he had established. It was certainly common for traders to sign their own names in other trading firms. For several weeks, these factors took their toll as Tony felt quite worn out by the end of the day.

At the end of the third week, Tony decided to approach Mr. Hickling about a few company policies so that he would have a clearer idea about how to approach certain items on his agenda. For example, Tony was still unsure about the limit of his signing authority for shipments to new customers. There was also the question of the firm's approach to selling odd-sized lots. On both issues, Tony had received conflicting opinions from the other traders. This may have been because they were in such diverse product lines and company policy might vary with the product. So Tony approached James Hickling directly for the answers.

Hickling's reply was hostile. "For God's sake, Tony!" he barked. "Can't you figure these things out for yourself? I haven't time for that trivia!"

Tony's initial feeling was that of embarrassment. Hickling spoke loud enough for all of the traders to hear, and several of them turned to find out what was going on. Embarrassment turned to anger, however, as Tony realized that his questions were not unreasonable. He turned on his heel and, without replying to Hickling, marched out of the room toward the records office. Hopefully, some of the answers might be found there in old invoices and other documents. Later that day, Tom Siu apologized to Tony for not warning him earlier about Hickling. Tom pointed out that most of the traders had received the same dress-down at one time or another and, therefore, avoided Hickling whenever possible. Hickling may have been one of the best traders in the city, but he wasn't easy to get along with.

The only exception was when Hickling had been drinking. It became increasingly apparent to Tony that Hickling and several of the traders were heavy drinkers. They almost always drank copious amounts of liquor at lunch. There was also a ritual of sharing a large bottle of rye or scotch whenever a major deal was finalized. Tony figured that at least one bottle was consumed openly in the office each week. Every trader had his or her own glass. Both an ice machine and liquor store were conveniently located around the block from the Hickling Associates offices. It was during these celebrations that Hickling became more personable with the traders, although the traders still watched what they said to him. Tony wasn't much of a drinker, but went along with the ritual and even broke out a bottle of scotch for the group one day in September when he signed up a major European customer. This office behaviour was quite different from Pisces Exporters Ltd. where drinking on the job was strictly forbidden.

The drinking habits of Hickling and the office staff (mainly the traders) paled against a more startling observation that Tony made after about a month on the job. James Hickling was married with three children, but Tony noticed him on several occasions leave for lunch with a female employee in the accounting group and not return until late in the afternoon. He quietly asked Tom Siu about this one day and was told that Hickling was having an affair with the woman. Tony was surprised at how casually Tom said this. Over the next few months, Tony learned about two other relationships in the office between traders and support staff. In both cases, one or both of the employees were married. All three affairs were generally known of and accepted throughout the firm. Apparently, other relationships had formed in the past, and when they dissolved one or both of the employees involved had left the company within a few months. Tony had difficulty accepting the moral standards of the office and couldn't understand how these affairs were condoned so easily by the other members of Hickling Associates Ltd.

After three months, Tony Azzara was beginning to feel a little more comfortable in his position at Hickling Associates Ltd. He hadn't received any feedback from Hickling, but had a fairly good idea that he was doing well by industry standards. The other traders were in diverse product areas and it was difficult to compare performance. Nevertheless, several of them congratulated Tony on the number of new customers he had signed up for the export of canned salmon and other seafood products. Tom Siu's excellent buying skills helped considerably, but in the tough European market, the traders knew that export sales would be the more difficult task.

Tony felt that his earlier contacts had really helped to increase sales. But he was not receiving the industry mail that used to come across his desk at Pisces Exports Ltd. This mail was important because it would inform Tony of upcoming functions in Vancouver and abroad. Instead, the mail was going directly to James Hickling's desk. On several occasions, Hickling attended these functions and Tony would not find out until after the event. In fact, Tony attended only two industry functions during the first year compared with the five or six events he had formerly attended annually.

Another major setback occurred in late November. Hickling had planned a trip to Europe and made arrangements to visit several of Tony's new customers. Tony was angry and frustrated. But when he approached his boss about this,

Hickling replied, "It doesn't make sense for both of us to travel." Two more trips were made in February and April 1984. On both of these occasions, Tony was told that he would be able to make these trips in the future. Meanwhile, Tony had to rely on the telephone and other forms of communication to make his important contacts for new business. On none of the trips that Hickling took did any new seafood export sales materialize.

The bonus and the final straw

At the end of six months of work, Tony Azzara had contributed over $425,000 in net profits to Hickling Associates Ltd. Seafood exports had more than doubled, and several new customers had been established in spite of the limitations that were placed on Tony. Hickling still hadn't provided any performance feedback but Tony had high expectations of the bonus, which was paid at the end of the year. In his final paycheque for 1983, Tony found a bonus in the amount of $10,000. It was a disappointment. He had worked harder than ever before and had personally generated record sales for the company. A few days later, when Hickling had returned from lunch and was in high spirits, Tony confronted Hickling about how the bonus was decided. Hickling looked rather awkward as he explained that it was based on a combination of overall company profitability and individual performance. He then promised Tony that if he sold as well in 1984, the bonus for that year would reflect this performance.

In February, when Hickling was out of town, Tony had the opportunity to talk about the bonus system with a few of the other traders. To his surprise, many of the traders had gone through a similar reaction to their first bonus. Most were still disappointed, but had resigned themselves to the fact that salaries would not be much higher than the base rate. As long as they avoided James Hickling and did their jobs, the traders accepted the situation. It was quite clear that they were doing enough to survive in the job and nothing more.

After a year on the job, Tony was feeling increasingly antagonistic to Hickling and the firm. He still had not been given the opportunity to visit his customers and make new contacts abroad. Tony even began rummaging through Hickling's mail to find out about upcoming industry events. He continued to sign his own name rather than the company's to most telex correspondence, but it was clear that Hickling wanted the customers to identify with him, not the traders. It was fairly easy at first to accept the drinking ritual. However, Tony later separated himself more from Hickling and the other traders when he realized how much alcohol he was drinking. In fact, it was his wife who first noticed this as Tony began to consume more liquor at home.

As the end of 1984 approached, Tony felt somewhat confident that his bonus would be at least as high as last year's. Sales had continued to climb and the seafood export component of Hickling Associates Ltd. represented a larger pro-portion of the business than ever before. The 1984 bonus was $5,000. Tony Azzara was shocked and upset. Neglecting the possibility of a loud confrontation, Tony again confronted Hickling. Hickling indicated that several other parts of the organization were not producing the expected levels of profit and, as a result, all bonuses were lower. He added that it was important to be part of the team at Hickling Associates Ltd. and share the profits and losses throughout the firm.

A few weeks later, Tony learned from sales records that none of the other trading areas in the company had suffered any serious drop in sales. In February

1985, Tony Azzara submitted his resignation at Hickling Associates Ltd. He accepted a position with a competing international merchant in Vancouver at a lower salary.

*© 1985 Steven L. McShane, Faculty of Business Administration, Simon Fraser University. All names and locations have been changed. Any similarity with current names and places is purely coincidental.

Case 6 **Pamela Jones, Former Banker***

Pamela Jones enjoyed banking. She had taken a battery of personal aptitude and interest tests that suggested she might like and do well in either banking or librarianship. Because the job market for librarians was poor, she applied for employment with a large chartered bank, the Bank of Winnipeg, and was quickly accepted.

Her early experiences in banking were almost always challenging and rewarding. She was enrolled in the bank's management development program because of her education (a B.A. in languages and some postgraduate training in business administration), her previous job experience, and her obvious intelligence and drive.

During her first year in the training program, Pamela attended classes on banking procedures and policies, and worked her way through a series of low-level positions in her branch. She was repeatedly told by her manager that her work was above average. Similarly, the training officer who worked out of the main office and coordinated the development of junior officers in the program frequently told Pamela that she was "among the best three" of her cohort of 20 trainees.

Although she worked hard and frequently encountered discrimination from senior bank personnel (as well as customers) because of her sex, Pamela developed a deep-seated attachment to banking in general, and to her bank and branch in particular. She was proud to be a banker and proud to be a member of the Bank of Winnipeg (B. of W.).

After one year in the management development program, however, Pamela found she was not learning anything new about banking or the B. of W. She was shuffled from one job to another at her own branch, cycling back over many positions several times to help meet temporary problems caused by absences, overloads, and turnover. Turnover—a rampant problem in banking—amazed Pamela. She couldn't understand, for many months, why so many people started careers "in the service" of banking, only to leave after one or two years.

After her first year, the repeated promises of moving into her own position at another branch started to sound hollow to Pamela. The training officer claimed that there were no openings suitable for her at other branches. On two occasions when openings did occur, the manager of each of the branches in question rejected Pamela, sight unseen, presumably because she hadn't been in banking long enough.

Pamela was not the only unhappy person at her branch. Her immediate supervisor, George Burns, complained that, because of the bank's economy drive, vacated customer service positions were left unfilled. As branch accountant, Burns was responsible for day-to-day customer service. As a result, he was unable to perform the duties of his own job. The manager told Burns several times that customer service was critical, but Burns would have to improve his performance on his own job. Eventually, George Burns left the bank to work for a trust company, earning $70 a month more for work similar to that he had been performing at the B. of W. This left Pamela in the position of having to supervise the same tellers who had trained her only a few months earlier. Pamela was amazed at all the mistakes the tellers made, but found it difficult to do much to correct their poor work habits. All disciplinary procedures had to be administered with the approval of Head Office.

After several calls to her training officer, Pamela was finally transferred to her first "real" position in her own branch. Still keen and dedicated, Pamela was soon to lose her enthusiasm.

At her new branch, Pamela was made "assistant accountant." Her duties included the supervision of the seven tellers, some customer service, and a great deal of paperwork. The same economy drive that she had witnessed at her training branch resulted in the failure to replace customer service personnel. Pamela was expected to pick up the slack at the front desk, neglecting her own work. Her tellers seldom balanced their own cash, so Pamela stayed late almost every night to find their errors. To save on overtime, the manager sent the tellers home while Pamela stayed late, first to correct the tellers' imbalances, then to finish her own paperwork. He told Pamela that as an officer of the bank, she was expected to stay until the work of her subordinates, and her own work, were satisfactorily completed. Pamela realized that most of her counterparts in other B. of W. branches were willing to give this sort of dedication; therefore, so should she. This situation lasted six months with little sign of change in sight.

One day, Pamela learned from a phone conversation with a friend at another branch that she would be transferred to Hope, British Columbia, to fill an opening that had arisen. Pamela's husband was a professional, employed by a large corporation in Vancouver. His company did not have an office in Hope; moreover, his training was very specialized, so that he could probably find employment only in large cities anyway.

Accepting transfers was expected of junior officers who wanted to get ahead. Pamela enquired at Head Office and learned that the rumoor was true. Her training officer told her, however, that Pamela could decline the transfer if she wished, but he couldn't say how soon her next promotion opportunity would come about.

Depressed, annoyed, disappointed, and frustrated, Pamela quit the bank.

*Source: C. C. Pinder, *Work Motivation* (Glenview, Ill.: Scott, Foresman, 1984), pp. 317–18.

Case 7 **Perfect Pizzeria***

Perfect Pizzeria in Southville, deep in southern Illinois, is the second-largest franchise of the chain in the United States. The headquarters is located in Phoenix, Arizona. Although the business is prospering, it has employee and managerial problems.

Each operation has one manager, an assistant manager, and from two to five night managers. The managers of each pizzeria work under an area supervisor. There are no systematic criteria for being a manager or becoming a manager trainee. The franchise has no formalized training period for the manager. No college education is required. The managers for whom the case observer worked during a four-year period were relatively young (ages 24 to 27), and only one had completed college. They came from the ranks of night managers, assistant managers, or both. The night managers were chosen for their ability to perform the duties of the regular employees. The assistant managers worked a two-hour shift during the luncheon period five days a week to gain knowledge about bookkeeping and management. Those becoming managers remained at that level unless they expressed interest in investing in the business.

The employees were mostly college students, with a few high school students performing the less challenging jobs. Because Perfect Pizzeria was located in an area with few job opportunities, it had a relatively easy task of filling its employee quotas. All the employees, with the exception of the manager, were employed part time. Consequently, they earned only the minimum wage.

The Perfect Pizzeria system is devised so that food and beverage costs and profits are set up according to a percentage. If the percentage of food unsold or damaged in any way is very low, the manager gets a bonus. If the percentage is high, the manager does not receive a bonus; rather, he or she receives only his or her normal salary.

There are many ways in which the percentage can fluctuate. Because the manager cannot be in the store 24 hours a day, some employees make up for their paycheques by helping themselves to the food. When a friend comes in to order a pizza, extra ingredients are put on the friend's pizza. Occasional nibbles by 18 to 20 employees throughout the day at the meal table also raise the percentage figure. An occasional bucket of sauce may be spilled or a pizza accidentally burned. Sometimes the wrong size of pizza may be made.

In the event of an employee mistake or a burned pizza by the oven person, the expense is supposed to come from the individual. Because of peer pressure, the night manager seldom writes up a bill for the erring employee. Instead, the establishment takes the loss and the error goes unnoticed until the end of the month when the inventory is taken. That's when the manager finds out that the percentage is high and that there will be no bonus.

In the present instance, the manager took retaliatory measures. Previously, each employee was entitled to a free pizza, salad, and all the soft drinks he or she could drink for every 6 hours of work. The manager raised this figure from 6 to 12 hours of work. However, the employees had received these 6-hour benefits for a long time. Therefore, they simply took advantage of the situation whenever the manager or the assistant was not in the building. Although the night managers theoretically had complete control of the operation in the evenings, they did not command the respect that the manager or assistant manager did. That was because night managers received the same pay as the regular employees, could not reprimand other employees, and were basically the same age or sometimes even younger than the other employees.

Thus, apathy grew within the pizzeria. There seemed to be a further separation between the manager and his workers, who started out to be a closely knit group. The manager made no attempt to alleviate the problem, because he felt it would iron itself out. Either the employees that were dissatisfied would quit or they would be content to put up with the new regulations. As it turned out, there was a rash of employee dismissals. The manager had no problem in filling the vacancies with new workers, but the loss of key personnel was costly to the business.

With the large turnover, the manager found he had to spend more time in the building, supervising and sometimes taking the place of inexperienced workers. This was in direct violation of the franchise regulation, which stated that a manager would act as a supervisor and at no time take part in the actual food preparation. Employees were not placed under strict supervision with the manager working alongside them. The operation no longer worked smoothly because of differences between the remaining experienced workers and the manager concerning the way in which a particular function should be performed.

Within a two-month period, the manager was again free to go back to his office and leave his subordinates in charge of the entire operation. During this two-month period, in spite of the differences between experienced workers and the manager, the unsold/damaged food percentage had returned to the previous low level and the manager received a bonus each month. The manager felt that his problems had been resolved and that conditions would remain the same, since the new personnel had been properly trained.

It didn't take long for the new employees to become influenced by the other employees. Immediately after the manager had returned to his supervisory role, the unsold/damaged food percentage began to rise. This time the manager took a bolder step. He cut out any benefits that the employees had—no free pizzas, salads, or drinks. With the job market at an even lower ebb than usual, most employees were forced to stay. The appointment of a new area supervisor made it impossible for the manager to "work behind the counter," because the supervisor was centrally located in Southville.

The manager tried still another approach to alleviate the rising unsold/damaged food percentage problem and maintain his bonus. He placed a notice on the bulletin board, stating that if the percentage remained at a high level, a lie detector test would be given to all employees. All those found guilty of taking or purposefully wasting food or drinks would be immediately terminated. This did not have the desired effect on the employees, because they knew if they were all subjected to the test, all would be found guilty and the manager would have to dismiss all of them. This would leave him in a worse situation than ever.

Even before the following month's percentage was calculated, the manager knew it would be high. He had evidently received information from one of the night managers about the employees' feelings toward the notice. What he did not expect was that the percentage would reach an all-time high. That is the state of affairs at the present time.

*Source: J. E. Dittrich and R. A. Zawacki, *People and Organizations.* (Plano, Texas: Business Publications, 1981), pp. 126–128. Used by permission of Richard D. Irwin.

Case 8 **Treetop Forest Products Ltd.***

Treetop Forest Products Ltd. is a sawmill operation located along the Fraser River near the British Columbia coast. The mill is owned by an international forest products company, but operates autonomously. It was built in 1979, and completely updated with new machinery in 1990. Treetop receives raw logs from the upper Fraser Valley area for cutting and planing into building-grade lumber, mostly 2-by-4 and 2-by-6 pieces of standard lengths. Higher grade logs leave Treetop's sawmill department in their finished form and are sent directly to the packaging department. The remaining 40 percent of sawmill output are cuts from lower grade logs, requiring further work by the planing department.

Treetop has one general manager, 16 supervisors and support staff, and 180 unionized employees. The unionized employees are paid an hourly rate specified in the collective agreement, whereas management and support staff are paid a monthly salary. The mill is divided into six operating departments: boom, sawmill, planer, packaging, shipping, and maintenance. The sawmill, boom, and packaging departments operate a morning shift starting at 6 A.M. and an afternoon shift starting at 2 PM. Employees in these departments rotate shifts every two weeks. The planer and shipping departments operate only morning shifts. Maintenance employees work the night shift (starting at 10 P.M.).

Each department, except for packaging, has a supervisor on every work shift. The planer supervisor is responsible for the packaging department on the morning shift, and the sawmill supervisor is responsible for the packaging department on the afternoon shift. However, the packaging operation is housed in a separate building from the other departments, so supervisors seldom visit the packaging department. This is particularly true for the afternoon shift, because the sawmill supervisor is the furthest distance from the packaging building.

Packaging quality

Ninety percent of Treetop's product is sold on the international market through Westboard Co., a large marketing agency. Westboard represents all forest products mills owned by Treetop's parent company as well as several other clients in the region. The market for building-grade lumber is very price competitive, because there are numerous mills selling a relatively undifferentiated product. However, some differentiation does occur in product packaging and presentation. Buyers will look closely at the packaging when deciding whether to buy from Treetop or another mill.

To encourage its clients to package their products better, Westboard sponsors a monthly package quality award. The marketing agency samples and rates its clients' packages daily, and the sawmill with the highest score at the end of the month is awarded a plaque. Package quality is a combination of how the lumber is piled (e.g., defects turned in), where the bands and dunnage are placed, how neatly the stencil and seal are applied, the stencil's accuracy, and how neatly and tightly the plastic wrap is attached.

Treetop Forest Products won Westboard's packaging quality award several times over the past few years, and received high ratings in the months that it didn't win. However, the mill's ratings have started to decline over the past couple of years, and several clients have complained about the appearance of the finished product. A few large customers switched to competitors' lumber, saying that the decision was based on the substandard appearance of Treetop's packaging when it arrived in their lumber yard.

Bottleneck in packaging

The planing and sawmilling departments have significantly increased productivity over the past couple of years. The sawmill operation recently set a new productivity record on a single day. The planer operation has increased productivity to the point where last year it reduced operations to just one (rather than two) shifts per day. These productivity improvements are due to better operator training, fewer machine breakdowns, and better selection of raw logs. (Sawmill cuts from high-quality logs usually do not require planing work.)

Productivity levels in the boom, shipping, and maintenance departments have remained constant. However, the packaging department has recorded decreasing productivity over the past couple of years, with the result that a large backlog of finished product is typically stockpiled outside the packaging building. The morning shift of the packaging department is unable to keep up with the combined production of the sawmill and planer departments, so the unpackaged output is left for the afternoon shift. Unfortunately, the afternoon shift packages even less product than the morning shift, so the backlog continues to build. The backlog adds to Treetop's inventory costs and increases the risk of damaged stock.

Treetop has added Saturday overtime shifts as well as extra hours before and after the regular shifts for the packaging department employees to process this backlog. Last month, the packaging department employed 10 percent of the work force but accounted for 85 percent of the overtime. This is frustrating to Treetop's management, because time and motion studies recently confirmed that the packaging department is capable of processing all of the daily sawmill and planer production without overtime. Moreover, with employees earning one and a half or two times their regular pay on overtime, Treetop's cost competitiveness suffers.

Employees and supervisors at Treetop are aware that people in the packaging department tend to extend lunch by 10 minutes and coffee breaks by 5 minutes. They also typically leave work a few minutes before the end of shift. This abuse has worsened recently, particularly on the afternoon shift. Employees who are temporarily assigned to the packaging department also seem to participate in this time loss pattern after a few days. Although they are punctual and productive in other departments, these temporary employees soon adopt the packaging crew's informal schedule when assigned to that department.

Case 9 Western Agencies Ltd.*

Western Agencies Ltd. is a manufacturers' agent representing Stanfields, McGregors, and several other men's fashion manufacturers in Western Canada and the Pacific Northwest of the United States. Jack Arthurs began his employment at Western as a warehouse worker in 1962. In 1965, he became a sales representative and was given responsibility for the company's business in the interior region of British Columbia. In 1973, he was transferred back to Vancouver and assigned several large accounts, including all Eaton's stores in the Lower Mainland.

Over the years, Arthurs bought shares in the company and, by 1979, held nearly one-third of the company's issued nonvoting shares. He also enjoyed a special status with the company founder and president, Mr. A. B. Jackson. Arthurs was generally considered Jackson's "number 1 man" and the president frequently sought Arthurs's ideas on various company policies and practices.

In 1980, the senior Mr. Jackson retired as president of Western Agencies and his son, C. D. Jackson, became president. C. D. Jackson was seven years younger than Arthurs and had begun his career in the warehouse under Arthurs's direct supervision. Arthurs had no illusions of becoming president of Western, saying that he had neither the education nor the skills for the job. However, he did expect to continue his special position as the top salesperson in the company, although this was not directly discussed with the new president.

Until 1987, Arthurs had an unblemished performance record as a sales representative. He had built up numerous accounts and was able to service these clients effectively. But Arthurs's performance began to change for the worse when Eaton's changed its buying procedures and hired a new buyer for Western Canada. Arthurs disliked Eaton's new procedures and openly complained to the retailer's new buyer and to her superiors. The Eaton's buyer resented Arthurs's behaviour and finally asked her boss to call Western Agencies to have Arthurs replaced. The Eaton's manager advised Jackson of the problem and suggested that another salesperson should be assigned to the Eaton's account. Jackson was aware of the conflict and had advised Arthurs a few months earlier that he should be more cooperative with the Eaton's buyer. Following the formal complaint, Jackson assigned another salesperson to Eaton's and gave Arthurs the Hudson Bay account in exchange. Jackson did not mention the formal complaint from Eaton's and, in fact, Arthurs believed that the account switch was due to an internal reorganization for the benefit of other salespeople employed at Western Agencies Ltd.

At about this time, several employees noticed that Arthurs was developing a negative attitude toward his clients and Jackson. He was increasingly irritable and rude to customers, and was making derogatory comments to Jackson. Arthurs even advised some of the younger employees that they should leave Western Agencies Ltd. and get into a sensible business. A phenomenon known as "pulling an Arthurs" became a topic of discussion around the office, whereby Arthurs would leave the office to go home in the midafternoon after announcing that he had had enough. Co-workers also noticed that Arthurs was becoming increasingly forgetful. He was often unable to remember stock numbers, colour codes, product lines, packaging modes, and other information essential for serving clients efficiently and completing orders accurately. These problems were subtle in 1987, but became quite pronounced and embarrassing over the next three years.

In May 1989, Arthurs and Jackson had a conflict relating to the purchase of a new company car. According to Jackson, Arthurs presented him with a quotation for a car which, in Jackson's view, included $2,500 in unnecessary options. Jackson informed Arthurs of his concerns and instructed him to find a car worth $13,000 instead of $16,000. Jackson then left town on business and when he returned was distressed to find that Arthurs had made his proposed car purchase with almost all of the unnecessary options. Jackson issued the cheque to pay for the car, but also included a note to Arthurs saying that he had lost confidence in the sales representative. It was about this time that Jackson contemplated firing Arthurs, but decided instead to be a "nice guy" and overlook the matter.

At the end of 1989, Jackson decided to reassign the North Vancouver independent accounts from Arthurs to another Western Agencies salesperson because the existing accounts had shown minimal growth and no new accounts were being added. Arthurs acknowledged that he had no time to find new accounts, but he denied Jackson's allegation that he was inadequately servicing the existing retailers in that area. At least one retailer later stated that Arthurs serviced his account well. Moreover, the salesperson assigned this territory added only a couple new accounts over the next two years.

In early 1990, the vice-president of marketing for Fields Stores called Jackson to say that Arthurs was not providing satisfactory service and that action should be taken if Western wanted to keep the Fields account. Arthurs had handled the Fields account for four or five years and there had been no problems until a new Fields buyer arrived. The new buyer complained that Arthurs was not providing sufficient promotional advice and assistance. She also expected Arthurs to take inventory counts, a practice that Arthurs resented and did not feel was properly part of his job. This was not the only retailer who expected Arthurs to count inventory, but Arthurs let them as well as Jackson know that he was an account builder, not an inventory stock counter. Eventually, the Fields buyer did not want to deal with Arthurs at all. In March 1990, matters were brought to a head when the Fields buyer and Arthurs had a major disagreement and Arthurs was not allowed back into any Fields stores. At this point, Jackson personally took over the Fields account and sales volume doubled within a few months.

A few months later, Western Agencies suffered several embarrassments over Arthurs's mishandling of the Work Wear World account. Arthurs had landed the Work Wear account a few years earlier when it was a small retailer with only two stores, but the company had subsequently grown into a regional chain of 10 stores. Problems began when Arthurs persuaded the Work Wear buyer to purchase a new line of stock by promising a manufacturer's allowance on an older line of goods. Arthurs had no authority to do this and, when the manufacturer refused to provide the allowance, Jackson had to personally explain that the allowance promise could not be honoured.

In late 1990, Arthurs mistakenly tripled a stock order for three of Work Wear's stores. This error was discovered when the second shipment arrived and Jackson instructed Arthurs to take immediate steps to cancel the third order. Arthurs failed to do so and Work Wear wound up with three times the inventory it had ordered. Work Wear's buyer subsequently gave Jackson the distinct impression that he should remove Arthurs from the account or risk losing Work Wear's business altogether.

For Jackson, Work Wear World's complaint was the last straw. In the spring of 1991, based on the series of incidents since 1987, Arthurs was dismissed from his job at Western Agencies Ltd.

Appendix A
Theory Building and Scientific Method

Appendix B
Vroom–Jago Decision Tree

Appendixes

Appendix A Theory Building and the Scientific Method

People need to make sense of their world, so they form theories about the way the world operates. A **theory** is a general set of propositions that describes interrelationships among several concepts. We form theories for the purpose of predicting and explaining the world around us.[1] What does a good theory look like? First, it should be stated clearly and simply as possible so that the concepts can be measured and there is no ambiguity regarding the theory's propositions. Second, the elements of the theory must be logically consistent with each other, because we cannot test anything that doesn't make sense. Finally, a good theory provides value to society; it helps people understand their world better than without the theory.[2]

Theory building is a continuous process that typically includes the inductive and deductive stages shown in Exhibit A–1.[3] The inductive stage draws on personal experience to form a preliminary theory, whereas the deductive stage uses the scientific method to test the theory.

The inductive stage of theory building involves observing the world around us, identifying a pattern of relationships, and then forming a theory from these personal observations. For example, you might casually notice that new employees want their supervisor to give direction, whereas this leadership style irritates long-service employees. From these observations, you form a theory about the effectiveness of directive leadership. (See Chapter 14 for a discussion of this leadership style.)

Theory testing: The deductive process

Once a theory has been formed, we shift into the deductive stage of theory building. This process includes forming hypotheses, defining and measuring constructs, and testing hypotheses (see Exhibit A–1). **Hypotheses** make empirically testable declarations that certain variables and their corresponding measures are related in a specific way proposed by the theory. For instance, to find support for the directive leadership theory described earlier, we need to form and then test a specific hypothesis from that theory. One such hypothesis might be: "New employees are more satisfied with supervisors who exhibit a directive rather than nondirective leadership style." Hypotheses are indispensable tools of scientific research, because they provide the vital link between the theory and empirical verification.

Defining and measuring constructs

Hypotheses are testable only if we can define and then form measurable indicators of the concepts stated in those hypotheses. Consider the hypothesis in the previous paragraph about new employees and directive leadership. To test this hypothesis, we first need to define the concepts, such as "new employees," "directive leadership," and "supervisor." These are known as **constructs,** because they are abstract ideas constructed by the researcher that can be linked to observable information. Organizational behaviour scholars developed the construct called *directive leadership* to help them understand the different effects that leaders have over followers. We can't directly see, taste, or smell directive leadership; instead, we rely on indirect indicators that it exists,

Theory
A general set of propositions that describes interrelationships among several concepts.

Hypotheses
Statements making empirically testable declarations that certain variables and their corresponding measures are related in a specific way proposed by a particular theory.

Constructs
Abstract ideas constructed by researchers that can be linked to observable information.

The Theory Building Process

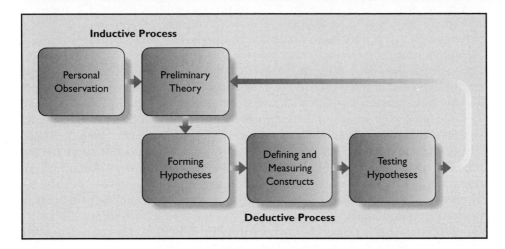

such as observing someone giving directions, maintaining clear performance standards, and ensuring that procedures and practices are followed.

As you can see, defining constructs well is very important, because these definitions become the foundation for finding or developing acceptable measures of those constructs. We can't measure directive leadership if we only have a vague idea about what this concept means. The better the definition is, the better our chances are of applying a measure that adequately represents that construct. However, even with a good definition, constructs can be difficult to measure, because the empirical representation must capture several elements in the definition. A measure of directive leadership must be able to identify not only people who give directions, but also those who maintain performance standards and ensure that procedures are followed.

Testing hypotheses

The third step in the deductive process is to collect data for the empirical measures of the variables. Following our directive leadership example, we might conduct a formal survey in which new employees indicate the behaviour of their supervisors and their attitudes toward their supervisor. Alternatively, we might design an experiment in which people work with someone who applies either a directive or nondirective leadership style. When the data have been collected, we can use various procedures to statistically test our hypotheses.

A serious concern in theory building is that some researchers might inadvertently find support for their theory simply because they use the same information used to form the theory during the inductive stage. Consequently, the deductive stage must collect new data that are completely independent of the data used during the inductive stage. For instance, you might decide to test your theory of directive leadership by studying employees in another organization. Moreover, the inductive process may have relied mainly on personal observation, whereas the deductive process might use survey questionnaires. By studying different samples and using different measurement tools, we minimize the risk of conducting circular research.

Using the scientific method

Earlier, we said that the deductive stage of theory building follows the scientific method. The **scientific method** is systematic, controlled, empirical, and critical investigation of hypothetical propositions about the presumed relationships among natural phenomena.[4] There are several elements to this definition, so let's look at each one. First, scientific research is systematic and controlled, because researchers want to rule out all but one explanation for a set of interrelated events. To rule out alternative explanations, we need to control them in some way, such as by keeping them constant or removing them entirely from the environment.

Second, we say that scientific research is empirical because researchers need to use objective reality—or as close as we can get to it—to test theory. They measure observable elements of the environment, such as what a person says or does, rather than rely on their own subjective opinion to draw conclusions. Moreover, scientific research analyzes these data using acceptable principles of mathematics and logic.

Finally, scientific research involves critical investigation. This means that the study's hypotheses, data, methods, and results are openly described so that other experts in the field can properly evaluate this research. It also means that scholars are encouraged to critique and build on previous research. Eventually, the scientific method encourages the refinement and eventually the replacement of a particular theory with one that better suits our understanding of the world.

Selected Issues in Organizational Behaviour Research

There are many issues to consider in theory building, particularly when we use the deductive process to test hypotheses. Some of the more important issues are sampling, causation, and ethical practices in organizational research.

Sampling in organizational research

When finding out why things happen in organizations, we typically gather information from a few sources and then draw conclusions about the larger population. If we survey several employees and determine that older employees are more loyal to their company, then we would like to generalize this statement to all older employees in our population, not just those whom we surveyed. Scientific inquiry generally requires researchers to engage in **representative sampling**—that is, sampling a population in such a way that we can extrapolate the results of that sample to the larger population.

One factor that influences representativeness is whether the sample is selected in an unbiased way from the larger population. Let's suppose that you want to study organizational commitment among employees in your organization. A casual procedure might result in sampling too few employees from the head office and too many located elsewhere in the country. If head office employees actually have higher loyalty than employees located elsewhere, then the biased sampling would cause the results to underestimate the true level of loyalty among employees in the company. If you repeat the process again next year but somehow overweight employees from the head office, the results might wrongly suggest that employees have increased their organizational commitment over the past year. In reality, the only change may be the direction of sampling bias.

How do we minimize sampling bias? The answer is to randomly select the sample. A randomly drawn sample gives each member of the population an equal probability of being chosen, so there is less likelihood that a subgroup within that population dominates the study's results.

The same principle applies to random assignment of subjects to groups in experimental designs. If we want to test the effects of a team development training program, we need to randomly place some employees in the training group and randomly place others in a group that does not receive training. Without this random selection, each group might have different types of employees, so we wouldn't know whether the training explains the differences between the two groups. Moreover, if employees respond differently to the training program, we couldn't be sure that the training program results are representative of the larger population. Of course, random sampling does not necessarily produce a perfectly representative sample, but we do know that this is the best approach to ensure unbiased selection.

The other factor that influences representativeness is sample size. Whenever we select a portion of the population, there will be some error in our estimate of the population values. The larger the sample, the less error will occur in our estimate. Let's suppose that you want to find out how employees in a 500-person firm feel about smoking in the workplace. If you asked 400 of those employees, the information would provide a very good estimate of how the entire work force in that organization feels. If you survey only 100 employees, the estimate might deviate more from the true population. If you ask only 10 people, the estimate could be quite different from what all 500 employees feel.

Notice that sample size goes hand in hand with random selection. You must have a sufficiently large sample size for the principle of randomization to work effectively. In our example of attitudes toward smoking, we would do a poor job of random selection if our sample consisted of only 10 employees from the 500-person organization. The reason is that these 10 people probably wouldn't capture the diversity of employees throughout the organization. In fact, the more diverse the population, the larger the sample size should be, to provide adequate representation through random selection.

Causation in organizational research

Theories present notions about relationships among constructs. Often, these propositions suggest a causal relationship, namely, that one variable has an effect on another variable. When discussing causation, we refer to variables as being independent or dependent. Independent variables are the presumed causes of dependent variables, which are the presumed effects. In our earlier example of directive leadership, the main independent variable (there might be others) would be the supervisor's directive or nondirective leadership style, because we presume that it causes the dependent variable (satisfaction with supervision).

In laboratory experiments (described later), the independent variable is always manipulated by the experimenter. In our research on directive leadership, we might have subjects (new employees) work with supervisors who exhibit directive or nondirective leadership behaviours. If subjects are more satisfied under the directive leaders, then we would be able to infer an association between the independent and dependent variables.

Researchers must satisfy three conditions to provide sufficient evidence of causality between two variables.[5] The first condition of causality is that the variables are empirically associated with each other. An association exists whenever one measure of a variable changes systematically with a measure of another variable. This condition of causality is the easiest to satisfy, because there are several well-known statistical measures of association. A research study might find, for instance, that heterogeneous groups (in which members come from diverse backgrounds) produce more creative solutions to problems. This might be apparent because the measure of creativity (such as number of creative solutions produced within a fixed time) is higher for teams that have a high score on the measure of group heterogeneity. They are statistically associated or correlated with each other.

The second condition of causality is that the independent variable precedes the dependent variable in time. Sometimes, this condition is satisfied through simple logic. In our group heterogeneity example, it doesn't make sense to say that the number of creative solutions caused the group's heterogeneity, because the group's heterogeneity existed before it produced the creative solutions. In other situations, however, the temporal relationship among variables is less clear. One example is the ongoing debate about job satisfaction and organizational commitment. Do companies develop more loyal employees by increasing their job satisfaction, or do changes in organizational loyalty cause changes in job satisfaction? Simple logic does not answer these questions; instead, researchers must use sophisticated longitudinal studies to build up evidence of a temporal relationship between these two variables.

The third requirement for evidence of a causal relationship is that the statistical association between two variables cannot be explained by a third variable. There are many associations that we quickly dismiss as being causally related. For example, there is a statistical association between the number of storks in an area and the birthrate in that area. We know that storks don't bring babies, so something else must cause the association between these two variables. The real explanation is that both storks and birthrates have a higher incidence in rural areas.

In other studies, the third variable effect is less apparent. Many years ago, before polio vaccines were available, a study in the United States reported a surprisingly strong association between consumption of a certain soft drink and the incidence of polio. Was polio caused by drinking this pop, or did people with polio have a unusual craving for this beverage? Neither. Both polio and consumption of the pop drink were caused by a third variable: climate. There was a higher incidence of polio in the summer months and in warmer climates, and people drink more liquids in these climates.[6] As you can see from this example, researchers have a difficult time supporting causal inferences, because third variable effects are sometimes difficult to detect.

Ethics in organizational research

Organizational behaviour researchers need to abide by the ethical standards of the society in which the research is conducted. One of the most important ethical considerations is the individual subject's freedom to participate in the study. For example, it is inappropriate to force employees to fill out a questionnaire or attend an experimental intervention for research purposes only. Moreover, researchers have an obligation to tell potential subjects about any potential risks inherent in the study so that participants can make an informed choice about whether or not to be involved.

Finally, researchers must be careful to protect the privacy of those who participate in the study. This usually includes letting people know when they are being studied as well as guaranteeing that their individual information will remain confidential (unless publication of identities is otherwise granted). Researchers maintain anonymity through careful security of data. The research results usually aggregate data in numbers large enough that they do not reveal the opinions or characteristics of any specific individual. For example, we would report the average absenteeism of employees in a department rather than state the absence rates of each person. When sharing data with other researchers, it is usually necessary to specially code each case so that individual identities are not known.

Research Design Strategies

So far, we have described how to build a theory, including the specific elements of empirically testing that theory within the standards of scientific inquiry. But what are the different ways to design a research study so that we get the data necessary to achieve our research objectives? There are many strategies, but they mainly fall under three headings: laboratory experiments, field surveys, and observational research.

Laboratory experiments

A **laboratory experiment** is any research study in which independent variables and variables outside the researcher's main focus of inquiry can be controlled to some extent. Laboratory experiments are usually located outside the everyday work environment, such as a classroom, simulation lab, or any other artificial setting in which the researcher can manipulate the environment. Organizational behaviour researchers sometimes conduct experiments in the workplace (called *field experiments*) in which the independent variable is manipulated. However, the researcher has less control over the effects of extraneous factors in field experiments than in laboratory situations.

Laboratory experiment
Any research study in which independent variables and variables outside the researcher's main focus of inquiry can be controlled to some extent.

Advantages of laboratory experiments

There are many advantages of laboratory experiments. By definition, this research method offers a high degree of control over extraneous variables that would otherwise confound the relationships being studied. Suppose we wanted to test the effects of directive leadership on the satisfaction of new employees. One concern might be that employees are influenced by how much leadership is provided, not just the type of leadership style. An experimental design would allow us to control how often the supervisor exhibited this style so that this extraneous variable does not confound the results.

A second advantage of lab studies is that the independent and dependent variables can be developed more precisely than in a field setting. For example, the researcher can ensure that supervisors in a lab study apply specific directive or nondirective behaviours, whereas real-life supervisors would use a more complex mixture of leadership behaviours. By using more precise measures, we are more certain that we are measuring the intended construct. Thus, if new employees are more satisfied with supervisors in the directive leadership condition, we are more confident that the independent variable was directive leadership rather than some other leadership style.

A third benefit of laboratory experiments is that the independent variable can be distributed more evenly among participants. In our directive leadership study, we can ensure that approximately half of the subjects have a directive supervisor, whereas the other half have a nondirective supervisor. In natural settings, we might have trouble finding people who have worked with a nondirective leader and, consequently, we couldn't determine the effects of this condition.

Disadvantages of laboratory experiments

With these powerful advantages, you might wonder why laboratory experiments are the least appreciated form of organizational behaviour research.[7] One obvious limitation of this research method is that it lacks realism and, consequently, the results might be different in the real world. One argument is that laboratory experiment subjects are less involved than their counterparts in an actual work situation. This is sometimes true, although many lab studies have highly motivated participants. Another criticism is that the extraneous variables controlled in the lab setting might produce a different effect of the independent variable on the dependent variables. This might also be true, but remember that the experimental design controls variables in accordance with the theory and its hypotheses. Consequently, this concern is really a critique of the theory, not the lab study.

Finally, there is the well-known problem that participants are aware they are being studied and this causes them to act differently than they normally would. Some participants try to figure out how the researcher wants them to behave and then deliberately try to act that way. Other participants try to upset the experiment by doing just the opposite of what they believe the researcher expects. Still others might act unnaturally simply because they know they are being observed. Fortunately, experimenters are well aware of these potential problems and are usually (although not always) successful at disguising the study's true intent.

Field surveys

Field survey
Any research design in which information is collected in a natural environment.

Field surveys collect and analyze information in a natural environment—an office, factory, or other existing location. The researcher takes a snapshot of reality and tries to determine whether elements of that situation (including the attitudes and behaviours of people in that situation) are associated with each other as hypothesized. Everyone does some sort of field research. You might think that people from some provinces are better drivers than others, so you "test" your theory by looking at the way people with out-of-province licence plates drive. Although your methods of data collection might not satisfy scientific standards, this is a form of field research because it takes information from a naturally occurring situation.

Advantages and disadvantages of field surveys

One advantage of field surveys is that the variables often have a more powerful effect than they would in a laboratory experiment. Consider the effect of peer pressure on the behaviour of members within the team. In a natural environment, team members would form very strong cohesive bonds over time, whereas a researcher would have difficulty replicating this level of cohesiveness and corresponding peer pressure in a lab setting.

Another advantage of field surveys is that the researcher can study many variables simultaneously, thereby permitting a fuller test of more complex theories. Ironically, this is also a disadvantage of field surveys, because it is difficult for the researcher to contain his or her scientific inquiry. There is a tendency to shift from deductive hypothesis testing to more inductive exploratory browsing through the data. If these two activities become mixed together, the researcher can lose sight of the strict covenants of scientific inquiry.

The main weakness with field surveys is that it is very difficult to satisfy the conditions for causal conclusions. One reason is that the data are usually collected at one point in time, so the researcher must rely on logic to decide whether the independent variable really preceded the dependent variable. Contrast this with the lab study in which the researcher can usually be confident that the independent variable was applied before the dependent variable occurred. Increasingly, organizational behaviour studies use longitudinal research to provide a better indicator of temporal relations among variables, but this is still not as precise as the lab setting. Another reason why causal analysis is difficult in field surveys is that extraneous variables are not controlled as they are in lab studies. Without this control, there is a higher chance that a third variable might explain the relationship between the hypothesized independent and dependent variables.

Observational research

In his recent book *The Creative Edge,* journalist Randy Scotland provides a rich account of life in the fast lane at Toronto advertising agency Vickers & Benson Advertising Ltd.[8] To collect his qualitative data, Scotland regularly visited the advertising agency's offices for almost one year, observing the comings and goings of people and events. Scotland's use of observational research was quite appropriate for his research objectives, because this method generates a wealth of descriptive accounts about the drama of human existence in organizations. It is a useful vehicle for learning about the complex dynamics of people and their activities.

Participant observation takes the observation method one step further by having the observer take part in the organization's activities. This experience gives the researcher a fuller understanding of the activities compared to just watching others participate in those activities.

In spite of its intuitive appeal, observational research has a number of weaknesses. The main problem is that the observer is subject to the perceptual screening and organizing biases that we discuss in Chapter 7 of this book. There is a tendency to overlook the routine aspects of organizational life, even though they may prove to be the most important data for research purposes. Instead, observers tend to focus on unusual information, such as activities that deviate from what the observer expects. Because observational research usually records only what the observer notices, valuable information is often lost.

Another concern, particularly with participant observation, is that the researcher's presence and involvement may influence the people whom he or she is studying. This can be a problem in short-term observations, but in the long term people tend to return to their usual behaviour patterns. With ongoing observations, such as Randy Scotland's study of Vicker & Benson Advertising Ltd., employees eventually forget that they are being studied.

Finally, observation is usually a qualitative process, so it is more difficult to empirically test hypotheses with the data. Instead, observational research provides rich information for the inductive stages of theory building. It helps us to form ideas about the way things work in organizations. We begin to see relationships that lay the foundation for new perspectives and theory. We must not confuse this inductive process of theory building with the deductive process of theory testing.

Notes

1. Kerlinger, *Foundations of Behavioral Research* (New York: Holt, Rinehart, & Winston, 1964), p. 11.

2. J. B. Miner, *Theories of Organizational Behavior* (Hinsdale, Ill.: Dryden, 1980), pp. 7–9.

3. Ibid. pp. 6–7.

4. Kerlinger, *Foundations of Behavioral Research,* p. 13.

5. P. Lazarsfeld, *Survey Design and Analysis* (New York: The Free Press, 1955).

6. This example is cited in D. W. Organ and T. S. Bateman, *Organizational Behavior,* 4th ed. (Homewood, Ill.: Irwin, 1991), p. 42.

7. Ibid. p. 45.

8. R. Scotland, *The Creative Edge: Inside the Ad Wars* (Toronto: Viking, 1994).

Appendix B **Vroom–Jago Decision Tree**

The Vroom–Jago model guides decision makers through the characteristics of a problem (called *problem attributes*) to determine the most appropriate level of employee involvement for that problem. There are five levels of employee involvement specified in the model. They are:

AI: You make the decision alone with no employee involvement.

AII: Subordinates provide information that you request, but they don't offer recommendations and they might not be aware of the problem.

CI: You describe the problem to relevant subordinates individually, getting their information and recommendations. You make the final decision, which does not necessarily reflect the advice that subordinates have provided.

CII: You describe the problem to subordinates in a meeting, in which they discuss information and recommendations. You make the final decision, which does not necessarily reflect the advice that subordinates have provided.

GII: You describe the problem to subordinates in a meeting. They discuss the problem and make a decision that you are willing to accept and implement if it has the entire team's support. You might chair this session, but you do not influence the team's decision.

The Vroom–Jago model consists of four decision trees. Two trees pertain to decisions affecting a team of employees, whereas the other two focus on individual problems. Within each pair, one emphasizes time efficiency and the other emphasizes employee development. Exhibit B–1 describes the time-driven decision tree for team issues, because it is the most frequently used in organizational settings. It consists of eight problem attributes that distinguish the characteristics of each decision situation. Each problem attribute is phrased as a question, and the appropriate answer directs the decision maker along a different path in the decision tree.

The decision maker begins at the left side of the decision tree and must first decide whether the problem has a high or low quality dimension. Most decisions have a quality requirement, because some alternatives are more likely than others to achieve organizational objectives. However, where all of the alternatives are equally good (or bad), the decision maker would select the low-importance route in the decision tree. He or she would then be asked whether subordinate commitment is important to the decision. This process continues until the path leads to the recommended participation level, ranging from AI to GII.

Exhibit B–1   Vroom–Jago Time-Driven Decision Tree

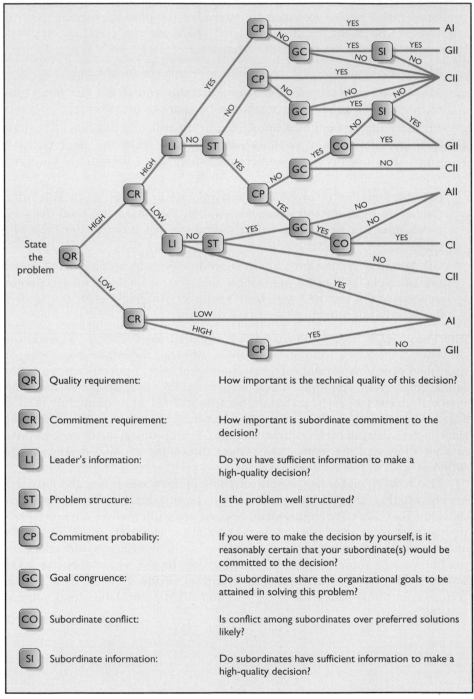

QR	Quality requirement:	How important is the technical quality of this decision?
CR	Commitment requirement:	How important is subordinate commitment to the decision?
LI	Leader's information:	Do you have sufficient information to make a high-quality decision?
ST	Problem structure:	Is the problem well structured?
CP	Commitment probability:	If you were to make the decision by yourself, is it reasonably certain that your subordinate(s) would be committed to the decision?
GC	Goal congruence:	Do subordinates share the organizational goals to be attained in solving this problem?
CO	Subordinate conflict:	Is conflict among subordinates over preferred solutions likely?
SI	Subordinate information:	Do subordinates have sufficient information to make a high-quality decision?

Source: V. H. Vroom and A. G. Jago, *The New Leadership: Managing Participation in Organizations* (Englewood Cliffs, N.J.: Prentice Hall, 1988), p. 184. © 1987 V. H. Vroom and A. G. Jago. Used with permission of the authors.

Glossary of Terms

Ability The learned capability and innate aptitude required to successfully complete a task. (2)

Action research A data-based, problem-oriented process that focusses on organizational diagnosis and action planning, implementation, and evaluation of an intervention to the system involved. (15)

Actor–observer error An attribution error whereby people tend to attribute their own actions more to external factors and the behaviour of others to internal factors. (7) (14)

Appreciative inquiry An organization development intervention that directs the group's attention away from its own problems and focusses participants on the group's potential and positive elements. (15)

Aptitudes Natural talents that help people learn specific tasks more quickly and perform them better. (2)

Artifacts The observable symbols and signs of an organization's culture, including its physical structures, ceremonies, language, and stories. (16)

Attitudes Relatively enduring emotional tendencies to respond consistently toward an attitude object. (8)

Attribution process A perceptual process whereby we interpret the causes of behaviour in terms of the person (internal attributions) or the situation (external attributions). (7)

Authoritarianism A personality trait referring to people who blindly accept authority and expect followers to do the same. (7)

Autonomy The degree to which a job gives employees the freedom, independence, and discretion to schedule their work and determine the procedures to be used to complete the work. (4)

Behaviourism A perspective that focusses entirely on behaviour and observable events, rather than a person's thoughts. (2)

Boundaryless career The idea that careers operate across company and industry boundaries rather than just within a single organizational hierarchy. (16)

Brainstorming A freewheeling face-to-face meeting in which team members generate as many alternative solutions to the problem as possible and no one is allowed to evaluate them during the idea-generation stage. (11)

Burnout The process of emotional exhaustion, depersonalization, and reduced personal accomplishment resulting from prolonged exposure to stress. (5)

Business ethics Societal judgments about whether the consequences of organizational actions are good or bad. (1)

Career A sequence of work-related experiences in which people participate over the span of their working lives. (16)

*The number in parenthesis denotes the chapter number.

Career anchor A person's self-image of his or her abilities, motivations, and attitudes relating to a particular career orientation. (16)

Centrality The degree and nature of interdependence between the power-holder and others. (12)

Centralization The degree that formal decision authority is held by a small group of people, typically those at the top of the organizational hierarchy. (17)

Ceremonies Deliberate and usually dramatic displays of organizational culture, such as celebrations and special social gatherings. (16)

Change agent A person who possesses enough knowledge and power to guide and facilitate the change effort. This may be a member of the organization or an external consultant. (15)

Coalition Two or more people who influence others about a specific issue by banding together to increase their power. (10)

Coercive power The capacity to influence others through the ability to apply punishment and remove rewards affecting these people. (12)

Cognitive dissonance A state of anxiety that occurs when an individual's beliefs, attitudes, intentions, and behaviours are inconsistent with one another. (8)

Cohesiveness The degree of attraction that members feel toward their team and their motivation to remain members. (10)

Communication The process by which information is transmitted and understood between two or more people. (6)

Concurrent engineering team A special cross-functional task force of designers, manufacturing engineers, marketing people, and others who work together to design products and services. (10)

Conflict Any situation in which people believe that others have deliberately blocked, or are about to block, their goals. (13)

Conflict management Any intervention that alters the level and form of conflict to improve organizational effectiveness. (13)

Constructive controversy Any situation in which team members openly debate different opinions regarding a problem or issue. (11)

Constructs Abstract ideas constructed by researchers that can be linked to observable information.

Content theories of motivation Theories that attempt to explain how people have different needs at different times. (3)

Contingencies of reinforcement The four types of events following a behaviour that increase or decrease the likelihood that the behaviour will be repeated. (2)

Contingency approach The idea that a particular action may have different consequences in different situations; that no single solution is best in all circumstances. (1)

Continuance commitment An individual's willingness to remain with an organization for purely instrumental (e.g., financial) rather than emotional reasons. (8)

Continuous reinforcement schedule A schedule that reinforces behaviour every time it occurs. (2)

Cost leadership strategy The strategy of maximizing productivity in order to offer popular products or services at a competitive price. (17)

Counterpower The capacity of a person, team, or organization to keep a more powerful person or group in the exchange relationship. (12)

Creativity Developing an original product, service, or idea that makes a socially recognized contribution. (9)

Decentralization The degree that decision authority is dispersed throughout the organization. (17)

Decision making A conscious process of making choices among one or more alternatives with the intention of moving toward some desired state of affairs. (9)

Delphi technique A structured team decision-making method that pools the collective knowledge of experts who do not meet face to face and might not know each other's identities. The information that experts initially submit on an issue is organized and fed back to them for further comment. This cycle is repeated until a consensus or dissensus is reached. (11)

Departmentation An element of organizational structure specifying how employees and their activities are grouped together, such as by function, product, geographic location, or some combination. (17)

Devil's advocacy A form of structured debate to encourage constructive controversy whereby one-half of the team looks for faulty logic, questionable assumptions, and other problems with the team's preferred choice. (11)

Dialogue A process of conversation among team members in which they learn about each other's personal mental models and assumptions, and eventually form a common model for thinking within the team. (10) (13) (15)

Differentiation A condition in which people hold divergent beliefs and attitudes due to their unique backgrounds, experiences, or training. (13)

Differentiation strategy The strategy of bringing unique products to the market or attracting clients who want customized goods and services. (17)

Discipline The act of formally punishing employees who violate an organizational rule or procedure. (4)

Discipline without punishment A behaviour change intervention that tries to avoid the use of punishment by counselling employees who have violated company rules and inviting them to participate in finding a solution to the problem. (4)

Discrepancy theory A theory that partly explains job satisfaction and dissatisfaction in terms of the gap between what a person expects to receive and what is actually received. (8)

Divisional structure A type of departmentation that groups employees around outputs, clients, or geographic areas. (17)

Dogmatism A personality trait referring to the extent that the person is open- or closed-minded about information contrary to his or her beliefs, and will tolerate others who deviate from organizational authority. (7)

Effort-to-performance (E→P) expectancy An individual's perceived probability that a particular level of effort will result in a particular level of performance. (3)

Electronic brainstorming Using computer software, several people enter ideas at any time on their computer terminals. Each participant can have his or her computer list a random sample of anonymous ideas generated by other people at the session to aid in thinking up new ideas. (11)

Empathy A person's ability to understand and be sensitive to the feelings, thoughts, and situation of others. (7)

Employee assistance programs (EAPs) Special counselling services to help employees cope with stressful life experiences and overcome ineffective coping mechanisms, such as alcoholism. (5)

Employee involvement Occurs when employees take an active role in making decisions that were not previously within their mandate. (11)

Employee share ownership plan (ESOP) A reward system that encourages employees to buy shares of the company. (4)

Empowerment A feeling of control and self-confidence that emerges when people are given power in a situation in which they previously were powerless. (11)

Equity theory A process theory of motivation that explains how people develop perceptions of fairness in the distribution and exchange of resources. (3) (8)

ERG theory Alderfer's content theory of motivation, stating that there are three broad human needs: existence, relatedness, and growth. (3)

Escalation of commitment Repeating an apparently bad decision or allocating more resources to a failing course of action. (9)

Evaluation apprehension An individual's tendency to withhold potentially valuable ideas that seem silly or peripheral because he or she believes that other team members are silently evaluating him or her. (11)

Expectancy theory A process theory of motivation, stating that employees will direct their work effort toward behaviours that they believe will lead to desired outcomes. (3)

Expert power The capacity to influence others by possessing knowledge or skills that they want. (12)

Extinction Occurs when the removal or withholding of a consequence decreases the frequency or future probability of the behaviour preceding that event. (2)

Feedback Any information that people receive about the consequences of their behaviour. (3)

Field survey Any research design in which information is collected in a natural environment.

Figure/ground principle A principle of organizing information whereby our perceptions of objects (figures) depend on the contexts (ground) in which they are perceived. (7)

Fixed interval schedule A schedule that reinforces behaviour after it has occurred for a fixed period of time. (2)

Fixed ratio schedule A schedule that reinforces behaviour after it has occurred a fixed number of times. (2)

Force field analysis A model that helps change agents diagnose the forces that drive and restrain proposed organizational change. (15)

Formal work team Two or more people who interact and mutually influence each other for the purpose of achieving common goals. Formal teams are explicitly formed to serve an organizational purpose. (10)

Formalization The degree that organizations standardize behaviour through rules, procedures, formal training, and related mechanisms. (17)

Frustration-regression process A basic premise in ERG theory that people who are unable to satisfy a higher need become frustrated and regress back to the next lower need level. (3)

Functional structure A type of departmentation that organizes employees around specific skills or other resources. (17)

Gainsharing plans A reward system usually applied to work teams that distributes bonuses to team members based on the amount of cost reductions and increased labour efficiency in the production process. (4)

General adaptation syndrome A model of the stress experience, consisting of three stages: alarm reaction, resistance, and exhaustion. (5)

Goal attainment approach Measuring organizational effectiveness in terms of progress toward organizational goals. (1)

Goals The immediate or ultimate objectives that employees are trying to achieve from their work effort. (3)

Grapevine The organization's informal communication network that is formed and maintained by social relationships rather than the formal reporting relationships. (6)

Group polarization The tendency for teams to make more extreme decisions (either more risky or more risk averse) than the average team member would if making the decision alone. (11)

Groupthink A situation in extremely cohesive teams in which members are so motivated to maintain harmony and conform to majority opinion that they withhold their dissenting opinions. (11)

Halo effect A perceptual error whereby our general impression of a person, usually based on one prominent characteristic, biases our perception of other characteristics of that person. (7)

Heterogeneous teams Formal or informal groups whose members have diverse personal characteristics, backgrounds, and values. (10)

Heuristic A rule of thumb (decision rule) used repeatedly to help decision makers evaluate alternatives under conditions of uncertainty. (9)

Hi–hi leadership hypothesis A proposition stating that effective leaders exhibit high levels of both people-oriented and task-oriented behaviours. (14)

Homogeneous teams Formal or informal groups whose members have common personal characteristics, backgrounds, and values. (10)

Hypotheses Statements making empirically testable declarations that certain variables and their corresponding measures are related in a specific way proposed by a particular theory. (Appendix A)

Impression management The practice of actively shaping our public images. (12)

Incremental change An evolutionary approach to change in which existing organizational conditions are fine-tuned and small steps are taken toward the change effort's objectives. (15)

Informal group Two or more people who group together primarily to meet their personal (rather than organizational) needs. (10)

Information overload A condition in which the volume of information received by an employee exceeds that person's ability to process it effectively. (6)

Inoculation effect A persuasive communication strategy of warning listeners that others will try to influence them in the future and that they should be wary about the opponent's arguments. (6)

Intergroup mirroring A structured conflict management intervention in which the parties discuss their perceptions of each other and look for ways to improve those perceptions and relationship with each other. (13)

Intuition The ability to know when a problem or opportunity exists and select the best course of action without the apparent use of reasoning or logic. (9)

Jargon Technical language understood by members of a particular occupational group, or recognized words with specialized meaning in specific organizations or social groups. (6)

Job characteristics model A job design model that relates five core job dimensions to three psychological states and several personal and organizational consequences. (4)

Job design The process of assigning tasks to a job and distributing work throughout the organization. (4)

Job enlargement Increasing the number of tasks employees perform within their job. (4)

Job enrichment Assigning responsibility for scheduling, coordinating, and planning work to employees who actually make the product or provide the service. (4)

Job evaluation Systematically evaluating the worth of jobs within the organization by measuring their required skill, effort, responsibility, and working conditions. Job evaluation results create a hierarchy of job worth. (4)

Job feedback The degree to which employees can tell how well they are doing based on direct sensory information from the job itself. (4)

Job rotation Moving employees from one job to another for short periods of time. (4)

Job satisfaction An individual's beliefs, feelings, and intentions regarding the job and the work environment. (8)

Job specialization The result of division of labour, in which each job now includes a narrow subset of the tasks required to complete the product or service. (4) (17)

Johari Window A model of personal and interpersonal understanding that encourages disclosure and feedback to increase the open area and reduce the blind, hidden, and unknown areas of oneself. (7)

Laboratory experiment Any research study in which independent variables and variables outside the researcher's main focus of inquiry can be controlled to some extent.

Lateral career development The perspective that career success occurs when employees fulfill their personal needs in different jobs across the organization rather than by moving through the organizational hierarchy. (16)

Law of effect A theory stating that the likelihood a behaviour will be repeated depends on its consequences. (2)

Leadership The process of influencing people and providing an environment for them to achieve team or organizational objectives. (14)

Leadership Grid® A model of leadership developed by Blake and Mouton that assesses an individual's leadership effectiveness in terms of his or her concern for people and production. (14)

Leadership substitutes Characteristics of the employee, task, or organization that either limit the leader's influence or make it unnecessary. (14)

Learning A relatively permanent change in behaviour (or behaviour tendency) that occurs as a result of study, practice, or any other form of experience. (2)

Learning organization The notion that an organization will excel if it is able to tap the commitment and capacity of all employees to continuously monitor and learn about the organization's environment. (2)

Legitimate power The capacity to influence others through formal authority, that is, the perceived right to direct certain behaviours of people in other positions. (12)

Locus of control A personality trait referring to the extent that people believe what happens to them is within their control; those who feel in control of their destiny have an internal locus, whereas those who believe that life events are due mainly to fate or luck have an external locus of control. (7) (14)

Machiavellian value A personal value held by some people who believe that deceit is a natural and acceptable way to influence others. (12)

Management by wandering around A management practice of having frequent face-to-face communication with employees so that managers are better informed about employee concerns and organizational activities. (6)

Matrix structure A type of departmentation that overlays a product-based structure (typically a project team) with a functional structure in an attempt to benefit from both designs. (17)

Mechanistic structure An organizational structure with a narrow span of control and high degrees of formalization and centralization. (17)

Media richness The data-carrying capacity of a communication medium; the volume and variety of information that it can transmit. (6)

Mixed consequences approach A behaviour change intervention that applies the four reinforcement contingencies—positive reinforcement, extinction, punishment, and negative reinforcement—at appropriate phases of employee performance. (4)

Motivation The internal forces that affect the direction, intensity, and persistence of a person's voluntary choice of behaviour. (2)

Motivator-hygiene theory Herzberg's content theory of motivation, stating that employees are motivated by characteristics of the work itself (called *motivators*) rather than the work context (called *hygienes*). (3)

Needs Deficiencies that energize or trigger behaviours to satisfy those needs. (3)

Needs hierarchy theory Maslow's content theory of motivation, stating that people have a hierarchy of five basic needs—physiological, safety, belongingness, esteem, and self-actualization—and that as a lower need becomes gratified, individuals become motivated to fulfill the next higher need. (3)

Negative reinforcement Occurs when the removal or termination of a consequence increases or maintains the frequency or future probability of the behaviour preceding that event. (2)

Negotiation Any attempt by two or more conflicting parties to resolve their divergent goals by redefining the terms of their interdependence. (13)

Network structure An alliance of several organizations for the purpose of creating a product or serving a client. (17)

Networking Cultivating social relationships with others for the purpose of accomplishing one's goals. (12)

Nominal group technique A structured team decision-making technique whereby members independently write down ideas, describe and clarify them to the group, and then independently rank or vote on them. (11)

Nonprogrammed decision The process applied to unique, complex, or ill-defined situations whereby decision makers follow the full decision-making process, including a careful search for and/or development of unique solutions. (9)

Norms Informal rules and expectations that groups establish to regulate the behaviour of their members. (10)

Ombuds officer Someone who formally investigates complaints as well as mediates the conflict. (13)

Open systems Organizations and other entities with interdependent parts that work together to continually monitor and transact with the external environment. (1) (13)

Organic structure An organizational structure with a wide span of control, very little formalization, and highly decentralized decision making. (17)

Organization development (OD) A planned systemwide effort, managed from the top with the assistance of a change agent, that uses behavioural science knowledge to improve organizational effectiveness. (15)

Organizational behaviour The study of what people think, feel, and do in and around organizations. (1)

Organizational behaviour modification A theory of learning and behaviour change that explains organizational behaviour in terms of the events preceding and following the behaviour. (2)

Organizational citizenship behaviours Employee behaviours that extend beyond the usual job duties, including altruism, courtesy, sportsmanship, civic duty, and conscientiousness. (2) (8)

Organizational commitment A complex attitude pertaining to the strength of an individual's identification with and involvement in a particular organization; includes a strong belief in the organization's goals, as well as a motivation to work for and remain a member of the organization. (8)

Organizational culture The basic pattern of shared assumptions, values, and beliefs governing the way employees within an organization think about and act upon problems and opportunities. (16)

Organizational design The creation and modification of organizational structures. (17)

Organizational effectiveness A multifaceted concept in which the organization "does the right things." This includes achieving organizational goals, adapting as an open system to the external environment, and addressing stakeholder needs. (1)

Organizational goals A desired state of affairs that organizations try to achieve. (1)

Organizational politics Attempts to influence others using discretionary behaviours for the purpose of promoting personal objectives; discretionary behaviours are neither explicitly prescribed nor prohibited by the organization and are linked to one or more power bases. (12)

Organizational socialization The process by which individuals learn the values, expected behaviours, and social knowledge necessary to assume their organizational roles. (16)

Organizational strategy The way the organization positions itself in its setting in relation to its stakeholders given the organization's resources, capabilities, and mission. (17)

Organizational structure The division of labour as well as the patterns of coordination, communication, work flow, and formal power that direct organizational activities. (17)

Organizations Social entities in which two or more people work interdependently through patterned behaviours to accomplish a set of goals. (1)

Parallel learning structure A highly participative social structure constructed alongside (i.e., parallel to) the formal organization with the purpose of increasing the organization's learning. (15)

Path-goal leadership theory A contingency theory of leadership based on expectancy theory of motivation that includes four leadership styles as well as several employee and situational contingencies. (14)

Perception The process of selecting, organizing, and interpreting information in order to make sense of the world around us. (7)

Perceptual defense A defensive psychological process that involves subconsciously screening out large blocks of information that threaten the person's beliefs and values. (7) (9)

Perceptual grouping The perceptual organization process of linking people and objects into recognizable and manageable patterns or categories. (7)

Performance standard A minimum acceptable level of job performance. (2)

Performance-to-outcome (P→O) expectancy An individual's perceived probability that a specific behaviour or performance level will lead to specific outcomes. (3)

Personality The relatively stable and consistent internal states of people that help to explain their behavioural tendencies. (7)

Persuasive communication The process of having receivers accept rather than just understand the sender's message. (6)

Positive reinforcement Occurs when the introduction of a consequence increases or maintains the frequency or future probability of the behaviour preceding that event. (2)

Postdecisional justification A perceptual phenomenon whereby decision makers justify their choices by subconsciously inflating the quality of the selected option and deflating the quality of the discarded options. (9)

Power The capacity of a person, team, or organization to influence others. (12)

Prejudice Negative feelings toward people belonging to a particular demographic group based on unfounded or blatantly incorrect beliefs. (7)

Primacy effect A perceptual error in which we quickly form an opinion of people based on the first information we receive about them. (7)

Procedural fairness Perceptions of fairness regarding the dispute resolution process, whether or not the outcome is favourable to the person. (13)

Process consultation A method of helping the organization solve its own problems by making it aware of organizational processes, the consequences of those processes, and the means by which they can be changed. (15)

Process theories of motivation Theories that describe the processes through which needs are translated into behaviour. (3)

Production blocking A time constraint in meetings due to the procedural requirement that only one person may speak at a time. (11)

Productivity The organization's efficiency in transforming inputs to outputs. (1)

Profit sharing A reward system in which a designated group of employees receives a share of corporate profits. (4)

Programmed decision The process whereby decision makers follow standard operating procedures to select the preferred solution without the need to identify or evaluate alternative choices. (9)

Progressive discipline An organizational discipline procedure in which the severity of punishment increases with the frequency and severity of the infraction. (4)

Projection A perceptual error in which we tend to believe that other people hold the same beliefs and attitudes that we do. (7)

Psychological contract The set of perceived mutual obligations that the employer and employee have about their exchange relationship. (16)

Punishment Occurs when the introduction of a consequence decreases the frequency or future probability of the behaviour preceding that event. (2)

Quality circle A small team of employees that meets on a regular basis to identify quality and productivity problems, propose solutions to management, and monitor the implementation and consequences of these solutions in its work area. (11)

Quantum change A revolutionary approach to change in which the organization breaks out of its existing ways and moves toward a totally different configuration of systems and structures. (15)

Realistic job previews Giving job applicants a realistic balance of positive and negative information about the job and work context. (16)

Reality shock The gap between pre-employment expectations and the perceived organizational reality that employees experience as they begin work. (16)

Recency effect A perceptual error in which the most recent information dominates our perception about the person. (7)

Referent power The capacity to influence others by virtue of the admiration and identification they have of the powerholder. (12)

Refreezing The introduction of systems and conditions that reinforce and maintain the new role patterns and prevent the organization from slipping back into the old way of doing things. (15)

Relations by objectives A structured conflict management intervention designed to improve labour–management relations that includes elements of intergroup mirroring. (13)

Representative sampling Sampling a population in such a way that we can extrapolate the results of that sample to the larger population.

Reward power The capacity to influence others by controlling the allocation of rewards valued by them and the removal of negative sanctions. (12)

Rituals The programmed routines of daily organizational life that dramatize the organization's culture. (16)

Role ambiguity A condition in which employees are uncertain about their job duties, performance expectations, level of authority, and other job conditions. (5)

Role conflict A condition in which individuals face competing demands, such as when obligations of the job are incompatible with the individual's personal values (person–role conflict) or when the individual receives contradictory messages from different people (intrarole conflict). (5)

Role perceptions A person's beliefs about what behaviours are appropriate or necessary in a particular situation, including the specific tasks that make up the job, their relative importance, and the preferred behaviours to accomplish those tasks. (2)

Satisfaction-progression process A basic premise in Maslow's needs hierarchy theory that people become increasingly motivated to fulfill a higher need as a lower need is gratified. (3)

Satisficing The tendency to select a solution that is satisfactory or "good enough" rather than optimal or "the best." (9)

Scientific management The process of systematically determining how work should be partitioned into its smallest possible elements and how the process of completing each task should be standardized to achieve maximum efficiency. (4)

Scientific method A set of principles and procedures that help researchers to systematically understand previously unexplained events and conditions. (Appendix A)

Selective perception The process of filtering (selecting and screening out) information received by our senses. (7)

Self-efficacy A person's beliefs and expectancies that he or she is able to perform a task effectively. (2)

Self-fulfilling prophecy A phenomenon in which an observer's expectations of someone causes that person to act in a way consistent with the observer's expectation. (7)

Self-managing work team A team of employees that completes a whole piece of work requiring several interdependent tasks and has substantial autonomy over the execution of these tasks. (11)

Self-monitoring A personality trait referring to the extent that people are sensitive to situational cues and can readily adapt their own behaviour appropriately. (7)

Self-serving bias A perceptual error whereby people tend to attribute their own success to internal factors and their failures to external factors. (7)

Sensitivity training An unstructured and agendaless session in which participants become more aware through their interactions of how they affect others and how others affect them. (15)

Shaping The strategy of initially reinforcing crude approximations of the ideal behaviour, then increasing reinforcement standards until only the ideal behaviour is rewarded. (2)

Situational contingencies Environmental conditions beyond the employee's immediate control that constrain or facilitate employee behaviour and performance. (2)

Skill-based pay (SBP) Pay structures in which employees earn higher pay rates with the number of skill modules they have mastered, even though they perform only some of the mastered tasks in a particular job. (4)

Skill variety The extent to which a job requires employees to use different skills and talents to complete a variety of work activities. (4)

Skunkwork A task force of employees borrowed from several functional areas of the organization to develop new products, services, or procedures, usually in isolation from the organization and without the normal restrictions. (10)

Social learning theory A theory stating that learning mainly occurs by observing others and then modelling the behaviours that lead to favourable outcomes. (2)

Social loafing The tendency for people to perform at a lower level when working in groups than when alone. (10)

Sociotechnical design A theory stating that every work site consists of a technological system and a social system, and that organizational effectiveness is maximized when these two systems are compatible with each other. (11)

Span of control The number of people directly reporting to a supervisor. This element of organizational structure determines the number of hierarchical levels required in the organization. (17)

Stabilization zone Any place where a person can rely on past routines to guide behaviour automatically; this is a stress management practice to temporarily withdraw from situations requiring constant vigilance in new surroundings. (5)

Stakeholder or multiple constituency approach Measuring organizational effectiveness in terms of how well the organization addresses the preferences of its stakeholders—groups with a vested interest in the organization. (1)

Stereotyping The process of using a few observable characteristics to assign someone to a preconceived social category and then assuming that the person also possesses other (usually less observable) characteristics of the group. (7)

Strategic choice The idea that an organization interacts with its environment rather than being totally determined by it. (17)

Stress An individual's adaptive response to a situation that is perceived as challenging or threatening to the person's well-being. (5)

Stressor Any environmental condition that places a physical or emotional demand on the person. (5)

Substitutability The extent to which those dependent on a resource have alternative sources of supply or can use other resources that would provide a reasonable substitute. (12)

Superordinate goal A common objective—such as an organizationwide goal—held by conflicting parties that is more important than the departmental or individual goals. (13)

Synergy A condition in which the interaction of two or more agents produces a greater result than if these agents had been operating independently. In employee involvement, synergy results when the quantity and/or quality of ideas generated from two or more people working together is greater than if these people had been working alone. (11)

Tacit skills and knowledge Abilities that are so subtle that they can only be learned by observing others and modelling their behaviours. (2)

Task identity The degree to which a job requires completion of a whole or identifiable piece of work. (4)

Task interdependence The extent to which work activities among people are interrelated. (10)

Task significance The degree to which the job has a substantial impact on the organization and/or larger society. (4)

Team-based (or lateral) structure A type of departmentation with a flat span of control and relatively little formalization, consisting of self-managing work teams responsible for various work processes. (10) (17)

Team building Any formal intervention directed toward improving the development and functioning of a work team. (10)

Team effectiveness The extent to which the team achieves its objectives, the needs and objectives of its members, and sustains itself over time. (10)

Theory A general set of propositions that describes interrelationships among several concepts. (Appendix A)

Third-party conflict resolution Any attempt by a relatively neutral person to help the parties resolve their differences. (13)

Time and motion study The process of systematically observing, measuring, and timing the smallest physical movements to identify more efficient work behaviours. (4)

Total quality management A philosophy and a set of guiding principles to continuously improve the organization's product or service quality. (1)

Transactional leadership Helping organizations to more efficiently achieve their current objectives, such as by linking job performance to valued rewards and ensuring that employees have the resources needed to get the job done. (14)

Transformational leadership One who transforms organizations by creating, communicating, and modelling a vision for the organization or work unit, and inspiring employees to strive for that vision. (14)

Type A behaviour pattern A behaviour pattern associated with people having premature coronary heart disease; Type A people tend to be impatient, lose their temper, talk rapidly, and interrupt others. (5)

Type B behaviour pattern A behaviour pattern of people with low risk of coronary heart disease; Type B people tend to work steadily, take a relaxed approach to life, and are even tempered. (5)

Unfreezing The first part of the change process whereby the change agent produces a disequilibrium between the driving and restraining forces. It typically includes making people aware of the need for change and providing them with the necessary skills, knowledge, and resources to execute the new role patterns. (15)

Utilitarianism A moral principle stating that decision makers should seek the greatest good for the greatest number of people when choosing among alternatives. (9)

Valence The anticipated satisfaction or dissatisfaction that an individual feels toward an outcome. (3)

Values Stable, long-lasting beliefs about what is important to the individual. (8)

Variable interval schedule A schedule that reinforces behaviour after it has occurred for a variable period of time around some average. (2)

Variable ratio schedule A schedule that reinforces behaviour after it has occurred a varying number of times around some average. (2)

Virtual corporation A hypothetically pure form of network structure in which the organization instantaneously reorganizes itself to create a product or provide a service at the moment the customer first wants it. (17)

Win–lose orientation A person's belief that the conflicting parties are drawing from a fixed pie, so his or her gain is the other person's loss. (13)

Win–win orientation A person's belief that a mutually beneficial solution can be found in a particular conflict with another person. (13)

Corporate Index

Name Index

Subject Index